THE

METAMORPHOSES

OF OVID

Also by Michael Simpson

Gods and Heroes of the Greeks:
The "Library" of Apollodorus

THE METAMORPHOSES

OF OVID

TRANSLATED WITH

AN INTRODUCTION

AND COMMENTARY BY

MICHAEL SIMPSON

University of Massachusetts Press

AMHERST AND BOSTON

Second, corrected, paperback printing, 2004
LC 00-069082
ISBN 1-55849-399-9 (paper)
Designed by Jack Harrison
Set in ITC Berkeley with Heraculaneum display by Graphic Composition, Inc.
Printed and bound by Sheridan Books

Library of Congress Cataloging-in-Publication Data

Ovid, 43 B.C.–17 or 18 A.D.
[Metamorphoses. English]
The Metamorphoses of Ovid / translated with an introduction and commentary by
Michael Simpson.
p. cm.
Includes bibliographical references and index.
ISBN 1-55849-309-3 (cloth : alk. paper)
1. Fables, Latin—Translations into English. 2. Metamorphosis—Mythology—Poetry.
3. Mythology, Classical—Poetry.
I. Simpson, Michael, 1934– . II. Title.
PA6522.M2 S48 2001
873'.01—dc21
00-069082

The publication of this book was supported by a grant from
the Cecil H. Green Distinguished Chair Endowment at
The University of Texas at Dallas, created by Mrs. Eugene McDermott.

For Katherine, Hannah, and Stephen

CONTENTS

BOOK SIX   94

BOOK SEVEN   109

BOOK EIGHT   128

BOOK NINE   147

BOOK TEN   165

BOOK ELEVEN   182

BOOK TWELVE   199

BOOK THIRTEEN   213

ACKNOWLEDGMENTS

I would like to thank Leone Stein, former director of the University of Massachusetts Press, for her kindness and encouragement many years ago. Bruce Wilcox, current director of the Press, has been steadily supportive throughout the decade or more that I've been working on Ovid.

Carol Dana Lanham read a draft of the translation and proposed many ways for me to improve it. Thanks to her, there are fewer errors and infelicities in it than there would have been otherwise. I would also like to thank Leo Curran for reading an early version of the translation and giving me helpful comments on it.

For the loving support of my wife, Katherine M. Sorensen (1951–2001), I shall always be grateful.

M. S.

THE
META
MOR
PHOSES
OF OVID

INTRODUCTION

The Roman poet Ovid (Publius Ovidius Naso) was born on March 20, 43 B.C., in Sulmo, modern Sulmona, a small town in the Abruzzi about ninety miles east of Rome.[1] His birthdate is almost exactly one year after the assassination of Julius Caesar on March 15, 44 B.C. The murder of Caesar in the Roman Senate by a group of conspirators who feared his power precipitated an intense struggle for control of Rome, a civil war that was only resolved in 31 B.C. At this time the forces of Octavian, Caesar's grandnephew and adopted son and heir, defeated the combined fleets of Caesar's former friend and supporter Marc Antony and Antony's lover and ally Cleopatra, queen of Egypt, in a naval battle off the town of Actium on the west coast of Greece. With this victory Octavian, who adopted the title Augustus, "the Revered," in 27 B.C., became Rome's first emperor and ruled the empire for almost all the rest of Ovid's life, dying in A.D. 14.

Ovid was born into an old, well-to-do family belonging to the order known as *equites* (knights), a wealthy class in the second rank of Roman nobility, just below the senatorial order. He had a brother who was one year older than he to the day. After their early schooling in Sulmo, their father sent his two sons to Rome for education in rhetoric, which would lead to a career in government or law, a typical pattern for provincial upper-class boys. While his brother had a natural gift for oratory, Ovid himself loved poetry. His father tried to discourage him by telling him that not even Homer had left any wealth behind. The boy tried to write prose, but poetry came of its own accord, he says, and whatever he attempted turned out to be verse. When Ovid was nineteen his brother died, and Ovid says he felt as though part of himself had died as well.

After his education in Rome, Ovid took the customary "grand tour" and traveled to Greece and Asia Minor, and also to Sicily, where he stayed for almost a year and visited famous sites.[2]

The poet-to-be next stepped onto the first rung of the ladder for a career in government[3] and could have continued by becoming a member of the Roman Senate, but he knew he had neither the inclination nor the stamina for the effort required. He decided instead to devote himself to poetry.

Ovid joined a circle of poets, whom he revered as though they were gods, he tells us, and attended poetry readings by Macer and Propertius. He reports that

1

he and his group were enthralled by Horace when they heard him read his poems. (The elegiac poet Propertius and the lyric poet and satirist Horace have works extant.) He only saw Virgil, Ovid says, and he adds that the early death of the elegiac poet Tibullus did not give them time to become friends. Both Virgil and Tibullus died in 19 B.C.

Ovid first read his poems in public when he was about eighteen,[4] and his poetic talent was quickly recognized, for younger poets revered him as much as he had revered older poets. He made his reputation as an elegiac poet, and he considered himself the immediate heir of Tibullus and so fourth in the succession of great Roman elegists, Gallus, Propertius, and Tibullus.

The poet tells us that he was married three times: the first time briefly, while he was still almost a boy, to someone "neither worthy nor useful,"[5] the second time to someone who had no faults, although the marriage was short-lived. His third wife remained with him to the end of his life. The poet's one child, a daughter (by which wife he does not say), had two children at a young age by two different men. Ovid's father died at ninety, his mother soon after.

Although the order of publication of Ovid's early poems is not certain, what is thought to be the earliest of his extant works, the *Amores*, or *Loves*, three books of love poems, was probably published "well after 20 B.C." With this first collection Ovid gained recognition as an up-and-coming poet.[6] Next came the *Heroides*, or *Heroines*, a series of fourteen letters by women characters in myth such as Penelope, Phaedra, and Medea to their absent husbands or lovers, a fifteenth from the Greek lyric poet Sappho to the mythical Phaon (if it is by Ovid), and three pairs of such letters, with replies from husbands or lovers. The *Ars Amatoria*, or *Art of Love*, probably published after the *Heroides*, around 1 B.C. to A.D. 1, is a handbook of seduction in three books in the manner of a didactic poem, or what we might call a "how-to" work. Of the *Medicamina Faciei Femineae*, or *Makeup for a Woman's Face*, also a didactic poem, only one hundred lines survive. The *Remedia Amoris*, or *Remedies for Love*, a didactic poem in a little over eight hundred lines, serves as an answer to the *Ars Amatoria*, with instructions on how to be "cured" of love. All of these poems are in the elegiac meter.

The *Metamorphoses*, a twelve thousand–line poem written in dactylic hexameter, the meter of epic, and divided into fifteen books, draws upon Greek mythology and Roman legend and tells of "transformations." It was completed, or virtually completed, in A.D. 8, just before Ovid was banished from Rome by the emperor Augustus and ordered to the eastern border of the Roman Empire. While working on the *Metamorphoses*, Ovid had also been writing a poem in elegiac meter on the calendar of Roman cults and festivals called *Fasti*, or *Calendar*, but the poet's banishment from Rome interrupted him, and he completed only six thousand lines, or half of the poem, the calendar for the months January to June.

In exile, from which he was never recalled, Ovid wrote several works, all in elegiac meter, all colored by or relating to the trauma of his banishment from Rome. The *Tristia*, or *Sorrows*, a collection of some fifty poems in five books, was sent back to Rome book by book in the first years of his exile. All seem to be open letters, many of them to his wife, others to both friends and enemies, though unnamed. Book 2 is a single poem, an open letter to Augustus. A second, later collection, called *Epistulae ex Ponto*, or *Letters from the Black Sea*, is composed of three books of thirty poems, the addressees of all but two of which are named, to which was added a fourth book of sixteen poems, all but two of which are also addressed to named individuals. The latest datable reference in this collection is to the consulship of Ovid's friend Graecinus in A.D. 16.[7] In these two collections, Ovid conducts an ongoing and unsuccessful campaign extending over seven or eight years seeking, if not to be allowed to return to Rome, at least to be given a place of exile not so harsh and remote.[8]

Ovid's *Ibis*, a curse in elegiac meter directed at an unknown enemy, probably fictitious, was also written in exile. Ovid wrote a tragedy called *Medea* before his exile, but it does not survive.[9]

Exile

In the summer of A.D. 8, when he had all but completed the *Metamorphoses*,[10] Ovid was summoned to a private meeting with the emperor Augustus, at which the emperor exploded in anger at the poet. He ordered him to leave Italy by a certain date and to proceed to Tomis, an outpost of the Roman Empire on the northwest coast of the Black Sea (Constantza in modern Romania) colonized by Ionian Greeks from Miletus, with a native population of Getae and Thracians. Ovid's poems were removed from Rome's three public libraries.[11]

Augustus' choice for Ovid's place of exile was exquisitely cruel.[12] The epithet most often used to describe this poet is "urbane," and the word does indeed define him: Ovid was a man of the city, the city was his life—and the city was Rome. Tomis, in its crudeness, its wildness, its dangers, even its climate, was, to a man of Ovid's sensibilities, as far from Rome as hell from heaven. His banishment, as Kenney says, was a spiritual death sentence.[13]

Why did Augustus do this? What had Ovid done to bring this on himself? What we know, we know only from Ovid himself (the *Tristia* and *Epistulae ex Ponto*), and he does not give us the whole story. He was exiled, Ovid tells us, because of "a poem and a mistake" (*carmen et error*).[14] The poem was the *Ars Amatoria*, published seven or eight years earlier.[15] This work, Ovid's playful handbook of seduction, which seemed to defy Augustus' program for moral reform at Rome, was very likely a cover for Augustus' more serious reason for banishing Ovid: his "mistake."[16]

Ovid says he must not reveal the "mistake," although he tells us that it was not something he said or did, but something he saw. "The picture that emerges," Kenney says, "from such hints as [Ovid] does give is that of involuntary complicity in some scandal, in which politics and morals were interlocked, affecting the Imperial house and Augustus in particular."[17]

Despite Ovid's pleading through all the years of his exile, both to Augustus and, after Augustus died in A.D. 14, to his successor, Tiberius, to lessen his wrath, to recall him from exile, or at least to change his place of exile from Tomis to a place less barbarous, less harsh, and less remote, he was answered only with silence.[18] These are the poet's last words from exile, to someone bent on attacking his poetry. "Jealous man, why tear in shreds the poems of Ovid, himself destroyed? . . . I, too, once had fame, when I was counted among the living." Then, after a roll call of poets he had known, naming them as though to reassure himself that he was once one of them, he ends, "[M]y Muse was famous, if it's right to say so, and among so many considered great I was read. So, Envy incarnate, cease cutting to pieces a man uprooted from his country! Don't scatter my ashes, cruel man! I have already lost everything. If I still live, it is only to know the sense and substance of sorrow. Why do you enjoy thrusting your sword into a body already dead? There's no place in me for a new wound."[19] Ovid died in A.D. 16 or 17 at the age of about sixty.

The *Metamorphoses*

In the opening lines or prologue of the *Metamorphoses*, Ovid declares that he is going to tell of metamorphoses ("forms changed to other bodies," 1.1–2),* beginning with the creation of the world and coming down to his own time (1.1–4), and in the next 11,982 lines he carries out this program so tersely described in the prologue. Creation of the world from Chaos, the first metamorphosis (1.5–88), is followed by a "purgative" flood and the re-creation of the world and the human race (1.89–451). These two parts serve as an introduction to the body of the poem, three long sections, the first more or less on gods (1.452–6.420), the second on heroes and heroines (6.421–11.193), and the third on "historical" personages (11.194–15.870). This last section begins with Troy and the Trojan War and ends with the emperor Augustus in Ovid's own time. In a brief epilogue, Ovid asserts the lasting value of his poem (15.871–879; for additional comment on the structure of the *Metamorphoses*, see translation n. 1).

By the end of the poem, everything that exists—almost—appears either to have undergone metamorphosis or to undergo continous change. The two are related but not identical, for metamorphosis, though obviously a change, would seem to be a one-time occurrence, while the change that occurs, for example, in the erosions caused by weather or in the cycle of seasons of the year is ongoing.[20] Yet the universe as it is here characterized, that is, created by metamorphosis from Chaos and then governed by endless change, provides

---

*The numbers refer to the Latin text of the *Metamorphoses* (books and lines).

the dynamic context necessary for metamorphosis in the poem to happen and to be real and believable.

Change, or metamorphosis, extends to the poem itself, for it gives us "endless change and variation of mood, tone, subject, and style both in individual stories and from one story to the next": "[M]etamorphosis is . . . the underlying principle for [its] form or structure."[21]

Ovid drew inspiration from a genre of poetry about metamorphosis in Hellenistic Greek literature, but what he created is original and unique: a poem epic in length and form, un-epic in its variety, and "modern" in its style. The narrator's "genial tone" enables him to sail unperturbed through tale after tale of love and loss, quests and battles, violence and suffering, human striving and human folly, always with wit and verbal adroitness. There is nothing else like the *Metamorphoses* in ancient Greek or Latin literature.[22]

Metamorphosis is, of course, the primary subject of the poem, but it is about other things as well. The claim has often been made that the *Metamorphoses* is an epic of love, but most of that love is one-sided, and Segal is closer to the truth when he says the work is more likely "an epic of rape." Kenney claims the poem's "real subject is the microcosm of human psychology," and Solodow adds a gloss: "In Ovid's world personal experience is recognized, and nothing larger."[23]

The *Metamorphoses* is also clearly about storytelling. Ovid himself is a master storyteller, and the "strong presence" of the narrator ("Ovid") gives the poem unity and invites reflection on the nature of storytelling.[24] The narrator repeatedly yields in the poem to other storytellers through a favored device, the embedded tale, the story within a story. There are even occasions of double embedding, a story within a story within a story, so that the poem, Conte says, "seems to be sprouting continually from itself." More than a third of the poem is made up of embedded tales, 4,422 lines out of 11,995 (see translation n. 49). Storytelling is "the most popular activity in the poem" and for Ovid "a fundamental means of comprehending the world."[25]

So many storytellers, each with his own story, his own version of reality, all versions welcome: this feature of the *Metamorphoses*, akin to its subject, metamorphosis and change, implies a tolerant mind and a pluralistic outlook at home with the variety, with the multiple realities in the world, and gives us a sense of Ovid as a deeply humane poet yet one with a "skeptical and rationalist disposition," as Kenney says. It was surely these qualities that put the man at odds with his time and place and its reigning Augustan ideology, but not in such a way as to make him an anti-Augustan dissident. Ovid was, rather, *non*-Augustan—"un-Augustan" Kenney calls him—and "react[ed] against the Augustan 'myth'" by "simply going his own way."[26]

The Translation

Kenney observes that Ovid's "diction is engineered to smooth and accelerate the verse" and that his style is "a transmitting, rather than, as with Virgil, a refracting medium."[27] I have tried to keep those observations in mind in making a prose translation in the rapid and direct American idiom while avoiding colloquialism on the one hand and academic translationese on the other. Readers will decide for themselves what success I have had in presenting Ovid in English to them.

I used the Miller-Goold edition of the *Metamorphoses* as the working text for the translation, and I indicate departures from that text in footnotes at the appropriate places.

The Notes

The translation's endnotes aim to shed light on the poem primarily for non-specialists, and composing them has been a way for me to deepen my own understanding of this poet. I have consulted the published writings of many scholars, but by no means claim exhaustive knowledge of Ovidian scholarship, and specialists will no doubt be able to name works or parts of works I should have referred to in preference to some I did.

META MOR PHOSES

BOOK ONE

My mind leads me to something new, to tell of forms changed to other bodies. Gods, inspire this poem I've begun (for you changed it, too),* and from the first origin of the world spin my song's fine thread unbroken down to my own time.

Before there were sea, earth, and sky (which covers everything), the face of nature was the same throughout the universe. They've called it chaos: a rough, disordered mass of elements, separate bits of matter jumbled together in a heap, heavy and inert.

No sun gave light to the world then; no crescent moon grew round and full; no earth floated in air, in perfect equipoise; no arms of the sea embraced the long shores of the world.

And though there were earth and sea and air, the earth gave no support, the sea no pathways, and the air no light. Nothing kept its form, and everything got in the way of everything else, for in a single body cold battled heat, wet fought the dry, the soft opposed the hard, things heavy fought things light.

Then a god, a superior kind of nature, broke up this strife, divided earth from heaven, sea from land, and moved the light-filled sky far from the hazy atmosphere.

After he sorted these out and removed them from the blind mass,† he set each in its own place, and fixed it there in peace and harmony with the others: Fire, lighter than air, belongs to the vault of heaven and leaped there and made a place for itself in the highest stronghold; just below it comes air, nearly as light. The earth, denser than either of these, attracts the larger elements and

---

*At 1.2: I read *illa* (translated "it" and referring to "beginning," *coeptis,* 1.2), following Kenney (1976) and Kovacs (1987) instead of *illas* (referring to "forms," *formas,* 1.1) with Miller-Goold and others. "for you changed it, too": Ovid is writing in hexameters instead of the usual elegiac meter.
†1.24: "blind mass," i.e., chaos (Anderson [1997] at 1.24, 155).

sinks by its own weight, while water flows to the lowest levels and hems in the solid earth.

When the god, whatever god it was, had thus laid out this mass of matter and divided it and formed the individual parts, he molded the earth into the shape of a great ball, taking care to make it perfectly round. Next, he ordered the seas to separate and swell with powerful winds and so surround the earth and lap its shores. Then he added springs, large ponds, and lakes and set rivers coursing seaward through their channels. Some rivers are swallowed by the earth, while others run down to the sea and join the vast and freer waters there and now wash against the shores instead of their own banks.

He also commanded plains to extend themselves, valleys to sink low, trees to put forth leaves, and mountains of stone to heave themselves into the air.

The god then divided the sky into zones, two on the right and two on the left, and a fifth that is hotter than these, and marked off the mass below the same way and divided the earth into the same number of regions. The middle region is too warm to live in; two are deep in snow; two he placed in between and made temperate regions, where heat and cold are mixed. Above these rests the atmosphere, heavier than fire to the same degree that water is lighter than earth. There he ordered fog to roll in and summoned clouds, and thunder, one day to terrify human minds, and winds, which make the crashing, brilliant lightning bolts.

The maker of the world did not allow the winds free run of the atmosphere, but gave each a separate region where it can blow at will. It is still hard, though, to keep the brother winds from tearing the world apart, so great is their discord.

The east wind withdrew to the land of the dawn, to Nabataea and the Persian kingdom and the mountain ridges touched by the rays of the morning sun. The evening star and the seashores warmed in the glow of the setting sun are nearest to the west wind; the sharp north wind invaded Scythia and the northern land of the Great Bear; the south wind soaks the southern land with constant clouds and rain. Above the winds he placed the clear and weightless upper air, without a trace of earthy residue.

The moment the maker of the world finished putting everything within set boundaries, stars, long hidden in dark mists, began to glow and burn throughout the entire sky.

Lest any region should be without its own inhabitants, stars and the gods occupied the heavens; water offered a place for gleaming fish to dwell; earth received wild beasts; and air with its shifting winds was home to birds.

A creature holier than these, with a more capacious mind than these, was lacking still, one able to dominate the rest. And so the human race was born, whether the creator of all things, the source of a better world, made us from a divine seed, or the fresh new earth, just now separated from the upper air, kept some seeds of its sister sky. This earth Prometheus mixed with rain and modeled in the shape of the gods who guide all things. Though other living things look downward, facing the ground, he set this creature's head upright and ordered it to lift its eyes to the stars and behold heaven. The earth, but lately crude and shapeless, was now transformed, for it was dressed in human figures, till then unknown.[1]

First came an age of gold, marked by trust and doing what was right, not by coercion but of one's own free will, without need of laws. Punishment and fear were things unheard of. Threatening words engraved on bronze were never read aloud in public places;* an anxious multitude never stood in fear before a judge: All lived safely and needed no protectors.

Pine trees had not yet been felled and carried down from their mountain homes to the sea to enable men to visit foreign lands: Mortals knew no shores except their own.

No deep defensive ditches then encircled towns; no long brass trumpets, no curved cornets called men to arms. There was no need for helmets nor for swords: All peoples were secure and lived in peace without maintaining armies.

The land itself, untilled, neither broken by the hoe nor turned by the plow, gave everything of its own accord. Content with food that no one forced to grow, humankind picked the fruit of the arbutus, mountain strawberries, cornel cherries, and blackberries hanging on brambly bushes, and gathered the acorns that dropped from the spreading oak of Jove.†

Spring was eternal; calm zephyrs and their soft currents caressed flowers that blossomed unsown. The earth gave its yield in season, though never plowed, and fields that never needed to lie fallow grew white with ripening grain. Rivers of milk flowed here, rivers of nectar there, and golden honey dripped from green oak trees.

When Saturn had been sent to the darkness of the underworld, and the universe was under Jove, a silver race came forth, worth less than gold but more valuable than bronze. Jupiter shortened the original spring and gave the year a cycle of four seasons: winter; summer; blushing autumn, with its changing weather; and now a briefer spring.

Then for the first time ever the air itself seemed to catch fire in the arid summer heat, while later on you could have seen icicles hanging, hardened by the winds. Then for the first time ever people lived in houses, made from caves, dense underbrush, and branches bound with strips of bark. Then for the first time ever seeds of grain were buried in the ground in long furrows, and oxen groaned as they struggled forward beneath the yoke.

---

*1.91–92: "threatening words engraved on bronze": "[L]aws, once they had been established, were posted in public places on tablets of bronze (as here) or stone" (Anderson [1997] at 1.91–93, 161).

†1.104–105: The fruit of the arbutus or wild strawberry tree and mountain strawberries were thought of "as the simple, natural food of early mankind," although in Ovid's time, "the arbutus was considered almost inedible." The cornel cherry "is almost all inedible pit" and the thorny branches on which blackberries grow "reduce their appeal" (Anderson [1997] at 1.104, 105, 162).

After that age there came a third, an age of bronze, more violent in character and readier to take up dreadful arms, but not a criminal age.

The final one was iron-hard: In this age of a baser metal every kind of forbidden crime was soon committed. Purity, truth, and trust all fled, and in their place came deceit and fraud, treachery and violence, and a criminal lust for possessions. Men now sailed on the winds, winds no sailor had known till now; and timbers that had long stood high on mountains now pitched in foreign sea-swells, while land that once was free as sunshine and fresh air surveyors now carefully marked with boundary lines. Not only was the rich earth made to serve up grain and other crops as though it was her duty, but men also dug down into her bowels and brought out the wealth she had hidden there, the source of all evils that she had buried deep in Stygian darkness.

Soon lethal iron came forth, and gold, more deadly than iron; war came forth, which needs both iron and gold for battles, banging weapons together in its bloody hands. People lived by stealing; no guest felt safe with his host, no father-in-law with his daughter's husband; and brotherly love was a thing of the past. A man hoped for his wife's early death, and she hoped for her husband's. Wicked stepmothers mixed their ghastly poisons; a son too soon asked his father how old he was: Family ties lay broken and defeated, and the maiden Justice was the last of the gods to leave the world, awash in bloody slaughter.

The highest part of the sky was no safer than the earth, for the Giants, they say, aimed to seize the kingdom of the gods and piled mountain on top of mountain, all the way to the stars. It was then that the father all-powerful hurled a lightning bolt and smashed Olympus, and knocked Pelion from Ossa underneath.*

The earth was soaked in blood from the horrible bodies of her sons now lying beneath this heap of shattered mountains, and she gave life to the hot gore, they say, turning it into human forms, to have something to remember her offspring by. But that race too was contemptuous of the gods, bloodthirsty and violent: They were clearly sons of blood.

Father Jupiter, Saturn's son, saw all this from his high summit and groaned, recalling something too recent to be widely known, the foul banquet at Lycaon's table. Consumed by rage, terrible rage, rage worthy of himself, he summoned the gods to a meeting, and, the summons received, they came at once.

High up in the open, peaceful sky you can make out a path called the "Milky Way," striking for its pure white glow. This was the route the gods took to the great Thunderer's royal palace: On the right and the left as you go stand the mansions of the noble deities, their doors thrown open to the throngs. Divinities lower down the scale live elsewhere. Here, though, the famous and power-

---

*1.154–155: "smashed Olympus, and knocked Pelion": As Homer tells the story, two giants, Otos and Ephialtes, tried to attack the gods in heaven by piling Mount Ossa on Mount Olympus and another mountain, Pelion, on Ossa, but Apollo killed them (*Odyssey* 11.305–320).

ful gods have set up their households, at a place which, if I may be so bold, I would not hesitate to call the Palatine of heaven.

So, when the gods had taken their seats in Jupiter's marble hall, the god himself, sitting on a throne above them and leaning on his ivory scepter, shook his terrible locks several times and made earth, sea, and all the stars tremble.

Then he opened his mouth to speak and voiced his indignation: "I was less anxious about my rule of the world when each of the snake-foot giants was about to throw his hundred arms around the sky and seize it. For though they were a savage enemy, that war was started by a single group and had a single origin.

"Now I must destroy the human race in every land throughout the world where waves of ocean break: I swear it by the river that glides through the Stygian grove beneath the earth! First, though, there must be a thorough examination, and whatever cannot be healed must be cut off, lest the healthy parts become infected. I have semi-gods, I have rural gods, I have nymphs, fauns, satyrs, and mountain-dwelling deities. Since we don't yet think they deserve the honor of living in heaven, we can at least let them inhabit this earth we've given them.

"But, my fellow gods, do you think they can be safe when Lycaon, notorious for his viciousness, has plotted to attack even me, wielder of the lightning and your king?"

They roared in anger and demanded that the one who dared to do such things be severely punished. It was the same when a godless band was raging to wash away the name of Rome with Caesar's blood: The human race was instantly filled with terror at such a disaster, and the whole world shuddered. Your people's devotion, Augustus, was as gratifying to you then as the gods' devotion was now to Jove.

He raised his hand and checked their outcry with a call for order, and all fell silent. When the noise had subsided under the weight of the king's authority, Jupiter broke the silence and spoke a second time: "He has indeed been punished. Rest assured of that. But let me tell you what his crime was and how he was punished.

"Stories of the infamy of that time had reached my ears. Hoping they were untrue, I slipped down from the heights of Olympus and traveled the earth, disguised as a human being. It would take too long to relate in detail all the corruption I found and where I found it: The truth was worse than what I had heard.

"I had crossed the Maenalian mountain range, where fearsome wild beasts have their lairs, and Mount Cyllene and the cool pine forests of Lycaeus. From there I made my way to that unfriendly house, the seat of the Arcadian tyrant, at dusk, when twilight ushers in the night.

"I gave a sign that a god had come, and the people began to offer prayers to me. Lycaon mocked their piety, however, and said, 'I shall make a public test to see if he's god or mortal—and there will be no doubt about the truth.' He was planning to murder me that night while I was sound asleep. This was his way to learn the truth.

"Not content with that, he took his sword and slit the throat of a hostage sent by the Molossian people and boiled part of the still-twitching limbs to make them tender and roasted the rest over the fire. The moment he set this on the table, I hurled an avenging thunderbolt and brought that house down upon its household gods, as guilty as their master.

"Lycaon himself fled in terror, and when he reached the silence of the countryside, he began to howl—he was trying to speak but he could not: His madness had been gathered in his mouth. His lust for slaughtered flesh made him attack flocks of sheep: He still loved to guzzle blood.

"His clothing turned to fur, his arms to legs: He was changed into a wolf, but kept some signs of his original form. The same grayness is there, the same violence in his face, the same glowing eyes, the same vicious look.

"One house fell, but not just that one house deserves to perish, for wild madness now rules everywhere on earth. You would think men were sworn to crime! So this is my decision: Let them all pay the penalty they deserve, immediately!" Some shouted their approval of Jove's speech, goading him to greater fury, others showed their support by clapping.

Still, the death of the human race saddens them all, and they ask, What will the earth be like bereft of mortals? Who will bring incense to their altars? Is Jupiter about to turn the earth over to wild animals to ravage? Responding to their questions, the king of the gods forbids them to worry (just leave it to him, he says) and promises them a human race from a miraculous source, totally unlike the old.

Jove was about to shower bolts of lightning over all the earth, but he was afraid that the sacred summit of the sky might be ignited accidentally from so much fire, and the universe's axis burn. It was also fated, he recalled, that at some future time the sea, the earth, and the palace of heaven would all catch fire, and the massive universe itself would be attacked by flames and threaten to fall. He put away his thunderbolts, made by the Cyclopes; he preferred a different kind of punishment: to bring torrential rains down from every quarter of the sky and so to drown the human race.

He immediately shut up in Aeolus' cave the north wind and all other gusts and blasts that scatter clouds and set the south wind free. This wind blew out on dripping wings, his frightening face wreathed in pitch-black clouds. His beard was soggy with rain, and water streamed from his white head; rain clouds clung to his brow, and his wings and clothes were soaking wet. He squeezed the overhanging clouds and made thunder crack and sheets of rain pour from the sky. Juno's messenger Iris, dressed in rainbow colors, then fed water to the clouds to make more rain.

The crops that farmers had so fervently prayed for now lay flat and scattered in the fields: The long year's labor was gone. Nor was Jove content to let his rage run only in the sky, and he called upon his sea-blue brother to help with more flood-waters. Neptune then summoned all rivers, and when they arrived at the palace of their king, he told them: "Now is not the time for a lengthy exhortation. Pour out your powers! That's what's needed! Open your rivery houses, take away all dams, give your streams free rein!"

Those were his orders. The rivers returned home and relaxed the curbs on the mouths of their springs and let their waters roll unbridled to the sea. Neptune himself struck the earth with his trident, and the earth trembled and opened paths for streams to come coursing through.

Rivers ran unchecked through open fields, sweeping crops and orchards, flocks and men, homes and shrines and household gods before them. If any house was left intact, able to resist such an onslaught and not be thrown down, an even bigger wave washed over its roof, and its towers sank out of sight beneath the flood.

And now land and sea were one: All was ocean, an ocean lacking shores. Here, a man clung to a hilltop; there, a man sat in a skiff and rowed over the tops of fields he recently plowed. Yet another guides his boat above his crops or past the roof of his sunken villa, while a fourth catches a fish in the highest branches of an elm. In a green meadow a ship drops anchor; keels of other ships skim a buried vineyard; and where graceful goats once grazed unsightly seals are lolling now.*

Sea nymphs are amazed to see woods, cities, and houses underwater. Dolphins swim in forests, brushing against high branches and shaking oak trees they bump into. A wolf paddles among sheep, and tawny lions and tigers are carried on the tide. The boar's tusks, powerful as lightning, do him no good now, nor do the stag's nimble legs help him when he's swept away. A wandering bird looks for land to light on and falls exhausted into the sea. Vast and unchecked, the ocean swallowed hills, and waves broke over mountain peaks, a sight strange to see. Most of the human race was carried away by the flood; those who were spared slowly starved to death from lack of food.

Phocis, a fertile land that separated Boeotia from the fields of Oeta while there *was* land, now was part of a sea, a broad plain of water that had suddenly appeared. A steep mountain there called Parnassus has twin peaks that penetrate the clouds and rise to the stars. Here Deucalion and his wife, Pyrrha, carried on a small raft, came to rest, for the floodwaters had covered everything else. They prayed to Corycian nymphs, to the mountain's deities, and to future-telling Themis, who held the seat of prophecy then.†

---

*1.300: "Modern taste might tend to regard the seal as a more attractive and graceful animal than the goat, but we have seen seals more frequently than did Ovid" (Anderson [1997] at 1.300, 180).

†1.320–321: 1.320: "Corycian nymphs" were nymphs who lived in a cave on Mount Parnassus (Anderson [1997] at 1.320–321, 182). 1.321: "the seat of prophecy" refers to Delphi, later the home of Apollo's oracle.

There was no better man than Deucalion at that time, none who loved justice more; and no woman was more in awe of the gods than Pyrrha. When
Jupiter saw the world submerged beneath great pools of standing water and
only one man surviving out of so many thousands, and only one woman surviving out of so many thousands, both blameless, both worshippers of the
gods, he scattered the clouds and, when the north wind had blown away the
storms, showed earth to heaven and showed heaven to earth.

The wrath of the sea subsided, and its ruler, Neptune, laid aside his trident
and calmed the waters. He summoned sea-blue Triton, who rose from the deep,
shoulders covered with purple shellfish, and ordered him to blow on his
conch-shell horn and signal the floods and currents to retreat.

Triton lifted up the hollow conch, great, spiral-shaped, and flared, which,
when it blares in the middle of the ocean, fills the shores from east to west with
its commanding sound. This time, too, when the god raised the horn to his
lips, wet from his dripping beard, and, as ordered, blew the call to retreat, all
the waters of land and sea heard the blast, and, when they heard it, all obeyed.

Now shores reappeared, now swollen streams returned to their beds, rivers
subsided, hills emerged, the earth rose, and dry ground spread as the flood
receded. Now, after so long a time, treetops were visible, rising out of the water,
leaves covered with mud. The world was restored.

When Deucalion saw it empty, lands desolated, enveloped in deep silence,
he said to Pyrrha, weeping: "O sister, wife, the one surviving woman, joined
to me by a common origin, a family tie, and then by marriage, now peril itself
unites us. In all the lands the sun beholds from dawn to dusk, we two are the
only people living still; the sea has claimed the rest, and even now there is no
certain guarantee that we shall continue to live; even now those storm clouds
terrify my mind.

"How would you now feel, poor dear, if fate had swept you to safety without
me? Could you bear your fear alone? Who would console you in your grief?
For I can tell you, my wife, if you were at the bottom of the sea, I would follow
you, and then I too would be at the bottom of the sea.

"If only I could use my father's art to create again the people of the world, if
only I could fashion figures out of earth and breathe life into them! Now the
human race survives in just us two. Such was the will of the gods. We are the
only specimens of humankind left on earth."

By the time he finished both were weeping. And now they decided they
should pray to the powers of heaven and look for guidance from the sacred lot.
They hurried together to the Castalian spring, still muddy, but flowing in its
familiar channel. When they had sprinkled water from it on their heads and
clothes, they made their way to the goddess' holy temple,* the pediments of
which were covered with green slime, the fires on its altars dead.

---

*1.373: The "goddess" is Themis, mentioned at 1.321.

When they reached the temple steps, they both fell to the ground and, trembling, kissed the cold stone and prayed: "If the powers of heaven can be swayed by righteous prayers and their hearts softened, if the wrath of the gods can be appeased, tell us, Themis, how our destroyed race can be restored and raise, kindest of goddesses, our sunken fortunes!"

The goddess was moved and answered with this oracle: "Leave the temple, cover your heads and loosen your garments, then toss the bones of your great mother behind you."

They stood for a long time, perplexed. Pyrrha broke the silence first. She could not obey the goddess, she said, and in a trembling voice asked her to forgive her, but she was afraid to offend her mother's shade by throwing her bones behind her. But they continued to ponder the words of the oracle, hard to understand, their meaning dark and hidden, turning them over together. Finally, the son of Prometheus calmed the daughter of Epimetheus, saying quietly: "Unless my mind deceives me, this is no impious oracle, urging us to do something that is forbidden: Our great mother is the earth! Yes, I'm convinced of it: Stones in the body of the earth are what she's calling bones. It's these we are commanded to toss behind our backs."

Although Pyrrha was swayed by her husband's interpretation, any hope she had was mixed with doubt; and neither one of them could really trust the goddess' instructions. But what would be the harm in trying? They came down from the temple, covered their heads, loosened their clothes, and threw stones behind them, as they had been ordered to do.

The stones—who would believe it, if antiquity did not attest it?—began to lose their hardness, their rigidity, began gradually to soften and, once softened, took new shapes, and as they grew and became more pliable, something resembling a human form could be made out, though still not well defined but rather like a marble statue just begun and not worked enough, more like a rough outline.

The moist and earthen part of the stones turned into flesh; the part that was solid and unbendable changed to bones; what were now veins stayed veins, and in short order, through the will of the gods, the stones cast behind him by Deucalion took on the likeness of men, those thrown by Pyrrha became women. From that we are a hard, enduring race and offer proof of our origin.

As the remaining moisture was warmed by the rays of the sun, and mud from the swamps swelled in the heat, the earth of itself created other living creatures with different forms. And teeming matter, fed by the life-giving soil as in a mother's womb, began to develop and gradually take on shapes of various kinds.

The same thing happens when the Nile recedes from flooded fields, and its waters return to their original bed: The mud newly deposited cooks in the sun, and farmers find a host of living things when they turn over the soil. Some of them they see at the very moment of their birth, some half-formed and lacking all their parts; and often in the same organism one end is alive while the other end is still raw earth. The reason is that moisture and heat, when they blend, conceive life, and from these two elements all things arise. Although fire is hostile to water, moist heat generates all things, and a "harmony of discord" is the right condition for producing life.*

And so when earth, coated with silt from the recent flood, grew hot again from the heat of the sun pouring down from the sky, she brought forth number-less forms of life, not only restoring creatures from before the flood, but also making strange new monsters.[2]

Although she would have preferred not to, at that time she gave birth to you, too, mighty Python, a serpent unknown till then. To the newly born people you were a thing of horror, so vast the area of Mount Parnassus that you cov-ered. Into this monster Apollo, god of the bow, emptied almost the entire con-tents of his quiver—deadly arrows till now used only on goats and fleeing deer—and killed it, finally, with a thousand shafts, whose sheer weight forced it to the ground, its black wounds streaming poison.

And lest the passage of time wipe out the fame of this exploit, Apollo founded sacred games, contests people flocked to, and he called them "Pyth-ian" from the name of the serpent. The young men victorious here in competi-tions of fists or feet or chariot received a crown of oak leaves as their prize. For the laurel did not yet exist, and the god crowned his long and handsome locks with leaves from any tree.

Apollo's first love was Daphne, Peneus' daughter, a love blind chance was not the cause of, but Cupid's savage anger. For the Delian god, proud of himself because of his recent victory over the serpent, saw Cupid drawing his bow and said to him: "What are you doing, you silly boy, with such a powerful weapon? A bow like that looks better on *my* shoulder, for I can hit anything—any ani-mal I hunt, an enemy—in fact, just now I killed the poison-bloated Python with more arrows than I can count, and he's flat on the ground, his rotting belly crushing numberless acres. Be satisfied to arouse a little passion now and then with your torch; you certainly should not consider yourself in the same class as me!"

The son of Venus in reply: "Well, Apollo, maybe you *can* hit everything you shoot an arrow at, but I'm going to hit you now with one of mine—and I'm better than you at archery to the same degree that all living creatures are infe-rior to you, a god!"

With that, he flew through the air on whirring wings and lighted at once on the shady peak of Mount Parnassus and drew two arrows from his quiver, of two quite different kinds. One drives love away, the other makes it happen; the one that makes it happen has a sharp and shining golden point, the one that

---

*1.433: "harmony of discord" translates Ovid's phrase *discors concordia,* a phrase used by Horace at *Epistles* 1.12.19 (*concordia discors*) to describe the way the universe works.

drives it away is blunt and tipped with lead. This is the one he shot at the nymph, Peneus' daughter, and shot the other at Apollo, wounding him all the way to the bone.

Immediately one was in love, the other ran from the very thought of love, delighting in her woodland haunts and in the skins of the animals she caught, tying a fillet around her head to hold her tangled hair in place and competing with Diana. Many boys pursued her, but she drove them off and roamed the solitary woods innocent of men, indeed, intolerant of them, no thought of weddings, love, or marriage. Often her father would say to her, "Daughter dear, you owe me a son-in-law." Often her father would say again, "You owe me grandsons, daughter dear."

But Daphne hated wedding torches as though they were crime itself, and, lovely of face, though shy and blushing, she twined her arms around her father's neck, beguiling him, and said: "Dear Papa, let me enjoy being unmarried, forever! Diana's father long ago granted this to her." Peneus did give in, but that loveliness of yours, Daphne, keeps you from having what you want, and your own beauty is at odds with your prayer.

Apollo sees her, loves her, wants her in his bed, and what he wants he hopes to have, and his own oracles fool him. As dry stubble burns in a field when the grain is cut, as a bush catches fire when a traveler accidentally brushes his torch against it or tosses it there at daybreak, so the god went up in flames, his whole heart burning, and fed his empty love on hope.

He saw her uncombed hair falling down around her neck and said to himself, "What if it were combed?" He saw her eyes, shining like stars, saw her lips (wasn't satisfied just to see them), admired her fingers, her hands, her arms, her shoulders, more than half bare, and what he didn't see he thought more lovely still.

But she ran away, swifter than a summer breeze, and kept on running when he called after her: "Nymph, please, daughter of Peneus, wait! I'm not your enemy! Wait, nymph! You're acting like a lamb fleeing a wolf, like a doe fleeing a lion, like a dove on trembling wing fleeing an eagle, when they're all trying to escape their natural enemies. But *love*'s the reason I'm chasing you!

"Oh dear me! I'm afraid you'll fall and scratch your legs on briars and it will be my fault! These are rough places you're going through. Please don't run so fast, slow down, and I won't chase you so fast!

"You should at least find out who it is that's trying to catch you: I'm no mountain yokel, no crude sheep herder out here tending sheep. You silly girl, you simply do not know whom you're running from, and that's why you're running.

"I'm the god that Delphi and Claros and Tenedos and Patara are all subject to! My father is Jupiter! Because of me what's going to happen, what has happened, and what's happening right now are all known. Because of me words and music make perfect harmony.

"My arrows always hit their target, it's true, but there's one arrow more accurate than mine, and it just now struck me in the heart—and I was fancy-free till now!

"Why, I invented medicine! I'm called healer throughout the world! Herbs and their power to cure are under my control. But, alas, there's not an herb in the world to cure love with, and the arts that I'm the master of, that help all others, don't help me now at all!"

He had much more to say, but the girl ran on, afraid, leaving him and his words trailing behind. Then, too, she was a lovely sight to see: Her garment fluttering open in the wind revealed her naked body, her hair was streaming behind her on the breeze, and running made her more beautiful still.

The youthful god could not endure to waste more breath on flattery—and love itself was urging him on—so he sped up and was hard on her heels: like a greyhound, when he sees a wild rabbit in an open field and runs for his dinner, the rabbit for his life: the hound so close—and yet, and yet, not quite— yet hoping, straining, his muzzle brushing the hopping feet. The rabbit, not sure if he's caught, snatches himself from the snapping teeth, pulls away from the jaws just grazing him. So the god and the girl both ran as fast as they could, he from hope, she from fear, but the one pursuing, sped by wings of love, ran faster, would not let up, hung on her back, was breathing on her hair, breathing down her neck.

Pale, exhausted, and overcome by the effort of running so far so fast, Daphne saw Peneus' waters. "Father, help me!" she cried. "If rivers have divine power—this beauty that has made me so attractive, rid me of it, change me!"

Even before her prayer was finished her legs were slow and heavy; a fine layer of bark covered her soft breasts; her hair turned to leaves; her arms became tree branches; her feet, just now so swift, were rooted in the ground; her head was now the top of a tree. Only her shining beauty stayed.

Apollo loved her still, and putting his hand on the trunk, he felt her heart still racing beneath the new bark. Throwing his arms around the branches as if they were limbs, he kissed the tree—and it shrank from his kisses, even though it was a tree.

"Well," he said, "since you cannot be my wife, at least you will be my tree: I'll wear you on my head, put you on my lyre and around my quiver, laurel, always!

"You will adorn Roman generals when joyful voices sing the hymn of triumph and the long processions ascend the Capitol. You will stand before the doors at the entrance to Augustus' palace, a faithful sentinel, and guard the crown of oak leaves there. And since I'm always young, and my hair is never cut, you, too, will always wear the glory of your foliage and be ever green." Before the Healer had finished, the laurel moved her new branches in reply, nodding the ones at the top as though nodding her head.[3]

There is a valley in Thessaly completely enclosed by steep, tree-covered slopes: They call it Tempe. Pouring from the foot of Mount Pindus, Peneus' foaming waters course through this valley, clouds of fine mist rise from his mighty falls and rain down on the trees below, and the sound of the roaring water can be heard far away. Here is the dwelling place, here the home, here the household gods of this great river. From a cave cut in these rocks he governs his waters and the nymphs living in them.

Here the local rivers gathered first, unsure whether to congratulate Peneus or to console him: the poplar-lined Sperchios, the turbulent Enipeus, the ancient Apidanus, the gentle Amphrysos, the Aeas, and soon the other rivers, as their currents carried them, bringing their weary wandering waters to the sea.

Inachus alone was absent. Hiding deep in his cave, he fed his waters with his own tears, poor fellow, grieving for his daughter Io, believing she was lost. He didn't know whether she was still alive or whether she was with the shades below, but since he couldn't find her anywhere, he thought she was gone and feared the worst.

Jupiter had seen Io returning from her father's stream and said to her: "You, girl! Jove deserves a girl like you. One of these days you'll make some mortal happy in bed, but for now, get yourself into the woods there, out of the heat of the noonday sun and into the shade"—he pointed to the woods and the shade he meant—"and if you're afraid to enter by yourself a place where wild beasts may lurk, know that you can safely go to the remotest part of any forest with a god as your protector—not a minor god, either, but the god who holds heaven's scepter in his mighty hand, the god who hurls down lightning from the sky—Hey! Come back here!" For she had run away.

Soon she had passed the pastures of Lerna and the woods and fields by Mount Lyrceum, but then the god enveloped the land in a sudden fog for miles around, stopped her in her tracks, and raped the innocent girl.

Juno, meanwhile, looked down into Argos, amazed that clouds had suddenly made it dark as night while there was daylight everywhere else. It wasn't river fog, she knew, and it didn't come from moisture in the ground. She looked around to see where her husband was, for she long had known about his furtive love affairs—had caught him at it many times. Not finding him at home in heaven she said, "Unless I'm wrong, I'm *being* wronged," and gliding down from the upper air touched ground and ordered the fog to lift.

Jupiter had already sensed his wife coming and had changed the daughter of Inachus into a sleek white heifer. (She made a beautiful cow, too.) Juno coolly appraised it, admired its beauty in spite of herself, and asked her husband whose it was and where it came from and what herd it belonged to, as if she didn't know the truth. Born from the earth, he said—a lie, of course, so she would stop asking who the original owner was. Juno asked if she could have it as a gift.

What to do? It's cruel to hand over his beloved, but it looks suspicious not to give her up: Embarrassment says hand her over; don't give her up, says love.

Love would have conquered embarrassment, but if he denied such a trifling gift as a heifer to a member of his own family, who even shared his bed, it would hardly seem to be just a heifer.

Though Jupiter's latest heartthrob now belonged to her, Juno's worries did not immediately go away. She was fearful of her husband and nervous about his secret love, until she gave Io to Argus, Arestor's son, to keep an eye on, or eyes on, for Argus had a hundred eyes all over his head. Only two ever slept at a time; the others stayed awake and watched. No matter which way he faced, Argus was always looking at Io; he had his eyes on Io even when his back was turned.

During the day he let her graze, but when the sun sank below the horizon he put a halter around her neck—adding insult to injury—and penned her up. She nibbled tree leaves, fed on bitter grass, slept on the ground, often the bare ground, poor thing, and drank muddy water. When she tried to hold out her arms to Argus to beg for mercy, she didn't have arms to beg for mercy with, and when she tried to wail, she could only moo and was frightened by the sound, terrified of her own voice!

She came to the banks of the river where she used to play, the banks of the Inachus,* her father, and when she saw her strange new horns reflected in the water, she was frightened and fled in terror from herself. Her sister nymphs didn't know who she was, nor did Inachus himself, but she trailed along behind her father and her sisters and let them pat her, offering herself to them to admire.

Old Inachus pulled up grass and fed it to her, and she licked his hands and kissed his hands and could not keep from crying. And if only she could make the words come, she would beg for help—and say her name and tell them what had happened to her. Instead of the words she could not speak, she traced letters in the dust with her hoof, spelling out her name and her sad change.

"Poor me!" her father cried, hanging on the groaning heifer's horns and snow-white neck, "Poor me! Are you the daughter I have searched for everywhere? I grieved for you less when you were lost than I grieve now, after I've found you! You don't say anything, you don't answer me, you only heave long sighs and, I suppose, do the only thing you can, moo back to me! In my ignorance I planned your wedding and hoped, first, for a son-in-law, then for grandsons. Now your husband has to come from a herd of cattle, and your son, too, has to come from a herd of cattle. I cannot simply die and end my sorrow. It hurts to be a god! And since the door of death is closed to me, my misery will last forever!"

As Inachus was bemoaning his state, eye-starred Argus, pushing him aside, seized the girl from her father and drove her into far-off pastures. He himself

---

*1.640: I read and translate *ripas*, "banks" (sc. *Inachidas*, "of the Inachus," 640), with the mss. (and Anderson [1982a], Haupt-Ehwald, LaFaye, and Lee), instead of *rictus*, Merkel's emendation, adopted by Miller-Goold.

climbed to the very top of a distant mountain where he could sit and look out in all directions.

The ruler of the gods could not bear Io's great distress, and so he summoned his son Mercury, whom shining Maia bore, and ordered him to kill Argus. Mercury took a moment to attach his wings to his feet, grab the wand that induces sleep, and put his cap on, and, ready now, leaped down to the earth from his father's stronghold. He took off his cap and removed his wings; all he kept was the wand: Pretending to be a shepherd, he used it to drive wild goats he had stolen on the way, while playing a tune on a set of pipes he had made.

Charmed by this music, which he had never heard before, Juno's watchman said: "You there, whoever you are, would you like to sit beside me on this rock? You won't find another place with grass more plentiful for your herd than it is here, and you can see how much shade there is. It's an ideal spot for shepherds."

Atlas' grandson sat down beside Argus and spent the day talking, whiling away the hours with story after story and trying to overcome the watchful eyes by playing on the pipes. But Argus fought the drowsiness that stole over him, and though some of his eyes were lulled to sleep, others stayed awake. He also asked how the pipes were made (for they had just been invented).

"At the foot of the mountains in cool Arcadia," the god began, "there was, among the Arcadian hamadryads, one without parallel: The nymphs called her Syrinx. She had escaped more than once from the satyrs and other gods of dark forests and fertile fields who chased her.

"Devoted to Diana, she kept herself a virgin for the goddess. She even dressed like Diana, and could have been taken for her, if her bow had not been made of horn and Diana's made of gold. Even so, she could certainly fool you.

"Now, Pan, wearing his pine-needle crown, once saw Syrinx coming down from Mount Lycaeus and said to her"—Mercury was about to repeat what it was Pan had said to her and to tell how the nymph spurned his entreaties and ran through untrodden ways till she came to the quiet waters of the sandy Ladon; how, since the river blocked her flight, she prayed to her sister nymphs in the stream to change her form; how Pan, just when he thought he had caught her, held marsh reeds in his hand instead of the nymph; how, as he sighed, his breath, moving through the reeds, made a high pure wailing sound; and how, charmed by this new instrument and the sweetness of its tone, the god had said, "I shall always make this music with you." And so, putting reeds of different lengths together, he fastened them with wax and thus preserved the girl's name, "Syrinx." Mercury was about to say all this, but he saw that every one of Argus' eyes was drooping, closing in sleep. He checked himself and deepened the sleep, caressing the creature's drowsy eyes with his magic wand, and then struck off the nodding head with his hooked sword, just where it joins the neck, and hurled the bloody thing from the rock they were sitting on, staining its steep sides with gore.

There you lie, Argus: The lights are out that lit a hundred eyes, and now a single darkness fills them all. But Juno took them and placed them in the plumage of her bird, in the feathers of its tail, like sparkling gems. She was furious, though, and in her anger quickly flung a terrifying madness into the eyes and mind of Jupiter's Argive sweetheart, burying goads deep in her heart, and drove her like a fugitive through the world.[4]

You, O Nile, became the end point for Io's great suffering. When she reached your banks she sank down on her knees, lifted up her head, and raised her eyes—she could raise nothing else—to the stars above, and with groans and tears and mournful mooing seemed to cry out to Jove and to beg him to end her misery. Jove then put his arms around his wife and asked her now, at last, to stop punishing Io, adding, "You don't have to worry any more; she will never again cause you unhappiness." And he called on the river Styx to witness his promise.

Juno softened, and Io got her original form back, became the same as she was before. The coarse hair fell from her body, her horns shrank, her eyes were no longer so round, her jaws receded, her hands and shoulders returned, and each hoof was divided into five nails. Nothing now remained of the cow she had been except her fair skin.

Relieved to have her two feet back again, the nymph stood upright, but was afraid to speak, lest she moo like a heifer, but then finally—timidly at first— she began to use the voice she had lost.

Now she is worshipped by the linen-wearing throngs as their most popular goddess. Epaphus was born to her, finally, from the seed of mighty Jove, people think, and in cities everywhere her son had temples beside his mother's.

Now Phaethon, the child of the Sun, was every bit the equal in age and spirit of this grandson of Inachus. Unwilling to defer to Epaphus, he proudly claimed Apollo as *his* father. One day Epaphus could bear Phaethon's boasting no longer and said to him, "You foolishly believe everything your mother tells you, and you puff yourself up with the notion that you have a father who is not your father."

Phaethon blushed and swallowed his anger, ashamed, but told his mother, Clymene, about Epaphus' insults, adding: "To make matters worse, Mother, as outspoken and quick-tempered as I am, I said nothing! I'm ashamed to take this kind of abuse and not fight back. So, Mother, if I really come from heavenly stock, give me some proof of such an exalted origin, grant me my place in heaven!" As he spoke he put his arms around his mother's neck and begged her, by his life and by her husband, Merops', life, by his sisters' marriages, for a convincing sign of who his father was.

It is not clear whether Clymene was moved more by Phaethon's prayers or by anger at the implied insult to herself, but, extending both arms to the sky and looking up at the Sun, she said: "I swear to you, my child, by this great light with its brilliant rays, this light that hears us and sees us, this Sun you're looking at, this Sun that regulates the world. From this Sun you were born! If this isn't true, let him forbid me to see him ever again, and let this daylight be the last I ever look upon!

"It won't take much of an effort on your part to find your father's house. The place where he rises is near the border of our land. If you want to, you can go there and ask him yourself."

At his mother's words, Phaethon sprang up eagerly, seeing the heights of heaven in his mind. He crossed his own land, Ethiopia, and India, lying just beneath the sun, and quickly came to the land where his father rises.[5]

BOOK TWO

The palace of the Sun rose high on lofty columns of bright gold and fiery copper-gold; its pediments glistened with ivory carvings; its silver doors gleamed with rays of light. The artwork on the doors surpassed its medium, for on them Vulcan had engraved the seas that surround the lands, the great globe of the earth, and the overarching sky. In the waters go the sea-blue gods: melodious Triton; ever-changing Proteus; Aegaeon, resting his hundred arms on the mighty backs of whales; and Doris and her daughters—some swimming, some sitting on a rock in the sun to dry their sea-green hair, some riding the backs of fish—not all the same, not entirely different, either, but with the family resemblance sisters have.

On land the craftsman god had fashioned men and cities, forests and wild animals, and streams and nymphs and other woodland deities. Above these he carved a gleaming sky and the signs of the zodiac, six on the door on the right, six on the one on the left.

When Clymene's son arrived here on the ascending path and entered the halls of the father he wasn't sure was his, he went at once into his presence but stopped a good way off, for if he came any closer he wouldn't be able to bear the light.

Wrapped in a purple cloak, Phoebus was sitting on a throne sparkling with emeralds. To his right and to his left stood the Day, the Month, the Year, the Centuries, and the Hours, stationed at regular intervals, and the new Spring, wearing a crown of flowers; Summer stood there, too, naked except for a garland made from ears of grain; and Autumn was there, stained by the grapes he had trampled, and icy Winter, bristling with snow-white hair.

In their midst the Sun who sees all things fixed his eyes on the boy, trembling at all the strange new sights, and asked: "Why have you come here? What are you looking for at this palace, Phaethon, my son?—for I'll never deny that I'm your father."

The boy replied, "O light common to the vast world, Phoebus—Father?—
if you'll let me call you Father, and if Clymene is not cloaking her guilt with a
false story: Give some sign, Father, to make people believe I'm truly your son,
and drive this doubt from my mind!"

When Phaethon had finished speaking, his father removed the crown of sun
rays shining all around his head and motioned him to come nearer. He embraced him saying: "You are indeed my son, and you deserve to be recognized
as my son. Clymene told you the truth about your birth. To remove all doubt,
ask for anything you want, and I shall gladly give it to you! Let the river the
gods swear by, the river I've never seen, be witness to this promise!"

The words were hardly out of his mouth when the boy asked for his father's
chariot and the chance to drive his winged horses for one day. The father instantly regretted his oath. Shaking his radiant head, he said: "It was a foolish
promise I made because of what you asked for; I wish I could take it back! Let
me tell you: This is the only thing I would deny you, my son. At least I can try
to talk you out of it. What you want is dangerous! This is a very large gift you
have asked for, Phaethon. It's beyond your powers; you're too young; you're
also a mortal; what you want is not for mortals. In your ignorance you want
something not even the gods can have. Though each may do as he pleases, not
one of them is strong enough to stand in that fire-bearing chariot except me.
Even the ruler of vast Olympus, the god who hurls the savage lightning bolts
with his terrible right hand, even *he* could not drive this chariot, and what do
we have more powerful than Jove?

"The way is very steep at the beginning, and the horses, fresh though they
are in the morning, can barely struggle up it. The path reaches its highest point
in the middle of the sky, and I myself am often afraid to look down on the land
and sea below, and my heart races with fear. At the end the path drops sharply
and requires steady control. Then, even Tethys herself, who receives me in her
waters, is always afraid I'll plunge headlong into the sea.

"The sky, moreover, is constantly turning, and it pulls the stars as it turns
and sets them spinning rapidly. I'm struggling, meanwhile, to go in the opposite direction, making my way against the motion of the swiftly rotating sphere
as it sweeps everything along with it. Suppose I give you the chariot. What will
you do? Will you be able to go contrary to the revolving poles and not let them
carry you away, as they swiftly move?

"Perhaps you imagine sacred groves up there, cities of the gods, and temples
filled with gifts. Not so. There are hidden dangers lurking along the route, and
images of wild beasts. Though you stay on the course and make no wrong
turns, you must nevertheless pass through the horns of Taurus, who stands in
your way, and through the bow of Sagittarius and the mouth of the raging Lion,
and Scorpio, who moves his vicious pincers in a mighty arc, and Cancer the
crab, who sweeps his claws in just the opposite direction. Nor will it be easy
for you to control those fiery horses, snorting flames from the fires that rage in

their breasts. I can barely control them myself when they're mad to run and fight the reins.

"Don't let me give you a fatal gift, my son, and while you still can, change your wish! I know you want clear proof so you can believe you were born of my blood. I am giving you clear proof by being afraid for you, and I am proving that I am your father by the father's fear I feel. Here, look at my face—and I only wish you could peer into my heart and see a father's sorrow there! Think of all the wealth the world possesses and ask for something from the great abundance of good things in the sky, the land, and the sea. I won't say no. This is the only thing I do not want to give you. It's really a punishment, not a present. Yes, Phaethon, a punishment is what you're asking for, not a gift!

"Why are you putting your sweet arms around my neck, foolish boy? Don't doubt it; it will be done! (I have sworn by the waters of the Styx.) You will get your wish, only wish more wisely!" Such was his warning. But Phaethon rejected it and kept to his intention, for he was on fire to drive the horses. So after delaying as long as he could, his father led the boy to the high chariot, the work of Vulcan. The axle was made of solid gold, the pole was golden, too, and rims of gold ran round arrays of silver spokes. The yoke was studded with rows of topaz and other precious stones that reflected Phoebus' own light back to him.

While noble Phaethon was admiring the various parts of the chariot and examining the craftsmanship, behold, in the brightening east, Dawn, already awake, threw open the crimson doors and the courtyard, filled with roses. The stars scattered, driven off by Lucifer, the last to leave his station in the sky.

As the Titan sun saw Lucifer heading for earth, the world becoming red, and the horns of the crescent moon beginning to fade, he commanded the Hours to be quick and yoke the horses. The goddesses hurried to obey his orders and from the mangers on high led the team, full of ambrosia and belching fire, and fitted them in the jangling harness.

Then the father coated his son's face with a sacred ointment, so he could withstand the searing heat, and placed his crown of rays upon the boy's head. Heaving a sigh from his anxious heart, a presage of sorrow, he said: "At least heed this warning from your father, if you can: Use the whip sparingly, son, and keep a powerful grip on the reins. The horses are naturally inclined to run; your task is to hold them back when they want to fly.

"Don't try to drive straight through the five zones of heaven! There is a broadly curving path cut at an angle and confined to the three middle zones that avoids both the south pole and the Great Bear where it meets the north wind. Follow this route—you'll see my wheel tracks clearly.

"So that heaven and earth can receive equal amounts of heat, don't take the chariot too low, nor climb up through the highest part of the sky. If you fly too high, you'll burn up the homes in heaven; go too low, and you'll burn up the homes on earth. The safest way is through the middle.

"Don't veer too far to the right, toward the coiled Serpent in the north, nor drive too far to the left, toward the Altar set low in the south. Maintain a course midway between them. The rest I leave to luck, and I hope it helps you and gives you better advice than you have given yourself.

"While I've been speaking, night that brings the dew has touched the markers set on the shore of the west, and we can wait no longer. We are summoned; dawn is gleaming, darkness fleeing.

"Hold the reins tightly in your hands, or if you can have a change of heart, take my advice—and not my team and car! While you still can, while you still stand on solid ground, before you step up into the chariot you want to drive in your ignorance—let me bring the world sunlight, and you can watch and be safe!"

But Phaethon climbed into the chariot, light with his boyish weight, and stood erect, delighted to grasp the slender reins, and thanked his father—who did not want his thanks.

Meanwhile, the winged horses of the sun—Torch, Dawn, Blaze, and Flame, the fourth—filled the air with their fiery whinnies and struck the barriers with their hooves. Then Tethys, unaware of what was waiting for her grandson, pushed the barriers back; and now before the team and driver lay the vast expanse of open sky.

Off at a run, the horses galloped through the air, parting the clouds before them. Climbing rapidly on their wings, they overtook the east wind, which had departed earlier from the same region of the sky. But the load was light and unfamiliar to the horses of the sun, the yoke without its usual weight. And just as ships that lack their normal cargo are much too buoyant and toss about in the sea, so the chariot, without its customary load, bounced and jolted high in the air as though it were empty.

Sensing this, the horses bolted, abandoned the well-worn path and ran out of control. Phaethon was terrified, for he didn't know how to slow the chariot, though the reins were now in his hands, nor did he know the way to go, and even had he known, he didn't know how to make the horses obey.

Then for the first time ever the frozen Bears were thawed by the rays of the sun and tried in vain to plunge into the sea, off limits to them. The Serpent, too, lying next to the icy pole, always sluggish from the cold and never a threat to anyone, now sweltered in the heat and felt a strange new wrath. You, too, Boötes, fled in alarm, so they say, though your wagon held you back and made you slow.

When poor Phaethon looked down from the summit of the sky at the earth far below, his eyes were blinded by all the light, and he turned pale and his knees began to tremble. He wished now that he had never touched his father's horses, was sorry now that he had learned who he was, sorry he had won out and gotten his wish. And now, longing to be called the son of Merops,* he was

---

*2.184: Merops is the husband of Phaethon's mother, Clymene (Bömer at 1.747–2.400, 1.221).

carried like a ship the north wind drives headlong, whose captain has given up the useless helm, abandoning the vessel to the gods and to his prayers.

What to do now? Vast reaches of sky lay behind him; much more stretched out before his eyes. In his mind he measured the distance each way, looking far ahead to the place where the sun was supposed to set, a place he would never reach, then looking back to where it rises. He had no idea what to do, was in a daze, couldn't let go the reins, yet wasn't strong enough to hold them, didn't even know the names of his horses. He saw images of monstrous beasts spread across the heavens and trembled at the sight.

There's a place in the sky where the Scorpion curves its claws into twin bows and, bending its arms and tail in opposite directions, extends its limbs across two signs of the zodiac. When the boy saw it, dripping with poisonous black sweat and threatening to lash him with its stinging tail, he froze, his mind went blank, and he dropped the reins.

The horses felt the slack traces lying on their backs and swerved from the path. With no one to restrain them, they raced down the air through a region unfamiliar to them, now running in this direction, now in that, wherever impulse drove them, crashing into stars fixed deep in the heavens, hauling the chariot across trackless space, one moment veering to the top of the sky, the next diving straight down to the earth. The moon was amazed to see her brother's horses running beneath her own, and low-lying rain clouds soon were scorched and smoking.

The heights of the earth burst into flame; other places, all moisture gone, grew hard and dry and cracked open, making fissures everywhere. White ash coated pasturelands, trees and leaves burned up together, and crops in dry fields fed the fire that killed them. But this was the least of it. Great cities and their walls burned to the ground; the conflagration reduced whole nations and their peoples to ashes. Mountains and forests burned: Mount Athos burned; Cilician Taurus, Tmolus, and Oeta burned; Ida, once filled with mountain springs, now dried up; Helicon, home of the maiden Muses, burned; and Haemus burned, not yet linked to Orpheus.

Aetna was ablaze with flames from two huge fires; Parnassus with its twin peaks, Eryx, Cynthus, Othrys, all burned, and Rhodope, too, its snows melted and gone at last. Mimas, Dindyma, Mycale, and Cithaeron (dedicated to the rites of Dionysus) were all on fire. Scythia's chill climate was useless: Fire raged on Caucasus; Ossa, Pindus, and Olympus, larger than either, burned. The Alps, towering in the air, and the cloud-covered Apennines were all on fire.

Phaethon saw all parts of the world in flames, and he could not endure such heat. The air he breathed seemed like a blast from a fiery furnace, and he felt the chariot glowing red hot. Enveloped in burning smoke, covered with clouds of soot, unable to bear the sparks and ashes spewing upward, he hurtled through the air at the mercy of the winged horses, not knowing where he was going, not knowing even where he was.

It was then, people believe, that the blood of the Aethiopians rushed to the surface of their bodies, and they turned black; then that Libya became an arid desert, when the heat carried off its waters; then that the nymphs let down their hair and wept for their lakes and fountains; and then that Boeotia looked for its Dirce, Argos for its Amymone, and Ephyre for the waters of Pirene.

Nor did rivers that happened to have wide banks remain safe: The waters of the Don, grand old Peneus, and Mysian Caicus were all boiling, and those of swiftly flowing Ismenus and Arcadian Erymanthus, too. Xanthus was on fire a second time; and yellow Lycormas burned, along with Meander, who delights in his stream as it curves back and forth. Thracian Melas, Laconian Eurotas, and Euphrates in Babylon all caught fire. Orontes, swiftly flowing Thermodon, Ganges, Phasis, and Danube all burned. Alpheus was boiling; the banks of Spercheus were in flames; the nuggets of gold that Tagus rolls along in its bed flowed molten now, and the singing swans that used to throng Cayster's banks were scalded in the middle of their stream. The Nile fled in terror to the ends of the earth and hid his head, and hides it still. His seven mouths lay dry and dusty, seven beds without a stream.

The same disaster dried up Thracian Hebrus, along with the Strymon and the western rivers: the Rhine, the Rhône, the Po, and our Tiber, which was promised power over the world. The earth gaped open with cracks everywhere, and light invaded Tartarus and struck terror in the king and queen of the underworld. The oceans shrank; what once was sea was now a sea of sand; and mountains underwater once now emerged and increased the scattered islands of the Cyclades.

Fish sought the lower depths, and dolphins dared not make their graceful curving leaps above the level of the waves. Dead seals floated belly-up on the surface of the sea, and even the sea god Nereus, his wife, Doris, and their daughters, so they say, hid in their underwater caves, now much too warm. Three times Neptune grimly dared to lift his arms and face out of the water, three times he was unable to endure the fiery air.

But the nurturing earth, surrounded by the ocean and amid the waters of the sea and her own springs (now only trickling and gone to hide in their mother's dark recesses), raised her scorched and weary head and, shielding her face with her hands, gave a great shudder, shaking the world, then sank back a little, below her normal posture, and in a cracked and breaking voice said: "If this pleases you, if I deserve this, then why, O mightiest of the gods, why don't you strike me with your lightning now? If I am going to perish by fire, let me perish by your fire. Make my death easier to bear with the thought that you're the cause! Indeed, I can barely open my mouth to say these words"— the smoke had forced her to keep it closed.

"Look at my singed hair! Look at the hot ashes in my eyes, all over my face! Is this my reward, the thanks I get for my fertility, for my service, for enduring the wounds of the crooked plow and the assaults of the hoe, for being worked all year long, for providing fodder for the flocks and grain for bread for the human race—even incense for you?

"But if I deserve this death, why do the seas deserve it? Why does your brother deserve it? Why are the waters, given to him by lot, shrinking and receding farther from the heights of heaven? And if you have no feeling for your brother or for me, at least take pity on your own sky! Look at the poles: Both are smoking! If this fire consumes them, your very palace will fall!

"Atlas himself is struggling now, barely able to hold the burning globe upon his shoulders! If the seas, if the earth, if the palace of heaven perish, we shall all be hurled back into ancient chaos! Please! Save from these flames whatever still survives! Show that you care about the universe!"

Earth stopped speaking now, for she could stand the heat no longer and was unable to say more. She hid her face deep in herself, in a cave near the underworld.

Then the father all-powerful called the gods to witness, especially the god who had given the boy the chariot, and said: Unless he came to the rescue, all that exists would die a terrible death. He then climbed to the top of heaven, where he always went when he wanted to cover the earth with clouds, set the thunder rolling, and hurl his quivering lightning bolts. But now he had no clouds with which to cover the earth, no storms to spill from the sky. He thundered instead, and hefting a lightning bolt in his hand, drew it back and hurled it at the chariot, and at one stroke blasted the life from the boy, the boy from the car, and stopped the raging fire with fire.

The horses reared in panic, leaped apart, threw off the yoke, sundering the traces, and left them far behind. Here lay the reins; there the axle, snapped off from the pole; over here spokes and the smashed wheels: bits and pieces of the wrecked chariot, scattered far and wide.

And Phaethon, tumbling headlong, his red hair streaming fire, fell in a broad arc through the air, like a shooting star that seems, sometimes, to fall down a calm, clear sky, but doesn't really fall. On the other side of the world, far from his fatherland, the great Eridanus received him, and bathed his burning face in his cool waters. His body, charred by lightning, nymphs of the west laid in a grave and then inscribed this poem on his tomb.

> *Phaethon lies buried at this spot;*
> *he yearned to drive his father's chariot.*
> *Though he lost control, fell far, and died,*
> *It was a great and daring deed he tried.*

His wretched father, heartsick and grieving, covered his face and hid himself away, and they say (if we can believe it) one whole day went by without the sun. Fires still raging made the only light, and so there was some benefit in that catastrophe.

After Clymene had said what has to be said at such a tragic time, she wandered the entire world, beside herself with grief, digging her nails into her breasts, searching at first for the lifeless limbs, and then only for his bones. And she finally found them, buried in a riverbank in a foreign land. She fell on the grave and filled the letters of his name cut in the marble with her tears and pressed her warm bare breasts on the cold tombstone. Phaethon's sisters, the daughters of the sun, wept bitterly, too, their tears an empty offering to their dead brother, and, beating their breasts, they flung themselves upon his grave and day and night called out, "Phaethon!"—but he could not hear their pitiful cries.

And now the crescent moon had grown round and full four times. The sisters of Phaethon had just finished the lamentation that was now their custom (for habit had made it custom), when Phaethusa, the eldest, trying to prostrate herself on the ground, cried out: Her feet would not move! Fair Lampetie tried to come to her, but was suddenly gripped by roots. When the third sister began to tear her hair—she pulled out leaves! Then Lampetie groaned when she saw her legs held by the trunk of a tree, while Phaethusa wept at the loss of her arms, for they were now branches. And as they watched in horror, bark covered their thighs and slowly spread over their wombs and breasts and shoulders and hands, till only their mouths remained, crying, "Mother!"

But what could their mother do but run in panic now to this one, now to that one, and kiss them while she could? Nor was that enough: She tried to tear their bodies away from their tree trunks—and broke off in her hands tender branches oozing blood, as from a wound.

"Stop, Mother! Please!" each one cried, in pain, "Stop! Please! You are tearing my body when you tear the tree, but now, farewell . . . ," and the spreading bark enclosed these last words. Their tears, dripping from new branches, hardened into amber in the sun, fell into the sparkling river, and were carried downstream, to be worn someday by the young wives of Rome.

Cycnus, son of Sthenelus, witnessed this miracle—he was a cousin on your mother's side, Phaethon, but closer still in friendship. He had abandoned his kingdom (for he had once ruled the Ligurian people and their great cities), and the sound of his weeping filled the grassy banks and waters of the Eridanus and the woods the sisters were now part of. As he wept, his deep voice grew thin and reedy, his hair turned into white feathers, his neck lengthened above his chest, membranes joined his reddening fingers, wings covered his sides, and a rounded beak replaced his mouth. Cycnus was now a new kind of bird, a swan, and will not commit himself to the sky and to Jove, for he remembers the lightning bolt the god unjustly hurled at Phaethon. Instead, he seeks out pools and wide lakes and, hating fire, chooses streams to dwell in, for they are the opposite of fire.

Meanwhile, Phaethon's father, pale, his radiance lost, as he is when he's in eclipse, hated the light, hated himself, hated the day, gave himself to his grief, added anger to his sorrow, and refused his obligation to the world.

"Enough!" he said "Since the beginning of time I've had no rest. I'm tired of toiling endlessly without any thanks! Let someone else—anyone else—drive my chariot and its cargo of light! If no one can be found, and all the gods say they cannot, let Jupiter himself drive it—at least while he's trying to he'll have to lay aside those lightning bolts that bereave fathers! Once he has felt the power of my horses and their fiery hooves, he'll know that the boy who couldn't control them did not deserve to die."

All the gods had gathered around the Sun while he was speaking and begged him not to cover the world in darkness. Jupiter, also, tried to justify the light-ning bolts he had hurled, and to his entreaties, king that he was, he added threats. Then Phoebus rounded up the still-trembling, frantic horses. Filled with grief and rage, he struck them with his goad and lashed them with his whip (for he was truly full of rage), rebuking them and blaming them, too, for his son's death.[6]

And now the father all-powerful made a tour of the mighty walls of heaven, inspecting them to see if any part of them might have been damaged by the fire and was about to collapse. When he saw that they were standing firm and strong, he looked down at the earth and the sufferings of the human race.

He was more worried about his own Arcadia than any other place: He re-stored its springs and rivers, reluctant to flow, put new grass on the ground, new leaves on the trees, and ordered the charred and blackened forests to be green again. As he traveled back and forth, he noticed an Arcadian girl, was taken with her, and the fire of passion, once kindled, burned to the very mar-row of his bones.

Not for her the task of carding wool or changing daily the way she wore her hair. With her tunic pinned up, a white ribbon on her head to keep her tousled hair in place, and a smooth javelin in her hand sometimes, sometimes a bow, she was a soldier of Diana. No girl who set foot on Mount Maenalus was more attractive to Diana than she was. But no preference lasts for long.

One day when the sun was high—a little past the midpoint of its course— Callisto (for that was the girl's name) entered a grove where the trees had never felt an axe, removed the brightly covered quiver from her shoulder, unstrung her limber bow, and stretched out in a grassy spot with her quiver as a pillow.

Jupiter saw her resting, with no one standing guard, and said to himself, "I'm pretty sure my wife won't find out about this little interlude, but if she does, it's worth a fight or two!"

At once he put on the features and dress of Diana and said to Callisto: "Dear girl, aren't you one of my companions? Where have you been hunting?" Jump-ing up from the grass, she replied, "Hail goddess, greater than Jove, as far as I'm concerned—and I don't care if he hears me!"

Jupiter *did* hear, and laughed, delighted that she preferred him to himself (so to speak), and kissed her—not a chaste kiss, not the way a girl should kiss another girl. As she was about to tell him where she had been hunting, he grabbed her (end of conversation), and with his assault gave himself away.

She fought, indeed she did, she fought as much as a girl can. If only you had seen it, Juno, you would have been easier on her. But whom can a girl fight against and win? Or who can fight against Jove and win? Her conqueror then returned to the lofty heights of the gods. Callisto, though, hated the grove and the trees that shared her guilty secret, and as she was leaving, she almost forgot to pick up her quiver full of arrows and pull down the bow she had hung on the limb of a tree.

Now came Diana with her band of nymphs, making her way along lofty Maenalus, proud of the game she had killed. She saw Callisto and called out to her. But when the girl heard her name she ran away, fearful at first that it was Jupiter again, posing as the goddess. But then, seeing the other nymphs with Diana, she realized it wasn't a trick and came up to the group.

Alas, how hard it is not to let the guilt one feels show in one's face! Reluctantly Callisto raised her eyes from the ground, but did not take her place at the goddess' side at the head of the band of nymphs (as she usually did), but was silent and by blushing scarlet gave every sign of the violence done to her innocence. And if Diana had not been a virgin, she could have sensed the girl's guilt in a thousand ways. They say the nymphs sensed it . . .

The crescent moon was growing round and full for the ninth time when the goddess left off hunting early one day, weary from her brother's rays, and found a cool grove where a rippling stream flowed over a bed of fine sand. She liked the place and, testing the water with her toe, liked the water, too. "Since no one can see us," she said, "let's take off our clothes and go for a swim in this stream."

All removed their tunics except Callisto, who blushed and hesitated, looking for reasons to delay. Her clothing was then stripped off, and now her naked body revealed her crime. Horrified, she tried to hide her belly with her hands. "Away from here at once! How dare you pollute this sacred stream!" Diana shouted, and ordered her to leave her and the other maidens.

The wife of the mighty thunderer had long been aware of her husband's love affair but waited to punish this girlfriend of his until the right time came. When Callisto gave birth to a son named Arcas (that in itself made Juno angry), there was no reason, the goddess thought, to delay the punishment any longer.

Glowering at the infant, she said to the girl: "This was no doubt your crowning touch, you whore, to get pregnant and have a child, humiliate me openly, and provide living proof of my Jove's disgrace. But you won't get away with it, you little fool: I'll take away that beauty of yours that you and my husband admire so much." And grabbing Callisto by the hair, she sent her sprawling to the ground. Extending her arms, the girl begged for mercy, but her arms bristled with shaggy black fur and her hands, growing, curved into claws and now worked like feet, and the lips Jove once adored widened into a broad snout.

To keep Callisto's prayers, her words of entreaty, from changing anyone's mind, Juno took away her power of speech: And now from her throat she gave out guttural, angry, threatening growls, enough to terrify a person. Her mind remained the same, though, after she became a bear, and her constant groaning bore witness to her wretched condition. Raising what hands she had to the sky, to the stars, she realized—though she could not utter the words—that Jove did not care. Not daring to rest in the lonely forest, how often did she find herself wandering in front of her own house and in fields that once were hers! How often did barking dogs drive her through rough and rocky places! A huntress, once, herself, she now fled in terror from other hunters.

Forgetting what she was, she often hid when she saw wild beasts. And though now a bear, she shuddered when she caught sight of other bears in the mountains, and was terrified of wolves, though her father, Lycaon, was now a wolf and ran with them.

One day she met her child, Arcas, now nearly fifteen and ignorant of who—or what—his mother was. He was hunting wild game and looking for suitable places in the Arcadian woods to lay his fine-meshed nets when he suddenly came upon her.

Callisto stopped when she saw him, seemed to recognize him, and as she stood there staring at him for an eternity, it seemed, he began to back away, frightened, not knowing who she was. She longed to come closer, and just as he was about to plant his deadly spear in her breast, all-powerful Jupiter stopped him, and in a single act the god lifted them up, removed the crime, sped them on the wind through the air, fixed them in the sky, and made them neighboring stars.

Juno, bursting with fury that the little bitch now shone among the stars, went down into the sea to white-haired Tethys and old Ocean, whom the gods themselves revere, and said, when they asked her why she had come: "You want to know why I, the queen of the gods, have come down here from my home in the upper air? I'll tell you why! Another woman has taken my place in heaven! Call me a liar if tonight, when darkness covers the world, you don't see stars recently raised to honor in the highest part of the sky at the farthest northern latitude, where the circuit around the pole is shortest. A deliberate insult to me!

"Is there anyone who would *not* want to hurt Juno—who will be afraid to—since I'm the only god it pays to injure? O what an achievement for me! Look how vast my power is! I wouldn't let her be a human being, so she was made a goddess! That's how I punish the guilty! That's my great power for you!

"Let him take away her animal face and give her back her original beauty, as he did before with Io! Why doesn't he just get rid of Juno, take *her* as his bride, put her in my bed, and have Lycaon as his father-in-law?

"If this scornful treatment of your foster daughter upsets you, keep those starry bears out of your deep blue sea, reject those stars now put in heaven as payment for fornication! Don't let that whore bathe in your pure waters!" And the gods of the sea gave their assent.[7]

Juno then made her way through the clear upper air in a light chariot drawn

by her brightly colored peacocks—peacocks brightly colored when Argus
was slain, at the time when you, O talkative raven, suddenly turned black,
though you had been white. For this bird once had feathers silvery like snow,
once was, in fact, the peer of doves in whiteness, not a bit less white than the
geese whose loud honking would one day save the Capitol, no less white than
the water-loving swan. His tongue was his undoing: Because of that wagging
tongue, his original white color is now the opposite of white.

Now in all of Thessaly there was no one more beautiful than Coronis from
Larissa. She was certainly attractive to you, Apollo, as long as she was faithful—or not caught being unfaithful. But Apollo's bird, the raven, discovered
her infidelity, and, relentless tattler that he was, flew straight to his master to
reveal her secret sin.

The gossipy crow flew along beside the raven, wanting to know all there was
to know, and when she heard the reason for the raven's journey, said: "This trip
will do you no good. Do not ignore the warning I'm about to give you! Consider what I was, look at what I am today, and ask me what I did to deserve it.
You will learn that loyalty ruined me.

"Pallas once took Erichthonius, a child born motherless, and shut him up
in an Attic wicker basket and gave him and the basket to the three virgin
daughters of twin-bodied Cecrops, forbidding them to look at the baby she was
keeping hidden. I kept out of sight in the dense foliage of an elm and watched
to see what they would do. Two of them, Pandrosos and Herse, guarded in
good faith the basket entrusted to them. The third, Aglauros, called her sisters
timid and undid the knots. Inside they saw an infant with a snake stretched
out beside it. I reported to the goddess what they had done. As thanks for this
I was dropped as Minerva's protégée and demoted to a place below the night
owl! My punishment can serve as a warning to other birds not to run risks by
talking. But, you see, I hadn't gone to her first to ask for anything:* She had
sought *me* out! You can ask Pallas herself, angry though she is, she won't deny
this just because she's angry.

"For I was born the daughter of Coroneus, who was famous in Phocis (this
is well known), and I was once a royal princess. Wealthy suitors wanted to
marry me—don't blame me for that—but my beauty ruined me. For one day
when I was strolling along a sandy beach at the shore, as I was in the habit of
doing, the god of the sea saw me and was consumed with flames of desire.
After he spent much time and many flattering words entreating me, he resorted
to force and began to chase me. I ran, leaving the hard-packed shore, and soon
exhausted myself struggling in soft sand. I then called on gods and men for
help. No one human heard my cries, but the goddess Minerva came to my
rescue, one virgin to another. As I held out my arms to heaven, they turned

---

*2.566: I read *nec quicquam* with LaFaye and Anderson (1982a), rather than *nequiquam* with
Miller-Goold.

into fine wings with black feathers; I tried to throw off my cloak, but it became plumage that drove its quills deep into my skin. I tried to beat my bare breasts with my hands, but now I had neither breasts nor hands to beat them with. I tried to run, and now the sand was no longer a drag on my feet, as before: I rose from the ground and was soon carried high on the wind and given to Minerva as a blameless companion. But what good did this do me, if Nyctimene, who was turned into a bird because of her terrible sin, has taken my place of honor?*

"Or have you not heard that well-known tale, told all over Lesbos? About how Nyctimene defiled her father's bed? She is indeed a bird, but she's filled with guilt and shrinks from being seen, avoids the light of day, and hides her shame in darkness, hounded from the sky by all."

The raven replied to the crow's sad tale: "Trying to hold me back, are you? I hope you come to grief for it! You can keep your useless warning to yourself, for I don't want it!" He continued on his way and told his master that he had seen Coronis in bed with a young man from Thessaly. When Coronis' lover Apollo heard she had been unfaithful, his jaw dropped, the laurel slipped from his head, the lyre-pick fell from his hand, and the color drained from his face. Swelling with rage, he grabbed his trusty bow, drew back the string—and the breast that had lain so often beside his own, that breast he now pierced with a deadly accurate arrow. Coronis groaned when the shaft struck her, and as she pulled it from the wound the rich red blood gushed down her fair white body, and she cried, "You could have waited to punished me, Apollo, until I had first given birth. Now two of us will die together." That was as far as she got, for her life drained away with her blood, and mortal cold invaded her body, from which her soul had fled.

Alas! The lover regrets his cruel punishment but regrets it too late and hates himself for listening to the raven and becoming so enraged, hates the bird for forcing on him the knowledge of the crime that caused his grief, hates his bow, hates his hand, and hates the arrow so rashly shot. He holds the limp Coronis in his arms and struggles to revive her, but his effort is too late, his medical skill applied in vain.

After these useless attempts, Apollo saw a pyre being readied and Coronis' body about to be burned in its final fire. Then he began to groan from the depths of his being (for a god was not allowed to wet his face with tears), just like a mother cow when she watches the heavy hammer, poised above the head of her nursing calf, bash in its fragile skull with one sharp blow.

As he poured over her breast the fragrant perfume she could not appreciate and embraced her and carried out the rites for an unjust death, Phoebus could not bear to think of his own seed likewise turning to ashes, and he snatched

---

*2.590: Nyctimene, who was changed into the owl (2.591–595), was said by the crow to have replaced her in Minerva's favor at 2.563–564.

his son from the mother's womb and out of the fire and brought him to the cave of the centaur Chiron. As for the bird, expecting a reward for his tale, which, after all, wasn't false, Apollo forbade it to continue as a white bird among white birds, and it's a black raven now.[8]

Meanwhile, Chiron was delighted to have a foster child from divine stock and took great pleasure in the combined honor and responsibility. And now here comes the centaur's daughter, her red hair falling over her shoulders, whom the nymph Chariclo once gave birth to on the banks of a fast-flowing river and named Ocyrhoe:* Not content simply to master her father's arts, the girl also made predictions about the future.

And so, when her mind was gripped by the prophesying madness and she burned with the god, whom she held enclosed in her breast, Ocyrhoe looked at the infant and exclaimed: "Grow, little child, bringer of health to the whole world! Mortals will often owe their lives to you, you will even be given the power to bring souls back from the dead. But after you dare this once and provoke the gods' wrath, your grandfather's thunderbolt will stop you from restoring anyone's life ever again, and you will change from god to corpse, then back to god again from the corpse you were, and so will twice make your fate new.

"You too, dear father, immortal now and by the law of your birth created to live forever: A time will come when you will be in agony from the poisonous blood of the vicious Hydra that has entered your body through a wound, and you'll wish that you could die; and then the gods will release you from divinity and give you death, and the three fates will cut the threads of your life."

Part of his future remained for Ocyrhoe to tell. But then, with tears suddenly filling her eyes and rolling down her checks, she sighed deeply and said: "The fates interrupt me; I am forbidden to say more, stopped from using my voice. The gift of prophecy, which has brought down the anger of the god upon me, has not been worth the price: I would prefer not to have known the future. Now my face seems to be changing, now I enjoy eating grass, now I have an impulse to run through the open fields: I am turning into a mare, into a form like my father's. But why all mare? My father is both horse and man."

The last part of her lament was barely intelligible, and her words were garbled and followed by a sound that neither a human nor a horse would make, but, rather someone imitating a horse, and in a moment she was actually whinnying and moving her arms in the grass. Then her fingers merged, and their nails fused to form fine, smooth hooves, her face and neck grew longer, her long cloak became a tail, the hair lying loose about her neck was now a mane: Her form and voice alike were changed. This wondrous transformation gave her a new name, too.

Her father, Philyra's son Chiron, was distraught and demanded help from

---

*2.638: The name Ocyrhoe means "fast-flowing."

you, Apollo, but in vain, for you could not rescind great Jove's decree, nor, if you could have, were you there to rescind it, for you were living then in Elis, in rural Messenia. That was the time you wore an animal skin for a shepherd's cloak and carried a staff you had cut in the woods in one hand and a reed pipe made with seven reeds in the other.

And while you were thinking only of love and soothing yourself with your pipes, your cattle, left unattended, wandered into the fields of Pylus, so they say. Mercury, son of Atlas' daughter Maia, saw them and stealthily led them away and hid them in the woods. No one knew about this theft except an old man well known in that part of the country, called Battus by all his neighbors.

Now, Battus kept watch over the woods and grassy pastures of wealthy Neleus and guarded his herd of fine mares. The god approached him and, putting a friendly arm around his shoulder, drew him close and said, "Whoever you are, friend, if someone should ask you about this herd of cattle, say you haven't seen it. And as thanks for your trouble, accept this lovely cow as your reward!" And he gave him a cow. Battus took it, replying, "Don't give it a second thought! Do you see that stone there?" And he pointed to a stone. "That stone will talk before I do." Mercury then pretended to go on his way. A few minutes later he returned—changed in appearance, with a different voice—and said, "My good country fellow, have you seen any cattle going down this path? Help me get to the bottom of this and I'll give you a cow and its own bull to go with it."

And now with a reward promised him that was twice as much as the earlier one, the old man replied, "You'll find them at the foot of yonder mountains." Find them he did, at the foot of the mountains Battus had indicated.

Laughing, Mercury said, "Well, well, my false friend, will you give me away to myself—or give myself away to me?" And he turned him and his lying heart into hard flint, which even now is called "Informer," branded with infamy it in no way deserves.

Mercury then rose up on his two pairs of wings and looked down from the air on the fields of Munychia, the land so pleasing to Minerva, and on the cultivated groves of the Lyceum, the seat of all learning.* It happened that on that day young girls, according to custom, were carrying purest offerings in flower-covered baskets on their heads to the festive temple of Pallas, and as the god flew along he saw them returning from the temple, and he changed course and began circling above them. As when a kite, most rapacious of birds, spies entrails on an altar below but fears the priests crowding around the sacrifice and wheels in a circle, not daring to fly away, constantly turning and greedily eyeing what it hopes to have, so Mercury turned above the Athenian citadel, nimbly

---

*2.709–710: 2.709: Munychia was the name of the citadel of Piraeus, the port of Athens, and here stands for Athens itself (Bömer at 2.709, 1.405). 2.710: The grove of the Lyceum, just northeast of Athens, was the home of Aristotle's Peripatetic school of philosophy. With the adjective "cultivated" (*culti,* 2.710) Ovid "pun[s] on [the Lyceum's] future as the seat of Aristotle's school" (Wilkinson [1955] 167).

circling in the air. And as the morning star gleams brighter than other stars, and the golden light of the moon shines brighter still, so Herse outshone the other maidens as she walked in the procession, the glory of the parade and the pride of her companions.

The son of Jove stared down at her beauty in amazement and while hovering above her began to burn like a lead bullet hurled from a Balearic sling that catches fire as it flies through the air and begins to glow as it travels. Mercury swerved, swooped down from the sky, and landed on the ground. He didn't bother to disguise himself, being totally confident of his own good looks, and rightly so, though attention to his appearance didn't hurt: He smoothed his hair and arranged his cloak to make it hang properly, so that its golden border was completely visible; then made sure his wand, the one that causes sleep, or prevents it, was well polished, his winged sandals were gleaming, and his feet were wiped clean.

In a remote part of the palace there were three rooms decorated with ivory and tortoiseshell. You, Pandrosos, had the room on the right, Aglauros the one on the left, and Herse the one in the middle. Now, Aglauros was the first to see Mercury coming, and she boldly asked the god his name and why he had come. The grandson of Atlas and Pleione replied: "I am the one who carries my father's orders through the air—my father being Jupiter himself. And I'll be perfectly honest with you—I only hope you're willing to be a true friend to your sister and to be called my child's aunt: Herse is the reason I'm here. Please help me, because, you see, I'm in love."

Aglauros regarded him with the same glint in her eye that she had when she looked on golden-haired Minerva's hidden secret,* demanded a huge sum of gold for her cooperation, and then made him leave the house until he brought the gold.

Minerva the warrior goddess then fixed her savage eye on Aglauros and began to breathe so violently that her powerful chest heaved, the aegis on it moving with each breath. She remembered it was Aglauros who had removed the cover on the basket and revealed its secret when she looked at the child of Vulcan, spawned without a mother, though forbidden by Minerva to do this. And now she was about to gain the favor of the god and her sister and become rich as well with all the gold she had so greedily demanded. So the goddess hurried at once to the house of Envy.

That house, dripping with slime, was hidden at the bottom of a deep valley, where it received no sun and no fresh air: It was a depressing place, invaded by bone-chilling cold, always lacking a fire, always filled with fog.

When the dread goddess, fearsome in war, arrived there, she stood in front of the house—divine law forbade her to enter it†—and banged on the door with the butt of her spear. The door swung open under her blows; inside she

---

*2.748–749: "Minerva's hidden secret": see 2.552–561.
†2.766–767: "divine law forbade her to enter it": "[f]or fear of contamination" (Lafaye 1.63 n. 2).

saw Envy, chewing on the flesh of poisonous snakes, feeding her vileness; and she averted her eyes.

Envy rose slowly from the ground, dropping the half-eaten carcasses of the snakes, and shuffled to the door. When she saw the goddess, so beautiful, so imposing in her armor, she grimaced, then groaned, and gave a deep sigh. Her face was ghastly pale, her body gaunt and wasted. She could never look straight at anyone; her teeth were black and rotten, her breast was green with bile she had slobbered on it, and she drooled venom from her lips. She never laughed, except when someone's grief amused her; never slept, but tossed and turned with worry; looked sourly on any human success, the sight of it gnawing at her; and, biting others with envy, she was bitten herself—she was her own punishment.

Minerva loathed her, and now, speaking rapidly, said what she had come to say: "Infect one of Cecrops' daughters with your rotting slime. That's what you have to do. Her name is Aglauros." She left without another word and vaulted on her spear into the air. Envy watched the goddess departing out of the corner of her eye and muttered to herself, grieving at the thought that Minerva's mission would be successful. She picked up her staff, around which a chain of thorns was wound, and, wrapping herself in black clouds, set out, trampling flowers wherever she went; scorching the grass; knocking the tops off trees; and polluting people, cities, and homes with the wind she raised as she passed. Finally she saw Minerva's city, green and flourishing with talent, wealth, and festive peace, and could hardly keep from crying, for she saw nothing there to cry about.

Carrying out Minerva's orders, Envy entered the bedroom of Cecrops' daughter and touched the girl's breast with her hand, which was covered with mold, filled her heart with sharp thorns, and breathed a noxious poison into her, a black venom she made seep into her bones and lungs. And to make sure Aglauros grasped the cause of her malady, she put before her eyes a vision of her sister, her sister's happy marriage, and the handsome god, and made it all seem great and wonderful.

Agitated by this vision, Aglauros was eaten by a hidden torment, nervous all night long, anxious all day long. She moaned and in her misery slowly began to dissolve and run like ice melting in a winter sun, and burned at the thought of Herse's happiness, like a smoldering fire beneath a pile of crabgrass that slowly burns it up without a flame. She often wanted to die so as not to have to see such happiness, often wanted to report it like a crime to their stern father. Finally, she sat in front of the door, to block the god's way when he returned. Arriving, he coaxed and pleaded and spoke to her ever so gently. "Stop!" she said. "I'm not going to move until I force you to leave."

"Agreed!" Mercury replied. "Let's stand by that," and he opened the door with his divine wand. When Aglauros tried to rise, she could not straighten up, as though a heavy weight pressed down upon her. Indeed, she struggled to stand, but her legs were locked. A numbing cold stole through her fingers and toes, and her veins, with the blood now gone, turned white. As a malignant cancer, widespread, inoperable, creeps through the body, invading healthy organs and adding them to the diseased ones, so a deathly cold entered Aglauros little by little and closed the passageways so vital to life and breath. She did not try to speak, nor, had she tried, would she have found a passage for her voice. Her neck changed to stone, her face grew hard, and she sat, a bloodless statue—but not a white one, for the darkness of her mind had stained the stone.

When Mercury had thus punished the girl for her reckless words and impious mind, he left the land called Athens and made his way on beating wings to the heights of heaven.[9]

His father took him aside and, without giving the reason (it was love), said to him, "My son, always so faithful to carry out my orders, be quick now and descend at once with your usual speed and go to the land that looks up from the left at your mother among the Pleiades (the natives call it Sidon) and drive to the shore the royal herd you see grazing in a mountain pasture some distance from the sea." Thus his command, and already the bullocks, driven down from the mountain, were heading to the shore Jove had indicated, where the great king's daughter would often play in the company of Tyrian maidens.

Two things never fit together well, can never abide in one and the same place: majesty and infatuation. But now the father and ruler of the gods, whose right hand is armed with triple-tongued fire, the god who shakes the earth when he nods his head, this god now dropped his scepter and took on the form of a bull. Mingling with the herd and lowing like a real bull, he strolled through the tender grass, a handsome creature, white as snow no heavy foot has plunged into nor rainy south wind melted. Muscles swelled in his neck, dewlaps hung from his shoulders; his horns, small and neatly curved, were clearer than fine crystal, and you could argue that they were made by hand. His brow was smooth; his eyes instilled no fear; his face was calm and peaceful.

Agenor's daughter, Europa, admired the bull because he was so beautiful and there was nothing menacing about him. Placid though he seemed to be, she was afraid to touch him at first, but soon came up to him and held out flowers to his snowy mouth. He was thrilled by this, for he was very much in love, and while he bided his time for the pleasure that was surely coming, he kissed her hands, but held back, held back kissing other parts of her. One moment he was doing a little dance, giving little leaps in the green grass, the next he was lying down on his side, so snowy white against the yellow sand. And as Europa became less timid, he offered his chest to her innocent little hand to pat and lowered his head so she could entwine fresh blossoms around his horns. Growing bolder, the royal girl climbed on the back of the bull, without any idea whom she was sitting on. And now the god moved slowly away from the grass, away from the shore, put his fake hooves into the water at its edge, then

stepped into it just a little more, and now was swimming through the open sea
with his prize.

Trembling, she looked back at the receding shore as she rode, gripping a
horn with one hand, resting the other on his back, her robe fluttering and
billowing in the wind.[10]

BOOK THREE

The god now dropped his guise as a bull and confessed who he was. They arrived in Crete about the time that Europa's father, not knowing what had happened, ordered his son Cadmus to search for the missing girl, threatening him with exile if he failed to find her, tender and cruel in the same act.

After wandering throughout the world—but who can catch Jove in one of his secret love affairs?—Cadmus did not return, now or ever, to his own country nor to his father's wrath. He was an exile now and consulted the oracle of Apollo as a suppliant to ask what land he could live in. "In a remote field you will come upon a heifer," the god replied, "that has never felt the weight of a yoke nor pulled a plow's curved blade. Take the path she leads you on, and where she stops to rest in a grassy field, there build the walls of your city and call the place Boeotia."*

Cadmus had just come down from the Castalian cave† when he saw a heifer ambling along untended and bearing on her neck no marks of servitude. He followed carefully in her tracks and silently blessed Apollo for showing him the way. The heifer had now forded the shallow Cephisus and passed through the fields of Panope when she stopped, lifted her handsome head with its spreading horns to the sky, and filled the air with her bellowing. Then, looking back at Cadmus and his companions, following behind her, she sank down and rolled over on her side in the tender grass. Cadmus gave thanks, kissed the foreign earth, and greeted the mountains and fields, which he had never seen till now. Preparing to sacrifice to Jove, he ordered his men to find water from a running spring for a libation.

In an ancient grove, a place untouched by the blade of an axe, there was a low-lying cave formed by a pile of stones in the shape of an arch and overgrown

---

*3.13: "Boeotia" means "the land of the heifer" (Miller-Goold 1.125 n. 1).

†3.14: "Castalian" refers to the oracle of Apollo at Delphi, some distance away from the Castalian spring (Henderson at 3.14, 43).

by thick underbrush. From this cave an underground spring was always flowing, and deep within it lived a dark blue serpent with a brilliant golden crest, the offspring of Mars. The serpent's eyes gleamed with fire, its body was swollen with venom, and from its mouth, filled with three rows of teeth, three tongues were flicking.

When the Tyrian exiles reached the grove on their mission, which would prove to be their undoing, and were noisily dipping their urns in the spring, the serpent raised its head from the depth of the cave and gave out horrendous hisses. The urns fell from their hands, and they turned pale and shook with fear. Coiling and uncoiling its scaly form, the serpent suddenly curved itself into a huge arc and reared up into the soft air to more than half its length and gazed down upon the entire grove, as gigantic, if you had seen the whole thing, as the constellation called "the Serpent" that separates the two Bears. It then attacked the Phoenicians, some as they were aiming arrows at it, others as they tried to run away, and still others who were too terrified to move: It caught up several of the men in its jaws and devoured them, crushed several others in its coils, and killed the rest with its deadly, poison-laden breath.*

The sun at noon had shortened all shadows, and Cadmus, wondering what was keeping his companions, set out to follow their tracks. He wore a lion's skin cloak and carried a lance tipped with shining iron, a javelin, and, more powerful than any weapon, a courageous heart. When he entered the grove and saw the corpses of his slain companions and their killer rearing over them with its huge bulk and—hideous sight—tasting their mortal wounds with its three bloody tongues, "Hearts so loyal," he cried, "either I shall avenge your deaths or join you!" and lifted an enormous stone and heaved it with all his strength. Although the force of it would have smashed a huge hole in the high walls and lofty towers of a city, the stone bounced off the serpent, for its scales and tough black hide protected it like a breastplate, and it stood unmoved.

But that same tough hide did not stop Cadmus' javelin, which he now thrust into the serpent's spine in the middle of its curving back, driving the iron spearhead deep into its gut. Wild with pain the creature twisted its head around, saw the wound, and bit the javelin lodged in its flesh. With a mighty effort it worked the shaft back and forth and slowly pulled it out, but the iron head remained embedded in the bone. Now indeed this fresh stimulus to the dragon's already powerful wrath made the veins at its throat swell to bursting, and clots of white foam dropped from its filthy jaws, its scales clacked loudly on the ground, and the black miasma issuing from its mouth as from the depths of hell infected the air with a foul and poisonous fog.

One moment it twisted its spiraling coils into a huge circle, the next it reared up straighter than a long wooden beam, and then, with a great onrush, like a

---

*3.49: I translate *hos necat* adflatu funesti *tabe veneni,* the text of Anderson (1982a), Bömer, Haupt-Ehwald, et al., instead of Miller-Goold's *hos necat* adflati funesta *tabe veneni.*

river roiled by rainstorms, hurled itself forward, crashing against the trees in its path.

Cadmus fell back a little, his lion's skin taking the worst of the serpent's attack, holding out his lance to ward off its lunging jaws. The serpent, raging, tried to crush the hard iron lance-head between its teeth, in vain. Blood now flowed from the roof of its mouth, where its poison sacs were, spattering the green grass, but the wound was slight, for the serpent kept drawing back from the jabbing lance, moving its injured neck away, and by yielding prevented solid blows from landing or piercing deeply.

But then Cadmus drove the iron into its throat, putting all his weight behind the thrust of the lance, and drove the serpent back until he slammed it into an oak on the point of his lance and pinned its neck to the tree. Bowed by the weight of the hanging serpent, the tree groaned, in pain for its trunk, now being lashed by the monster's tail.

As Cadmus, victorious, surveyed his conquered foe in all its bulk he suddenly heard a voice—where it came from he could not tell—but he heard it say: "Why, son of Agenor, are you staring at the serpent you have slain? Someday you will be a serpent at whom someone else will stare." Cadmus stood shaking, his mind a blank, his face drained of color, his hair standing on end, frozen with terror. Then suddenly his patron Minerva dropped down from heaven and stood before him and ordered him to turn up the ground and plant the serpent's teeth, and, she said, a people would spring up. Hurrying to obey, Cadmus made a furrow with a plow as ordered and sowed the serpent's teeth, the seeds of mortals to come. Then (hard to believe!) the soil began to stir. First spear points appeared from the furrow, followed by helmets with colored crests nodding, then shoulders, chests, and arms holding the spears came into view: A crop of men armed with shields was springing up. In just this way in the theater on holidays, when the curtain is raised, the figures painted on it begin to rise, showing their faces first, then gradually their remaining parts until, the curtain now smoothly drawn up, they are totally visible, down to their feet at the bottom edge.

Terrified by this new enemy, Cadmus was about to seize his weapons. "Don't do it!" shouted one of the men the earth had just created. "Do not get caught up in our civil war!" With that the man stabbed one of his earth-born brothers nearby with his sword and was then struck down himself by a spear hurled from a distance. The one who had killed him lived no longer than he did and expired with the first breath he had drawn.

Soon the entire group was battling furiously in the same way, and the new-found brothers were falling from the wounds they gave one another as they warred among themselves. The youths, granted such short lives, struck the bloody ground—their mother's warm breast—like blows raining down upon it, till only five remained, one of whom was Echion. At Minerva's command he threw down his arms and made a mutual pact of peace with his brothers. These the Sidonian émigré* had as his comrades when he founded the city mandated by the oracle of Apollo.

Thebes was now standing, and it should have been possible for you to be happy in your exile, Cadmus. You had Mars and Venus as your father- and mother-in-law; to this add a posterity from your noble wife: so many sons and daughters, and, sweet pledges of love, grandsons as well, these, too, now grown. But, as is always the case, you must wait to see someone's last day on earth, and no one ought to be called happy until he dies and his funeral is over.[11]

Amid so much prosperity, so much happiness, Cadmus, your grandson was the first cause of grief—the strange horns that grew on his forehead, and you, his dogs, slaking your thirst with your master's blood. But if you look closely, you will find the fault was fortune's; it wasn't Actaeon's crime, for how can a simple mistake be called a crime?

There is a mountain soaked in the blood of wild game of all kinds, and now it was midday there, when the sun stands halfway between morning, where it started, and evening, and shadows have grown short. Young Actaeon called out happily to his hunting companions wandering through the woods: "Our nets now drip with the gore of wild game, my friends, and our spears are bloody: Enough good luck for one day. When Dawn in her rosy chariot brings us first light tomorrow, we'll return to our work. Now the sun stands midway between morning and evening, and its rays are parching the fields. Let's gather up our nets and stop for the day." The men did as he ordered, and they left off hunting.

In a valley called Gargaphie, filled with sharp-needled pine and tapering cypress and sacred to the huntress Diana—in the remotest part of this valley, hidden by trees, there was a cave no human art had made, for nature with its own genius had imitated art and created a natural arch from native pumice and porous tufa. On the right, clear springwater trickled into a pool surrounded by a grassy border. Here the goddess of the woods often swam when she was tired from hunting, refreshing her virgin limbs in the cool water.

Coming there now, she handed her spear to one of her nymphs, her weapons-bearer, and passed her quiver and unstrung bow to her. Another nymph held out her arms for her cloak, as she took it off, and two nymphs untied the thongs of her sandals.

Ismenus' daughter, Crocale, more practiced than these, gathered up Diana's hair, lying about her neck, into a bun, though her own hair lay loose. Nephele, Hyale, Rhanis, Psecas, and Phiale† filled large urns with water and poured it over the goddess, and while she was having her customary bath, look at this:

---

*3.121: "the Sidonian émigré," that is, Cadmus.

†3.169–172: The names of the servant nymphs who attend Diana—all of which are Greek—are associated with water or liquid: "Crocale" (3.169) = "sea pebble"; "Nephele," "Hyale," etc. (3.171–172) = "cloud," "crystal," "raindrop," "drizzle," and "saucer." They obviously sound better in Greek. Bömer comments on the provenance of these names at 3.169, 1.494–495; and 3.171–172, 3.496.

Cadmus' grandson, having finished his work for the day, wandered through unfamiliar woods, unsure of the way, and stumbled into the grove. That is where the fates were leading him.

The instant he entered the grotto with the flowing spring the nymphs saw him and, naked as they were, began to beat their breasts and fill the entire woods with sharp cries. They surrounded Diana and hid her from his eyes with their bodies. The goddess, however, was a head taller and towered over them all. Seen without her clothes, she turned the color of clouds tinted by the rays of the setting sun or the color of the rosy dawn.

Though shielded by her companions, who crowded around her, she crouched down nevertheless. If only she had her bow and arrows in her hands! But she did have water, and scooping some up in her hands, she threw it in Actaeon's face, drenching his hair with its avenging drops, and added these words as a forecast of the disaster about to happen to him: "Now you can say that you saw me with all my clothes off—if you can say anything at all!"

She then made the antlers of a full-grown stag sprout from his dripping head, lengthened his neck and drew his ears into a point, changed his hands into hooves and his arms into nimble legs, and covered his body with a dappled hide. She made him skittish, too, and Autonoe's son bounded away, marveling at his speed.

When he saw his face and antlers reflected in water, he tried to say, "O wretched, wretched me!" but he had no voice, and he groaned instead: That was the only sound he could make, and tears ran down a face that was not his own. Only his mind remained unchanged.

What could he do? Should he go home to the royal palace or hide in the woods? Shame kept him from doing the first, fear, the second. While he was hesitating, his dogs spotted him, and Blackfoot (with Spartan pedigree) and crafty Tracker (a Cretan hound) first alerted the pack with their baying. Then the rest raced after him, swifter than a whistling wind: Devourer, Gazelle, and Mountain Ranger, all three Arcadian dogs; then brave Fawn Slayer, savage Hunter, and Hurricane; Wing, valued for speed, and Trapper, for her nose; fierce Woody, recently slashed by a boar; Dale, part wolf; and Shep, a sheep dog; Seizer, with two of her pups running with her; and Sicyonian Ladon,* so lean in the flanks; and Runner, Gnasher, Spot, and Tiger; Valiant and Whitey with his snowy coat and Soot with his black fur; powerful Spartan and Cyclone, relentless in pursuit; Swifty and speedy Wolf with her brother Cyprian; Eager, marked by a white spot in the middle of his black forehead; Blackie and shaggy Shaggy; and Fury and White Fang, both the get of a Cretan father by a Spartan mother; Barker, who bayed with the best; and others it's too tedious to name. This pack, slavering for its prey, pursued Actaeon past cliffs, crags, pathless rocky stretches, and places where the trail was difficult or didn't even exist.

---

*3.216: Ladon is the name of a river in Arcadia.

And Actaeon ran from them, ran through places where he himself had often chased game. Horrible! He ran from his own dogs!

He tried to shout, "It's me, Actaeon! Don't you know your master?" But the words would not come; only the yelping of the dogs filled the air.

Blackfur struck him first, burying her teeth in his back, Beast Slayer next, and Mountain Pup bit into his shoulder and hung on. They had started late but took a shortcut over the mountain and got ahead of the pack. While they were dragging their master down, the rest of the hounds appeared and sank their teeth into his body; soon there was no place left to sink teeth into.

Actaeon groaned, a sound that, though not human, was not like any groan a stag would make, and filled the familiar hills with heartrending cries. Sinking to the ground on his forelegs like a suppliant, he turned his mute and pleading face like a pair of outstretched arms from comrade to comrade. But his companions in their ignorance urged on the vicious pack with the usual cries, looking around for him and shouting "Actaeon!" again and again as though he were absent—he swung his head toward the sound of his name each time—annoyed that he wasn't there and able to watch the kill, since he was so slow. He would have preferred not to be there, but there he was; he would have preferred to watch, not feel, the fierce attack of his own dogs.

They came at their master, now a stag, from all sides, burying their snouts in his flesh and tearing him to pieces. Nor was the huntress Diana's lust for vengeance satisfied, they say, until, after countless wounds, he died.[12]

In the talk about it afterwards there were two opinions: To some the goddess seemed more cruel than was right, while others applauded what she had done and said she had lived up to her reputation as a severe and unforgiving virgin. Each side found reasons to support its view.

Jove's wife alone neither praised nor blamed Diana, but simply took pleasure in the tragedy that had struck Agenor's house, for her stored-up hatred for Jove's little Tyrian sweetheart* now extended to the other members of the family line.

And Juno had a fresh reason now for hating them to add to the earlier one: Semele was pregnant from the seed of mighty Jove, and the goddess was once again enraged. Preparing to have it out with her husband, she said to herself: "What have I ever gained by fighting with him? I ought to go after the girl herself. In fact, I'll destroy her—if I'm truly great Juno! If I'm really entitled to hold the jeweled scepter! If I'm indeed queen, Jove's sister and wife—his sister, anyway.

"Am I to believe that she'll be satisfied with a brief affair? Am I to believe she won't go on violating our marriage bed? But she's gotten herself pregnant! That does it! Now her crime is there for all to see in that big belly she carries around. She's so confident in her looks that she wants only Jove to make her a

---

*3.258: "little Tyrian sweetheart," that is, Europa.

mother. Why, that has only happened to me a few times. But I'll see to it that her looks do her in. If she doesn't sink to the bottom of the Styx—thanks to her precious Jove—then I'm not Saturn's daughter!"

With this she rose from her throne, wrapped herself in a yellow cloud, and came to Semele's door. Before she dispersed the cloud she changed herself into an old woman: She added some gray hair, made her skin wrinkled, walked bent over with halting steps, and adopted an old woman's voice. Now she was Beroë herself, Semele's nurse from Epidaurus.

So, then, one day they began talking and were deep in conversation when Jove's name came up. Juno sighed and said: "I only hope it's really Jupiter, but I worry constantly. So many men have gotten into the beds of innocent girls by calling themselves gods. Saying he's Jove is not enough. He should give some proof of his love if he is really Jove. So ask him to put on all his power and glory and come to you and make love to you the way he is when exalted Juno takes him in her arms!" Thus she worked on Cadmus' unsuspecting daughter.

Semele then asked Jove for a gift, without being specific. "Name something!" he replied. "I won't say no, and if you don't believe me, let the raging Styx be my witness, the god that even the gods are afraid of."

Happy in her doom, too successful in getting what she wanted, and about to die from her lover's generosity, Semele said, "You know the way you are when Juno takes you in her arms and you make love to her? Make love to me like that!"

The god wished he could close her mouth even as she was speaking, but she had spoken quickly and the words had rushed out. He groaned, for she couldn't take back her wish, nor he his oath. And so it was a very sad Jove who ascended to the lofty heights of heaven and summoned clouds and added rainstorms to them, sheet lightning mixed with winds, thunder, and the lightning bolt that never missed. Even so, he tried as much as he could to tone down his power. He didn't arm himself with the fire he used to blast the hundred-handed Typhoeus, for it was much too fierce. He had another, lighter kind of thunderbolt, to which the Cyclopes who forged it had given less savagery, flame, and wrath, a shaft the gods call medium-sized. With this he entered Cadmus' palace.

But Semele's human frame could not withstand even these lesser fireworks from on high, and she burned to a crisp from the gifts Jove brought his "bride."

The still-growing baby was snatched from its mother's womb, and (if you can believe it) the dear thing was sewn up in its father's thigh and came to term as though it were still with its mother. Ino, his mother's sister, reared the infant boy in secret and later gave him to nymphs of Mount Nysa, who hid him in their cave and gave him milk.[13]

While all this was taking place on earth by the laws of fate—and the twice-born baby Bacchus was safe and secure—it happened that Jove (so they say), mellow from drinking nectar, put serious matters aside and began to tease Juno (who was in a relaxed mood herself): "I'll bet you that women get more pleasure from making love than men do." She declared it wasn't true. They decided to get an opinion from learned Tiresias: He knew lovemaking from top to bottom, so to speak, for he had once seen two huge snakes copulating in a green wood, struck them with his staff, and, amazingly, was changed from a man to a woman. He lived seven years that way and in the eighth year saw the same snakes again and said, "If the force of the blow I gave you was so great that it could change the one who gave it into the opposite sex, I'll strike you again." And when he struck them now he regained his earlier form and his original sex.

Drafted, then, to decide their mock dispute, Tiresias supported Jove. Juno, they say, took this much harder than she should have or was called for and cursed her own judge with everlasting blindness. But the father omnipotent, to compensate Tiresias for losing his eyesight (for no god can nullify the action of another god), allowed him to know the future and so softened the punishment with this special privilege.[14]

And so Tiresias, renowned throughout the cities of Boeotia, gave responses that could not be faulted to all who sought him out. Cerulean Liriopé was the first to put his gift of prophecy to the test. Now, the river Cephisus had once enveloped Liriopé in his stream, overpowered her, and raped her while she was caught in his waters. This very beautiful, very pregnant nymph gave birth to a baby you could fall in love with even then, and she called him Narcissus.

When she asked Tiresias whether Narcissus would live to see a ripe old age, the seer replied, "If he never knows himself." This answer made no sense for a long time, but the way things turned out—Narcissus' strange obsession and the way he died—proved the prediction to be true. For when the son of Cephisus was sixteen and could seem a boy—or a young man—or both boy and man—many young men desired him, many young women, too, but in this soft and tender beauty there was such steely pride that no young man could touch him, and no young woman, either.

That nymph who loved to talk saw him one day driving frightened stags toward his nets, the nymph who didn't know how to be quiet when someone else was speaking nor could say anything herself, unless someone else was speaking, ever-mimicking Echo.

She still had a body then, she wasn't just a voice; and, loquacious as she was, she could only talk the way she does now, could only repeat the very last words she heard someone say.

Juno had made her like this, for whenever the goddess was about to catch some nymph or other lying on some mountain beneath her Jove, Echo would engage the goddess in a lengthy conversation on purpose until the nymph could wriggle out from under the god and get away.

When Juno realized this she decreed: "From now on, you'll be barely able to wag that tongue you tricked me with, and your voice will only work for brief periods of time!" She made good her threat, for now Echo can chime in only at the end when someone is talking, and can only repeat the last words she hears the person say.

So then, when Echo saw Narcissus wandering through the countryside, she fell madly in love with him and began secretly following him, and the more she followed him, the hotter the flame that consumed her. In the same way sulfur (which catches fire so easily) when smeared on the tops of torches ignites if a flame even comes near it.

How often Echo wanted to use her charm on him, to be seductive and enticing, but her condition held her back and wouldn't let her begin. What it did allow she was ready to do, and that was to take up anything he said and repeat it back to him, word for word.

One day Narcissus happened to be separated from his friends in the woods and called out, "Anyone here?"

" . . . here!" Echo replied.

Amazed, he spun around and shouted, "I'm over here!"

" . . . over here!" she answered.

He looked all around, and when no one came he cried out again, "Why are you avoiding me?" And heard the same words again, after he said them. He stood still, puzzled by what seemed to be a voice answering his own "Come here," he called out.

To no other words would Echo ever reply more happily. "Come here!" she repeated, and joyfully obeyed her own command and emerged from the woods and ran up to him, eager to throw her arms around his neck. Narcissus fled, shouting as he ran, "Keep your hands off me! I'd die before I'd give myself to you!"

" . . . I'd give myself to you!" she answered only.

Rejected, Echo hid in the woods and buried her face in leaves, burning with shame, and lived in lonely caves from that time on. But she loved Narcissus still, and her sadness at being spurned only made her love him more. Miserable and heartsick night and day, she wasted away, her skin shriveled, and her sweet young body simply vanished in the air. Only her voice and bones were left, and then just her voice. (Her bones, they say, turned to stone.) From that time on she hid in forests and was seen no more in the mountains, though everyone could hear her, for her voice (and nothing more) lived on.

That was the way Narcissus treated Echo, the way he treated other mountain nymphs and water sprites, and the way he had treated young men, too, before that. Then some rejected lover, raising his hands to heaven, prayed, "Let *him* love as we have; let him succeed in love as we have!"* And the goddess Nemesis granted his prayer, for it was surely just.

---

*3.405: I accept Kovacs' suggestion for line 3.405 ([1994] 247–248) and read (and translate) *sic amet ipse, precor, sic et potiatur amato!* instead of *sic amet ipse licet, sic non potiatur amato!* with Miller-Goold and other editors.

There was a spring with a pool of silvery, sparkling water free of mud and fallen branches, that no shepherds, no mountain goats, nor any cattle had ever touched, no bird or beast had ever disturbed. The grass around the pool was watered by the spring, and trees provided shade that kept the place cool. One day, when he was hot and tired from hunting, Narcissus lay down here, drawn by the natural beauty of the place and by the spring. And while he was eagerly quenching his thirst, another thirst began to grow. For as he drank from the pool he was caught by his image in the water and fell in love and longed for something that was not real: He thought his reflection was someone real.

He lay on the ground, perfectly still, like a statue carved from Parian marble, staring at his mirror image, himself amazed at himself. He gazed at his eyes, like twin stars; gazed at his hair, like the hair of Bacchus, even like Apollo's; gazed at his smooth cheeks; at his neck, like ivory; at the lovely shape of his mouth; at the color of his skin, snow white and rosy pink. And he admired all those features for which he was admired.

He wanted himself, not knowing it was himself he wanted, cast appraising glances—and received appraising glances himself, was subject and object of his own desire and aroused the very passion that he burned with.

How often he kissed the deceiving water, but in vain! How often he plunged his arms into the pool, reaching for the neck he saw there, but couldn't embrace himself! He didn't know what he saw, but he burned for what he saw, and the very illusion deceiving him invited him to look.

Naive boy, why do you try so hard to grasp a fugitive form? What you want does not exist; what you're in love with—turn away, and it's gone! It's an image, a reflection in the water that you see and nothing else. It comes when you come, it stays while you stay, and it will go away when you go away—if only you could go away!

But neither hunger nor craving for sleep could draw him away from the pool. Collapsed on the grass in the shade, he gazed at the false image, never got his fill of gazing, and perished through his own eyes.

Raising himself a little and holding out his arms to the trees above, he cried: "Was there ever anyone, O trees, more cruelly in love than I am? Surely you must know, for you have been a secret place for countless lovers to meet. And since you have lived so many centuries, do you remember anyone ever wasting away like me?

"He is so alluring, and I can plainly see him! But what I can plainly see and is so alluring, I still cannot reach"—so bewitched is the boy in love!

"And to make it worse, it's not a vast sea that separates us, not an endless highway, not a mountain range, not city walls with locked gates. It's only the surface of this pool that keeps us apart!

"He himself wants me to kiss him, for whenever I move my lips to the clear, still water, he strains toward me with upturned mouth. You would think I could touch him, so slight the barrier between us.

"Whoever you are, come out! Why do you tease me, you wonderful, strange boy? Where do you go when I try to reach you? Surely it isn't my face or youth you run away from; even nymphs have been in love with me!

"You lead me on with your inviting look, and when I reach out to you, you reach out to me. When I smile at you, you smile back at me. And I've often seen your tears, too, whenever I'm weeping. You nod to me when I nod to you, and to guess from your moving lips, you answer me, but your words never reach my ears . . .

"Why, you're me! Now I see. My reflection has deceived me! I'm in love with myself! I light the fire that I feel! What am I going to do? Wait for him to make the first move? Make it myself? How can I make the first move *now*? What I want, I've got; what I've got, I want. Oh! If only I could leave my body! Here's a new prayer for a lover: 'Go away, my love!'

"Sadness robs me of my strength, and I have so little life left, and I'm so young—yet I'm dying! But death is not so awful, for my grief will end when I die. If only the one I love could live a while longer. But now two hearts, beating as one, will cease to beat, as one."

Half out of his mind with grief, he looked again at the face in the pool, and his tears, splashing into the water, broke up the reflection. "Where are you running away to?" he cried, when he saw the image disappearing. "Stay with me, heartless boy! Don't leave the one who loves you! At least let me look at you, even if I cannot touch you, and let me feed this wretched passion!"

As he wept he tore open his tunic at the neck and beat his naked breast with hands that were white as marble, and his skin colored beneath the blows, like apples turning white and red as they ripen, like clusters of grapes not yet ripe and slowly becoming purple.

Seeing his face in the water when it was calm and clear again, he could endure it no longer, and as yellow wax over a small flame runs, or as frost fades in the warm morning sun, so he slowly melted away, consumed by love as though by a hidden fire. The skin that once was pink and fair was deathly pale now, and his strength and liveliness were gone; gone were the limbs so lovely, once, to see; gone the body Echo once had loved. And when she saw him, though she was angry, though it was painful to remember, whenever the unhappy boy cried, "O poor me!" she cried, "O poor me!" And whenever he struck his shoulders with his hands, she echoed the sound of the blows. Gazing into the water, as always, he uttered these last words: "Alas, dear boy, loved in vain!" and the place gave back the words; and when he said, "Good-bye!" "Good-bye!" said Echo, too.

He laid his weary head in the grass, and death closed his eyes, still gazing at their master. And when he entered the house of the dead, there, too, he would often gaze at himself in the river Styx.

His sister naiads beat their breasts and cut their hair for him and put it on his bier. Dryads beat their breasts, too, and the blows were heard twice, thanks to Echo.

And now the pyre, the torches, the bier were all prepared, but the body was nowhere to be seen. They found instead a flower, white petals ringed around a yellow cup.[15]

The news of this brought well-deserved fame to Tiresias throughout the cities of Greece, and his reputation grew immensely. Nevertheless, Echion's son Pentheus, contemptuous of the gods, rejected the seer—the only one to do so—mocked the old man's prophecies, and taunted him for his blindness— and for the unfortunate event that led to his loss of sight.

Shaking his old gray head, Tiresias replied: "How happy you would be if you, too, were deprived of the light, so you would never see the rites of Bacchus! For the day will come, a day I predict is not far off, when Semele's son, the new god, Liber, will arrive here in Thebes, and if you still think he's not worth honoring with a temple, you will be torn apart and your body scattered far and wide, and your blood will stain the trees of the forest, your mother, and her sisters. It will happen! For you *won't* think he's worth honoring, and in sorrow you will acknowledge that in this darkness of mine I saw only too clearly." Pentheus drove him out even while he was still speaking, but what he said came true. The seer's prediction was fulfilled.

And now Liber had arrived! The countryside was filled with festive howls. People rushed out in throngs—mothers, daughters, and their husbands, nobles and commoners alike—all hurrying off to the strange new rites.

"What madness, Serpent-born children of Mars, has blasted your wits?" cried Pentheus. "Do clashing cymbals, Asian flutes, and magic tricks have such power that women's cries, wine-frenzy, lewd crowds, and hollow tambourines can conquer those whom battle swords, the sound of trumpets, and massed troops with threatening spears never terrified?

"How can I admire you elders, who sailed across vast seas, built a new Tyre here, and established your gods here, when now you let yourselves be taken without a fight? And you, young men, more vigorous and closer to my own age, should I admire you? You would look better bearing arms, not Bacchus' wand, and wearing helmets on your heads, not grape leaves.

"Remember, I beg you, the stock you come from and put on the courage of that Serpent who by himself destroyed so many! He died fighting for the waters of a spring; but I say to you: Conquer for the sake of your name! He killed many brave souls; but I say: Repel these unmanly men and safeguard the honor of your fathers!

"If fate were forbidding Thebes to stand for long, it ought to be missiles and men that demolish our walls! The only sounds we ought to hear are swords clashing, fires roaring! We would then be in a miserable state, but above reproach! We would mourn our fate, but not conceal it! We would shed tears, yes, but we would be unashamed!

"And now Thebes will be captured by an unarmed boy without the help of weapons, spears, or horsemen, but using only the myrrh dripping from his locks, soft garlands, and garments bright with purple and embroidered with gold. If you will get out of my way, I will force him at once to admit that he claims a father who is not his father, and that his sacred rites are a lie.

"Was Acrisius once courageous enough to condemn this false divinity and close the gates of Argos against him, and yet this interloper will now terrify Pentheus and all of Thebes? Go quickly!" (he commanded his slaves). "Go and drag this leader here in chains! No lingering or delay for these orders!"

His grandfather Cadmus, his brother-in-law Athamas, and his friends and relations all crowded around Pentheus and argued vehemently with him and tried to stop him, but it was no use. Their warnings only made him fiercer still; their attempt to restrain his madness only inflamed it and made it grow. Their effort to delay him had the opposite effect.

Thus have I seen a mountain torrent running calmly and with a moderate roar, so long as nothing checked its flowing. But where it was choked with rocks and trees, it foamed and raged and coursed more violently because of the obstructions.

And now, look! They returned spattered with blood, and when their master asked where Bacchus was, they said they had not seen him. "We caught this one, though, a companion of his and a minister of his rites," they said, handing over a man with his hands tied behind his back, a Tyrrhenian, who practiced the rites of Bacchus.

Pentheus stared at him, his eyes bulging with rage and, though reluctant to put off punishment, said to him, "Oh, you're going to die, all right, and provide a lesson to others by your death, but first you're going to tell me your name, the names of your parents, your country, and why you practice the rites of this strange cult."

Without a trace of fear the stranger began: "My name is Acoetes. I am from Maeonia, and my parents were of humble origin. My father left me no fields nor hardy oxen to plow with, no flocks of sheep, no herds of any kind. He was poor, like me, and spent his days fishing with hook and line, catching the leaping fish with his rod. This skill was his entire estate. When he passed it on to me he said, 'Such wealth as I have is yours, for you are heir and successor to my profession,' and when he died he left me nothing except the waters he fished in. That was all the patrimony I had.

"But so as not to be stuck forever in the same place, I soon taught myself to pilot a ship, and I began to observe the stars, the rainy constellation of the Olenian She-Goat, Taygete, the Hyades, and the Bear,* and I learned the winds and where they came from and the harbors best for ships.

"Making for Delos once, I was driven by chance to Chios, and, coming about

---

*3.594–595: "the Olenian She-Goat, Taygete, the Hyades, and the Bear": the Olenian She-Goat is a star in the constellation Auriga, whose "appearance coincides with the coming of rain"; Taygete, a star in the constellation of the Pleiades, "a group [of stars] on which sailors of the Mediterranean much relied"; the Hyades, a constellation of five stars "whose rising and setting synchronized with rain." The Bear (née Callisto) "helped sailors determine north" (Anderson [1997] at 3.594–596, 397–398).

to port, I put in to shore, leaped lightly from the boat, and landed on the wet sand. I spent the night there. When the dawn sky had just begun to redden, I arose, urged my men to fetch fresh water, and showed them a path which led to a spring. From the top of a hill I was myself looking to see which way the wind was blowing, and I summoned my companions and headed back to the ship.

"'Here we are,' said Opheltes, the leader of the crew, who had stumbled upon a lucky find (or so he thought) in a remote field, a young boy as pretty as a girl, whom he was leading along the shore. The boy appeared a little drunk and seemed to stagger and to have trouble following. I looked at his clothes, at his face, and watched the way he walked: I saw nothing there that would make me think he was mortal. When I realized this, I said to my companions: 'I'm not sure which god is in this boy, but that there is a god in him I have no doubt! Whoever you are, show us your favor and help us in our difficulty. Grant your grace to these men, too!'

"'Stop praying for us!' cried Dictys, the fastest man to climb up to the highest yardarm and come back down by the halyard. Libys gave his support to this, and blond Melanthus added his (he stood watch at the prow); Alcimedon agreed with them, and Epopeus, who called the strokes for the rowers, urging them on, joined in; and all the others supported it, too, so blind is the lust for gain.

"'No matter what you say,' I cried, 'I will not allow this ship to be polluted by forcing this sacred person to come on board. I am the one in command here,' and I blocked the gangway. Lycabas, the rashest man in the entire crew, was enraged. He had been driven from his Tuscan city and forced into exile as punishment for a vicious murder. As I stood in his way, he smashed me in the throat with a powerful blow of his fist and would have knocked me overboard, thrown me right into the sea, if I had not grabbed a rope and clung to it, dazed though I was. That godless rabble cheered him for this.

"Finally, Bacchus—for that is who it turned out to be—as though the shouting had awakened him and he was sobering up from the wine he had drunk, said: 'What are you doing? What is this uproar? Tell me, sailors, how did I get here? Where are you getting ready to take me?'

"'Don't worry,' said Proreus. 'Just tell us what port you want to reach and you'll be put ashore there.'

"'Naxos!' Bacchus replied. 'Set your course for Naxos! That's my home; you'll be welcome in that land!' Those liars swore by the sea, by all the gods, that so it would be, and they ordered me to get the ship under way.

Naxos lay on the right. As I set our course to starboard they all shouted, 'What are you doing, you lunatic? Acoetes, what madness possesses you? Steer to port!' Most signaled with a nod what they wanted me to do; some whispered in my ear.*

*3.643: I read *aure susurrat* with Anderson (1982a), Bömer, Haupt-Ehwald, and LaFaye, rather than *ore susurro* with Miller-Goold.

"I was dumbfounded. 'Let someone else take the helm,' I said, moving away and refusing to let my skill serve their crime. All raised their voices against me, and a growing murmur spread through the crowd. A member of the crew named Aethalion said, 'As if our entire welfare rested in your hands alone!' and stepped up to the helm himself, took over my job, abandoned the course to Naxos, and turned the ship in a different direction.

"Then the god looked out over the sea from the curved deck, pretending to weep (he was making fools of them, as though he had just now caught on to the deception), and said, 'These are not the shores you promised me, sailors; this is not the land I asked you to bring me to! What have I done to deserve this? What pride can you take in deceiving a boy, so many of you against just one?'

"I was weeping—had been for some time—but that godless band laughed at my tears and smacked the sea faster and faster with their oars. I swear to you now by the god himself (for no god is more present than he), what I am about to tell you is as true as it is unbelievable: The ship suddenly stood still in the water, as though it were high and dry in a shipyard.

"The crew, astonished, kept on beating the water with their oars and also unfurled the sail, trying to make headway by these twin means, but the oars became entangled with ivy creeping in all directions, entwining itself around everything, and draping heavy clusters of berries over the sail. The boy's brow, too, was crowned with grapes, and he brandished a wand covered with leafy vines.

"Around him lay phantom tigers, lynxes, and fierce, spotted panthers. The men jumped up, whether from madness or fear I cannot say, and first Medon turned black all over, and his back was curved into an arc. 'What strange thing are you becoming?' said Lycabas, and as he spoke his own jaws widened, his nose was rounded, and his skin hardened with scales. Then Libys tried to ship the oars, which were holding us back, but saw his hands suddenly shrink— they were hands no longer; now you could call them flippers.

"Another member of the crew tried to grab the rigging with his arms but had no arms, and with his body now bent like a bow, jumped into the water. The end of his tail was sickle-shaped, like the crescent moon.

"Now they all leaped into the sea with a great splash, surfaced, then dived down again, doing this over and over, moving like a group of dancers, cavorting with their bodies, drawing in water and spouting it from their nostrils. Of the original crew of twenty that the ship had carried, I alone remained.

"I was terrified and cold, trembling all over and scarcely myself, but the god reassured me, saying, 'Stop being afraid and head for Dia!'* Arriving there, I joined in the rites of Bacchus, and I've practiced those rites ever since."

"I listened to your long, winding tale," Pentheus said, "to let my wrath cool

---

*3.690: Dia is the ancient name for Naxos, where the god had originally said he wanted to go (at 3.636).

down. . . . But now: Seize him at once, servants! Torture him in all the fiendish ways you can think of and then dispatch him to the dark of Stygian night!"

Tyrrhenian Acoetes was immediately taken away and shut up in a thick-walled prison. While iron and fire were prepared, cruel instruments for the death Pentheus demanded, the prison doors swung open of their own accord, the story goes, and of their own accord the chains fell from Acoetes' arms—no one removed them.

But the son of Echion persisted. This time, however, instead of ordering someone else to go to Mount Cithaeron, he went himself to the place chosen for celebrating the rites, where one could now hear chanting and the piercing cries of Bacchantes.

As a spirited horse whinnies and cries, and his eagerness for battle grows when the army trumpeter sounds the call to attack, clear and melodious, on his brass horn, in the same way the long drawn-out howls that filled the air excited Pentheus, and the cries rekindled his wrath.

About halfway up the mountain there was a field ringed by forest but clear of trees itself and open to view on all sides. Here the first to see Pentheus watching the sacred rites with profane eyes, the first aroused to a mad attack, the first to hurl her staff at him and hurt him—her own son—was his mother, who shouted, "Here, sisters, both of you, come here! That boar, the huge one that wanders in our fields—I'm going to kill that boar!"

The entire throng in a frenzy hurled itself at that lone man; massed together they ran him down, and he was quaking with terror, yes, quaking with terror now, not so violent now in what he had to say, condemning himself now, confessing now how wrong he had been. Torn and bleeding, he cried, "Help me, Aunt! Autonoe! The ghost of your son Actaeon should make you pity me!" She had no idea who Actaeon was and pulled off Pentheus' right arm even as he begged for help, while Ino tore off the left. Now he had no arms, poor fellow, to reach out to his mother with and, showing the gaping holes where his arms had been, he said, "Look, Mother!"

At the sight she threw back her head and, tossing her hair, let out a howl, then, wringing his head from his neck and holding it between her bloody hands she shouted, "Look, comrades! What I've done means victory for us!"

Leaves touched by the chill of autumn and lightly clinging to a lofty tree are plucked by the wind no more quickly than the man's body was ripped apart by unspeakably brutal hands. Warned by such an example, the daughters of Ismenus performed the new rites, offered incense, and worshipped Bacchus at his sacred altars.[16]

BOOK FOUR

But Minyas' daughter Alcithoe did not think the god's rites had to be accepted and, even more rashly, denied that Bacchus was the son of Jove. Her sisters shared her impious attitude.

Now, the priest had ordered the people to celebrate the god's festival: He ordered servants, who had been released from their work, ordered their mistresses, too, to put on animal skins, remove their headbands, wear garlands in their hair, and take up leafy wands in their hands. He warned them that if the god were insulted, his wrath would be savage.

The women young and old obeyed, put aside their weaving and the baskets of wool waiting to be spun, offered incense, and invoked the god as Bacchus, Bromius, Lyaeus, as fire-born, twice-born, the only god with two mothers. To these names they added Nyseus; Thyoneus with uncut hair; Lenaeus, planter of the vine, source of joy; Nyctelius, father Eleleus, Iacchus, Euhan, and all the other names you have, Liber, throughout the cities of Greece. Your youth is never consumed; you are boy eternal, admired as the most handsome god to be seen in all of heaven. When you appear before us without horns, your head has the innocent grace of a young girl's. The Orient is under your power, even as far as dusky India, watered by Ganges at the world's edge.

You killed Pentheus, O revered one, and Lycurgus, too, who once wielded the axe with double blade, because of their sacrilege; and you threw the Tyrrhenian sailors into the sea.

You guide your pair of lynxes with brightly colored reins, and Bacchantes and satyrs follow in your train—old, drunken Silenus, too, supporting his wobbly legs with a stick and clinging precariously to a sway-backed ass. Wherever your procession goes, one hears the shouts of young men and the cries of women mingled with the sound of the tambourines they strike with their palms, the clash of bronze cymbals, and the melodious tones of boxwood flutes.

"Be present to us, O god, and be gentle and kind to us," the Theban women prayed, and performed the sacred rites as they had been ordered to do. Only the daughters of Minyas stayed indoors and profaned the feast day by doing Minerva's work, for it wasn't the right time to do it. They drew out the wool, spun the threads, or wove on the loom, and kept the servant girls at their tasks, too. And one of them said, as she spun: "Well! The other women have stopped their work to attend those bogus rites. Since Minerva, a far better god, keeps us at home, let us make our work, useful as it is, easier for ourselves by talking about different things—let's take turns and tell stories to make the time go by and to have something to listen to."

Her sisters agreed and asked her to go first. Which story to tell? she asked herself (for she knew many) and wondered whether to narrate the tale about you, Dercetis of Babylonia, who the Palestinians believe turned into a fish and now, covered with scales, swims about in a pool; or, better, the one about Dercetis' daughter, who grew wings, became a dove, and spent the last years of her life in a white dovecote; or the one about the naiad who used incantations and powerful herbs to turn young men into silent fish, until she suffered the same fate; or the one about the tree that used to have white berries but now has black ones, after being splashed with blood. She preferred the last because it wasn't commonly known and began to tell the story as she spun her wool into yarn.

"Pyramus and Thisbe—the handsomest boy and the most beautiful girl in the Orient—lived in houses side by side in Babylon, the city Semiramis is said to have enclosed with a high wall of fired brick. They met as next-door neighbors, fell in love, and their love grew with time. They would have married, too, but their fathers had forbidden it. But one thing their fathers could not forbid: Each had captured the other's heart, and each burned with the same passion. No one shared their secret; they communicated by nods and signs, and the longer they kept their feelings hidden, the hotter their passion burned.

"There was a small crack in the wall between the two houses that had been there since the wall was built. This fault, unnoticed for generations, you two were the first to see—doesn't love see everything?—and you made it a passage-way for your voices: Through it your softly whispered words of love could safely go.

"Often Thisbe on one side of the wall and Pyramus on the other would catch the breath from the other's mouth and would then cry out: 'You mean old wall! Why do you stand in the way of two people in love? How easy it would be for you to let us embrace completely, or if that's too much to ask, at least you could open wide enough for us to kiss! Not that we don't appreciate you: It's thanks to you, we know, that our words go back and forth to loving ears.' With these hopeless complaints from their different places they would say 'Farewell' at nightfall, and kiss their own sides of the wall—kisses that went nowhere.

"The next day's dawn had made the fiery stars of night fade away, and the

rays of the morning sun had dried the frost on the grass: Pyramus and Thisbe
met at their usual place. After lamenting their sad state in quiet whispers, they
decided they would try to slip past their guards in the wee hours of the coming
night and steal out of their houses and, once outside, leave the city, too. And
lest they miss each other wandering in the countryside, they agreed to meet at
the tomb of Ninus, and the first to arrive would wait there in the shadow of a
tree—there was a tree near the tomb filled with white berries, a tall mulberry
tree beside a cool spring. They were very excited by these plans.

　"The sun, though seeming to take forever to set, finally sank into the sea,
and night emerged from the same waters. Thisbe quietly eased the door of her
house open in the dark, and went through it and out into the night. Covering her head with a shawl, she made her way to the tomb and sat down beneath
the tree where they had agreed to meet. (Her passion had made her daring.)

　"Now came a lioness, her jaws smeared with the blood of cattle she had just
killed, her mouth foaming with blood. She wanted to quench her thirst in the
water of the nearby spring. Babylonian Thisbe saw her from a distance by the
light of the moon and, frightened, ran into a dark cave, her shawl slipping from
her shoulders as she ran. When the savage lioness had slaked her thirst with
great draughts of water and was returning to the forest, she came upon the fine
shawl (without the girl) and tore it with her bloody mouth.

　"Leaving his house later, Pyramus saw the fresh tracks of the lioness in the
thick dust, and his face turned white. When he found the bloodstained shawl
he cried: 'One night will destroy two lovers, though it was she who most deserved to live. It's all my fault! It was I who killed you, poor girl, I who insisted
that you come at night to this place so full of danger without coming here first
myself. You lions who live among these rocks! Rip my body in pieces and let
your savage jaws devour my guilty flesh! But it's a timid man who only wishes
for death.'

　"He picked up Thisbe's shawl and took it with him to the tree in whose
shadow they had agreed to meet, and as he wept all over the familiar article
and covered it with kisses, he said, 'Now you can lap up my blood, too!' and
drove the sword he was wearing into his belly and—now dying—drew it out
of the gushing wound. As he lay flat on the ground, the blood spurted upward
in an arc, like water that shoots from a hole in a pipe where the lead's worn
through and jets into the air in a hissing stream. Spattered with gore, the fruit
of the tree turned dark, and the roots, soaked in blood, tinged the hanging
berries a deep purple.

　"And now, Thisbe, still fearful, returns to the tree, lest she miss her lover,
and looks around eagerly for her young man, longing to tell him what terrible
dangers she has just escaped. Although she recognized the place and recognized the tree by its shape, the color of the berries made her uncertain; she
wasn't sure if it was the same place.

　"As she stood there, debating with herself, she saw Pyramus' body flopping on the bloody ground. She jumped back, suddenly paler than boxwood, and shuddered like the sea when a light breeze ruffles its surface. It took her a moment to recognize her beloved, and then she began to beat her arms—too young and innocent for such sharp blows—and tear her hair, and she took the body of her beloved in her arms and wept over his wound, pouring her tears into it and mixing them with his blood. Covering his cold face with kisses she cried: 'Pyramus! What has taken you from me? Answer me, Pyramus! Your dearest Thisbe is speaking to you. Listen to me! Lift up your head!'

"At the name 'Thisbe,' Pyramus opened his eyes, now heavy with death, and closed them again. Recognizing her shawl and seeing the empty scabbard, Thisbe said: 'Your own hand killed you, and your love for me, poor boy! I, too, have a hand brave enough for this one thing, and I have my love for you, too: This will give me strength for the blow. I shall follow you, though you are dead, and I shall be called both cause and companion of your end. Only death could snatch you from me—but death won't snatch you from me!

"'O miserable fathers—mine and his—we make this last request. We, whom steadfast love, whom our last hour joined together—do not begrudge us burial in the same tomb. And you, O tree, whose branches now spread above one wretched body and soon will spread above two: Preserve the signs of our death and always bear fruit that is dark, fruit that is proper for grief, in remembrance of the blood of us both.'

"Thisbe then placed the point of the sword beneath her breastbone and fell upon the weapon, still warm from the blood of Pyramus. Her prayer, though, touched the gods and touched their parents, too; and now the mulberry, when it ripens, is black, and their ashes rest in a single urn."

This was her story. After a brief pause Leuconoe began a tale, and her sisters fell silent and listened. "Love possessed another, too," she said, "the star whose light governs all things, the Sun, I mean. I shall tell a story about the loves of the Sun.

"This god, people think, was first to see Venus committing adultery with Mars. This god sees everything first. Pained by what he saw, he told Venus' husband, Juno's son Vulcan, about the pleasure stolen from his bed, and showed him the bed. Shocked, Vulcan let the artwork he was making fall from his skillful hands. Straightway he fashioned from tiny links of bronze a net invisible to the eye to use as a snare, handiwork finer than the finest thread, finer than a spiderweb hanging from a ceiling, and arranged it carefully above the bed, setting it to drop at the slightest touch, the smallest movement.

"When his wife and her lover made love in the bed, they were caught in each other's arms, fastened to each other by this new kind of net designed by a husband's art. Vulcan immediately threw open the ivory doors of the bedroom and let in the gods. There the lovers lay, body bound to body—a shocking sight—and various gods (all amused) wished out loud that *he* could be part of a shocking sight like that. It gave them all a good laugh, and for a long time this was the most repeated story in all of heaven.

"Venus never forgot the embarrassment and demanded punishment for it, and the Sun, who ruined her secret love affair, she ruined in turn through a love affair. And so, son of Hyperion, what good to you now are your beauty, your brilliance, and your luminous rays? For though your fire burns all lands, you yourself are now burned by a strange new fire; and though you ought to look upon everything everywhere, you now gaze only at Leucothoe and fix upon a single girl the eyes you owe the world. Now you're rising earlier in the eastern sky, now you're setting later in the western waters, and by gazing long you lengthen the hours of winter. Sometimes you go into eclipse when the disquiet in your soul spreads to your rays and, darkened then, you terrify human hearts. Nor is it only when the moon passes between you and the earth that your face turns pale: Your passion for Leucothoe creates this wan hue as well. You love her only. Clymene doesn't attract you; nor Rhodos; nor Aeaean-born Circe's beautiful mother; nor Clytie, who still longs to make love with you, though you rejected her, and who still feels deeply wounded, even now. Leucothoe has made you forget all other girls.

"She was the daughter of Eurynome, the most beautiful woman in the land of aromatic spices.* But when the daughter grew up, she surpassed her mother in beauty, just as her mother had once surpassed all others. Her father, Orchamus, ruled over the cities of Persia, seventh in the line of descent from ancient Belus.

"Now, the pasture the Sun's horses graze in lies under the western sky; here, instead of cropping grass, they feed upon ambrosia, which restores their bodies, wearied from their daily round, and revives them for new toil. And while his team was there, eating this fabulous food of the gods, night came on, and the god put on the form of Eurynome, Leucothoe's mother, and entered the bedroom of his beloved. He saw her in the lamplight with her twelve servants turning the spindle and spinning fine thread, and he kissed her, like a mother kissing her dear daughter, and said to the servants, 'Servants, this is between us two, so please leave us now and don't hinder a mother's wish to speak to her daughter in private.' They obeyed, and with no witnesses in the room now the god said, 'I am the one who measures out the year, who sees all things, the one by whom the earth sees all things, the eye of the world—and you're a very pleasing sight indeed.'

"Leucothoe trembled and in her fright let the distaff and spindle slip from her slack fingers: Even her fear became her. Unable to wait any longer, the god resumed his true form, his natural splendor, and the girl, though terrified by the unexpected sight, was overwhelmed by this splendor and submitted without complaint as he forced himself upon her.

"Clytie was filled with jealousy (for she had always loved the Sun madly), and, aroused to fury at his new girlfriend, she spread the story of their love-making all around and made sure Leucothoe's father, Orchamus, knew about

---

*4.209: "the land of aromatic spices," that is, the East.

her disgrace. He was a savage man with an ungovernable temper, and even as Leucothoe was pleading with him and pointing to the Sun and saying to her father, 'He forced me to, against my will,' Orchamus buried his daughter deep in the ground, barbarous man that he was, and heaped a mound of heavy sand upon her. The Sun bore into this with his beams of light and made it crumble, giving you a way to move your buried head, dear nymph, but still you couldn't lift it, for it was pressed down by the dead weight of the earth. And there you lay, a lifeless corpse.

"The driver of the winged horses, they say, never beheld anything sadder than that, except when his son Phaethon was burned up. He even tried to see if he could warm her cold, cold limbs by the strength of his rays and bring her back to life. But fate opposed such an effort, and so he sprinkled scented nectar on her body and on the place where she lay and, after much railing against fate, said, 'You will rise through the air, even so.' And immediately her body, drenched with divine nectar, dissolved and soaked the earth in its fragrance, and a shoot of frankincense began to put out roots and rise gradually through the soil until it broke through the top of the mound.

"As for Clytie, though passion could excuse her for being bitter, bitterness for exposing the affair, the author of light no longer came to her and made love to her no more. She wasted away after that, driven mad by her passion. For, unable to endure the company of her sister nymphs, she sat out in the open on the bare ground night and day, her head uncovered and her hair uncombed, and went without food and water for nine whole days, sipping only a little dew and her own tears, and remaining on the ground, not moving, only watching the god, following him with her gaze as he crossed the sky. They say her limbs grew into the ground. The part of her that was pale and wan changed into bloodless leaves, while her face, the part that was tinged with red, became a flower most like the violet. Though she is held fast by her roots, she always turns to face the sun, and though she has been transformed, she loves him as much as ever."*

This was Leuconoe's story, and the amazing account gripped all those listening. Some denied it could have happened, others said real gods could do anything—only Bacchus was not a real god. The sisters insisted Alcithoe tell a story and then fell silent.

"I won't tell of the passion of Daphnis, the shepherd on Ida," she began, as she ran the shuttle back and forth on the loom, "for it's too well known how a nymph, furious because of her rival, turned him to stone. Such jealousy consumes lovers! Nor shall I say how, by a strange quirk of nature, Sithon's sex once became uncertain, and he was now a man and then a woman. Nor shall I tell how Celmis, now hardened steel, was once so devoted to the baby Jove;

---

*4.270: Clytie became the heliotrope, "a delicate small plant, violet-like in some species" (Anderson [1997] at 4.268–270, 440).

nor how the Curetes were born from a mighty rainstorm; nor how Crocos was turned into a tiny flower, along with Smilax—I'll skip over these and give you a charming and novel tale to think about.

"Do you know how Salmacis got her bad reputation? Do you know how she weakens and softens the bodies of men who touch her enervating waters? Listen and learn. Well, *how* it happens nobody knows, although her spring and its power are notorious.

"To Mercury the goddess Venus bore a son, whom naiads reared in a cave on Mount Ida. You could see both his mother and his father in his face, and his name, too, he took from them.* When he turned fifteen, he left his native mountains, moved away from Ida, where he was reared, and enjoyed wandering in places unknown to him and seeing rivers likewise unknown. His love of travel overcame all hardships.

"He even visited the cities of Lycia, and Caria, the country near Lycia. There he found a pool with water so clear you could see to the very bottom of it. No marsh reeds were in it, no useless algae, no sharp-pointed rushes. The pool was absolutely clear. Around it ran a border of grass that was always green. A nymph lived there who cared neither for hunting, nor shooting the bow, nor competing in foot races, the only one of the naiads not known to fleet-footed Diana. Her name was Salmacis.

"Often, the story goes, her sisters would say to her, 'Salmacis, you ought to get a javelin or a bow and quiver and devote some of your leisure time to hunting: good outdoor exercise.' But she wanted neither a javelin nor a bow and quiver, nor did she wish to devote any of her leisure time to hunting, good outdoor exercise though it might be. Instead, she preferred bathing in her pool and carefully washing her lovely limbs and combing her hair with her boxwood comb and consulting her reflection in the water to see what made her most attractive. Occasionally she would wrap herself in a cloak made from some sheer material and lie down on a bed of soft leaves or grass. Often she gathered flowers. And that is what she happened to be doing when she saw Hermaphroditus—and wanted him as soon as she saw him. Eager though she was to approach him, she took a moment to compose herself, survey her cloak, make her face attractive—all done to appear truly beautiful. Now she was ready to speak to him: 'Dear boy—oh, you could so easily be taken for a god! If you are a god, perhaps you're Cupid; or if you're mortal, how lucky the parents who gave birth to you, how happy your brother, too, and how truly fortunate your sister is, if you have a sister, and the nurse who gave you her breast! But the happiest of them all by far is the girl engaged to you, if there is one, if you've found the right girl to marry. If there really is someone else, then let my pleasure with you be our secret, but if there is no one, let me be yours—let's lie down together, right now!'"

*4.291: The son of Mercury and Venus is named Hermaphroditus, a combination of the Greek forms of his parents' names (Hermes and Aphrodite).

"The naiad stopped and was silent. The boy turned red in the face (for he didn't know what love was), and he was handsome even blushing, his face the color of apples on a tree aglow in the sun, or the color of tinted ivory, or of the moon, shining red beneath its silvery light when men bang bronze pots to help her (but in vain).*

"When the nymph insisted that he kiss her, at least like a brother, and kept on putting her arms around his beautiful ivory neck, he cried: 'Stop! Or else I shall run away and leave this place and leave you, too.' Alarmed, Salmacis said, 'The place is yours,' and turned, pretended to leave (but looked back even so), and disappeared behind some bushes where she crouched down and hid.

"And now, thinking he was all alone in the grass and that no one was looking, he leaped about in sheer delight and then dipped first his toes and then his feet up to the ankles in the dancing water. Taken with the mild and inviting pool, he slipped the fine clothes off his slender body—and then he was attractive indeed—and Salmacis burned with longing for his naked beauty. Her eyes were glowing, too, just like the sun's reflection in a mirror, bright and pure and round. She could hardly bear to wait, could hardly now postpone her pleasure, wanted to take him in her arms now, could scarcely contain herself now, wild with desire. The boy slapped his sides in glee, quickly dived into the pond, and swam arm over arm, his body gleaming in the bright water like an ivory statue or white lilies within fine crystal. 'I have won! He's mine!' the nymph exclaimed and, throwing off her clothes, jumped into the pond, too, and held him as he tried to fight her off; kissed his lips, as he resisted; reached down underwater and fondled him; stroked his unwilling chest; and rubbed herself against him, now on one side, now on the other.

"Finally, as he struggled, trying to wriggle free of her, she wrapped herself around him: like a snake an eagle has caught and carried off into the sky (dangling, it twists itself around the eagle's head and talons and winds its tail around its outspread wings), or like ivy twining around the trunk of a tall tree, or like an octopus, enveloping its prey underwater, sliding its tentacles around it from all directions. Mercury's son stood firm, denied the nymph the pleasures she was hoping for, but she held him fast, pressing her entire body against his, clinging to him, saying: 'Fight all you want, you naughty boy, you won't get away from me. Make it so, gods, and let no day take him away from me or me away from him.'

"Her prayer found its own gods to answer it: For their two bodies, pressed so closely together, now were fused, and they appeared to be a single person, as if someone should graft a branch of a tree onto another under the same bark and observe them growing and uniting as they grew. And so, after their limbs were joined in a tight embrace, they were no longer two, nor a form

*4.332–333: "[T]he narrator refers to the moon in eclipse, when superstitious people would anxiously beat bronze cymbals to 'help' recover its white form" (Anderson [1997] at 4.331–333, 448).

of doubleness, nor were able to be called either girl or boy, and seemed to be neither and both.

"When Hermaphroditus saw that the water he had entered as a male had made his limbs soft, had made him half the man he was, he lifted his hands and prayed in a voice now an octave higher: 'Mother! Father! Grant this gift to your son, who carries both your names. Let whoever enters this pond as a male turn suddenly soft when its water touches him and emerge from it half a man!' Each parent was moved, and they answered the prayer of their twin-sex son and infused the water with a drug that makes one's sex uncertain."* That was Alcithoë's story.

The daughters of Minyas continued working, spurning the god and profaning his festal day. Suddenly the crash and rattle of unseen drums broke upon them, and the sound of shrill Asian flutes and clashing cymbals. The air was filled with the odor of myrrh and saffron and—a thing unbelievable—the cloth they were weaving on the looms began to turn green; what was already woven and hanging down sprouted leaves and changed into ivy, and part of it became grapevines. Spun yarn turned into tendrils, little leaves sprouted from the threads on the loom, and balls of purple yarn were gleaming grapes.

Now the day was over, and it was the hour you could say was neither dark nor light, the border of coming night with just a trace of the waning day. Suddenly the foundations of the house seemed to shake, torches rich with resin appeared to blaze more brightly and light up the halls in their red glow, and phantom images of wild beasts howled. The sisters had already scattered to different parts of the smoky house to hide and escape the fire and light. And as they sought the dark, a delicate membrane spread over their limbs, now become very small, and enclosed their arms in fine wings.

The darkness kept them from knowing precisely how they had lost their original shape. It wasn't wings with feathers that lifted them in the air; they flew instead on translucent wings the membranes had made. And when they tried to speak, their voices were tiny (in keeping with their size), and they uttered their complaints with little squeaks. They crowd together in houses instead of woods; and hating daylight, they fly at night and take their name from the evening.[17]

Then all of Thebes did indeed speak of Bacchus as divine. Ino, aunt of the new god, told of his great power everywhere and alone of all her sisters was free from sorrow, except for her sadness at their sorrow. Juno then looked down on Ino, sublimely happy and proud of her sons, proud of her marriage to Athamas, and proud of the young god she was rearing, and she could not bear it. "Could that son of Jupiter's whore," she said to herself, "change the form of the Maeonian sailors and throw them into the sea, allow a mother to tear her

---

*4.388: I read *incerto* with Anderson (1982a), instead of *incesto* with Miller-Goold and others. See Anderson (1997) at 4.387–388, 455–456, for comment.

own son's flesh apart, and cover Minyas' three daughters with a new kind of wings, while Juno can only weep for the injury she has suffered, injury that is unavenged? Am I to be satisfied with that? Is that all the power I have? Yet Bacchus himself teaches me—and it's right to learn, even from an enemy—for with Pentheus' slaughter he has made the power of madness very clear indeed. So why not let Ino be driven crazy, too, and in her madness go the way of her sister?"

There is a downward-sloping path, darkened by funereal yew trees, that leads through soundless silence to the homes of hell. Here the Styx is stagnant, and mist and fog rise from it. By this path descend the recent dead, the shades of those laid to rest just now in the grave. The pallor and chill of winter lie over these rough places, and new souls are ignorant of the way to the city on the Styx and the grim palace of black Dis. This huge city has a thousand entrances and gates, wide open everywhere, and just as all the world's rivers flow into the sea, so this place receives all souls. There is room here for a population of any size, and the crowds streaming in are hardly noticed. Here spirits wander, bereft of bodies and bones. Some visit the forum; others flock to the palace of the king of the dead; still others practice different arts, imitating their lives of long ago. Fitting punishments torment a different group of souls.*

Juno, daughter of Saturn, forced herself to leave her home in heaven and travel here, willing to go that far to gratify her hatred and her wrath. As the goddess crossed the threshold, which groaned beneath her divine tread, Cerberus raised his three heads and barked once from all three mouths. Juno called out to the sisters born from night, punishing and implacable goddesses, who were sitting in front of the bolted steel doors of hell, combing the black snakes from their hair.

When they made her out in the shadows and mist, the goddesses all rose from where they were sitting, called the Seat of Crime: This is the place where Tityos, his body spread over nine acres, exposes his bowels to be torn; the place where you, Tantalus, cannot scoop up any water to drink, while the tree hanging above you always moves just out of your reach. Sisyphus, you struggle here to push that rock of yours uphill, or run back after it when it tumbles down to the bottom again. Here Ixion whirls on a wheel, chasing himself round and round; and here the daughters of Danaüs, who dared to plot their husbands' deaths (their own cousins!), endlessly fill jars with water that endlessly runs out again.

Juno took them all in with her fierce-eyed gaze, staring first at Ixion, and then, turning from him, at Sisyphus, and said, "Why does he, out of all his brothers, suffer eternal punishment, while Athamas the proud, along with his

---

*4.446: I have added to the Latin text and translated this line (*exercent, aliam partem sua poena coercet*), which Miller-Goold reject, persuaded by Anderson, who calls it "ably conceived" and "worthy of Ovid" ([1997] at 4.443–446, 462).

wife, has always rejected me, yet lives on in a luxurious palace?"* And she explained to the Furies the reasons for her hatred, why she had come, and what she wanted. What she wanted was this: She wanted the sisters to draw Athamas into madness and crime and the house of Cadmus to fall.

Rolling imperial command, promises, and prayers into one, Juno compelled the goddesses to give her their help: When she finished speaking, Tisiphone shook her head with its tangled white locks, pushed the snakes out of her face, and said, "No need for a lengthy discussion; consider it done, whatever you want; now leave this loathsome kingdom and go back to the healthier air of the world above." Juno returned happy, and just before she entered heaven, Iris, Thaumas' daughter, washed her with a cleansing rain.

Implacable Tisiphone at once took up her blood-soaked torch, put on her cloak, red with dripping gore, knotted a coiling snake around her waist, and left her house, taking with her Grief, Fright, Terror, and Madness with her twitching face. She paused on the threshold of Athamas' palace, and the door-posts trembled, they say, the maple doors blanched, and the sun fled from the sky. Ino, Athamas' wife, was terrified by these apparitions; Athamas was terri-fied, too, and both tried to run from the palace, but the malevolent Fury stood in the doorway and blocked their path. Tisiphone held out her arms, looped about with snakes coiling and uncoiling, and shook out her snaky locks, and the scales of the serpents rattled and clicked as she swung them back and forth. Some of them lay on her shoulders and some fell around her breasts, hissing and vomiting pus and flicking their tongues.

Then she yanked two snakes from her hair and with a toss of her filthy hand threw them at the pair. They slithered inside the garments and down the chests of Ino and Athamas and breathed their morbid breath upon them, but did not wound their bodies: It was their minds that felt the savage blows. Tisiphone had also brought a monstrous mixture of deadly poisons: foam from Cerberus' mouths, venom from the monstrous Echidna, the wandering blankness of a darkened mind, crime, tears, and an insane craving to kill, all ground up to-gether, mixed with fresh blood, boiled in a bronze vat, and stirred with a green stick cut from a hemlock tree. While Athamas and Ino cowered there, she ladled this concoction causing madness into both their breasts and deranged their hearts' core. Next, she swung her torch rapidly round and round and kindled a ring of fire from the whirling brand.

Successful in carrying out her orders, Tisiphone now returned to the empty kingdom of Dis and removed from her waist the serpent she had worn as a sash.

Athamas immediately went raging in the palace courtyard, shouting: "Ho! Comrades! Lay out your hunting nets here in these woods, for I just spied a

---

*4.465–469: Sisyphus and Athamas were both sons of Aeolus and thus brothers (Apollo-dorus 1.9.1–3).

lioness with her two cubs!" Now insane, he stalked his wife as though she were a wild animal, snatched little Learchus from his mother's breast, the infant smiling and holding out his tiny arms, and swung him round and round in the air like a sling and bashed his dear, soft head against a rock. Then Ino, the baby's mother, hysterical now, either from grief or from Tisiphone's poison, let out a howl, and, her hair in tangles, ran with you in her arms, little Melicertes, out of her mind and crying, "Euhoe, Bacchus!" At the name of Bacchus, Juno laughed and said, "Benefits like this may you always have from your foster son!"

There was a cliff jutting out over the sea, and its base, eaten away by the action of the waves, made a kind of shelter below from the rain, while the brow at the top extended over the water. Ino reached the top of this cliff (madness had given her strength) and without a moment's hesitation threw herself and her precious burden into the sea. White foam rose from the impact.

Venus, meanwhile, pitying her granddaughter's suffering, so undeserved, approached her uncle Neptune: "O great divinity of the waters," she said, flattering him, "to whom power has been given second only to heaven's: Dear Neptune, I have a favor to ask; a large one, I'll admit. Please pity my dear ones, whom you see tossing on the huge Ionian sea, and add them to your divinities. There ought to be some goodwill toward me in the deep if it is true that I was once formed from foam in the sea and my Greek name comes from that."*

Neptune granted her prayer and took away the mortal parts of Ino and Melicertes. He planted in them the awesome majesty of deity, changed their forms, and gave them new names, pronouncing mother and son the gods Leucothea and Palaemon.

Ino's Theban friends followed her footprints as far as they went and saw them stop at the edge of the cliff. Believing mother and child dead without a doubt, they beat their breasts in grief for the house of Cadmus, tore their hair and ripped their clothes, and cried out their hatred of the goddess for being too unjust and too cruel to her husband's mistress.†

Juno would not endure this abuse: "I'll make you yourselves the greatest monument to my cruelty," she said, and she did just that, for when the friend of Ino who loved her most ran to the edge of the cliff to jump off, saying, "I shall follow my queen into the sea," she found she was rooted to the spot and could hardly move at all. Another friend, trying to beat her breast in the customary way, felt her arms grow rigid in the attempt. Yet another, who, as it happened, had stretched out her hands toward the sea, turned to stone with her hands still stretched out toward the sea. A friend who was tearing out her

---

*4.536–538: Bilingual Venus knows her Greek name, Aphrodite, and refers to its folk etymology, generally accepted in classical antiquity, as "foam-born" (Hesiod, *Theogony* 190–199; *aphros* in Greek means "foam"). The name is not Greek. See M. L. West, introduction in his edition of Hesiod, *Theogony*, to 154–210, 211–213; and at 197, 223. See also Bömer at 4.537–538, 2.175.

†4.547: "her husband's mistress": Semele, Ino's sister, Juno's hatred of whom has extended to Ino (see 4.430–431) and her friends.

hair by the roots—you would have seen her fingers suddenly harden in her hair. Each remained frozen in the movement she was caught in. But some were turned into birds and even today fly over that water, skimming the waves with their wingtips, once women of Thebes.

Agenor's son Cadmus was unaware that his daughter and small grandson were now gods of the sea, and so, overcome by grief from the long train of disasters and by the signs he had seen,* he abandoned his city, though he was its founder, as if it were the city's misfortunes and not his own that were crushing him. After wandering for a long time, he and his wife reached the borders of Illyria. And now, weighed down by afflictions and bent with age, the couple recalled the very first troubles of their house and talked about their sufferings. "Was it a sacred serpent that I pierced with my spear so long ago, after I left Sidon, the serpent whose teeth I sowed, those strange seeds?" Cadmus asked. "If this is what the gods are avenging with such relentless anger, then I pray that I myself may turn into a serpent with a serpent's body."

As he spoke, his body lengthened into a snake with a long underbelly; he felt scales growing on his skin, now become hard; and saw his skin mottled black and blue. He fell onto his belly, and his legs, joined together, gradually extended themselves into a smooth and slender tail. His arms still remained, and he stretched forth those arms, while they remained and while he was still human, and said to his wife, tears streaming down his face, "Come, poor wife, come and touch me while there's something left of me to touch, and take my hand, while it's still a hand, before I become all snake." He intended to say more, but his tongue was suddenly split in two and his words trailed off even as he attempted to speak; every time he tried to cry out, he hissed instead. This was the voice nature left him.

Beating her bare breasts with her hands, his wife cried out: "Cadmus, wait! Poor man, change back from this monster! What is this, Cadmus? Where are your feet? Where are your shoulders, your hands, your color, your face and— even as I'm speaking—where's *any* of you at all? Oh, me, too, gods! Turn me into a serpent, too!"

Cadmus was licking the face of his dear wife and now made his way inside her garment to her dear breasts, as to a place he knew, entwining himself around the neck so familiar to him. Everyone present was terrified (and there were friends present), but Harmonia stroked the slippery neck of the crested snake—and suddenly there were two. And then with coils entwined, they slithered along the ground until they reached a hiding place in a wood nearby. Now they neither flee nor ever try to strike a human being, and, peaceable serpents, remember what they once were.[18]

But even so it was a great consolation to them in their changed form to think of their grandson Bacchus, whom India worshipped after it was conquered and

*4.565: It is not known what "signs" Ovid refers to. See Bömer at 4.565, 2.180–181.

whom all Greece honored in the temples built for him. Only Abas' son Acrisius, king of Argos, who traced his ancestry to the same origin,* continued to shut the god out of his city. Refusing to believe that Bacchus was a son of Jove, he took up arms against him. He also refused to believe that Perseus, whom his daughter Danaë had conceived in a golden rain, was Jove's son. But such is the power of truth that Acrisius soon regretted his offense to the god and his failure to recognize his own grandson, for the one now has a place in heaven, while the other, fanning the air with his rustling wings, brought back the head of the snake-haired monster, Medusa—a memorable trophy.

While he hovered above the sands of Libya in triumph, drops of blood from the Gorgon's head fell to the ground below and sprang to life as snakes of many kinds, and that is the origin of the reptiles infesting that land. From there he was driven through the sky by raging winds, blown this way and that like a cloud, as he flew over the entire world and from his great height looked down on the lands far below. Three times he saw the frozen Bears, three times the claws of Cancer, borne now toward the setting sun, now toward the rising sun.

As day was dying, Perseus, afraid to entrust himself to the night, halted in the region of the west, the kingdom of Atlas, and sought a little rest there until the morning star called forth the lights of dawn, and dawn, in turn, the chariot of the sun. Here lived Iapetus' huge son Atlas, larger by far than any human being. He ruled this remotest part of earth and the sea there, which offers its waters to the sun's hard-breathing horses and receives the weary chariot.

Now, Atlas possessed a thousand flocks of sheep and as many herds of cattle, which roamed his grassy pastures, and didn't have a single neighbor encroaching upon his land. He also owned a tree whose leaves of shining gold hid golden branches hung with golden apples. "Stranger," Perseus said to Atlas, "if illustrious origins impress you, Jupiter is the founder of my line; or if you admire great achievements, you will certainly admire mine. I ask you for hospitality and a place to rest."

Atlas remembered an ancient prophecy Themis once gave at Delphi: "A time will come, Atlas," she had said, "when your tree will be robbed of its gold, and a son of Jove will have the distinction of owning this treasure." Fearing this, Atlas had surrounded his orchard with a thick wall, stationed a huge dragon there to guard it, and closed his borders to all foreigners. Perseus, too, he ordered to leave: "Go away, far away," he said, "lest those glorious achievements—which I'm sure you lied about—lest even Jupiter help you not at all!" And he added force to his threats and tried to push Perseus out.

But the hero resisted, mixing threats with gentle appeals. Obviously inferior in strength (for who can equal the strength of Atlas?), he said, "Well, then, since my effort to be friendly is worth so little to you, here's a present for you!"

*4.607: "the same origin," that is, the same origin as Bacchus, not Cadmus (LaFaye 1.116 n. 1 and *contra* Anderson [1997] at 4.604–803, 478, and at 4.607–609, 480).

Turning his face away, Perseus thrust out the hideous head of Medusa with his left hand. Huge as he was, Atlas instantly changed into a mountain. His beard and hair became forests; his shoulders and hands, ridges on the mountain; what was formerly his head was now the mountain's peak; and his bones hardened into stone. Expanding on all sides, he became even more huge (such, gods, was your will), and the entire heavens with all their stars now rested upon him.*

Aeolus, son of Hippotes, had now confined the winds in their prison beneath Aetna, and Lucifer, the brightest star in the sky, had risen, summoning men to toil: Perseus took up his wings, tying a pair on each foot, and fastened his hooked sword at his waist. Then, wings whirring, he streaked through the clear bright air and had passed over countless nations, spread out below, when he caught sight of the people of Ethiopia and the land of their king, Cepheus. There the pitiless oracle Ammon had unjustly ordered Andromeda to pay for the sins of her mother's tongue with a punishment she did not deserve.

When Perseus first saw the girl, with her arms chained to solid rock, he would have taken her for a marble statue had it not been for the light breeze lifting her hair and the hot tears pouring from her eyes. Though he did not know it, he was on fire for her. He was so astonished, so taken with this vision of loveliness, that he almost forgot to flap his wings as he flew. The instant he landed, "O," he said, "O Girl-so-undeserving-of-*these*-chains-but-rather-those-that-bind-eager-lovers-to-each-other! Tell me your name and the name of your country and why you are wearing these chains."

Silent at first and not daring to speak to a man, the virgin girl would have covered her face with her hands out of modesty if she hadn't been bound to the rock. She could weep, though, and her eyes filled with tears. Perseus continued to press her, and, lest she appear unwilling to admit some misdeed of her own, she told him her name and the name of her country and told him, too, how self-confident her mother was in her own beauty, and had not finished relating the story when the ocean was filled with a mighty sound and a monster appeared heading right at them, looming above the vast expanse of water, its chest covering the broad sea. The girl looked up and screamed. Her father appeared from nearby, heartsick, her mother appeared, too—both distraught, her mother more so, neither able to help, both weeping and beating their breasts—certainly the right time for that—and clinging to their daughter, chained to the rock.

"You'll have time for tears later," Perseus said, "right now we've only a few moments to help her. If I should ask you for her hand—I am Perseus, the son of Jove and the woman he filled with his golden seed when she was shut up in a box; Perseus, I say, the conqueror of the Gorgon with the snaky hair, who

---

*At 4.660–662 Ovid "catches up with the anachronism" at 2.296–297, where Atlas is described as "barely able to hold the burning globe upon his shoulders!" (Anderson [1997] at 4.660–662, 484).

dared to fly on beating wings through the windy regions of the sky—if I should ask you for her hand, I'm sure I would be preferred as a son-in-law to any other. I'll try now to add a real benefit to such great qualities, if only the gods will help me: I propose that she be mine, if my heroism can save her." Her parents accepted his terms (who could refuse them?) and begged him to help them, promising their kingdom as dowry in addition.

And now . . . look! As a speeding ship shoots forward on the sweat and muscle of its youthful crew, and its jutting prow cuts through the water, so the monster divided the waves with its thrusting chest. When it was as far from the rock as a Balearic sling can hurl a lead bullet through the sky, Perseus suddenly sprang high into the air with a mighty thrust and disappeared in the clouds. Catching sight of the hero's shadow on the water, the monster attacked it savagely.

As an eagle, the bird of Jove, sees a snake in an open field sunning its blue back and seizes it from behind and, to keep it from twisting its savage head around, digs its powerful talons into the reptile's scaly neck, so Perseus dove straight down through the air with lightning speed, landed on the monster's back, and buried his sword up to the hilt in its right shoulder. Screaming with pain from the savage wound, the serpent now reared high in the air, now plunged into the sea, now turned round and round like a ferocious boar terrified by a pack of snarling dogs that has it cornered.

Using his quick wings, Perseus flew out of reach of the snapping jaws and, wherever he found an opening, struck with the sickle-shaped sword, now stabbing its back, encrusted with hollow conch shells, now slashing its ribs, now hacking at the slenderest part of its tail, where it turns into a fin. The monster vomited seawater mixed with crimson gore, drenching Perseus' wings with the bloody spray, weighing them down. The hero dared not rely on them any longer, since they were now soaking wet, and so, catching sight of a rock, the top of which stood above water when the sea was calm, but underwater when the sea was rough, he rested on this, holding on to the top of it with his left hand, while with his right he plunged his sword into the monster's belly, driving it in again and again.

The shore was filled with cheering and applause that rose to the homes of the gods on high. Cassiope and Cepheus, rejoicing, greeted Perseus as their son-in-law and acknowledged that he was the mainstay, the salvation of their house. Released from her chains, the girl, the cause of this great struggle (and also its prize) came to join them.

Perseus scooped up water to wash his victorious hands and, to keep from injuring the snaky head of Phorcys' daughter Medusa in the coarse sand, made a soft bed of leaves on the ground, spread seaweed on top, and placed the head upon it. The seaweed, freshly gathered, pliant, and still moist inside, absorbed the power of the monstrous head and began to harden from its touch, feeling a strange new rigor in its leaves and branches.

Sea nymphs attempted this miracle with more seaweed and were delighted to see the same thing happen again, and they made the seaweed grow and spread by tossing petrified pieces of it like seeds into the water. And coral still has this same quality, becoming hard on contact with air, and though it's a plant underwater, when it's out of water it turns to stone.

Perseus set up three altars made from turf to three gods: The one on the left he dedicated to Mercury; the one on the right to you, Minerva, virgin warrior; and the altar in the middle to Jove. He sacrificed a cow to Minerva, a calf to winged Mercury, and a bull to you, Jove, mightiest of the gods, and then took possession of Andromeda, his prize for so great an achievement, declining the promised dowry.

Hymenaeus and Love, leading the procession, waved the wedding torches; the altar fires were blanketed with incense; garlands were strung from the ceiling; and everywhere there was singing and the music of lyres and flutes, happy signs of joyful hearts. The doors of the palace were thrown open, revealing the entire golden atrium, and the princes of Ethiopia entered for the king's banquet, laid out with a beautiful service.

When they had finished feasting and now reclined at their ease with cups of wine, the gift of noble Bacchus, Perseus asked about the people who lived there, about their way of life, and about the character and spirit of the men. When Cepheus had answered his questions, he said, "Now, Perseus, my intrepid friend, tell us, if you will, how much courage and skill it took to remove this head that has snakes for hair?"*

The son of Agenor then described a place lying at the foot of frozen Atlas and protected by a mass of solid rock, in the entrance to which lived twin sisters, both daughters of Phorcys and sharing a single eye. He acquired the eye by a clever trick, he said, carefully sticking out his hand for it when it was being passed from one sister to the other, and then made his way through remote and impassable places, across rocky ground bristling with rough patches of growth, until he reached the home of the Gorgons. Everywhere in the fields and along the roads he saw statues of men and animals that had been turned to stone at the sight of Medusa. Nonetheless, he said, while Medusa and her snakes were in a deep sleep, he had caught her horrible reflection in the polished surface of the bronze shield he carried in his left hand and, looking at her there, had struck off her head from her neck. Swift-winged Pegasus and his brother Chrysaor were born from the drops of their mother Medusa's blood.

He told also of the dangers—all real!—of his long journey, the seas, the

---

*Two lines, 4.767a and 768, that "do not appear in any major early MSS, but have been added in the margin of some by later hands" (Anderson [1997] at 4.767a–768, 493) and that are usually printed but "bracketed," are considered spurious by Bömer and omitted by Miller-Goold. See Anderson, ibid., and Bömer at 4.767a–768, 2.220. If there is a lacuna after 4.767, as some editors assume (see Bömer, ibid.), in the missing line or lines Cepheus answers Perseus' questions (Haupt-Ehwald at 4.769, 1.248) and at 4.769–771 questions him in turn.

lands below him that he had seen from the air, and the stars his beating wings
had brushed against.

His listeners waited to hear more, but he fell silent. One of the princes then
asked why Medusa, alone of her sisters, had snakes mixed in with her hair.
Their guest replied. "That's a story worth telling in itself. Here's the answer to
your question: Medusa was quite famous for her beauty and had many suitors,
all jealous, all hoping to win her. Of all her features none was more striking
than her hair. This I learned from someone who claimed to have seen her then.
Neptune, king of the sea, is said to have raped her right in the temple of Minerva. The goddess turned away, covered her chaste eyes with the aegis, and,
unwilling to let Medusa go unpunished, changed the Gorgon's hair into loathsome snakes."* And now, too, in order to drive her enemies mad with fear, the
goddess wears upon her breast the serpents she created.[19]

---

*4.801: I end Perseus' narration at 4.801 because he still possesses the head of Medusa, which
he will use in the next book, and so cannot say (in the next sentence) that Minerva "wears upon
her breast the serpents she created" (4.803). The anachronism is solved if the next sentence
("And now, too, . . . ") is given to the narrator (Anderson [1997] at 4.802–803, 496).

BOOK FIVE

While the hero Perseus, son of Danaë, was telling this story amid the assembled gathering, the shouts of a noisy crowd filled the hall. It was not the kind of clamor one hears at a wedding party, but the sort that heralds fierce fighting, and the banquet, degenerating suddenly into an angry mob scene, you could compare to a calm sea that violent, raging winds whip up into furious waves.

The leader of this mob and the reckless instigator of conflict was Phineus, who was brandishing an ash spear with a bronze head and crying out: "Yes, it's me, come to avenge my stolen wife. Your wings can't snatch you from me now, nor can that Jupiter who turned himself into false gold!"

As he was about to hurl his spear, Cepheus shouted: "Phineus! What are you doing? What delirium, my brother, drives you to this crime? Is this the proper thanks for such a courageous act? Is this the gift you offer Perseus for saving my daughter's life? He did not take her away from you, if you want to know the truth. It was the mighty god of the Nereids; it was horned Ammon;* it was the sea monster, coming to gorge himself upon my very heart!

"She was taken from you at the moment she was going to die. Is that what you wanted, cruel man, for her to die? And would you have been consoled by my grief? It's not shameful enough, I see, that while she was being chained to the rock you simply looked on and made no move to help her—and you her uncle, even her fiancé! After that, are you sorry that someone did save her, after all, and will you take away his reward? If it's so important to you, you should have tried to save her when she was bound to that rock. Now let the man who did save her have her, as he deserves and as we agreed, the man who has freed my old age from grief and loss; and understand that I prefer him, not so much to you as to my daughter's otherwise certain death."

*5.17: "horned Ammon": The reference is to the "god of the oracle of Cyrene, [who] was represented as having ram's horns" (Anderson [1997] at 5.16–19, 500).

Phineus said nothing. Looking from Cepheus to Perseus and back to Cepheus, he could not decide whom to attack first. After hesitating a moment, he threw his spear at Perseus with all the strength his rage gave him, but missed: The spear stuck in the couch on which the hero was lying. Then, finally, Perseus leaped up and, furious, hurled the spear back at him, and would have shattered Phineus' chest had he not ducked behind an altar that offered the criminal protection he did not deserve. The weapon was not cast in vain, though: Its point lodged in Rhoetus' forehead. After he fell and the spear was wrenched from his skull, he gave a convulsive kick and spattered the banquet-laden tables with his blood.

Then the mob burned with an unconquerable wrath and hurled their spears, and some said that Cepheus ought to die along with his son-in-law; but the king had slipped out of the palace, calling on justice, good faith, and the gods of hospitality to witness that this battle had started despite his effort to prevent it. Now Pallas the warrior goddess appeared and protected her brother Perseus with her aegis and gave him courage.

There was a certain Athis from India, to whom, they say, the Ganges' daughter Limnaee had given birth beneath her clear waters, a strong and healthy, very handsome boy, sixteen years old, whose costly clothes enhanced his looks, for he was wearing a purple cloak with a golden border, a gold chain around his neck, and a curved head band over his hair, which was drenched in myrrh. Although he had been taught to hit a distant target with a spear, he was even more skillful with a bow and was on the point of drawing his when Perseus struck him with a smoking log from the altar fire and smashed his face into bits of flesh and broken bone. When Athis' closest friend, the Assyrian Lycabas, who loved him with a true and unfeigned love, saw the beautiful face jerking in spasms in its own blood, he wept bitterly, and as Athis lay dying from the horrible wound, he snatched up the bow his friend had aimed at Perseus and said: "Now fight with me! You won't rejoice for long at this boy's death, which wins you more hatred than glory"—as Lycabas said all this he shot an arrow straight at Perseus, but missed, and the shaft hung in the folds of the hero's robe. Perseus turned on him with his hooked sword, tempered in the blood of Medusa, and drove it into his heart. Dying, his eyes swimming in darkness, Lycabas looked around for Athis, fell against his friend, and as he went to the shades below took comfort in the fact that they had died together.

Now Phorbas of Syene, son of Metion, and Amphimedon of Libya were eager to fight, but they slipped and fell in the hot blood the ground was soaked in, and, trying to get up, they, too, met Perseus' sword, which the hero drove between the ribs of Amphimedon and into Phorbas' neck.

Deciding not to rely on his sword against Actor's son Erytus, whose weapon of choice was a broad-edged double-bit axe, Perseus raised a massive wine bowl high over his head with both hands, a bowl with figures carved in relief, and brought it down upon the man. Vomiting crimson gore, Erytus fell backward, all but dead, his head drumming on the ground.

Then Perseus killed Polydegmon, of the line of Semiramis; next, Abaris from Caucasus; then Lycetus, descended from the river god Spercheus; then long-haired Helix; then Phlegyas; then Clytus; and now he was stepping on the bodies of the dead, lying in heaps.

Not daring to fight his enemy hand to hand, Phineus hurled his spear at Perseus instead, striking Idas by mistake, who had remained neutral and taken no part in the battle, but in vain. Glaring savagely at cruel Phineus, Idas said, "Since you force me to take sides, Phineus, defend yourself against the enemy you've just made and pay me wound for wound!" And he wrenched the spear from his chest in order to hurl it back, but he had lost too much blood and collapsed and died.

Then Hodites, first in rank after the king, fell to the sword of Clymenus; Hypseus struck down Prothoenor; Perseus, Hypseus.

There was a very old man among them named Emathion, who feared the gods and followed the right, and, since his age prevented him from going to war, he fought with words; and now he assailed these criminal arms, cursing them bitterly.* As the old man clung to the altar with trembling hands, Chromis struck off his head with his sword, and it fell on the altar fire, where his tongue, still alive, continued to utter curses and then expired in the midst of the flames.

Next, the twins Broteas and Ammon, champion boxers both—if only fists could conquer swords—fell by the hand of Phineus, and Ampycus, too, a priest of Ceres, wearing the priest's white headband. You also fell, Lampetides, though you had not been invited for this, but rather to play the lyre and to sing, a peaceful pursuit: You had been told to enliven the festive banquet with your song. Now he was standing off to the side, holding a harmless plectrum, when Pedasus, with a mocking laugh, said, "Sing the rest of your song to the spirits of the dead by the waters of the Styx," and stabbed him in the temple with his sword. He fell, yet his dying fingers kept on strumming the lyre and with his fall played a pathetic tune on the strings.

Fierce Lycormas did not let the singer's death go unpunished: He seized the oakwood bar from the right door and slammed it into Pedasus' neck, and Pedasus crumpled to the ground like a slaughtered ox. Libyan Pelates was trying to pull the bar from the left door, but as he did so, Corythus of Marmarica nailed

---

*Lines 5.101–102 read in Latin: *loquendo / pugnat et incessit scelerataque devovet arma.* Bömer (at 5.102, 2.253) and modern translators, for example, Humphries, Melville, and Miller-Goold, take *incessit* as the perfect tense of *incedo* ("came forward," Humphries; "striding forwards," Melville; "strode forward," Miller-Goold), rather than as the present tense of *incesso,* "assail," for example, with words, as I have translated it (see *OLD* s.v. *incesso* 2a), and as Ovid uses it at 13.232–233. Aside from the fact that the present-tense *pugnat* and *devovet* (5.102) on either side of *incessit* should make the perfect of *incedo* suspect, *incessit,* "he assails," here makes a nice bridge between *pugnat* and *devovet.* Moreover, in the next line Emathion is said to cling to the altar with trembling hands (*amplexo tremulis altaria palmis,* 5.103), an action that seems incongruous with "striding forwards." Haupt-Ehwald takes the verb as the present of *incesso,* saying that *scelerata . . . arma* (5.102) is the object of both *incessit* and *devovet* (at 5.102, 1.258).

his hand to the door with the point of his spear, pinning him to it. While he was fastened there, Abas stabbed him in the side; yet he did not fall, but hung by his hand from the door, dying.

Melaneus was also killed (he was on Perseus' side) and Dorylas, the richest man of the land of Nasamonia and rich *in* land. No one owned property as far and wide as he nor could heap up as many piles of incense as he. A thrown spear pierced his groin at an angle and hung there, a fatal spot. When Halcyoneus of Bactria, who had made the wound, saw him gasping out his last breath, saw his eyes rolling back in his head, he said, "Out of all the lands you own, you'll have only this much, the plot of ground you'll lie in!" and strode away from the lifeless body.

Avenging him, Perseus, wrenched the spear from the still-warm wound and hurled it at Halcyoneus: The spear struck him in the nose and emerged from the back of his neck, sticking out of his head in front and back. While luck was with him, Perseus cut down Clytius and Clanis, sons of one mother and dying from two different wounds, for, hefting an ash spear in his powerful arm, he drove it through both of Clytius' thighs at the same time, while Clanis bit down on the javelin he suddenly found between his teeth.

Celadon from Mendes died. Astreus died; his mother was from Palestine, his father was unknown. Aethion died, very acute, once, in seeing what was coming, this time deceived by a false omen. Thoactes, the king's armor bearer, also died; and Agyrtes, notorious for murdering his father.

Though many had been killed, many more remained, all with a single intent, to overwhelm one man. Thus united, the band attacked him from all sides, opposing Cepheus' pledge and rejecting Perseus' merit. His father-in-law, earnest, but no help to him, was on his side, and his new wife and her mother were, too, and they filled the hall with their wailing, which the clanging of weapons and groans of the dying drowned out, and at the same time the war goddess Bellona was splashing great quantities of blood on the household gods, polluting them with it, stirring up the fighting, keeping it going.

Perseus, meanwhile, was alone, surrounded by Phineus and a thousand of his followers; spears were flying thicker than winter hail, whizzing past him on both sides, past his eyes and ears. Planting his back against a large stone column to protect his rear and facing the horde in front of him, he fought them off as they pressed him: Molpeus of Chaonia threatening him on his left, Ethemon the Nabataean on his right. And like a tigress driven by hunger who hears cattle lowing in two different valleys and cannot decide which to attack first—and burns to attack both—so Perseus could not decide whether to hurl himself to the left or to the right. He drove Molpeus back, stabbing him in the leg, content to let him get away, for Ethemon was upon him, raging, swinging his sword wildly, trying to slash him in the neck: He struck the column instead and shattered the blade, and a piece of steel flew back and was driven into his own throat. The wound was not severe enough to kill him, however, and as he stood there, powerless and trembling, holding out his hands for mercy, Perseus ran him through with his hooked sword, the gift of Mercury.

When the hero felt his strength failing before such numbers, he called out, "Since you force me to it, I shall call on an enemy for help; any friend who is here, turn away and don't look!" And he held up the Gorgon's head.

"Find someone else to terrify with your magic," said Thescelus, but as he was about to hurl his deadly spear he froze in his position, a marble statue now. Ampyx, beside him, aimed his sword at the courageous breast of Perseus, and his hand hardened in mid-swing, unable to move at all. Now Nileus, who had lied about his origin, claiming to be the son of the Nile with seven mouths and engraving on his shield the river's seven branches, some in silver, some in gold, said, "Behold Perseus, the origin of my line. Take with you to the silent shades the comforting thought that you died by the hand of such a great man . . ." His last words were cut off in mid-sentence, and with his mouth open you would think he was trying to speak but could not make the words come.

Then Eryx rebuked them: "It is cowardice, not the Gorgon's power, that is paralyzing you. Come on! Let's charge together and bring down this youth who fights with magic weapons!" He was about to charge, but the earth gripped his feet, and, stock-still, he stayed there, an armed stone statue.

These at least suffered a punishment they deserved, but Aconteus, one of Perseus' soldiers, while fighting for his leader glanced at the Gorgon and in an instant turned to solid rock. Astyages thought he was still alive and struck him with his sword, and the blade clanged, ringing sharply. And while he stared, amazed, he himself turned to stone, a look of surprise fixed on his marble face.

It would take too long to give the names of the men from the rank and file who died: Two hundred survived the battle, two hundred looked at the Gorgon and hardened into stone.

Phineus now regretted starting this unjust war, but what was he to do? He saw statues in different poses, recognized them as his own men, called each by name and begged for help. Not believing his eyes, he touched the forms nearest to him: They were marble. Turning his face away from Perseus, he acknowledged defeat and extended his hands and arms as a suppliant, sideways, saying: "You win, Perseus! Get rid of this monstrous thing of yours, take away the face of your Medusa, whoever she is, that turns men to stone, take it away, please! It wasn't hatred and lust for power that drove me to war. I took up arms for my bride! You deserve her more than I do, but I was there before you were. I am not ashamed to give in. I ask you for nothing except my life, you take the rest." While he spoke, Phineus dared not turn and look at the man he was begging for his life.

Perseus replied: "O most fearful Phineus! One thing I *can* grant, a great favor for a fainthearted fellow—fear not, Phineus!—I'm going to grant it. My sword won't touch a hair of your head. I shall create instead a monument that will

last for ages, and you will always be on display in my father-in-law's house so
my wife can console herself with the image of her former fiancé."

With this he thrust the Gorgon's head in front of Phineus' face, which was
turned away in terror, and even as he tried to avert his eyes his neck grew rigid,
the tears in his eyes hardened into stone, and the quivering lip, the pleading
look on his face, the praying hands, the cowering body—all were caught in
marble.

Perseus, triumphant, entered his native city with his bride, and as champion
and avenger of Acrisius, his wronged grandfather, attacked Acrisius' brother
Proetus, who had defeated Acrisius in battle, forced him to flee, and gained
possession of the city. Now neither force of arms nor stolen city enabled Proetus to overcome the fierce eyes of the snake-haired monster.

As for you, Polydectes, ruler of little Seriphos, neither Perseus' courage,
which he showed in so many achievements, nor his sufferings had softened
you. Hard and unrelenting, you kept on hating him. There is simply no limit
to an unjust wrath. You even scoffed at the honor he was paid and insisted that
the slaying of Medusa was a fiction. "I'll prove it to you," Perseus said, and
warning his companions, "Protect your eyes!" with Medusa's head made the
king's face bloodless stone.[20]

Up to now, Minerva had been a companion to her brother, born of gold, but
now she cloaked herself in a cloud and departed from Seriphos, and with Cyth-
nus and Gyarus dropping away on her right, she flew over the sea by the shortest route to Thebes and Mount Helicon, home of the virgin Muses.

When she reached the mountain she came to earth and addressed the learnéd
sisters*: "I've heard about a new spring, which Medusa's child, the winged
horse Pegasus, made with a sharp blow of his hoof. This is the reason I've
come. I want to see this marvelous creation; Pegasus himself, born from his
mother's blood, I've already seen.

The Muse Urania replied: "Whatever the reason you've come to our home,
goddess, you are very dear to our hearts and most welcome! What you've heard
is true. Pegasus did create this spring," and she led Minerva to the sacred waters. After admiring for a long time the spring made by the blow of a hoof, the
goddess looked around at the shade in the ancient forest, the grottoes, the
grassy meadows stippled with thousands of wildflowers, and declared the
daughters of Memory happy in work and home alike.

One of the sisters then said to her: "O Minerva, if only your excellence had
not led you to greater achievements, you would have been part of our chorus.
What you say is true, and you rightly praise our art and the place where we
live, and ours is indeed a happy lot—if only we can remain safe! But—for no
crime is forbidden here—everything terrifies the hearts of innocent girls. Sav-

---

*5.255: Ovid calls the Muses "learnéd" (*doctas*), thus enduing them with "the ideal asset
of contemporary Roman poets," erudition "in the Alexandrian tradition" (Anderson [1997] at
5.253–255, 521).

age Pyreneus haunts my mind, and I'm still not quite myself again: That wild man with his Thracian army seized Daulis and the fields of Phocis and ruled them unlawfully. As we were going to the temple on Mount Parnassus he saw us coming and, feigning a worshipful attitude toward us as divinities, said: 'Daughters of Memory' (for he knew who we were), 'stop! Please don't hesitate to come in under my roof and get out of this foul weather' (for it was raining). 'Gods have often entered the houses of lesser folk.'

"Persuaded by his words (and by the weather), we accepted his invitation and stepped into the hall of his house. When the rain stopped and the wind shifted around to the north and the dark clouds were fleeing and the sky was clearing, we were ready to go, but Pyreneus locked his doors. He intended to rape us, but we sprouted wings and escaped. He himself stood high up on the citadel as if to pursue us, and said, 'I shall go the same way you did,' and, madman that he was, threw himself from the top of the tower, fell headfirst, and crashed to the ground, shattering his skull and soaking the ground with his violent blood."

The Muse was still speaking when the sound of flapping wings filled the air, and from high in a tree a chorus of voices cried out, "Hel-lo!" Minerva looked up to see where this greeting came from, so distinct and clear, thinking that it was human voices she had heard. But it was a flock of birds: In the branches of the tree, lamenting their fate, sat nine magpies, who mimic everything. When Minerva marveled at this, the Muse said to her, speaking goddess to goddess: "These have only recently joined the bird kingdom, after being defeated in a contest. Pieros, a wealthy landowner in Pella, was their father; their mother, Euippe of Paeonia. She gave birth nine times, calling on Lucina, the powerful goddess of childbirth, each time.

"This crowd of stupid sisters, swollen with pride in their numbers, traveled here through all the cities of Thessaly and Achaea to challenge us to a contest, on these terms: 'Stop deceiving the ignorant masses with your syrupy songs,' they said, 'and compete with us—if you have the courage—O goddesses of Thespiae.* We will not be outdone, neither in our voices nor in our art, and there are just as many of us as there are of you. If you lose, cede to us the Boeotian springs of Medusa and Aganippe, and if we lose, we'll give you the Macedonian plains as far as snowy Paeonia. Let the nymphs decide the outcome.'

"It was shameful to compete with them, but even more distasteful to give up without a fight. The nymphs who were chosen as judges took oaths by their rivers and sat down on rock that offered them a natural seat. Then, without waiting for the lot to decide who would go first, the Pierid sister who had initiated the contest began to sing about the battle between gods and giants, giving undeserved honor to the giants and making the great deeds of the

---

*5.310: "goddesses of Thespiae": Thespiae was a city in Boeotia at the foot of Mount Helicon that was the ancient site of the cult of the Muses (Haupt-Ehwald at 5.310, 1.271).

mighty gods look small. She told how Typhoeus emerged from the depths of the earth and terrified the gods, all of whom turned and fled until, exhausted, they took refuge in the land of Egypt and the Nile with its seven mouths.

"Here, too, she continued, came earth-born Typhoeus, and the gods concealed themselves by adopting false shapes and, she said, 'Jupiter became a ram, the leader of a flock, and because of that as Libyan Ammon he is even now depicted with horns; Apollo became a raven; Semele's child, Dionysus, a goat; Apollo's sister, Diana, a cat; Juno, a snow-white cow; Venus disguised herself as a fish; Mercury as a winged ibis.' So she sang, accompanying herself on the lyre.

"Then we Muses were called upon to sing—but perhaps you're in a hurry and don't have time to listen to our song . . ."

"No, no," said Minerva, "do begin and sing your song for me from beginning to end," and settled herself on the ground in the gentle shade of the grove. The Muse resumed. "We put all the responsibility of competing on just one of us, on Calliope. She rose, put an ivy crown on her head to keep her long, flowing hair in place, strummed a plaintive chord on the lyre, and sang this song as she plucked the strings:

"'Ceres was the first to turn the soil with the plow, the first to give the sweet nourishing fruits of the earth to the world, the first to make laws. Everything is the gift of Ceres, and of her I must sing. I only wish my song were worthy of the goddess, for the goddess is most worthy of my song!

"'The huge island of Sicily had been heaped upon the body of Typhoeus, and it pressed down on the giant, confined beneath its massive weight, for he had dared to aspire to a home in heaven. He struggled beneath the island and fought continually to rise up again, but his right hand was pinned by Ausonian Pelorus, his left by you, Pachynus, and his legs were held down by Lilybaeum.* Mount Etna's mass pressed heavily on fierce Typhoeus' head, and as he lay on his back beneath it, he spewed molten sand from his mouth and belched out flame. He labored constantly to throw off the weight of the earth and roll the towns and huge mountains from his body. Then the earth would quake and the king of the silent dead himself would be thrown into a panic, lest the ground crack wide open, his kingdom lie exposed, and daylight pour in and terrify the trembling shades.

"'Fearing this catastrophe, the ruler of the underworld left his shadowy home and in a chariot drawn by black horses drove around the foundations of Sicily, carefully inspecting them. After he had satisfied himself that nothing had fallen and, fears allayed, was wandering about, Venus saw him from her mountain home and took her winged son in her arms and said, "My son—my weapons, my hands, my power—dear Cupid, take those swift arrows with which you conquer everyone and bury them deep in the heart of the god whose

---

*5 350–351: Pelorus, Pachynus, and Lilybaeum are three headlands or spits of tricornered Sicily, in the northeast, south, and west, respectively. See Bömer at 5.350, 351, 2.315.

fortune it was to receive the third and last of the kingdoms of the world. You can subdue the gods in heaven and Jupiter himself, the deities of the sea and the king who rules them: Why not the underworld, too? Why not extend your mother's empire, and your own? A third of the world is at stake; and besides, in heaven we are spurned—we've just had to endure it—and love's power has been diminished, along with mine. Have you not noticed that Minerva and spearwoman Diana have no use for me? And Ceres' daughter Proserpina will remain a virgin, too, if we let her, for she hopes to be like them. But on behalf of the kingdom we share, if it means anything to you at all, join the young goddess to her uncle."

"'So Venus. Cupid then opened his quiver and, obeying his mother, selected from his thousand arrows just one, but the one that was sharpest, most accurate, and most responsive to his bow; next, he braced the supple instrument against one knee to string it and then drew it into an arc and shot Dis in the heart with the barbed arrow.*

"'Not far from the city walls of Henna there is a deep lake called Pergus. You can hear as many swans singing there as you can on the lazy waters of the river Cayster. Trees surround this lake on all sides, their leaves and branches, like an awning, shade the place from the rays of the sun and keep it cool, and purple flowers blossom on the moist ground. Here it is always spring.

"'One day, while Proserpina was playing in this grove and picking violets here, white lilies there, and in her girlish eagerness filling both her flower basket and the folds of her robe, trying to outdo her playmates in gathering flowers, in a single instant, almost, she was seen, loved, and raped by Dis. (Love is always in such a hurry!) The goddess, terrified, wailing, cried out for her mother, for her friends, but mostly for her mother, and since she had ripped open her robe,† the flowers she had tucked in it tumbled out, and she was so young and innocent that losing them also made her cry.

"'Her abductor then got his chariot under way, urging on his horses, each by name, shaking the rust-colored reins on their necks and manes, and they were off, running through deep lakes and the pools of the Palici, stinking with sulphur and bubbling up through cracks in the earth, and past the place between two harbors of unequal size where the offspring of Bacchus, a line that sprang up in Corinth, had laid their walls.‡

---

*5.383–384: 5.383: "[Cupid] braced the supple instrument": As Bömer notes, Ovid, perhaps influenced by Lysippos' statue of Eros drawing his bow, confuses—conflates, really—two actions: *drawing* the bow to shoot it and *stringing* the bow. No one, Bömer continues, can draw a bow with the knee, hold it drawn, fit an arrow to it, and then shoot it, although one would use one's knee and lower leg to help in stringing a bow (at 5.383, 2.323–324). The translation expands Ovid's Latin (*oppositoque genu curvavit flexile cornum*, 5.383) by describing two separate (and successive) actions, Cupid's stringing the bow with the help of his knee and then drawing the bow to shoot it. 5.384: Dis is another name for Pluto, god of the underworld.

†5.398: "'and since she had ripped open her robe'": "a conventional gesture of grief" (Anderson [1997] at 5.396–399, 540).

‡5.407–408: "the place between two harbors" refers to Syracuse. See Haupt-Ehwald at 5.407f, 1.282.

"'Between the springs of Cyane and Arethusa of Elis lies a gulf, enclosed between narrow points of land. Here Cyane lived, the most famous of the Sicilian nymphs, for whom the spring-fed pool was named. Rising out of the water as far as her waist, she recognized the young goddess and shouted at Dis, "Stop right there! You cannot become Ceres' son-in-law against her will. Proserpina must be wooed and won, not carried off and raped! And if I may compare small things with great, I too was loved, by Anapis, but I was courted properly and did not, like this girl, marry in a state of terror!" And spreading her arms wide, she blocked their way.

"'Saturn's son could restrain his rage no longer, and, urging on his terrible horses, with his mighty arm he whirled the royal scepter and flung it into the water. The earth opened a way to the underworld where the scepter struck it and swallowed the hurtling chariot in the chasm.

"'Grieving for the goddess who had been stolen away and for the contempt shown to her spring and its rights, Cyane nursed in her silent heart an inconsolable wound and, completely consumed by her tears, dissolved into those waters whose great goddess she had just now been. You would have seen her limbs soften, her bones become pliant, and her nails lose their hardness. First, the slenderest parts of her body became liquid, her sea-blue hair, fingers, legs, and feet. (For it doesn't take long for the thinner parts to turn to water.) Next her shoulders, back, sides, and breasts all melted away into rivulets. Then water ran in her dissolving veins instead of warm blood, and there was nothing left of her to grasp.

"'Meanwhile, Ceres, fearful for her daughter, searched for her in every land, on every sea, but in vain. Dawn coming up from ocean at the break of day with hair still damp saw Ceres looking everywhere, and Hesperus, the evening star, saw her at dusk, looking still. She lit torches made of pine from Mount Etna and carried them in each hand through the frosty night, never resting, and when nurturing day once again blotted out the stars, she was still searching for her daughter, searching from the rising of the sun to its going down.

"'Exhausted and thirsty from her effort, she had found no spring where she could wet her lips. Then she happened to see a hut roofed with straw and knocked at its small door. An old woman emerged, saw the goddess, who asked for water, and gave her a sweet concoction topped with roasted barley. While she was drinking, the old woman's son, a vulgar, impudent boy, stood staring at the goddess, then burst out laughing and called her greedy. Angered, Ceres flung what was left of the barley mixture in the boy's face, while he was still speaking. As the drops sank into his skin, what he had just now moved as arms he now wiggled as legs, a tail grew from his changing body, and lest he have great power to do harm, he was reduced to the form of a lizard, but a smaller-than-ordinary lizard.

"'Astonished and in tears, the old woman tried to touch the strange new creature, but he scurried away from her and sought the dark. His body is starred with bright spots, and he bears a name that matches his shameful behavior.*

"'It would take too long to tell all the lands the goddess passed through in her wandering and all the seas she crossed. There was now no place left in the world for her to look, so she returned to Sicily and, traversing it again in her search, came eventually to Cyane.

"'Had the nymph not been changed, she would have related everything, but though she longed to tell all she knew, she had neither mouth nor tongue nor way to speak. She was able, nevertheless, to communicate by signs, and she pointed to Proserpina's sash. The goddess immediately recognized it. It happened to have slipped from the girl's waist at that very spot in the sacred pool and was floating on the surface. When she saw the sash, the goddess realized that her daughter had been raped, and she tore her already disheveled hair and beat her breast again and again. She still did not know where Proserpina was, but even so she rebuked all the lands of the earth, calling them ungrateful, not deserving the gift of grain, Sicily above all, where she had found the traces of her lost daughter. And with a sharp blow of her hand she smashed the plows that turn the soil in Sicily, and in her rage killed farmers and oxen alike and ordered the fields to turn against the seeds the farmers planted, while she herself destroyed the seeds they sowed.

"'The land of Sicily, known throughout the wide world for its rich soil, lay barren. The grain died when the first blades appeared, scorched by too much sun or rotted by too much rain. Weathers and winds worked their harm, and birds carried off the seeds that were planted, while darnel, thorns, and ineradicable, relentless wire grass choked the grain at harvest time.

"'Then Arethusa, beloved of Alpheus, raised her head from her waters (which flowed from Elis), brushed her dripping hair from her eyes, pushed it behind her ears, and said to Ceres, "Mother of grain and mother, too, of the girl you've hunted the whole world for, stop your futile searching and do not inflict your violent rage on an earth that has been so faithful to you. It deserves none of this, it opened itself to her abductor unwillingly.

"'"I am not pleading for my fatherland. I came here as a stranger. My country is Pisa, and I began life in Elis. I now live in Sicily as a foreigner with the name Arethusa, but this land is dearer to me than any other. My household gods are here, my home is here. Be merciful and spare it. Why I crossed such a mighty sea and came to Sicily—but I'll tell you my story at another, more suitable time, when you're not so worried, don't appear so downcast. The earth gave me passage underground, and I was carried through its cavernous depths until

---

*5.460–461: The boy has been turned into a gecko (small lizard) the Latin word for which, *stellio,* not used here—Ovid uses instead the word *lacerta* (5.458)—also means "a treacherous or deceitful person" (see *OLD* s.v. *stellio*). Ovid says the lizard is *stellatus* (5.461), "starred," thereby suggesting *stellio,* which is derived from *stella,* "star" (Anderson [1997] at 5.459–461, 546).

I lifted up my head here and saw again the stars I had forgotten. As I made my way beneath the earth, like another Styx, I saw Proserpina with my own eyes. She was still very sad, and fear still showed in her face, but she was a queen, even so, ruling now in the world of darkness, the powerful consort now of the king of hell."

"'Ceres was quiet for a long time, like a stone, like someone stunned by a blow, in profound shock at what she had heard. And then her shock gave way to profound grief, and she drove in her chariot to the heights of heaven. She stood before Jove, hair in disarray, face dark with despair, smoldering with hostility. "I come, Jupiter, as a suppliant, on behalf of my daughter—and your daughter, too," she said. "And if her mother is out of favor with you, then your daughter's plight should move her father, and you should not be indifferent to her simply because she has me as her mother.

"'"Well, I have found her now, after looking for her for so long, if you call 'finding her' the certainty of losing her, if you call 'finding her' merely knowing where she is. That she was raped—that I will try to bear. But he must bring her back! And if she's no longer *my* daughter, well then, *your* daughter does not deserve a rapist for a husband."

"'Jupiter replied. "The daughter you and I had together is both a bond between us and a responsibility we share. But if we can just call it by its right name, what happened was not a violation, it is, in fact, love. He's not a son-in-law we'll be ashamed of, if only you, goddess, give your consent. Though he may lack other things, what an advantage it is to be the brother of Jove! But have you considered this: that he is in no way deficient, in no way inferior to me, except in his station in life, which was decided by lot? Yet if you truly want them to separate, Proserpina will return to heaven, but only on the strict condition that no food has touched her lips in the underworld. For this proviso is stated in the law of the fates."

"'Jove had spoken. Ceres was still determined to get her daughter back, but the fates would not allow it, for the girl had indeed eaten something. While innocently strolling in the well-kept gardens in the underworld, she had picked a red pomegranate from a low-hanging branch, peeled the deadly skin, taken seven seeds, put them in her mouth, and eaten them. The only one who saw this was Ascalaphus, whom Orphne, one of the best-known nymphs of Avernus, is said to have borne to Acheron beneath a tree in a black forest. Ascalaphus saw it, reported it, cruel boy, and kept her from returning.

"'Learning this, the queen of darkness groaned and turned the informer into a sinister kind of bird, for she sprinkled water from the river Phlegethon on his head, giving him a beak and feathers and large eyes. Losing his original self, Ascalaphus was cloaked in tawny wings, became almost all head,* and his

---

*5.547: "became almost all head": Ascaphalus "grows into his head as it becomes a larger part of his [screech owl's] total body" (Anderson [1997] at 5.546–550, 554).

nails curved into long talons. Covered with feathers, hardly stirring his slug-gish limbs, he was now a bird with loathsome features, a messenger of grief to come, the slothful screech owl, an omen of dread for mortals.

"'He can easily seem to deserve this punishment because of his tattling tongue. But you, daughters of Achelous, where did you get your birds' feet and your feathers, since you have girls' faces? Was it because, O Sirens, learnéd singers, you were with Proserpina when she was picking spring flowers? For you were with her, and after you searched in vain for her throughout the world, you wanted to be able to hover over the waves on wings so the waters would sense your sorrow. The gods were merciful to you, and you suddenly saw yellow feathers growing on your limbs. Yet, lest their song, made to soothe all who heard it—such a great gift—lose the tongues it needs for singing, they kept the faces and voices of the girls they had been.

"'Mediating between his brother and his stricken sister, Jupiter divided the year into two parts of equal length, and now the goddess Proserpina, a deity belonging to two worlds, spends the same amount of time each year with her mother and with her husband. In an instant, her state of mind changed, her expression lightened, and her face, which had seemed so gloomy, even to Dis, shone with joy, like the sun when it emerges from rain clouds that had hidden it.

"'Ceres the nurturing mother, free from sorrow after regaining her daughter, now asked you, Arethusa, the reason for your flight, why you are a sacred spring. The spring fell silent, and then its goddess raised her head from its depths, pressed the water from her green hair with her hand, and told the story of the long-ago love of Alpheus, the river of Elis. "I was one of the nymphs of Achaea," she began, "and no other nymph roamed the upland woods more constantly than I nor set out the hunting nets more frequently. Though I never wanted to be thought a beauty, and though I was brave and strong, I was considered quite beautiful all the same. I received too much praise for my looks, and it made me unhappy, and the features other girls are delighted to have only embarrassed me, for I was a country girl, and I thought being beautiful was a crime.

""Once I was returning exhausted from the Stymphalian forest (I remember it well), it was a hot day, and the fact that I was tired made it seem twice as hot. I came upon still water, flowing so silently that it hardly seemed to move and so clear that you could count every pebble on the river bottom. Silver willows and poplars fed by the stream provided natural shade for its sloping banks. I walked down to the water's edge and tested it with my toes, then waded in up to my knees. Not content with that, I undid my fine soft tunic and threw it across the overhanging branch of a willow and plunged into the stream naked.

""While I was splashing in the water and scooping it up and moving my arms as I swam, I heard something like a murmuring sound coming from the bottom and was frightened and jumped out on the bank I was closer to. 'Where are you going in such a hurry, Arethusa?' said Alpheus in a husky voice from his waters, and again, 'Where are you going in such a hurry?' I fled just as I was, without my clothes (for they were on the opposite bank), but just as quickly he came after me, becoming aroused as he chased me, and because I was naked, I seemed easier for him to take. And so I ran, like a dove flapping her wings as she flees a hawk, and so he was hot after me, like a hawk swooping down on a trembling dove.

""'I even ran past the walls of Orchomenos, past the walls of Psophis and the foot of Mount Cyllene, through the valleys of Mount Maenalus, past cool Mount Erymanthus, past Elis.* He couldn't catch me, but I couldn't keep up this pace for long, for my strength wasn't equal to his, while he had the stamina for a long, long chase. Even so, I ran on, across plains and tree-covered mountains, over rocks and crags, through open country.

""'The sun was at my back, and suddenly I saw a great shadow looming over me—unless I imagined it in my fear. The sound of Alpheus' running feet terrified me, and his heavy panting breath fluttered my headband. Exhausted from the effort to escape him, I cried: 'Help me, Diana! I've been caught! I'm your arms-bearer, whom you've allowed so many times to carry your bow, your quiver, and your arrows!'

""'Moved by my plea, the goddess enveloped me in a thick mist that she parted from a mass of clouds. Alpheus kept circling the mist, puzzled, looking for me all around the fog that enclosed me. Twice he went right past the spot where the goddess had put me, not knowing I was there, and twice called out, 'O Arethusa, O Arethusa!'

""'How do you think I felt then, frightened as I was? How does a lamb feel when, deep within the sheepfold, it hears wolves howling outside? How does a rabbit hiding in a thicket feel, when it sees excited dogs, noses to the ground, sniffing all about and dares not move a muscle? Alpheus wouldn't go away, for he didn't see footprints leading on. He kept his eye on the cloud, watching the place.

""'I felt trapped and broke out in a cold sweat. Azure drops ran down my entire body, and wherever I moved my foot, a pool formed. Water trickled from my hair, and in less time than it takes me to tell you, I was changed into a spring. But Alpheus recognized me in the spring, dropped his guise as a man, and turned back into his own stream in order to mingle his waters with mine.

""'Then Diana broke open the ground, and I sank down into dark caverns and was carried to Ortygia, which is dear to me because it bears one of my goddess' names, and there I first came up into the open air.'" That was Arethusa's story.

---

*5.607–609: "I even ran . . . past Elis": "a fantastic chase route" that covers "more than 150 miles and a variation between lowest and highest points of a mile and a half" (Anderson [1997] at 5.607–609, 561).

"'Ceres then yoked twin serpents to her light chariot, forced the bits into their mouths, and drove through the sky between heaven and earth, guiding the chariot to Athens. There she gave it to Triptolemus, along with some seeds, half of which she ordered him to sow in ground never tilled before and half in earth that had lain fallow for a long time.

"'Now borne in the goddess' chariot high over Europe and Asia, the young man made his way to Scythia, where Lyncus was king. He entered the king's palace, and when he was asked where he came from, the reason for his journey, and his name and homeland, he answered, "My country is renowned Athens, my name, Triptolemus. I came neither by ship through the sea nor overland by foot. The sky was open to me, and I came that way. I bring with me gifts from Ceres, which, when scattered through your broad fields, will grow fruitful crops and make sweet harvests."

"'The barbarian king envied him for this, and since he wanted to be the source of so great a gift himself, he welcomed Triptolemus warmly and when he was sound asleep attacked him with a sword. As Lyncus was about to stab him in the heart, Ceres turned the king into a lynx, and ordered the Athenian youth to drive her sacred team back through the air.'

"Calliope, our greatest singer, had ended her learnéd song, and the nymphs with one voice declared us goddesses of Mount Helicon the winners in the contest. When the losers began to abuse us, I said, 'Since it is apparently not enough for you to deserve punishment for challenging us to a contest, and you now add insult to injury, and since our patience is not limitless, we shall punish you as our wrath dictates.' The Macedonian women just laughed, scoffing at these threats, and as they tried to speak and, with loud shouts, tried to reach out to scratch us, they suddenly saw feathers sprouting from their fingernails, saw down covering their arms, saw one another's faces stiffening into hard beaks, and were added to the forest as new birds. They wanted to beat their breasts, but when they moved their arms, the Pierides rose up and hovered in the air, magpies now, noisy denizens of the woods. The old talkativeness stayed with them as birds, their garrulousness, their inborn passion for chattering."[21]

BOOK SIX

Such was the story Minerva heard, and she applauded the Muses' song—and their anger, too, for she thought it was entirely justified. Then she said to herself, "There's not enough praise here; we ought to be praised, too, nor should we let our divine power be scorned with impunity"; and she began to think about how to punish Arachne of Lydia, who, she had heard, saw no reason at all to yield to the goddess in the art of weaving wool.

Now, Arachne was undistinguished both in place of origin and in family line; her fame lay in the art of weaving. Her father, Idmon of Colophon, was a dyer of wool who liked to use Phocaean purple. Her mother was dead, but she had been a commoner, too, on the same level as her husband. Though born in a small house in the small village of Hypaepa, Arachne had nevertheless acquired quite a reputation for her talent at the loom throughout the cities of Lydia. Nymphs on Mount Tmolus often abandoned their vineyards, and nymphs of the river Pactolus often left their waters, just to come and look at her wonderful handiwork. And it was a pleasure not only to examine her finished tapestries but also to watch her weaving, her artistry was so beautiful. Whether shaping the raw fleece into balls, or using her fingers in one continuous motion to make the wool soft and fluffy and pull it out for spinning; or whether she was keeping the polished spindle turning with a light touch of her thumb, or creating a colorful pattern as she wove: You would know she had learned her art from Minerva.

But Arachne denied this, offended at the idea of being taught by so great a teacher as the goddess. "Let her have a contest with me," she declared. "If she defeats me, she can do what she likes with me."

Minerva disguised herself as an old woman and put on a wig of gray hair, took up a cane, as if her limbs were infirm, and came to Arachne and said to her: "Not everything about old age should be despised. Advancing years bring *some* advantages, so don't reject my advice. Compete with mortals for the greatest mortal reputation in making wool, but yield to the goddess and humbly

94

beg her forgiveness, reckless girl, for your rash words. She'll forgive you if you ask her to."

Giving her a hard look, her face working with anger, Arachne let go the threads she had taken up and almost slapped the disguised Minerva's face. "You senile old fool," she cried, "with one foot in the grave! You've lived too long for your own good! Save your words for your daughter-in-law, if you have one, or your daughter. I can give myself advice. Don't think your warning has had any effect on me. My opinion hasn't changed. Why doesn't your goddess come here herself? Why is she avoiding a contest with me?"

"She *has* come!" Minerva declares, taking off her disguise and revealing herself as the goddess. The nymphs who are there, as well as the Mygdonian women, prostrate themselves before the divinity; Arachne alone is unafraid. But she blushed even so, and her face turned deep red for just a moment, against her will, even as the sky turns purple at dawn but quickly brightens as the sun comes up. Nonetheless, she persists in her plan and rushes into ruin from a thick-headed lust for glory. For the daughter of Jove does not decline her challenge, nor repeat her warning, nor put off the contest.

Without further delay they set up two looms opposite each other, and on the cross-pieces that joined the uprights of each loom they string the fine threads of the warp, keeping them separate by means of reeds, and then, using their fingers to free the threads from a skein for the woof, they insert these with sharp needles among the threads of the warp and weave them through and tap them into place with the notched-tooth combs that weavers use.

They both work quickly, their robes wrapped tightly around them, moving their arms expertly, their skill concealing their effort. They weave in purple dyed in Tyrian vats and subtle shades of slightly different colors, as when the rays of the sun are interwoven with the falling rain, and a vast curving rainbow paints the sky. Though a thousand hues are shining there, the eye cannot tell where one color ends and the next begins. They seem the same where they touch, yet are clearly different at the rainbow's edges.

Fine gold is also intertwined among the threads, and old tales are woven down the web. Minerva fashions the Hill of Mars on the Acropolis at Athens and that long-ago contest to name the land.* The twelve celestial gods sit in august majesty on their lofty seats: An exact rendering identifies each one like a signature, Jove's the very image of kingliness. She weaves in the god of the sea standing and striking a jagged rock with his trident, and salt water gushes from the gash in the rock. With this the god makes his claim to the city. To herself she gives a shield, a sharp spear, a helmet, and the aegis that protects her breast. And she depicts the earth, struck by her spear and producing the olive tree, silvery green and heavy with olives, to the astonishment of the gods. She completes the scene with the figure of Victory.

So that Arachne, competing with her for recognition, may understand by

---

*6.70–71: "Ovid here confuses the Acropolis with the Areopagus" (Miller-Goold, n.1, 1.293).

examples the price she can expect to pay for her reckless daring, Minerva adds
four contests to the four corners of her tapestry, weaving in small figures, each
with its own bright colors.

One corner has Thracian Rhodope and Haemus, who took for themselves
the names of the highest gods and now are frozen mountains, though they
once had human forms. Another corner has the wretched fate of the pygmy
woman,* whom Juno defeated in a contest, changed into a crane, and forced
to make war on her own people. In the third corner she fashioned Antigone,
who once dared to contend with Jove's consort, royal Juno. Juno turned her
into a bird. Neither her city Ilium nor her father Laomedon could keep Antigone from becoming a stork with white wings and applauding herself with her
clacking beak. The remaining corner has Cinyras, desolated, lying on temple
steps made from the bodies of his own daughters, hugging the stones and
weeping.

Minerva frames her work with a border of olive branches, the emblem of
peace, and so ends with the image of her own tree.

Now Arachne depicts Europa, deceived by the semblance of a bull. You
would think it was a real bull swimming in a real sea. Europa herself seems to
look back at the land she has left and to cry out for her friends and, fearing the
touch of the lightly splashing waves, to draw up her nervous feet.

Arachne also made Asterie in the grip of the eagle that struggles with her,
made Leda lying beneath the wings of the swan, and added Jupiter: how as a
satyr he made beautiful Antiope pregnant with twin sons; how as Amphitryon
he took you, Alcmena; how as golden rain he fooled Danaë; as fire, Aegina; as
a shepherd, Memory; as a speckled snake, Proserpina.

You, too, Neptune, she placed in the scene, changed into a fierce bull for
love of the girl Canace. As the river Enipeus you engender the sons of Aloeus,
Otus and Ephialtes; as a ram you deceive Theophane. The flaxen-haired goddess, most gentle mother of grain, felt you as a stallion; the snake-haired
mother of the winged horse felt you as a bird; Melantho felt you as a dolphin.
All these Arachne rendered, each with its own likeness, and the places, exactly.

Phoebus Apollo is there, first as a farmer, then wearing the feathers of a
hawk and then a lion's skin; next she showed how as a shepherd he fooled
Isse, daughter of Macareus; how Bacchus deceived Erigone with false grapes;
and how Saturn as a horse created the centaur Chiron, both horse and man.†
The edge of her tapestry has a narrow border of flowers interwoven with twining ivy.

Minerva could not fault the work—not even Envy herself could fault it—
but Arachne's success rankled with her, and she ripped apart the figured cloth
and its crimes of the gods and began beating the girl on the head with the

---

*6.90: Bömer gives the pygmy woman's name as Oinoe or Gerana (at 6.90, 3.32–33).
†6.126: Ovid does not name Saturn's victim here, but she was Philyra, mother of Chiron.
(Haupt-Ehwald name her at 2.630, 1.127.)

boxwood shuttle she still held in her hand. Unable to endure this, the unfortunate Arachne, still defiant, slipped a noose around her neck and hanged herself.

Then Minerva pitied her, as she hung there, and, lifting her up, said, "Live on, shameless girl, but hang forever, even so, and think not that this curse ends with you, for I decree the same punishment for your entire line and all your descendants!" and as she left she flung at Arachne juice pressed from one of Hecate's herbs. Touched by those magic drops, Arachne's hair fell out; her nose and ears dropped away; her head became tiny; her whole body shrank; and slender, finger-like limbs grew from her sides as legs. The rest of her was belly, from which she spins a thread to weave as she wove before, for she is a spider now.[22]

All Lydia was in an uproar, and the story of what had happened spread to all the towns of Phrygia and created talk throughout the great world. Now, when Niobe was a young girl, still unmarried and living in Maeonia near Mount Sipylus, she had known Arachne, but the punishment of her countrywoman had not taught her to submit to the gods and not insult them. Niobe did have much to be proud of, and while her husband's art, their family lines, and the large kingdom they ruled all made her happy, they did not make her as happy as her children did, and she would have been called the luckiest mother ever had she not thought so, too.

Now, Tiresias' daughter Manto, who always knew in advance what was going to happen, had gone into the streets of Thebes, possessed by divine power, and had prophesied: "Women of Thebes, hurry, all of you, to Latona's temple. Wear laurel in your hair and offer her and her two children incense and your holy prayers. So Latona orders me to say."

All the Theban women hastened to obey, adorning their heads with laurel wreaths, as Latona had ordered, throwing incense on the sacred fire, and reciting the words of the prayers. And now came Niobe, surrounded by a throng of attendants, magnificent in a robe of Phrygian purple and gold brocade, as beautiful as her anger would allow her to be.

Tossing her fine head, her hair falling around her shoulders, she stopped, looked round with an imperious gaze, and said: "What madness is this, to prefer the gods in heaven, of whom you've only heard, to what is right in front of you? Why is Latona worshipped at altars everywhere while my godhead still lacks incense? My father was Tantalus, who alone of mortals was allowed to sit at the table of the gods. My mother's sisters are the Pleiades, mighty Atlas, who supports the vault of heaven on his shoulders, is one of my grandfathers. Jupiter is my other grandfather, and I take pride in the fact that he is also my father-in-law. The people of Phrygia live in fear of me. Cadmus' royal house is under my power. The people and city of Thebes, whose walls were formed by the music of my husband's lyre, are governed both by him and by me.

"Wherever I turn my eyes in my house I see enormous wealth. I myself am just as beautiful as any goddess. To that, add my seven daughters and seven sons and my sons-in-law and daughters-in-law, soon to come! Now ask why I'm so proud! Now prefer Latona, the child of some Titan or other, Coeus, I think, to me—if you dare! Why, the earth, as huge as it is, once denied her even one small corner to give birth in! Neither land nor sea nor sky accepted your goddess. She was an exile from the world until the island Delos pitied her homeless state, saying to her, 'You wander the earth, I wander the sea, each of us strangers,' and gave her a precarious refuge.

"She became the parent of two—that's one-seventh the number of children from my womb. I have everything my heart desires—who can deny it? And I'll keep it, too! Who is there to doubt it? My fertility has given me security. I possess too much for fortune to be able to hurt me, and even if it took much away, I would still have much more left. I'm too well-off ever to have to worry about anything.

"Suppose one—or even more—of my flock of children was taken away? Robbed though I was, I would never be down to two, the size of Latona's . . . *crowd.* With only two she might as well have none. Away! Enough of this sacrificing! And take off that laurel!"

The women quickly removed their wreaths, left the sacrifices unfinished, and did the only thing they could do: They prayed to the goddess under their breath.

Outraged, Latona stood on the summit of Mount Cynthus and spoke to her two children: "Look at me, your mother, so proud to have brought you into the world, yielding to no goddess, except to Juno. But am I a goddess? I really don't know. I'm to be barred from the altars where I've been worshipped for ages, unless you help me. And that is not my only complaint. Tantalus' daughter has added insult to injury, has had the audacity to rank you behind her own children and has called me practically childless—may it happen to her!—and she has shown her father's penchant for blasphemy."

After this tale of woe, Latona began pleading with Apollo for help. "Stop!" he said, "the longer you complain, the more you delay the punishment!" Diana agreed, and they dropped through the air and alighted, wrapped in clouds, on the citadel of Thebes.

Near the city walls there was a broad, open, level field, constantly pounded by galloping horses, whose hooves—and the wheels of countless chariots— had ground the earth to dust. Some of Amphion's seven sons often mounted spirited horses decked in Tyrian purple and rode them there, guiding their chargers with heavy golden reins. Ismenus, the first son to be carried in his mother's womb, was turning his horse around in a tight circle, hauling back on the bit in the animal's foaming mouth, when he cried out in pain, an arrow fixed in his chest. The reins fell from his dying hand, and he slowly slid sideways down the horse's right shoulder to the ground. Sipylus, nearest to him, hearing a quiver rattling in the air, urged on his horse the way the captain of a ship, when he spies a cloud and senses a storm, unfurls the sails to catch every breeze, but the inescapable arrow caught him as he spurred his horse and lodged, quivering, in the back of his neck, its iron head emerging from his throat. He was leaning forward, and now he rolled over the horse's neck and down among the pounding hooves, staining the ground with his warm blood.

Unlucky Phaedimus and Tantalus, named for his grandfather, had just finished their riding practice and now, glistening with oil, had gone to the gymnasium to wrestle. They were locked in a hold and struggling chest to chest when an arrow shot from a taut bowstring pierced them both, each in the other's grip. With one voice they groaned, doubled over with pain and toppled to the ground as one, lay there, looking their last on the light of day as one, and breathed their final breath, as one.

Alphenor saw it happen. Beating and tearing his breast, he flew to them to lift them up and untangle their cold limbs. In this pious act he fell, for Apollo shot him clean through the chest with a deadly arrow, and when Alphenor tried to yank it out, he pulled out a portion of lung on the arrowhead, and his blood gushed out, his life along with it. More than one wound brought down long-haired Damasicthon, for he was first hit by an arrow in the bend of the knee, where the tendons are gathered, and while he was trying to draw out the deadly shaft, another arrow struck him in the throat, driving up to the feathers at the end of the shaft. Blood forced it out and spurted out after it, piercing the air and shooting up high in a broad arc.

The last son, Ilioneus, had raised his arms to heaven in a useless prayer, "O gods, all gods together" (not realizing he did not need to pray to them all), "spare me!" And the archer god was moved, but the flying shaft could not be recalled. Nevertheless, Ilioneus died with the slightest wound possible, for the arrow struck his heart, but did not go in deep.

Rumors of a disaster, the sight of people in shock, and a sobbing household made the mother Niobe aware of the sudden catastrophe. She was astounded that the gods could do all this and enraged that they had dared to do it, that they had so much power. As for Amphion, the children's father, he had fallen on his sword and died, his grief ending with his life.

Alas! How very different was this Niobe from the Niobe who had just now driven people from Latona's altars and who had moved through the city with her head thrown back, envied then by her own people, but now to be pitied, even by an enemy! Bending over the cold bodies of her sons she kissed them all, over and over, one after another—and for the last time.

Turning away from them she raised her bruised arms to heaven, arms black and blue from blows of grief, and cried: "Feed, cruel Latona, feed on my sorrow, and gorge your heart with my misery! Your wild heart! Gorge it! To seven funerals add mine, too. You've won, hateful enemy; enjoy your triumph! But why do I say you've won? I'm better off miserable than you are happy. Even after so many deaths, I'm still the winner!"

And then "Twang!" went a bow string, and the sound terrified everyone but Niobe herself. Her tragedy had made her even more arrogant. Her daughters, wearing black, their hair let down in mourning, were standing in front of their brothers' biers. One of them, trying to pull an arrow from her abdomen, fell down dead, her face upon her brother's. Another, attempting to console her weeping mother, was suddenly silent, and doubled over from an unseen wound.* Still another daughter collapsed, trying in vain to run away. A fourth tumbled down dead on top of her. One was hiding; you could see another trembling.

With six daughters now dead from different wounds, one last girl remained. Covering her with her robe and shielding her with her body, Niobe cried, "Leave me just one, my littlest girl, out of all my children I ask for just the littlest girl, just one." And while she was pleading, the one she was pleading for dropped, dying, to the ground.

Completely bereft, Niobe sank down among the bodies of her sons and daughters and husband, rigid with grief. Not a hair on her head moved in the air. Her face was pale, drained of blood. Her eyes staring, her expression anguished, she seemed to be lifeless. Her tongue itself was frozen, her palate hard. Her veins ceased to pulse; her neck could not bend, nor her arms move, nor her feet walk. Her inner organs were stone, too. She was weeping, though, and now she was caught up in a powerful whirlwind and carried off to the land of her birth. Fixed on a mountain peak there, she dissolved into tears, which still flow down the face of the marble.[23]

Then indeed all the people, men and women alike, feared Latona's wrath, which had been shown so clearly, and they worshipped the great power of the goddess, mother of twins, more earnestly than before. And as often happens, accounts of recent events led to earlier stories, and one of the men said: "Long ago in Lycia, too, the farmers who tilled the fertile fields there scorned the goddess, and they paid the price for it. The story is not well known because of the humble origins of the men, but it's an amazing tale even so. I have been there and seen both the lake and the place made famous by the miraculous event.

"For my father had ordered me to go to Lycia, select cattle there, and drive them back. (He was then an old man and not able to make the journey.) Before I left he himself provided me with a Lycian guide. As we were crossing some fields, I suddenly saw an ancient altar, black with the remains of burnt offerings, standing in the middle of a lake, around the border of which reeds swayed in the wind. My guide stopped and in a frightened voice murmured, 'Have mercy on me!' and I murmured the same thing: 'Have mercy!'

"I asked him, nevertheless, whether the altar was sacred to the naiads, or to Faunus, or to a local god, and this is what he said 'My son, this altar belongs

---

*6.294: This line, *oraque compressit nisi postquam spiritus ibat* (and she compressed her lips until her last breath left her), is bracketed by Miller-Goold as spurious and has been omitted from the translation.

to no mountain deity. That goddess claims it to whom Jove's royal wife once made the world off-limits, the one whose prayer wandering Delos just barely granted when that small island was itself drifting. It was there that Latona, bracing herself against two trees, an olive and a palm, gave birth to twins, against the will of their stepmother. From there, too, they say, the new mother fled Juno, carrying the two little gods, her infants, at her breast.

"'When she arrived in Lycia, home of the Chimaera, the sun was beating down on the fields, and the goddess, exhausted from her long journey and parched from the summer heat, had a terrible thirst. (Her eager infants had long since drained her breasts of milk.) She happened to see a small lake in a valley not far away. There farmers were gathering twigs from bushes, reeds, and sedge grass, which likes to grow in swamps.

"'Latona came to the lake and knelt down at its edge to scoop up cool water to drink. The farmers crowded in front of her to keep her from drinking. As they stood in her way the goddess said to them: "Why do you want to keep me from drinking some water? Water belongs to us all. Nature did not make the sun one person's property, nor air, nor water, cool and clear. This lake I've come to is free to all, but even so, like a supplicant, I'll petition you to let me have some water to drink. I was not intending to bathe and so refresh myself here, weary though I am, but just to quench my thirst. My mouth is so dry, my throat so parched, that even as I'm speaking I can hardly talk. A drink of water will be nectar to me, will restore me at once. You'll give me life if you give me water. Let these children, holding out their tiny arms from my lap, move you, too." (They happened to be holding out their arms.)

"'Who could fail to be moved by the goddess' plea? In spite of it, however, the men persisted in blocking her from the water, threatened her with harm if she did not take herself off, and added insults to their threats. Not satisfied with that, they even began splashing the water itself, smacking it with their hands and kicking it with their feet, out of pure meanness stirring up the muck from the bottom of the lake.

"'Latona's wrath overcame her thirst. She stopped trying to appease these worthless folk, no longer made herself utter words beneath a goddess. Raising her hands to the sky she said, "Live in this lake forever!" And that is exactly what happened. Now they love being in the water. One minute they dive down in it, the next they raise their heads above it, and then swim on the surface. Often they sit on the bank of the lake, often jump back into the cool water. But now, too, they wag their quarrelsome, foul tongues and even underwater try to croak their raucous insults.* Their voices, too, are harsh; their necks swell with their huffing and puffing; and the stream of abuse issuing from their mouths has stretched them wide. Now their necks are squat; their heads rest

---

*6.376: "and even underwater": Ovid portrays the sound of the frogs croaking with "probably [his] best known onomatopoeia" (Bömer at 6.376, 3.106): quamvis *sint* sub aqua, sub aqua *maledicere temptant*.

on their shoulders; their backs are green; their bellies white—they're mostly belly now, and they hop about in muddy ponds, new creatures: frogs.'"

And so, after whoever it was had narrated the destruction of the Lycian farmers, someone else remembered the satyr whom Latona's son Apollo punished after he defeated him in a contest with the flute, Minerva's invention. "Why are you tearing me from myself," he cried. "Oh! Oh! Oh! I'm sorry! I'm so sorry! The flute isn't worth this," he screamed, as his skin was ripped from his body, and he was nothing but one huge wound. Blood ran everywhere, his muscles were totally exposed, his naked arteries throbbing, and you could count his quivering organs as they pulsed and the glistening sinews in his chest. Country-dwelling fauns, gods of the forests, wept for him, his brother satyrs wept, and the boy Olympus, still dear to him, also wept. Nymphs, too, and all who grazed their woolly flocks and horned herds in those mountains— all these also grieved for him. The rich earth was bathed in falling tears, and it soaked them up and let them drain down into its deepest veins, where they turned into water and were sent out again into the open air as a stream now rushing between steep banks to the sea and called the Marsyas, Phrygia's clearest river.[24]

After these tales the people returned to the present and mourned for Amphion, dead with all his line. They all hated the mother, Niobe, though one person was said to have wept for her even then, her brother Pelops, who tore open his robe and revealed his left shoulder, made of ivory. At birth he had his own left shoulder, flesh-colored, like his right one. But his father carved him up, they say, and the gods restored him, and though all his other parts were found, a piece of him was missing between his neck and the top of his left arm. Here a shoulder carved from ivory was fitted, in place of the one that was gone, and with that Pelops was whole again.

The neighboring princes assembled, and the people in the nearby cities begged their kings to go and offer the Thebans consolation: Argos, Sparta, and Mycenae, city of the sons of Pelops; Calydon, not yet hateful to savage Diana; fertile Orchomenos; Corinth, famous for its bronze; fierce Messene, Patrae, low-lying Cleonae; Pylos, ruled by Neleus; Troezen, not yet ruled by Pittheus; and the other cities south of the isthmus that faces two seas, and those north of the isthmus and visible from it.

Only you, Athens—who could believe it?—failed to appear. War interfered with duty, for a barbarian host from across the sea, camped outside your walls, had been terrifying the city. Tereus of Thrace had come to the aid of Athens and routed the besieging army, and his victory had made him famous.

Now, Tereus was rich and powerful and traced his line all the way back to the great god Mars. Pandion, king of Athens, had made Tereus an ally by giving his daughter Procne in marriage to him. But Juno, the divine matron of honor, did not attend that wedding, nor did Hymenaeus, god of marriage, nor the Graces. Instead, the Furies held aloft the wedding torches, snatched from a funeral procession, and the Furies made up the marriage bed. A sinister screech owl settled on top of the house, perching on the roof of the wedding couple's bedroom.

Under this bird of ill omen Procne and Tereus were united; under this bird of ill omen they had a child named Itys. Thrace congratulated them, to be sure, and they themselves gave thanks to the gods and proclaimed as feast days both the anniversary of Procne's marriage to the illustrious ruler and Itys' birthday. So seldom do we see what is best for us!

The Titan sun had led the seasons of the year through five autumns when Procne, sweetly coaxing her husband, said: "If you love me, let me go to my sister, or let my sister come to me; you can promise our father that she will return soon. To let me see my sister would be the greatest gift you could give me."

Tereus ordered a ship to put to sea, and, powered by sail and by oar, it carried him to the port of Athens, touching land at Piraeus. When he was shown in to his father-in-law, the king, they clasped hands—a friendly beginning that augured well for their meeting. Tereus had begun to say why he had come, delivering his wife's request and promising to send the girl back home soon, when, lo and behold! Philomela entered, beautifully dressed, but even more beautiful herself: like naiads and dryads, as we hear, when they walk in the forest—if, that is, they are as well turned out and as tastefully adorned as Philomela was.

Tereus was inflamed with passion when he saw the girl, like a field of dry straw someone puts a match to, or a pile of leaves or a barn full of hay someone sets on fire. Her beauty was indeed striking, but Tereus' inborn lust also aroused him—and the people in his land are prone to sexual passion: He burned because of his own weakness and that of his race. His first impulse was to corrupt her companions and their devotion to her, to subvert her nurse's loyalty, and to entice the girl herself with expensive gifts—to spend the wealth of his entire kingdom—or to seize her and carry her off, and then fight fiercely for his prize. There was nothing that Tereus, gripped by a passion that could not be curbed, would not dare to do. His heart could not control the fire within, and now, impatient of any delay, he fervently renewed Procne's request, expressing his own wishes as though they were hers. Love made him eloquent, and when he went too far in his pleading, he claimed he was carrying out Procne's wishes. He even added tears, as though she had ordered him to cry.

O gods! The darkness that fills the hearts of men! His very effort, wicked though it was, made Tereus seem kind and good, and his evil intentions won him praise. As for Philomela, she wanted the same thing, and hugged her father tenderly and begged him to let her go see her sister, she herself working both for and against her own welfare.

Tereus watched her and in his mind had his hands all over her, and when he saw her slide her arms around her father's neck and kiss him—this excited him, and fueled and fired his lust, and every time she embraced her father, he wished he were her father, though his thoughts would have been no less impure. Their father finally gave in to the entreaties of both his daughters, and Philomela was overjoyed and lavished thanks upon him, poor girl, and thought it had turned out so well for them both, though it would be very sad for them both.

And now the sun had but a little labor left to do, and his horses' hooves were pounding on the downward path of heaven. The tables were laid with a royal feast, and golden cups were filled with wine. From here, stuffed with food and drink, they gave themselves to peaceful sleep.

But the king of Thrace, though he, too, had gone to bed, lay smoldering with passion for Philomela, recalling her face, her hands, the way she moved, imagining those parts of her body he hadn't yet seen, feeding his lust himself, his desire keeping him awake the whole night long.

Finally, morning light appeared, and Pandion clasped Tereus' hand as he was leaving and with tears in his eyes handed over to him his companion for the trip back to Thrace. "Dear son-in-law," he said, "because I love my girls so much and feel I must—and so they wish (and you do, too)—Tereus, I put into your hands this daughter of mine, and I beg you in the name of trust, in the name of the bond between us, in the name of the gods, watch over her with a father's love and send back to me as soon as you can this sweet comfort of my fretful old age. Any absence will be too long.

"You, too, Philomela, if you love me, come back as soon as you can—it's bad enough that your sister is far away." Pandion was kissing his daughter as he gave her these instructions and weeping softly as he spoke. To seal their promise he insisted they give him their right hands, and he held them in his own and begged them to remember him to his absent daughter and grandson. And now, sobbing uncontrollably, he could barely say good-bye, and a sense of foreboding filled him with fear.

As soon as Philomela was on board the ship with its decorated prow and they had rowed out to sea, leaving land behind, Tereus exclaimed: "I have won! I have it! My heart's desire!" Beside himself with joy, he could barely control himself, barely put off his pleasure, barbarian that he was. He never took his eyes off the girl, like an eagle, Jove's bird of prey, when it drops a hare from its hooked talons into its lofty nest. The creature is trapped, and the predator gazes hungrily upon its prize.

The journey was now over, and when they had wearily disembarked from the ship onto Tereus' home shore, the king dragged Pandion's daughter to a remote hut hidden in an ancient forest, and there he shut up Philomela, pale, trembling, and terrified, weeping, asking him where her sister was. And now he told her the unspeakable thing he was about to do to her, and while she cried out for her father, over and over, but in vain, cried out for her sister, over and over, cried out above all for the mighty gods, he raped her, a girl, and alone.

She was shaking, like a frightened, wounded lamb dropped from the jaws of a gray wolf and not yet aware it is still alive, or like a dove, its feathers all bloody, still shivering and in terror of the powerful talons that had gripped it.

As soon as she regained her senses, she tore her hair and beat her arms like a woman in mourning and pointed at Tereus and cried: "You fiend! What a terrible thing you have done! Animal! Not my father's request, not his loving tears, not your feelings for my sister, not my innocence, not your marriage vows—nothing stopped you! You have broken every law there is. You have made me a whore for my sister's husband, made yourself the husband of two women, forced Procne to be my enemy!

"Why not kill me too, treacherous man, and leave no crime uncommitted? If only you had, before you forced me to do this unspeakable act. Then I would not have a soul full of guilt in the afterlife. But if the gods see this, if the gods exist at all, if all that is right and just did not perish when I did, sooner or later you will pay! I will cast my shame aside myself and tell the world what you have done. If I get the chance, I will go before the people; if I am kept shut up in the forest, I will fill the forest with my story, and the stones themselves will cry out when they hear. Heaven on high will learn of it, and if there is any god in heaven, he will hear it, too!"

Her words aroused the tyrant to a savage fury, and to fear no less than fury, and, goaded by both fear and fury, he drew his sword from the scabbard at his thigh, grabbed Philomela by the hair, twisted her arms behind her back, forced her hands together, and bound them tightly. When she saw the sword, Philomela bared her throat and hoped to die. But Tereus seized her tongue with a pair of tongs and, as it resisted, as it called "Father!" again and again and struggled to speak, hacked at it hard, hacked it out of her mouth with his sword. The stump remaining quivered, while the tongue itself lay trembling on the bloody ground, whimpering, and just as the tail of a snake that has been cut in two twists and turns, so her tongue wriggled its way to the feet of its mistress, and there it died.

After this bestial act Tereus is said—though I can hardly believe it—to have gratified his lust upon the girl's mutilated body again and again. And after committing these atrocities he even had the gall to return to Procne.

When Procne saw her husband, she asked him where her sister was. He pretended to groan and contrived a story about her death, and his tears made her believe him. Procne tore from her shoulders the shawl with a bright border of gold she was wearing, dressed herself in black, set up an empty tomb, made offerings to a nonexistent shade, and mourned her sister's fate, which was certainly to be mourned, but not in the way she thought.

The sun-god had traveled through the twelve signs of the zodiac, and a whole year had passed. What was Philomela to do? Guards kept her from escaping, the walls of her hut, built from solid rock, stood immovable, her mouth, made tongueless, had no way to tell the deed.

But pain breeds ingenuity, and cunning comes when things are at their worst. Philomela hung a piece of cloth on a Thracian loom and—clever girl!—wove red signs across its white threads, spelling out the crime. When she had finished, she rolled up the cloth and put it in the hands of a servant and, using gestures, asked her to take it to her mistress. The servant did as she was asked and brought the material to Procne, not knowing what was on it.

The wife of the savage tyrant unrolled the cloth, read the account of her sister's pitiful fate,* and—a wonder she was able to—said not a word: Grief closed her mouth, and though her tongue sought ways to express her outrage, words would not come. Nor was there time for tears. Confusing right and wrong, she plunged ahead, obsessed with the revenge she imagined for Tereus.

It was the time appointed for the young women of Thrace to perform the rites of Bacchus, celebrated every other year under the friendly cover of darkness (and during the night Mount Rhodope would ring with the sharp bronze sound of cymbals). The queen left the palace after dusk, dressed for the god's rites, taking with her the things that were used in Bacchic frenzy: She covered her head with grapevines, draped the left side of her body in a deerskin, and balanced a light spear on her shoulder. She then hurled herself through the forest with a throng of attendants, a fearsome sight, driven by a furious grief, O Bacchus, that she pretended was your fury, and came at last to the hut in the woods where Philomela was imprisoned and began to howl, crying, "Eu-ho-e-e!" and broke down the door and seized her sister and dressed her like a worshipper of Bacchus, hiding her face with vines of ivy, and dragged her off in a state of shock to the palace and led her inside.

When Philomela realized she was in that evil house, she turned pale, let out a wail, and began to shake. Procne found a safe place in the palace, removed the various items Philomela had worn for the rites, uncovered her pitiful face, filled with shame, and took her in her arms. But the poor girl could not bear to look her sister in the eye, for she still thought of herself as the whore of her sister's husband. Staring at the floor, wanting to swear, to call the gods to witness that he had forced her to do this shameful act, she could only say it with her hands and not her voice.

Consumed with a rage she could barely contain, Procne ordered her sister to stop weeping: "Tears will accomplish nothing! No, we must use steel, or something stronger than steel. I am ready, sister, for any crime: Either I will set the royal palace on fire, burn it to the ground, and in that flaming inferno incinerate Tereus, who contrived this evil; or I will cut out his tongue, or gouge out his eyes and hack off that member of his that robbed you of your virginity, or I will stab him a thousand times and drive out that guilty soul! What it will be I do not yet know, but it will be terrible, whatever I do."

---

*6.582: "the account of her sister's pitiful fate." I read *carmen miserabile* (pitiful poem) with Anderson (1982a), Bömer, Haupt-Ehwald, and LaFaye, instead of *miserabile fatum* (pitiful fate) with Miller-Goold, although I translate a version of Bömer's gloss of *miserabile carmen,* "die 'Nachricht über das traurige Schicksal'" (at 6.582, 3.158).

While Procne listed possibilities, Itys came in to his mother, and seeing him gave her an idea. Staring at him with cold eyes she said: "Ah! How very like your father you are!" And without another word, still seething with silent rage, she conceived a horrible crime, and when the boy came up and said hello to his mother and put his little arms around her neck and kissed her and worked his boyish charms upon her, the mother in her was indeed moved and her rage was checked. Tears flooded her eyes, against her will, but as soon as she felt her resolve weakening from too much love for her son, she turned away from him and back to her sister's face, and then, looking from one to the other, said: "Why is it that he can utter his winning words, but she is silent, her tongue cut out? If he can call me 'Mother,' why can she not call me 'Sister'? See, daughter of Pandion, the man you're married to! You're forgetting your own kin! Any feeling for Tereus would be a crime!"

And like a Bengal tiger dragging a doe's suckling fawn through the dark forest, she dragged Itys off to a remote part of the great palace, and as he held out his hands, staring at his own death now, crying "Mother! Mother!" and reaching for her neck, Procne looked into his eyes and plunged a sword into his side. One wound would have been enough to kill him, but Philomela then took the sword and slashed his throat with it, and while there was life still in him, they tore his body apart. Part of him bubbled and surged in a boiling cauldron, part of him hissed on spits. The room was awash in gore.

Then Procne set this dish before her husband, Tereus, who was totally unaware, and pretending it was a sacred meal at which, according to her country's custom, only her husband could be present, she dismissed friends and servants. Tereus himself, sitting high on his ancestral throne, ate thereof, stuffing his belly with his own flesh and blood.

And then, so dark was the night in his soul, he said, "Fetch me Itys here!" Unable to conceal her savage joy and eager now to give him the news of his own destruction, Procne replied, "The one you're calling for, he's here, *inside.*" Looking around, Tereus asked, "Where is he?" And as he was searching for him and calling him again, Philomela suddenly leaped forth, her hair still spattered with gore from the mad slaughter, and thrust the bloody head of Itys in the face of his father. Never at any time had she wanted so much to be able to speak and express in words the joy she felt.

With a scream of utter horror, the king of Thrace thrust the table away and summoned the snaky-haired sisters from the valley of the Styx. One moment he was longing to cut open his body, if only he could, and disgorge the horrible feast, the half-digested flesh; the next he was weeping uncontrollably, calling himself the miserable tomb of his own son. And now, with sword drawn, he pursued the daughters of Pandion.

You would have thought the two Athenian women hung in midair on wings: They *were* hanging on wings. One sought the woods, the other flew up under the eaves, both still bearing the signs of the murder on their breasts, their plumage streaked with blood. Driven by grief and lust for vengeance, Tereus himself turned into a crested bird called the hoopoe, with a huge protruding beak, like the point of a sword, and a face that seems like a weapon.

Grief sent Athens' king, Pandion, to the shades of the underworld before his time, before the last years of an advanced old age. The kingdom and control over its affairs then passed to Erechtheus, whose power was derived as much from his sense of justice as his military might. He had now begotten four sons and four daughters, two of whom were equal in beauty. Of these two, Aeolus' grandson Cephalus was fortunate to have you, Procris, as his wife.

But the reputation of Tereus and his fellow Thracians hurt Boreas, and for a long time the god had no success with Orithyia, the other beautiful sister, as long, that is, as he was content to court her politely, with entreaties, rather than use force with her. But when he got nowhere with his charm, bristling with rage (all too customary, all too normal for that wind), he said to himself: "Serves me right! Now why did I ever rule out these weapons of mine, savagery and violence, rage and a menacing attitude? Why did I try entreaties, which I'm not good at? Violence suits me better. I use violence to drive threatening clouds from the sky, with violence I whip up the sea and uproot gnarled oaks, turn snow to ice and batter the earth with hail. It's the same when I encounter my brothers in the open sky (for that's my arena): I fight them so hard that the air thunders with our clashing, and lightning bursts from the clouds in jagged streaks. And it's the same when I blow down into the chasms in the earth and force my way through its deepest caverns: I upset the spirits of the dead and the whole world, too, with the tremors and quakes I cause. This is the kind of violence I ought to have used when I wanted to marry, and I should simply have forced Erectheus to become my father-in-law, not asked him to be."

Having said this, or something like this, Boreas shook out his wings, and their movement sent a cold wind over all the earth and roiled the surface of the sea. And now Orithyia's would-be lover drew his dusty cloak across the highest mountain peaks, swept it over the lowlands, and, wrapped in fog, enfolded the trembling girl in his tawny wings. As he flew, the flames of his passion, fanned by the wind, burned brighter still, nor did the abductor check his flight through the air until he reached the Ciconian people and their city. There the Athenian girl married the king of the icy wind and bore twin sons, who were like their mother in other ways, but had their father's wings.

But people say the two boys, Calais and Zetes, were not born with wings, did not have wings at all, until their beards began to grow below their golden hair. Eventually, though, like birds, they grew wings from their shoulders, just at the time blond wisps appeared upon their cheeks. And when their boyhood years had passed, they went with the Minyans in search of the sheep's skin with the bright, shining fleece in the first ship ever to cross the sea, which was then unknown.[25]

BOOK SEVEN

And now the Minyans were cutting through the sea in their Thessalian ship. They had seen Phineus,* dragging out his old age, impoverished, in endless darkness, and the sons of Boreas had driven off the winged creatures with girls' faces that hovered around the mouth of that poor old man. After many hardships at sea under the command of the illustrious Jason, they had finally reached the swift waters of the muddy Phasis.

They appeared before King Aeetes of Colchis to demand the golden fleece, and he imposed great and dangerous labors upon them as a condition. Then it was that Aeetes' daughter Medea conceived a powerful passion for Jason. She struggled against it for a long time, but when she could not conquer her madness with reason she said to herself: "Medea, you are fighting something, but to no avail; some god is opposing you, and I wonder if this—or something very like it—is what is called being in love? Why else do the labors my father ordered them to perform seem to me to be too hard? Well, they *are* too hard! Why else am I so afraid that this man I've only just now seen will die? What is the reason for such fear? Beat out the flames raging in your innocent heart, poor girl, if you can! I would be a lot saner if I could. But some strange force is drawing me on, against my will. Desire pulls me one way, my mind another way. I see clearly which is better, and I know it is right, yet I follow the way that is worse.

"Why, royal girl, are you on fire for this stranger, and why do you dream of a wedding halfway around the world? This land, too, can give you someone to love. Whether Jason lives or dies is in the hands of the gods. But let him live, O gods! I don't have to be in love to pray for that. What wrong has he done?

*7.2–4: "They had seen Phineus": This is obviously a Phineus different from the brother of the Ethiopian king Cepheus, whom Perseus battles and turns to stone at 5.1–249. For the blind seer Phineus whom the Argonauts encounter on their way to Colchis, see Apollodorus 1.9 21–22.

109

Who but the most hard-hearted would not be moved by his youth, by his breeding, by his courage? Even if he had nothing else to offer, who would not be affected by his beautiful face? He has certainly touched my heart! Unless I help him, he will be blasted by the bulls' fiery breath;* he will fight a crop of warriors that he himself planted, enemies sprung from the earth, or he will be delivered up as prey to that wild and famished serpent. If I let this happen, then I shall have to admit that I was born from a tigress, that I have flint and iron in my heart!

"But why don't I just watch him die—and involve my eyes in the crime by looking on? Why not goad the bulls against him, and those fierce earth-born creatures, and the never-sleeping dragon?

"Gods forbid that I should do such a thing! Right now I must act, not pray. And yet—shall I betray my father's kingdom and help save some utter stranger so that thanks to me he can sail away without me and marry someone else, while Medea's left behind to face the consequences? If he can do this, if he can prefer someone else to me, then let him die, the ungrateful wretch!

"But I don't see that in his face; his heart is nobler than that; there is too much grace in him for that. I need not fear betrayal; I need not fear that he would forget what I had done for him. He will give me his word beforehand, and I shall compel the gods to witness our agreement. Why are you afraid when there is nothing to be afraid of? You should get ready; there is no time to lose.

"Jason will always owe his life to you, he will join you to himself in holy matrimony, and throughout the cities of Greece you will be hailed by scores of mothers as the savior of their sons.

"Shall I therefore leave my sister, brother, father, gods, my native land, and be gone with the wind? Oh yes! Yes! For my father is a savage, my country is barbaric, my brother is still a baby, my sister's prayers are with me, and the greatest god of all is in my heart! There's nothing here for me; everything is there, where I'm going: acclaim for saving the youth of Greece, the pleasure of knowing a better land, towns that are famous even here, their civilization, their arts, and a man I would give everything in the whole world to have, Jason, son of Aeson. When he marries me, my happiness will be complete; the gods will bless me; my head will touch the stars.

"But what about the clashing rocks they say are in the middle of the ocean? What about Charybdis, hostile to ships, sucking up the sea and spewing it out again? What about Scylla in the waters of Sicily, quick to strike, with that girdle of savage dogs growing from her groin, and howling like a dog herself?† No matter, for holding Jason, clinging to my love, I can sail anywhere. With him in my arms I have nothing to fear, or if I fear anything, I'll be afraid only for my husband.

---

*7.29: "Unless I help him": see 7.104ff.

†At 7.64–65 I have added "growing from her groin," which is not in the Latin here but describes Scylla's condition later in the poem. (See 13.732 and especially 14.59–67.)

"But do you consider this marriage, Medea? Aren't you concealing your guilt under a false name? Look what a terrible wrong you're about to do! Flee this crime while you still can!" Before her eyes Righteousness, Duty to her parents, and woman's Virtue all took their stand, and Desire was defeated, turned, and fled.

Medea was now on her way to ancient altars of Perse's daughter Hecate, hidden away in a sunless grove in a remote forest, full of resolve now that she had resisted her passion and subdued it. But then she saw Jason, and the flame she had managed to put out blazed up again. Her cheeks reddened; her whole face burned; and as a tiny spark, hidden in ashes, is fed by the wind, begins to glow, and as it's fanned leaps into flame again, as strong as ever, so now Medea's love, which had died down, which you would think was fading away, burst into flame at the sight of the young man, when she saw him face to face.

Jason seemed more handsome than ever that day, and you could forgive Medea for being in love with him. She gazed at him, her eyes fixed on his face as if she were seeing him for the first time, and in her stricken state she thought she was seeing a god and could not turn away. As he began to speak and took her hand in his and humbly asked for her help and promised to marry her, Medea replied, tears streaming down her face: "I see what I am going to do; it won't be ignorance of the truth that deceives me, but love. I will help you, and you shall be saved, and once you are safe—do what you promised!"

Jason swore by the rites of the goddess with three forms, by the divine power of the grove they were in, by the father of his father-in-law-to-be, the god who sees all things; by the success he expected to have; by the great dangers he faced. Medea believed him and gave him magic herbs right then and there and taught him how to use them, and he returned to his lodging happy.

When dawn the next day drove away the twinkling stars, the people gathered at the sacred field of Mars and sat down on the heights above it. The king himself, wearing a purple robe and distinguished by his ivory scepter, was sitting amid his retinue.

And now came the bulls with hooves of bronze, snorting fire from nostrils made of steel, setting the grass on fire with their breath. As a wood-filled furnace roars, or as limestone melted in an earthen kiln and sprinkled with water bursts into flame, so the bulls' chests, so their scorched throats, thundered with the fire that rumbled in them.

The son of Aeson went out to meet them, nevertheless, and as he approached, they swung their fierce heads and iron-tipped horns around to face him, pawed the dusty ground with cloven hooves, and filled the air with smoke and bellowing. The Minyans were frozen in fear.

Jason advanced on the bulls, not feeling their fiery breath (such was the power of the magic herbs), boldly stroked their hanging dewlaps, led them under the yoke, and forced them to pull the heavy plow and break up the hard-packed ground with the iron plowshare. The Colchians were dumbfounded, while the Minyans shouted encouragement and urged him on.

Next, Jason took the serpent's teeth from his bronze helmet and planted them in the furrows the bulls had plowed. The soil softened these "seeds," which were filled with a powerful poison, and the planted teeth began to sprout and to grow into strange new forms.*

As an infant acquires a human face in its mother's womb, develops within itself, and does not emerge into the light of day until it is time, so here, human forms took shape in the belly of the gravid earth and sprang up in the rich soil and, what is more astonishing, brandished arms created at the same time they were.

When the Greeks saw these creatures poised to hurl their sharp spears at Jason's head, their hearts sank in dread, and they could not bear to watch. Medea herself was frightened, too, though she had made Jason invulnerable, and when she saw the lone youth the target of so many enemies, she turned pale and suddenly sat down, cold and about to faint. Fearing that the magic herbs she had given him were not powerful enough, she began to chant an additional spell to help him, calling upon her secret arts. But Jason hurled a heavy stone into the midst of the armed men, diverting the battle from himself, and made them turn upon themselves. The earth-born brothers then died from wounds they gave one another, falling in a civil war. Cheering, the Greeks surrounded Jason and embraced him and clung to him. You, too, barbarian girl, wanted to enfold the victor in your arms, but your shyness stopped you; still, if only you could have. . . . But no, concern for your reputation held you back. Nevertheless, you rejoiced silently, thanking the spells, thanking the gods who gave them to you.

Jason's final ordeal was to put an ever-wakeful serpent to sleep with magic herbs. This serpent guarded a golden tree and was a fearsome sight with its crest, triple-forked tongue, and curved fangs. But when Jason sprinkled on it the juice of an herb gathered from beside the river Lethe and uttered three times the words that bring on sleep—words able to calm an angry sea and force floodwaters to subside—those eyes that had never closed before now slept, and Jason, victorious, possessed the gold.† Exulting in his prize and taking with him the giver of this gift, a second prize, he reached the harbor of Iolcus with his new bride.

Thessalian mothers and community elders brought gifts to the gods for the return of their sons, heaped incense on the altar fires, and sacrificed an ox, whose horns had been wrapped in gold leaf, as they had promised in their prayers.

But Aeson was absent from the rites of thanksgiving, worn out with old age now and close to death. His son Jason said to Medea: "Dear wife, to whom I

---

*7.121–124: The teeth came from the serpent Cadmus slew and were given to Aeetes by Minerva (Apollonius Rhodius, *Argonautica* 3.1176–1184). The poison is thus the serpent's venom. See also *Metamorphoses* 3.102ff.

†7.155–156: "possessed the gold," that is, the golden fleece.

confess I owe my life: Although you've given me everything, and all you've done for me is beyond belief, if your magic can do one more thing—for what can it not do?—then take some of my years from me and give them to my father!" and he burst into tears.

Medea was moved by Jason's request and by his love for his father. She thought of her own father, Aeetes, whom she had abandoned, though her feelings for him were nothing like Jason's devotion to his father. Not admitting this, however, she asked Jason: "What blasphemy is this you've uttered, dear husband? Do you really think I can give someone else a portion of your lifespan? Hecate would not allow it, nor is it right for you to ask for this. But I shall try to give you a gift that is greater than the one you've asked me for. I shall make an attempt to renew your father's life, not by taking years from yours, but by magic—if only the goddess in three persons will come and help me and give her blessing to this huge and daring task."

Three nights remained until the horns of the growing moon would join to make the shining sphere. When, finally, it gleamed in all its fullness and its bright round face gazed upon the earth, Medea left her house, her garments loose about her, her feet bare, her hair uncovered and falling on her shoulders, and wandered alone through the mute silences of midnight: Men, beasts, and birds lay dissolved in deep pools of quiet. No bush rustled; no leaf stirred. The night air was damp and still; only the stars were flickering.

Holding out her arms to them, Medea turned around three times, then scooped up water from a stream three times and let it trickle onto her hair, then threw back her head and howled three times. Next, kneeling on the ground, she prayed: "O night, faithful friend of mysteries; and you, golden stars and moon, who follow the fiery star of day; and you, Hecate, goddess with three forms, who know my designs and come to strengthen my spells and magic arts; and you, earth, who offer your potent herbs to magi; and airs, winds, mountains, streams, and lakes, and all you woodland gods, and all you gods of the night: Be present now. Thanks to you, rivers amaze their banks and flow back to their sources, thanks to you, with my spells I calm the sea when it rages and arouse it when it's still; thanks to you, I gather clouds, drive clouds away, summon and dismiss the winds, shatter the viper's fang with magic words, dislodge natural rock, pluck oak trees from their native ground, move forests, and bid mountains tremble, earth to roar, and ghosts to come forth from their tombs!

"You, too, O moon, I draw down, though Temesaean cymbals seek to ease your struggle.* My charms can make the sun turn pale, my poisons bleach the dawn! You helped me blunt the flames of the fire-breathing bulls and fit the yoke for the curved plowshare on necks that had never felt its weight. You gave

---

*7.207–208: "Temesaean cymbals": Temese (also called Tempsa) was a town on the west coast of Bruttium in southern Italy noted for its copper mines (*OLD* s.v. *Temese*).

bloody war among themselves to the warriors born from the serpent's teeth; you put the guardian of the golden fleece to sleep for the first and only time, and while he dozed you snatched the fleece and sent it to the cities of Greece.

"Now I need magical juices that can renew an old man, return him to his prime, restore his early years; and I know that you will give them, for the flashing stars answer my prayer—and here now is the chariot drawn by the winged serpents," for the chariot, sent from heaven, had arrived.

Medea mounted and, patting the necks of the harnessed serpents, gave a shake to the reins and was aloft at once and looking down on the valley of Tempe spread out below. She guided the serpents over regions she knew and surveyed the herbs growing in them—on Ossa, on high Pelion, on Othrys, Pindus, and Olympus (much larger than Pindus), and some of the herbs she sought she pulled up by the roots, and some she cut with a sickle made of bronze. Many herbs she gathered from the banks of the Apidanus and the banks of the Amphrysus; nor did she overlook you, Enipeus. The river Peneus; the waters of the Spercheus; and the shores of Boebe, where rushes grow, of-fered yet more herbs. From Anthedon, across from Euboea, she plucked an herb that gives long life, though it was not as well known now as it would be later, after Glaucus was transformed.*

For nine days and nights she flew low over a host of fields in the chariot drawn by flying serpents and then returned to Iolcus. The serpents had not touched the herbs, only breathed their aroma, yet they shed their aging skins. Arriving at the palace, Medea stopped in front of the palace doors, and with only the open sky for cover, avoiding all contact with men, she set up two earthen altars, one to Hecate on the right, one to Youth on the left, and draped them both with leafy branches.

Nearby she dug two broad trenches in the ground and performed a sacrifice above them, plunging a knife into the throat of a black sheep and letting its blood run into them. Next, while spilling clear honey from one goblet and warm milk from another, she uttered a profusion of magic words, summoning the powers beneath the earth and beseeching the king of the shades and his stolen queen not to take away so quickly the breath of life from the old man.

After murmuring this lengthy prayer and asking the gods' blessing, she or-dered the enfeebled Aeson to be brought outside, put him into a deep, death-like sleep by means of a spell, and laid him on a bed of magic herbs. She then ordered Jason and the servants of Aeson to stand back and instructed them to keep their profane eyes averted from these mysteries. They did as they were told and moved away.

Then, disheveling her hair like a Bacchant, Medea walked in a circle around

---

*7.231–233: 7.231–232: Boebe and Anthedon are not rivers but, respectively, a village on a lake named Boebeis (Anderson [1972] at 7.228–231, 269) and a harbor town in Boeotia oppo-site the island of Euboea (Lewis and Short s.v. *Anthedon*). 7.233: "after Glaucus was trans-formed": For the story of Glaucus' metamorphosis, see 13.917–965.

the altars and the altar fires, dipped torches of split kindling in the trenches black with blood, lit them at the twin altars, and purged the old man three times with fire, three times with water, and three times with sulfur.

Meanwhile, in a bronze cauldron set over a fire a powerful concoction was boiling and bubbling, roots cut from the valley of Thessaly along with seeds and flowers and black juices; and white foam was spilling over the top and running down the sides of the vat. Medea stirred in precious stones brought from the remotest part of the Orient and sand washed by the ocean's ebb tide. She added frost that had fallen from the nightlong moon, the foul wings and flesh of a screech owl, and the inner organs of a werewolf, which can change its ferocious features into those of a man. She next tossed into the cauldron the scaly skin of a slender Libyan water snake, along with the liver of an elderly stag, and dropped in the eggs and head of a crow nine generations old.

Having added these and a thousand other nameless ingredients to her more-than-mortal mixture, the barbarian Medea stirred the brew thoroughly with the dried-out branch of an olive tree, blending it from top to bottom. But look! The ancient olivewood stick moving in the steaming vessel turns green, sprouts leaves, and suddenly is laden with fat, ripe olives. And wherever the foam boiled over and steaming clots fell on the ground, flowers and tender grass sprang up in little spots of springtime. Seeing this, Medea opened a vein in the old man's throat with a sword, let his watery, agéd blood run out, and replaced it with some of the mixture from the vat.

As the liquid flowed into Aeson's veins—and when he had drunk some of it, too—the gray left his hair and beard, and they were black again. His thin and shriveled form disappeared, the pallor and decay of old age were gone; flesh was added, deep wrinkles were smoothed out, and his limbs became robust. Aeson was amazed, remembering that this was the way he had looked some forty years before. Bacchus beheld this miracle from heaven and, seeing that his nurses' youth could be restored, sought this benefit from the woman from Colchis.

Medea also used her magic for revenge, for, pretending to quarrel with her husband, she ran to the palace of Pelias and took refuge there as a suppliant.* And because Pelias himself was burdened with old age, his daughters took her in.

In no time at all the cunning Medea deceived them into thinking she was their friend. Telling them how she had removed the ravages of Aeson's old age and claiming this as her greatest achievement, dwelling on it, she planted the hope in Pelias' innocent daughters that she could also make their father young

---

*7.294–297ff.: 7.294–296: Bacchus' "nurses": "We do not know exactly what nurses Ovid refers to, but the story is clearly not terribly important here" (Anderson [1972] at 7.294–296, 275). 7.297ff.: Medea's revenge on Pelias: Pelias was king of Iolcus, where Jason was born, and fearing Jason because of a prophecy had sent him on the quest for the golden fleece, hoping, no doubt, that he would never return (Apollodorus 1.9.16).

again with the same magic. They asked Medea to do it and told her to set any price she wished. She was silent for a few moments, seeming to hesitate, keeping them in suspense after they made their request with a false air of gravity. Finally she agreed and said, "So that you will have confidence in what I'm about to do, my magic mixture will now turn the oldest ram in your flocks into a lamb." Immediately, an ancient, feeble ram was dragged forth by one of the horns that spiraled around his hollow temples. The sorceress jabbed a Thessalian knife into the old sheep's flabby throat, spotting the blade with a few scant drops of the animal's thin blood. She then stuffed its body into a bronze kettle and poured in her powerful liquids. These began to shrink its limbs, eat away its horns, and consume its years along with its horns. Then they heard a faint bleating from inside the kettle, and suddenly, while the girls were marveling at the sound, a little lamb leaped from the vessel and frisked about, looking for a milky teat. The daughters of Pelias were dumbfounded, and now that Medea's promises were confirmed, the girls pressed her all the harder.

Three times Phoebus had removed the yoke from his horses' necks after they plunged into the western sea, and the brilliant stars were shining on what was now the fourth night. Wily Medea placed plain water and strengthless herbs over a blazing fire. The king and his guards now lay inert, sound asleep, dead to the world from the powerful magic spells Medea had uttered. Following her orders, Pelias' daughters entered his bedroom with her and surrounded his bed. "Well," she said, "what are you waiting for, you lazy girls? Draw your knives and drain the ancient blood from his veins so I can fill them up again with fresh new blood! You now hold your father's life, his age, in your hands. If you love him, if you're not simply filling yourselves with empty hopes, see to your task. Take your knives and let the weak and watery blood flow and rid him of his old age!" Urged on by Medea, Pelias' daughters, because they loved their father, vied with one another to commit the crime (and it seemed criminal to them not to). Still, none of them could bear to watch as they stabbed him, and so, turning their heads and looking away, they struck blindly with savage hands—again and again.

Full of cuts and gashes and bleeding from them all, the old man raised himself on one elbow, trying to rise from the bed, stretched out his bloodless arms amid the plunging blades, and cried: "What are you doing, daughters? Who gave you knives to kill your father?" Their hearts sank; their hands fell. He was about to say more when Medea cut him off—cut his throat, that is—and plunged his mutilated body into the boiling water. And if she had not risen into the air on her winged serpents at that very moment, she would not have escaped punishment for what she had done.

She fled through the sky, over shady Pelion, the home of Philyra, and over Othrys and the place that is famous for what happened to old Cerambus. For when in Deucalion's time the earth was inundated by swollen seas, Cerambus was borne into the air on wings the nymphs gave him and escaped the flood unharmed.*

She next flew over Aeolian Pitane on her left and the stone image of the long serpent and the grove on Mount Ida, where Bacchus hid the bullock his son had stolen, giving it the form of a stag. Continuing on her way, she passed over the place where Paris, the father of Corythus, was buried beneath a small mound of sand, over the countryside Maera terrified with her strange barking, over the city of Eurypylus, king of Cos, where the Coan mothers wore horns at the time Hercules and his troops were withdrawing, over the island of Rhodes, dear to Apollo, and over the Telchines of Ialysos, whose eyes were able to destroy something just by glancing at it. But Jupiter despised those eyes and sank them beneath the waters of his brother's sea.

Medea also flew over the walls of ancient Carthaea on Ceos, where Alcidamas would later show astonishment that a gentle dove could be born from his daughter's body. Next, she saw Lake Hyrie and Tempe, the valley where Cycnus lived that was made famous by his sudden transformation into a swan. For it was there that Phylius, who loved Cycnus, gave him birds he himself had tamed and a fierce lion he had subdued when the boy demanded them. When Cycnus ordered Phylius to overpower a bull, he did that, too; but then, furious because his love had been rejected so many times, he refused to give this final prize, the bull, to Cycnus when he demanded it. Outraged, Cycnus said, "You will wish you had given it," and jumped from a cliff. Everyone thought he had fallen and died, but he was changed into a swan and hovered in the air on snow-white wings. His mother, Hyrie, not knowing he had been saved, dissolved into tears and became the lake that bears her name.

Adjacent to this lake lies Pleuron, where Ophius' daughter, Combe, fled her son's attacks on trembling wings. From there Medea looked down upon the fields of Latona's sacred island, Calaurea, which had seen its king and queen transformed into birds. On her right lay Cyllene, where Menephron would one day sleep with his mother, the way wild animals do. Far in the distance she saw Cephisus, bewailing the fate of his grandson, whom Apollo changed into a large, fat seal, and she also saw the house of Eumelus, who grieved for his son, now a bird. Finally, the flying serpents brought her to Ephyre,† daughter of the spring, Pirene. Here, in the first age of the world, the ancients say, men were born from mushrooms that sprang up after a rain.

When Jason's new bride was consumed in the flames ignited by Medea's poison and the seas on either side of Corinth saw the royal palace burning, this godless mother stained a sword with the blood of her sons, and after taking this horrible revenge on Jason, escaped his soldiers.

---

*7.354–356: "Cerambus, friend of the nymphs, was changed into a winged creature, presumably a bird, and so escaped death in the Great Flood. This story is unique here" (Anderson [1972] at 7.354–356, 281).

†7.391: Ephyre is the ancient name of Corinth.

From Corinth she was borne away in a serpent-drawn chariot sent by the Sun and came to Athens, Minerva's city, which saw you, most righteous Phene, and you, too, old Periphas, flying side by side, and which had also seen Polypemon's granddaughter when she first tried out her new wings. Aegeus took Medea in, the only thing he ever did he could be blamed for, nor did he stop with offering her hospitality, for he married her as well.

And now Aegeus' offspring, Theseus, who had used his strength and courage to pacify the Isthmus that faces two seas, arrived in Athens—a son his father did not know he had. Medea tried to kill Theseus by putting aconite in his wine. She had brought the poison with her from the shores of Scythia long ago. Now, aconite, they say, came from the saliva of Cerberus, Echidna's offspring: There is a hidden cave that leads to a dark chasm with a steep downward path, and up this path Hercules dragged Cerberus on a steel chain, the monstrous dog resisting all the way, blinking from the light, turning his eyes away from the sun's bright rays, enraged, filling the air with barking from all three mouths at once, and spattering the green fields with drops of foamy saliva. The saliva hardened, people think, and, fed by the rich and fertile soil, became a lethal poison. And because it was formed and grows on hard stones, farmers call it "aconite."

This poison Theseus' father, Aegeus himself, was tricked by his wife into giving to his son as though he were an enemy. When Theseus, unsuspecting, took the poisoned wine that was offered to him, his father recognized the family crest on the ivory hilt of his son's sword and struck the deadly cup from his lips. Medea escaped death by concealing herself in clouds she summoned with an incantation.

Although Aegeus rejoiced that his son was safe, he was shocked nevertheless that he had come so close to committing a terrible crime. To thank the gods, he lit fires on their altars and showered them with gifts, while priests brought down axes on the powerful necks of bulls with fillets wound round their horns. They say no day dawned more brightly for the Athenians than that day. Nobles and citizens of middle rank alike celebrated with banquets and, inspired by wine, sang this hymn: "You, great Theseus, Marathon praises for shedding the blood of the Cretan bull. Thanks to the deed you performed for the farmers of Cromyon, they now plow their fields, safe from the boar. Epidaurus saw the club-wielding son of Vulcan fall at your hands, the shores of the Cephisus watched fierce Procrustes fall, and Eleusis dear to Ceres witnessed the death of Cercyon. Sinis also fell; he used his great strength cruelly, for he would bend down two pine trees, forcing their tops all the way to the ground, and when he released them, they would spring up and scatter far and wide fragments of the bodies he had tied to them.

"The way to Megara, ancient home of the Lelegeians, lies open, now that Sciron has been subdued, and earth and sea have denied a final resting place to the robber's scattered bones. Long tossed about, these bones they say the passage of time hardened into rocky cliffs. (And to these cliffs the name of Sciron is attached.)

"If we added up your honors and the years of your life, your deeds would far outnumber your years. And now, our valiant hero, we solemnly declare our gratitude to you, and we drink to your health." The people's shouts of approval and the prayers of well-wishers rang out in the royal palace, and there was not a gloomy corner in the entire city.[26]

Nevertheless—for how true it is that no pleasure is unalloyed, and trouble of some kind always interrupts our rejoicing—nevertheless, Aegeus did not enjoy perfect happiness after he found his son, for Minos, king of Crete, was preparing for war. Although his army, and especially his navy, made him powerful, his greatest resolve came from his anger as a father, and he set out to avenge the death of his son Androgeos in a just crusade.

First, however, Minos wished to acquire allies, and so he sailed the seas with his swift fleet (the source of his power), on that expedition recruiting Anaphe and Astypylaea (the one by promises, the other by threatening war). Next, he added to his forces low-lying Myconos; the chalky fields of Cimolus; Syros, flourishing with thyme; Seriphos with its plains; Paros, rich in marble; and Siphnos, which godless Arne betrayed: When that grasping girl received the gold she demanded, she became a bird that still loves gold, a jackdaw, with black feathers and black feet.

But Oliaros; Didyme; Tenos; Andros; Gyaros; Peparethos, filled with shimmering olive trees—none of these allied themselves with Minos and his fleet.

Sailing west from there, King Minos made for Oenopia, the kingdom of Aeacus. The ancients called it Oenopia; but Aeacus himself named it Aegina, after his mother.* A crowd rushed to the shore, anxious to see such a famous man. Telamon and his younger brother, Peleus, and Aeacus' third son, Phocus, also ran down to meet the king from Crete. Aeacus made his way to the shore, too, moving slowly because of old age, and he asked Minos why he had come.

Reminded of his grief, the ruler of a hundred cities sighed and answered him thus: "I ask you to take up arms with me on behalf of my son and join this just expedition. I demand consolation for him in his grave."

Aeacus, grandson of Asopus, replied "Your request is made in vain; it is one my city cannot grant, for no other land is more closely allied with the Athenians than my own. Such is our treaty with them." Minos went away sadly, saying only, "This treaty will cost you dearly," for he thought it was better now simply to threaten war than to wage it and use up his forces there ahead of time.

---

*7.471ff.: "Sailing west from there": Ovid actually says, "Sailing to the left from there." But since the island Peparethos is due north of Aegina, and the island Euboea and the southern part of Attica lie between the two islands, a ship would have to sail *around* Euboea and Attica, that is, in a southeasterly direction first and then in a southwesterly direction (skirting the southern tip of Euboea and Attica), then west-northwest into the Saronic Gulf to Aegina. Or the poet may simply have included Peparethos among the just-named islands, belonging to the Cyclades, from which one would sail "to the left" or west to reach Aegina.

The Cretan fleet, sailing away, was still visible from the walls of Aegina when a ship from Athens appeared under full sail and entered the harbor of its ally, bringing Cephalus with a message from his city. Many years had passed since the sons of Aeacus had seen Cephalus, but they recognized him and welcomed him ashore and led him to their father's palace. Still handsome and retaining even now signs of his original beauty, the hero entered carrying the branch of an Athenian olive tree and flanked by two younger men, Clytos and Butes, sons of Pallas.

After he exchanged formal greetings with Aeacus, Cephalus carried out Aegeus' instructions and requested aid, recalling the treaty between them and the agreements their forefathers had made, adding that Minos sought to bring all Greece under his control. His eloquence aided his cause, and when he had finished delivering the message entrusted to him, Aeacus, leaning on the scepter in his hand, said: "You don't need to ask for aid, Athenians, but simply to take it. Consider this island's forces yours, without a doubt, and—I pray this remains true for me!—military strength is not lacking: I have enough manpower left, and this is, thanks to the gods, an opportune time and one that allows no excuses."

"I hope things continue this way," Cephalus replied, "and that your city grows. Indeed, on my way here just now I rejoiced at such an attractive procession of young men, all the same age, coming to meet me. Nevertheless, there were many I missed, many I remember seeing when your city welcomed me once before."

Aeacus groaned and in a sad voice said: "Better luck followed an unfortunate beginning. I wish I could tell you about the one and forget the other! But I'll relate it all in sequence. To come straight to the point, bones and ashes they lie, those you remembered and asked about, yet how small a part they were of all my losses!

"A deadly plague fell upon my people because of Juno's wrath, and she was unjust in this. She hated this land because it was named after one of her rivals for Jove's affection. As long as we thought the pestilence had natural causes, and the source of so lethal an epidemic lay hidden, we battled it with all our medical knowledge. But the mounting deaths overwhelmed our efforts and finally defeated them.

"At first, a thick fog settled upon the land, trapping oppressive heat. Four times the horns of the moon had joined to make its sphere, four times the waning moon unmade that sphere, and for all that while the south wind breathed over us its hot and poisonous breath. As a result, contagion infected the springs and lakes, and thousands of reptiles crawled over untilled fields to pollute the rivers with their venom.

"We saw the first signs of the deadly plague in the sudden deaths of scores of animals—dogs, birds, sheep, cattle, and wild beasts. Plowmen, poor souls, were dumbfounded to see their powerful oxen collapse while pulling the plow and fall in the middle of the furrow. Flocks of sheep bleated pitifully as their

wool fell off mysteriously and their flesh melted away. The horse that was once
so spirited, so famous on the dusty racecourse, was now too sick to try to gain
a victory and, forgetting his earlier honors, groaned in his stall, passively waiting to die. The boar forgot to rage, the doe to trust her fleetness, bears to attack
the mettlesome herds.

"All were possessed by languor; rotting bodies lay in woods, fields, and
roads, fouling the air with their stench. And, strange to say, neither dogs,
hungry vultures, nor gray wolves would touch this flesh which, as it decom-
posed, turned to liquid and gave off noxious gases, spreading the contagion far
and wide. The plague took an even heavier toll among the wretched farmers
and raged unchecked within the walls of our great city.

"It began with a burning sensation in the bowels; other symptoms of lurking
infection were a rash and labored breathing. Fever made the tongue rough and
swollen; the mouth, become dry, lay open to the warm, disease-laden winds
as victims gasped for breath. Wearing clothes, even being covered they found
unbearable and pressed their naked bodies into the ground, though the earth
did not cool them: Their bodies heated it instead.

"No one could check the spread of the epidemic. In fact, the disease, raging,
broke out among the doctors themselves, and the healing arts were a danger
to those who practiced them. The nearer one came to a victim of the plague
and the more loyally one ministered to him, the quicker one caught it oneself
and died. And since there was no hope of recovery, and people saw death as
the only outcome of their sickness, they abandoned themselves to their in-
stincts and lost all interest in what might help them, for nothing could help
them.

"Throughout the city they crowded shamelessly around fountains, streams,
and large cisterns, but could not kill their thirst before they killed themselves
drinking water. Many became so bloated they couldn't get up and died in the
water itself. Someone else would come along and drink from it anyway.

"The sick became so weary of the beds they loathed that they would leap
up, or, if they were too weak to stand, would roll their bodies onto the ground
and flee their own houses, for their homes seemed to each one like a tomb;
and since the cause of the disease was unknown, the house itself was blamed.
Some you could see staggering half-dead through the streets for as long as they
could stand upright, others you would see weeping and lying on the ground
exhausted, rolling their eyes in one last effort and holding out their arms to
the stars, to the sweltering sky, here, there, and everywhere seized by death
and breathing their last.

"What was I feeling then? Just what you would expect me to feel: I hated
life and wanted to share my people's fate. Everywhere I looked the ground was
strewn with bodies, like rotten apples fallen from swaying branches or acorns
from an oak tree someone has shaken.

"Do you see that temple facing you, high up, reached by that long flight of
steps? That is a temple of Jupiter. There wasn't a soul who didn't burn incense

at its altars, but it did no good. Wives were constantly praying for their husbands, and fathers for their sons, and they died at these altars, their prayers unanswered, unused incense still in their hands.

"As priests recited prayers over bulls that had been led to the altars to be sacrificed and poured pure wine between their horns, the animals fell down dead without waiting for the blow of the axe. And once when I myself was making a sacrifice to Jove on behalf of myself, my country, and my three sons, the victim bellowed fearfully and suddenly collapsed, though not yet struck, with only a small trace of blood found on the knife used to cut its throat.

"The entrails, too, filled with disease, had lost all signs of truth and the will of the gods. The foul sickness reached that far! I saw corpses flung down in front of temple doors, and some of those who were stricken made their deaths even more revolting by hanging themselves in front of the altars, dying to escape the fear of death, going to meet the fate that was coming to meet them.

"Nor were the dead carried out in the customary processions, for the city gates could not accommodate so many funeral corteges, and corpses either piled up on the ground unburied or were thrown onto huge pyres without funeral rites at all. And now there was absolutely no respect for the dead, as men fought over pyres and burned bodies in fires meant for others.

"There were none to mourn the dead, who wandered unwept, the souls of sons and fathers, men young and old; no place for their graves, and not enough trees for fires. Caught up in such a whirlwind of misery and in a state of shock, I cried out, 'O Jupiter, if what they say is true, if you really entered the arms of Aegina, Asopus' daughter, and you are not ashamed, great father, to be my father, either restore my own to me or consign me also to the tomb!'

"And Jupiter sent omens—lightning followed by confirming thunder. 'I take these as clear signs,' I said, 'and pray that they portend a favorable will. I claim as an omen what you have just now given to me.' I happened to be standing beside an oak with magnificent spreading branches that had grown from an acorn from the oak tree at Dodona and was sacred to Jove. On this tree we saw a long line of ants carrying bits of grain, huge burdens for their tiny mouths, but keeping their single file across the rough and uneven bark. Marveling at how many there were, I said, 'Father, highest of the gods, grant to me the same number of citizens to fill my empty city!' The lofty oak trembled and sighed, its branches rustling, though there was no breeze. I shuddered with fear, and my hair stood on end. Nevertheless, I kissed the ground, kissed the oak, and though I dared not say in words what I hoped for, I was hoping, nevertheless, and repeating my fervent prayer in my heart.

"Night came on, and sleep invaded my careworn limbs; the same oak seemed to stand before my eyes, with the same number of branches and the same number of ants on its branches, and it seemed to tremble with the same movement and to scatter the army of ants carrying the grain onto the ground below. Suddenly, they appeared to grow and to become larger and to raise themselves from the ground, stand upright, shed their thin bodies, their many legs, and their black color, and take on human form.

"Sleep left me, and now, fully awake, I cursed my dream, sadly lamenting the lack of help from the gods. But then there was a loud murmuring in the palace, and I seemed to hear human voices, though I was long since unaccustomed to them. And while I was thinking that these were part of my dream, Telamon came running and threw open the doors and shouted: 'Father, come outside! You will see more than you could ever hope for, something beyond belief!' I went outside and looked and there I recognized the same men I seemed to have seen in my dream. They approached me and hailed me as their king. I carried out my promise to Jupiter and divided up the city among these new people and assigned them the fields left vacant by the original farmers, and I called them Myrmidons, their name preserving their origin.* You've seen what they look like, and they still have the character they had before: a frugal, hardworking race, holding on to what they've acquired and storing it up for the future. All the same age and equal in courage, they will go off to war with you as soon as the wind blowing from the east, which brought you here so quickly"—for the east wind had brought them—"changes around to the south."²⁷

And so they spent the entire day in conversation on this and other subjects. The evening was given to dining, the night to sleep.

When the golden sun again brought forth its light, the east wind was blowing still, and the sails, set for the return, remained slack. The sons of Pallas came to Cephalus, their elder, and together they went to King Aeacus, but he was still sound asleep. His son, Phocus, met them at the door of the palace, for Telamon and his brother Peleus were recruiting men for the war. Phocus led the Athenians inside to a beautifully furnished apartment and sat down with them. He noticed that Cephalus, grandson of Aeolus, was carrying a spear with a golden point, made from a kind of wood he did not recognize. After a few pleasantries Phocus said: "I'm a dedicated woodsman and hunter, and I've been wondering for some time in what forest you cut the shaft of the spear you're carrying. Now, if it were ash, it would be sandy-colored. If it were cherry, the shaft would have knots. I don't know where it comes from, but I have never seen a handsomer spear."

One of the two brothers from Athens† replied, "If you saw it in action you would be even more impressed than you are by its beauty, for it always strikes its target, is never guided by luck, and always returns bloody, of its own accord." Then Phocus, grandson of Nereus, wanted to know all about the spear, who gave it, and why—where such a fine gift came from. Cephalus himself

---

* 7.654: The name Myrmidons (Myrmidones) is supposedly derived from myrmeˆx, the Greek word for "ant." "Note [Ovid's] typical concern," Anderson says, "to connect the name of a thing with its metamorphosis" ([1972] at 7.654, 311).

†7.681: The "two brothers from Athens" are Clytos and Butes, sons of Pallas. See 7.499f.

was silent for a long time and then, moved by grief* for the wife he had lost, he said, with tears in his eyes: "Goddess-born, it is this spear that is making me weep (who could believe it?), and it will continue to for a long time to come, if fate gives me a long time to live. It destroyed me and my dear wife. I wish it had never been given to me!

"Procris was the sister of Orithyia—if Orithyia's name is more familiar to you—who was raped, but if you compared the two in beauty and character, Procris herself was the one more likely to be raped. Her father, Erechtheus, joined her to me in marriage, and love bound her to me, too. People said I was lucky, and I was. But the gods had other plans, or I would still be lucky, perhaps.

"One morning, two months after our marriage, I was spreading my deer nets on Mount Hymettus, where flowers are always blooming, when Aurora, goddess of the golden dawn, saw me after she drove away the darkness, and carried me off against my will. I pray the goddess won't be offended when I tell you the truth: That her face shone with a rosy glow, that she held in her power the boundaries of day and night, that she lived on nectar—of all that there was no doubt. But I loved Procris; Procris was in my heart; Procris' name was always on my lips. I spoke continually of our recent wedding, our sacred marriage, our love as man and wife, still new for us, and invoked the sanctity of the marriage bed, now abandoned.

"The goddess was furious: 'Stop complaining, you graceless fool! Keep your Procris. But if I know anything about the future, you will wish you had not.' And in a rage, she sent me back to her.

"As I was returning home I thought over what the goddess had said, and I began to fear that my Procris had not been faithful to her marriage vows. Her youth and beauty led me to suspect adultery, though her character opposed my suspicions. Even so, I had been away, and the one I was returning from was herself an example of infidelity—but we lovers fear everything. I decided to try something I would bitterly regret: to assault my wife's faithfulness with a bribe. Aurora fed my anxiety and changed my appearance. (I seemed to sense it happening.)

"I entered Athens incognito and proceeded to my house. The members of my household were themselves above reproach, gave every sign of being completely honest, and were anxious about their missing lord. It was only with great difficulty and after an endless number of ruses that I was able to approach the daughter of Erechtheus.

"When I saw her I was overcome and almost abandoned my plan to test her fidelity. I could barely restrain myself from revealing the truth, could barely keep myself from kissing her—I should have done both! She was very sad (but

---

*For lines 7.687–688 I have translated the text suggested by Tarrant 110: *at silet ipse diu Cephalus tactusque dolore*, one line replacing two.

no one could be more beautiful than she was, even though she was sad), and she was pining away, longing for her lost husband. Just imagine, Phocus, how very beautiful she was, this woman whose beauty grief itself enhanced.

"Why tell you how many times she rejected my attempts to seduce her, because of her faithfulness to me, how many times she said, 'I am keeping myself for one man; wherever he is, I am reserving my pleasure for one man.' What sane person would not have been satisfied by such a test of fidelity? But I was not satisfied, and I fought to wound myself until, by promising that I would make her rich if I could have just one night with her, and then increasing the amount, I finally made her hesitate. 'I've got you!' I exclaimed in bitter triumph, 'It's a fake adulterer you see, you shameless woman! I am really your husband! You have been caught in the act, and I am the witness!'

"She said not a word. Instead, silent, defeated, and filled with shame, she fled the treacherous house and her evil husband. Despising me and hating the entire male sex, she wandered in the mountains, devoting herself to Diana's pursuits.

"After she left me, a fire more violent still ate into my bones. I then begged her to forgive me, admitted that I had wronged her, said that I, too, with gifts offered to me, gifts such as these, might have yielded to a similar temptation.

"After my confession she came back to me, now that she had avenged the injury I had done to her honor, and we spent sweet years together in perfect harmony. In addition she gave me—as if she herself weren't gift enough—a dog that her dear Diana, when she gave it to her, claimed could outrun all other dogs. She also gave me a spear, the one you see in my hand. Would you like to know what happened to the first gift? Listen: It's a bizarre story and will astound you.

"Oedipus, son of Laius, had solved the riddle men before him could not answer, and the dark diviner had hurled herself into an abyss and lay there, forgetful of her own obscure sayings. Boeotian Thebes was immediately afflicted with another plague, a wild fox.* The country people kept it well fed, at the cost of their own lives and their livestock. We, the young men of the neighboring country, came to help, and we ringed the broad fields, but the swift creature leaped lightly over our nets, sailing over the highest cords of the snares we laid. Then we unleashed the dogs, but, swifter than a bird, the beast outran the pack, making fools of them all. A shout went up for me to bring out my Hurricane. (That was the name of Procris' gift.) For a long time he had been struggling to get free of the chain around his neck, straining against it. The moment we let him go we couldn't tell where he had gone. We saw his tracks in the hot dust, but he himself was out of sight, as swift as a javelin,

---

*7.762–764: 7.762 is bracketed as spurious by Miller-Goold and other editors, and I have omitted it from the translation. 7.763–764: Ovid does not identify the creature he calls simply "another plague" (*altera . . . / pestis*), but according to Apollodorus 2 4.6–7, the wild beast was a fox.

as swift as a bullet hurled from a sling, as swift as a light arrow leaping from
a Cretan bow.

"There was a low hill rising above some fields. I climbed to the crest to watch
this strange chase in which the creature seemed now to be caught, now to
escape Hurricane's snapping jaws by a hair. He was canny enough not to run
in a straight line across an open space, but instead tricked his pursuer by running in circles to keep him from springing.

"The hound was right on top of him (both running at the same speed), almost had him, didn't quite have him, bit the air. I picked up the javelin to help
and looked away while I balanced it in my right hand and tried to slip my
fingers into the leather thong. When I looked back, there in the middle of the
field (incredible!) I saw two marble figures, one about to escape, the other
poised to seize. The god no doubt wanted both to survive the contest undefeated, if indeed a god was helping them." Cephalus fell silent.

"But what about the spear? What do you blame it for?" Phocus asked. Cephalus then told him what the spear had done. "What began in joy, Phocus, ended
in sorrow. First the joy: It is such a pleasure to recall that blessèd time, son of
Aeacus, those first years when I was as happy with my wife as a man could be,
and she was happy with her husband. We shared an affection that was mutual,
a bond of love that held us both. She would not have preferred the bed of Jove
to my love, and there was no one who could have captivated me the way she
had, not even Venus herself, if she had come to me. The flames in both our
hearts burned equally strong.

"Full of youthful spirits, I used to go hunting in the forest when the morning
sun was just striking the mountain peaks with its first rays. I took no servants
with me, no horses, no keen-scented hounds, and I brought no nets; my spear
was all I needed. But when my spear-arm was tired and I had had enough of
killing wild game, I would seek out a shady spot where a breeze might be
blowing from the cooler valleys below. I was always looking for a light breeze
in the stifling heat, always waiting for a breeze to refresh me after hunting.
'Breeze, come to me,' I remember I used to call out, 'make me happy, slip into
my heart, delightful breeze, and cool me off, as only you can do, for I'm on
fire.' Maybe I added more flattering words (for my fate was drawing me on),
perhaps I said something like, 'You've given me such pleasure, you caress me
and restore me and make me love the forest, this solitary place, and your breath
always lingers on my face.'

"Someone, I don't know who, heard these ambiguous words, was deceived
by them, and thought the 'breeze' I so often called to was the name of a
nymph—believed I was in love with a nymph named Breeze. And then this
foolish person went straight to Procris about my adulterous affair—a figment
of his imagination—and whispered in her ear what he had heard.

"Love is such a naive thing. Procris fainted, collapsing on the spot out of
grief. (So I was told.) When she was finally revived, she cried out in her misery,

said how unfair it was, complained bitterly about my faithlessness, upset by a crime that never happened, and feared something that did not exist, feared a name that belonged to nobody, the poor woman, and grieved as though I really had a mistress. Even so, she was doubtful by turns and hoped in her wretchedness that she had been deceived, said she did not believe the story, said she was not going to condemn her husband unless she saw for herself.

"When the light of dawn the next day drove the night away, I went out into the forest to hunt, had a successful morning, and afterwards lay in the grass and called out, 'Breeze, come, soothe me after my labors!' Suddenly, while I was speaking, I thought I heard someone groaning. As I continued to call out, 'Come, dearest one,' there was a slight rustling of fallen leaves. I thought it was a wild animal and hurled my spear. But it was Procris! Clutching her chest where the spear struck her, she cried out, 'Oh! I'm hit!' I recognized the voice of my faithful wife and ran blindly toward the sound, beside myself.

"I found her dying, her clothes soaked in blood, and (to my horror) she was pulling from her wound her own gift to me. I held her close, the one who was dearer to me than I was to myself, cradled her tenderly in my arms, cut away her clothing from her chest, bound the wound—a savage one—tried to stop the bleeding, and begged her not to die and abandon me, guilty though I was.

"Growing weaker by the moment and now on the point of death, she forced herself to say these last few words: 'By our marriage vows, by the gods above and now by mine below, by whatever I meant to you, and by the love that caused my death but is living still, even as I die, please don't let Breeze become your wife and share our bed!'

"Now at last I realized the mistake she had made about the name, and I explained it to her. But what good did explaining do? She was slipping away, and what little strength remained was ebbing with her blood. While she could still look at anything at all she looked at me and breathed on me her last unhappy breath, which I caught and then, with a faint smile, she seemed to die content."

There were tears in Cephalus' eyes as he related this, and his listeners were weeping, too. Then Aeacus entered with his two sons and the newly formed and well-equipped army, of which Cephalus now took command.[28]

BOOK EIGHT

And now as the morning star unveiled the shining day and drove the hours of night away, the east wind fell, moist clouds appeared in the sky, and, with a steady south wind blowing, Cephalus and the soldiers of Aeacus could set their course for Athens. Running swiftly before this wind, they reached the port they were making for ahead of time.

Minos, meanwhile, was ravaging the coast of Megara and testing his army's strength against the city of Alcathous,* ruled by Nisus, who had a lock of shining purple hair on his head amid the venerable grey, the source and guarantee of his sovereignty. The horns of the rising moon had come together six times now, and the outcome of the war still hung in the balance. (For a long time victory had flown back and forth on uncertain wings between the two opposing armies.)

A royal tower had been built above the city wall, a musical wall, as it happened, for Apollo had once rested his golden lyre upon it, they say, and the music of the lyre passed into the stones of the wall. Nisus' royal daughter would often climb to the top of the tower, when peace still reigned, and toss small pebbles at the melodious stones. During the war she would also often watch the relentless clash of arms from the wall, and because the conflict had gone on for so long, she had come to know the chieftains' names, their armor, their horses, their battle dress, and even their Cretan quivers.

The face she recognized above all others was that of their commander, Minos, Europa's son. She more than recognized it; she knew it very well indeed. When Minos donned his helmet with its feathered crest, she thought he was so very handsome! Or when he held his gleaming bronze shield, he looked truly elegant to her. When he raised his arm to hurl his limber spear, the girl admired the fusion of strength and skill. When he laid an arrow on his bowstring and drew the bow into an arc, she swore that Apollo stood just so when

*8.7–8: The "city of Alcathous" is Megara.

he shot his arrows. When he removed his helmet and revealed his face and, dressed in purple, sat astride his brightly caparisoned white stallion and hauled back on the bit in its foaming mouth, Nisus' daughter was hardly herself, barely able to keep her wits about her. "How lucky the spear he touches!" she thought. "How lucky the reins he holds in his hands!" She had the impulse— if only she had the nerve!—to make her innocent way through the enemy line, or to hurl herself from the highest tower right into the Cretan camp, or to open the bronze gates of the city to the enemy, or to do anything Minos might want her to do.

As she sat gazing down at the white tent of the Cretan king, she said to herself: "Should I rejoice, or should I lament because of this sad war? I say 'lament,' because Minos is the enemy of someone who loves him, yet, if there had not been a war, I would never have known him! At least, if I became a hostage, he could end the war. I would be by his side—and I would also be a guarantee of peace!

"If your mother, most handsome of kings, was as beautiful as you yourself are, then I can understand why a god was on fire for her. O, I would be happy three times over if I could sail through the air on wings and land in the camp of the king of Crete, say who I was, confess my love, and ask how large a dowry it would take to buy him—only he mustn't demand my father's kingdom! It would be better for this marriage I hope for to perish than for me to get what I want through treason!—although for many, a gentle victor's clemency has often made defeat a good thing.

"There's no doubt he is waging a just war—on behalf of his murdered son— and he is powerful, both in his cause and in the arms he has to fight for his cause. We shall be defeated, I think, and if that is the fate that awaits my city, why should his forces, and not my love, breach my city's wall for him? He can have a better victory without a slaughter, without a long siege, without shedding his own blood. Then, at least, Minos, I won't have to fear that someone will wound you by accident, for who would be so cruel as to aim his deadly spear at you on purpose? The plan I've made seems best, and my mind is made up: I'll hand over to him both myself and my country (as my dowry) and put an end to this war.

"But wishing is not enough! Sentinels guard the gates, and my father holds the keys. Him alone I fear, I am sorry to say; he alone stands in the way of what I want. If only the gods would make me fatherless!

"Each person is truly his own god: Fortune opposes the prayers of the timid. Another woman burning with desire as great as mine and for as long as I have would happily destroy whatever stood in the way of her love. And why should some other woman be stronger than I? I would gladly go through fire and sword—but no fire or sword is needed for this: All I need is a lock of hair from my father's head! That to me is more precious than gold; that purple lock will make me very happy; it will enable me to get what I want."

As she was speaking, night came on, which calms our anxious minds, and in the dark her daring grew. The first hours of rest were now at hand, when sleep holds human hearts, weary with the worries of the day. Silently the daughter of Nisus entered her father's bedroom and (such a terrible crime!) robbed him—her own father!—of his vital lock of hair. With that forbidden prize in her possession, she passed through the enemy lines (so great was her confidence in what she had done) and came before the king. He was horrified to hear her say: "Love justified my crime. I am Scylla, Nisus' royal daughter, and I now hand over to you mine and my country's gods. The only reward I ask is . . . you. Here, take this purple lock as a token of my love and understand that what I now give you is not simply a lock of hair, but my father's life!" and she offered him the wicked gift.

Minos shrank from her outstretched hand, shocked at the idea of this outrageous crime, and replied: "May the gods drive you from the universe, infamy of our age; I pray that you have no place on land or sea! I will certainly not let Crete, Jove's cradle and my domain, be touched by such a monster."

After imposing the fairest of terms upon the defeated enemy, Minos ordered the lines mooring his fleet to be cast off and the rowers to get the bronze-clad ships under way.

When Scylla saw the vessels launched and putting out to sea, saw Minos offering her no reward for her crime, her pleas now exhausted, she flew into a violent rage and, filled with fury, her hair disheveled, threw up her hands and cried out: "Where are you running to, abandoning your benefactor, you whom I preferred to my own country, whom I preferred to my father? Where are you running to, O heart of stone, whose victory was both my crime and my claim upon you?

"Did neither the gift I gave you nor my love move you? Nor the fact that I set all my hopes on you alone? Where shall I turn, now that you've deserted me? To my country? It lies conquered! But imagine it still stood: Because of my treachery it is closed to me! To my father? Whom I delivered to you? The citizens hate me, and rightly so; neighboring countries fear my example. I am cast out, deprived of all the world, and Crete alone is open to me. If you keep me from there, too, and abandon me, ungrateful man, your mother wasn't Europa, but hostile Syrtis, Armenian tigresses, and Charybdis, churned by the south wind. Nor are you Jove's son, nor in the guise of a bull did he carry off your mother. The story of your birth is false! It was a real bull, a wild bull seized with passion for no heifer, that was your sire.

"Nisus, Father, punish me! Rejoice in my downfall, city I have just now betrayed! I confess I deserve it and ought to die. But let one of those who was injured by my betrayal kill me!

"You conquered, Minos, thanks to my crime. Why do you punish me for it? Consider this unpardonable offense against my father and my country a benefit for you! That adulteress who deceived the fierce bull with a wooden contraption and carried its monstrous offspring in her womb, she truly deserves you as her husband!

"Does what I am saying reach your ears, or do the winds that bear your ships away, you ingrate, scatter my useless words? Now I know, now it's no wonder to me why Pasiphae˜ preferred the bull to you: You are fiercer.

"O, woe is me! He orders the crews to put on more speed! The sea resounds with oars beating the water, and my land and I recede together from your sight! It will do you no good; in vain do you forget my benefits! I shall pursue you against your will, hang on to the stern of your ship, and let it pull me through the vast sea."

With these words she leaped into the water and, gaining strength from her obsession, caught up with the Cretan vessel and clung to it, a hateful companion. When her father saw her (for he had just been turned into an osprey and was hovering in the air on tawny wings), he dived down to tear at her with his hooked beak as she held fast to the ship.

Terrified, she let go, and as she fell, a light breeze seemed to catch her and keep her from touching the water. No: It was plumage: Scylla had sprouted feathers and changed into a bird called the ciris. She was given this name because she had sheared the lock from her father's head.*[29]

When Minos arrived back home and disembarked from his ship on Cretan soil, he paid his vow to Jove by sacrificing a hundred bulls and then adorned his palace walls with the spoils he had taken.

His family's disgrace had grown, for the monstrous hybrid offspring made plain its mother's bestial adultery. Minos was determined to remove this shame from his household and to shut up the Minotaur in its own dark and labyrinthine lair.

Daedalus, known throughout the world for his genius in the art of building, created that lair, setting up false markers and devising multiple winding passageways that in their twists and turnings led one's eyes astray. Just so the river Meander wanders through the fields of Phrygia, now one way, now back the other way, turning upon itself to see its waters coming down, the uncertain stream now flowing back to its source, now running onward to the open sea. So Daedalus made an endless maze of wandering corridors and—so perfect the deception—could barely get back to the entrance himself.

There Minos confined the half-bull, half-human monster, which gorged itself twice on Athenian blood from the first and second lots that were chosen and sent to Crete, nine years apart. It was finally subdued when the third lot came. For Aegeus' son Theseus, aided by the girl Ariadne, rewound the thread and made his way back to the lost door no one had ever before returned to.

He then swept up Minos' daughter and sailed at once to the island of Dia and on that shore cruelly marooned his faithful companion. The god Liber

---

*8.150: I accept the manuscripts' reading, *pluma fuit: plumis in avem,* etc., translated, "No: It was plumage [*sc.* "that was holding her up": Hollis at 8.150, 53]: Scylla had sprouted feathers and changed," with Anderson (1982a), Bo˜mer (at 8.150, 4.54), and Hollis (at 8.150, 53), rather than *pluma subit palmis,* "Plumage covered her hands," read by Miller-Goold. "Ciris" is from Greek keiris, "shearer" (keirô, "I shear").

offered his aid—and his embrace—to the forlorn and weeping girl and, wishing to pour light upon her from the everlasting stars, took the crown from her head and hurled it into the sky. As it flew through the air its precious stones turned into brilliant stars, which kept the shape of a crown and were fixed in the heavens between the Kneeler and the Serpent-holder.

Daedalus, meanwhile, hated Crete and his long exile there and longed for his native land, but he was cut off from it by the water that surrounded him. "Minos can block my path by land and sea," he thought to himself, "but the sky at least lies open. That's the way we'll go! Let him rule all else—he doesn't rule the air!"

He now turns his mind to arts unknown and makes nature anew.* For he places feathers in a row, beginning with the smallest, so you would think they grew on a slope† or resembled a shepherd's pipe, where each reed is slightly longer than the one next to it. Next, he ties the row of feathers down the middle with stout twine and fastens their ends in wax. And then he curves the row of feathers slightly, to make them like a real bird's wings.

His son Icarus stood at his side and, unaware he was handling something that would be deadly for him, now caught at feathers floating in the air, now molded the yellow wax with his thumb, getting in the way of his father's amazing work as he himself played.

When the creator of the wings had put the finishing touches on them, he tried out his own pair, moving them up and down—and hovered in the air! He also gave his son instructions: "Icarus," he said, "be sure to take a middle course, for the water will drag on your wings if you go too low, and the sun will burn them up if you go too high. Fly in between! Don't look at Boötes or the Great Bear or Orion with his drawn sword. Let me lead the way and follow me!"

As the old man fitted the unfamiliar wings on his son's shoulders and explained to him how to fly, tears streamed down his cheeks as he worked and his hands trembled. He kissed his son—it would be for the last time—and, rising on his own wings, flew in front, and was anxious for his companion, like a mother bird that launches its tender fledgling into the air from its lofty

---

*8.189: "makes nature anew": As did James Joyce (or so he hoped) in his novel *A Portrait of the Artist as a Young Man* (1916), as an epigraph for which he used the preceding line (8.188: "He now turns his mind to arts unknown").

†The Latin text of 8.189b–191a reads: *nam ponit in ordine pennas / a minima coeptas, longam breviore sequenti, / ut clivo crevisse putes* ("For he places feathers in a row, beginning with the smallest, with the shorter following the long, so that you think they have grown on a slope"). The second half of 8.190 (= 8.190b), "with the shorter [feather] following the long," reverses the order of the first half, "beginning [sc. "feathers beginning"] with the smallest," and various solutions have been proposed: Bömer retains 8.190b, noting Marahrens' view of "a change of perspective" but thinking himself that Ovid was merely careless with his details (at 8.190, 4.72–73). Anderson says that 8.190b should perhaps be "daggered," that is, considered suspect ([1972] at 8.190–192, 351). Hollis (following Merkel) deletes the entire line (8.190), judging 8.190b as not authentic (at 8.190, 59). I have omitted 8.190b from the translation.

nest, and looked back at him often, urging him to stay close behind, teaching him the destructive art, while keeping himself aloft.

A man with a fishing pole quivering with the fish that had taken the bait, a shepherd leaning on his crook, a ploughman resting on his plough—all saw the pair passing overhead and were astonished: They believed they were gods because they could fly through the air.

Juno's island, Samos, was on their left (they had already flown past Delos and Paros), and Lebinthos and Calymne, rich in honey, were on their right, when the boy grew daring and began to delight in flying, abandoned his guide, lured on by desire for the open sky, soared higher, and came too near the burning sun. The fragrant wax that held the wings together turned soft and melted, and now he was moving bare arms; but, lacking wings, he felt no wind, and the blue sea filled his mouth as he cried "Father!" and got its name, Icarian, from him.

His father, desolate, called, "Icarus! Icarus! Where are you, Icarus? Where must I look for you?" kept calling, "Icarus!" and then saw feathers on the water, cursed his art, laid his son's body in a tomb, and named the land for the boy he buried there.

As Daedalus put his poor son in his final resting place, a garrulous partridge looked up from a muddy ditch, clapped its wings, and expressed its glee by warbling a song. A singular creature then, not seen in former years and only recently become a bird, it was a lasting reproach to you, Daedalus. For the artist's sister, not knowing the fate in store for her son, had entrusted him to Daedalus to be taught. A boy of twelve with a bright and eager mind, he had once observed the backbone in a fish, used it as a model, cut a continuous row of teeth in an iron blade, and so invented the saw. He was also the first to tie two iron legs together, fix one in place, and describe a circle around it with the other, while keeping them the same distance apart.

Envious of the boy, Daedalus threw him down from Minerva's sacred citadel headfirst, then said that he had fallen. But the goddess, who protects all those with genius, caught him and covered him with feathers in midair, and so turned him into a bird. The vigor of his mind, once so quick, went into his wings and legs. He kept the name that he had before.* Yet this bird never flies high in the air nor makes its nest in branches at the top of a tree. Instead, it skims over the ground, lays its eggs in bushes, and, remembering its ancient fall, fears all high places.

An exhausted Daedalus now reached the land of Sicily and found a kind protector there in Cocalus, who took up arms on behalf of his suppliant.[30]

Now, too, Athens ceased to pay its sad tribute to Crete, thanks to Theseus' glorious achievement. Its temples were decked with garlands, and the people

---

*8.247–255: 8.247–249: "He was also the first . . . ," that is, he invented the draftsman's compass. 8:255: "the name that he had before": Daedalus' nephew was named Perdix, which is also the Latin word for "partridge."

invoked the warrior goddess Minerva, Jove, and other gods, and honored them with caskets of incense and the blood sacrifice they had promised.

The story of the hero's exploits had spread his name throughout the cities of Greece, and so the people living in this wealthy land* appealed to him for help with their great dangers. The Calydonians also sought his help, although they had Meleager, and came as anxious suppliants to plead for aid.

The reason for their mission was a hog, the avenging servant of a hostile Diana. For they say that Oeneus in a year of bountiful harvests gave the first fruits of the grain to Ceres, gave wine to Bacchus, and gave olive oil to Minerva with the yellow hair. And so the honors the gods covet were paid first to the deities of farming, and then to all the other gods. Only Diana's altars were ignored and left without incense, they say, and she was passed over. But gods, too, can feel wrath. "We shall not simply submit to this and do nothing," the goddess said, "and though we are dishonored, let it never be said we fail to get revenge."

And to punish Oeneus' neglect, she sent a boar to ravage the fields of Aetolia, a boar larger than the bulls of Sicily, as large, in fact, as those in grassy Epirus. Its eyes flashed blood and fire, and bristles stood erect on its neck like spears stuck in the ground. Its tusks were huge, like the tusks of an Indian elephant, and when it screamed, hot foam flecked its great shoulders, lightning darted from its mouth, and leaves and grass burst into flames from the heat of its fiery breath.

First, it trampled the growing grain in the blade, then cut down the crop ripe for harvesting that the farmer had put his hopes on (though he was now in tears), destroying the gift of Ceres in the ear. In vain the threshing floor, in vain the granaries waited for the promised harvest. Ripening grapes were strewn on the ground, trailing their vines, and olives still on leafy branches were scattered everywhere.

The boar then attacked flocks of sheep, and neither shepherds nor their dogs could defend them, nor could fierce bulls protect their herds.

The people scattered, fleeing the countryside, believing that only within the city walls would they be safe, until Meleager and a band of young men he had chosen gathered together, eager to win glory: the twin sons of Tyndareus, one spectacular in boxing, the other as a horseman; Jason, builder of the first ship; Theseus and Pirithoüs, a happy pair of friends; the two sons of Thestius; the son of Aphareus; Lynceus and swift Idas; Caeneus, no longer a woman;† fierce Leucippus; Acastus, outstanding with the javelin; Hippothoüs; Dryas; Phoenix,

---

*8.268: Ovid says, "the people living in wealthy Achaea" (*dives Achaia*), which I have translated as "this wealthy land," following Bömer, who notes that Achaia here stands for all of Greece (at 8.268, 3.92).

†8.301–305: 8.301: The "twin sons of Tyndareus" are Castor (the horseman) and Pollux (the boxer). 8.304: The "two sons of Thestius" are Plexippus and Toxeus (named at 8.440 and 441), who are brothers of Meleager's mother, Althaea (Miller-Goold 1.427 n. 1), and thus his uncles. 8.305: For "Caeneus, no longer a woman," see 12.189ff. and 459ff.

son of Amyntor; the twin sons of Actor; and Phyleus, sent from Elis. Telamon was there, along with Peleus, the father of great Achilles; Admetus, son of Pheres; Boeotian Iolaus; the energetic Eurytion; Echion, unbeatable on the race track; Locrian Lelex; Panopeus; Hyleus; fierce Hippasus; and Nestor, now in his youth—all these were there as well. And more came: the sons of Hippocoon, sent from ancient Amyclae; Laertes, Penelope's father-in-law; Ancaeus from Arcadia; Mopsus, son of Ampyx, with his keen mind; Amphiaraus, son of Oecles, not yet murdered by his wife; and a Tegean girl, the glory of the Arcadian forest.* Her robe was fastened at the top with a polished pin; her hair was simply arrayed, for she had gathered it in a bun at the back of her head; an ivory quiver rattling with arrows hung from her left shoulder; and she carried a bow in her left hand. Thus was she dressed and fitted out; her face you could say was a girl's face on a boy's body—or was it a boy's face on a girl?

As soon as he saw her, the Calydonian hero† desired her (though the gods were opposed), and a hidden fire stole into his heart. "How happy the man," he said, "whom she considers good enough to be her husband!" But it was not the moment to say more (and his modesty would not allow him to). The more pressing task, the great contest, was now upon him.

A dense forest in which no tree had ever fallen stands on level ground and commands a view of downward-sloping fields. When the men arrived there, some spread the hunting nets, others unleashed the dogs, still others followed the tracks of the boar intently, each group eager to find the danger for themselves.

Below, there was a hollow with standing water after a rain. At the bottom of this marshy place grew supple willows, light sedge, swamp rushes, osier, and tall rushes, with shorter reeds beneath. Aroused from here, the boar hurled itself violently into the midst of its enemies, like lightning leaping down from colliding clouds. Trees the boar crashed into cracked and snapped and lay strewn on the ground from its onslaught.

The young men shouted and aimed their spears, the broad iron spearheads glinting in the sunlight. The boar charged furiously at the dogs, scattering those in its path with sidelong thrusts as they stood barking.

The first spear, hurled by Echion, missed the boar but lightly gashed the trunk of a maple tree. The next seemed about to fasten itself in the boar's back but was hurled too hard and flew over its target. Jason of Pagasae threw that one. Then Mopsus prayed to Phoebus Apollo: "If ever I served you and serve you still, let my spear hit its mark!" The god granted his prayer, as far as he could: Mopsus did indeed hit the boar, but he didn't wound it, for Diana broke off the iron head as the spear sailed through the air, and the shaft arrived without a point.

---

*8.317: The "Tegean girl" is named Atalanta, although Ovid never gives her name. She is not the Atalanta who is the subject of a tale at 10.560–707.

†8.324: The "Calydonian hero" is Meleager.

The beast's wrath was now loosed, and it raged like forked lightning, shooting flames from its eyes and breathing fire from its snout. As a boulder flies when flung by a sling at city walls or towers filled with soldiers, so the boar, hooking and slashing with its deadly tusks, hurled itself into the midst of the young men, cutting down Hippalmos and Pelagon, who were guarding the right flank. Their comrades quickly hauled them away.

But Enaesimus, son of Hippocoon, did not escape a fatal goring. As he turned in terror to run away, the boar slashed the tendons behind his knees, and he felt his legs fail. Even Nestor from Pylos might well have perished before the Trojan War, but he thrust his spear into the ground for purchase and vaulted into the branches of the nearest tree, whence he gazed down in safety at the enemy he had just escaped.

Now the creature angrily sharpened its curved tusks on the trunk of an oak, intent on dealing death, and then, trusting in its renewed weapons, buried one of them in the thigh of the mighty son of Eurytus.

The twins Castor and Pollux, not yet stars in the sky, both conspicuous, both riding horses whiter than snow, brandished their spears together and together sent them flashing through the air. They would have given twin wounds to the bristly beast, had it not slipped into the dark woods just then, to a place too dense for spears or horses. Telamon pursued the boar, but in his zeal not watching where he ran, tripped over the root of a tree and fell flat on his face. While Peleus was setting him on his feet, the Tegean girl laid a swift arrow on her bowstring, drew it all the way back, and sent the arrow flying, but it only grazed the back of the boar, hanging beneath one ear and reddening the bristles with a trace of blood.

Happy as she was at the success of her shot, Meleager was happier still and was the first to see the blood, people think, and the first to point it out to his companions and to say to her, "You deserve the prize for valor!"

The men grew red in the face and urged one another on, working up their courage as they shouted, and flung their spears all at once and in disorder. But the jumble of weapons ruined the throws and made the javelins miss their target.

Now see Arcadian Ancaeus, armed with a double axe, his rage hastening his fate, shouting: "Learn, you men, how superior a man's arms are to a woman's, and make way for me! Let Diana herself, if she wants, protect this beast with her weapons. But no matter what Diana does, I'm going to kill it!"

With that inflated boast, the arrogant Ancaeus raised his axe above his head with both hands and, rearing on his toes, was about to bring it crashing down on the boar, but it checked him in this act of daring and drove both tusks into his abdomen, the quickest route to death. Ancaeus fell, and his bowels slithered out in a wet and bloody heap on the ground, now soaked in his gore.

Then Ixion's son Pirithoüs went after the boar head on, brandishing his powerful hunting spear in his hand. Theseus, son of Aegeus, shouted at him: "Back, O heart of my heart, dearer to me than I am to myself! A little distance is the better part of valor. Reckless courage just killed Ancaeus," and he hurled his heavy bronze-tipped spear. Well aimed, it would have fulfilled his vow, but the leafy branch of an oak tree got in the way.

Jason, son of Aeson, threw his spear, but it missed its target and fatally struck an innocent hound instead and, passing through its belly, stuck in the ground.

The luck of Meleager's hand was mixed. Of two spears he hurled, the first hit the ground, but the second ripped into the middle of the boar's back. The creature went into a frenzy, whirling around and around, spewing fresh blood and foam from its mouth. And then the giver of the wound was upon it, goading the boar into a rage, and, facing it, buried his gleaming spear between its shoulders.

His comrades gave a mighty cheer, shouting out their joy, and each sought to clasp the victor's hand in his own. They gazed in wonder at the huge beast, spread out over several square yards of ground, thinking it wasn't safe to touch it yet, each dipping his spear in its blood, nevertheless.

Meleager himself stood with one foot resting on the menacing head. "Atalanta," he said, "take the spoils that are mine by rights, and let me share my triumph here with you." And then and there he gave her the stiff and bristly hide, as well as the head, magnificent with its great tusks.

She was delighted with both the giver and the gifts, but the other hunters begrudged them, and a murmur of protest spread through the crowd. Grabbing at the spoils, the sons of Thestius shouted, "Put them down, woman, and don't try to make off with the honor that belongs to us men, nor let your confidence in your looks lead you astray, lest your benefactor, smitten though he is, be unable to help you." And so they denied her the spoils and denied him the right to give the spoils away.

Meleager, son of Mars, could not endure this. Swelling with rage and grinding his teeth, he shouted: "So you want to steal another's glory? Well, learn the difference between threats and deeds!" and—unspeakable act!—plunged his sword into the chest of Plexippus, who certainly wasn't expecting this. Toxeus, unsure what to do, wished to avenge his brother, yet feared his brother's fate. Meleager did not allow him to be unsure for long, and he heated again with kindred blood the blade still hot from killing the first brother.

Althaea was taking gifts to the temples of the gods in thanksgiving for her son's victory when she saw her dead brothers as they were borne back home. Beating her breast, she filled the city with the sounds of her lamentation and changed her golden robe to the black of mourning. But when she learned who their killer was, her grieving stopped, completely, and she turned from tears to a passion for revenge.

Many years before, when Althaea was recovering from the birth of Meleager, the three sisters put a log on the fire and said, as they spun his fate, pressing the thread with their thumbs, "We give you a life span, O newborn babe, that will last as long as it takes this log to burn." With this decree the goddesses departed, and Meleager's mother snatched the burning brand from the fire and doused it in water.

For a long time the log remained hidden in the innermost part of the house and, itself preserved, young man, it preserved your life. Now his mother brought out the log and ordered servants to make a pile of sticks and kindling, and when they had done that, she started a deadly fire. Four times she tried to put the log on the fire, started to do it, then held back four times, the mother and sister at war within her, two names pulling her single heart in two directions. Often she turned white from fear of the crime she was about to commit, but just as often her seething rage shone red in her eyes. One moment her face had a cruel and threatening look, the next a pitying one. When the raging anger in her mind had dried her tears, new tears sprang up, and, like a ship that the wind pulls one way, the tide another, while the vessel feels both forces and, faltering, obeys them both, so Althaea, awash in uncertainty, veered from one feeling to the other, calmed her wrath and then revived it again.

The sister in her nonetheless began to overcome the mother, and to soothe her kinsmen's shades with blood, she gave her full devotion to a godless act. For when the deadly fire had caught and began to burn, she said, "Let these flames be a funeral pyre to consume my flesh and blood." Then, holding in her cruel hand the fatal log, she stood downcast before the altar of death and prayed: "Eumenides, triple goddesses of vengeance, look upon these rites offered to you! I thus avenge—and I commit—a crime. Death must be paid with death, outrage added to outrage, slaughter to slaughter. Let this godless house perish beneath its load of grief! Why should Oeneus enjoy the sight of his victorious son while Thestius is bereft of his two sons? Better for you both to mourn.

"Shades of my brothers, new souls among the dead, observe my service to you, and accept this funeral offering prepared at a great cost, this unhappy pledge from my womb!

"Oh, woe is me! What is happening to me? Brothers! Forgive a mother! My hands will not move. I know he deserves to die, but why should I be the cause of his death?

"But will he then go unpunished and, alive, victorious, and swollen with success, rule Calydon, while you, my brothers, lie dead—ashes and icy ghosts?

"I won't allow it! Let the criminal die and take with him his father's hope, his kingdom, and the downfall of his country!

"Oh, where is the mother's heart in me? Where is the sacred obligation to the burden I carried nine long months?

"I wish you had burned as a baby in that first fire! I wish I had suffered through it then! But you lived then, thanks to me. Now, thanks to yourself, you will die! Receive this—it is what you get for what you did. Give me back the life I gave you twice, first when I bore you, then when I snatched the log from the fire—or else put me in my brothers' tomb with them!

"I want to do it, but I cannot. What am I going to do? Over and over I see my brothers' wounds before my eyes—a vision of terrible murder! But now a mother's love, the very name of mother, breaks my will! How wretched I am! You will win a terrible victory, brothers, but go ahead and win it!—provided that I myself join you and the one I give to you as consolation!"

With trembling hand—but unable to look—she threw the fatal log upon the fire. As it was enveloped by reluctant flames and began to burn, it groaned, or seemed to groan. Far away and unaware, Meleager was ignited by the same fire, felt himself burning from unseen flames deep within himself, and tried to overcome the terrible pain by sheer courage. It grieved him, though, to die a slow and bloodless death, and he thought Ancaeus lucky in his wounds. With his dying breath he groaned and called out to his aged father, his brothers, his loyal sisters, his wife, and perhaps his mother, too. The fire, far away, and his pain flared up together, together they died down, together they went out; and his spirit gently entered the soft, still air, as white ash slowly covered the fading ember.

Lofty Calydon was laid low. Young and old were grieving, commoners and nobles wept, and Calydonian mothers, dwellers by the Evenus, cut their hair and beat their breasts. Meleager's father lay prostrate on the ground, fouling his hair and agéd face with dust, crying out against his long life. As for Meleager's mother, she punished herself with the same hand that was guilty of such a terrible deed and drove a sword through her belly.

Not even if a god should give me a hundred singing tongues, great genius, and all the music on Mount Helicon, not even then could I recite the sad fate of Meleager's grieving sisters. Forgetting decorum, they not only beat their breasts black and blue, but before the body was burned they embraced it again and again and kissed it again and again and kissed the bier when it was laid upon the pyre, and after it was burned gathered the ashes and hugged them to their breasts. They threw themselves upon Meleager's grave and lay there, trying to embrace the name cut in the stone, and filled the letters incised there with their tears. Finally, Diana, well satisfied with the destruction of the house of Parthaon, made feathers grow on the sisters' bodies (except for Gorgé and the daughter-in-law of noble Alcmena*), raised them up and gave them wings down the length of their arms, made their faces into beaks, and sent them thus transformed through the air.[31]

Theseus meanwhile, after doing his part in the common effort to kill the boar, was hurrying to the city of Erechtheus, Minerva's city, when the river Achelous, swollen with rain, blocked his way and delayed him. "Famous son of Cecrops," the river-god said, "come into my house and don't expose yourself to these violent waters of mine that often sweep away huge tree trunks and tumble boulders so thunderously down my stream. I have seen great barns by the river's edge swept away, cattle and all. Once they are caught in the cur-

---

*8.543–544: "the daughter-in-law of noble Alcmena," that is, Deianira, wife of Hercules, son of Alcmena.

rent, strength is no use to a herd nor speed to a horse. And when the river
rages with melted snow from the mountain, its swirling eddies have sucked
many a young man to the bottom. It is better for you to rest here until the river
runs in its normal course again, until my waters abate and flow in their usual
channel."

Theseus agreed: "I'll accept both your advice, Achelous, and your invitation," and he did just that and entered the river's dwelling, which was made of
porous pumice stone and rough tufa, its floor covered with damp moss, its
ceiling studded with rows of conch and murex shells.

And now when the sun had measured out two thirds of his light for the day,
Theseus and the comrades of his toils reclined on couches: Pirithoüs, son of
Ixion, lay on one side; Lelex, the Troezenian hero, a little gray at the temples,
lay on the other, along with the rest of Theseus' companions, whom the Acar-
nanian river-god honored in the same way, delighted to have such an important
guest. Barefoot nymphs appeared immediately and heaped food on the tables
and, when the feast was taken away, served wine all around in jeweled goblets.

Then the great hero looked out at the sea in the distance and, pointing with
his finger, asked: "What place is that? It seems to be an island. Tell me, what
is the name of it? Indeed, there appear to be several islands."

"That's right; it's not just one island you see," the river-god replied; "there
are five, but the distance makes it hard to tell them apart. And to make you
wonder less about the way Diana reacts when she's spurned,* let me tell you
that these islands used to be naiads, and once, when they slaughtered ten bullocks and invited gods of the countryside to their sacred banquet, they danced
and celebrated with no thought of me. I swelled with wrath and rain, grew as
huge as I become in full spate, uprooted trees from the forest, tore a piece of
earth from the fields, and swept it and the nymphs together into the sea. They
remembered me then! Our waves, mine and the sea's, broke up that single
piece of ground and created the islands of the Echinades, which you can see
out there in the water. And as you yourself can tell, one island has moved quite
far out, one I'm particularly fond of. Sailors call her Perimele. I fell in love with
her and robbed her of her virginity. Enraged by this, her father, Hippodamas,
hurled his daughter from a cliff into the sea to drown, but I caught her, kept
her afloat, and prayed to Neptune: 'O trident-bearing god, whose portion is the
restless sea, the second kingdom of the world, help this girl, who was nearly
drowned by her father's savagery, and make a place for her, or let her become
a place herself.' And while I was speaking, new land enfolded her limbs in the
water,† her body changed, and from it a solid island grew.'"

---

*8.579: "the way Diana reacts when she's spurned": Achelous is referring to Diana's punishing
the Calydonians with the wild boar after Oeneus neglected to honor her (8.271ff.), this boar the
object of the hunt from which Theseus is now returning.

†Twelve of the fourteen lines between 8.596 and 8.609 (excluding those lines, and there are
two 600s and two 601s) are considered spurious and are usually either bracketed or omitted
altogether, as Miller-Goold have done. These lines have been omitted from the translation. See
Hollis at 8.595ff., 102ff., for a clear explanation of the problem.

The river then was silent. The miracle had moved them all. But Pirithous, the son of Ixion, laughed at them for believing it, and since he was an arrogant man and contemptuous of the gods, he said, "You made that story up, Achelous, and you allow the gods too much power if you think they give bodies their forms and take those forms away."

All were astonished at Pirithoüs and disapproved of such talk, especially Lelex, an older man, a man of experience, and he said to him: "The gods' power is immense and has no limit; whatever they want is done. Do you doubt this? Well, in the Phrygian hills there's an oak that stands beside a linden tree, both surrounded by a low wall. I've seen the place myself, for Pittheus once sent me to the fields of his father Pelops, the former king of Phrygia. Close by there's a marshy lake, land that was habitable long ago; now gulls and coots flock to its waters. Jupiter came here once in human form with his son (and Atlas' grandson) Mercury, the wand-bearer, who had removed his wings. They knocked on a thousand doors, looking for a place to rest, and a thousand doors were slammed in their faces and locked.

"One home, though, received them, a small one, it's true, a hut roofed with straw and marsh reeds. An old woman, god-fearing Baucis, and her husband, Philemon, the same age as she, were married in that hut when they were young, grew old in it together—and made a light thing of their poverty by accepting it and bearing it with equanimity. No need to ask if there were masters and servants in that house; those two were the entire household. They gave the orders, and they obeyed them.

"When the heaven-dwelling gods arrived at this modest home, stooping to pass through the low doorway, old Philemon drew up a bench and invited them to rest their weary limbs. Baucis hurried to throw a coarse blanket over the bench, stirred the warm ashes in the fireplace, reviving the fire from the day before, fed it with dry leaves and bark, coaxed it into flame with puffs of an old woman's breath, pulled down split kindling and dry branches from the rafters, broke them up and put them under a small bronze pot of water, and stripped the outer leaves from a cabbage her husband had picked in the garden they kept so well watered. With a two-pronged fork Philemon lifted down from a blackened roof-beam a side of bacon, long-preserved and dingy with smoke, and from it cut a thin slice that he dropped into the pot of water to boil, along with the cabbage.

"Meanwhile, they made conversation to fill up the time as they shook out a mattress of soft marsh grass that lay on a couch with frame and legs of willow and covered the mattress with a spread they never used except on festal days, an old, cheap coverlet, just right for the willow couch. On this the gods reclined.

"With her skirt tucked up, and trembling a little with age, Baucis brought out a three-legged table, one leg of which was shorter than the other two. She put a piece of broken pottery beneath it to make the table level, then wiped the top with green mint. Next, she put on the table some fresh olives that were not yet ripe and so still partly green; some autumn cherries preserved in wine lees; endive; radishes; cheese; and eggs, lightly roasted in warm ashes, all in earthen dinnerware. Next she got out a wine bowl, as fine as the dinnerware, and wine cups carved from beechwood and coated on the inside with golden wax.

"Shortly, a steaming banquet was served from the hearth, and then the wine (not a vintage one), which had been taken away during the main course, was brought back, but was put a little to one side, sharing the table with a dessert of nuts; dried figs, mixed with dates; plums; a large basket full of sweet-smelling apples; ripe grapes, just picked; and, in the middle, a gleaming honeycomb. To all these, kindly faces and an attentive and gracious welcome were added.

"They noticed, meanwhile, that the wine bowl filled itself as often as it was emptied, and the wine rose to the top by itself. Astonished by this strange happening and quaking with fear, Baucis and Philemon lifted their hands in prayer and begged forgiveness for the simple meal and the inelegant service.

"The couple possessed a single goose, the guardian of their tiny holding, which they were preparing to kill for their divine guests. It was swift on the wing and wore them out as they chased it, old and slow as they were, continually eluding them till finally it seemed to take refuge with the gods themselves, who told the couple not to kill it, saying: 'We are gods, and your impious neighbors will get the punishment they deserve; our gift to you is this: You will not be touched by their disaster, but you must leave your house and come with us, and go to the top of yonder mountain!' They both obeyed and struggled to make their way up the long slope, putting their weight on their canes. When they were but a single bowshot from the summit, they looked back and saw everything below covered by water, except their house, which was still visible, and while they stared in astonishment, weeping at the fate of their countrymen, their ancient cottage, small even for its two owners, turned into a temple: Columns replaced the forked uprights supporting the gable; the straw on the roof turned yellow—the roof now seemed to be made of gold; the doors were engraved; and the earthen floor was covered with marble.

"Then Jupiter said to them in a kind and reassuring voice, 'Tell me, righteous old man, and you, old woman, worthy of a righteous husband, what would you like to have?' Philemon spoke briefly with Baucis and then reported their joint decision to the gods: 'We ask to be priests and to have charge of your temple; and because we have spent our lives together in harmony, we ask that the same moment take us both away: Let me never see my wife's grave, nor let her ever have to bury me.' Their prayer was granted: They became the custodians of the temple for the rest of their lives.

"And then one day as they were standing in front of the temple steps, quite old and feeble now, and, as it happened, telling how the temple came to be, Baucis saw leaves growing from Philemon, and old Philemon, in turn, saw leaves growing from Baucis, too. They spoke with each other for as long as they could, while the trees they were changing into rose toward their two faces and then cried out, 'Farewell, beloved,' at the same moment, and at the same moment leaves grew over their mouths and covered them.

"Even today the inhabitants of Bithynia point out the tree trunks standing side by side that were once their two bodies.* The old men who told me this story were not simpleminded, nor was there any reason they should want to lie to me. Indeed, I saw garlands hanging from the branches, and, as I was placing fresh ones on them myself, I said, 'May those whom the gods love be gods themselves, and those who honored the gods be honored themselves.'" Such was Lelex's tale. Both the story and its teller had moved them all, especially Theseus.

And now, because Theseus wanted to hear about the wondrous things done by the gods, the Calydonian river, leaning on one elbow, said: "There are some, O bravest of friends, whose forms were once changed and who then remained in their new shapes. There are others who have the power to change into many forms, like you, Proteus, who dwell in the earth-embracing sea. For people have seen you as a young man at one moment and as a lion at another; once you were a raging wild boar, then a snake men were afraid to touch; horns once made you into a bull; often you turned into a stone, often, too, into a tree; sometimes, imitating water, you were a river and sometimes fire, the opposite of water.

"The wife of Autolycus, Erysichthon's daughter, has this power, too. Her father was a man who scorned the gods and refused to burn incense on their altars. He is even said to have taken an axe to a grove sacred to Ceres and to have desecrated this ancient wood by chopping down its trees.

"Among them stood an ancient oak with a huge trunk, a tree that was a grove all by itself, decorated with ribbons, commemorative tablets, and garlands, tokens people had left for prayers answered. Dryads often danced their festive dances beneath this tree; often, too, they joined hands and encircled the mighty trunk, which measured fifteen cubits around.† The oak towered above the other trees in the grove to the same extent that they towered above the grass beneath. But that did not stop Erysichthon from taking an axe to this sacred tree. He ordered his servants to cut it down, and when he saw them hesitate to carry out his order, bent on committing a crime, he snatched an axe from one of them. 'I don't care whether the goddess loves it or whether it is the goddess herself,' he said. 'The top of this tree will soon touch the ground.' And when he raised the axe to strike the tree, Ceres' oak trembled and uttered a

---

*8.720: "the tree trunks standing side by side": These are the oak and linden trees mentioned at the beginning of the story at 8.620–621.

†8.748–749: "fifteen cubits around": I have translated the Latin word *ulna* (8.748), "forearm" or, as a measure of length, "ell," as "cubit," following Bömer's citation of Kiessling-Heinze: "*ulna* or *cubitus* = 45 centimeters," that is, about 18 inches, fifteen of which give a circumference of 22.5 feet. (Bömer at 8.748–749, 4.243–244; Hollis [at 8.748, 135] agrees).

groan, its leaves and acorns turned pale, and its great branches took on the same pallor.

"As Erysichthon's godless hand made gashes in the trunk, blood poured from the mangled bark, just as blood gushes from the severed neck of a mighty sacrificial bull when it is struck down before an altar. All the servants were dumbfounded, and one of them was bold enough to try to stop this outrage and prevent more blows of the savage axe. Thessalian Erysichthon, glaring at the man, said, 'Here's your reward for piety,' raised his axe, lopped off the man's head, and resumed chopping down the tree.

"From deep within the oak there came a voice: 'I am one of Ceres' dearest nymphs, and I live inside this tree. Though I am dying, I predict that punishment for this awaits you—consolation for my death.' But Erysichthon persisted in his crime, and the oak finally fell from the countless blows of the axe and the ropes attached to it and crashed to the ground, crushing much of the forest beneath its weight.

"The other tree nymphs, shocked by the destruction of the grove and the injury to themselves (they were all sisters of the oak tree nymph), approached Ceres in their grief, wearing black, and begged her to punish Erysichthon. The goddess, a vision of loveliness, agreed with a nod of her head that shook the fields full of grain ripe for harvesting. She devised a kind of punishment that would have made Erysichthon pitiable, if it hadn't been for the fact that no one felt pity for him because of what he had done: She intended to torture him to death with omnivorous Hunger.

"Since the goddess herself could not approach Hunger (for the fates do not allow Ceres and Hunger to meet), she spoke to one of the mountain divinities, a country nymph: 'There is a place in the remotest part of frozen Scythia, a gloomy region, a sterile, barren, treeless land. Numbing Cold lives there, and Pallor, Trembling, and empty Hunger. Go tell Hunger I said to bury herself deep in the criminal gut of that blasphemous man and to let no amount of food whatsoever overcome her, and tell her to fight against my powers in him—and defeat them! And if you're afraid because of the distance you have to travel, take my chariot and serpents and drive them there through the sky,' and she turned the serpents over to her.

"Borne through the air in Ceres' chariot, the mountain nymph descended into Scythia and landed on a frozen mountaintop (called Caucasus). As she lifted the yoke from the serpents' necks, she caught sight of Hunger, the object of her journey, in a stony field pulling up the sparse grass with her nails and teeth. Her hair was matted, her eyes hollow, her face pale, her lips gray from disuse, her jaws scabrous with mold, and her skin stretched so tight that one could see her organs. Her bones, too, were visible beneath the skin at the curve of her hips, and instead of a belly she had only a place for a belly, and you would think her breasts were attached to her spine and hung down from it. Emaciation made her joints appear large: Her knees looked swollen, and her ankles seemed to be great bulges.

"Viewing her from a long way off (for she dared not come closer), the nymph repeated the goddess' orders—and almost immediately, although she was some distance away, although she had only just come there, she nevertheless began to feel exceedingly hungry herself, and she turned the chariot around and drove the serpents back through the sky to Thessaly.

"Hunger obeyed Ceres' orders, though she is always opposed to what the goddess does, and let the wind carry her through the air to the house where she had been ordered to go. She immediately entered the bedroom of that violator of the sacred wood and wrapped her arms around him, sound asleep (for it was night), and breathed herself into the man, filling his mouth, throat, and chest with her breath and spreading hunger throughout his veins, now empty of all nourishment. And so, having carried out her orders, she abandoned the fertile world and returned to her impoverished home, her familiar cave.

"Gentle sleep was still wafting Erysichthon on its quiet wings, but now in a dream he looks for something to eat and works an empty mouth, teeth chewing on teeth, and his throat, deluded, swallows food that is not there and instead of a meal gulps down drafts of empty air.

"After the dream drove his sleep away, a powerful urge to eat gripped him, all the way from his starving jaws to his burning belly, and drove him mad. He called for fruit of the sea, of the earth, of the air, complained at table of being hungry, and looked around for more to eat, even while he was eating. Food that would satisfy cities, even an entire people, was not enough for one man, and the more he shoveled into his stomach, the hungrier he became.

"Just as rivers from all over the earth feed the ocean, but the ocean itself never has water enough and swallows up the streams of faraway countries, and just as a roaring fire never refuses more fuel, but burns up countless logs, and the more it is fed the more it demands and the hungrier it becomes from the very mass of wood, so wicked Erysichthon, while calling for still more food, at the same time stuffed anything edible into his maw. Each bite demanded another, and constant eating made him feel constantly famished.

"And now because of the bottomless pit in his starving stomach he had seriously reduced his inherited wealth without reducing his relentless hunger at all, and the fire in his implacable gullet raged on. Finally, when all his assets had been converted to food and loaded into his belly, he was left with his daughter, who surely deserved a better father. Her, too, he sold in his desperate need, but, coming from noble stock, she refused to have a master. Stretching out her hands toward the nearby sea, she cried to Neptune, 'Deliver me from slavery; you possessed the prize of my stolen virginity'—for it was Neptune who had stolen that prize.

"The god did not reject her prayer. Her new master had just caught sight of her and was running her down when she suddenly changed her form and now had a man's face and wore a fisherman's outfit.

"Seeing her, her owner said: 'I say, you there with the fishing pole, fixing bait on a hook you're about to cast into the water: May the sea be ever calm for you and the fish be ever trusting and not feel the hook until they're caught. A girl, shabbily dressed, her hair in disarray, just now stood on this shore (for I *saw* her standing on the shore!)—tell me where she went, for her tracks stop here.'

"And she, realizing that the gift from the god really worked, and enjoying it, that she was asked about herself, answered him thus: 'I'm sorry, whoever you are; I've been intent on my fishing and haven't looked up from the water at all. And if you don't believe me, as the god of the sea aids my arts, I swear there has been no one on the shore except me for quite a while—and certainly no woman.' The man did believe her, turned around, and trudged back through the sand, completely fooled, and she regained her original form.

"When the father realized that his daughter could change her form whenever she wanted to, he sold her to one master after another, and she escaped from them all, now as a mare, now as a bird, then as a cow, or as a stag, and thus furnished her starving father with ill-gotten food. But when his powerful affliction had eaten everything in sight and there was nothing left for his relentless disease to consume, he began to bite off mouthfuls of his own flesh, and the poor wretch ate himself to feed himself.

"But why take up time talking about others? For indeed, I, too, young man, have the power to change myself into a certain number of shapes, for one moment I appear as who I now am, and then I can turn into a snake, then as king of the herd I put all my strength into my horns—O my horns! While I could I did," he added, with a groan. "Now one of them is missing, as you can see."[32]

BOOK NINE

When the hero Theseus, son of Neptune, asked Achelous why he had groaned and how he lost his horn, the Calydonian river-god, his tangled locks held in place with a crown of reeds, replied: "You've asked me a question that's painful to answer, for who wants to recall a battle that he lost? Nevertheless, I shall tell you what happened, but let me say that it was more honorable to have fought than disgraceful to have been defeated, and I am greatly consoled when I recall how formidable my opponent was.

"Tell me, have you ever heard of a girl named Deianira?* She was very beautiful and once had many suitors vying for her, all hoping to win her. I was one of those suitors myself, and when I went with them to her father's house, I said to Oeneus, 'Son of Parthaon, choose me as your son-in-law.' Hercules said the same thing. The other suitors then yielded to the two of us. Hercules listed what he had to offer: Jove as a father-in-law, the renown he had acquired from his labors, and his triumph over his stepmother's commands.

"Countering that, I said, 'Oeneus, it's disgraceful for a god to yield to a mortal'—for Hercules was not yet a god. 'You see in me the lord of the waters that wind through your kingdom. With me you won't have a stranger come from foreign shores as a son-in-law, but a native of this land and part of your domain. Don't let royal Juno's lack of hatred for me hurt my chances, nor the lack of orders to perform labors as punishment—don't let that hurt me, either.'

"'As for your boast, son of Alcmena, that Jupiter sired you, it's either a lie and he's not your father, or if he is, then you're the product of an illicit union: It's only because of your mother's adultery that you can claim him as your father. So decide: Either you made it up that Jove's your father, or, if he really is, then you were born in shame.'

*9.8–9: "a girl named Deianira": Theseus and his companions should have heard of her, since she is the sister of Meleager of Calydon, whence they have just come, as Anderson notes ([1972] at 8.8–9, 418).

"While I was speaking, Hercules had been staring at me with a fierce look on his face, seething, barely able to control his rage, and finally he burst out: 'My fists are more powerful than my tongue. Go on, win the debate—as long as I win the fight'; and he came at me, threatening me.

"I was ashamed to back down after the insulting things I had said to him, so I threw off my green robe, put up my hands, holding them in front of my chest like a wrestler, and got ready to do battle with him. He scooped up dust and threw it at me, and I in turn gave him a taste of yellow sand. Coming at me now from every direction, he grabbed my neck, my legs, my private parts—or you would have thought he grabbed them. But his attacks all failed: My size protected me like a breakwater that waves crash down on with a mighty roar, while it stands steadfast because of its mass. We broke apart for a moment, then closed with each other again and stood our ground, both determined not to yield, foot jammed to foot, chest to chest, our fingers locked, head pressed to head.

"In just this way I have seen powerful bulls clash when they battle to win the most beautiful cow on the range for a mate. The herd looks on and trembles, not knowing which of the two victory and a great kingdom await. Three times Hercules tried to shove me away as I thrust my chest against his, but he could not budge me. On the fourth try he managed to loosen my arms, which held him in a tight grip, and to break my hold, and as I lurched forward he quickly spun me around (I'm bound to tell the truth) and jumped on my back, heavy as he was.

"Believe me—and I'm not trying to glorify myself by making this up—he felt like a mountain on my back, weighing me down. With an effort I managed to work my sweating arms inside his, which were around my chest, and with another effort broke his hold. But as I tried to catch my breath, he was at me in an instant, not letting me recover, and got an armlock around my neck. Then, finally, my knees touched the ground, and I got a mouthful of sand.

"No match for Hercules' strength, I used trickery and slipped from his grasp by changing myself into a snake, and when I coiled myself and hissed savagely, flicking my forked tongue at him, he only laughed and made fun of me, saying: 'I defeated serpents in my cradle, Achelous, and though you may outsnake other snakes, you realize, don't you, that you're but a single serpent, only a fraction of the hydra at Lerna? She flourished from her own wounds, and every time I chopped off one of her hundred heads, two more grew back and made her twice as strong. This self-sprouting monster, reproducing from my very efforts to kill it and growing from its loss, I overpowered, and once I had overpowered it, I ripped it open. And what do you think I'm going to do to you, now that you've turned yourself into a false snake, concealing yourself in a form that's not your own and using defenses you're not accustomed to?'

"Then he wrapped his fingers around the top of my neck like a chain. I was being choked, as though my throat were caught in a pair of tongs, and I was struggling to wrest my neck from his thumbs. Defeated here, too, I had one last form to use, that of a fierce bull, so I changed myself into a bull and renewed the fight, but coming at me from the left, Hercules threw his arms around my neck and, as I hurled myself forward, wrestled me down, landed on top of me, and pinned my horns to the ground, laying me out in the deep sand. Nor was he satisfied with that, for, gripping one of these mighty horns in his powerful hand, he broke it off, leaving a bloody hole in my forehead. Wood nymphs then filled the horn with fruit and sweet-smelling flowers and blessed it, and now it has enriched the goddess Bona Copia."*

Just as Achelous finished speaking, one of his serving girls, a nymph dressed like Diana, with her hair loose about her shoulders, entered bearing the horn, filled to overflowing with luscious fruit, the bounty of autumn, as their dessert.

At daybreak, as the first rays of the morning sun were striking the mountaintops, the young men departed, not waiting for the floodwaters to recede completely and the river to return to its placid course. Achelous then hid beneath his stream his homely face and his head with its scar where the horn had been. Though the loss of this ornament, now gone, grieved him, he was otherwise whole, and the injury to his head he was able to conceal by wearing a crown of willow or of reeds.

But you, Nessus, were destroyed by your fierce lust for the same girl† when Hercules shot you in the back with a winged arrow. For the hero was returning home with his new bride when he reached the raging waters of the Evenus, swollen by winter rains beyond its normal size and full of swirling eddies, and found it impossible to cross.

The son of Jove felt no worry for himself, but he was afraid for his wife. Then the powerful centaur Nessus, experienced at fording the river, approached him and said: "Let me put her on the opposite bank for you, grandson of Alcaeus. Use your strength to swim across!" So Hercules handed over to Nessus his wife, Deianira, pale and trembling, fearing him as much as she feared the water. Without more ado and just as he was, wearing his quiver and lion's skin (for he had thrown his club and bow across to the other side), Hercules plunged in, saying, "I've just defeated one river, and I might as well conquer another." Nor did he make for the place where the stream flowed gently, for he refused to let it carry him across by yielding to its currents.

As he reached the opposite bank and was collecting his bow, he heard his wife cry out, and he shouted to Nessus, who was on the point of violating his trust: "Foolish faith in the speed of your hooves has robbed you of sense, you violent scoundrel! It's you, Nessus, you double-bodied monstrosity, I'm talking

---

*9.88: Thus the creation of the Cornucopia or Horn of Plenty. The goddess Copia (an embodiment of the abstract idea of "abundance") was known and probably worshipped at Rome but was not one of the deities of the official state cults (Bömer at 9.1–88, 4.277).

†9.99–101: 9.99–100: "a crown of willow or of reeds": At 9.3 Ovid calls it simply a crown of reeds. 9.101: "lust for the same girl," that is, for Deianira.

to! Hands off my property! If respect for me hasn't stopped you, then the wheel might have inhibited this forbidden rape—your father's wheel.* You won't get away with this, trust in your strength as a horse though you may. I can hit you from right here without taking a step," and he made good his threat by shooting the centaur in the back with an arrow as he galloped away. The iron barb emerged from his chest, and when he yanked the arrow out, blood mixed with the poisoned gore of the hydra spurted from both wounds. Nessus collected this and smeared it on his tunic, saying to himself, "I shall not die unavenged!" and calling the bloodstained garment a love charm, he gave it to his victim.

During the long interval that followed, Hercules' great deeds filled the earth and satisfied his stepmother's hatred. Then, fresh from victory in Oechalia, the hero was performing sacred rites to Jove at Cenaeum, when scurrilous gossip—which likes to mix the false with the true and from the tiniest grain of fact swells through its own lies—this gossip, Deianira, reached your ears, that Hercules was gripped by a passion for the princess Iole.

Loving him, Deianira believed the talk of a new amour and was terrified by it, and at first gave herself to fits of weeping and tried to drown her grief in tears. But then she said to herself: "Why all this crying? It will only make my rival happy. Since she'll soon be here, I must hurry and come up with something now, while I can, before someone else occupies our bed. Shall I make a scene? Or keep silent? Return to Calydon? Or stay here? Shall I leave the house, or, if nothing else, at least make it hard for her? What if, Meleager, remembering that I'm your sister, I plan a crime, and by cutting her throat testify to how far a woman's outrage and sense of injury can go?"

Her mind raced in different directions. Of all the possibilities, she preferred to send Hercules the tunic stained with Nessus' poisoned blood, hoping it would revive his dying love for her. And so, not knowing what it was she gave, she herself put into the hands of Lichas, who was as ignorant as she was, a gift that would cause her great sorrow, poor woman, and begged him to take it to her husband.

Unaware, the hero accepted the gift, put the tunic on, and so pulled over his shoulders the poison of the hydra of Lerna. He had just built a fire and was sprinkling incense on it, saying a prayer and pouring wine from a saucer on the marble altar, when the poison's power, heated by the fire, was released and spread through his body.

With the courage that came naturally to him, Hercules held in his groans for as long as he could, but when his agony overwhelmed his ability to endure it, he shoved the altar away and filled the groves of Oeta with his screams. He tried to tear off the deadly garment, but when he tugged at it, his skin came away with it, and, horrible to tell, the tunic either stuck to his body as he

---

*9.123–124: "your father's wheel": Nessus' father, Ixion, tried to rape Juno and was punished by being tied to a wheel that spins eternally (Apollodorus, *Epitome* 1.20).

pulled it or exposed his torn muscles and huge bones. His blood hissed and bubbled with the burning poison like a white-hot knife blade dipped in cold water, and there was no limit to the pain. Hungry flames devoured his organs, black sweat ran down his body, and his burning sinews crackled. As the marrow of his bones melted from the hidden poison, he raised his hands to the stars and cried: "Feed on my destruction, Juno! Behold my torment from on high, cruel one, and feed on it! Let your savage heart have its fill! Or if I'm pitiable even to an enemy—to you, I mean—take this life, sick with torment, hateful to me, and born only for suffering. Death would be a gift, a gift fitting for a stepmother to give.

"Was it for this that I overcame Busiris, who fouled his temples with the blood of strangers? That I deprived savage Antaeus of his mother's nourishment? That I never feared the triple-bodied shepherd of Spain nor you, three-headed Cerberus?

"Was it for this, my hands, that you wrestled the powerful horns of the Cretan bull to the ground? That Elis, the Stymphalian waters, and the grove of Parthenius all offer proof of your achievements? Was it for this that your might brought back the sword belt engraved with gold from Thermodon and the apples guarded by the never-sleeping serpent?

"Was it for this that neither the centaurs nor the boar that ravaged Arcadia could withstand my attack? Was it for this that the hydra failed to thrive on loss—failed to get back twice her strength?

"And did I not, when I saw the Thracian horses grown fat on human blood, when I saw their stalls filled with mangled bodies—did I not overturn those stalls and slaughter the horses and their master, too? Does not the massive Nemean lion lie dead, strangled by these arms? Did I not bear up the sky on this neck?

"The savage wife of Jove grew weary of giving me orders; I never grew weary of carrying them out. But now I have a strange new affliction, which neither courage nor weapons can resist. A fire is devouring my lungs and eating its way through my body. Yet Eurystheus flourishes! Can anyone still believe the gods exist?"

Hercules staggered along the heights of Mount Oeta, ravaged with pain, like a bull that carries a spear planted deep in its body, and the hunter who wounded it has run away. You would have seen him groaning at one moment, shrieking in agony the next, and trying again and again to tear off the tunic, knocking trees to the ground, raging against the mountain, or stretching out his arms to his father's heaven.

He caught sight of Lichas, hiding in terror in the hollow of a rock, and with pain-driven fury cried: "It was you, Lichas, wasn't it, who gave me this deadly gift? And it will be you, won't it, who will be the cause of my death?" Lichas turned white and, trembling, tried to explain in a halting voice. Even as he was speaking and embracing the legs of Hercules, the grandson of Alcaeus seized

him, whirled him around three times, four times, and flung him faster than a
bullet from a sling toward the Euboean Sea. As Lichas flew through the air he
began to harden, and just as rain, they say, freezes in icy winds and turns to
snow, and the soft snow, swirling, is compressed and forms hard round hail-
stones, so Lichas, hurled through space by Hercules' powerful arms, all color
drained from his body, all moisture gone, now turned to stone—or so an earlier
generation said. Even now in the Euboean Sea there is a small rock rising out
of the water that shows traces of a human form and that sailors are afraid to
step onto, as though they think it can feel their tread, and they call it Lichas.

But, renowned son of Jove, when you had felled trees on Oeta's steep slope
and piled them in a heap to make your funeral pyre, you ordered Poeas' son*
to take your bow, your capacious quiver, and the arrows that would see the
Trojan kingdom once again, and to light the fire. As flames raced through the
wood and engulfed the pyre, you spread out your lion's skin upon it and lay
down, resting your head on your club and looking for all the world as though
you were reclining at a dinner among cups full of wine with a garland on
your head.

The fire, roaring fiercely now, had enveloped the pyre and was beginning to
lick at the limbs of Hercules, who lay composed, contemptuous of the flames.
The gods, however, were fearful for the earth's champion, and Jupiter, Saturn's
son, sensing their fear, addressed them, clearly gratified: "Gods and goddesses,
I am pleased to see that you are afraid for Hercules, and I am also pleased to
be called the father and guide of a remembering people and for my offspring
to be the beneficiary of your favor. For though your concern stems from his
great achievements, since I'm his father I am in your debt, nevertheless.

"But let not groundless fear trouble your loyal hearts. Ignore the flames on
Oeta! He who has conquered all else will also conquer the fire you see there,
and he will not feel the powerful heat of Vulcan, except in that part of him that
comes from his mother! What he has from me is immortal, exempt from and
immune to death, and it cannot be consumed by fire. That part, freed from the
world, I shall receive in heaven, and I am confident that my action will please
all the gods.

"If, nevertheless, it makes anyone here unhappy for Hercules to become a
god, if there's someone who doesn't want him to receive this honor, that someone will, I trust, come to realize that Hercules deserves it, and will have to
accept that he's going to get it, like it or not."

The gods agreed. The royal wife, too, seemed to take Jove's words calmly
enough, except for the last part, which made her frown, for she was irritated
at the implied threat, clearly aimed at her.

Meanwhile, whatever parts of Hercules could be destroyed by fire the fire
had burned away. There was no recognizable likeness of him in what remained,

---

*9.233: "Poeas' son" is Philoctetes.

nor anything that had come from his mother's form; he kept only the signs of his father, Jove.

Like a snake, when it sheds its skin: Along with the skin the years fall away and the snake is young again and revels in its new and glistening body—so Hercules, when he lost his mortal flesh, grew strong in the better part of himself, seemed grander, seemed to become an awesome, august, weighty figure. His all-powerful father swiftly carried him above the clouds in a chariot drawn by four horses and placed him among the shining stars, and Atlas felt the increased weight.[33]

Eurystheus, son of Sthenelus, had not yet exhausted his wrath, however, and he now directed his fierce hatred for Hercules against the hero's children. Alcmena of Argos, anxious and worried for so long, now had Iole to complain to and to talk to about her son's labors, to which the whole world bore witness—or about her own troubles. For Hyllus, at his father's command, had taken Iole to his heart—and to his bed—and had planted his noble seed in her. To her Alcmena thus began: "May the gods be kind to you at least and shorten your labor when you're ready to bear a child and call upon Ilithyia, protector of women fearful of childbirth, though she made it hard for me in order to please Juno. For when the day was at hand for me to give birth to Hercules, destined to toil (the sun stood in the tenth sign of the zodiac), my womb was swollen and heavy, and the baby I carried was so large that you could truly call Jove the father of the weight inside me. Soon I could no longer endure the pain—cold fear grips me now as I speak of it, and it hurts me even to remember.

"I was in agony for seven days and nights, I was exhausted, and I raised my arms to heaven and with a loud cry called upon Lucina and her companions, the goddesses of childbirth. She came, but Juno had bribed her beforehand, and Lucina was willing to hand my life over to Juno, who hated me.

"Lucina heard me groaning and sat down on the altar in front of my house. Crossing her right leg over her left and clasping her hands, with her fingers tightly interlaced, she stopped me from delivering. She also muttered spells under her breath, and they, too, held up the baby's birth, which had already begun. I was struggling and raving and shouting insults at Jove, that ingrate! but to no avail. I wanted to die, and my weeping and wailing would have melted the hardest stone. Theban mothers came and stood beside me, offering their prayers and encouraging me, as I lay in agony. One of my servants, a blond-haired lower class girl named Galanthis, was attending me and carrying out my orders quickly and energetically, and I loved her for all she did for me. She sensed that Juno's hostility had kept me from giving birth, and while going in and out the door she saw Lucina sitting on the altar with her arms around her knees and her fingers intertwined. Galanthis then said to her: 'Whoever you are, congratulate my mistress! Alcmena's labor is over. Her prayer has been answered, and she's had her baby!'

"The goddess with dominion over the womb leaped up in fear, loosening her hands, and I was at that moment freed from the bonds that held me. It is said that Galanthis laughed at having deceived Lucina, and as she was laughing Juno grabbed her savagely by the hair and began dragging her along the ground, holding her down as she tried to get up, and changed the girl's arms into forelegs. The old quickness, the old energy, remained, and the fur on her back kept the color of her hair, but her form was different from what it was before. Because she came to my rescue by telling a lie when I was giving birth, she gives birth through her mouth, and as before, she has the run of my house."*

Alcmena was moved as she remembered her former serving girl and uttered a groan. Then her daughter-in-law Iole said to her as she sat grieving: "The loss of her human form by someone not even related to us by blood moves you. But suppose I tell you about my sister's fate, so unbelievable, though my sorrow, my weeping, may interfere, and I won't be able to speak.

"My sister's mother had just the one daughter (my father had me by another woman), who was the most beautiful of all the girls in Oechalia and was named Dryope. Though she was raped by the god who dwells in Delphi and Delos and thus no longer a virgin, a certain Andraemon accepted her as his wife and was considered fortunate to have her.

"There is a pond whose shore, gently sloping, makes a kind of beach, crowned by myrtles at the top. Dryope had come here quite innocently and, to increase your outrage, in order to offer garlands to the nymphs there, and in her arms she was carrying her baby boy, a sweet burden, not yet a year old, whom she was feeding at her breast with her warm milk. Near the pond grew an aquatic lotus tree, blooming with purple blossoms, a sign that it was about to bear fruit.

"Dryope plucked some of the blossoms and gave them to her son to play with, and I was about to do the same thing—for I was there, too—when I saw blood dripping from the flowers and the branches trembling in horror. It was the nymph Lotis, who, the farmers now told us—too late—had changed herself into this tree when she fled the obscene advances of Priapus, but had kept her name. My sister had not known this, and when in terror she tried to back away from the tree, pay homage to the nymphs, and leave, her feet had taken root in the ground.

"She struggled to pull them out but could only move the upper part of her body, and now bark was slowly growing on her from below, creeping up her groin. Seeing this, she tried to pull out handfuls of her hair, but only filled her hands with leaves: Leaves now covered her entire head.

"Her son, Amphissos (his grandfather Eurytus had given him this name),

*9.323: "she gives birth through her mouth": Galanthis was changed into a weasel, which "[s]ome Greeks and Romans . . . believed . . . gives birth through its mouth" (Anderson [1972] at 9.322–323, 440).

felt his mother's breast harden and no milk coming despite his sucking. I could only watch your cruel fate happen to you, dear sister, I could not help you, but even so I threw my arms around the growing trunk and branches and tried as hard as I could to slow them down, and I confess I wanted that same bark to cover me.

"Suddenly her husband, Andraemon, appeared and our poor father, too, looking for Dryope, asking, Where was Dryope? I showed them the lotus tree and they kissed the trunk, still warm, and threw themselves upon the roots at the base of the tree, now their own, and clung to them. All of my dear sister was now a tree, except her face, and tears trickled down the leaves that had sprouted from the poor girl's body.

"As long as she was able to talk, as long as her voice could find a passage through her mouth, she poured out a stream of pathetic laments: 'If anyone puts faith in what the wretched have to say, I swear by the gods I do not deserve this unspeakable treatment. I am being punished for a crime I never committed. I have lived a blameless life. If what I say is untrue, let my leaves wither and fall, let me be cut down with an axe and burned! But take my baby from his mother's arms—her branches—and give him to someone else to nurse. Make sure she comes beneath my tree when she suckles him, and let him play beneath my tree. And when he learns to talk, see that he speaks to his mother, and let him sadly say, "My mother is hidden within this tree." Let him fear all ponds and never pluck blossoms from a tree, and let him believe that the body of a goddess lives in every one.

"'Farewell, dearest husband, and you, dear sister, and you, too, Father, farewell! If you love me, protect my leaves from the sharp blades of pruning hooks and from cattle browsing. And since I cannot bend down to you, rise up to me and come where I can kiss you while I can still be kissed, and lift up my little boy to me, too!

"'I cannot say more, for now the smooth bark creeps up my fair neck and I am vanishing into the branches at the top of the tree. Don't close my eyes. Hold off this last duty of yours and let the spreading bark cover my fading vision.' Her mouth ceased to exist at the moment she ceased to speak, and the new branches kept the warmth of her body long after she became a tree."

While Iole was telling this wondrous tale, and Alcmena was wiping tears from the girl's eyes with her thumb (and weeping herself), something very strange checked their sadness: Iolaus stood upon the high threshold, almost a boy, with the first signs of a beard upon his cheeks, his appearance restored to the years of his youth. Juno's daughter Hebe had given him this gift, moved by the prayers of her husband, Hercules. And when she was about to swear an oath that after Iolaus she would never again make such a gift to anyone, Themis would not allow it, "For Thebes is now caught up in a civil war," she said, "and Capaneus can only be defeated by Jove; their mortal wounds will make the brothers Polynices and Eteocles equal, and when the earth opens beneath the seer Amphiaraus, he will behold his own shade, though he's still alive, and his son Alcmaeon will kill a parent* to avenge a parent, blessed and damned by the same deed.

"Horrified by the evil he has done, driven from his wits and from his country, too, Alcmaeon will suffer torment from the Furies and his mother's ghost until his wife demands from him the fatal necklace of gold, and the sword of Phegeus is plunged into his side. Then at last will Callirhoe, daughter of Achelous, beg great Jove to add those years† to her infant boys lest the avenger's murder go unavenged. Moved by her prayer, Jupiter will ordain for her ahead of time the gifts of his stepdaughter Hebe, who is also his daughter-in-law, and though the sons of Callirhoe are children still in years, he will make them men."

When Themis, who knew what was to come, had finished her prophecy, the gods were in an uproar, clamoring to know why others could not have these same gifts. Aurora, Pallas' daughter, complained that her husband was ancient; bountiful Ceres, that her Iasion's hair was turning gray. Vulcan demanded that his son Erichthonius be allowed to live his life over again. Venus, too, was worried about the future and tried to arrange for Anchises' life to be renewed. All the gods, in fact, had someone to make a case for and shouted in support of their favorites. Tempers flaring, they were about to come to blows, when Jupiter opened his mouth to speak:

"Have you no respect for me? Where will this end? Do some of you think you are so powerful that you can even conquer fate? By *fate* Iolaus was able to live again the years he had lived before. By *fate* Callirhoe's infant sons could suddenly become young men—not by politicking or going to war. Fate also rules you, and (if it is any consolation to you) fate rules me as well. If I had the power to alter fate, the weight of years would not have bent my son Aeacus, and Rhadamanthus would forever possess the fresh flower of youth, and so would my son Minos, who is now despised because of the bitter burden of old age and no longer has the respect as ruler he once had."

Jove's words moved the gods, and no one could bear to complain when he saw Rhadamanthus, Aeacus, and Minos, all weary with age, Minos especially, for in his prime his name alone had struck terror in the hearts of great nations. But now he was old and feeble, and he greatly feared Miletus, son of Deione, who took pride in his youthful strength and in having Apollo as his father.

Although Minos believed Miletus was leading an insurrection against his rule, he lacked the courage to exile him from his home and country. But you fled of your own accord, Miletus, crossing the Aegean Sea in a swift ship, and in Asia you founded the city that bears your name. Here you made love to

---

*9.407–408: "will kill a parent," that is, his mother, Eriphyle.

†9.411–415: 9.411: "until his wife": that is, his second wife, Callirhoe, daughter of Achelous. 9.412: Phegeus is the father of Alcmaeon's first wife, Arsinoe. (For the complex myth of Alcmaeon, see Apollodorus 3.7.5–7.) 9.413–415: "to add those years": the years "removed," as it were, from Iolaus when Hebe made him young again. Callirhoe wants these years added to her sons' ages so they can avenge Alcmaeon (Anderson [1972] at 9.413–414, 446).

Cyanee, the beautiful daughter of the river Meander, who continually doubles back on himself, while she was walking along her father's curving bank, and in time she gave birth to twins named Byblis and Caunus.[34]

Now, Byblis is a warning to girls to fall in love in the way that's allowed, the normal way, for she was possessed by desire for her twin brother, Apollo's grandson. She loved him not as a brother, not in the way a sister ought to love a brother. Indeed, at first she did not recognize the fire inside herself, saw nothing wrong with kissing her brother so often and holding him close, her arms around his neck, and for a long time she deceived herself with what seemed to be sisterly devotion, but was not. Little by little her affection changed to desire, and she would dress up to go see her brother, wanting too much to seem beautiful to him, and if someone more beautiful was there, she was jealous of her. She was not yet aware of her true feelings, and they did not yet lead her to desire him consciously, though she smoldered inwardly.

But then she began to call him her hero, hated the word brother, wanted him to call her Byblis rather than sister. Even so, when she was awake, she dared not allow herself lustful fantasies.

When she was asleep, though, she often saw what she loved and wanted: She seemed even to join her body to her brother's, and she would blush, though sound asleep. Then she would wake up and lie quietly for a long while, trying to dream her dream again and, divided and confused in her mind, would cry out: "Oh woe is me! What does this dream in the middle of the night mean? I don't want it to be real! Why do I have these dreams? He's so handsome, even to hostile eyes, and so desirable, and if he weren't my brother I could make love to him, and he would be meant for me.

"It's too painful to be his sister. As long as I don't try to do anything like this when I'm awake, I can have these dreams as often as I want when I'm asleep! Nobody sees your dreams, and they give pleasure that's almost real.

"O Venus! O Cupid, your mother's wingéd son! What delights I have tasted! Such a feeling—so intense! How totally limp I was, lying there afterwards! How delicious to remember!—though the pleasure was too brief and the night went by too swiftly, as though it envied what I was doing.

"If only I could change my name and marry you! What a good daughter-in-law, Caunus, I could be to your father. What a good son-in-law, Caunus, you could be to mine! If only the gods would let us have everything in common except forebears. (I would only want you to be nobler than I am!) And so, my darling, you'll make some girl a mother. But to me, whose bad luck it is to have the same parents as you, you'll never be anything but a brother. What stops us is the one thing we shall always share.

"What do my dreams mean, then? What weight do they carry? Do dreams carry any weight? Gods forbid! But the gods have certainly made love to *their* sisters. Saturn took his sister Ops to be his bride; Ocean took Tethys; and the lord of Olympus took Juno.

"But the gods have their own laws. Why am I trying to make human ways correspond to the gods' ways, which are different? Either this forbidden passion will be driven from my heart, or, if I cannot drive it from my heart, let me die before I go astray, let me be laid out dead upon my bier—and let my brother kiss me as I lie there.

"Yet *this* is something two must want to do! Suppose I'm eager to do it. It will seem wicked to him.

"But the sons of Aeolus weren't afraid to sleep with their sisters! Where did this example come from? Why did I mention them? What is wrong with me? Leave me alone, obscene passion, let me love my brother only as a sister should!

"And yet, if he had fallen in love with me first, I could perhaps abandon myself to my passion for him.

"Shall I, then—since I wouldn't have rejected him had he made advances to me—shall I myself, then, make advances to him? Will you be able to speak? Will you be able to confess your love?

"Oh yes! I *will* be able to. Love will force me to! Or if shame will keep my lips shut tight, a secret letter will confess my hidden passion."

She liked this idea; it overcame her divided and confused mind. She rolled over on her side and propped herself on one elbow and said: "I'll confess my mad love. Let him decide!" And then, "My god! Where am I falling? What is this passion my heart conceives?"

Hands trembling, she began to compose some carefully chosen words, holding a stylus in her right hand, a blank tablet in her left.

She starts, then stops; she writes, then rejects what she has written; she puts words down, then she erases them, makes changes, then criticizes—then she likes what she's said, picks up the tablet, puts it down, picks it up again. She doesn't know what she wants to say; she's about to write something, but doesn't like it, her face a mixture of daring and shame.

She had written, "Your sister," but decided to erase it, and after smoothing out the wax, inscribed the following words: "What she herself will not have unless you give it—good health, I mean—a lover wishes for you. But she is ashamed, oh, how ashamed she is, to give her name, and if you ask what I want, I would like to be able to plead my case without giving my name, and not be acknowledged as Byblis until I am sure my prayers will be answered.

"Here are signs of a wounded heart you could have seen: my wan color, my haggard face, my eyes so often filled with tears, endless sighs with no apparent cause, and frequent embraces and kisses, which, if you happened to notice, could never be considered a sister's.

"I myself, though wounded to the heart's core, though a fiery passion rages inside me, did all I could (as the gods will testify) to keep my sanity. I struggled for a long time to escape Cupid's cruel shafts without success, and I endured far worse than you could imagine a girl could suffer. I am forced to admit that

I am defeated; I am forced, with this timid entreaty, to beg you for help. You alone have the power to save or destroy the one who loves you. Choose which you will do. She is not an enemy who pleads for this, but someone who, though as close to you as she can be, wants to be closer still, wants to be bound to you with a more intimate tie.

"Leave questions of morality to old men; let them investigate what's allowed, what's right and what's wrong; let them uphold the fine points of the law. Youth is the time for reckless passion, and I am just the right age for it. What limits there are we don't yet know. We believe everything is allowed, and we are guided by the example of the great gods. A father who is harsh cannot stop us, nor concern for reputation, nor fear. But if there is some reason to be afraid, we shall conceal our secret pleasure by calling it the love of brother and sister.

"I am free now to speak with you in private, and we now embrace and kiss each other openly. What is lacking? Pity me for confessing my love to you— and I would not confess it if the strength of my passion did not force me to— don't let it be inscribed on my tomb that you were the cause of my death."

She ran out of space as she was writing this (O how futile it was!) and put the last line in the margin. She immediately sealed her sinful letter and pressed the wax with her seal ring, moistened by her tears. (Her mouth had become quite dry.)* Blushing as she did so, she summoned one of her servants and in a honeyed voice said to the fearful man, "Loyal and trustworthy friend: Will you please take this to my"—she paused, then added—"brother." As she handed the tablet to him, it slipped from her hands and fell to the floor. Though disturbed by this omen, she sent the letter anyway.

The servant waited for the right moment and then approached Caunus and gave him the letter with its secret message. The youthful grandson of Meander received it, began to read it, and then, instantly enraged, hurled it from himself. Barely able to keep his hands from the throat of the trembling servant, he shouted: "Get out of my sight while you still can, you criminal instigator of forbidden lust! If your death would not bring exposure and shame to us, I would have killed you on the spot for this!"

The servant fled in terror and reported Caunus' outrage to his mistress. Hearing this, that you had been rejected, Byblis, you turned deathly pale and began to tremble with a glacial chill.

Nevertheless, when she recovered from the shock, her mad passion returned as well, and in a weak and barely audible voice she said: "It serves me right! Why was I so foolish as to give any sign of this pain? Why was I in such a hurry to write and send a letter and say things in it that should have been kept secret? I ought to have dropped some hints beforehand to find out how he felt about it. To make sure the wind was with me I should have tested it first by

---

*9.567: "Her mouth had become quite dry": "[I]t was customary to dampen the signet before applying it so that it would not stick" (Anderson [1972] at 9.566–567, 457).

letting out part of the sail and then put out to sea on a sea that was safe, instead of allowing winds I hadn't tested to fill the sails. I'm now blown back on the rocks! Capsized! Sunk in the depths of the ocean! And my sails can't bring me home.

"Wasn't there also a clear omen to keep me from yielding to my passion, when the tablet fell out of my hand as I was giving it to the servant and made my chances fall with it? Shouldn't I right then have decided on another day, or changed my whole plan? But better to have changed the day: A god himself was trying to warn me, was giving me signs, clear to see, had I not been so mad.

"Even so, I should at least have spoken myself instead of confiding my feelings in a letter; I ought to have revealed my passion to him in person. He would have seen my tears, would have seen the face of the one who loves him. I could have said more to him than I was able to write in my letter. I could have put my arms around his neck, unwilling though he may have been, and if he had rejected me, I could have made it seem I was about to die, could have embraced his feet, could have prostrated myself and begged for my life. I would have done everything in my power, and if any one thing by itself couldn't soften his hard heart, everything together might have.

"Maybe it's the fault of the servant I sent. I don't think he approached him in the right way, nor chose the right time, nor looked for the right moment, when my brother had nothing on his mind. That's what hurt me, for Caunus wasn't born from a tigress; he doesn't have a heart made of stone or solid iron or steel; he didn't suckle a lioness. He will be conquered! I must try again! And once I begin I won't give up as long as breath remains.

"If I could undo what I have done, the best thing would be never to have started this, but since I did, next best is to fight to the bitter end. And even if I renounce my passion, he will never be able to forget what I dared to do, and because I'll have retreated, I shall seem to have wanted him in a casual way, or even to have tested him, or sought to trap him. He will surely think it was lust and not a god that overpowered me and set my heart on fire and drove me on. I cannot avoid the fact that I did a wicked thing: I made advances to him in a letter. My passion stands revealed, and though I go no further, I cannot be called innocent. And so I may as well go after what I want; I have nothing left to lose."

So great is the conflict in a confused heart that Byblis, ashamed of herself for having tried, was eager to try again. And now she put off all restraint and exposed herself to rejection again and again. Since there seemed to be no end to it, Caunus finally fled his country, fled from incest, and built a new city in a foreign land. Then it was, they say, that Miletus' daughter, in despair, went totally insane; then it was she ripped open the front of the garment she was wearing and in her fury beat her arms and shoulders.

And now she was mad for all to see and openly declared her hope for the forbidden love. She abandoned her hated home and country and followed the trail of her fleeing brother. And, Bacchus, son of Semele, just as the Bacchants of Ismaros, excited by your wand, celebrate your rites anew every other year, so the mothers of Bubassus saw Byblis go howling across the broad fields. From there she wandered through the land of the Carians, the home of the militant Leleges, and through Lycia.

She had now put Mount Cragus behind her, the city Limyra, the river Xanthus, and the ridge that's the home of the Chimaera, which has the chest and head of a lion, the tail of a serpent, and fire in its belly. As you reached the end of the forest, Byblis, you fell, exhausted from pursuing Caunus, and there you lay, your hair spread out on the hard earth, pressing your face into the fallen leaves.

The Lelegeian nymphs repeatedly tried to lift her in their arms, repeatedly told her how she could be cured of her passion, and offered their sympathy, but she closed her mind to their consoling words. She lay silent, clawing at the green grass with her nails, soaking the grass with a river of tears.

Beneath these tears, they say, water nymphs created a spring that would never dry up. For what better gift could they give her? Just as resin drips from a slash in the bark of a tree; or just as sticky tar oozes from the bulging ground; or ice, frozen solid, melts in the sun when the west wind gently blows, so Byblis, Apollo's grandchild, consumed by her own tears, turned into this spring, and even now in that valley it keeps the name of its mistress and flows from the base of a black oak tree.[35]

The story of this strange new wonder would have filled a hundred Cretan cities, perhaps, if Crete itself had not recently produced a marvel of its own when Iphis was transformed. For in the Cretan countryside, near Knossos, there once lived a man named Ligdus, not from a prominent family, but a free commoner. His fortune was on a par with his class, but he was an honest man and led a blameless life. When his wife, Telethusa, was pregnant and about to give birth, he gave her these instructions: "I'm hoping and praying for two things, that your labor will be free of pain, as much as it can be, and that you give birth to a boy. The other sex is so much more trouble, and fortune denies me the means to rear a girl. But if, gods forbid, you happen to have a baby girl, then—against my will I must insist on this; forgive me, family Piety—let her be killed."

His face was bathed in tears as he laid down the law, and so was hers, to whom he laid the law down. Even so, Telethusa again and again begged her husband not to stifle her hopes. But it was no use; Ligdus had made up his mind.

She had reached the point where she could hardly endure the weight of her baby, soon due, when she saw Io in a dream in the middle of the night, or thought she saw her, standing beside her bed with a sacred band of attendants. On her brow were horns like crescent moons, and on her head she wore a shining garland of golden ears of grain and a royal diadem. Barking Anubis;

holy Bubastis; many-colored Apis; Horus, who shushes voices, motioning for silence with his finger at his lips; and Osiris, ceaselessly sought, were gathered around her, and she also had with her the rattles used in her rituals and a foreign serpent with sleep-inducing venom in its fangs.

Seeing everything clearly, as though she had just awakened, she heard the goddess say: "Telethusa, one of my own, cease to be so anxious and ignore your husband's commands. When Lucina delivers you, do not hesitate to accept the child, whatever its sex. I am a helping goddess, and I bring aid when asked. You will never complain of worshipping an ungrateful deity." Thus the goddess instructed her, and vanished from her bedroom.

Cretan Telethusa rose joyfully from her bed and, raising to the stars hands free from stain, prayed for her dream to come true. Soon her labor pains increased, and the baby entered the world. It was a girl—but the father did not know.

The mother ordered her baby to be taken up and reared and gave out that it was a boy. This was accepted as the truth, and no one was aware of the fiction except the nurse. The father fulfilled the pledge he had made to the gods and named the child Iphis, after his grandfather. The mother was delighted with the name, for it was common to both sexes and she wouldn't deceive anyone with it. And so the lie told as an honest deception went undetected. The child was dressed like a boy; and its face, whether you gave it to a boy or a girl, would have been attractive in either sex.

You had just turned thirteen, Iphis, when your father arranged for you to marry golden-haired Ianthe, the daughter of Telestes of Crete and considered the most beautiful of all the girls in Phaestus. The two were equal in age, equally lovely, and had learned their ABCs, the first skills children acquire, from the same teachers. And so love touched the innocent hearts of both girls, giving each the same feelings, though their expectations were not the same. Ianthe looked forward to her wedding day and to marriage with the man she believed would be *her* man. Iphis, though, loved a girl she could never hope to possess, and this itself fanned the flames of her desire, a girl who burned with love for another girl.

Fighting back tears she said: "What will become of me? I'm in the grip of a passion that no one has ever felt before, a strange, a monstrous passion. If the gods wanted to spare me, they should have spared me. But if not, if they wanted to destroy me, they should at least have given me a natural affliction, one that was normal.

"Cows don't fall in love with cows, nor mares with mares. A ram wants a ewe; a doe belongs to her stag. Birds mate the same way, and in the entire animal kingdom no female has ever been seized by desire for another female. Oh how I wish I weren't a girl!*

"In order for Crete to surpass all other places in producing monstrosities,

*9.735: Also, "I wish I didn't exist!" The Latin, *vellem nulla forem,* can be taken both ways.

Pasiphaë, daughter of the sun, made love to a bull. But it was still a female loving a male. To be honest, my passion is more insane than hers. Yet she was driven on by the hope of making love; and with a stratagem, a hollow wooden heifer, she offered herself to the bull, and the lover she tricked was male.

"Even if skilled artificers from all over the world should gather here, even if Daedalus himself flew back here on his wings of wax, what could he possibly do? Could he turn me into a boy with his learned skills? No! Could he change you, Ianthe? No! So, harden yourself, Iphis; pull yourself together and shake off this senseless, stupid passion. Accept what you were born as—unless you're deceiving yourself, too. Do the right thing and love what you as a female ought to love! It is hope that creates love, hope that feeds it. But what you are deprives you of hope. True, there is no guard set over the one you love that keeps you from embracing her; there's no anxious husband, no stern father. She won't deny herself to you if you approach her. But even so, she is not to be yours, nor can you be happy, no matter what is done for you, not even if gods and men should work on your behalf. Even now none of my prayers have gone unanswered, and the gods have readily given me everything they could. My father wants what I want; she herself and my would-be-father-in-law, they want it, too. But nature does not want it. More powerful than all those put together, nature alone is against me.

"And now the wished-for time approaches, the wedding torches are here, and Ianthe will soon be mine—but I won't have her. With water all around me, I'll be dying of thirst. Why are you here, Juno? And you, Hymenaeus, why have you come to this ceremony, when there's no bridegroom, and we're both brides?"

With this she fell silent. The fires of passion raged in the other girl as violently as ever, however, and she prayed, Hymenaeus, for you to come quickly.

But what Ianthe was so eagerly looking forward to, Telethusa dreaded, and she postponed the wedding at one point, later feigned illness to delay it, often cited omens and dreams as reasons for waiting. But the time came when she had told every lie she could think of, and the wedding, put off for so long, was at hand, only one day away.

Telethusa tore off her daughter's headband and her own and with her hair down embraced the altar and cried: "Isis, you who dwell in Paraetonium, in the fields around Lake Mareotis, in Pharos, and at the Nile with its seven mouths: Help me, I beg you, and free me from my fear! You, goddess, and your attributes I once saw, and I recognized them all, the sounds and the bronze rattles, and I engraved your commands in my memory. This child lives, and I have escaped punishment, thanks to the advice you gave me. Pity the two of us and grant us your help!" And she burst into tears.

It seemed to her that the goddess made the altar move. Yes! She had made it move! Then the temple doors shook, the moon-shaped horns gleamed, and the rattles sounded loudly.

Not entirely certain, but happy nonetheless because of the favorable omen,

Telethusa left the temple, and as Iphis walked along beside her, the girl took longer strides than she usually did, her face was not as fair, she seemed stronger, her features were sharper, her hair was shorter and uncombed, and she had more vigor than a female usually does: For though you were a girl a moment ago, you're a boy now! Carry gifts to the temple! Don't be timid, but believe and rejoice!

And they did carry gifts to the temple and added an inscription, composed of these brief lines:

> *The vow that Iphis as a girl once made,*
> *This vow Iphis, now a boy, has paid.*

When the rays of the morning sun brought light to the wide world the next day, Venus and Juno and Hymenaeus joined the procession of wedding torches, and the boy Iphis possessed his Ianthe.[36]

BOOK TEN

Hymenaeus then put on his saffron cloak and flew through the immense sky, making his way from Crete to the land of the Cicones, called by the voice of Orpheus, though it was a futile summons. The god did indeed arrive, but he brought neither solemn words nor happy faces nor lucky signs. The wedding torch that he held, moreover, kept hissing and smoking and making eyes water, and it would not ignite, even when he waved it in the air.

What happened next was worse than this omen, for while the new bride was walking through the grass in the company of her fellow naiads, she was bitten on the ankle by a serpent and fell dead.

After the Thracian bard* had mourned her death long enough in the world of the living, in order to work on the shades in the world below he dared to go down to the realm of the Styx (through the Taenarian gate) and made his way through the ghostly crowds, the images of those who lie in the grave, and stood before Proserpina and the lord of the dead, the ruler of this joyless kingdom.

Accompanying himself on the lyre he said: "O gods of the world beneath the earth, where all of us born mortal come: If I may lay aside the poet's stock of flowery, false phrases and speak the simple truth (and if you will allow me to): I did not come down to the twilight of Tartarus to see what I could see, nor did I come to chain Medusa's three-headed monster, covered with snakes. The reason I am here is—my wife; she stepped on a viper, and he shot his poison into her and snatched away her life when she was young and blossoming still.

"I wanted to be able to bear it; I won't deny that I've tried to: Love defeated me. This god is well known in the land above. Whether he's as well known here, I cannot say, but I would guess that he is, and if the story of that long-ago abduction is not false, Love joined the two of you as well.†

---

*10.8–12: 10.8–9: the "new bride," that is, Eurydice. 10.11–12: the "Thracian bard," that is, Orpheus.

†10.21–28: 10.21–22: "Medusa's monster" is the three-headed dog, Cerberus, watchdog of the underworld; he is called "Medusa's monster" because "a glance at him turned one into stone"

165

"I beg you by this place so full of fear, by this great void and the silence of your vast domain, undo the death of Eurydice, for it came too soon, and spin her fate again. You own us, entirely, and though we may delay a little, sooner or later as we hurry on we come to this one place. We are all heading here, this is our final home, and your reign over the human race is the longest reign of all. When the years that are hers have come and gone and she is old enough to die, she, too, will belong to you by law. I'm only asking you to lend her to me for a little while. And if the fates deny this favor to my wife, I know I do not want to go back up above. Rejoice in the death of us both."

The souls of the dead were weeping as he spoke and plucked the strings of his lyre: Tantalus ceased trying to get a drink of the water that always dropped away from him, and Ixion's whirling wheel was stunned, and stopped. The vultures looked up from the liver they were eating,* the Danaids left their jars untended, and you, Sisyphus, sat down upon your now still stone.

They even say that for the first time ever tears ran down the cheeks of the Furies, overcome by the song. Neither Pluto's royal wife nor the king of the dead himself could bear to say no to Orpheus and deny his prayer, and they called Eurydice. Among the recent dead, she came, walking slowly, limping from her wound.

And now she was with him again, but on this condition, that the Thracian hero not turn and look at her until they had emerged from the valley of Avernus, or else the gift would be taken back.

The couple picked their way through deathly silent places along a steep upward path, enveloped in thick fog and hard to see, and they had just reached the edge of the upper world when Orpheus, fearing Eurydice would fail and eager to see her, turned, loving her, to look, and at once she fell away, and then, struggling to grasp her hands grasping at his, alas, he seized only empty air.

Dying now a second time, Eurydice blamed her husband not at all (for what could she blame him for, except for loving her?) and saying a last "Farewell," which Orpheus could barely hear, was whirled back down to the same place again.

Orpheus was stunned by the second death of his wife, just like the man who saw the three-headed dog (with a chain around its middle neck) and was terrified and whose terror did not leave him until his life did, when his body froze into stone; and just like Olenos, too, who took his wife, Lethaea's, crime upon himself and wished to be considered guilty of it; and like you, unhappy Lethaea, too sure of your own beauty: two hearts once joined completely, and now two stones on Ida's rainy summit.

Though Orpheus prayed to cross the river Styx again, it was no use: Charon

---

(Anderson [1972] at 10.19–22, 477). 10.28: "the story of that long-ago abduction": Pluto's rape of Proserpina is told by the Muse Calliope, Orpheus' mother, at 5.341ff.

*10.43: The "liver they [the vultures] were eating" belonged to Tityos (Anderson [1972] 10.40–44, 478).

the ferryman blocked his way. Nevertheless, for seven days the singer sat on the riverbank, unwashed, unkempt, not eating, his only food his love and grief, washed down with his tears. Then, complaining bitterly against the cruel gods of the underworld, he withdrew to towering Rhodope and to Haemus, battered by the north wind.

Three times the sun had brought the year to a close in Pisces.* And now because it had ended sadly for him, or because he had vowed to be faithful, Orpheus fled the love of females. Yet many women longed for unions with the bard, and many grieved when he rejected them. He even taught the men of Thrace to turn their desire to tender males and so to pluck the first blossoms boys offer in that brief springtime before they become young men.[37]

At the top of a hill there was a broad and open field, grassy and green. The field was lacking shade, but the seer, born of a god, sat down there and plucked the sweet strings of his lyre, and shade came: the Chaonian oak tree; a grove of poplars, the Heliades; the Italian oak, with leaves all the way to the top; the gentle linden tree; the beech; the still unmarried laurel; the delicate hazel; the ash, source of excellent spears; the smooth fir; and the ilex, laden with acorns: all these came.

The genial plane tree and the many-colored maple came; and with them willows from riverbanks and lotus trees from lakesides; the boxwood, ever green, and slender tamarisk trees came; both the two-colored myrtle and the viburnum with its dark blue berries came; and, ivy, you came too, with your spreading shoots, and grapevines and vine-covered elms came with you.

Mountain ash and pitch pines came; and with them came the strawberry tree, heavy with sweet red fruit; the supple palm tree, whose branch is the victor's prize; and the umbrella pine, with its swept-up look and bristling needles at the top, the tree cherished by Cybele, mother of the gods, ever since her beloved Attis changed his human form and hardened into wood and became this tree.

Amid this forest of trees stood the cypress, straight and tall as the turning post on a racecourse. It was now a tree, but once it was a boy loved by the god whose fingers pluck the strings of the lyre and the bow. For at one time in the fields around Carthaea† there lived a great stag, sacred to the nymphs there, whose lofty, wide-branching antlers, gleaming with gold, provided shade for its head. A necklace strung with precious jewels hung from its smooth and shining neck and rested on its shoulders. A silver amulet on a leather thong lay on its forehead, and beads of shining bronze were pendent from each ear about its temples.

Lacking natural fear, the skittishness deer have, this stag often approached human dwellings and offered its neck to be stroked. But you, Cyparissus, most

---

*10.78: Pisces (the Fish), the twelfth sign of the zodiac, mark the end of the year (Anderson [1972] at 10.78–82, 481).

†10.109: Carthaea was a city on the island of Ceos (Haupt-Ehwald at 10.109, 2.135).

handsome boy of the Cean race, you loved the stag more than anyone else. It was you who would lead it to fresh pastures and clear springs, you who twined flowers through its antlers, and you who mounted its back like a knight and rode it joyfully all around, guiding it with purple reins.

It was noon on a summer day, and the curved claws of the Crab, who once lived by the sea, were burning in the heat of the sun. Weary, the stag lay down in the grass beneath a tree to cool off in the shade. Without looking first, the boy Cyparissus pierced it with his spear, and when he saw what he had done, saw the stag dying from his cruel wound, he resolved to die himself. Apollo tried to comfort him in every way he knew, urged him not to give way to his sorrow, urged him to grieve in proportion to the object of his grief. But the boy continued to weep, nevertheless, and asked the gods as a supreme favor to let him mourn forever.

And now, after endless tears, his blood was nearly gone,* and his arms and legs began to turn green. His hair, lying across his smooth white forehead, grew shaggy and stiff and shaped itself into a slender point that gazed at the starry sky. Groaning, the god said, sadly, "I shall always mourn for you—and in the future you will mourn for others and share the grief of those who grieve."³⁸

Such was the forest of trees the seer had drawn to himself, and there he sat, amid a gathering of beasts and a flock of birds. First he plucked the strings of the lyre with his thumb and listened to be sure it was properly tuned and its chords were in harmony, then he began: "Inspire me now, Muse, mother of mine,† and let me begin my song with Jove, for his kingdom is over all, and his power I have often sung before. Once in a more solemn key I sang of Giants and Jove's lightning bolts raining down in victory on the Phlegraean plain. Now I need a lighter melody, so let us sing of boys loved by gods and girls gone mad with forbidden desire and rightly punished for their lust.

"The king of the gods once burned with love for Phrygian Ganymede and cast about for a form to take that he preferred to his own. The only bird it wasn't beneath his dignity to become was the one that could carry his lightning bolts.‡ And instantly, beating the air with a pair of wings he'd put on, he carried off the Trojan boy, who still today mixes nectar for Jove and serves it to him, under the hostile eye of Juno.

"Apollo would have placed you in heaven, too, Hyacinthus, son of Amyclas, if the grim fates had relented and granted you your entire life span. You are immortal, even so, in the way you are allowed to be, and as often as spring drives winter away and Aries takes the place of rainy Pisces, you rise out of the ground and blossom upon the green earth. My father, Apollo, loved you above all others, and Delphi, the center of the world, was without its guardian god

---

*10.136: "his blood was nearly gone": "The . . . physiological notion that prolonged and violent weeping leads to loss of blood is probably an invention of Ovid's, by means of which he seeks to explain the transition to the gray-green color of the cypress" (Bömer at 10.136, 5.59).

†10.148: "Muse, mother of mine," that is, Calliope.

‡10.157f.: "The only bird," that is, the eagle.

while he visited Eurotas and unwalled Sparta, neglecting both his lyre and his bow. For he forgot who he was and happily carried your nets or held your dogs on a leash or followed you across steep mountain ridges, and fed his passion by going with you everywhere.

"Once, when the sun was half the distance from the night before and the night coming on and stood midway between the two, the boy and the god stripped off their clothes and, their bodies oiled and shining, competed with the discus. Apollo, whirling around, hurled it first and, showing off his strength and skill, flung the discus high into the air, where it scattered the clouds in all directions, and then, after a long interval, finally fell heavily back down to earth. The Spartan boy, carried away by the fun of the game, ran at once to pick it up, not thinking—and it bounced up from the hard ground, Hyacinthus, and struck you full in the face.

"The god, himself as pale as the wounded boy, gathered the limp form in his arms and tried to revive you, Hyacinthus, then tried to stop the horrible bleeding, then applied herbs, trying to hold on to your life, ebbing away. But his medical skills were useless. The wound was beyond healing.

"When someone snaps the stem of a violet or a slender poppy in a garden, or a lily bristling with its yellow stamens, these flowers instantly wither, their shriveled heads droop, and, unable to straighten up, they gaze at the ground: So the dying boy's head, too heavy for his strengthless neck, lolled upon his shoulders. 'I feel you slipping away from me, my Spartan, cheated of your youth!' Apollo cried. 'I see your wound, my doing; you are my grief, but also my crime. My right hand will be branded forever with your death. I'm the reason your life is ending.

"'But how am I to blame? Unless it's the fun we've had together that's to blame, unless it's love that is to blame. If only I could give up my life and die with you! But since I am bound by a law of fate, you will always be in my heart, your name will always be upon my lips, and it's you my lyre, it's you my songs will sing. As a new flower you will have markings on your petals that describe my sadness, and a time will come when the bravest hero of all will use these same markings on this flower as the letters of his name.'

"While Apollo uttered these words, true-spoken—look! Hyacinthus' blood had dripped on the ground and streaked the grass and was ceasing to be blood, and from it a flower was springing up, brighter than Tyrian dye and resembling a lily, if it hadn't been purple, and if lilies weren't silvery white. But this wasn't enough for Apollo (for he devised this honor). He himself inscribed his lamentations on the petals, tracing the letters 'AI AI,' on them, spelling out his grief.

"Sparta is proud to be the birthplace of Hyacinthus, and to this day his fame endures there. Each year, they celebrate the festival of the Hyacinthia in the time-honored way with a solemn procession.

"But should you ask Amathus rich in ores whether it wanted to give birth to the Propoetides, it would say no, nor to the people whose brows once sprouted twin horns, from which they take the name Cerastae. Now, in front of their gates stood an altar to Jupiter, God of Visitors, stained with blood, and if some stranger who was ignorant of their crime had seen this altar, he would have believed that nursling calves and lambs from Amathus had been slaughtered on it. But no! A human visitor was killed there.

"Outraged by this unspeakable sacrifice, nurturing Venus herself was about to abandon her own cities on Cyprus as well as the countryside around them. 'But,' she asked herself, 'what wrong have these dear places done? What sins are my cities guilty of? What crime have they committed? Better to let the impious race that did this be punished with exile, or death, or something between exile and death. And what can that be, except the punishment of a changed form?'

"While she was deciding what to turn them into, she noticed their horns, and it occurred to her that she could leave the Cerastae with these, and so she changed their hulking bodies into raging bulls.

"The whorish Propoetides, nevertheless, had the nerve to deny that Venus was a goddess. For this, they say that she, in a fury, made them the first to offer their beauty—their bodies—for sale.* As their modesty retreated and their faces hardened, it took but a slight change for them to turn to stone.

"Because he had seen the Propoetides living such depraved lives and was shocked by all the vices the female mind was naturally given to, Pygmalion lived as a wifeless bachelor, sleeping night after night alone, with no one to share his bed. Meanwhile, delighting in his wondrous art, he carved a statue from snow-white ivory and gave it beauty no woman could ever be born with—and conceived a passion for his own creation.

"She looked like a real girl, and you could believe she was alive and would like to move, if it weren't for her modesty, so artfully was the art concealed. Pygmalion gazed at his work spellbound, as liquid fire for the body of the girl that seemed so real poured into his heart. He often felt the statue with his hands, to see if it was flesh, or ivory still, and then no longer admitted it was ivory.

"He kissed his statue and was sure it kissed him back; he spoke to it and held it in his arms. When he touched its limbs, he really believed his fingers sank into them and worried lest he bruise them. One moment he whispered tender words of love in her ear; the next he brought her gifts girls always like— seashells, smooth stones, small birds, flowers with a thousand colors, lilies, gaily decorated balls, and tears of the Heliades that had fallen from a poplar tree.†

"He also dressed his statue, put rings with precious stones on her fingers, a long strand of beads around her neck, pearl earrings in her ears, and a pendant

---

*At 10.240 I read *forma* with Anderson (1982a), Bömer, and Haupt-Ehwald, instead of *fama* with Miller-Goold. Bömer glosses the Latin *corpora cum forma* at 10.240 with *corpora formosa* (at 10.240, 5.92).

†10.263: "[T]ears of the Heliades" are amber. See 2.364–366.

on her chest. She was so beautiful then!—and no less beautiful when she was naked. He laid her down on sheets dyed with Sidonian purple, called her his wife, and put down pillows under her head, as though she could feel them.

"And now it was the day of the most popular festival of Venus on all of Cyprus. Heifers, their curved horns wrapped in gold leaf, fell from the axe blows that struck their snowy necks, and the odor of smoking incense filled the air.

"After he made his sacrifice, Pygmalion stood at the altar and prayed in a timid voice: 'O gods, if you can really give all things, let my wife be'—he didn't dare say, 'let my wife be the ivory girl,' but, rather, 'let my wife be *like* the ivory girl.' Golden Venus, present herself at the festival, understood what his prayer meant, and as a friendly sign from the goddess, the fire on the altar flared up, and a tongue of flame leaped into the air three times.

"When he returned home, Pygmalion took the statue of his girl and lay down on his bed with it and began to kiss it. She seemed to grow warm: he kissed her some more and felt her breasts with his hands. As he touched them, the ivory softened; its hardness no longer resisted but yielded to his fingers the way beeswax from Hymettus turns soft in the sun and is worked by the hand and formed into many shapes, made usable from use itself.

"Amazed, unsure whether to rejoice, afraid of being tricked, Pygmalion like a lover touched and felt and caressed this answer to his prayers. She was real, and alive! He could feel the veins throbbing beneath his thumb! Then indeed the Paphian hero thanked Venus again and again and pressed his lips to lips that were real at last. The girl felt the kisses and blushed, and when she shyly raised her eyes, the first thing she saw was her lover.

"The goddess attended the wedding she had made possible, and when the horns of the crescent moon had come together nine times to make the round and gleaming sphere, the girl gave birth to a daughter, Paphos, from whom the island takes its name.[39]

"Now, Paphos bore Cinyras, who could have been counted among life's lucky ones, if only he had been childless. It's a dreadful story I'm about to tell. It's not for you, daughters; and it's not for you, either, fathers—or, if you cannot resist my song, don't put any faith in this part of it, don't believe it happened; or if you *do* believe it, then believe the punishment that followed. But if nature *does* allow a horror like this to happen, I congratulate this land for being far from the region that spawned such an unspeakable thing.* Let the land of Panchaia be rich in cardamom, let it have its cinnamon and costum, its incense oozing from incense trees, let it have all its other flowering spices, as long as it keeps its myrrh: The price for having this strange new tree was much too high.

"Cupid himself denies that *his* shafts harmed you, Myrrha, and he also ac-

---

*I have omitted 10.305 from the text of the translation, considered an interpolation by Miller-Goold and printed in brackets in their text. It reads: *gentibus Ismariis et nostro gratulor orbi,* "'I congratulate the Thracian people and our part of the world.'" See Bömer's discussion of the line at 10.304–305, 5.118–119.

quits his torches from complicity in the crime you're charged with. It must have been one of the three sisters with her Stygian torch and venom-bloated snakes who breathed her breath on you. It's a sin to hate one's father, but love like this is a greater sin than hatred.

"Princes chosen from all over the world desired you; young men from the entire Orient came to compete to share your bed. Choose one man from all these to be your husband, Myrrha, provided that one man is not among all these.

"Myrrha did indeed recognize her vile passion, and fought against it, saying to herself: 'Where is my mind leading me? What am I about to do? Dear gods, and family ties, and sacred rights of fathers, prevent this wicked act, I beg you, oppose the sin I'm contemplating—if indeed it is a sin. But it's not true that family ties condemn this kind of love. Other living creatures come together freely, as they choose. No one thinks it shameful for a heifer to be mounted by her father; a stallion takes his daughter for his partner; a he-goat enters the females of the herd that he has sired; a bird conceives from the seed of the bird it was itself conceived by. Happy are those creatures that are free to do this! Human scruples have made mean laws, and these hateful laws forbid what nature allows.

"'Even so, in other countries, they say, mothers mate with sons and fathers with their daughters, and family ties are strengthened by this doubled love. Bad luck for me, since I wasn't born in one of them—it was my misfortune to be born here! But why go over this again and again? Forbidden hopes, depart! He deserves to be loved, but only as a father. And so, if I were not the daughter *of* great Cinyras, Cinyras I could sleep *with*. Now, though, because he's already mine, he isn't mine, and our close tie dooms me. I would have a better chance if I were a total stranger.

"'I would be willing to go far away, to abandon my fatherland, if I could avoid this crime. But an evil passion keeps me from leaving, keeps me here so I can see Cinyras and touch him and talk to him and kiss him—if more is not allowed.

"'But do you really expect anything more, you guilty girl? Don't you realize how many laws you're confounding, how many names you're confusing? Will you become your mother's rival and your father's mistress? Will you be called the sister of your son and the mother of your brother? Aren't you afraid of the Furies with their black and snaky locks, whom guilty hearts see aiming savage torches at their eyes and mouths? Since you haven't let this unspeakable union happen in fact, don't imagine it in your mind. Don't foul great nature's compact with this forbidden sex! You think you want to? The act itself forbids it! He's a moral man, and he knows what's right—but O how I wish that he was on fire with a passion like mine!'

"So Myrrha to herself. Cinyras, meanwhile, was faced with a host of worthy suitors. Not knowing what to do, he recited their names to his daughter and asked her which one she wanted for her husband. Myrrha was silent at first, and then, her eyes lingering on her father's face, her chest began to heave and her eyes filled with tears.

"Thinking this was only a sign of a young girl's fear, Cinyras told her not to cry, dried the tears on her cheeks, and kissed her, a kiss Myrrha enjoyed too much, and when her father asked her what kind of man she wanted to marry, 'Someone just like you,' she said. He approved of her answer, though he didn't understand it, saying, 'I hope you will always be such a loving daughter!' At the words 'loving daughter,' Myrrha dropped her eyes, thinking about her wicked desire.

"It was midnight: People everywhere were sound asleep, minds freed from care. The daughter of Cinyras lies awake, unconquerable lust gnawing at her, obsessed with her insane passion. One moment she's in despair, the next she wants to offer herself to her father; then she's filled with shame; then she wants him; then she can't think what to do.

"When a mighty tree is being felled, you cannot tell before the final blow of the axe which way it will come down; it could fall in any direction. So Myrrha's mind, weakened by repeated blows, swayed back and forth, aiming now this way, now that way. She can find no end to her desire, no respite from it but death—and she longs for death.

"She sat up in bed and decided to put a noose around her neck and end it all. She tied her sash to the top of the door-frame and whispered: 'Farewell, dear Cinyras! Understand the reason for my death!' and slipped the sash over her head and around her pale and slender neck.

"They say that her last words, barely audible, reached the sharp ears of the faithful nurse guarding her door. The old woman sprang up and opened the door and, seeing Myrrha getting ready to die, began to scream and beat her breast and tear her clothes, all at the same time. She yanked the sash from around Myrrha's neck and tore it to pieces. Then, finally, she was free to weep, to take the girl in her arms and ask her why she wanted to hang herself.

"Myrrha was silent, saying nothing. She stared at the floor, not moving, bitterly regretting that she had been caught, that she had been too slow in trying to kill herself. The old woman implored her to say something and, baring her white head and her withered breasts, begged her by her very cradle, by the first milk she had given her, to tell her what had made her so unhappy.

"The girl turned away, moaning. The nurse, however, was bent on finding out and promised not only to keep secret what Myrrha told her, but also said: 'Tell me what it is and let me help you. I'm not yet that far gone in old age. If it's madness, I know a woman who can cure it with charms and herbs.* Or if someone has put an evil spell on you, I know a magic rite that will purify you.

---

*10.397: "I know a woman" etc.: I follow Lafaye, who translates the line *habeo, quae carmine sanet et herbis,* "je sais une femme qui a des incantations et des plantes pour te guérir"; also, cf. Bömer, who comments: "*quae,* 'a woman, who': Magic is women's business" (at 10.397, 5.141).

Or if it's a god's anger, it can be appeased with sacrifices. What else can it be? At least all is safe and well with you, with your family. Both your mother and father are still alive . . . ' At the word 'father' Myrrha heaved a deep sigh, but the nurse still suspected nothing unspeakable—though she sensed even so that whatever it was, it had something to do with love. Determined to discover what was the matter, she begged Myrrha to tell her, pulled her weeping onto her bony lap, and put her weak old arms around her and said: 'I think you're in love! But don't worry, I'm ready and willing to help you, and your father will never find out.'

"Beside herself, Myrrha jumped from the nurse's lap, buried her face in her bed, and cried: 'Go away! Please! Spare me what shred of miserable innocence I have left!' As the nurse kept on insisting, Myrrha kept on repeating: 'Go away! Or stop asking me why I'm so upset. What you're trying to find out is wicked, wicked.'

"The old woman shuddered, reached out her hands, trembling with age and with fear, and fell down like a suppliant at the feet of the child she had reared, begging her one moment, trying to frighten her the next, threatening to show the noose and expose her attempted suicide if she did not tell her whom she was in love with—and promising to help her if she did.

"Myrrha raised her head from the bed and now hid her face, wet with tears, in the nurse's breast. She tried to speak, then checked herself, until, finally, ashamed, covering her face with her robe, she cried, 'O Mother, how lucky you are in your husband! . . . ' That was all she said, and then she groaned.

"An icy shiver shook the nurse's body and pierced her bones, and her white hair stood on end all over her head, for she understood what Myrrha meant. She then said whatever she could think of to shock the girl out of her dreadful passion.

"Myrrha knew everything the nurse said was true, but she was still determined to die if she could not have the man she loved. 'O live!' the nurse said, 'you will have . . .'—she could not bring herself to say 'your father,' and so fell silent, but she sealed her promise with an oath.

"The women—wives and mothers—were celebrating the annual festival of holy Ceres, at which, wearing snow-white robes, they offer the goddess the first fruits of the harvest and garlands made from ears of grain and for nine nights are forbidden to make love with their husbands or to let them touch them. Cenchreis, the king's wife, was with the women, taking part in the secret rites. And so while his lawful wife was absent from his bed, the meddling fool of a nurse, coming upon King Cinyras when he'd had too much to drink, told him he was someone's true love—and gave a false name and praised her beauty to the skies. When he asked how old the girl was, the nurse replied, 'Myrrha's age.' Ordered to produce her, she went back home and said to Myrrha: 'Rejoice, my child! We've won!' But the poor girl was not filled with joy, for a sad foreboding crept into her heart. So great was the conflict in her mind, though, that she did rejoice a little, even so.

"It was the time of night when all is silent, and Boötes has guided his wagon between the two Bears and onto the downward slope. The girl made her way in the dark to her evil deed, for the golden moon had fled from the sky, black clouds covered the hiding stars, and the night lacked all its natural light. You, first, Icarus, hid your face, and Erigone, too, made holy by her pure love for her father.

"Three times Myrrha stumbled, a sign to turn back; three times a baleful screech owl uttered its mournful cry, an omen for sure. But on she went, and the darkness, the blackness of the night, lessened her feeling of shame. Holding the nurse's hand in her left hand, she felt her way along in the dark with her right: Now her foot touches the threshold of her father's bedroom; now she opens the door; now she is led inside. But her knees are shaking and her legs give way and the color drains from her face and she feels as if she is going to faint as she moves to the bed. The closer she comes to the awful deed, the more frightened she is; she deplores what she is daring to do and wishes she could turn around and go back without being recognized. She was hanging back, but the old crone pulled her forward with her hand and pushed her toward the lofty bed and handed her over, saying, 'Take her, Cinyras, she's all yours,' and so united the curséd bodies.

"Her father received his own flesh and blood into his obscene bed, and he tried to lighten an innocent girl's dread, tried to calm her fears. Perhaps, too, since she was so young, he called her 'daughter,' and she called him 'father'— lest their sin lack names.* Myrrha left her father's bed filled with his guilty seed, carrying it in her monstrous womb, conceiving there the fruit of their crime.

"The next night the evil deed was doubled, nor did it end there. Finally, Cinyras, eager to know his lover after so many nights of sharing his bed with her, brought in a light and saw his daughter—and his crime.

"Mute with shock and dismay, he snatched his gleaming sword from its scabbard, hanging beside the bed, but Myrrha ran and, thanks to the darkness, gift of the night, escaped an early death. Stumbling across broad fields, she made her way out of Arabia with its palm trees and out of the Panchaean country and wandered for nine months until, finally, exhausted, she stopped to rest in the land of Saba,† barely able to carry the weight in her womb. Then, caught between weariness with life and fear of death and not knowing what to pray for, she composed this prayer: 'If any gods hear sinners when they confess: I deserve a bitter punishment, and I do not shun it, but let me not by living violate the living nor by dying defile the dead. Banish me from both realms! Change me! And so deny me life and death!'

"There is indeed a god who hears a sinner's prayer, and last requests do have

---

*10.468: "lest their sin lack names": In this context, "daughter" and "father" add up to the "sin" (*scelus,* 10.468) of incest.

†10.480: Saba is in the southwestern part of Arabia. "Its riches were proverbial" (Kenney [1986] 435).

their own divinities, for as she spoke, earth began to cover her legs, her toes split open, and roots from them shot down into the ground, supporting her long trunk; her bones changed to hard wood, the marrow remaining deep within; her blood changed to sap; her arms turned into great branches, her fingers into leafy twigs; and her skin hardened into bark.

"The tree as it grew had enclosed her heavy womb, swallowed up her breasts, and now was gradually covering her neck. Its progress was too slow for Myrrha, though, and she sank down into the wood as it spread upward and buried her face in its bark. Although she lost all feeling as her body disappeared, she was weeping still, and her hot tears ran down the trunk of the tree. But there is honor even for tears, and now from the bark myrrh drips—and keeps its mistress' name and will spread it far and wide in time to come.[40]

"But the infant, so unfortunately conceived, had continued to grow inside the tree and now sought a way to leave its mother and get free. The heavy belly within the trunk began to swell as her burden stretched its mother's womb, but the pain it felt had no words to cry out with, no voice, as Myrrha gave birth, for calling upon Lucina. The tree was now doubled over like a woman in labor, groaning continually and drenched by a flood of falling tears. Then gentle Lucina stood by the branches tossing in agony, laid her hands upon the tree, and spoke the words that hasten birth. The trunk split open and through a fissure in the bark brought forth its living burden, a baby boy, wailing. Naiads laid it on a bed of soft grass and bathed it in its mother's tears. Even Envy would have admired its beauty, like that of the naked Cupids artists paint. Indeed, give it a little quiver—or take Cupid's away—and you could not tell them apart.

"Time glides by so quickly and quietly, and nothing is swifter than the passing years: That child, the son of his own sister and grandfather, enclosed in a tree till recently, a newborn infant a moment ago, just now a most beautiful baby, already a boy, now a young man, now even more beautiful than himself—and now he delights the eye even of Venus and avenges his mother's passion.

"For Cupid, wearing his quiver, was showering his mother with kisses and accidentally pricked her breast with an arrow. "Ouch!" she said and pushed her son away. But the wound was deeper than it appeared to be and fooled even Venus at first. Soon she was captivated by the young man's beauty and no longer cared for the shores of Cythera; no longer sought Paphos-by-the-Sea; nor Cnidos, where fishes play; nor Amathus, rich in metals.

"She even stayed away from heaven—preferred Adonis to heaven. She clung to him, went everywhere with him, and though more accustomed to lounging in the shade and to making herself look ever more beautiful, she now wanders across mountain ridges, hikes through forests, scrambles over rocks, and picks her way through brambles. She wears her dress pulled above her knees like Diana's, urges on the dogs, chases scampering rabbits or stags with spreading antlers or gentle does—all harmless prey—but keeps away from raging boars and stays clear of bloodthirsty wolves, sharp-clawed bears, and lions gorged on the meat of the cattle they hunt down.

"Venus warns you, too, Adonis, to beware of these—if warnings can do any good—and says: 'Face those beasts that are easily frightened and run away. Toward the fearless, fearlessness is not a good idea. Your rashness can hurt *me*! Don't let it! Don't provoke those creatures nature has armed, lest you win glory at a price too high for me. Neither your youth, nor your beauty, nor all those other charms of yours that have aroused Venus will move lions and bristly boars and bewitch the eyes and hearts of savage animals. Fierce boars have lightning in their tusks; tawny lions are filled with rage and always poised to spring. I hate the entire breed of lions!'

"Adonis asked her why. 'I'll tell you why,' she said, 'and you'll marvel at the incredible thing that happened because of an ancient offense against me. But all this action I'm not used to has exhausted me, and look, that poplar there with its shade is so inviting, and the grass beneath it is just like a bed. Let me lie down with you here,' and she lay down.

"Reclining on the grass—and on Adonis, too, with her head in his lap— she began to tell him the story, pausing often to raise her head a little just to kiss him.

"'Have you heard of the woman who could outrun even the fastest men in a footrace? The story was not made up, for she did outrun them, and you really couldn't say whether she was more renowned for the excellence of her feet or the glory of her beauty. When she consulted an oracle about a husband, "Husband?" the god replied. "Atalanta, you don't need a husband. Run from the very idea of a husband—yet I predict you won't run from it, and though still alive, you'll lose your self."

"'Terrified by the god's prediction, Atalanta went off to live, unwed, in the darkest part of the forest, and she drove away the hordes of suitors who pressed her to marry them with the dangerous condition that she set. "You cannot have me," she would tell them, "unless you defeat me in a race. Bid for me with your feet! To the swift, my hand and my bed will be the prize; to the slow, the prize is death! That's the condition you must accept for the contest!" A harsh rule, indeed, but her beauty was so compelling that a heedless crowd of suitors rushed to submit to it.

"'Hippomenes had come to watch this uneven contest and, contemptuous of the young men's reckless passion, had asked himself, "Why would anyone ever take such a risk to get a wife?" But when he saw Atalanta's face and, after she took off her clothes for the race, saw her body—like my body, Adonis, or like yours, if you became a woman—he stared in amazement and raised his hands to heaven and cried, "Forgive me, all you men I scorned just now! I did not know what a prize you were competing for." And so it was that Hippomenes, admiring Atalanta's beauty, fell in love with her himself. He hoped that none of the suitors could run faster than she, he was jealous of them, and he feared one of them would. "But why shouldn't I try my luck in this contest, too?" he asked himself "God himself favors the bold!"

"'While Hippomenes was musing thus, the girl ran by on winged feet. And though she seemed to the Boeotian youth faster than a Scythian arrow, he admired her beauty even more than her fleetness: Running itself made her beautiful. The wings on her speeding feet flew on the wind, her hair was lifted from her ivory shoulders, bright ribbons at her knees streamed behind her, and her fair skin glowed with a rosy hue like the tinted shade a crimson awning makes on a marble floor.

"'While the stranger at the race was taking all this in, the final lap was run, the crown of victory was placed on Atalanta's head, and the losers, groaning, paid the penalty called for by the rules of the contest.

"'Undaunted by their fate, young Hippomenes approached the girl on the field, fixed his gaze on her, and said: "Why do you seek easy victories by defeating such lazy runners? Race against me! If I'm lucky enough to win, you won't be ashamed to lose to someone like me. My father was Megareus of Onchestus, his grandfather was Neptune. I am the great-grandson of the king of the sea. My prowess is no less than my lineage. If I lose, you will acquire a great and memorable name for yourself by defeating Hippomenes."

"'Atalanta, daughter of Schoeneus, gazed at him softly as he spoke, unsure whether she wanted to win or lose: "What god," she thought, "can be so hostile to the handsome that he wants to destroy this lad by commanding him to try to marry me at the risk of his own dear life? If you ask me, I'm not worth it. Nor am I so touched by his good looks (though I *could* be touched by them)— but he's still a boy! He himself doesn't move me, but his young and tender age does. And what about his courage? He has no fear of death at all! And then there is his family line. He's only four generations away from his origin in the sea. And what about this: He loves me. He wants to marry me so much he's willing to die if hard luck denies me to him.

"'"Oh go away, my friend, while you can! Give up the idea of a marriage soaked in blood! Marrying me is a cruel thing to want to do. There isn't a girl alive who wouldn't like to be your wife; any girl with any sense will want you. But why do I worry about you, when so many have already died?

"'"Let him find out! Let him die, then, if he won't be warned by the deaths of so many suitors and has now grown tired of living. But will he therefore die, simply because he wanted to live with me? His death—undeserved—the price he pays for love? I'll be hated for my victory, and I won't be able to bear it. But I can't help it; it's not my fault.

"'"If only you would withdraw, or, since you've lost your senses, if only you were faster! What an innocent face that boy has. O poor Hippomenes! I wish you had never seen me! You deserved so much to live. And if I were luckier, if a perverse fate were not denying me marriage, you would be the one person I would want to share my bed with." Those were Atalanta's thoughts. Since she was inexperienced, and this was the first time she had ever been touched by desire, she fell in love without knowing it and wasn't aware that it was love.

"'When the people and her father now demanded the customary race, Hippomenes, scion of Neptune, was worried and prayed to me: "I ask Venus to be with me in what I am daring to do and to aid the passion she ignited." An accommodating breeze brought this touching prayer to me, and I was moved, I confess, and my help wasn't long in coming.

"'There is a place on Cyprus the inhabitants call Tamasus, the nicest part of the island, which the elders long ago consecrated to me, ordering it to be attached to my temple property as a gift. Here, in the middle of a field, a tree of gold stands gleaming, its golden leaves and golden branches clicking in the wind.

"'I was coming from there, carrying in my hand, as it happened, three apples of gold I had picked from that tree, and I appeared to Hippomenes—only he could see me—and I showed him how he could use them.

"'When the trumpets sounded, both shot forth headfirst from the starting line, their speeding feet barely touching the sandy track. You would think they could skim across the waves of the sea without wetting those feet or run through a field of ripening grain and leave it unstirred.

"'The crowd cheered Hippomenes on, increasing his will to win, shouting: "Give it all you've got, Hippomenes! Run! Use all your strength! Faster! You're going to win!"

"'It's hard to say who was more thrilled to hear these words, the hero, son of Megareus, or Schoeneus' daughter. How many times, when she could have passed him, Atalanta held back, just to gaze at his face for a moment, then reluctantly sped on by him!

"'Hippomenes, exhausted, his throat dry, was gasping for breath—and the goal was far away. Then, finally, the descendant of Neptune threw down one of the apples from the golden tree. The girl was amazed and, eager for the shining fruit, swerved off the track and picked it up as it rolled like a golden ball; Hippomenes ran on by, and the stands went wild with applause.

"'Atalanta made up for her lost time with a burst of speed and again left the young man behind. She slowed once more when he tossed the second apple down, but caught up and passed him again. And now only the last few yards of the race remained.

"'"Be with me now, goddess, giver of these gifts!" Hippomenes prayed, and he threw the third gleaming apple hard and to the side, toward the edge of the field, where it would take Atalanta longer to run back from. The girl seemed to hesitate: Should she go after it? But I forced her to pick it up, and I made it heavier than it was, and so I slowed her down with the weight of the apple and the time she lost.

"'And, lest the story go on longer than the race itself—he outran the girl and, being the winner, led his prize away. Did I not deserve to be thanked, Adonis? Did I not deserve to be offered incense? But he didn't do either one, didn't thank me or offer me incense.

"'Instantly furious and seething at the slight, I went after them both and made an example of them to keep anyone from ever scorning me again.

"'They were passing by a temple built by illustrious Echion to fulfill a vow he had made to the mother of the gods, a temple that was hidden away deep in a forest.* After traveling for so long, they thought it was an inviting place to rest.

"'There Hippomenes was possessed by desire to make love to Atalanta—it was the wrong time and place for it, but it was desire my power had aroused. Near the temple there was an inner recess, like a cave, that had a roof of natural rock and let in little light. It was a place long hallowed, where the priest had stored a number of wooden statues of the ancient gods. Hippomenes entered this sacred cave with Atalanta and desecrated it by a scandalous and forbidden act. The statues turned their eyes away, and the tower-crowned mother of the gods wondered whether she ought to drown the guilty pair in the river Styx then and there. But that punishment seemed too light. Instead, tawny manes now covered their smooth necks; their fingers curved into claws; their shoulders turned into forequarters; all their weight went to their chests; now they had tails they swished over the sand; their faces showed menacing rage now, and they uttered growls instead of words; now they mated in the forests, instead of the marriage bed; and, though feared by others, they bit down on Cybele's curb in their mouths, her tame lions now.

"'And so, my dearest, run from these and every other kind of beast that offers its chest to battle but not its back to flight, lest your fearlessness hurt us both!'

"Thus she warned Adonis, then made her way through the air in her swan-drawn chariot. But his fearlessness stood opposed to such a warning. It happened that his dogs followed the tracks of a boar one day and drove it from its lair. As it fled the woods, the young grandson of Cinyras struck it with his spear, but at an angle, and, shaking the bloody spear point from its snout, the raging boar turned to attack the terrified Adonis, who tried to run away, and buried its tusks in the boy's groin and laid him out on the yellow sand, nearly dead.

"Venus, meanwhile, had almost reached Cyprus in her light car when she heard the groans of the dying boy far away. She turned her white swans around and, from high in the sky, saw him tossing in his own blood, close to death. Diving down to earth, she ripped her garments, tore her hair, beat her breasts—meant to be touched, but not like this—and cried out to fate: 'One thing, at least, will escape your law: A monument to my grief, Adonis, will stand forever, and your death reenacted yearly will commemorate my sorrow. Your blood will become a flower—or will you be allowed, Proserpina, to turn a girl's limbs into fragrant mint while I cause resentment for changing this hero, grandson of Cinyras?'

"With these words she sprinkled scented nectar on the blood, which, as the nectar touched it, began to swell in the way an opalescent bubble often rises

---

*10.686: Echion was one of the "sown men" (sown by Cadmus): 3.126. The mother of the gods is Cybele (Miller-Goold 2.113 n. 1).

from yellowy mud, and in no more than an hour's time a flower had sprung up, red as the blood of Adonis and like the blossom of the pomegranate, which hides it seeds beneath its tough skin.

"Our delight in this flower is brief, though, for the wind that gives it its name soon tears off the light and lightly clinging, easily falling petals of the anemone."*[41]

*10.738–739: The anemone takes its name from *anemos,* the Greek word for wind.

BOOK ELEVEN

With this song the Thracian bard had gathered trees and animals around him, and even boulders bumped along to join them.

But suddenly, Ciconian women, dressed in animal skins and raving mad, spied Orpheus from the top of a hill as he plucked his lyre, and one of them, hair flying in the wind, cried, "Look! Look! There he is, the man who hates us!" and hurled her wand like a spear at the mouth of Apollo's poet, even as he sang. But the leaves were still on the wand, and it failed to break the skin and only left a mark. Another woman heaved a rock at him, but as it flew through the air it was overcome by the sweet harmony of his voice and lyre and came to rest at his feet like a suppliant seeking forgiveness for such a mad attack.

And now the women grew more daring, and the violence increased. Nothing held them back, for they were possessed by an insane Fury. Yet all the angry weapons would have been soothed by Orpheus' singing if the shouting, if the shrill cry of Phrygian flutes with flared bells, if the rattle of drums, the clapping of hands, the wailing, and the howling had not drowned out the sound of his lyre. But finally the stones no longer heard the poet as he sang, and they grew red with his blood. First, the Maenads seized countless birds and snakes and a horde of beasts, his adoring audience* and enchanted still by the sound of his voice still singing, and tore them apart. Next, they turned on Orpheus with their bloody hands. They swooped down on him like birds when they see a night owl wandering blindly in daylight, while Orpheus was like a stag in the arena in the morning, about to be killed by dogs. They ran toward him, hurling their leafy wands at him, wands not made for this. Some threw clods of dirt,

---

*At 11.22 I read and translate *theatri* with Anderson (1982a), Bömer, and Haupt-Ehwald (and the MSS) instead of *triumphi*, Merkel's emendation, adopted by Miller-Goold, the phrase *titulum . . . theatri*, glossed by Bömer, "'der Ruhm, der in der Zuhörerschaft der Tiere bestand,'" "the fame he had won among his animal audience" (at 11.20–22, 5.244).

others, branches torn from trees; still others threw stones: Whatever they found became weapons for their fury.

Oxen happened to be close by, plowing the earth, and near them farmers spading up the hard ground with their powerful arms, by their sweat getting it ready for planting. When they saw the mob of women, the farmers ran away, leaving their tools, their hoes, heavy rakes, and long-handled mattocks, scattered about in the empty fields. These the women seized and then, after tearing apart the oxen with threatening horns,* ran back to slaughter the poet. As he stretched out his arms to them and for the first time ever spoke in vain and moved nothing with the sound of his voice,† these sacrilegious women killed him. O Jupiter! From the mouth that stones had listened to and wild beasts understood, the breath of life flew out and into the wind.

Dear Orpheus, grieving birds wept for you, wild beasts wept for you, stones wept for you, and forests, which had so often come to hear your songs, they wept for you, too. Trees shed their leaves in mourning for you. Rivers, they say, were swollen with their own tears. Naiads and dryads donned robes edged in black and disheveled their hair. The parts of Orpheus' body lay widely scattered, but you, O Hebrus, received the head and the lyre, and (amazing!) as they floated downstream the lyre made some kind of tearful sound, the lifeless mouth murmured something tearful, and from the banks of the river a tearful echo came. The head and the lyre were swept out to sea from their native stream and washed ashore at Methymna on the isle of Lesbos. As the head lay exposed on the foreign sands with its wet and dripping hair, a savage snake glided toward it, but Apollo appeared at last, stopped the serpent as it was about to strike, and froze its wide-open mouth and hardened its gaping jaws into stone, just as they were.

The shade of Orpheus then went down to the underworld, where he saw again all the places he had seen before. Searching through the fields of the blessed, he found Eurydice and clasped her tightly in his loving arms. Here now they stroll together side by side, and sometimes she leads the way and Orpheus follows her, or sometimes he goes in front. But now Orpheus can safely look back at his dear Eurydice.

Bacchus did not allow this murder to go unpunished, however, and, grieving for the priest of his rites, now lost, immediately tangled in roots the feet of all the Thracian women in the forest who had witnessed this horrible crime. Indeed, the path itself that each had taken in her pursuit tugged at her toes, forcing the ends of them down into the solid ground. When a bird steps into a snare hidden by a cunning hunter, feels its leg caught, and frantically flaps its

---

*At 11.37 I read and translate *minaci* (sc. *cornu*) with Anderson (1982a), Bömer, Haupt-Ehwald, and Murphy, instead of *minaces* (sc. *boves,* 11.38) with Miller-Goold. See Murphy's note at 11.37, 45–46.

†11.39–40: "for the first time ever spoke in vain" (*primum/inrita dicentem*). At 10.3 Ovid says that the god Hymen was "called by the voice of Orpheus, though it was a futile summons" (*Orphea nequiquam voce vocatur*).

wings and tightens the strings, so each of the women, caught and rooted in the ground, struggled in terror to get free, but in vain, for her feet were entangled in supple roots that held them fast when she tried to leap up, and as first one and then another looked for her nails, for her toes, for her feet, she saw her smooth legs harden into the trunk of a tree; and when she tried to beat her thighs in grief, she struck wood. The women's breasts also turned to wood, and their shoulders were wood, too. You would think their outstretched arms* had become long branches, and you wouldn't be wrong to think so.[42]

But this was not enough for Bacchus. He also abandoned the land itself and with a better troop of followers sought the vineyards of his own dear Mount Tmolus and the river Pactolus (though it was not then flowing with gold or prized for its precious sand). Here his usual band of satyrs and Bacchants gathered around him. Silenus, though, was absent, for, staggering along because of his age (and too much wine), he fell behind and was seized by Phrygian peasants, who crowned his head with garlands made from flowers and brought him to King Midas.

Now, Orpheus had instructed Midas in the rites of Bacchus along with Eumolpus of Athens, and when Midas recognized Silenus as a companion of the god and a devotee of his rites, he was delighted to have such a guest and celebrated his arrival with a festival that lasted ten whole days and nights. On the eleventh day, after the new light of morning had ushered the host of stars from the sky, the king was happy to travel to Lydia and restore Silenus to his young charge.†

Rejoicing at the return of his foster father, the god as a reward allowed Midas to choose whatever he wanted for a gift—a reward that did him no good, for the king, who was going to use his gift foolishly, said, "Make whatever I touch turn to burnished gold." Bacchus granted Midas what he asked for and gave him the gift, harmful though it was, but he was sorry that Midas had not asked for something better.

The Phrygian hero went away happy, delighting in his unfortunate gift, and tested the god's promise to see if it was genuine by touching everything he saw: Not really believing it, he broke off a green twig from a low branch of an oak tree, and the twig turned to gold! He picked up a rock from the ground, and the rock, too, gleamed pale gold! He touched a clod of dirt and look! at his touch the clod became a gold nugget. He plucked some ears of grain: a harvest of gold! He picked an apple from a tree and held it in his hand: You would think it was a gift from the Hesperides. When he brushed his fingers across the palace's lofty doorposts, the doorposts shone brightly. And when he washed his hands in clear water, the water flowing from his hands would have fooled Danaë.‡

---

*At 11.83 I read *porrecta* (sc. *bracchia*), "outstretched arms," with Bömer, Haupt-Ehwald, and Murphy, instead of *nodosa*, "knotty," with Miller-Goold.

†11.99: "his young charge," that is, Bacchus.

‡11.116–117: Zeus (or Jupiter) appeared to Danaë in a shower of golden rain, impregnating her with Perseus (Apollodorus 2.4.1–2).

He imagines everything golden—and hardly accepts his own hopes himself. Rejoicing at the thought, he sat down at a table his servants had set for him, heaped high with roasted meat and bread baked from toasted grain, but when he took a piece of bread in his hand, the bread turned hard, and as he was about to sink his teeth with pleasure into a juicy slice of the roast, he found himself taking a bite of meat that was gold-plated. When he mixed pure water with wine, made by the god who gave him this gift, you would see liquid gold flowing between his open lips.

Shocked by this strange and horrible state of affairs, rich and wretched, Midas longed to escape his newfound wealth, and he hated now what he had only recently prayed to have. No amount of riches could relieve his hunger, and his dry throat burned with thirst.

Tormented by this unwelcome gold—and deserving to be!—he raised his hands and gold-clad arms to heaven, praying, "Forgive me, father Bacchus, for I am guilty of great wrongdoing. Pity me, I beg you, and deliver me from this golden hell!"

The will of gods can soften. Since Midas acknowledged his offense, Bacchus canceled the gift he had given to fulfill his promise, restored the king to his former self, and said: "To remove the gold your foolish desire has gilded you with, go to the river near the great city of Sardis, climb the slope beside it, and make your way upstream until you come to its source. There, where a bubbling spring gushes from the ground, submerge yourself completely and wash your silly crime away."

King Midas obeyed the order, and when he entered the water, his power to turn all things to gold flowed from his body and into the river, dyeing it golden. The grains of the ancient gold were absorbed by the fields near the stream long ago, yet even today the fields gleam with a golden crust.

Despising his wealth, Midas took to the fields and forests, where he worshipped Pan, who always dwells in mountain caves. But he was as thickheaded as ever, and, as before, his foolish notions were going to get him into trouble again.

Now, Mount Tmolus rises solid and sheer with a steep ascent, commanding a view far over the sea, its north slope extending to Sardis, its south slope to the little town of Hypaepa. Once, when Pan was showing off with his reed pipe to a group of impressionable nymphs, playing them a simple tune, he dared to compare Apollo's music unfavorably to his own and soon found himself in an unequal contest, to be decided by Tmolus.

The ancient god took his seat as judge on his own mountain and cleared the trees from his ears; only a garland of oak leaves remained, crowning his dark blue hair, acorns from it dangling around his sunken temples. Looking at Pan he said, "I'm ready to judge the contest whenever you're ready to play."

The god of the herds then played a crude tune on his country pipes, and charmed Midas, who happened to be there. When he finished, the honorable Tmolus turned around to face Phoebus Apollo; his forest swung around with him. Apollo was wearing a laurel crown from Mount Parnassus on his golden head, and his rich purple cloak swept the ground. In his left hand he held his lyre, inlaid with ivory and studded with precious stones; and in his right he held his plectrum: the very image of an artist. His accomplished fingers plucked the strings, and Tmolus, charmed by the sweetness of his melody, ordered Pan to lower his pipes in defeat before the lyre.

The decision rendered by the god of the mountain pleased everyone but Midas, who spoke out against it, calling it unjust. Apollo could not allow ears as dull as those of the king to keep their human form, so he stretched them out and covered them with gray fur and made them floppy and able to wiggle. And so Midas now had the long ears of a lazily walking ass. But only his ears were singled out for punishment; the rest of him remained human.

Ashamed of his grotesque appearance, Midas wanted to hide his ears, and so he tried to keep his head covered with a purple cap. But the servant who regularly cut the king's hair had seen those ass's ears, and though he did not dare expose the king's disgrace, he couldn't keep quiet about it, either. Since he wanted to bring it to light, he went outdoors, dug a hole in the ground, and in a low voice described the ears he had seen on his master, whispering all this into the hole. He then put the dirt back, covering over the words he had spoken, and when he had filled in the hole, he stole away.

A thick stand of rustling reeds sprang up there and a year later, now grown tall, betrayed this planter of words. For when the reeds swayed in a light south wind, they whispered the buried message and so revealed the secret of the king's ears.[43]

Now properly avenged, Apollo left Tmolus, flew through the air, and came to land just this side of Helle's narrow sea in the country of Laomedon. On the coast of Troy between the promontories of Sigeum and Rhoeteum there is an ancient altar sacred to Jupiter the Thunderer, Creator of Prophecy. There Apollo saw Laomedon beginning to build the walls of the new Troy, saw this enormous work going forward only with the greatest effort and demanding enormous resources, and so, together with Neptune, trident-bearing father of the deep sea swells, he put on human form and made an agreement with the king of Troy to build the walls for a sum of gold.

When the walls were finished and standing, the king refused to pay the agreed-on price and, crowning this treachery, even denied he had made an agreement. "You'll soon regret this," said the lord of the deep and diverted all his waters to the shores of miserly Troy and made a sea out of the plains, burying the fields beneath mountains of water and robbing the farmers there of their sustenance. Nor did this punishment satisfy him, for he demanded that the king offer his daughter to a monster from the sea. She was chained to a rock, but Hercules freed her and then asked for the reward he had been promised for saving her, some horses he was told he could have. When this recompense for so great a labor was also denied, he breached the walls of Troy and conquered the city ruled by this two-time liar.

His comrade-in-arms Telamon retired from the field with a prize, for he was given Hesione,* whom he kept for himself, since his brother Peleus was already famously married to a goddess and was just as proud of having Nereus for a father-in-law as he was of having Jupiter for his grandfather. For it was hardly singular to be Jupiter's grandson, but to have a goddess for a wife—now that was singular indeed!

Old Proteus had once said to Thetis: "Goddess of the sea, conceive! You will become the mother of a young man who, when he reaches his prime, will surpass his father's exploits and be called greater than he." And so to prevent the world from having anything greater than himself, Jupiter fled from a liaison with the sea nymph Thetis, though his passion for her was hardly lukewarm, and he ordered his grandson Peleus to take his place and do what he had wanted to do himself, enter the arms of this girl of the sea.

There is a cove in Thessaly curved like a sickle, and it would make a fine harbor if only it were deeper. But the water is shallow here, and the sea barely covers the sand. The beach is free from seaweed, and its hard-packed surface preserves no footprints nor slows anyone down who walks on it. A grove of myrtles with their black-green berries grows nearby, and in the middle of it there is a cave—formed by nature or made by the hand of an artist? It's hard to say: More likely an artist made it. Here, Thetis, you often used to rein in the dolphin you rode naked; and here Peleus grabbed you one day as you lay sound asleep and, when you fought him off despite his begging and pleading, tried to force you to have sex with him, wrapping both his arms around your neck. If you hadn't used all the tricks you knew and kept on changing your shape, he would have possessed the one he dared to attack. First you became a bird, but a bird that Peleus caught nevertheless and held on to; next, a solid tree trunk, and Peleus still hung on, now to a tree trunk. And then your third form: You were a striped tigress! And now he let go of you in a hurry, terrified.

Peleus then prayed to all the gods of the sea, pouring wine on their waters, offering them sheep's entrails, and burning incense to them until Proteus, the Carpathian seer, appeared from the deep and said: "Son of Aeacus, you will have the marriage you wish for. Now, pay attention to what I tell you: When Thetis lies asleep in her cave, take a rope and wind it around her several times before she realizes what's happening and tie her up tight. Don't let her fool you with the hundred or so forms she will pretend to be, but cling to her, whatever she becomes, until she turns back into her own self." As he said this, Proteus sank back down into the sea, his last words bubbling up from underwater.

The Titan Sun, homeward bound in his descending chariot, was touching down in the western ocean when Nereus' lovely daughter emerged from the cove and came to nap at her usual place. Peleus had just thrown himself on top of the girl when she began changing into one form after another, until she realized she had been tied up with her arms stretched out. Then at last she

*11.217: Hesione was the daughter of Laomedon.

groaned and said, "You couldn't have overpowered me without a god's help," and, giving up, became Thetis again. Now that she had yielded, the hero fully embraced her, satisfied his desire, and filled her womb with mighty Achilles.[44]

Happy twice over because of his son and his wife, Peleus had all the good luck one can have, if you overlook the crime of cutting his brother Phocus' throat. Guilty of murder, he was banished from his father's house and found refuge in the land of Trachis.

Here King Ceyx, son of the morning star, ruled his kingdom without violence or bloodshed, his father's brilliance shining in his face. But at this time he was not his usual self, and his countenance was dark with grief, for he was mourning the loss of his brother.

Peleus arrived in Trachis, careworn and weary from travel. He left the herds of sheep and cattle he was driving in a shady valley not far from the city walls, entered Trachis with a few companions, and was granted an audience with the king. Holding a suppliant's olive branch covered with wool, Peleus approached King Ceyx and told him who he was and where he came from, omitting only his crime and lying about the cause of his exile. He asked the king if he could settle himself either in the city or somewhere in the country.

The Trachinian ruler replied kindly: "Even ordinary folk, Peleus, can benefit from what our kingdom has to offer, nor are we inhospitable. Disposed as we are to welcome strangers, you add powerful claims that incline us to help you even more: your illustrious name and your grandfather Jupiter. Don't spend another moment making supplication. Your petition is entirely granted. Consider what you see here, such as it is, in part your own. I only wish you could see something better." And he began to weep.

Peleus and his companions asked him why he was so sad, and he told them this story: "You may think the bird that feeds off prey and terrifies all winged creatures has always been a bird, but it was once a man named Daedalion, and so constant is his character that even then he was fierce and warlike and inclined to violence.

"We were both sons of the star that summons the dawn, the star that is last to leave the sky. While I thought only of living in peace and loving my wife, my brother delighted in war and war's savagery. His martial spirit, which now in his changed form makes him harry the doves of Thisbe,* led him then to subject kings and peoples to his power.

"Daedalion had a daughter Chione, whom nature endowed with such beauty that she had a thousand suitors by the time she was fourteen and ripe for marriage. One day Apollo and Mercury, Maia's son, were returning home, the one from his temple at Delphi, the other from Mount Cyllene, when they saw Chione at the same instant and at the same instant burned with lust for her. Now,

---

*11.300: Thisbe is a town in Boeotia that Homer at *Iliad* 2.502 describes as "dove-haunted" (Murphy at 11.300, 59).

Apollo put off his hope of having sex with her until nightfall, but Mercury could not bear to wait and touched the girl's face with the wand that causes sleep. One tap from that powerful wand and Chione was unconscious and unable to resist the god's assault. And now it was night, and the sky was sprinkled with stars: Apollo adopted the form of an old woman and took his pleasure after Mercury.

"When Chione had come to term and was ready to give birth, from the seed of the winged god a cunning child was born named Autolycus, who had a natural talent for every kind of trick and was able to change white to black and black to white, a not unworthy heir of his father's artfulness. Chione also bore a son to Apollo named Philammon (for she gave birth to twins), who achieved fame for his singing and lyre-playing.

"But what good did it do her to bear two sons, give pleasure to two gods, and be the daughter of a valiant father herself and granddaughter of a brilliant star? Glory itself harms many, does it not? It certainly harmed her! She had the gall to rate herself above Diana, calling the goddess' beauty flawed. Infuriated, Diana said, 'Let's see how she likes this,' and instantly drew her bow, shot an arrow from the string, and pierced the girl's offending tongue. The tongue was still, and neither voice nor words would come, though she urged them to, and while the girl was trying to speak, her life drained away with her blood. In despair, I held her in my arms as she was dying, bore her father's grief in my heart, and consoled him as well as I could, for my brother loved his daughter so! He heard me the way a cliff hears the murmuring sea, lost in mourning for his dead child.

"When he saw her body burning on the funeral pyre, he tried four times to enter the flames. Flung back four times by the heat, he ran off in a frenzy, like a bull stung by hornets, head lowered, charging in all directions. He seemed to me even then to run with more than human speed—you would think his feet had grown wings. And so Daedalion escaped from us all and, driven on by his longing for death, reached the summit of Mount Parnassus. When he hurled himself from its rocky height, Apollo pitied him and changed him into a bird, lifting him up on sudden wings, and gave him a hooked beak and curved talons, gave him his old warlike spirit, too, and strength far greater than the size of his body. Now he's a hawk, friend to no bird, savage toward them all, and, grieving himself, a cause of grief to others."

While the son of the morning star was relating this incredible story about his brother, Peleus' herdsman, Onetor of Phocis, ran up, shouting, "Peleus! Peleus!" and struggling to catch his breath. "Something terrible has happened!" he cried. "That's why I've come!" Peleus ordered him to tell him what it was; even the king of Trachis himself was in suspense, a look of fear on his face.

"I had driven the weary cattle down to the shore at midday," the herdsman began, "when the sun is highest in the sky and can see that the space he's crossed is the same as the distance he has still to go. Some of the cows had knelt down on the yellow sand and lay gazing out at the broad expanse of sea; others were wandering idly about here and there; still others were swimming, holding their heads up out of the water.

"By the sea stands a temple gleaming neither with marble nor with gold and shaded by a thick grove of ancient trees. It is sacred to Nereus and his daughters, gods of those waters,* according to an old fisherman who was drying his nets on the beach. One side of the temple faces a marsh made by the overflow from the sea and dense with willows. Here a huge beast, a wolf, was crashing about in the underbrush, terrifying all who lived nearby, and now he emerged from the reeds in the marsh, his jaws, like lightning, smeared with foam and spattered with blood and his eyes glowing red with fire.

"This monstrous creature was raging both from its own ferocity and from fierce hunger, but clearly more from ferocity, for it had no desire to eat the cattle it slaughtered and so satisfy its hunger, and instead attacked the entire herd of cows and savagely killed them all. Some of us, too, while fighting off the wolf, were ripped open by its deadly fangs and died. There was blood on the shore, blood in the water at the sea's edge, and blood in the marsh, which was filled with animals bellowing.

"Any delay will be deadly!" the herdsman cried. "We cannot wait! While we still have some of the herd left, get your weapons! We must all run and get weapons and attack this monster together."

Peleus was undisturbed by the loss of his herds, for he remembered his crime, and he reckoned that Nereus' daughter Psamathe, the bereaved mother of Phocus, had sent this destruction upon him to appease the ghost of her murdered son.

The king, however, ordered his men to put on their armor and take up their spears and was preparing to go with them himself, when his wife, Alcyone, aroused by all the shouting, leaped out of doors, her hair half undone, and now, letting it all down, clung to her husband's neck and in tears begged him to send the men without him and preserve two lives in one.

The son of Aeacus then said to her: "Your fears, dear queen, are a touching sign of your concern, but lay them aside. I am most grateful for the aid that you and the king have offered me, but I prefer that no one take up arms on my behalf against this strange monster. We must instead pay honor to the god of the sea!"

At the highest part of the citadel there was a lofty tower serving as a lighthouse that weary sailors were always glad to see. They climbed to the top of it and viewed with dismay the dead cattle lying scattered on the shore and saw their savage killer, its mouth smeared with gore and its fur matted with blood. There Peleus stretched out his hands toward the open sea and prayed to deep-

---

*11.361–362: "gods of those waters," that is, "of the straits extending from the Malian Gulf between Euboea and Thessaly" (Haupt-Ehwald at 11.361f., 2.205).

blue Psamathe to end her wrath and grant them her aid. She was not swayed by his prayer, but her sister Thetis interceded on behalf of her husband and received Psamathe's forgiveness.

Although the goddess called off the wolf from its fierce slaughter, it continued to rampage, excited by the sweet taste of blood, until she changed the monster to marble as it hung on the neck of a heifer it was tearing apart. The body of the wolf was completely preserved except for its color, which is now the color of marble and shows that it is no longer a wolf, no longer to be feared.

Fate, nevertheless, did not allow the exiled Peleus to settle in this land, and he wandered to Magnesia as a refugee, where he was purified for the murder of Phocus by Acastus of Thessaly.[45]

Ceyx, meanwhile, was anxious and troubled by these bizarre events, his brother's transformation and the one that came after it. And so he decided to go to Apollo's temple at Claros to consult the god's sacred oracle, which offers consolation for the woes of humankind, for the impious Phorbas and his Phlegyans were then blocking the road to Apollo's temple at Delphi.

But Ceyx told you his plans, Alcyone, most loyal of wives, before he departed. Hearing them, she turned pale, the color of a boxwood tree, and felt a chill in the marrow of her bones, and tears streamed down her cheeks. Three times she tried to speak, three times her mouth was flooded with tears, until, finally, she asked in a plaintive voice, choking with sobs: "What have I done, my beloved Ceyx, to make your feelings for me change? Where is the love you used to have for me? Can you now so easily abandon your Alcyone and go away? Does the thought of a long journey appeal to you now? Do you now care more for me when I'm not with you? But I suppose you'll travel by land, and so I'll only be sad, but not afraid; I'll miss you, but I'll feel no fear. For it's the sea I'm terrified of; the very thought of it upsets me. Recently I saw shattered ship's timbers that had washed ashore, and I've often read the names on empty tombs.

"You mustn't let the fact that my father is Aeolus give you false confidence, though he can shut up the powerful winds and calm the sea when he wants to, for once the winds are released and free to range over the water, nothing can stop them. Land and sea are at their mercy, they drive clouds together, and their wild collisions in the sky loose red lightning in all directions. Knowing the winds as I do—and I know them well, for when I was a girl I often saw them in my father's house—I know how much they must be feared.

"But if, dear husband, your mind cannot be swayed by any of my pleas and you are so set on going, take me with you! At least we'll be buffeted together, and then I'll not fear dangers I won't be suffering myself. Together we'll bear whatever happens; together we'll be borne over the wide sea."

Alcyone's words and her tears greatly moved her husband, the son of the morning star, for his love for her burned no less fiercely than her love for him. But since he wanted neither to forgo the journey over the sea that he had planned nor to expose Alcyone to danger, he said everything he could think of to console her and ease her fears; despite all that he said, however, he could not convince her. Then he added this promise, which alone calmed his beloved and changed her mind: "Any time we spend apart is much too long, but I swear to you by the light of my father's star, if only fate allows me to return, I shall be back before the second full moon."

When with this promise Ceyx had planted hope for his return in Alcyone's mind, he ordered his ship to be brought out of dry dock, put into the water, and fitted with all its gear for sailing. Alcyone became fearful all over again when she saw the ship, as though foreseeing the future, and tears welled up in her eyes and rolled down her cheeks. In despair, she embraced her husband and managed to murmur "Farewell" in a small voice, then collapsed on the ground. Though Ceyx looked for ways to delay his departure, the twin banks of young rowers were already pulling the oars to their powerful chests, striking the water in unison with the oar blades and cutting it evenly with their strokes.

Alcyone, bereft, raised her tearful eyes, and at first she was able to see her husband standing on the deck and waving to her, and she waved back.* As the distance between them grew, and she was unable to make out his face, she followed the receding ship with her eyes as long as she could. As this, too, became harder for her to see as it moved out of sight, she fixed her gaze on the sails fluttering at the top of the mast. When she could no longer see the sails, she sought her empty bed, anxious and afraid, and flung herself upon it. But the bed and the bedroom reminded her of the part of herself that was gone and brought on fresh tears.

Now the ship had cleared the harbor, and the wind was humming through the halyards. The sailors brought their oars to the side, then raised the yards to the top of the mast and unfurled the sails to catch the stiffening wind.

They had sailed perhaps halfway to the destined port, no more than that, with land far off in either direction, when, as night was falling, a powerful east wind began to blow violently and the sea to heave with foaming swells. "Lower the yards straightway," the captain shouted, "and reef all sails." Such were his orders, but blasts of wind hurled back his words, and the crashing waves drowned out his voice. Some of the sailors hurried on their own to pull in the oars, others closed the oar-holes and sealed leaks in the sides of the ship, still others reefed the sails. One was bailing water, pouring sea back into sea; another quickly took hold of the lowered yards. Amid this confused flurry of action on deck the violence of the storm increased and the winds attacked fiercely from all directions, roiling the angry sea.

The captain himself was terrified and confessed he did not know how things

---

*11.464–466: 11.464: "Alcyone, bereft": I read *relicta* (sc. *illa,* 11.463, that is, Alcyone) with Anderson (1982a), Bömer, Haupt-Ehwald, and Murphy rather than *recurva* (sc. *puppe,* 11.464) with Miller-Goold. 11.466: "at first": I read *prima* (again sc. *illa,* 11.463, that is, Alcyone) with Anderson (1982a) Bömer, and Haupt-Ehwald rather than *prona* with Miller-Goold.

stood with his ship, nor what orders to give, nor what he wanted to do,* so
great the danger massed against him, so much more powerful than his skill.
Men were shouting, halyards creaking, waves crashing on waves, and the sky
roared with thunder. Billows, rearing upright, seemed to touch the sky and
dash the gathered clouds with spray. One moment the sea ran yellow with sand
churned up from its depths; the next it was blacker than the Styx, then flat and
white with hissing foam.

Hurled about in this tumult, the Trachinian ship, now lifted up, seemed to
look down into valleys from a mountain peak, even into the bottom of an
abyss; then, plunged down and towered over by gigantic walls of water, it
seemed to peer up at the vault of heaven from seas of hell. Constantly pounded
by waves, the ships' sides groaned and cracked, battered like the walls of a
citadel smashed by an iron battering ram or a bullet-slinging catapult.

And just as fierce lions, coiled to spring, leap chest-first at bristling swords
and spears, so the waves, roused to fury by the winds and looming over the
ship, crashed against its hull. The wedges keeping the planks in place worked
loose, and, with the caulking gone, cracks appeared and let in deadly water.

Suddenly the clouds opened, spilling rain in sheets, and you would think
the entire sky had come down into the sea and the swollen waters of the deep
had risen to the sky. The sails of the ship were sodden, and rain and sea were
mixed to make all water one. The fiery stars were doused, and the night, already dark, grew darker still from the blackness of the storm, though flashes
of lightning shot through the black, making a blazing light that seemed to set
the sea on fire.

Waves now leaped into the hollow ship: As a soldier, braver than his comrades, attempts again and again to jump up onto the wall of a city under siege
and finally succeeds and, fired with love of glory, alone among a thousand men
occupies that wall, so when waves had nine times battered the resisting hull,
the tenth wave, surging vaster still, crashed down upon the ship, not ceasing
to attack the weary vessel until it had poured over its walls and captured it.
Part of the sea was trying still to invade the ship, part was now inside.

And the sailors trembled the way a city trembles when soldiers outside its
walls tunnel beneath them while others inside hold the walls from within.
Their seamanship failed, their courage drained away, and the multitude of on-
coming waves seemed like so many deaths bursting in and breaking over them.

One sailor wept without restraint; another stood dazed, yet another called
those blessed who could look forward to a decent funeral. One seaman lifted
his eyes in vain to a sky he could not see, prayed to the gods, and vowed
offerings, begging for deliverance; another thought of his brother and his parents; a third thought of his children, his home, and all he was leaving behind.

---

*11.493: I read (and translate) *iubeatve velitve* with Anderson (1982a), Bömer, Haupt-Ehwald,
and Murphy rather than *iubeatve vetetve* with Miller-Goold.

Alcyone alone moved Ceyx. No name but Alcyone's was on his lips, and though he longed for her and no one else, he was glad she wasn't there. He would have liked to see the shores of his country, to look upon his home for one last time, but he didn't know where he was, for the raging sea was a maelstrom, with murkiness pouring down from the pitch-black clouds, obscuring the entire sky and doubling the darkness of the night.

A rain-soaked whirlwind snapped the mast in two and smashed the rudder. Next, a cresting wave, like a warrior vaunting over his spoils, looked down at the waves below, and then with the weight of an Athos or a Pindos, should someone pluck these mountains from their base and drop them into the open sea, crashed thunderously down, its weight and the force of its fall driving the ship to the bottom of the sea.

Most of the men were sucked under by the sinking ship and never rose to the surface again, meeting their fate below. Others clung to floating bits of wreckage. Ceyx himself held on to a fragment of the broken ship with the hand that used to hold a scepter, calling aloud to his father and father-in-law, but in vain.

But the name that was most on his lips as he tried to keep afloat was Alcyone's. Remembering her, he called her name again and again and longed for the waves to wash his lifeless body home to her so she could bury him with her loving hands. Struggling and gasping in the water, as often as the sea would let him he called Alcyone, so far away, even murmuring her name when he was underwater.

Suddenly, a black wave crested high above the swells, then broke and buried him beneath its flood. At dawn that day Ceyx's father, the morning star, was dark, and difficult to see. Because he could not leave the sky, he hid his face in a bed of clouds.

Aeolus' daughter Alcyone, meanwhile, unaware of the disaster that had engulfed her husband, was counting the nights and hurrying to finish the robe she was weaving for Ceyx to wear when he came home and the one she was weaving for herself, too, while she dreamed of his return, and dreamed in vain. She devoutly offered incense to all the gods, but returned again and again to the temple of Juno, approaching the altar of the goddess on behalf of her dear husband, who was no more, praying that he would be safe, praying that he would return to her, would love no one but her—but of all her prayers only the last was answered.

The goddess, though, could not endure Alcyone's supplication for her dead husband any longer, and to rid her altar of these beseeching hands to which death clung, she said to Iris: "Most faithful messenger of my words, go, go quickly to the drowsy home of Sleep and order him to send the ghost of the perished Ceyx to Alcyone in a dream to tell her what has happened." At Juno's command, Iris donned her cloak of a thousand hues and, trailing the brilliant colors of the rainbow down the sky, came to the palace of the king of slumber, hidden beneath the clouds, as Juno had ordered her to do.

Near the land of the Cimmerians a hollow cave runs deep into a mountain, the home and sacred hearth of idle Sleep, a place never touched by the rising sun, nor by the light of noon, nor by the rays of the sunset. Swirling mist and fog rise from the ground here and meet the dusk of an ever-fading day.

No watchful, crested cock calls the dawn with his crowing here, no restless dogs pierce the silence with their barking; no geese, more alert than dogs, shatter it with their honking. Here there are no wild beasts, no flocks, no branches rustling in the breeze, no babble of human voices. Deep silence lives here: There are only Lethe's murmuring waters, flowing from the base of a rock and rippling over a bed of pebbles, inviting sleep.

At the cave's entrance poppies and countless herbs were blooming, and from their juices night distilled sleep and scattered it with the dew through darkened lands. There wasn't a single door in the entire cave, lest hinges creak, nor a guard in the open doorway.

In the middle of the cave stood a high bed made of ebony, on which was spread a feather bolster covered with a dark counterpane, and on this bed the god himself lay sleeping, exhausted, dead to the world. Around him swirled ghostly dreams of all kinds, as many as the kernels of corn at harvest time or leaves in a forest or grains of sand on the seashore. Here Iris entered, brushing aside the dreams floating around her, her gleaming cloak lighting up the austere dwelling.

Slowly, with an effort, the god lifted his heavy eyelids, but then nodded off, letting his chin drop on his chest, then finally shook himself awake, raised himself on one elbow and asked Iris—for he recognized her—why she had come.

"Sleep," she began, "the world's repose, O Sleep, gentlest of the gods, you who are the soul's peace, whom worry flees, you who give bodies exhausted with grinding toil their ease and restore them for new labor: Summon the dream that can liken itself to living beings and order it to go in the form of King Ceyx to Alcyone in Hercules' city, Trachis, and put before her there a vision of the king's shipwreck. This by order of Juno."

Her mission accomplished, Iris left quickly, for she could no longer resist Sleep's power and felt drowsiness stealing over her, and so she fled, returning along a rainbow, the way she had come.

From his thousand sons Sleep chose to awaken Morpheus, the most artful imitator of the human form. None is more skilled than he in contriving a person's walk or voice or expressions. He can adopt the habits of dress and ways of speech of anyone at all, but he imitates human beings only. There's another son of Sleep who can become a wild animal, a bird, or a coiling serpent. This one the gods call Icelos, but mortals Phobetor. There is also a third, named Phantasos, with a different skill. He can change into earth or rock or water or wood—anything inanimate. These three dreams appear at night to kings and chieftains; other dreams wander among the common folk.

Their father, Sleep, passed over these and from all the brothers chose Morpheus alone to carry out the orders Iris brought. Then he lay back down, sinking into the depths of his bed, overcome by a delicious weariness.

Morpheus flew through the darkness of night on silent, soundless wings and quickly arrived in Trachis. Removing these, he assumed the figure of Ceyx and in that guise, ghastly pale like a corpse and stripped of clothing, stood over the bed of the king's poor wife, his beard sopping wet and water streaming down his head.

Then, leaning over her, tears running down his cheeks, he said: "Do you recognize your Ceyx, my poor darling? Or has death so changed my appearance? Take a good look: You know me, but instead of your husband you see your husband's ghost. Your prayers did not help me, Alcyone. I am dead! Don't count on my return: You will be disappointed.

"A stormy south wind seized my ship in the Aegean Sea, buffeted it with mighty blasts and broke it up, and waves filled my mouth as I called your name in vain. A trustworthy source brings you this news; you are not hearing idle rumor. It is I myself before you, telling you what happened to me. Come, wake up, shed tears for me, put on your mourning clothes, and let me not go down to the barren world below unwept!"

The voice Morpheus used in saying this sounded to Alycone exactly like her husband's. He also seemed to cry real tears, and his gestures were just like Ceyx's, too.

Groaning and weeping, she held out her arms to him in her sleep, trying to embrace him, but embraced only air, and cried out: "Wait! Please don't leave me! We shall go together!"

Awakened by the sound of her own voice and the vision of her husband, she sat up and looked around to see if he was there (servants, hearing her cry out, had brought in a light), for she had just now seen him. Finding him nowhere, she began beating her face with her fists and ripped open her nightgown and beat her breasts, too. Not bothering to let her hair down, she tore it out as it was, and when her old nurse asked her why she was so upset, she cried: "Alcyone's life is finished! Finished! She has died with her Ceyx! Don't try to console me! He has perished at sea! I saw him and I recognized him!

"I reached out my hands and tried to hold him as he left me. He was only a ghost, but even as a ghost it was clear who he was, the actual ghost of my husband. He did not look the way he usually does, it's true, nor did his face light up as it normally does. He was deathly pale and naked, and his hair was still dripping—oh, how awful a sight it was—when I saw him. In that wretched state he stood right there, himself!" And she looked around to see if there was any sign of him.

"It was this I had a premonition of, it was this I was afraid of, and I begged you, dearest husband, not to leave me and follow the winds. Since you were going away to die, you should at least have taken me with you. It would have been better for me to go with you, for then I would not have spent a moment of my life away from you, nor would we have died apart.

"Now I, too, have died, though far away; though far away, I, too, am tossed on the waves, and the sea holds me, too, though I am here. My heart would be more cruel than the sea itself if I struggled to prolong my life and fought to survive such grief! But I will not fight to live, and I will not abandon you, poor husband; and now, at least, I shall come to you as your companion, and one inscription on our tombstone will unite us, if not one urn. If my bones cannot lie with yours, at least my name will touch your name." Grief prevented more. She had punctuated every word with a blow to her breast while groaning from the depths of her stricken heart.

When morning came, Alcyone left the palace for the shore, returning sadly to the place where she had watched Ceyx sail away, and lingered there, saying to herself, "Here he cast off; here he kissed me good-bye." And as she recalled what had happened at each place and was gazing out to sea, she saw something far out that seemed like a body floating in the water, though she wasn't sure at first what it was. When a wave washed it a little closer (though it was still far away), it was clear it was a body. Not knowing who it was, she nevertheless took it as a sign, for it was some sad shipwrecked soul, and as though weeping for someone all unknown, in tears she said, "O you poor man, whoever you are, and your poor wife, too, if you have a wife."

The body drifted closer on the waves. As Alcyone continued looking at it, she became more and more disturbed. Oh! Now it was carried near the shore, now she saw it clearly enough to recognize it: It was her husband! "It's him!" she wailed, and tore her cheeks, her hair, her clothes, all at the same time, and reaching out with her trembling hands to him she wailed, "Is this the way, dearest husband, is this the way, poor one, that you return to me?"

A jetty had been built out into the water to break the angry assault of the incoming waves and check the force of the tide. Alcyone leaped up on this and—a miracle—she was flying! Beating the air with newborn wings, she skimmed the waves, a piteous bird, uttering plaintive, piercing cries from her slender beak as she flew.

She touched the mute and bloodless corpse, embracing the beloved limbs with her wings and kissing the cold lips with her hard beak, but in vain—or did Ceyx feel her kissing him? Was it merely the motion of the waves that made him seem to lift his head? It was hard for people there to say, but surely he did feel it, and at last, since the gods pitied them, they were both turned into birds.

Their love survived this change in their fate and still abides, and they are united still, even as birds. They mate and bear young, and for seven tranquil days in winter Alcyone broods on her nest floating on the water. At that time of year the sea is calm, for Aeolus guards the winds and keeps them in his cave, making sure that the sea is placid for his grandsons.[46]

An old man watched them flying over the wide sea together and spoke with admiration of the love they preserved to the end. Then someone nearby—or perhaps it was the same old man—said, "The bird you see there with the slender legs, gliding over the water" (pointing to a long-necked gull) "is of royal descent, and if you want to trace its ancestry back to the beginning, its forebears were Ilus, Assaracus, Ganymede, whom Jove carried off, old Laomedon, and Priam, whose bad luck it was to see Troy's last day.

"This bird was Hector's brother, and had he not met a strange fate when he was so young, perhaps his name would have been no less famous than Hector's, whose mother was Hecuba, daughter of Dymas, while the mother of Aesacus (the name of his brother) was Alexirhoe, daughter of twin-horned Granicus. She is said to have given birth to him in secret in the forests on Mount Ida.

"Aesacus hated cities and stayed away from his father's elegant court, preferring to live an unpretentious life in the country, in remote mountain areas, and appeared only rarely at gatherings in Ilium. But he wasn't a country lout, nor was his heart invulnerable to love, for he had often chased the river Cebren's daughter Hesperia through the forest.

"One day he caught sight of her drying her luxuriant hair in the sun by the banks of her father's river. As soon as he saw her, she ran away like a frightened doe fleeing a tawny wolf, or like a mallard, caught far from its home pond, that flees a hawk. The Trojan prince went after her, and while she ran from fear, he ran from love, staying right behind her. Suddenly, a snake hiding in the grass bit her on the foot as she sped by, injecting its venom into her, and she fell dead, her flight thus ended.

"Beside himself with grief, Aesacus took her lifeless body in his arms and cried bitterly: 'Oh why did I ever pursue you? I never feared this happening. It wasn't worth it, this conquest. Two of us killed you, you poor dear. The snake bit you, but I gave it the chance to. Consider me the guiltier of the two—unless by my death I console you for yours.' And he leaped from a cliff, the base of which had been eaten away by the pounding surf, into the sea.

"But the goddess Tethys pitied him, softened his fall, and covered him with feathers as he floated on the waves, and so he did not get the chance to die, as he wanted to do. Enraged that he was forced to live against his will, that an obstacle was placed before his soul when it wished to leave its wretched home, the young lover flew up on his new wings and again hurled himself into the water, but they lightened his fall.

"Furious, Aesacus dove headfirst into the sea again and again, trying to kill himself. His passion made him lean: His legs became long and jointed, his neck was lengthened, his head raised far above his body. Now he loves the sea and has acquired the name of 'diver' from always diving into it."[47]

BOOK TWELVE

Priam, father of Aesacus, went into mourning for his son, not knowing that he now had wings and was living still. Hector and his brothers, also grieving, needlessly offered sacrifices at the empty tomb that bore Aesacus' name. Paris, though, failed to appear for his sad duty. He soon returned, however, bringing to his country the wife he had stolen—and a lengthy war. For a thousand ships sailed after him, bearing the united forces pledged by the Pelasgians.*

They would have taken their vengeance sooner, if fierce winds had not made it impossible to cross the sea and held the fleet in Boeotia at the fishing port of Aulis as the fleet was about to sail. Here the Danaans† had prepared sacrifices to Jove, following the custom of their forebears, and when the fire on the ancient altar burned hot enough to make it glow, they saw a dark blue serpent slither up into a plane tree growing near the place where the sacrifices were being made. In a nest at the top of the tree there were eight baby birds, and all watched in amazement as the serpent seized them and greedily swallowed them down, along with the mother bird, hovering near her doomed brood.

But the seer Calchas, Thestor's son, understood the meaning of this sign and said: "Rejoice, Pelasgians! We shall conquer! Troy will fall, though we shall labor long and hard there," for he read the nine birds as nine years of war. The serpent, meanwhile, had coiled around a green branch of the tree and in that position turned to stone, the stone preserving the serpent's form.

A violent north wind went on blowing over the Boeotian waters and would not carry the war across to Asia. Some believed that Neptune was sparing Troy because he had built the city's walls, but not Calchas. For the seer knew the truth and would not keep silent: The wrath of the virgin goddess had to be placated by the blood of a virgin.

---

*12.7: "Pelasgian" refers to the indigenous people of Greece and was often applied to the Greeks generally (Haupt-Ehwald at 7.49, 1.358).

†12.13: "Danaans" is another name for the Greeks and often appears in the *Iliad*.

And so the common cause conquered a father's love; the king in Agamemnon conquered the father; and Iphigenia stood before the altar with the weeping priests, ready to let her innocent blood be shed. Then at last the goddess
was overcome, and she fashioned a cloud so no one could see, and during the
ritual, amid the crowd thronging the sacrifice, the babble of praying voices,
she put a doe, they say, in place of the Mycenean girl.

When Diana was appeased by this more suitable sacrifice, her wrath and the
wrath of the sea subsided together. Favorable winds then came to the thousand
ships, and after enduring much hardship they arrived at the Phrygian shore.*

There is a place in the middle of the universe, at the boundary shared by the
three parts of the world, earth, sea, and sky, where everything that happens can
be seen, no matter how far away, and where every voice reaches listening ears.
Rumor lives here, at the highest point, in a house she has chosen for herself.
She has given it numberless entrances and a thousand openings for windows,
but no windows or doors, and it lies wide open day and night. Built entirely
from clanging bronze, it echoes with every sound, repeats every voice, and
sends back everything it hears. There's no quiet at all inside this house, not a
bit of silence in any part of it, but there's no uproar either, only the constant
hum of voices, like the murmuring of the sea when you hear it far away, or
the rumble of rolling thunder when Jupiter tumbles black clouds one on top
of another.

A crowd of rumors jams the entrance hall, a floating multitude coming and
going, and thousands of them, false mixed with true, mill around and toss out
garbled accounts of things. Some of these rumors pour their stories into idle
ears; others carry their tales elsewhere, tales that grow as each adds something
new to what he has heard. There Gullibility dwells, and reckless Error, baseless
Joy and frantic Fears, fresh Faction, and Whispers of uncertain origin. Rumor
herself keeps her eye on the entire universe and sees all that happens on land,
at sea, and in the sky.

She had spread the word that Greek ships were approaching Troy with a
powerful force on board, so when the hostile army arrived, no one was surprised. The Trojans, guarding their shore, opposed the Greeks as they tried to
land, and there, Protesilaus, you fell to Hector's spear, fated to be the first to
die. The battle the Greeks fought that day cost them many men, and a brave
warrior's death introduced them to Hector. But the Trojans, too, with not a
little of their own blood shed, got a taste of what Greek power could do.

Soon the Sigean shore was red; soon Cycnus, Neptune's son, had sent a thousand men to their deaths; soon Achilles was upon the Trojans in his chariot,
and cut down entire battalions with thrusts of his ash spear from Mount Pelion.
Searching through the line for either Cycnus or Hector, he came upon Cycnus
and engaged him in battle. (Hector's death was delayed until the tenth year.)

---

*12.38: "the Phrygian shore": The kingdom and city of Troy were located in the region of
Phrygia.

Urging on his horses, making them strain their snowy necks against the yoke, Achilles aimed his chariot at the enemy and, brandishing his spear with his powerful arm, shouted, "Whoever you are, young man, console yourself as you die with the thought that you were slaughtered by Achilles from Thessaly!" Such was the boast of Aeacus' grandson, and his hefty spear followed hard upon his words. But though his aim was true and the spear went straight to its mark, the sharp iron point failed to pierce Cycnus, as though it were dull, and it only bruised his chest.

Then Cycnus: "Goddess-born—for I know you already from rumors that arrived before you did—why are you surprised that I have no wound?" (For Achilles *was* surprised.) "This helmet you see, with its tawny horsehair plume, this curved shield I hold in my left hand—these don't protect me. I only carry them for show. The god of war bears arms for the same reason. Even if I take off the armor that covers me, I'll still leave the field unscathed. It's worth something to be the son, not of a daughter of Nereus, but of the god who rules over Nereus, over his daughters, and over the entire sea."

With this he hurled his spear at Achilles, and it struck his curved shield and pierced the bronze surface and the first nine layers of cowhide, halting at the tenth and hanging there. The hero shook it off and again, with a powerful cast, threw a quivering shaft at Cycnus. Again, he was unhurt, unwounded. Not even with a third spear, not even with Cycnus standing exposed and offering himself as a target, could Achilles manage even to scratch him.

Now Achilles raged like a bull in the arena when it lowers its fearsome horns and lunges at the red cloak driving it mad—and learns it has missed it again. He examined the end of his spear to see if the iron head had fallen off: It was still there. "Is my arm so weak? Have I used up all the force I had before against this one man? For I certainly had great strength when I pulled down the walls of Lyrnesus; when I filled Tenedos and Eetion's city, Thebes, with the blood of their inhabitants; when the river Caicus ran red from the slaughter of its people; and the two times Telephus felt the work of my spear. Here, too, I've killed multitudes—I can see the pile of corpses I've heaped up on the shore—and I can kill still more."

And as though he hardly believed he had done these things, he hurled his spear at a common soldier, a Lycian named Menoetes standing in front of him, and the weapon punched through Menoetes' breastplate and pierced the chest beneath it. He was dead before his head hit the ground. Achilles wrenched his spear from the warm wound and exclaimed: "Now *that's* my hand! *That's* my spear! And now I'm going to use them on Cycnus, with this prayer: Let them have the same effect!" He threw his ash spear at Cycnus again, and did not miss, for the weapon thudded squarely against that hero's left shoulder but bounced off, as from a wall or solid rock. Seeing a trace of blood where the point of the spearhead had struck Cycnus, Achilles exulted, but for no reason: There was no wound: It was Menoetes' blood!

Achilles then jumped down from his chariot, roaring in his fury, his sword gleaming in his hand, ready to fight his ever-so-cool enemy hand to hand. He saw the holes his sword had made in Cycnus' shield and helmet—and he saw that he was dulling the blade against Cycnus' hard flesh. He could stand this no longer and raised his shield and began to beat the man in the face and over the head with his shield and the hilt of his sword, driving him back, keeping up the attack, confusing him, all over him without letup, stunning him.

Cycnus was trembling, his eyes swimming in darkness, and as he retreated, step by step, he backed up against a rock in the middle of the field. Lunging forward, Achilles bent him over it, spun him around violently, and knocked him to the ground. Then pinning him down with his shield, and with his knees in his chest, he jerked the chin strap of Cycnus' helmet beneath his chin, cutting off his air and choking him to death. He prepared to strip the corpse, but he saw that the armor was empty, for the god of the sea had changed Cycnus into the snow-white bird whose name he bears.*[48]

The battle and the toll it took required a respite of many days, and so each side laid down its arms and observed a truce. While Trojan sentries on the alert were guarding Trojan walls, and Greek sentries, likewise alert, were keeping watch over their trenches, a feast day occurred, and Achilles, to celebrate his victory over Cycnus, slaughtered a heifer and offered its blood to Pallas.† When he had placed its entrails on the altar fire, and their savor, pleasing to the gods, had risen to heaven, part of the meat was claimed for the sacrifice, while the rest was set out on tables.

Reclining on cushions, the chieftains gorged themselves on roasted flesh and banished both cares and thirst with wine. Then they diverted themselves, but not with the music of the lyre, nor with songs, nor by listening to the boxwood flute. Instead, they prolonged the evening in conversation, with courage as their subject. They recalled past battles, their own and their enemies', and took pleasure in telling and retelling, each in turn, stories about dangers met and overcome. For what else would Achilles talk about? What else would anyone talk about at great Achilles' lodging?

His recent victory over Cycnus was the foremost topic. It seemed fantastic to them all that no spear could break the young man's skin, that he could not be wounded, that his body dulled the blade that struck it. As the other Greeks and Achilles himself were wondering about this, Nestor said: "Cycnus is the only one in your time who was scornful of steel and impervious to any blow. But long ago I myself saw a man, Caeneus of Thessaly, take a thousand cuts and suffer not a scratch; yes, Thessalian Caeneus, who lived on Mount Othrys and was famous for his great feats. But what is even more amazing about him is that he was born a girl."

His listeners were struck by this strange phenomenon and asked Nestor to

---

*12.144–145: "the snow-white bird whose name he bears": *Cycnus* is the Latin word for "swan."

†12.151: Pallas is another name for Minerva.

relate the story, especially Achilles, who said: "Come tell us, for we all want to hear about it, my eloquent old friend, voice of wisdom in our time. Who was this Caeneus? And why was his sex changed? What campaign do you know him from? What battle? Who vanquished him, if anyone ever did?"

"Although the burden of old age makes it difficult for me to remember," the old man replied, "and I've forgotten much that I saw when I was young, even so there is much I can still recall, and nothing has remained in my mind longer among all the things that have happened in war and peace.* And if it's true that a long old age makes you a witness to a multitude of events, well, I've lived two hundred years and I'm now in my third century.

"Elatus' daughter, Caenis, was famous for her beauty. She was the loveliest of all the girls throughout Thessaly and the cities near yours, Achilles—including yours as well, for she came from your city. Many suitors prayed for her to be theirs, but in vain. Peleus, too, would perhaps have tried to marry her, but he was either already married to your mother or she had been promised to him; at any rate, Caenis remained unmarried.

"One day, while she was walking along a deserted stretch of seashore, Neptune, the god of the sea, raped her (so the story goes), and since he had enjoyed making love to someone he had never made love to before, he said to her: 'Make a wish; I won't refuse it. Go ahead; ask for whatever you want!' And according to the same story Caenis replied, 'What you've done to me demands something extraordinary: I don't ever want this to happen to me again: I don't want to be female anymore. Give me that, and you'll give me all I'll ever want.' Her last words were in a deeper voice, a voice that could have been taken for a man's, as indeed it now was, for the god of the sea had already granted her wish and had also made it impossible for *him* ever to be wounded or to be killed by the sword.

"Thessalian Caeneus departed, rejoicing in his gift, and spent his days roaming the countryside around the Peneus River, doing the things men do.

"Now, when Pirithoüs, son of Ixion the foolhardy, married Hippodame, he invited the cloud-born beasts, the centaurs, to the wedding feast. They reclined at tables set up in a cave that trees gave shade to. The chieftains of Thessaly were there, as was I myself, and the festive palace echoed with the sounds of the thronging guests. The wedding hymn was sung, the entrance hall was filled with the smoke of wedding torches, and then the bride appeared, surrounded by her attendants, mothers and young wives, and she was more beautiful than them all.

"We told Pirithoüs how fortunate he was to have her as his wife—and nearly ruined the wedding's good omens. For you, Eurytus, most savage of the savage centaurs, were already heated with wine, and when you saw the girl you be-

---

*12.184–186: "nothing has remained in my mind longer," that is, longer than the story of Caeneus.

came twice as drunk with lust. In an instant the tables were overturned, the wedding feast was thrown into an uproar, and the new bride was brutally seized by the hair and carried off.

"It was Eurytus who seized Hippodame; and then each of the other centaurs grabbed any woman he took a liking to—or any woman he could grab—and the place looked like a captured city. The house was filled with the sound of women shrieking. We all jumped up at once, and Theseus, the first to speak, cried: 'Eurytus! What madness drives you to this? Do you think you can insult Pirithoüs with this outrage while I live? Don't you know that in attacking him you attack me?' To back up his words, he rushed into the midst of the raging centaurs, seized Hippodame, and carried her away.

"Saying nothing (for there was no way he could defend such actions), Eurytus went after the girl's noble protector and began beating him in the face and chest with his fists. An antique wine bowl carved with figures in high relief happened to be standing nearby. This wine bowl Theseus hoisted up—huge as it was, he himself was huger still—and brought it down squarely on Eurytus' head. Blood, brains, and wine spewed from his mouth and spurted from the wound, and the centaur fell on his back on the wet sand, legs kicking in the air.

"Enraged that their brother had been killed, all the centaurs shouted with one voice, 'Get him! Get him!' Wine gave them courage, and as the battle began, the air was filled with flying goblets, fragile wine jars, and round cauldrons, things originally made for banquets, now used for war and killing.

"Amycus, son of Ophion, led the way to the sanctuary of the house and without a moment's hesitation stripped it of the offerings there and, taking the lead again, seized a blazing candelabra from the shrine, raised it above his head the way a priest raises the sacrificial axe to bring it down on the bull's gleaming white neck, and bashed in the forehead of the Lapith Celadon, leaving his face an unrecognizable mass of shattered bone: His eyes popped out of his head, the front of his skull was crushed, and his nose was driven up into the roof of his mouth.

"Then Pelates of Pella broke off the leg of a table made from maple and knocked Amycus to the ground with it. As he lay on the floor with his chin driven into his chest, spitting teeth mixed with blood, Pelates hit him again and sent him to the underworld.

"Gryneus, standing nearby, fixed his fearsome gaze on the smoking altar and said to himself, 'Why not use this?' Picking it up, fire and all, he hurled it into the midst of the Lapiths, crushing two beneath it, Broteas and Orios. The mother of Orios was Mycale, who, people believed, when the crescent moon sought to rise, forced it to sink by means of incantations. 'You won't get away with this,' cried Exadius, 'if only I can find a spear!' And he did find a kind of spear, the antlers of a stag fastened to a tall pine tree as a votive offering. He stabbed Gryneus in both eyes with the twin branches of the antlers and pulled his eyes out, one eye stuck on an antler, the other rolling down onto his beard and hanging there in a clot of blood.

"Next, Rhoetus snatched a blazing plumwood brand from the middle of an altar and with it struck Charaxus a glancing blow on the right temple. The blond hair covering it caught fire and burned like a dry wheat field. The blood in the wound made a terrible sizzling sound, like red-hot iron when a blacksmith takes it from the forge with his curved tongs and plunges it into water: The iron sizzles and hisses and heats the water it's dipped in.

"In agony, Charaxus shook his head to put out the fire in his hair, then pulled the cave's stone threshold right up out of the ground (it weighed at least a ton) and hoisted it onto his shoulder: It was so heavy, in fact, that he couldn't heave it at his opponent, but dropped the massive stone instead on his companion, Cometes, who was standing closer to him. Laughing out loud Rhoetus said, 'I hope the rest of your comrades are as mighty as you are!' and renewed his attack with the half-burned firebrand and landed three or four solid blows on Charaxus' head and shattered his skull and drove it into his brain.

"Victorious, Rhoetus next attacked Euagrus, Corythus, and Dryas, and as Corythus fell—he was a boy with his first growth of beard—Euagrus cried, 'What glory have you won by killing a child?' Rhoetus didn't let him finish, but rammed the flaming torch into his open mouth even as he was speaking and buried it deep in his chest.

"Rhoetus pursued you, also, savage Dryas, swinging another torch around his head, but the outcome was different, for as he came at you, exulting in a string of slaughters, you stabbed him in the neck with a fire-hardened stake, at the place where the neck joins the shoulder. Screaming, he wrenched the stake from the bone with an effort and fled, soaked with his own blood.

"Orneus fled, too; and these also fled: Lycabas; Medon, who had been wounded in the right shoulder; Thaumas; Pisenor; Mermeros, who only recently had defeated all comers in a footrace (because of a wound he was running more slowly now); Pholus; Melaneus; Abas, a hunter of wild boars; and the seer Asbolos, who had tried to persuade his companions not to fight, but without success. Now he taunted Nessus, who was afraid of being wounded and who was also fleeing: 'You need not run away, Nessus; you're being saved for one of Hercules' arrows.' But Eurynomus, Lycidas, Areos, and Imbreus did not escape death: They were all killed fighting Dryas. You, too, Crenaeus, were hit facing your foe, so to speak, for though you had turned to flee, you looked back and were at that instant struck right between the eyes, at the place where nose and forehead meet.

"Amid this uproar Aphidas lay peacefully stretched out on a shaggy Ossaean bearskin sound asleep, a wine goblet about to slip from his limp fingers. But his absence from the battle helped him not at all, for, seeing him from a distance, Phorbas thrust his fingers in his spear thong and shouted, 'From now on you'll mix the water of the Styx with the wine you drink!' and hurled the shaft at the young centaur. The ash spear's iron head drove into his neck as he lay on his back, and he was dead and didn't know it, blood gushing from his throat onto the cushion he was lying on and into the goblet itself.

"I saw Petraeus trying to uproot an oak tree. He had put his arms around it and was shaking it this way and that, pulling and tugging and working it out of the ground, when Pirithoüs drove a lance between his ribs and pinned his chest to the tree as he wrestled with it.

"Lycus also fell, they say, at the hand of Pirithoüs, and Chromis fell, too, but Pirithoüs' victory over these brought him less glory than his victories over Dictys and Helops. He thrust his javelin in Helops' right ear, and it passed through his head and came out his left ear. As for Dictys, he slipped and fell from a mountain precipice while fleeing in terror from Pirithoüs, who was hot on his heels, and crashed headlong into a huge ash tree, breaking it and impaling himself on the splintered trunk. He had an avenger in Aphareus, who pulled up a boulder from the same mountain, intending to hurl it at Pirithoüs; but just as he was about to throw it, Theseus struck him on his mighty arm with the trunk of an oak tree, shattering his elbow.

"Without bothering to kill the crippled centaur, Theseus next leaped on the back of the imposing Bienor, where no one but the centaur himself was accustomed to ride and, digging his knees into the creature's flanks, grabbing his hair and winding it around his left hand, and pulling back the centaur's head, bashed it in with his gnarled club, shattering his face with its menacing scowl.

"Theseus then clubbed to the ground Nedymnus and Lycopes, the spear thrower; Hippasos, too, who had a beard down to his chest; Ripheus, who towered above the trees; and Thereus, who often trapped bears in the mountains of Thessaly and brought them home alive—and deeply offended.

"Demoleon could no longer endure Theseus' successes in battle and tried as hard as he could to uproot the thick trunk of an ancient pine to attack him with. Not succeeding, he broke off the top of the tree and hurled it at Theseus, but his opponent dodged the flying missile, warned by Pallas—or so he wanted people to believe. The tree, however, did not hit the ground in vain, for it sheared off tall Crantor's head and neck from his chest and shoulder. He had been your father's armor bearer, Achilles, whom Amyntor, king of the Dolopians, had given to Peleus as a pledge and guarantee of peace after your father defeated him in war.

"When Peleus, some distance away, saw Crantor cut in two with this hideous wound, he cried out: 'Crantor! Most cherished of young men! Here is a funeral offering for you,' and with all the power of his right arm hurled his ash spear straight at Demoleon, his wrath giving it added force. The spear punched through Demoleon's rib cage and hung there among his ribs, quivering. With a great effort he pulled out the shaft, but without the head, which was caught in one of his lungs.

"Pain itself fueled Demoleon's rage, and despite his wound he reared and struck at Peleus with his hooves. Protecting himself, his helmet and shield ringing from the blows raining down on them, Peleus raised his spear and thrust it through the centaur's forequarters and pierced its two chests.

"Peleus had already killed Phlegraeos and Hyles from a distance and Iphinous and Clanis up close. Now he added to these Dorylas, who, instead of carrying a savage spear, wore on his head a wolfskin cap fitted with curved bull's horns that were now very bloody. I had challenged Dorylas (for anger increased my strength): 'Test your horns against my spear!' and sent it flying. Unable to avoid it, he raised his hand to shield his head from the wound approaching, and the spear pinned his hand to his forehead. A shout went up, but Peleus (nearer to him than I was) stabbed him in the belly with his sword as he stood there, stuck to himself, immobilized by this awful wound. Dorylas leaped forward and with his free hand began savagely pulling his intestines out and onto the ground and trampling them with his hooves and tearing them apart, and he got his legs tangled in them and fell to the earth on his empty belly.

"Cyllaros, your beauty—if we grant that a creature like you can be beautiful—your beauty could not save you when you were fighting. Your beard was just beginning to grow—a golden beard—and golden hair hung down over your shoulders to the middle of your flanks. There was a graceful vigor in your face, and your neck, shoulders, hands, chest, and whatever else of yours was a man seemed like a beautiful sculpture. The horse beneath the man was no less perfect, no less handsome. Give it the head and neck of a horse, and it would be worthy even for Castor to ride, so inviting its back to sit on, so muscular its chest. It was black all over, blacker than pitch, except for its snow-white tail and gleaming white legs.

"Many females of his race wanted to possess him, but one alone had won his heart, and that was Hylonome, loveliest of the lady centaurs dwelling in the forest. She alone, by pleasing him, loving him, and always telling him she loved him, held Cyllaros' affection. The careful attention she gave to making herself attractive—to the degree a centauress can make herself attractive—also won his heart: the way she made her hair so smooth when she combed it; the way she tucked rosemary in it or violets or roses, or occasionally wore white lilies in it; the way she washed her face twice a day in the spring that fell from Pagasa's wooded summit and twice a day bathed her body in this stream; or the way she wore only the choicest and most becoming animal skins, draping them over her shoulder or her left flank.

"Equally in love, they roamed the mountains together, explored grottoes together, and at that time had entered the house of Pirithoüs together, and now were fighting fiercely, side by side.

"A spear came from the left—thrown by whom I don't know—and struck you in the chest, Cyllaros, just below the neck. Though a small wound, it was in the heart, and your heart went cold along with your entire body when the spear was pulled out.

"Hylonome rushed to cradle the dying form in her arms, covering the wound with her hand, and pressed her lips to his, trying to prevent his soul from escaping. But when she saw that her husband was dead, she said something that the uproar kept me from hearing and fell upon the spear that had just been pulled from his chest and died with her arms around him.

"I can also see before my eyes the figure of the centaur Phaeocomes, who had sewn together six lion skins to cover himself, man and horse. He hurled a tree trunk that a double yoke of oxen would have trouble budging and hit Tectaphos, son of Olenus, on top of his head, splitting it wide open. Through his mouth, nose, eyes, and ears Tectaphos' soft brain ran out, like curdled milk through a wicker basket or a pulpy liquid forced through the holes of a fine sieve.

"But I—as the centaur was about to strip the armor from the man lying at his feet (your father knows this well)—I buried my sword deep in his groin. Chthonius, too, and Teleboas fell to my sword, the former wielding a two-pronged branch, the latter a spear—in fact, he wounded me with that spear: Look! Here is the sign of it, the old scar from that wound, still visible.

"It was then I should have been sent to capture Troy; it was then I would have been able, if not to defeat great Hector, at least to slow him down. But Hector wasn't born then, or was just a boy, and now old age has taken its toll on me.

"Why tell about Periphas, who killed the centaur Pyraethus? Or about Ampyx, who drove his cornel spear without its point into the face of the centaur Echeclus? Macareus planted a crowbar in the chest of Erigdupus from Pelethronium and killed him, and I also remember how Nessus buried a hunting spear in the groin of Cymelus.

"Don't ever believe that all the son of Ampyx could do was tell the future—Mopsus, I mean. Oh no: Mopsus hurled his javelin, and the centaur Hodites found himself flat on the ground, trying to speak, his tongue pinned to his chin, his chin to his throat.

"Caeneus killed five centaurs in a row: Styphelus, Bromus, Antimachus, Elymus, and axe-wielding Pyracmus. I don't remember where he wounded them, but the number and the names are fixed in my mind.

"Then a centaur came speeding toward me at a gallop, wearing armor he had stripped from Halesus from Macedonia, whom he had just killed. It was Latreus, the largest of all the centaurs, with a huge body, huge arms, and huge legs. He was middle-aged but as strong as a man half as old, though gray at the temples. Commanding attention with Halesus' shield and sword and Macedonian pike, he wheeled in a tight circle, facing each side in turn, clashing these arms together and pouring a stream of taunts into the air. 'Eh! Caenis,* must I put up with you? To me you will always be a woman, to me you will always be—*Caenis*. Have you forgotten what you were at birth? Has it slipped your mind what you were rewarded for? What it cost you to take on the false appearance of a man? *Girl!* Remember what you were born as, what happened to you,

---

*12.470: Latreus calls Caeneus by the feminine form of his name, Caenis, which he bore as a girl. See 12.189ff.

girl! and go, take your distaff and basket of wool and do your spinning. Leave war to men.'

"As Latreus taunted him with insults, Caeneus let fly his spear, and it dug into the centaur's side, exposed as he turned around, where the man was joined to the horse. Furious with pain, Latreus struck the Thessalian youth in the face, which was unprotected, with his pike. But the pike bounced off, like hail from a roof, or a pebble dropped on the head of a drum. Latreus then galloped forward to attack him at close quarters and struggled to bury his sword in Caeneus' side, but it was unyielding, impervious to the weapon. 'You won't get away, even so!' he shouted. 'Since the point is dull, I'll carve you up with the blade!' And extending his arm he held the sword aslant and hacked at Caeneus' midsection with its sharp edge, and the blade clanged as though it had struck a marble statue and shattered against his hard skin.

"Invulnerable though he was, when he felt he had had enough from an astonished Latreus, Caeneus cried, 'Come now, let me try my steel on you!' and sank his deadly sword up to the hilt in the centaur's flank and turned and twisted the sword buried deep in his gut, making a new wound in the first one. With a fierce shout all the centaurs attacked Caeneus, enraged, hurling their spears or slashing him with their swords, but their weapons fell to the ground, the edges blunted: Not one of them had broken his skin, not one had drawn a drop of his blood.

"This amazing state of affairs left the centaurs stunned. 'What a disgrace!' Monychus exclaimed. 'We, an entire people, are being beaten by just one man, and hardly a man at that! Well, I concede he's a man, but we, we're weak as water, we're what he was! These mighty limbs of ours—what are they good for? What good is our double strength, the twin natures that unite in us the most powerful creatures on earth? I cannot believe our mother was a goddess, our father was Ixion, a man so daring he expected to conquer towering Juno. We are being beaten by an enemy who is only half a man! Roll boulders on him! Tree trunks! Entire mountains! Heap whole forests on him and smash that life that keeps on living! Crush his head beneath that mass and let its weight serve for wounds!'

"He found a tree that had been blown down by the furious blasts of the south wind and hurled it at his powerful foe. The other centaurs hurled trees, too, and soon Mount Othrys was bereft of forests and Mount Pelion bare of shade.

"Buried beneath the trees heaped upon him, Caeneus, sweltering in the heat, struggled to lift them with his hardened shoulders. But after the pile had grown above his face and head and he could no longer breathe, he began to weaken, though at times he would still make a feeble effort to raise himself above the trees and throw them off, and he would move them, just like Mount Ida— look, we can see it from here—whenever its steep slopes are shaken by an earthquake.

"As for what happened next, no one knows for sure. Some say Caeneus' body was forced down by the mass of trees into the underworld below. Mopsus, son of Ampyx, disagreed, for he said he saw a bird with tawny wings rise free from the heaped-up trees into the air, a bird that I myself caught sight of then for the first and only time. Mopsus watched it circling slowly above its comrades, making loud cries, and as he followed it with his eyes, focusing on it, he cried: All hail, glory of the Lapith nation, once the greatest of men, but now a singular bird: Caeneus, hail to you!'

"Because it was Mopsus who said it, we believed it, and we were now enraged that so many had joined in crushing just one man, sorrow feeding our wrath. Nor did we cease venting our rage with our swords until we had killed many of the centaurs. The rest stole away in the night."

When Nestor finished the story of the battle of the Lapiths and half-human centaurs, Tlepolemus, angry that his father Hercules, grandson of Alceus, had been overlooked and unable to hide his anger, cried out, "I'm amazed, old sir, that you could have forgotten to pay homage to my father, Hercules, because he certainly told me many, many times that he had defeated the cloud-born centaurs."

Nestor replied, sadly: "Why do you force me to recall troubles from the past, to lay bare sorrows buried by time, and to mention my hatred for your father and the harm he did to me? God knows he accomplished things that are beyond belief, and the world is full of his benefactions—I would prefer to deny it if I could, but I cannot.

"But neither are we singing the praises of Deiphobus or Polydamas or Hector himself, for who would want to praise his enemy? That father of yours once demolished the walls of Messenia, destroyed the cities of Elis and Pylos for no reason, and subjected my own home to fire and sword. And without mentioning others whom he killed—there were twelve of us, sons of Neleus, outstanding young men all, and all twelve fell at the hands of Hercules, except for me alone—and although I accept their defeat, Periclymenus' death was truly astonishing. For Neptune, father of Neleus' line, had given Periclymenus the ability to assume any shape he wanted and then to change back into his own self once again. After trying every conceivable form to no avail, he turned himself into the bird that carries the thunderbolt in his claws, the favorite bird of the king of the gods, and, using all his eagle's strength, flew at Hercules' face, attacking him with wings, hooked beak, sharp talons, everything.

"The Tirynthian aimed his all-too-accurate bow at him as he soared high among the clouds and hung there, and hit him where one of his wings joined his body, not a serious wound, but the arrow struck a tendon and tore it, and he could not flap his wings and fly. Without lift from his failing wings, he fell to the earth, and the slender arrow was driven into his body by the impact and emerged from the left side near his throat.

"Do you *still* think I am obliged to proclaim the exploits of your father, Hercules, illustrious admiral of the fleet from Rhodes? But except for keeping silent about his mighty deeds I seek no vengeance for my brothers. My friendship with you, is firm." Thus the eloquent Nestor. After the old man's story, they drank another round of wine, then rose from their couches and gave the rest of the night to sleep.[49]

But the god who controls the sea with his trident was brooding in his father's heart about his son Cycnus, turned into a swan, Phaethon's bird, and in his hatred of savage Achilles nursed a wrath that was unforgetting, a wrath beyond anything human.

With the war drawn out for almost ten years now he addressed Apollo, the long-haired Sminthian god*: "You whom I love most of my brother's sons, you who built the walls of Troy with me—wasted labor! Are you not sad when you look upon this citadel, about to fall any moment now? Do you not grieve for all the many thousands killed defending these walls? And—not to mention everything—do you never think of Hector, who was dragged around his own city after he was killed?

"Yet that ferocious man, Achilles, crueller than war itself, destroyer of our handiwork—this Achilles still lives! Just let him face me: He'll see what my trident can do! But since I'm not allowed to fight my enemy hand to hand, Apollo, *you* kill him with an unseen arrow when he least expects it!"

Apollo agreed, and in order to carry out his uncle's intentions—and his own—wrapped himself in a cloud and entered the ranks of the Trojans. In the midst of the slaughter he caught sight of Paris, shooting an arrow occasionally at one Greek or another. Revealing himself as a god, Apollo said to him: "Why waste your arrows on the rank and file? If you have any feeling for your own flesh and blood, attack Aeacus' grandson, Achilles, and avenge your slain brothers!" Pointing out the son of Peleus, busily cutting down Trojans with his sword, he aimed Paris' bow for him at the Greek champion and with deadly accuracy guided an arrow right to its mark.

If anything could make Priam happy after Hector's death, this death could. And so, Achilles, conqueror of such great heroes, you were yourself conquered by the cowardly ravisher of a Greek wife! But if you had to die in battle with a woman, you would prefer to have fallen under the axe of Penthesilea.

Now this terror to the Trojans, the glory and the protector of the Pelasgian people, grandson of Aeacus, hero invincible in war, was committed to the flames, and the god who forged his armor in fire, this same god now burned his body in fire, and great Achilles is ashes now, and little remains of him, hardly enough to fill an urn. But his fame lives on, and it fills the entire world. His fame gives the true measure of the man; through it he remains what he was and does not feel the emptiness of Hades.

---

*12.585: "Sminthian god": Sminthian is an epithet of Apollo that appears first at *Iliad* 1.39 (and rarely thereafter) and refers either to a town called Sminthe in the region around Troy or to the Mysian word *sminthos*, "mouse," and to Apollo's role as "'mouse-god' or protector against mice" (Kirk [1985b] at *Iliad* 1.39, 57).

Even his shield itself—so you can know whom it once belonged to—started a war, and men took up arms over his arms. Neither Diomedes nor Ajax son of Oileus dared to demand them, nor Atreus' younger son, nor his elder son, the greater warrior, nor any others. Only the sons of Telamon and Laertes* believed, each one, that he alone deserved so great an honor.

Tantalus' descendant, Agamemnon, removed from himself the hateful burden of chosing between the two warriors and, ordering the Greek chieftains to take seats in the middle of the camp, handed over to them the judgment of the case.[50]

*12.624–625: The son of Telamon is the Greater Ajax, thus to be distinguished from the Lesser Ajax, son of Oileus, just mentioned (12.622). The son of Laertes, of course, is Ulysses.

BOOK THIRTEEN

The chieftains then sat down, while the common soldiers stood in a circle behind them. Ajax, lord of the sevenfold ox-hide shield, then rose up before them, trembling with rage and scowling fiercely. Looking out toward the Sigean shore and the fleet drawn up there, he pointed to the ships and exclaimed: "By Jupiter! Here I am making my case in front of our ships—and to think that Ulysses contends with me! He certainly wasn't slow to fall back before Hector and the fire he brought to these ships, but I faced Hector's flames, and I turned them away from the fleet. It's safer to wage war with words you've invented than to take up real arms and fight. Well, speaking doesn't come naturally to me, nor action to him! My strength you will see in battle where the fighting's most fierce, his strength—in talking.

"I don't think I need to recall to you all I've done, my fellow Greeks, for you've seen it. But let Ulysses tell you what he's done, for his deeds have no witnesses—except the night! Without a doubt, the prize I'm seeking is a great one; but a contender for it like him destroys its value. No matter how great it is, Ajax takes no pride in winning what Ulysses hopes to win. Yet he's already earned a reward for this contest, for when he loses, he will be known for competing with me.

"Now, if my courage were in doubt, I could still point to my noble ancestry: son of Telamon, who, under the command of brave Hercules, took Troy, then sailed to the shores of Colchis on board the *Argo*; and grandson of Aeacus, who renders justice to the silent multitudes in the place where Sisyphus struggles against his heavy stone. Most high Jupiter acknowledges Aeacus, accepts him as his own offspring: So Ajax is the great-grandson of Jupiter. Nor, Greeks, will this line of descent help my case if great Achilles is not included in it: He was my cousin; I seek what was my cousin's! Why, O son of Sisyphus—just like your father in theft and fraud—why are you planting an alien family's name into the line of Aeacus?

213

"Or will I be denied Achilles' arms because I joined the army first, because an informer did not force me to serve? Will Ulysses win them then, a man who joined the army last, tried to get out of serving by pretending to be mad till someone craftier than he—Palamedes—but more harmful to himself exposed the ruse of a cowardly mind and hauled him off to the war he tried to avoid? We cannot let him wear the finest armor there is, can we, when he wanted to wear none at all? And am I to go without honor, be deprived of an inheritance from my cousin, because I faced the dangers of war from the very first?

"I can only wish that his madness had been real—or believed—and that he had never come with us to the citadel of Troy, this instigator of crime! Then, Philoctetes son of Poeas, we would never have been guilty of abandoning you on Lemnos, where even now, they say, hiding deep within your cave in the forest, you move the very stones with your cries of agony and call down on the son of Laertes the punishment he deserves—punishment, if the gods exist, that you will not have called down in vain. Even now that poor man who took the oath of war along with the rest of us, one of our own chieftains, inheritor of the bow of Hercules—that man is even now broken by disease and hunger, wears the feathers of the birds he eats, and uses up arrows to hunt them that were intended for bringing down Troy. He's still alive, though, *because* he didn't come here with Ulysses.

"Poor Palamedes would certainly prefer to have been left behind. He would still be living, too—or at least would have died without being accused of a crime he did not commit. Ulysses, however, never forgot that Palamedes—at risk to his own life—exposed his madness, and made up a story that he had betrayed the Greek cause. As proof of this crime that never occurred, Ulysses 'discovered' gold that he himself had planted earlier in Palamedes' tent. And so he has weakened the strength of the Greeks, by exile or by murder. That's the way Ulysses fights, that's the way he strikes terror in our enemies!

"Even if his eloquence outshines that of loyal old Nestor himself, he will never make me believe that deserting the veteran warrior was not a crime. Slow to leave the battlefield because of a wounded horse and exhausted because of his age, Nestor begged Ulysses to help him, but was betrayed by his comrade-in-arms. Diomedes knows I'm not inventing this outrage, for he berated his cowardly friend over and over, by name, rebuking him for running away.

"The gods look upon human actions with just eyes. Yes, they do! For the very one who would not help another later needed help himself, and just as he deserted Nestor, so he should have been deserted. He himself had made the rule that applied to him. But when he cried out to his comrades, I was at his side in an instant and saw him trembling, ashen with fear, and terrified that he was going to die. I held my huge shield over him, covering him as he lay on the ground, and saved his cowardly life. (No glory in that!)

"If you insist on competing with me, let's return to that time and place. Let's bring back the enemy, your wound, and your usual cowardice. Hide under my shield once more and there contend with me!

"He couldn't even stand because of his wound, but as soon as I saved him he got up and ran—his wound didn't slow him down then.

"When Hector appeared, bringing his gods into battle with him, and went on the attack, you weren't the only one terrified, Ulysses; brave men were, too: Such was the fear he inspired. As he exulted in his bloody slaughter, I hurled a huge stone at him and knocked him flat on his back; and when he demanded that someone fight him hand to hand, I alone dared to face him. In fact, Greeks, you prayed for the lot to choose me, and your prayers were answered. As for the outcome of our duel—he didn't defeat me.

"And now the Trojans attacked, brought steel, brought fire, brought Jupiter to the Greek ships. Where now was Ulysses with his facile tongue? Oh no, I was the one who took my stand in front of a thousand ships, your only hope of returning to Greece. Award me the arms for all these ships! And to tell the truth, the honor is greater for the arms than it is for me. It is actually a single glory for us both, and the arms are seeking Ajax, not Ajax the arms!

"To these actions of mine let the Ithacan compare his own: Rhesus and faint hearted Dolon, killed; Priam's son Helenus, captured, the Palladium, stolen; nothing done in daylight, nothing without Diomedes. If you're going to award the arms for exploits so second-rate, divide them up and let Diomedes have the larger share. What good are they to the Ithacan, who always does what he does in secret, without weapons, and uses tricks to get the better of an enemy not on his guard? The very brilliance of Achilles' gleaming gold helmet will reveal the traps Ulysses sets and give him away in his hiding place.

"But his neck won't even support the weight of Achilles' helmet, and the Pelian spear is too heavy for his puny arms. As for Achilles' shield, it has the whole world in its vastness engraved upon it and does not suit a coward's hand, made for stealing. This prize, in short, will wear you out; so why do you want it, O greedy man? And if a blunder by the Greeks gives you Achilles' arms, the enemy will have the chance to strip you of them, not fear you because of them. And when you run off the battlefield, the one thing you do better than anyone else, you master of cowardice, it will take you a lot longer, weighed down by such heavy gear.

"On top of all this, your shield, so rarely exposed to combat, is in mint condition, while mine has a thousand holes from all the spears that have struck it and needs to be replaced with a new one. But why do we have to debate this? Observe us in action! Heave that brave man's arms into the midst of the enemy, order us to go get them, and when they're brought back, award them to the one who brings them back." Thus the son of Telamon. An approving murmur rippling through the rank and file followed his last words.

The son of Laertes now stood up, studied the ground for a moment, then looked up at the chieftains, and in the voice they knew so well addressed them with grace and eloquence: "Oh my fellow Greeks, how I wish my prayers and yours had been answered! Then there would be no doubt about who should possess the great legacy now being contested, and you would have your arms,

Achilles, and we would have you. But now, since an unjust fate has taken him from me, and from you" (and with these words he made as if to wipe tears from his eyes), "who better should get the arms of great Achilles than the one who got great Achilles for the Greeks?

"But don't let this man here win points for appearing to be dense, which in fact he is, nor let it be counted against me, Greeks, that my brains have always served you well. My talent for words, such as it is—at the moment this talent is being used on behalf of the one who possesses it, but it has often been used on your behalf. So let no one resent it; a man should use the gifts he has.

"Now, as for birth and ancestors and things we did not ourselves do, I really don't think we ought to invoke them as somehow our own, but since Ajax has declared that he is the great-grandson of Jupiter, well, Jupiter is the founder of my line, too. I, too, am a great-grandson of the god, for Laertes was my father, Arcesius his, and Jupiter his—and neither was ever convicted of a crime or exiled. From my mother I have another claim to nobility in Mercury; so both my parents are descended from gods.

"But it isn't because I'm of higher birth on my mother's side, nor because my father is innocent of shedding his brother's blood that I lay claim to the arms we contend for here. Judge us on our merits, yes, but don't let it count in Ajax's favor that Telamon and Peleus were brothers: Don't let blood relations decide to whom you will award these arms taken from Achilles' body. No, let honor decide, honor and courage!

"Or if it's kinship, if it's the next-of-kin you're looking for as the heir, there's his father, Peleus; there's his son, Pyrrhus. Where does Ajax fit in? Let the arms be taken to Phthia, or to Scyrus! And isn't Teucer Achilles' cousin, just like Ajax? He isn't laying claim to the arms, though, is he? If he did lay claim to them, he wouldn't win them, would he?

"Since, therefore, this is strictly a contest about things we've done, I have indeed done more than I can easily cover in my words here; nevertheless, in telling about my achievements I shall let myself be guided by the order they occurred in.

"Achilles' mother, Thetis, daughter of Nereus, knew in advance of her son's death and disguised him by dressing him like a girl. She fooled everyone, including Ajax. But then I put some weapons among items strictly for girls, weapons I knew would surely arouse a man's heart, and when Achilles grabbed the sword and the shield—though he hadn't yet thrown off the dress he was wearing—I said to him, 'Goddess-born, Pergamum reserves herself for you to destroy! Why do you hold back from overturning mighty Troy?' And I laid my hand upon him, and I sent forth this brave young hero to do brave deeds.

"The things he's done, therefore, belong to me. And so it was I who brought down Telephus with a spear, and, when he was beaten and begged for his life, it was I who spared him. Thebes fell, because of me. Put the capture of Lesbos down as mine, also; and Tenedos, Chryse, and Cilla, Apollo's cities; and Scyrus, too. Say it was my hand that smashed the walls of Lyrnesus and leveled them with the ground. And—not to mention everything—I gave you the man who was able to kill fierce Hector, famous Hector. Hector lies dead now, thanks to me! In return for the arms I used to find Achilles, I now claim Achilles' arms. When he was alive I gave him those; now that he's dead, I ask for these.

"When all Greeks felt one man's grievous loss,* and a thousand ships filled the harbor at Aulis, winds long awaited never came, or came from the wrong direction for the fleet. A grim prophecy then ordered Agamemnon to offer his innocent daughter to cruel Diana. He refused, enraged at the gods themselves: This king was very much a father still. But I talked to him, managed to change his tender feelings toward his daughter and made him think of the common good. Indeed, I'll admit it now—and Agamemnon, please pardon me for this admission—I had a difficult case to make and a hostile judge to make it to; but, nevertheless, the people's interest, his brother, and his own absolute power moved him to trade his daughter's life for the coming glory.

"I was also dispatched to Iphigenia's mother. I did not have to ask her, only lie to her, but if the son of Telamon had gone there, our sails would still be waiting for winds.

"Later I was sent as an envoy on a daring mission to Ilium's citadel. I saw the senate house of lofty Troy, entered it while it was still full of warriors, and, without fear, presented our case to them, as the Greek nation had instructed me to do. I accused Paris and demanded that Helen and the treasure he had stolen be returned. My words moved Priam and also Antenor, who agreed with him, but Paris, his brothers, and those who joined him in abducting Helen could barely keep their criminal hands off me, as you well know, Menelaus, and that was the first time you and I faced danger together.

"It would take too long to remind you of all the counsel I gave you and all I did myself to help our cause, as the war dragged on. After our first engagements with the enemy, the Trojans kept themselves shut up inside their city walls for a long, long time, so there was no chance for open warfare. We fought, finally, in the tenth year. During all that time, Ajax, what did you do? Combat is all you know. What good were you? If you ask me what I did, I can tell you: I laid ambushes for the enemy; I fortified our trenches with a wall; I gave encouragement to my fellow soldiers to help them bear a long and dreary war with equanimity; I showed them how we were to provision and equip ourselves for battle; in short, I went where I was needed.

"And consider this: At the behest of Jupiter, our king—deceived by a dream—commands us to stop fighting and give up the war effort, can justify his order as coming from the god. Ajax should not allow this, should insist that Troy be destroyed, ought to do the one thing he can do: He should fight! Why won't he stop the men when they're about to go home? Why does he not

---

*13.181: The phrase "one man's grievous loss" refers to Menelaus' loss of Helen.

put on his armor and set an example for them to follow, since they're confused? Surely this was not too much for someone who never speaks except to boast! And can you believe it? He ran away himself! I saw you, Ajax, and it was an embarrassing sight to see, when you cut and ran and shamefully began to hoist your sails. I shouted to my comrades immediately: 'What are you doing? What madness drives you to abandon Troy when it's already captured? What will you carry home after ten years—except disgrace?' Using such words and others like them (despair itself made me eloquent), I led the deserters back from their ships, which were ready to sail away.

"Agamemnon assembled the terror-stricken allies. Even then the son of Telamon did not dare open his mouth. But Thersites dared—he dared to assail the kings, although, thanks to me, he paid for his impudence! I rose to my feet and rallied the quaking troops against the enemy and summoned back their lost courage. From that time on, whatever brave acts my opponent may possibly seem to have done I can take credit for, since I dragged him back when he took to his heels.

"Finally, Ajax, who among the Greeks praises you or seeks you out? Yet Diomedes includes me in all his actions, thinks highly of me, and is always confident when Ulysses goes with him. It's worth something to be the one picked out by Diomedes from so many thousands of Greek soldiers—nor was I chosen by lot and compelled to go! I scorned the dangers of the night and the enemy even so, and killed the Phrygian Dolon, who had boldly set out on a mission just like ours, but not before I forced him to betray his country and found out what the treacherous Trojans were getting ready to do. And now I had learned all I wanted to know, and there was no need to continue on. I could have returned then and claimed the honor I had been promised. But I wasn't satisfied, so I went on to the place where Rhesus had pitched his tents and slaughtered him in his own camp, and slaughtered his comrades, too. And then, after doing all I had set out to do, I mounted the chariot I had captured from Rhesus and drove it back to our camp as though I were leading a victory parade. Deny me the arms of Achilles, whose horses Dolon had demanded as a reward for his night patrol, and Ajax will turn out to be more generous than you.*

"Why mention Sarpedon's battalions, which I carved up with my sword when I brought down in bloody deaths Coeranus, son of Iphitus, Alastor, Chromius, Alcander, Halius, Noemon, and Prytanis; and when I killed Thoön, Chersidamas, Charops, and Ennomus, driven on by a harsh fate, and others less illustrious, who fell by my hand beneath the city walls?

"And I have wounds, too, fellow citizens, honorable ones, and they're in the right place. But don't take my word for it: Look!"—and pulling up his shirt—

---

*13.254: "Ajax will turn out to be more generous": At 13.102 Ajax had said, sarcastically, "[D]ivide them [the arms] up and let Diomedes have the larger share."

"See?" he said: "This chest has been in action for your sake! But Ajax has never, after all these years, lost one drop of his own blood for his comrades—has not received so much as a scratch! So what if he says that he fought both Trojans and Jupiter to protect the Greek ships? I grant it. He did fight. I am not mean-spirited; it is not my way to disparage what he's done for us. But he ought not to claim as his alone achievements we have all had a hand in. Let him give you some credit, too. For the record: Patroclus, safe in the armor of Achilles, pushed the Trojans back from the ships when they were about to go up in flames, along with Ajax their defender.

"He even supposes that he alone dared to meet Hector in battle, forgetting our king, other chieftains, and me as well, himself the ninth to volunteer for this duty, and then, when he was chosen, it was by the lot. Nevertheless, the outcome of your battle, O bravest of the brave, what was it? I will tell you: Hector left the field without a mark on him!

"But oh! How sad it is for me to be forced to recall the day that Achilles, the wall of the Greeks, fell! Neither tears nor grief nor fear stopped me from lifting his body from the ground and carrying it off the battlefield. On these shoulders, *these* shoulders, I say, I carried him, his armor with him, armor that now, too, I'm struggling to carry away. Heavy as it is, I have the strength for it, and I am sensitive enough, rest assured, to appreciate the honor you will confer upon me.

"Did the azure goddess solicit these gifts from heaven for her son so that a crude and unfeeling soldier could put on works made with such art? For Ajax is incapable of recognizing the engraving on the shield, the ocean and lands and stars in the lofty sky; the Pleiades and Hyades; and Arctus, which never dips into the sea; and so many different cities; and Orion's shining sword. He demands that he be given a set of arms he cannot even begin to understand!

"As for accusing me of avoiding service in a brutal war and of entering late in a struggle already begun, does he not realize he is maligning noble Achilles? For if you call pretending a crime, well, we both pretended. If we're to be blamed for coming late . . . I was here long before Achilles was. My loving wife detained me; his loving mother detained him. The first days of the war we gave to them, the rest to you. I shall hardly fear a charge, even one I cannot deny, when I share it with such a great man. In any case, Achilles was found out by the cleverness of Ulysses, but not Ulysses by the cleverness of Ajax.

"Let us not be surprised at the stream of stupid abuse he aims at me. He has shamefully insulted you as well. For let me ask you this: Was it despicable of me to accuse Palamedes falsely, but right and proper for you to condemn him? But he was unable to prove he was innocent of a crime at once so terrible and so obvious, nor were you relying on hearsay. You saw the evidence of his treason right there in the gold that was found.

"As for Philoctetes' confinement on Lemnos, I don't deserve to be accused of that; defend yourselves against that charge, for you agreed to it. I won't deny that I urged him to remove himself from an exhausting voyage and the toil of war and to try to rest and ease his fierce pain. He agreed, and he is alive today! My advice was sincere, and it was fortunate, too, though it's enough that it was sincere.

"The seers all say Philoctetes must be here for Troy to be destroyed, but don't ask me to go get him! Better to let Ajax go. Let him use his eloquence to mollify a man who is mad with pain and rage, or think up some clever ruse to bring him here! Well, Simois will flow backward, Mount Ida will stand treeless, and Greece will offer aid to Troy, before Ajax—should I cease to work on your behalf—before Ajax and his dull brain benefit the Greeks. Granted, hard-hearted Philoctetes, that you bitterly detest your comrades, the king, and me; granted that you curse me, would send me to hell forever, and in your present suffering long to get your hands on me and spill my blood, long for the chance to do to me what I did to you: I shall go after you, nevertheless, and make every effort to bring you back. With a little luck I'll possess your arrows, just as I got and held the Trojan priest, just as I revealed the will of the gods and the fate of Troy, just as I stole the image of Trojan Minerva from its sanctuary in the midst of the enemy.

"And Ajax contends with me?

"We all know the fates would not let us capture Troy unless we had that image. Where was brave Ajax then? Where were the mighty words of this great hero? What were you afraid of? Why was it Ulysses who dared to move out beyond our sentries and give himself to the night, cross the enemy lines, and not only pass inside the walls of Troy but even penetrate the heart of the citadel, seize the goddess from her temple, return through the enemy lines, and bring her back here? If I had not done all that, the son of Telamon would have borne his sevenfold ox-hide shield in vain. On that night, victory over Troy was won—by me, and I conquered Troy then, when I made it possible for Troy to be conquered.

"Stop making faces and whispering and pointing to my friend, Diomedes. Yes, he shares honors with me for that. You weren't alone, either, when you raised your shield to defend the allied fleet. Comrades by the score were massed at your side; only one stood at mine. And if Diomedes did not already know that a warrior eager to fight is less valuable than a thinking warrior, and that the prize is not automatically awarded to an invincible right arm, he himself would also be claiming these arms; the other Ajax, more modest than you, would claim them; and fierce Eurypylus; and Thoas, son of the illustrious Andraemon; and Idomeneus as well; and his countryman Meriones; and Menelaus, Agamemnon's younger brother—they would all lay claim to them. Why not? They are all brave men, as good as I am in war, but they yield to me in stratagems.

"Your right arm serves you well enough in battle, but your mind needs me to guide it. You use your great strength without thinking; I am always thinking about what's going to happen next. You know how to fight, but Agamemnon consults me on when to fight. You're valued for your great strength; I for my brains. I surpass you in the same way the captain of a ship ranks higher than the rowers, in the same way the general of an army is more important than the ordinary soldier. That is true of individuals, too: Brains are more powerful than brawn; true strength lies in the mind.

"And so, chieftains, award these arms now to your ever-watchful sentinel. Confer this honor in recognition of what I have done for you, for all the anxious years I have lived in constant worry. Our labor here is nearly finished. I have removed the obstacles fate put in our way, and by making it possible for Troy to be taken, I have taken Troy. And so I beg you—by our now common hopes, by the walls of Troy soon to fall, by the gods I recently took from our enemies, by whatever remains to be done that must be wisely done—if there is some bold and sudden stroke still to be looked for, if you think something is yet required for Troy's downfall, remember me! Or if you will not give the arms to me—give them to her!" And he pointed to the dread statue of Minerva.

The chieftains were moved, and their decision made it clear what eloquence could do, for a skillful speaker carried off a brave man's arms, and the warrior who faced Hector all alone, who withstood fire and sword and even Jupiter so many times, could not withstand his own anger; and grief and outrage now defeated an undefeated hero. He drew his sword and cried: "This, at least, is mine, or does Ulysses demand it for himself also? And now I must use this sword so often wet with Trojan blood upon myself; and it will now be wet with my blood, for no one but Ajax conquers Ajax." And he drove the deadly sword into his chest at a place where it was exposed—its first wound ever. No one could pull the great sword out, so deeply was it buried; the blood of Ajax itself expelled it, and from the earth soaked red with his gore the purple flower bloomed that first sprang up from the wound of Hyacinth. Its petals were marked with letters for the boy and the man, the lament of the one, the name of the other.*51

After his victory Ulysses sailed to the island of Lemnos, the domain of Hypsipyle and renowned Thoas and a place infamous for the murder of men long ago, to get the bow and arrows of Hercules. After he brought them and their owner† to the Greeks at Troy, a final effort was made to end this war at last. And now Troy fell, Priam fell, and Priam's poor wife, having lost everything else, now lost her human form and filled the air of a foreign land at the place where the narrows of the Hellespont begin with her terrible, strange barking. Ilium was burning, the fires had not yet gone out, and old Priam's meager blood

---

*13.392–398: 13.392: I read *ferro* with Anderson (1982a), Bömer, Haupt-Ehwald, and LaFaye, instead of *ferrum* with Miller-Goold. 13.394–398: The "purple flower" referred to is the hyacinth, which was inscribed with the letters *AI AI*, Apollo's lament (in Greek) and, when written together (*AIAI*), also the name of Ajax in the vocative case in Greek. See book 10.214–216.

†13.402: The "owner" of Hercules' bow is Philoctetes.

had trickled onto the altar of Jupiter. Apollo's priestess Cassandra, hauled out by the hair, was lifting her hands helplessly to heaven. The Trojan women remained in the burning temples as long as they could, embracing the statues of their country's gods, until the victorious Greeks, quarreling over their prizes, dragged them away. Astyanax was thrown down from the very tower where he used to watch his father, when his mother would point him out, fighting for his son, defending his ancestral kingdom.

And now the north wind invited the Greeks to depart, the sails of the ships were flapping in the freshening breeze, and the helmsmen ordered them to take advantage of the winds. "Farewell, my Troy!" the women cried, "We are being torn away from you," and they kissed the ground and left behind the smoking ruins of their fatherland. Hecuba was the last to go on board, so sad to see, discovered by Ulysses among her children's graves and pulled away, clutching at the gravestones, kissing the remains—though she managed to scoop up in her hands the ashes of one child, her son Hector's, and carry them with her in the folds of her robe. She left on his grave tufts of gray hair, torn from her head, a useless offering to his shade, gray hair and tears.

Thracians live in the land across from Phrygia, where Troy once was, and in that land stood the opulent palace of their king, Polymestor, to whom your father Priam entrusted you, Polydorus, to be reared in secret, far from Troy and the war, a wise precaution, if Priam had not also sent a large sum of gold to Polymestor, a temptation for a greedy soul, his for the price of murder. When Troy fell, the impious king of the Thracians seized a sword and buried it in the neck of his young ward and then, as though he could make the crime vanish with the corpse, hurled the lifeless body from a cliff into the sea.

Agamemnon had moored his fleet off the Thracian coast until the waters were calm and the winds more friendly. Here, suddenly, the ground broke open and from it Achilles emerged, as huge as he was in life, with the same threatening look on his face as on the day he made his wild and lawless attack upon Agamemnon.* "Greeks!" he cried, "You are sailing home without a thought for me; you buried your gratitude for my courage when you buried me! Stop! Don't let my grave go without its honor due: Kill Polyxena to soothe the shade of Achilles!"

His comrades obeyed the pitiless spirit, snatched Polyxena from her mother, Hecuba's, arms—the only child she had left to warm her heart—and led the brave, unlucky girl, whose courage they had never seen in a woman before, to Achilles' grave, and at this dreadful monument slaughtered her like an animal.

But she never forgot who she was, and when she was made to stand before the cruel altar, and it dawned on her that the barbaric ritual had been prepared for her, and when she saw Neoptolemus, waiting, sword in hand, his eyes fixed

---

*At 13.444 I read *iniusto*, sc. *ferro*, "lawless attack," with Bömer, Anderson (1982a), Haupt-Ehwald, and LaFaye, instead of *iniustum*, sc. *Agamemnona*, "lawless Agamemnon," with Miller-Goold.

on her face, she said: "Go ahead: Shed now this noble blood. Plunge your sword in my neck or in my breast!" (She bared her neck and breast as she spoke.) "For surely you know that I, Polyxena, would hardly wish to be any-one's slave, though with a sacrificial victim like me I doubt there's any god you will appease! I only wish my death could be kept from my mother. It is the thought of her that lessens my joy in dying, though it is not my death that should make her tremble, but her own life.

"You men, let me join the shades of the underworld a free woman. Stand away, I ask you; do not touch my virgin body with your male hands! The blood of one who is free will be more acceptable to whoever it is you are preparing to appease by slaughtering me. And if the last words I shall ever speak can move any of you (the daughter of King Priam makes this request, not some captive woman), return my body to my mother without ransom. Let her pay only with her tears for the sad right to bury her dead. Do not make her pay with gold!"

Thus Polyxena; and those present could not hold back their tears, though she held back her own. The priest himself was weeping as he drove the iron blade unwillingly into the breast she bared for him. She sank to the ground as her knees gave way, but with a look of high courage on her face to the very end she was careful even as she fell to keep herself covered and preserve her dignity and modesty.

The Trojan women gathered up her lifeless form and counted the number of Priam's children they had mourned, the many lives one house had lost to bloodshed. They wept for you, dear girl, and for you, Hecuba, once called royal wife and royal mother, once the image of Asia flourishing. Now you have the bitter luck to be a prize of war. The victor Ulysses would not have wanted her for himself had she not given birth to Hector. Hector paid a high price to find a master for his mother!

Hecuba took in her arms the body now bereft of such a brave spirit, and tears she had wept so many times for her country, for her sons, for her husband, she wept for this child, too. She let them fall in the wound, pressed her daughter's mouth to her own, beat her breasts, by now so used to blows, and, pulling out her gray hair, stiff with blood, she cried out again and again and finally this, as she tore her breasts with her nails: "Child of mine, your mother's final grief— for what have I left? O child of mine, there you lie, and I see your wound— my wound, too. Is it not clear to see? Lest I should lose a child to something else besides slaughter, you, too, have your wound.

"I thought that you, because you were a woman—I thought that you would be safe from the sword, but you fell by the sword, woman though you were. The very one who killed so many of your brothers killed you, too: Achilles, Ilium's destroyer—he has made orphans of us all.

"After he fell to the arrows of Paris and Apollo, I told myself that now, at least, we need not fear Achilles. But now, too, I see I ought to have feared him.

His very ashes, buried though he is, assault our race. We have felt his hatred, even from the grave. For Achilles I bore children!

"Mighty Ilium lies in the dust. With its sad fall the city's destruction ended, but it did end. For me alone does Troy still stand, and my grief goes on.

"Only yesterday I was at the height of fortune because of my husband, my sons, my sons' wives, and my sons-in-law. Today I am pulled away from the graves of my children and dragged into exile, helpless, a gift for Penelope, who will point me out to the wives of Ithaca as I card the wool I'm given every day. 'This is the famous mother of Hector,' she will say, 'and the wife of Priam.' After all those children I have lost, now you, who alone could lighten a mother's grief—you, too, have been killed, as a sacrifice at an enemy's tomb! I gave birth to a death gift for an enemy's shade. Why does this iron self live on? Why do I linger? Why, great age, do you keep me alive? Why, cruel gods, do you draw out an old woman's life, already too long, except to make me see new deaths?

"Who would think that Priam could be called a happy man after Troy was destroyed? But in his death he is happy! For he did not live to see you killed, my child, and he gave up his life and his kingdom at the same time. Your funeral will be your dowry, royal girl, and your body will be laid in an ancestral tomb. But that would be too lucky for this house. The only burial gift you will receive will be your mother's tears and a handful of foreign dust!

"I have lost everything. The only reason I can bear to live any longer is my one surviving child, dearest to my heart, once the youngest of my sons but now my only son, Polydorus, whom we sent to this land and put into the hands of the king of Thrace. But why am I so slow to clean these cruel wounds and wash from Polyxena's face the blood so brutally spilled?" And pulling at her white hair, she made her way to the shore with an old woman's halting step.

In a sad and pitiful voice she asked the women of Troy to give her an urn to draw water with. Then she saw the body of Polydorus, washed up on the shore, saw the gaping wounds that a Thracian sword had made. The women of Troy screamed, but Hecuba was mute with grief; grief itself choked her voice and swallowed the tears that welled up in her; and she froze, hard and still as stone, stared at the ground one moment, thrust her face, wild-eyed, toward the sky the next, then looked at the face of her son lying dead, and then looked at his wounds, especially his wounds. She armed herself with rage, put on rage like armor. As the fire of her wrath blazed, she resolved to get revenge, as though she were still a queen, and became the living image of punishment.

As a lioness rages when she has lost her nursing cub, finds the trail of the enemy she hasn't seen, and tracks him down, so Hecuba, her grief compounded now with wrath, recalled her courage, forgot her age, went to find Polymestor, who had committed this brutal crime, and asked to speak to him. She wanted, she said, to show him where gold was hidden that she intended for her son. The Thracian king believed her story and, drawn by his lust for loot, went with her to a remote place. Suave and cunning, he said to Hecuba:

"Hurry now, and give me this gold for your son. I swear by the gods in heaven, all you give me will go to him, just as it did before."

As he spoke, swearing falsely, she was glaring at him like a wild animal, and then, exploding with rage, she seized him and called the band of captive women to help her as she dug her fingers into his treacherous eyes and tore them from their sockets (rage gave her strength) and then plunged her hands, dripping with the villain's blood, into the sockets and gouged out, not his eyes, for they were gone, but the place where his eyes had been.

Enraged at the horrible violence done to their king, the Thracians attacked Hecuba with spears and stones, but she, with a low growl, tried to bite the rocks they threw at her and then, opening her mouth to speak, tried to speak, but barked instead. The place still exists and takes its name from what happened there.* As for Hecuba, long remembering her past suffering, she went howling pitifully through the fields of Thrace.

Her fate moved the Trojans, her own people, moved her enemies, the Greeks, and moved all the gods, too, yes, all of them, and even Juno herself, wife and sister of Jupiter, said Hecuba did not deserve what had happened to her.

But Aurora, though she had favored the Trojan cause, could not mourn Troy's downfall and Hecuba's misfortune, for she was racked by personal sorrow and grieved for Memnon, the son she had lost. The saffron goddess of the dawn had seen him go down on the plains of Troy beneath the spear of Achilles, saw it happen, and the color she reddens early morning with turned gray, and the sky was hidden in clouds. She could not bear to see Memnon laid on the funeral pyre for burning, and just as she was—her hair in disarray—she fell at the knees of great Jupiter without any shame and, weeping, said: "I am lower down in the scale than all the goddesses in golden heaven, and I have only a few temples throughout the world, but even so I am a goddess, and I've come, not to ask you to give me shrines and holy days for sacrifices to me and altars with fires burning on them. Still, if you would consider how much I, a woman, do for you when at first light every day I set a limit to the night, you would realize you ought to reward me in some way. But this is not what Aurora cares about right now, nor does she kneel before you to demand the honor she deserves. I have lost my son Memnon; that's why I'm here. He fought bravely for his uncle, King Priam, but in vain, and he died in the first years of his life at the hands of powerful Achilles—such was your will. O most high ruler of the gods, bestow upon him, I beg you, honor of some kind as solace for his death, and heal a mother's wounds!"

Jupiter granted her request. Instantly Memnon's towering pyre, engulfed in flames leaping high in the air, crashed to the ground. Thick smoke then bil-

---

*13.569–570: "The place . . . takes its name from what happened there": The name of the place in Greek is *Kynos sêma*, "Sign of the Dog" (Bömer at 13.569–570, 6.345).

lowed upward, darkening the sky like a dense fog that rises from a river and blots out the sun. Dark ashes, swirling, came together, formed a body, took shape, and drew heat and life from the fire. Its own lightness gave the figure wings, and at first like a bird, then as a real bird, it noisily flapped its wings, and then, with countless sister-birds formed in the same way and flapping their wings, too, this flock flew around the pyre three times, and three times the sound of their wings, beating in unison, rose on the air; the fourth time around they parted, made two groups, and like two warlike peoples flew at each other from opposite directions and fought, venting their rage with beak and talon, until their wings were exhausted as they battled breast to breast. As funeral offerings to Memnon and his ashes the kindred bodies fell, remembering their creation from so brave a man, who gave his name to these suddenly formed birds, called Memnonides, after him. And now every year, when the sun has traveled across the twelve signs of the zodiac, they battle each other once more and die, just as their father did.

And so, while Hecuba's barking seemed especially sad to others, Aurora was lost in her own sorrow and even now weeps for love of her son and bathes the entire world in the dew of her tears.[52]

Yet the fates did not allow all hope to be lost when Troy fell, for Aeneas, son of Venus, carried his sacred gods on his shoulders from the city, and carried something else sacred, his father, a venerable burden. From all the wealth of Troy the devoted son selected these as his share of the spoils and with his beloved son Ascanius escaped by sea from Antandros with a band of refugees on board a fleet of ships.

He sailed past the guilt-stained dwellings of Thrace and the ground soaked in the blood of Polydorus, and, helped by favoring winds and waves, he and his comrades entered Apollo's city.* There Anius, king of the people and priest of Apollo, received him at his temple and his palace and showed him the city, its famous shrines, and the two trees Latona once held on to when she was giving birth. After sprinkling incense on the flames of the altar fire, pouring wine on the incense, and duly burning the entrails of slaughtered cattle, they returned to the royal palace, where they reclined on cushions piled high, and made a meal of bread and wine, the gifts of Ceres and Bacchus.

Then devout Anchises said, "O worthy priest of Phoebus, am I mistaken, or did you not have a son and, as I recall, four daughters the first time I came to this palace?"

Sadly shaking his head, bound with the snow-white fillets of a priest, Anius replied: "No, you're not mistaken, great hero. You saw me then as the father of five children, and now—so much uncertainty buffets the affairs of human-kind—you see me nearly bereft of them all. For what good to me is my absent son, who lives now on the island Andros, named for him, and rules there in

---

*13.631: "Apollo's city" is on the island of Delos.

my place and on my behalf? Apollo gave him the gift of augury; Bacchus gave other gifts to my daughters, gifts greater than anyone could desire or believe possible, for everything they touched turned to grain, pure wine, and oil from Minerva's silvery tree, and our wealth was overflowing.

"But Agamemnon, sacker of Troy, learned about this—understand now that we, too, felt some part of the storm that broke over you—and he tore my daughters from me by force, against their will, and ordered them to feed the Greek fleet with their divine gift. They escaped, each going where she could, two to Euboea, two to their brother's island, Andros. Soldiers came there and threatened war if they were not delivered up. Fear conquered Andros' devotion to his sisters, and he surrendered them to the Greeks for punishment.

"You could forgive the timid brother. There was no Aeneas here to defend him, no Hector, who enabled you to hold out against the Greeks for ten long years. Just as the soldiers were about to bind the arms of the captive girls in chains, they raised their hands, still free, to heaven, crying, 'Father Bacchus, help us!' And the giver of their special gift did help them, if losing their human form in some strange way can be called 'helping.' I have never been able to find out how they were changed, nor can I tell you now, but I do know the unfortunate outcome: Growing wings, they turned into snowy doves, the birds that are so dear to your wife."*

While they ate they spoke of this and other matters, and after dinner the tables were removed, and they retired for the night.

Arising at daybreak, the Trojans went to consult the oracle of Phoebus Apollo, who ordered them to seek their ancient mother and their ancestral shores. The king sent them on their way and gave them gifts as they departed: a scepter for Anchises, a riding cape and quiver for his grandson, and for Aeneas a wine bowl, which a guest, Therses of Thebes, once brought to the king from Boeotia. Therses was the giver, but Alcon of Hyle had hammered it out and engraved an elaborate scene upon it: a city whose seven gates you could see; these were in place of its name and showed what city it was. In front of the city a funeral procession, burial mounds, fires and funeral pyres, mothers with hair down and breasts bared—all these signified mourning. Nymphs, too, seemed to weep and to bewail their dried-up springs; trees stood leafless and bare; goats gnawed at dry stones.

In the middle of Thebes (for that was the city), look, Alcon fashioned the two daughters of Orion: here, cutting their throats—not a wound for a woman—there, bravely stabbing themselves in the heart and dying for their people. Then they are carried through the city in a magnificent funeral cortege and cremated at a place where throngs have gathered. Lest the line die out, from the girls' still glowing ashes twin youths arise, to whom fame has given

---

*13.673–674: "birds that are so dear": Doves were sacred to Venus (Bömer at 13.673–674, 6.380).

the name "Coronae," and they lead the procession to inter their mothers' remains. Such were the figures gleaming on the antique bronze bowl; the top
was overlaid with a rugged border of gold acanthus leaves. In return, the Trojans offered gifts just as valuable. They gave the priest of Apollo a little box for
incense, a shallow bowl for pouring libations, and a gleaming golden crown
studded with precious stones.

Remembering their origin from the line of Teucer, the Trojans set sail for
Crete, but were unable to endure the island's climate for long. So they left
Crete's hundred cities, eager to reach the ports of Italy. Battered at sea by a
raging storm, the men took refuge in a harbor of the Strophades, though it
proved treacherous, for the winged harpy Aello drove them in terror from the
island. They now sailed past Dulichium, Ithaca, Samos, and Neritos and its
houses, all the kingdom of cunning Ulysses. They saw Ambracia, over which
the gods fought a contest, and also the stone into which the judge of the contest was changed. Ambracia now is famous for the temple of Actian Apollo.

They saw the land of Dodona with its talking oak, and the Chaonian bay,
where the sons of Munichus, king of the Molossians, escaped a violent and
fiery death on sudden wings. Next, they sailed toward the land of the Phaeacians, lush with orchards, and came to Epirus and the city of Buthrotum, a
second Troy, ruled by the Trojan seer Helenus.

Certain of their future after Helenus, the son of Priam, foretold it, they sailed
from there to three-cornered Sicily. One corner, Pachynos, faces the rainy
south; another, Lilybaeum, lies open to gentle west winds; and the third, Pelorus, looks toward the north wind and the Bears, which never touch the sea.
Here was the Trojans' landfall. Rowing with a favorable tide, they reached the
sandy shore of Zancle as night came on.[53]

The coast on the right is plagued by Scylla, the coast on the left by seething
Charybdis, which seizes ships and sucks them down, then spews them up
again. Now, Scylla, her belly disfigured by a girdle of fierce dogs growing from
it, has the face of a girl and actually was a girl at one time, if the tradition the
poets have left us is not entirely false. She had many suitors then but rejected
them all and would go to the nymphs of the sea (who were always delighted
to see her) and tell them about all the young would-be lovers she had eluded.

One day, Galatea, spreading her hair for Scylla to comb, heaved a sigh and
said: "You, dear girl, are pursued by the kind of men you would hardly consider
uncouth, and you can say no to them, as you do, without a second thought.
But consider my case: My father is Nereus; my mother, sea-blue Doris; and I
have a group of sisters who protect me; yet I was unable to escape the love of
a Cyclops without suffering for it," and her voice choked with sobs. The girl
wiped away Galatea's tears with a hand white as marble and consoled her, saying, "Tell me about it, dearest, don't hide your sorrow—you can trust me."

The nymph replied to Scylla, daughter of Crateis: "Acis was the son of Faunus and a nymph who was the daughter of Symaethus, and he was a source of

great joy to his father and mother, but an even greater joy to me, for he alone
had captured my affection. He was sixteen, with a trace of fine down on his
delicate cheeks, and very handsome. I pursued him, and the Cyclops pursued
me—day and night. And if you asked me, I really could not say which consumed me more, hatred of the Cyclops or love of Acis. My feelings were evenly
balanced. But oh, Venus! How powerful your dominion! For this crudest of
creatures, who made whole forests shudder, whom no stranger ever beheld
except at his own peril, and who had nothing but contempt for Olympus and
all its gods, this creature could feel love and burned with a powerful desire,
oblivious of his flocks and caves.

　"And now, Polyphemus, you pay attention to your appearance and try to
make yourself attractive. You comb your coarse and dirty hair with a rake and
happily trim your shaggy beard with a sickle; you look at your face in the
water, and your fierce expression softens. Your lust for killing, your brutish
nature, your mighty thirst for blood all subside, and ships now safely come
and go.

　"Telemus, meanwhile, sailed to the coast of Sicily, to the foot of Mount
Aetna, Telemus, son of Eurymus, who had never once misread a flight of birds.
He now approached the fearsome Polyphemus and said: 'That single eye you
have in the middle of your forehead: Ulysses is going to steal that eye from
you.' The giant laughed and replied: 'O dumbest of seers, how wrong you are!
Someone else—a girl—has stolen it already.' And so he mocked Telemus, who
was telling him the truth (though it did no good), and lumbered down the
shore, making huge tracks in the sand, and returned to his dark cave when he
grew tired.

　"A promontory extended out into the sea, shaped like a wedge and ending
in a long and narrow point, along each side of which waves washed to shore.
The brutish Cyclops climbed to the top (his woolly flocks followed of their
own accord), sat down, and, laying at his feet the pine tree he used for a staff—
so large you could fit it with yardarms and use it for a mast—took up his
shepherd's pipe, which he had made by fastening a hundred reeds together,
and now all the mountains and all the waves in the sea were deafened by his
shrill and whistling pipes. And I, lying hidden beneath a crag with my head in
the lap of my Acis, heard him singing miles away, and this, I remember, is the
song that he sang:

　"'O Galatea, fairer than snow-white leaves of privet, fresher than a meadow,
taller than the slender alder, brighter than crystal, friskier than a tender kid,
smoother than shells forever polished by the sea, more welcome than winter
sun or summer shade, fleeter than a gazelle, more striking than a lofty plane
tree, more brilliant than ice, sweeter than a ripened grape, softer than the down
of a swan, and smoother than the smoothest cream cheese, and, if you won't
run away from me, lovelier than a well-watered garden: Yet you, the same Galatea, are more savage than an untamed bull, harder than ancient oak, more

fickle than the sea, tougher than a willow branch or a bryony vine, harder to budge than these rocky cliffs, more violent than a river, prouder than a praised peacock, more painful than fire, pricklier than a thornbush, more ferocious than a she-bear with cubs, deafer than the ocean, angry as a snake that's been stepped on, and—what I wish so much that I could cure you of—not only quicker to flee than a nervous stag at the cry of dogs coming closer, but more fugitive than summer winds and a winged breeze.

"'But if only you knew me, you would be sorry you ran away, you would curse yourself for putting me off, and you would try hard to hold on to me. I have a natural cave, part of a mountain, made of hanging rock, where I feel neither the midsummer sun nor winter's cold. I have apples hanging heavy from their branches; I have grapes on the vine the color of gold; I have purple ones, too, and I'm saving both for you. With your own hands you will gather strawberries ripening in the forest shade and pick cherries in autumn and plums, too, not just purple ones with their dark juice, but also the finer ones, yellow as new wax.

"'When I'm your husband, you'll never lack for chestnuts or go without the fruit of the arbutus tree. Every tree, in fact, will be there to serve your pleasure. This entire flock of sheep belongs to me, and many more wander in the valleys. Still others are sheltered in the forest; many are penned in my caves. I couldn't tell you the number of sheep I have, not even if you asked me: Only a poor man counts his flocks! You may not believe me when I sing their praises, but once you're here you can see for yourself how, when they walk, they can barely swing their legs around their swollen udders.

"'And I have younglings, little lambs in cozy sheepfolds, and kids, too, the same age, in other folds. I always have a fresh supply of snow-white milk; some I set aside to drink, the rest I let rennet harden into curds.

"'I'll never give you easy-to-find pets, the ordinary kind of gifts: gazelles, hares, and goats or a pair of doves, or a nest taken from high in a tree. I found a set of twins on top of a mountain for you to play with, so much alike you can hardly tell them apart, the cubs of a shaggy mother bear. When I found them I said, "I'll keep these for my mistress."

"'Now raise your pretty head from the deep blue sea and come to me, Galatea—don't despise my gifts! Yes, I know what I look like, for I recently saw my reflection in water—I liked myself when I saw me! See how huge I am? Jupiter in the sky isn't any bigger than that—you're always mentioning some Jupiter who rules there.

"'A mass of hair hangs down over my wild and fearsome face and shades my shoulders like a grove of trees, and I'm hairy all over, from head to toe. You ought not think that's ugly. A tree without leaves is ugly; a horse is ugly without a mane spreading over its tawny neck. Birds are covered with feathers; sheep are dressed in wool. A beard and a hairy body look good on a man.

"'I have a single eye in the middle of my forehead, but it's like a huge shield.

What of it? Does not the great sun look down from the sky on all there is? Yet the sun has only a single eye.

"'And don't forget that my father rules the sea you and your sisters live in. I give him to you as your father-in-law. Only pity me and listen to me, begging you like a suppliant! For I've succumbed to your charms only; and I, who scorn Jupiter and heaven and his piercing thunderbolt, fear you, daughter of Nereus—your wrath is a lot fiercer than any thunderbolt. Yet I could endure your contempt if you said no to everyone. But why do you reject Cyclops and love Acis and want Acis to hold you in his arms instead of me? He may think he's attractive, and you may think he's attractive, Galatea, though I wish you didn't.

"'Give me half a chance and he'll realize my strength matches my size! I'll rip his living guts out, tear his arms and legs off, and scatter them over land and sea—your sea. (Let him make love to you then!) For I'm on fire, and passion spurned burns hotter still. I seem to carry Aetna, with all its raging heat, in my heart, and you, Galatea, are not the least bit moved.'

"After this long and useless lament he heaved himself to his feet (for I saw it all) and, like a bull in a fury because its cow has been taken away, could not stay in one place and went crashing through familiar forests and mountain pastures. When, as he raged, he saw Acis and me, unsuspecting and certainly fearing nothing like this, he bellowed, 'I see you two, and I'm going to make this the last time you'll ever make love!' His voice was as loud as an enraged Cyclops' voice can be, and Aetna trembled at the sound.

"I was terrified and dove into the sea nearby, but Acis turned and ran, crying: 'Help me, Galatea! Mother! Father! Help me! Mother! Father, save me! He's going to kill me!' And the Cyclops, running after Acis, broke off part of a mountain as he ran and hurled it at him, and though only a corner of the huge rock hit him, it crushed him completely. As for us, we did the only thing the fates would let us do. We enabled Acis to acquire the strength of his ancestors, and as his dark red blood flowed from under the massive mountain fragment, the redness faded, and first it became the color of a river churned by a rainstorm, and after a time ran clear. Then the mass split open, and a tall green reed sprang up through the gap, and from the cleft in the rock came the sound of gushing water. Then, wonder of wonders, a young man suddenly appeared, standing waist-deep in a stream, with pliant reeds wound round his new horns, and except that he was taller and his entire face was blue like the sea, it was Acis, but Acis now become a river, and the river has kept his name from that time so long ago."[54] When Galatea had finished her story, the gathering broke up and the Nereids swam away through the placid waters.

Scylla returned to the shore (for she did not dare entrust herself to the open sea) and either wandered naked along the wet sand, or, when she grew tired, found a remote inlet and there cooled off in its waters. Now, skimming over the waves, came Glaucus, a new inhabitant of the deep recently transformed in Anthedon opposite Euboea.* He saw the girl, was transfixed by desire, and said everything he could think of to keep her from running away. She ran away even so, and, sped on by fear, reached the top of a height near the shore, a huge mountain right by the sea that rose up into a single tree-covered summit extending far out over the water. Here she stopped and, feeling safe, and unsure whether Glaucus was monster or god, looked in awe at his sea-blue color, at the hair covering his shoulders and falling down his back, and at the lower part of his body, with the smooth and sinuous form of a fish.

Glaucus sensed what she was thinking and, resting on a large rock, said: "Girl, I'm no prodigy, no wild beast, but a god of the sea, and neither Proteus nor Triton nor Palaemon, son of Athamas, has more power in the deep than I do. I was once a mortal, but because I was bound for the sea, no doubt, even then the sea was the center of my life, and when I wasn't hauling in nets filled with fish, I was sitting on a jetty and fishing with a pole and line.

"There is a place where the shore is bordered by a green meadow: On one side is the sea, on the other, grass that heifers have never grazed on nor you, gentle sheep and shaggy goats, have ever cropped. No busy bee has ever gathered pollen from the flowers there, nor has the place ever yielded joyful garlands for anyone's head; nor have any hands ever swung a scythe there. I was the first to sit down in that meadow, while I dried my dripping nets, and in order to count the fish I had caught I laid them out in a row on the ground, those that chance had driven into my nets or naïveté onto my hook and line.

"As for what happened next—it sounds like something I might have made up, but why make up a story like this? As soon as the fish I had caught touched the grass, they began to move, to flop from one side to the other, and to wriggle on the ground the way they do in the water. And while I stopped and stared in amazement, my entire catch escaped back into the sea whence they had come, leaving behind their new master and the shore.

"I was dumbfounded and for a long time could not believe my eyes, and I asked myself whether some god had done this or whether it was the juice in the grass. 'What grass has the power to do this, anyway?' I wondered to myself and pulled up a handful, stuffed it in my mouth, and began to chew it. I had just swallowed some of the grass and its mysterious juice when I felt my heart beating wildly in my chest, and I was seized with a longing for a different nature. Unable to resist, I cried out: 'Farewell, earth! I shall never seek you again!' and dove into the water. The gods of the sea received me and honored me as one of them and asked Ocean and Tethys to take away my mortal qualities. These cleansed me by repeating a magical formula over me nine times to rid me of all my human impurities and then ordered me to immerse myself in a hundred rivers. At once, streams from every corner of the earth—whole seas

---

*13.905–906: "Glaucus, . . . recently transformed": Ovid mentions the metamorphosis of Glaucus at 7.232–233.

of water—rolled down over my head. What happened up to this point I can relate to you; up to this point I can remember; as for the rest, my mind's a blank.

"When I came to, I was changed: My entire body was different from what it had just been, nor was my mind the same. Then for the first time I saw this beard, the color of verdigris, saw this hair, which trails behind me in the sea, saw my huge shoulders and sea-blue arms, and saw my legs, which had fused and, tapering at the ends, become the tail of a fish.

"And yet, what good is this form, what good is it to be a pleasing sight to the gods of the sea, what good is it even to be a god, if you are not moved by this?" As Glaucus was speaking, as he was about to say more, Scylla left him and was gone. Furious, enraged by her rejection, he headed at once to the wondrous house of Circe, daughter of the Sun.[55]

BOOK FOURTEEN

And so Euboean Glaucus, now at home in the billows of the sea, had left behind Mount Aetna, hurled down, once, upon the giant's head, and the fields of the Cyclopes, untouched by hoe or plow and never trod by teams of oxen. He had also left Zancle behind, the walls of Rhegium opposite Zancle, and the perilous strait running between the twin shores that form the borders of Ausonia* and Sicily. From there his powerful strokes carried him across the Tyrrhenian Sea and brought him to Circe, daughter of the Sun, whose house, built on a grassy slope, was filled with wild animals of every kind. Seeing her, he greeted her and said: "Goddess, pity a god, I beg you! For you alone can bring to life this love of mine—if I seem worthy of it. No one, O daughter of the Sun, knows the power of your herbs better than I, for I was changed by them.

"This is the reason I'm angry (in case you don't already know): On the Italian shore, opposite the walls of Messene, I caught sight of Scylla, and I'm embarrassed to repeat the promises I made, the entreaties, the flattery I used, all the things I said—all of which she scorned. But if your sacred magic spells have any power, utter one for me; or if an herb of yours would be more likely to conquer her resistance, use its proven and effective power on my behalf. I'm not asking you to cure me and heal my wound. There's no need to end this passion; just make her share it."

No woman or goddess is more susceptible to love than Circe, either because of her nature or because Venus, angry at Circe's father for exposing her own indiscretion, made her that way, and now Circe replied: "It would be better for you to pursue someone who is willing, someone who wants the same things you do, someone overcome by a desire as strong as yours. Scylla should have made advances to you; you certainly deserve them, and if you held out a little hope, believe me, someone would make advances to you.

*14.6–7: Ausonia is a poetical name for Italy, from Ausonians, the primitive peoples who were the original inhabitants of Campania. (See *OLD* s.v. *Ausones*.)

234

"Trust in your own good looks; do not doubt them; for though I am a goddess, the daughter of the shining Sun, and though I can do much with spells and herbs, I want only to be yours. Reject the girl who has rejected you, love the one who loves you, and so with one stroke give each what she deserves." Such was Circe's response, an effort, really, to get Glaucus to love her.

He replied thus: "Trees will grow in the sea and seaweed on the mountaintops before my love will change, while Scylla lives."

Deeply offended, but unable to punish Glaucus—nor did she wish to, since she loved him—and hurt, too, by his rejection of her love, Circe turned her wrath on Scylla, whom he preferred to her. She set to work crushing some of her notorious herbs, the juices of which had frightening powers, while uttering a magic spell to blend with the mixture. She then donned a sea-blue cape and, passing through the horde of wild beasts fawning upon her, left her courtyard and headed for Rhegium, opposite the rocky shore of Zancle. Stepping onto the heaving swells, she walked on them as though on solid ground and so hastened over the sea with dry feet.

There was a small inlet, curved like a bow, a quiet place that Scylla loved, where she would often go to escape the restless sea and the sweltering sky when the sun, midway through the heavens, was at its highest and hottest and made the smallest shadows. Arriving before Scylla, the goddess poisoned this inlet with a virulent, monster-producing liquid that she had pressed from a noxious root and now sprinkled over the water, while repeating thrice nine times a magic spell, which she made unintelligible by scrambling its strange words.

Scylla came and waded into the water up to her waist. Looking down, she saw monstrous barking dogs underwater all around her body and, not realizing at first that they were attached to her, jumped back and tried to push them away, frightened by the vicious mouths. But when she moved, they moved with her, and feeling over her body—her thighs, her legs, her feet—instead of those familiar parts, she felt jaws like those of Cerberus and found herself standing on snarling dogs, her groin and abdomen grotesque, deformed by these creatures growing from them.

Glaucus wept at the sight, for he loved her, and fled from marriage with Circe, who had used the power of her magic herbs so cruelly. Scylla, however, remained in the inlet, and out of hatred for Circe snatched up several of Ulysses' companions when she had the chance to. Not long afterwards she would have sunk the Trojan fleet had she not been changed before then into a crag that rises from the sea and stands there still. As a rock, too, sailors avoid her.

When the Trojan ships had safely rowed past Scylla and ship-devouring Charybdis and had almost reached the Italian coast, they were driven by winds to the shores of Libya. There the Sidonian woman took Aeneas in—into her home and into her heart—and could not easily bear to lose her Phrygian husband. And so she erected a pyre as though to perform a sacred rite, climbed upon it, and fell on a sword and, herself deceived, deceived her own.[56]

Fleeing Dido's new city and sandy kingdom, Aeneas came back to Sicily, to the land of Eryx and to loyal Acestes and there performed a sacrifice to honor his father's grave. He then weighed anchor in ships that Iris, at Juno's command, had nearly destroyed by fire and sailed past Aeolus' kingdom, where fumes of burning sulfur rise from the ground, and past the rock of the Sirens, daughters of Achelous. After losing its helmsman, Aeneas' ship made its way past the islands of Inarime, Prochyte, and Pithecusae, dominated by a barren hill and taking its name from its inhabitants.* Because the father of the gods hated the fraud, deceit, and other crimes of the Cercopes, a treacherous people, he once changed the men into ugly animals, making them seem both like and unlike human beings: He shortened their legs, flattened their noses and turned them up, furrowed their faces with the wrinkles of old age, and covered their entire bodies with a shaggy coat of reddish hair. Jupiter sent them to this place, depriving them also of words and language, which they had once used for their wicked lies. He left them able only to screech and scream.

When Aeneas had passed by their dwellings and sailed past the walls of Parthenope on the right and the burial mound of musical Misenus, son of Aeolus, on the left, and the reed-filled marshes of the Cumaean shore, he entered the cave of the ancient sybil and asked her to let him go down through Avernus and visit his father's spirit. She fixed her eyes on the ground for a long time, then looked up and, filled with the prophesying fury of the god, spoke at last: "This is a great thing you ask me for, O doer of greatest deeds, whose fighting strength has been tested in battle, whose devotion to duty in the flames of Troy. Yet, Trojan, fear not. You will get what you are seeking. With me as your guide you will see the houses of Elysium and the world's final kingdom and come face to face with the shade of your dear father. No road is blocked for the brave."

She showed him the golden bough gleaming in the forest of Avernian Juno† and ordered him to pluck it from the tree on which it grew. Aeneas obeyed the sybil and then beheld the wealth of dreaded Pluto, saw his own forebears, and met the shade of his old father, noble Anchises. He learned, too, the laws that govern this place and the dangers he must face in new wars.

From there he climbed the ascending path, step by weary step, easing the toil by conversing with his Cumaean guide as they moved up the fearsome way through the dim twilight: "Whether you're actually a goddess or someone dear to the gods," he said, "I shall always think of you as godlike and always acknowledge my debt to you for letting me go to the home of the dead and, once I had seen them, come away again. In return for what you have done for me, when I reach the air above I shall raise a temple to you and burn incense in your honor."

*14.90: "Pithecusae . . . taking its name from its inhabitants": The name is from Greek *pithêkos*, "ape" or "monkey"; see Bömer at 14.88–90, 7.37.

†14.114: "Avernian Juno": The sybil refers to Proserpina, queen of the underworld (Haupt-Ehwald at 14.114, 2.364).

Looking back at him the priestess said with a sigh: "I am not a goddess, nor must you consider a human being worthy of sacred incense. Do not, in your ignorance, make that mistake about me: Phoebus Apollo loved me once and would have given me life eternal and without end if I had given myself to him. While he still hoped to have me and sought to overcome my resistance with gifts, he said to me, 'Girl of Cumae, ask me for anything, whatever you want; you will have your wish.' I scooped up a handful of dust and showed it to him and foolishly asked to live as many years as I held particles of dust in my hand. It did not occur to me to ask to remain young all those years. He granted my wish and said he would add eternal youth if I would let him make love to me. I rejected this second gift and remained a virgin. And then a happy life for me was gone, bitter old age with its halting step came in its place, and I have endured it and must still endure it for years to come. For I've now lived seven centuries, but to equal the particles of dust I must see three hundred more harvests, three hundred more vintages of new wine.

"A time will come when the endless number of my days will wear me down from what I am now, and my body, ravaged by age, will waste away almost to nothing. Nor will it seem then that I was once loved by a god, that a god once found me attractive. Apollo himself, perhaps, will not even recognize me then, or will deny he ever loved me, so much shall I have changed. Though no one will be able to see me, I'll still be known by my voice; only my voice will the fates leave me." And so, while they were making their way up the steep path, the sibyl told Trojan Aeneas her story, and then they emerged from the underworld at Euboean Cumae. After making the proper sacrifice, Aeneas approached the shore that was yet to be named for his agéd nurse.[57]

There Macareus from Neritos, a companion of that veteran Ulysses, had stayed behind after long and wearisome journeying. He recognized Achaemenides, abandoned once among the rocks of Aetna.* Coming upon him so unexpectedly, and surprised he was alive, Macareus asked him: "What chance, or what god, saved you, Achaemenides? Why is a Greek traveling aboard a barbarian vessel? What port is it making for?"

No longer wearing animal skins held together with thorns, and restored to his old self, Achaemenides replied: "May I once again see Polyphemus and those jaws of his, dripping with human blood, if I prefer my homeland and Ulysses' ship to this ship,† if I honor Aeneas less than my own father. For I can never repay him enough, even if I could offer him the world. That I'm alive and speaking to you and see the sky and the light of day—how could I ever be so ungrateful as to forget that? It was because of Aeneas that my life did not

---

*14.160–161: Achaemenides, "recognized" by Macareus, was a Greek who, as Virgil tells it, was left behind by Ulysses in the land of the Cyclopes after his encounter with Polyphemus (*Aeneid* 3.588–654).

†At 14.169 I read *Ithaci,* "the Ithacan's," that is, Ulysses', sc. "ship," with Anderson (1982a), Bömer, Haupt-Ehwald, and LaFaye, rather than *Ithace,* that is, "my homeland and Ithaca," with Miller-Gould.

end in the Cyclops' mouth, and even if I should die today, I would be buried in a grave—or at least not in that monster's belly.

"What do you think my state of mind was then, after I was left behind and saw you heading for the open sea—except that terror had taken away all sense and feeling? I wanted to cry out, but I was afraid I would give myself away to that fiend. As it was, Ulysses' shouting nearly sank your ship. I saw the Cyclops break off a great crag from a mountain and hurl it far out into the sea. I saw him throw with that giant arm of his another huge rock, which flew through the air like a missile launched from a catapult, and I was also terrified lest a wave or wind sink the ship, forgetting I was no longer on board.

"After all of you escaped from certain death, the Cyclops, groaning, stumbled his way over Aetna, groping through forests, blindly blundering into rocks,* and, pointing toward the sea with bloody hands, he cursed the Greek race: 'If only luck would somehow bring Ulysses back to me, or one of his companions for me to loose my wrath upon, I would eat his guts raw, tear his body in pieces, guzzle his blood, and grind his trembling limbs between my teeth. Then how light a thing, or nothing at all, would be this loss, my sight gone!' This and more from the fierce giant. I blanched in horror as I looked at his face, still smeared with blood from his feasting, looked at his cruel hands, looked at his empty, lightless eye, his body, and his beard, encrusted with human blood. Death was staring me in the face, but death itself was the least of my troubles. I was sure the Cyclops was going to snatch me up now and stuff my innards into his own, and an image was fixed in my mind: I saw the bodies of my comrades, smashed, two at a time, three and four times on the ground, while he himself, lying over them like a shaggy lion, greedily gobbled down their organs, their flesh and bones and marrow and arms and legs, still twitching. I was shaking all over, pale as a ghost, and in deep shock as I watched him chewing bloody pieces of human meat and spitting out gristle and belching up gobbets of wine-soaked flesh. I imagined he was preparing such a fate for me, and I hid for many days, trembling at every sound, fearing death, yet wishing to die, staving off hunger with nuts and grass mixed with leaves, alone, helpless, hopeless, and giving myself up to death.

"After a long time I saw this ship far out at sea and ran down to the shore and waved my arms, desperately signaling them to rescue me, and I moved them to pity. A Trojan ship took me, a Greek, on board! But now you too, dearest of friends, tell me what happened to you and your leader and to that collection of Greeks who entrusted their lives to the sea with you."

Macareus then told Achaemenides how Aeolus the son of Hippotes, who rules the Tuscan Sea and keeps the winds shut up in a prison, stuffed the winds into a leather bag and gave them, a memorable gift, to the Dulichian† leader,

---

*14.188 is a fine example of onomatapoeia: *ille quidem totam gemebundus obambulat Aetnam.*
†14.226: "Dulichian" refers to Dulichium, one of the islands in Ulysses' kingdom.

Ulysses, who then sailed with a favorable breeze for nine days and came in sight of his long-sought land. But when the tenth day dawned, his crew, overcome by greed and lust for booty and thinking that the bag with the winds was full of gold, untied it, the winds flew out and carried them back through the sea they had just now sailed across, and the ship returned to the harbor of the Aeolian tyrant.

"Next," he said, "we came to the ancient city of Lamos the Laestrygonian. Antiphates was the ruler of that land. Two other men and I were sent to him, with one of whom I barely escaped to safety; the blood of the other reddened that Laestrygonian's godless mouth. Antiphates then roused a group of men and came after us as we ran away, and together they hurled rocks and tree trunks at us, sinking nearly all our ships and drowning the men on board, except for the one ship that escaped, the ship that carried us and Ulysses himself. Grieving over the loss of our companions and weeping uncontrollably, we sailed to the island you can see in the distance. (Believe me, now that I've seen it up close, I can say that island should only be seen from a distance!)

"And now you, Aeneas, most fair-minded of all the Trojans, goddess-born—since the war is over I must not call you an enemy—I urge you, stay away from Circe's shores! When we anchored our ship at her island, we remembered Antiphates and the savage Cyclops and were unwilling to disembark. But a group of us was chosen by lot to approach that mysterious place, and I and loyal Polites, Eurylochus, and Elpenor—he was overfond of wine—and eighteen other crew members were sent to Circe's house. When we reached it and stood waiting at the door, a thousand wolves, she-bears, and lionesses ran up to us, terrifying us, but there was nothing to fear, for not one of them was even going to scratch us. In fact, they wagged their tails affectionately and followed us, rubbing up against us, while servant girls welcomed us and led us through the marble-roofed atrium to their mistress.

"Circe was sitting in a beautiful alcove on a magnificent throne, wearing a dazzling cloak, over which she had draped a shawl embroidered with gold. Nereids and nymphs, instead of carding wool and spinning thread with their nimble fingers, were sorting out plants and taking flowers and herbs of various colors from a heap and putting them into different baskets. The goddess herself oversaw the work they were doing. She knew what each of the leaves was to be used for and how to blend them in the proper proportions, and she carefully examined the herbs after they were weighed out.

"When she saw us, she greeted us with a smile and gave every sign of giving us whatever we wanted. She immediately ordered something for us to drink, a mixture of wine, honey, roasted barley grains, and grated cheese. The sweetness of the drink concealed the taste of the herbal extracts Circe secretly added to it. We took the cups she held out to us in her divine hand, and as soon as we had drained them—we were dying of thirst and our throats were parched—the cruel goddess lightly touched the tops of our heads with her wand, and, ashamed though I am to say it, I began to sprout bristles and was unable to talk; instead of saying words I could only grunt, and I found myself bent forward and facing the ground, felt my mouth hardening into a curved snout and the muscles in my neck swelling; and the hands that recently held the cup I was drinking from now made prints on the ground. I was shut up in a pigsty with my companions, who had suffered the same fate (so powerful were Circe's potions). The only one we saw who wasn't changed into a pig was Eurylochus. He alone avoided taking one of the cups Circe had given us, and if he hadn't refused it, I would still be part of that bristly herd of swine, and Ulysses would never have learned from him about our terrible misfortune and come to Circe to pay her back for this.

"Mercury, bringer of peaceful solutions, gave Ulysses a white flower with a black root that the gods call 'moly,' and, protected by this and armed with the god's warning, he entered Circe's house, where he was offered a cup of the treacherous mixture. When Circe attempted to touch his head with her wand, he shoved her away, drew his sword, and frightened her into submission. They then pledged not to harm each other and shook hands to seal their pledge.

"When Ulysses entered Circe's bedroom, he demanded that his comrades be restored as his 'wedding present.' So Circe sprinkled us with the juice of an unknown (but more powerful) herb, tapped us on the head with the other end of her wand, and uttered words to undo the original spell. As she intoned them, we began to rise from the ground and stand erect, our bristles fell away, the split in our cloven hoofs was healed, our shoulders returned, and our forearms reappeared beneath our upper arms. Weeping, we now embraced Ulysses, who was also weeping, and, hanging on his neck, with our very first words we thanked him profusely for rescuing us.

"We were delayed there for a year, and over such a long period I saw and heard many things, including a story told to me in secret by one of the four servants whom Circe had trained in her magic. For one day, while Circe and our leader were alone together, this servant showed me a white marble statue of a young man with a woodpecker on his head standing in a sacred shrine and adorned with many wreaths. Out of curiosity I asked who it was, why he was worshiped in a sacred shrine, and why he had a bird on his head. The servant replied: 'Listen, Macareus, and learn just how powerful my mistress is. Now pay attention to what I'm about to say.

"'Picus the son of Saturn was king in Ausonia and devoted himself to rearing horses for war. He looked just like that statue of him there. Observe how handsome it is, and in the carved image see the true one of the boy. His soul was just as beautiful. He was not quite old enough to have seen the quinquennial games in Elis four times,* but already dryads from the mountains of Latium

*14.323–325: At 14.323 I read *veram* (sc. *imaginem* from *imagine*) with Anderson (1982a), Bömer, Haupt-Ehwald, and LaFaye instead of *verum* with Miller-Goold. 14.325: "the quinquennial games in Elis": These are the Olympic games (an anachronism, since they were considered

had their eyes on him—on his handsome face. Already spring nymphs were pursuing him, and naiads, too: those from the river Albula and the waters of Numicius; from the Anio and the Almo, which flows but briefly; from the swiftly coursing Nar and the shady waters of the Farfar; and those naiads who live in the woodland pond of Scythian Diana and in the lakes nearby. He, though, disdained all these and loved one nymph alone, whom Venilia is said to have borne to Janus, who has two faces, on the Palatine.

"'As soon as this nymph had reached the age for marriage, she was betrothed to Laurentian Picus, whom she preferred to all others. She was a rare beauty, but rarer still was her gift as a singer, for which she had been given the name Canens.* With her songs she could move woods and rocks, soothe wild beasts, stop rivers from flowing, and make birds pause in their flight overhead.

"'One day while she was singing in her sweet girl's voice, Picus left their house and went to the Laurentian fields to hunt the boars that roam there. He rode a spirited horse, carried two hunting spears in his hand, and wore a purple cloak fastened with a clasp of yellow gold. Now, the daughter of the Sun had left the fields of Circe (named for her) and come into these same woods to gather new herbs from the lush hillsides. Hiding in a thicket, she saw the young man and was overcome by the sight of him. The herbs she had gathered fell from her hands and a flame seemed to penetrate to the very marrow of her bones. As soon as she recovered from this powerful surge of desire, she was about to confess her love to him, but the speed of his horse and his retinue all around him made it impossible for her to approach him. "You won't get away from me," she said, "even if you're carried on the wind—if I know myself, if the magic power of my herbs hasn't all vanished and my charms don't fail me."

"'She then fashioned an image of a boar and made it run in front of the king and then seem to enter a densely wooded grove where the underbrush was thickest and a horse could not get through. Not knowing it was a phantom, Picus was after the quarry at once, jumping down from the back of his foam-flecked horse and running into the forest on foot, pursuing a false hope. Circe then began conjuring with prayers, uttering magic words, and summoning mysterious gods with the equally mysterious spells that she always used to hide the face of the snow-white moon and draw a curtain of rainclouds across her father's face. Now, too, as she chanted a magic spell, the sky was filled with clouds, fog rose from the ground, and Picus' attendants, stumbling on paths they could not see, were no longer able to guard the king. Having now arranged the time and place, Circe said, "I beg you by those eyes of yours that have

---

to have begun—were reorganized, actually—in 776 B.C.), held every four years. Counting by Olympiads was a traditional way of reckoning time in antiquity. As Bömer notes, a *quinquennium* denotes, with reference to Greek festivals, a *pentetêris,* that is, a period of four years, for example, the Olympic games in Elis. Ovid, however, Bömer says, counts five years for a *quinquennium* at *Metamorphoses* 12.584 and 4.292 and reckons an Olympiad as five years at *Tristia* 4.10.95–96. In other words, Bömer concludes, Picus is about nineteen years old (at 14.324–325, 7.114–115).

*14.338: Canens means "singer" (from *cano,* "I sing").

captured mine, by those looks of yours, my beautiful one, that have made me, a goddess, your slave, indulge my passion, take the all-seeing Sun as your father-in-law; do not be hard-hearted and disdain a Titan's daughter."

"'But Picus vehemently rejected her and her prayers, adding: "Whoever you are, I don't belong to you. Another has captured my heart, and I pray she keeps it forever. Nor shall I injure our marriage bond by loving someone else, as long as fate keeps Janus' daughter Canens safe for me." Circe pleaded with him over and over, but in vain. "You'll pay for this," she said; "you'll never see Canens again, and you will learn the hard way what someone you've injured—what a lover, what a woman—can do, especially when that lover, when the one you've injured, when that woman is . . . *Circe!*"

"'She then turned twice toward the west, twice toward the east, touched Picus with her wand three times, and chanted three spells. Picus fled and was amazed to see himself running faster than he had ever run before. Then he noticed wings on his body and, outraged that he had suddenly become a new bird in the woods of Latium, began to hammer the trunk of a tough oak with his hard beak and in his fury drilled holes in the tree. His wings took on the purple color of his cloak, the golden clasp he had fastened it with turned into yellow feathers around his neck, and nothing of Picus' original self remained except his name.*

"'His companions, meanwhile, kept shouting "Picus" through the woods and fields, but in vain, for he was nowhere to be found. They found Circe instead (for she had cleared the air by allowing the winds and the sun to scatter the clouds), and they crowded around her, making accusations—rightly—and demanding that she produce their king. They threatened her with violence and were about to attack her with their deadly spears when she sprinkled them with noxious liquids and poisonous juices, summoned night and the gods of night from Erebus and Chaos, and prayed to Hecate with long howling cries. Trees in the forest (this was bizarre!) uprooted themselves; the earth groaned; an orchard nearby turned white; the plants she had sprinkled with her poisons dripped blood; stones seemed to bellow hoarsely; dogs barked; the ground crawled with black snakes; and ghostly spirits of the silent dead flitted all around them.

"'Picus' attendants were thunderstruck by these apparitions and quaked with fear. As they stood trembling, she touched their amazed faces with her poison-tipped wand, and from this touch monstrous wild beasts of all sorts entered the young mens' bodies, and not one of them retained his original form.

"'The setting sun had scattered its evening light on the shores of southern Spain: Canens watched and waited in vain for her husband to appear. Her own slaves and people from the town spread out through the forest, lanterns in hand, searching for Picus. Nor was the nymph satisfied to weep and tear her

*14.396: *picus* is Latin for "woodpecker."

hair and beat her breast. All this she did, and she also hurled herself out of doors and wandered distraught through the countryside of Latium for six days and nights without eating or sleeping, stumbling along the ridges and down the valleys, anywhere and everywhere chance led her.

"'Tiber was the last to see her. Worn out with loss and wandering, she flung herself down on his wide bank and there, weeping, poured out a stream of words in a high quavering voice, the voice of grief itself, as often a swan, soon to die, will sing a dirge. Finally, the very marrow of her bones dissolved into water from her deep sadness, and she melted and slowly disappeared like a vapor on a gentle breeze. Memory of her is kept alive by the place, which the ancient Muses* properly called "Canens," from the name of the nymph.' Such were the many stories I heard or things I saw during a long year.

"Idle now, and slow to get under way again because of our idleness, we were ordered to put out to sea. Circe had told us that a perilous course lay before us, an endless journey through the dangers of the savage sea. I was terrified, I admit, and when I reached this shore I planted myself here." Macareus had finished his tale.

The ashes of Aeneas' nurse Caieta were now placed in a marble urn, and this brief epitaph was inscribed upon her gravestone:

> *Here am I, Caieta: The boy I reared, known for his devotion,*
> *Saved me from the fire of the Greeks and burned my remains*
> *In their final fire, as it was his duty to do.*[58]

The Trojans loosed the hawsers from the grassy riverbank, left far behind the treacherous place where the notorious goddess lives, and made for the groves where the shady Tiber churns the yellow sand as it rushes into the sea. There Aeneas received from King Latinus, son of Faunus, both a warm welcome and the hand of his daughter in marriage, but not without resorting to arms. War was waged against a fierce people, whose leader, Turnus, battled furiously for the wife that had been promised to him.

All of Etruria entered the conflict against Latium, striving for a costly victory in a long and hard-fought campaign. Each side increased its forces with outside troops, and many came to reinforce the Rutulian camp, many the Trojan camp. Although Aeneas' journey to Evander's city was not in vain, Venulus traveled in vain to the stronghold of Diomedes, who was living in exile.

For Diomedes had founded a powerful city under the protection of Apulian Daunus and controlled the surrounding lands, a wedding gift from the father of his wife.† But when Venulus, carrying out the orders of Turnus, asked for help, the Aetolian hero declined, offering as an excuse his lack of forces. He

---

*14.434: "Muses" translates Ovid's *Camenae*, "Italian water deities . . . early identified with the Greek Muses," whose "name has in reality nothing to do with *cano* [I sing] or *carmen* [song], though the etymology was traditional" (Kenney [1986] 456).

†14.458–459: Diomedes' city is Arpi, north and east of Naples and about twenty miles from the Adriatic coast.

did not want to commit himself or his father-in-law's people to battle, he said, nor did he have men of his own country whom he could arm for war. "And lest you believe that I've invented this excuse, I'll force myself to tell you the entire story, though recalling it will only reawaken bitter grief.

"After lofty Troy had burned to ashes and Pergamum had fed the Greek flames, and after Locrian Ajax had seized a virgin from the care of a virgin* and brought down on us all the punishment he alone deserved, we Greeks were seized by the winds and scattered over hostile seas. We suffered lightning, the darkest of nights, storms, the wrath of sky and sea, and the crowning disaster, Caphereus—and lest I take up time with a long account of all our sad misfortunes, let me say only that Greece then could have made even Priam weep.† Even so, Minerva, the warrior goddess, cared about me and snatched me from the ocean swells and saved me. But again I was driven from my father's lands, and nurturing Venus, remembering how I had wounded her long ago, punished me for it now.‡ I endured so much in trials at sea and so much in battles on land that I have often called those happy whose ship a storm and fatal Caphereus wrecked, and I wish that I had been with them then.

"After suffering the worst that war and the ocean's waves can do, my comrades lost their courage and begged for an end to their wandering, and Acmon of Pleuron, impetuous by nature and at that moment greatly agitated by all the disasters we had suffered, cried: 'What is left for your endurance to refuse to bear after this, men? What can Cytherea do to us—what more can she do to us—if she wants to? For as long as we fear something worse, there's a reason to pray. But once our luck runs out, we can cast our fears aside and calmly face the worst. Let Venus herself hear me; I don't care. Let her hate all of Diomedes' companions—as she does. We feel only contempt for her hatred, and her great power does not seem so great to us.'

"With talk like that Acmon revived Venus' wrath and goaded her to fury. A few agreed with what he had said, but most of his friends rebuked him, including me. He was about to reply, but his throat narrowed, his voice grew small and thin; his hair turned to plumage, his neck (changing its shape), his chest, and his back were covered with down; his arms sprouted feathers; his elbows curved into slender wings; his feet were webbed; and his face, hardening into horn, turned into a sharp beak.

"Lycus, Idas, Nycteus, and Rhexenor stared at Acmon in amazement, and

---

*14.468: "a virgin ['seized'] from the care of a virgin" refers to Cassandra, daughter of Priam, who was dragged from the temple of Minerva at Troy by Locrian Ajax (so named to distinguish him from the other Ajax) and raped (Apollodorus, Epitome 5.22).

†14.472: Caphereus is a headland on the northeastern coast of southern Euboea onto whose rocks the returning Greek fleet was lured by a fire signal lit by Nauplius, father of Palamedes, in revenge for his son's execution by the Greeks at Troy after Ulysses falsely accused him of accepting a bribe from the Trojans to betray the Greek cause. See *Metamorphoses* 13.34–39, 56–60, and 308–312. For Nauplius' revenge, see Apollodorus, Epitome 6.7–11.

‡14.477–478: "Venus, remembering how I had wounded her long ago": For Diomedes' wounding of Venus, see *Iliad* 5.330–342.

while they were staring took on the same form, and then most of my troops flew up into the air and circled the rowers, flapping their wings. If you asked me what these instant birds looked like, I would say that their form, while not that of a white swan, was very close to a swan's form. And now it is difficult indeed for me as Daunus' son-in-law to hold this city and the arid fields around it with only a fraction of my men." Thus the grandson of Oeneus.

Venulus then departed from Diomedes' Calydonian kingdom, passing by the Peucetian bay and the fields of Messapia. There he saw a cave shaded by a thick stand of trees and hidden by slender reeds, which the half-goat god Pan now occupies, but which at one time belonged to a group of nymphs. Once an Apulian shepherd frightened them suddenly, and they fled in terror from the place. Soon afterwards, though, they recovered their senses and were filled with contempt for the shepherd who had made them run away, and they formed a circle and began to dance, pounding out the rhythm with their feet. The shepherd mocked them, mimicking their dancing with crude movements, and added insults in foul language, spewing out a stream of obscenities. Nor did he stop until his throat was filled with a tree, and that is what he is now. You can tell the kind of tree it is from its fruit. It is, in fact, the oleaster,* and its bitter olives exhibit the mark of his tongue: The harshness of his words passed into them.

When the envoys returned from Diomedes with the news that Aetolian arms had been denied them, the Rutulians, deprived of those forces, nevertheless waged the war they had prepared for, and each side shed much of the other's blood.

And now Turnus hurled blazing torches at the pine-wood ships, and those whom the sea had spared now feared fire. Soon pitch and wax and anything else that could burn was burning; the flames traveled up the tall mast to the sails; and the rowing benches were smoking. Then the sacred mother of the gods remembered that these ship timbers had been cut from the top of Mount Ida.† She filled the atmosphere with the sound of clashing cymbals and the murmur of boxwood flutes and drove her tame lions through the air to Turnus and said, "It's a sacrilege to hurl these firebrands and useless as well, for I will save these ships; I will not let fire burn to ashes this wood that once was part of my forests."

As the goddess was speaking, thunder rumbled, and close on the thunder heavy rain and bouncing hail began to fall. The brother winds, sons of Astraeus, rushed into battle, buffeting the air and churning the sea, swollen by their sudden clashing. The caring goddess used the force of one of these winds to break the hempen cables with which the Phrygian ships were moored, pointed their stems down, and sank them in the sea. The hard wooden timbers

---

*14.525–526: The oleaster is the wild olive.
†14.536: The "sacred mother of the gods" is Cybele (Bömer at 14.535–538, 7.178–179).

softened into flesh; the beak-like prows turned into heads, the oars into swimming legs and feet. Their sides remained as they were, but the keels beneath
the ships were now spines; the rigging became fine hair; and the yards changed
into arms. Their color was deep blue, as before.

And now as nymphs they play the games that young girls like to play, splashing in the waves they once were so afraid of. Though born in hard and rugged
mountains, they now live in calm and gentle waters, and nothing remains
of what they once were. The nymphs have never forgotten all the dangers
they faced so many times at sea, however, and often, when ships are pitched
and tossed by the waves, they place their hands beneath them to hold them
steady—except when a ship carries Greeks. Remembering the Trojans' defeat,
they hate all Greeks. And so they smiled when they saw the wreckage of Ulysses' ship floating in the water; and as they watched the ship of Alcinous hardening and its timbers slowly turning to stone, they smiled again.

When the ships were changed into sea nymphs, there was hope that Turnus,
frightened by this prodigy, would stop fighting, but he battled on. Each side
had its gods, and what is the same as gods, its courage. They no longer sought
a kingdom promised as dowry, nor the scepter of a father-in-law, nor even you,
Lavinia; they wanted simply to win, and they waged war because they were
ashamed to lay down their arms.

Finally, Venus saw her sons' forces victorious, and Turnus fell. Ardea fell,
too, a city called powerful while Turnus was alive.

After the invaders' fire burned Ardea to the ground and it lay buried beneath
the still-warm ashes, a bird never seen before flew up from the smoking ruins,
stirring the cinders with its flapping wings. Its cries, its ravaged form, its pallor—all the features of a devastated city—and even its name came from Ardea,
and now as a heron Ardea mourns, beating its breast with its wings.*

The valor of Aeneas had now compelled all the gods, even Juno herself, to
put an end to their ancient wrath. Since the power of Iulus, nearly grown now,
was firmly established, the hero, son of Venus, was ready for heaven. The goddess had paid a call on each of the divinities and then, putting her arms around
her father's neck, had said: "Dear father, you're never cruel to me, ever: Be kind
to me now. Grant my Aeneas—my son and your grandson—O best of fathers,
make him a god of some kind, even if it's only a little one! It's enough for him
to have seen the loveless kingdom once, just once to have crossed the waters
of the Styx."

The gods agreed—nor did Jupiter's royal consort remain unbending, for,
now placated, she nodded in agreement. Then the father replied: "You deserve
this divine gift, both you who seek it and the one you seek it for. Receive your
wish, my child."

Venus, rejoicing, thanked her father and, carried on the winds by her pair of

---

*14.574–580: *Ardea* is the Latin word for "heron."

doves, came to the Laurentian shore, near the place where the river Numicius flows under a cover of reeds, winding its way to the sea. She ordered that stream to scour away the parts of Aeneas marked for death and bear them down in its silent course to the waters of ocean. The horned river god carried out Venus' command and poured his waters over Aeneas, cleansing him of all that was mortal until only his best part remained. His mother now anointed his purged body with a divine perfume, touched his lips with ambrosia and nectar, and made him a god, whom the people of Quirinus call Indiges and receive at their temple and altars.[59]

Then Alba and the Latium kingdom came under the rule of Ascanius, also called Iulus.* Silvius succeeded him, and when Silvius' son inherited the ancient sovereignty, he adopted the name Latinus, now used again. Illustrious Alba came after Latinus, and Epytus followed him. After Epytus came Capetus and Capys, Capys preceding. Tiberinus received the kingdom from them; he drowned in the waters of the Tuscan River, thenceforth called Tiber, after him. He had two sons, Remulus and Acrota the fierce. Remulus, the elder, was killed when he tried to imitate lightning and was himself struck by lightning. Acrota, more restrained than his brother, passed the scepter to Aventinus the brave, who lies buried on the hill from which he ruled and to which he gave his name. And now Proca held power over the people of the Palatine.

It was during Proca's reign that Pomona lived. No other wood nymph in Latium tended her garden as well as Pomona tended hers, and none paid more attention to her fruit trees, whence her name.† She cared for neither forests nor rivers, loving instead tilled fields and trees bearing lush and abundant fruit. Nor did she burden herself with a javelin but carried instead a curved sickle, with which she pruned her trees and cut back their limbs, spreading in all directions, or split the bark of a tree and grafted a cutting onto it, offering sap to the foreign shoot. She never let her fruit trees feel the effects of drought, for she led water in furrows to their gnarled and thirsty roots. This was her passion, her only interest; she had no desire for romance. Even so, fearing violence from her crude country neighbors, she enclosed her orchards, blocked entry to them, and shunned the male sex. Dance-loving satyrs; Pans, who crown their horns with pine-wreaths; Silvanus, always younger than his age; and the god who frightens thieves away with his sickle or his private parts‡—what did they not do to possess her?

Vertumnus surpassed them all in his passion for Pomona, but he was no luckier than they. How often, dressed like a rough field hand, did he bring her ears of grain in a basket—and he was the very image of a harvest worker! And

---

*14.609: Ovid actually calls Ascanius "double-named," *binominis.* At Virgil, *Aeneid* 1.267–268, Jupiter gives Ascanius his cognomen or surname, Iulus.

†14.625–626: "fruit trees, whence her name": Pomona's name is cognate with *pomus,* Latin for "fruit tree," and *pomum,* Latin for "fruit."

‡14.640: "the god who frightens," that is, Priapus (Bömer at 14.637–641, 7.204).

often, with freshly cut clover in his hair, he would seem to have come from turning the new-mown hay. He often carried a goad in his calloused hand, and you would swear that he had just unyoked a team of weary oxen. Appearing with a sickle, he was a pruner of trees or a trimmer of grapevines; with a ladder on his shoulder you would think he was an apple picker; with a sword he was a soldier; carrying a rod, a fisherman. In short, with his many disguises he frequently found a way to approach Pomona so he could enjoy gazing at her beauty.

He even tied a bright kerchief around his head, stuck white hair on his temples, and, leaning on a cane, pretended to be an old woman. And now he was able to enter her well-kept garden! After admiring Pomona's apples he said, "You're even prettier!" and, continuing to compliment her, kissed her as no real old woman would ever have kissed anyone. Then, bent as though with age, he eased himself to the ground and looked up at the branches, weighed down with autumn's fruit. Nearby was an elm, adorned with clusters of shining grapes. He cast an appraising glance at the tree and its companion vine and said: "This tree, if it stood unwedded to the vine, would have nothing but its leaves to make it attractive. This vine, too, now resting on the elm it twines around, would trail on the ground if it weren't trained to the tree. Yet I see that you're unmoved by this example; you shy away from sharing your bed and don't care to commit yourself to anyone. How I wish you did want to! Then not even Helen herself would have been beset by more suitors, nor the one who caused the battle of Lapiths and centaurs,* nor the wife of Ulysses, who was too slow in coming home. Even now, though you turn your back on those who court you, though you run away from them, a thousand men desire you, nevertheless—and so do gods and demigods and all the divinities that dwell in the Alban hills.

"But if you're wise, and if you want to make a good choice—and if you're willing to listen to an old woman who loves you more than all those others, more than you think—reject marriage with some ordinary fellow and choose Vertumnus to share your bed! Take my word for it. I know him better than he knows himself, and he is neither prone to wander the wide world over—he lives here, and here only—nor, like most suitors, does he fall in love with every girl he sees. You will be his first flame and his last, and he will devote all the years of his life to you alone. He's a young man, too, and nature, as a gift, made him handsome. He can also assume any form he chooses, and anything you order him to turn into, no matter what it is, he will turn into that. And what about this: You both like the same things; the apples you grow he is the first to receive; and when you give them to him, he's delighted to have them.

"But now he doesn't want fruit from your trees, nor the sweetly flavored herbs that grow in your garden, nor anything at all, except you. Pity him, for

---

*14.670–671: "the one who caused," that is, Hippodame; see book 12.210ff.

he's on fire for you, and believe that the one who wants your love is here himself and appeals to you through me. Beware of avenging gods and Idalian Venus, who hates hard hearts, and beware of Nemesis, too, who has a long memory when she's angry. And so that you'll have a healthy respect for them, let me tell you a story—for I've had a long life and learned many things. It's a story that's well known all over Cyprus, and it will enable you to soften your heart and more easily give in.

"A man of humble origin named Iphis once saw Anaxarete, a noble girl of the ancient line of Teucer—saw her and loved her with every fiber of his being. He struggled with his passion for a long time, but when he wasn't able to overcome it with reason, he came as a suppliant to her door. First, he confessed his unhappy love to her nurse and begged her, by the hope she had in her dear charge, not to be hard toward him. Next, he flattered her host of servants and begged each one of them to do him a special favor. Often he wrote down sweet and tender messages on tablets for the servants to take to her. Sometimes he would decorate her door with floral wreaths, well watered with his tears, and lay himself gently down on the hard stone threshold and berate the barred door in a mournful voice.

"But she was more savage than the surging sea when the Kids are setting* and harder than fire-hardened Norician steel, harder even than natural rock embedded in the ground. She rejected him and laughed at him and, cruel as she was, added arrogant insults to her pitiless actions and deprived the lovesick Iphis even of hope.

"Unable to bear the torment of pining for her endlessly, Iphis uttered these last words at her door: 'You win, Anaxarete. You won't have to put up with me any longer. Have yourself a parade and enjoy your triumph! Sing a paean for your victory! Crown your head with shining laurel! For you have truly won, and I gladly die. Come, iron-hearted girl, rejoice! And yet, there's surely *something* that will make you appreciate my love, *something* about me that's attractive to you, *something* you'll admit makes me worthy of you . . . Remember also that I loved you as long as I lived, and when my love was lost, so was my life. It won't be a rumor of my death that comes to you. Oh no, I'll be there myself, in person, believe me, so you can feast your cruel eyes on my dead body. Still, gods above, if you see what mortals do, remember me. (I don't have the strength to offer a longer prayer.) Let my story be told down through the ages, and give the time you've taken from my life to my memory!'

"Lifting eyes filled with tears and raising pale arms toward the door he had so often adorned with wreaths, he said, as he tied a noose to the top of it, 'I hope *this* garland pleases you, cruel and heartless girl!' And he put his head in the noose, turning toward her, even then, and hanged himself, poor devil, and

---

*14.711: The constellation of the Kids sets in mid-December; its setting indicates winter rainstorms (Haupt-Ehwald at 14.711, 2.410).

broke his neck and died. His jerking feet banged against the door, like someone demanding to be let in, and when the door was opened it revealed the deed. The servants cried out and cut him down, but it was too late. They carried him back to his mother's house (for his father was dead), and she pulled him up on her lap and held his cold body in her arms. After she had uttered the words grief-stricken parents say and done the things grief-stricken mothers do, she led the cortege of weeping mourners through the city, bearing the pale corpse on a bier to be burned.

"Anaxarete's house happened to be on the street the tearful procession was going down, and the sound of mourners beating their breasts came to the ears of the hard-hearted girl, whom an avenging god was now leading on. Troubled, she nevertheless said, 'Let me see this wretched funeral,' and went upstairs to an open window. As she looked down at Iphis, laid out on the bier, her eyes hardened, the warm blood drained from her face, and she became deathly pale. She tried to step back but was rooted to the spot; she tried to turn her face away, but this, too, she could not do, and gradually the stone that had been in her heart for so long spread throughout her body. And if you think I've made this up, Salamis still has a statue that looks just like Anaxarete, the model for it, and a temple, too, called the temple of Venus-Looking-Out.

"Mindful of this, my gentle nymph, do put away your stubborn pride, I beg you, and give yourself to the one who loves you. And, if you do, may frost in spring never nip your apples when they first appear, nor violent winds blow them off the trees when they're getting ripe!"

After the god in the form of the old woman had said all this, but to no avail, he removed his disguise, became his youthful self again, and appeared to Pomona like the brightest image of the sun when it breaks through an overcast sky that blocked its light and shines again, undarkened by a single cloud. He was about to take her by force, but there was no need of force, for the nymph was swept away by the god and his beauty and felt the same wounds of love as he.

Next after Proca,* the unjust Amulius ruled in Ausonia by military force, and then the aged Numitor, with the help of his grandson Romulus, regained his lost kingdom. On the festal day of the shepherd-goddess Pales, the walls of Rome were built; Tatius and the Sabine fathers then waged war; and Tarpeia, after revealing the way to the citadel, died beneath the arms that were piled on top of her, a punishment she deserved.

Then the Sabine men, like silent wolves, crept up on the sleeping Romans without a sound, making for the gates that Ilia's son had shut and made fast with heavy wooden bars. One of the gates, however, Juno herself opened, not letting it creak when it turned on its hinges. Venus alone sensed that the bars

---

*14.772: Ovid returns to the list of early Roman kings he left at 14.622 to tell the story of Vertumnus and Pomona.

of the gate had fallen and would have closed it, except that gods are never permitted to reverse the actions of other gods.

Ausonian water nymphs happened to occupy places connected by the gated Janus-crossing and made wet with water from an icy spring. Venus asked them for help, and the water nymphs did not turn a deaf ear to the goddess and her just request. From deep underground they brought up the streams that fed their spring. But the way through the open Janus-gate was still not impassable; the spring had not blocked the path. The nymphs then put yellow sulfur deep in the rushing water and set its underground streams on fire with smoking pitch. Vapors from these and other powerful substances penetrated to its depths, and you, O currents, till now daring to rival alpine cold, grew as hot as fire itself. The two gateposts began to smoke from the burning water splashed on them, and the gate, promised in vain to the rugged Sabines, was closed off by the new spring until the Roman soldiers could arm themselves.*

Romulus then went on the offensive, and soon the Roman ground was strewn with Sabine bodies and those of its own men, and godless weapons mingled the blood of sons with that of their fathers-in-law. Finally, though, both sides agreed to end the war with a treaty of peace, instead of prolonging the clash of arms to the bitter end, and they also agreed that Tatius would have a share in the royal power.

After Tatius died, Romulus, you were making one set of laws for both peoples, when Mars removed his war helmet as a sign of his peaceful intention and addressed the father of gods and men: "Now that the Roman state rests on a strong foundation, Father, and no longer depends upon one man to protect it, the time has come to grant the reward promised to me and your worthy grandson and to remove him from earth and establish him in heaven. You once said to me in the presence of the assembled gods—I recall your solemn promise, fixed forever in my memory†: 'One man there will be, whom you will lift up to heaven's azure. . . .' Let your will, as then declared, now be done!"

All-powerful Jupiter assented with a nod, darkened the day with clouds, and terrified the world with thunder and lightning. The intrepid Gradivus took these as signs for the promised ascension of his son and, vaulting into his chariot on his spear, cracked his whip and lashed his horses forward beneath the bloody yoke and shot down through the air, coming to rest on the summit of the wooded Palatine. There he caught up Romulus as he was making fair judgments for his people, the Quirites.‡ His mortal body burned away in the air,

---

*14.778–799: For discussion of the topography of the place in Rome that Ovid alludes to here see Holland 103–107 and Richardson s.v. *Ianus Geminus* 207–208.

†14.813: "I recall" translates Kovacs' proposed *memini*, corrupted, he says, to the MSS *memoro*, "mention," "relate" ([1994] 248–249).

‡14.820–823: 14.820: Gradivus is another name for the god Mars. 14.823: I read *non regia iura*, lit. "not royal judgments," with Anderson (1982a), Bömer, Haupt-Ehwald, and LaFaye, instead of *iam regia iura* with Miller-Goold. Haupt-Ehwald, commenting on *non regia*, say, "not tyrannical [*non regia*], because his rule was based on a constitution and the rule of law" (at 14.823, 2.418).

just as a lead bullet, shot from a sling, melts as it hurtles through the sky. A beautiful form appeared in its place, more worthy of the couches of the gods in heaven, a form like that of berobed Quirinus.

His wife, Hersilia, was mourning him as lost when royal Juno commanded Iris to descend by her rainbow to the widowed queen and give her this command: "Lady, so highly esteemed among both the Latin and Sabine peoples, most worthy once to have been the wife of such a great man, now just as worthy to be the wife of Quirinus: Cease weeping. If you wish to see your husband, follow me to the woods that grow on the Quirinal hill and shade the temple of the Roman king."

Iris obeyed, glided down to earth along her brightly colored rainbow, and conveyed Juno's command to Hersilia. Hardly able to raise her eyes and look at Iris, Hersilia shyly said: "O goddess—for you are clearly a goddess, though I cannot say who you are—take me to my husband. Please take me to him and show me his face. If fate will let me see him one more time, I'll say that is heaven enough for me!"

She then went straightway with Thaumas' virgin daughter to the hill of Romulus. There a star streaked down from the sky and fell to earth. Hersilia's hair burst into flames from its light, and with the star she vanished in the air. Rome's founder received her in the arms she knew so well. He changed her name along with her form and called her Hora, and now as a goddess she is joined to Quirinus.[60]

BOOK FIFTEEN

A search was on, meanwhile, for someone to bear the weight of so great a task and to succeed so great a king. Then Fame, herald of truth, destined the illustrious Numa for power.

Now, Numa was not content to know the customs of the Sabine people only. He conceived for his capacious mind a far greater inquiry and sought to learn the nature of the universe. His passion for this knowledge led him to abandon his native Cures and make his way to the city that had once received Hercules.* When he asked who had founded this Greek city on the shores of Italy, one of the older inhabitants, who knew the history of past ages, told him this: "They say that Hercules, Jupiter's son, returning from Ocean a rich man because of cattle he had acquired in Spain, safely reached the Lacinian shore and, while his cattle grazed in the grassy fields, entered the house of great Croton, who offered him hospitality. And there he rested after his long journey. As he was leaving he said to his host, 'In the time of your grandchildren a city will stand here,' and his prediction came true.

"For the Argive Alemon had a son named Myscelus, whom the gods loved more than any other man of that time. One night while Myscelus was sound asleep, Hercules the Club Bearer bent over him and said: 'Get up and leave your native land. Go and seek that faraway river, the Aesar, with its rocky bed!' and threatened him with fearful punishment if he did not obey. The god then withdrew, and the son of Alemon woke up. Arising from his bed, he went over his recent dream in his mind for a long time, his thoughts at war with themselves. The god had ordered him to depart, but the laws of his country forbade him to leave, and death was the penalty for anyone wishing to abandon his native land.

---

*15.7–8: 15.7: Cures was an ancient town of the Sabines (*OLD* s.v. *Cures*). 15.8: "the city that had once received Hercules" is Croton, located in the far south of Italy near the "instep" of the Italian "boot" and a little north of the promontory of Lacinium, referred to at 15.13 as "the Lacininan shore."

"The shining sun had hidden its bright face in Ocean, and darkest night had raised its starry head, when the god appeared in a second dream, gave him the same instructions, and threatened him with punishment even more severe if he did not obey. Myscelus was now thoroughly frightened, and he prepared at once to move his household gods to a new country.

"There was murmuring in the city, and Myscelus was accused of breaking the laws. When the prosecution's case was laid out and the charge, being evident, was considered proved (and the testimony of a witness, therefore, not necessary), the accused, who appeared in court shabbily dressed, with dirt in his hair,* raised his face and extended his hands to the gods and cried, 'You to whom the Twelve Labors gave the right to enter heaven, I pray to you for help, since you are the author of my crime.'

"Following an ancient custom, the people there used black pebbles to convict a defendant and white ones to free him from guilt. Now, too, the verdict was given in this way, and it was a lethal one, for every pebble dropped into the pitiless urn was black. But when the urn was overturned and the pebbles were poured out to be counted, they had all changed from black to white. A favorable verdict was thus rendered, by the divine will of Hercules, and the son of Alemon was acquitted.

"He gave thanks to his savior, the son of Amphitryon,† crossed the Ionian Sea with favoring winds, and sailed past Neretum, the city of the Sallentines; past Sybaris; Lacedemonian Tarentum; the Bay of Siris; Crimisa; and the Iapygian shores. Just beyond the lands that look upon these waters he found the mouth of the Aesar, whither fate had called him; found a grave not far from there, in which the sacred bones of Croton were buried; laid the foundations for a city at that place, as he had been ordered to do; and gave it the name of the hero interred therein." Such, according to the well-known tradition, was the first beginning of that place and the ancient origin of that city built in the land of Italy.[61]

A man lived there who was Samian by birth but who had fled Samos and its masters and become an exile of his own free will because he hated tyranny.‡ He drew near to the gods, remote though they are, by pure thought alone, and what nature denies to human sight he took in with the eyes of his mind. After giving himself to careful study and gazing on all that exists, he passed his knowledge on to others, teaching those gathered about him in silent awe at his words the first beginnings of the great world, the causes of things, what nature is, and god, whence snow, the origin of lightning, whether it is Jupiter or the winds that thunder when clouds break up, why earthquakes occur, what law governs the stars as they move, and whatever else lies hidden.

He was the first to speak out against serving animal flesh at meals, the first,

---

*15.38: Myscelus appears in this condition in order to arouse sympathy in the judges (Haupt-Ehwald at line 15.37, 2.424).

†15.49: The son of Amphitryon is Hercules.

‡15.60–62: The man is Pythagoras.

too, to express sentiments—learnéd, indeed, but not believed—like these: "Refrain, mortals, from polluting your bodies with forbidden food! There are cereals and grains; there are fruits that bend down branches of trees with their weight; there are grapes ripe to bursting on the vine; there are greens, some sweet when fresh, others that cooking makes tender and delicious. You have milk in abundance and honey, scented with thyme, and the earth, lavish with its bounty, heaps upon you savory foods and offers you feasts without blood and slaughter.

"Wild beasts satisfy their hunger with meat, though not all do, for horses, sheep, and cattle live on grass, but those with natures wild and untamed— Armenian tigers, ferocious lions, bears, and wolves—these enjoy feasts rich in blood. But O what a terrible crime it is for animal to eat animal, for one body to fatten itself by stuffing another down its gullet, for one being to live by the death of another! Amid the plenty that best of mothers the good earth bears, will nothing please you but to sink your savage teeth in helpless flesh and imitate the practice of the Cyclopes? Can you not satisfy the hunger of your ravenous and ill-mannered belly without destroying some other living creature?

"That long-ago age we call 'golden' was blessed with fruit that fell from trees, with crops the earth brought forth on its own; and none defiled their lips with blood. Then birds flew safely through the air, a hare could hop about in fields unafraid, and no fish ever hung from a hook because of its trusting nature. The world was free of snares, none feared hidden traps, and peace reigned over all.

"But then some begetter of destruction envied lions for the meat they devour and crammed his greedy gut with flesh and opened the way for crime, and for the first time swords grew warm and dripped with blood from the slaughter of wild beasts. That should have been enough, and I agree that animals trying to kill us were dispatched in good conscience. But though they ought to have been killed, they should not have been eaten.

"From there crime went further, and the first animal thought to deserve slaughter as a sacrificial victim was the sow, because it rooted up seeds with its curved snout and so cut off hope for the year's harvest. And because the goat ate Bacchus' vines, the god led it to the altar and sacrificed it there, avenging his loss.

"These two were to blame for their own deaths! But you, little sheep, O gentle creatures born to look after the human race, who bring us your udders filled with nectar, who offer us your wool for our soft warm cloaks, who help us more by living than by dying, what were you guilty of? What were cattle guilty of, animals free of deceit and guile, simple and harmless, born to endure toil? That man had no memory at all and deserved none of the fruits of the earth who could unyoke from the plow his fellow tiller of the soil and slaughter him, who could strike with an axe the neck rubbed raw with toil, the neck that had renewed the hard earth so many times, that had given so many harvests.

"Nor is it enough that such unspeakable acts are committed: Men have enlisted the gods themselves in their crimes and believe the powers in heaven rejoice at the slaughter of a weary ox! A victim without blemish, peerless in its beauty—its beauty is its undoing—and adorned with ribbons and gold is brought to the altar, hears the prayers of the priest, not knowing what it hears, sees the grain placed on its brow between its horns, grain it cultivated, and is then struck and stains with its blood the knife it may have seen reflected in water.* The entrails are then pulled from the still-living body and pored over by priests looking for signs of the will of the gods. From there, O mortal race, you dare to eat! (So starved is humankind for forbidden food!) Do not do it, I beg you! Heed my warning! Know and understand that when you fill your mouth with meat of the cattle you have killed, you are chewing on the flesh of your fellow workers.

"Since a god gives me voice, I shall follow him carefully as he enables me to speak and reveal the spirit of Delphi within me. I shall bring to light the secrets of the universe itself, and make known the oracles of an august mind.† I shall sing of great mysteries never delved into by the genius of ages past and long hidden from humankind. It is thrilling to go past the stars, thrilling to leave behind the still earth and rise up on a cloud to the powerful shoulders of Atlas, where I can look down on human beings far below as they scurry now here, now there without plan or purpose, trembling with dread at the thought of death, and can reassure them and reveal to them the fated course of things.

"O race of mortals, thunderstricken by the icy fear of death, why do you dread the Styx? Why are you afraid of the dark, the names of things unreal— the stuff of poets—and the dangers of a world that does not exist? Whether the flames of the funeral pyre or time's decay consumes our bodies, do not suppose that they can ever suffer any harm.

"Dying never, our souls live on in new homes, always, after they leave their former seats, abiding in the places that receive them. I myself—for I remember it clearly—was Panthous' son Euphorbus at the time of the Trojan War, in whose chest Menelaus once lodged his heavy spear. Recently in the temple of Juno in Argos, Abas' city, I recognized the shield I had carried on my left arm!

"Everything changes; nothing dies: The spirit wanders here, wanders there, enters anyone's body, passes from beasts to human beings and back to beasts again, but never perishes.

"As soft wax is molded into different figures, remains neither as it was nor keeps the same shape, yet is still the same substance, is still wax, so I declare that the soul is always the same, although it migrates to different forms. There-

---

*15.131–135: 15.131: An animal to be sacrificed had its horns wrapped with gold leaf. See 7.161–162 and Haupt-Ehwald at 7.161, 1.366. 15.135: "While the priest, following an ancient custom, passed the knife over the forehead and back of the animal, it saw the knife [reflected] in the water in the vessel in front of it that was used in the offering" (Haupt-Ehwald at line 15.134f., 2.433).

†15.145: Ovid's phrase, *augusta mens,* here translated "august mind," may allude to the emperor Augustus, but it is not clear what to make of the allusion.

fore, lest your reverence for life be conquered by your belly's lust, let me give you a solemn warning: Do not drive kindred souls from their homes by the unspeakable act of killing; do not let blood be fed with blood!

"And since I am under way on a mighty sea, and the wind is filling my sails: There is nothing in the world that stays the same. All things are flowing, and every form takes visible shape as it wanders. Time, too, glides in endless motion, like a river; for a river cannot stop, nor can one passing hour. But as wave drives on wave, the same one as it rolls urging on the wave ahead and urged on by the wave behind, so time runs on, and time pursues, and time is always new. For what was here is gone, what never was now comes to pass, and every moment is made anew.

"You can see how night, fading, turns to day, and bright sunlight follows the darkness of the night. Nor is the color of the sky the same when weary creatures lie asleep in the middle of their rest as it is when the morning star goes forth on his shining white horse; and it changes again when dawn, the morning's messenger, bathes the world in her glowing hues as she gives the day to Apollo. The shield of the sun god itself burns red in the morning when it rises above the rim of the earth, shines red again at evening, when it sinks below earth's rim, but is blinding white at its highest point, for the sky is purer there, far from the world's defiling touch. Nor can the moon ever remain as it is, for when it's waxing, it's smaller today than it will be tomorrow, but larger when it's waning.

"And do you not see the year change before our eyes four times, one season after another, imitating our lives? For the new spring is gentle and mild as milk, very much like a little child: Fresh and delicate shoots, burgeoning yet tender, give farmers joy and hope of harvest. Then all things bloom, and the rich fields dance with colors, though their leaves aren't yet as hardy as they will be. After spring, the year becomes more robust as it passes into summer, like a strong young man. No season is more robust than this, none more fertile, none hotter. Then, when the fervor of youth has gone, autumn arrives, ripe and sweet, a calm season, midway from youth to age, though its temples are sprinkled with gray. Next, winter, old and shivering, shuffles in, most of its hair now gone and the hair it has left turned white.

"Our bodies are always changing, too, without any respite, nor shall we be tomorrow what we were, or even what we are today. At one time we lay hidden in our first mother's womb, merely seeds, only a hope for humankind. Then nature touched us with her artful hands, not wanting our bodies to be cramped and hidden in our mother's swollen belly, and sent us from our first home into the open air.

"Brought forth into the light of day, the infant lies weak and helpless. Soon, though, the baby crawls on all fours, as animals do, and little by little, shaky at first and a little wobbly in its knees, it stands upright, holding onto things for support. The child becomes strong and swift and strides through the space of youth, and then, when the middle years are past and gone, we slip down the declining path of old age, which wears away and finally ruins the vigor of earlier years.

"Milo grown old wept to see his strengthless biceps, once a mass of solid muscle like those of Hercules, now soft and sagging. Helen also wept, when she beheld her ancient, wrinkled face in a glass and asked herself how she could ever have been carried off twice.*

"O time devouring everything! And you, hateful, unrelenting years! You destroy all things! For all things are caught in the grinding ages and eaten away, little by little, in a slow death!

"What we call the elements, these, too, do not endure. Listen to me, and I shall tell you about the changes they go through. The eternal world contains four kinds of matter. Two of them, earth and water, are heavy and sink by their own weight down to the lower regions. The other two, air and fire (which is finer than air), have no weight at all, and since nothing holds them down, they rise to the upper regions.

"Though these four elements sit apart in space, all things are made from them and change back into them. Earth, dissolving, thins to water; moisture turns to vapor and then to wind and air. With a further loss of weight, air, when most rarefied, leaps up to ethereal fire. From these they return, but the order is reversed: Fire, condensing, changes into air, heavier than fire; air into water; and earth is forced from water that's compressed.

"Nothing keeps its original shape, and nature, ever renewing the world, creates new forms from old ones endlessly. Believe me when I say that nothing perishes, ever, anywhere in the world. Rather, things change; they make their forms anew; and 'to be born' simply means that something is other than it was before; 'to die,' that it has ceased to be what it was. While things can change from one state to another, now to this one, now to that one, the sum of things stays constant.

But truly, nothing keeps the same form for long, or so I believe. Thus it is, O ages past, that you have gone from gold to iron; thus it is that the fortunes of different places have changed so many times.

"I have seen what was once the most solid earth turn into sea; and I have seen land that was made from ocean. Sea shells have lain far from water, and an ancient anchor has been found on a mountaintop. Water coursing down from a height has made what was once a plain into a valley, and floods have washed hills into the sea. Marshy ground has dried to desert sand, and arid land has turned to watery marsh.

---

*15.229–233: 15.229–231: Milo of Croton was "the most famous athlete of antiquity," and his career "extended over more than 30 years." Six Olympian, six Pythian, ten Isthmian, and nine Nemean victories are recorded for him. He and his wife were supposedly students of Pythagoras (*Der Kleine Pauly* 3.1303–1304, s.v. *Milon* 2). 15.232–233: Helen was first abducted as a child by Theseus; see Apollodorus 3.10.7–8 and Epitome 1.23.

"Nature has sent forth new springs in one place and dammed them in another, and tremors deep in the earth make rivers leap forth or else dry up and disappear. And so the Lycus, swallowed by a fissure in the ground, comes out far from there, reborn at another place. And so the Erasinus is drunk down into the earth, flows underground, and returns as a mighty river in the fields of Argos. In Mysia, the Caicus, weary of its source and original banks, they say, now flows somewhere else. The Amenanus sometimes surges, roiled with Sicilian sand, and sometimes dries up when its springs are reduced to a trickle.

"At one time you could drink the water of the Anigrus, but you would not want to touch it now, after the centaurs washed their wounds in it, wounds made by the bow of club-bearing Hercules (if you believe what the poets say). And consider this: The Hypanis, which rises in the mountains of Scythia and was once sweet tasting—isn't it bitter now, ruined by salt? Antissa, Pharos, and Phoenician Tyre used to be surrounded by water, but none is an island now. Leucas was a part of the mainland in the time of its first inhabitants; now water surrounds it. Zancle, too, they say, was joined to Italy at one time, until the sea carried off their common border, and the strait between them pushed back the land on both sides. Should you look for Helice and Buris, cities of Achaea, you would find them underwater, and sailors still point out those sunken towns and their submerged walls.

"Near Troezen, where Pittheus ruled, there is a steep and treeless rise, once an open field, completely flat, but now a hill. For—a story terrible to tell— savage and powerful winds, shut up in an airtight cavern underground, sought a way out and struggled in vain to reach the open sky. Since there wasn't a single fissure in their entire prison, no exit for winds, they stretched the earth above them and made it swell, just as one can use one's breath to blow up a bladder or a goatskin bag. The ground there remained forever swollen in the shape of a high hill, which grew hard over time.

"Many more examples that I've known and heard about come to mind, but I shall mention only a few. Isn't it true that water gives new forms to things and also changes, itself? Your spring, O horn-bearing Ammon, is ice-cold at midday, but hot at dawn and again at dusk, and it's said that during the last phase of the moon, the Athamanians can ignite wood by pouring water on it from the Ammon. The Ciconians have a river that will turn your stomach to stone if you drink from it, and it forms a layer of marble over anything it's poured on. In our own land the river Crathis and, near it, the Sybaris turn hair to golden amber. And what is even more amazing, some waters can change not only people's bodies but their minds as well. Who hasn't heard of the Salmacis and the disgusting movement of its waters* or of the lakes in Aethiopia? Those who drink from them either go mad or fall into a strange and heavy sleep.

"People who quench their thirst from the Clitorian spring avoid wine ever

*15.319: For the pool of Salmacis, see 4.285ff.

after, happily preferring pure water only. Either there's something in the spring that works against the power of wine, or, as the natives say, after Melampus, son of Amythaon, delivered Proetus' crazed daughters from their madness by means of herbs and spells, he threw the curatives he had used into the spring, and ever since it has created an aversion to wine in whoever drinks from it.

"The water of the Lyncestius River has the opposite effect, for anyone gulping it down without restraint staggers away as if he had been drinking pure wine, unwatered. There's a place in Arcadia called Pheneus that people in ancient times were suspicious of because of its treacherous waters. Avoid them at night, for they are poisonous then; but you can safely drink from them during the day, for then they are harmless. So lakes and rivers have many different characteristics.

"At one time the island Delos moved around in the sea; now it stays in one place. The Argo's sailors feared the clashing of the Symplegades, always wet with spray from the waves they smashed, though now the rocks stand immovable and resist the winds.

"Aetna, burning now in its sulfurous crater, wasn't always on fire, nor will it always be. For if the earth is a living creature and has airways in many places for exhaling flames, it can change these passages for its breathing as often as it moves, can close up caverns here and open others there. Or if swift and powerful winds are confined in caves deep underground and hurl rocks together that have a fiery material in them and burst into flame on impact, the caves will be left cold when the winds subside. Or if it's pitch on fire beneath the earth, or yellow sulfur (which makes hardly any smoke when it burns), then, certainly, as the earth stops providing a rich supply of fuel for the flames, and they gradually die down, the fire, starved of fuel, will go out and so desert those burned-out places.

"There are said to be men in Pallene, in the far north, who, after diving into the Lake of Minerva nine times, come out covered with fine feathers. I can hardly believe this. Scythian women are also said to undergo the same change by sprinkling themselves with a magic substance.

"If we are to accept as true facts long established, corpses rotting because of delay in being buried or from exposure to heat, which makes them decompose—you do see, don't you, that these corpses turn into tiny living creatures? And we know from experience that if you throw the carcasses of slaughtered bulls into a ditch, bees spring up everywhere from their putrefying innards and begin looking for flowers and, like the animals they were born from, live in the fields, like to work, and toil for the future. Hornets come from warhorses buried in the ground. If you pull off a crab's claws and cover the crab with sand, a scorpion will emerge from the buried part and threaten you with the stinger in its tail. Caterpillars, which spin their white cocoons around leaves, change into tombstone butterflies (something farmers have observed).

Mud has seeds that generate green frogs: Limbless trunks at first, they soon have legs for swimming; and to be fit for hopping and jumping about, the back legs are longer than the ones in front.*

"When a mother bear gives birth to a cub, at first it is just a ball of furry flesh, barely alive. But by licking it she fashions its limbs and gives it the shape that she herself has.

"And do you not see that the larvae of honeybees, inside the six-walled bees-wax cells in the hive, are born as bodies without limbs and only later acquire legs and wings?

"Juno's peacock, with stars in its tail; Jupiter's armor-bearing eagle; the doves of Venus; and every kind of bird—who would think they could come from eggs, if you didn't already know that's where they come from?

"Some people believe that when the human spine decomposes in a sealed tomb, the marrow changes into a snake.

"All these creatures owe their first origins to other animals. There is one bird, however, that by itself renews and even reproduces itself; the Assyrians call it the phoenix. It eats neither grain nor grass, but lives instead on the gum of the incense tree and fragrant balsam extract. As soon as it completes its life cycle of five hundred years, it uses its talons and beak, which it has cleansed from all impurities, to build a nest for itself in the branches at the top of a swaying palm. And after lining the bottom of its nest with bark of the cassia tree, spikes of mild nard, bits of cinnamon, and yellow myrrh, it lays itself upon this bed and ends its life amid these scents. Then, they say, a small phoenix is born from its father's body, destined to live the same number of years. When the newborn has grown large and strong enough to bear the weight of the nest, it lifts it up from the branches of the tree and with loving care carries its own cradle and its father's tomb through the clear air to the city of the Sun and places it before the sacred doors of his temple.†

"If in all these wonders there is anything truly amazing, let us then be amazed at the hyena, which changes its sex and, just now a female that let itself be mounted by a male, now becomes male itself. Consider this too: The creature that lives on wind and air immediately turns the color of whatever it touches.‡

"When India was conquered, it gave vine-crowned Bacchus the lynx, and they say that whatever this animal voids from its bladder hardens and turns to

---

*15.372–378: 15.372–374: Butterflies were frequently represented on tombstones as a symbol of the soul (Haupt-Ehwald at 15.374, 2.452), hence Ovid's reference at 15.374 to "tombstone butterflies" (*ferali . . . papilione*). 15.376–378: In these lines Ovid uses alliteration of the letters t, p, d, and b to simulate hopping and jumping:

> *et generat truncas pedibus, mox apta natando*
> *crura dat, utque eadem sint longis saltibus apta,*
> *posterior partes superat mensura priores.*

†15.406: The "city of the Sun" is Heliopolis, in lower Egypt, the city of the sun god Ra, who had his widely famous temple there (Haupt-Ehwald at 15.406, 2.454).

‡15.411–412: "The creature that lives on wind and air" is the chameleon.

stone when it meets the air. Coral, too, at the moment it's exposed to air, grows hard, though underwater it's pliant seaweed.

"The day will end and Phoebus Apollo's panting horses will plunge into the sea before I can name all the things that are transformed into different shapes. So we see times changing and some nations growing strong while others decline. And so it is that Troy once was great in wealth and heroes and for ten years was able to lose so much of its blood. Leveled to the ground, it now has only ancient ruins to show, and its only riches are the tombs of its forefathers.

"Sparta was once an illustrious city, great Mycenae flourished, and Athens and Thebes flourished as well, the citadels of Cecrops and Amphion. But now Sparta is worthless ground, noble Mycenae has fallen, and what is the Thebes of Oedipus, except a name? What is left of Pandion's Athens, except a name?

"Now, too, I have heard, Trojan Rome is rising, her great task to lay the foundations of empire by the waters of Tiber, flowing down from the Apennines. And thus she changes her form as she grows and will, one day, be the capital of the vast world! So, they say, the prophets declare in their far-seeing oracles; and as I well recall, Priam's son Helenus said the same thing to Aeneas, when he was in tears and uncertain of his welfare as Troy was collapsing: 'Goddess-born, mark well what I foretell: You are saved; Troy, therefore, will not entirely fall! Fire and sword will give way to you, and as you pass through them you will gather up Pergamum and bear it away, until you find for Troy and yourself a foreign soil more welcome to you than your own fatherland. I behold, too,* that your Trojan heirs are destined to build a city greater than any city now, greater than any city will ever be, greater than any city seen in ages past. As the centuries go by, its other princes will increase this city's power, but it will be a son of Iulus who will make Rome rule the world, and after the earth has enjoyed his presence, the halls of heaven will have the pleasure of his company, and there his final resting place will be.'

"Thus Helenus prophesied to Aeneas as he carried his gods away. I repeat his words as I remember them, and I rejoice that my native city flourishes,† that the victory of the Greeks was a blessing for the Trojans.

"Now, lest our horses forget to run to the finish line and lead us far off the track: The sky and all beneath it, the earth and all within it, change their forms. We, too, a part of this world, since we are not bodies only but winged souls as well and can make our homes in beasts and dwell in our own herds, let us revere all flesh and keep it safe, for perhaps it has held our parents' souls, or our brothers', or souls bound to us by some other tie, or if not, at least other human souls; and let us not gorge ourselves on meat from Thyestes' table!

"What an evil habit he creates, how easily he takes the next step and sheds

---

*15.444 I read *etiam* with Anderson (1982a), Bömer, Haupt-Ehwald, and LaFaye, rather than *et iam* with Miller-Goold.

†15.451: Pythagoras calls Rome his "native city" (*cognata moenia*) because as Euphorbus in a previous life he was a Trojan citizen (Haupt-Ehwald at 15.451, 2.458; see 15.160–164).

human blood without a second thought, the man who slashes a bullock's throat with a knife, unmoved by its pitiful bellowing; or the man who can cut the vein of a kid that's whimpering like an infant; or the man who can kill and eat a bird that he himself has fed! What difference is there between such acts and full-blown crime? Where do they lead us? Let an ox pull his plow and attribute his death to advancing years; let sheep arm us against the cold north wind; let nursing goats offer their teats to human hands for milking! Away with nets and traps and snares—all those invidious skills! Stop catching birds with limed twigs! Stop trapping deer with lines tied with frightening feathers!* Stop hiding fishhooks in bait! Kill those animals that harm you, yes, but kill them only; keep their flesh from your mouth; consume only the food that is gained by gentle means!"

They say that Numa stored these and other teachings in his heart, returned to his fatherland and, called to govern by the Latin people, accepted the reins of power. Happy with a nymph for his wife and guided by the Camenae, he taught his people the rites of sacrifice and, accustomed though they were to the savagery of war, converted them to the arts of peace.[62]

When the agéd Numa's life and reign had come to an end, all the Latin people—young mothers, ordinary folk, and ruling elders—mourned his death. His wife now left the city and hid herself in dense woods in the Valley of Aricia, where her groans and lamentations halted the rites of Diana, established by Orestes. Oh! How often the nymphs of the groves and lakes there urged her not to carry on so and offered her words of consolation! How often the hero, son of Theseus, said to her as she wept: "Put a limit to your grieving, for you are not the only one with misfortunes to weep over; have respect for others with troubles like your own! You'll then bear yours more easily. I wish it weren't my own story that could lighten your sadness! But mine can, I know.

"If you've heard of a certain Hippolytus and how he came to die because of his father's credulity and his stepmother's criminal deception, you will be amazed to learn—though I doubt I can prove it to you—I am he. The daughter of Pasiphaë once tried to make me defile my father's bed with her, but I refused. She then contrived a story that it was I who wanted what she wanted and so turned the guilt around and accused me—whether fearing exposure or offended by rejection, who can say? And though I was totally innocent, my father exiled me from the city and called down a curse upon my head as I was leaving.†

*15.474–475: 15.474: The phrase "limed twigs" (*viscata . . . virga*) refers to the practice of catching small birds by smearing branches or twigs with a sticky substance called bird-lime (see *The American Heritage Dictionary* s.v. *bird-lime*) and was "the primary method of catching birds" in antiquity (Haupt-Ehwald at 15.474, 2.459). 15.475: The phrase loosely translated as "lines tied with frightening feathers" (*formidatis . . . pinnis*) refers to the practice of tying feathers on cords and stringing the cords around a hunting area so that the fluttering of the feathers would frighten deer and drive them toward the hunters (Haupt-Ehwald at 15.474, 2.459).

†15.500–505: 15.500: "The daughter of Pasiphaë" is Phaedra. "Hippolytus does not want to mention the (hated) name of Phaedra" (Bömer at 15.500–504, 7.387). 15.504–505: The city

"Now a fugitive, I started out in my chariot for Pittheus' city, Troezen, and as I made my way along the shore of the Gulf of Corinth, the sea rose up, and an enormous mass of water, swelling, seemed to curve into a mountain, bellowing all the while, and then spill open as it crested, and from the breaking wave the head and chest of a horned bull burst into the soft air, seawater gushing from its mouth and nostrils. My companions were terrified, but I stayed calm, thinking of my exile.

"But now my spirited horses, frightened by the monster, turned their heads toward the sea, ears erect, then shuddered and bolted, dashing the chariot on the jagged rocks, while I struggled with powerless hands to tighten the curbs, now smeared with white foam, hauling back on the reins until I was nearly level with the ground. The horses' mad frenzy would never have overwhelmed my strength had not a wheel, where it turns around the axle, struck the stump of a tree and flown apart, smashed to pieces. I was thrown from the chariot and entangled in the reins, and you would have seen my viscera dragged over the ground, my muscles wrapped around the trunk of a tree, my arms and legs either hurled along or caught and left behind, my bones cracking as they snapped in two, my exhausted soul expiring, and no part of my body that you could have recognized: It was one huge wound.

"Surely, nymph, you cannot, you dare not, compare your injury to mine, can you? I also saw the lightless kingdom and soothed my torn flesh in the river Phlegethon. My life would never have been restored without the powerful medicine of Apollo's son.* Thanks to strong herbs and Apollo's aid I received back my life, over the angry objection of Hades, and Diana then covered me in thick clouds, lest the sight of me arouse envy because of her gift. And then, to keep me safe and enable me to show myself without risk, she added years to my age and changed my face, made it less recognizable. For a long time she pondered whether to settle me on Crete or Delos, but finally she rejected both Crete and Delos, put me here, ordered me to accept a change of name, since my own could remind me of horses, and said to me, 'You who were Hippolytus, now be Virbius!' Since then I have inhabited this grove, and as one of the lesser gods I take refuge in the divine power of my mistress and am enrolled in her service."

Another's loss, however, could not lighten Egeria's grief. She lay at the foot of a mountain, melting into tears, until Diana, Phoebus' sister, moved by the devotion of the grieving woman, changed her body into a cool spring, dissolving her limbs into its ever-flowing waters.

This strange occurrence touched the nymphs, and the son of the Amazon†

---

from which Hippolytus is here exiled is Athens. From there he heads for Troezen, of which his grandfather Pittheus is king. Ovid follows the version of the myth that Euripides uses in the first of his two plays on the subject, the *Hippolytus Kaluptomenos* (*Hippolytus Veiled,* not extant), the setting of which is Athens (Haupt-Ehwald at 15.504, 2.462).

*15.533: "Apollo's son" is Aesculapius.

†15.552: The "son of the Amazon" is Hippolytus-Virbius, the son of Theseus by the Amazon Antiope, who is alternatively named Hippolyte.

was astonished—like the Etruscan plowman who in one of his fields once saw a lump of earth, marked by fate, of its own accord, with nothing making it move, first shed its form as earth and then assume human shape and open its newly formed mouth to speak of things to come. The natives called him Tages, and he was the first to teach the Etruscan race how to open the secrets of the future.

Hippolytus was also just as astonished by Egeria's change as Romulus when he saw his spear, which he had planted in the ground on the Palatine hill, suddenly sprout leaves and, held now by its new roots and not by the head of the spear driven into the ground, continue to stand and give unexpected shade to an amazed people, not a weapon now but a tree with willowy branches.

Hippolytus was likewise as astonished as Cipus when he saw his horns reflected in a river (for so he did) and, believing he ought not trust his eyes, repeatedly touched his brow with his fingers—and felt what he had seen. No longer blaming his vision, he stopped as he was returning home victorious after defeating an enemy and raised his eyes and extended his arms to the heavens and prayed, "O gods, whatever is meant by a sign like this, if it's a happy one, let it be for my country and the people of Quirinus, but if it's a threatening omen, let it be for me alone." Then he built an altar from sods of grass and sought to placate the gods by burning incense on it. Next, he poured a libation of wine from a saucer and then examined the still-quivering entrails of a sheep he had slaughtered for the signs they could give him.

When the high priest of the Etruscans viewed the entrails, he did indeed see great things to come, though not yet completely clear. Peering intently at the sheep's innards and then at Cipus' horns, he said: "Hail to you, O King! For this place, and the city of Rome, will obey you, Cipus, you and your horns. But delay no longer and hasten to enter the open gates! Thus does fate decree, for when you are received in the city, you will be king, and you will possess authority, securely and forever."

Cipus stepped back and turned away from the walls of the city with a grim expression on his face and said: "May the gods forbid any omen like this ever to come true! It would be far better for me to spend my life in exile than for the Capitoline to see me as king." He immediately convened a meeting of the people and that solemn body, the Senate. Before addressing them, however, he covered his horns with a laurel wreath, the symbol of peace. He then stepped up on a mound his soldiers had made and, after offering the customary invocation to the ancient gods, said: "There is one person here who, unless you drive him far from the city, will become king. I shall indicate who he is by a sign rather than by name: He has horns on his brow! The man whom the high priest points out to you will make you slaves if he enters Rome. Indeed, he could have burst in through the open gates just now, but I blocked his way—though no one is more closely connected to me than he is. Keep this man out of your city, Quirites! Or, if he deserves it, bind him with heavy chains; or put an end to your fear by sentencing this would-be tyrant to death!"

Like umbrella pines murmuring when a fierce east wind blows through them, or like the pounding of ocean waves when you hear them from afar— such was the sound that arose from the people. And then, above the confusing roar of the noisy crowd, a single voice was heard to shout, "Who is it?" And they looked at everyone's forehead, searching for the telltale horns. Addressing them again Cipus said, "The one you are looking for is here in front of you," and removed the laurel wreath from his head as the people tried to stop him, and revealed his temples, marked by the pair of horns. All lowered their eyes, groaning in dismay (who could believe the sight?), unwilling to look at that head, so deserving of its fame. Allowing him no longer to be stripped of honor, they put the festal wreath back on his head.

Since you were forbidden to enter the city, Cipus, out of respect for you the senators offered you as much land as you could plow a furrow around with a team of oxen between sunup and sundown. They also carved an image of the wondrous horns on the bronze post of a city gate to be a memorial through the ages.*

Reveal to me now, Muses, divine powers always present to poets (for you know the story, nor does the ancient past elude you), how deep Tiber's island admitted the son of Coronis into the sacred number of the gods of Rome.†

A terrible plague once infected the air of Latium, wasting its victims and encrusting their bodies with sores. Weary from burying the dead and seeing that human efforts did nothing and all medical skills came to nothing, the Romans sought divine aid and went to the oracle of Apollo at Delphi, the center of the world. They asked the god to help them in their miserable condition and give them a favorable response and end the suffering of so great a city. The temple, the laurel, and the quiver that Apollo carried all began to tremble at the same time, and from the priestess sitting on the tripod in the lowest part of the shrine came a voice that made their hearts quake with fear. "What you are seeking here, Roman, you should have sought in a place nearer to you. Do so now! You do not need Apollo to lighten your grief, but the son of Apollo. Go with good omens and summon my offspring."

After the senators had listened carefully to the god's instructions, they sought to learn what city the son of Apollo lived in and then commissioned men to sail there, to the shores of Epidaurus. As soon as the keel of their curved ship touched bottom, the envoys presented themselves to the council of Greek elders and asked them to give them the deity whose presence would put an end to the deaths of the Ausonian people, or so a trusted oracle had told them. Opinions varied, and there was disagreement in the council. Some thought aid

---

*15.620–621: The image was carved either on the posts or on the door itself of the Porta Raudusculana (Bömer at 15.620–621, 7.416–417), a gate located, Richardson says (308), "in the depression between the Aventinus Maior and the Aventinus Minor (modern Viale Aventino at Piazza Albania)."

†15.624: The "son of Coronis" is Aesculapius, whose father was Apollo (see 2.542–547 and 596–632; and 15.533).

should not be denied, many argued that they should keep their resources at home and not send them out nor deliver up the god and his power.

While they were debating, twilight banished the late light of day. When night had brought darkness to the world, the healing god seemed, Roman, to stand beside your bed, but in the form in which he appears in the temple.* Holding his rustic staff in one hand and stroking his beard with the other, he uttered these words in a calm voice: "Fear not! I shall abandon my usual form and come with you. Look at this serpent, coiled around my staff, and regard it carefully, so you can recognize it! I shall turn myself into this, but I shall be larger, of a size that gods must be when they take on other forms."

He then ceased speaking and vanished, sleep vanished with him, and a new day followed the flight of sleep. When the burning stars had fled before the coming dawn, the council of elders, uncertain what to do, gathered at the imposing temple of the god and asked him to show them by divine signs the place where he wished to dwell.† Scarcely had they finished speaking when the god, in the form of a golden serpent with a lofty crest, announced his presence by hissing, and with his appearance his statue, the altars, the doors, the marble floor, and the gilded ceiling all began to shake. He halted in the middle of the temple, erect to half his length, and, fire flashing from his eyes, surveyed the scene. The crowd gathered there was quaking with terror. The priest, who was wearing a white fillet around his venerable head, recognized the deity and cried: "The god! The god is here! Incline your hearts to him and keep silence, all who are present! Manifest yourself to us, O most beautiful one, for our benefit, and grant your aid to those who worship at your sacred altars!"

All bowed their heads to the divinity in adoration, as ordered to do, repeating the words of the priest, and the sons of Aeneas also paid homage to the god in thought and word.‡ He acknowledged their prayer and then, shaking his crest and hissing three times with his darting tongue to confirm his pledge, slithered down the shining steps, turned his head and looked back at the ancient altars as he was about to depart, and bade farewell to the temple home where he had lived so long.

The mighty serpent then flowed across the blossom-strewn ground, curving himself into spiraling coils as he made his way through the middle of the city to the harbor and the curving jetty that protected it. Here he stopped and with a serene expression seemed to dismiss his entourage, the devoted throng following him in procession. Then he went up on the Italian ship, which dipped beneath the divine weight and rode lower in the water with the god on board.

The sons of Aeneas rejoiced and, after sacrificing a bull on shore, hung gar-

---

*15.654: The "Roman" addressed by the narrator is Q. Ogulnius Gallus, the head of the delegation (Bömer at 15.653–655, 7.428).

†15.666: These are the Greek elders of Epidaurus referred to at 15.645 (LaFaye 3.143 n.2).

‡15.682: The phrase "sons of Aeneas," translating *Aeneadae,* is a synonym for "Romans." The word recurs at 15.695.

lands of flowers about the ship and cast off the lines. A light breeze drove it along, the god towering above it as he rested his neck on the curved stern and gazed down into the blue waters. Crossing the Ionian Sea on moderate winds, he reached Italy at dawn on the sixth day, sailed past the Lacinian promontory, known for its temple of the goddess, and the shore of Scylaceum.* Leaving Iapygia behind, he avoided the Amphrisian rocks on the left and the Cocin-thian cliffs on the right; coasted by Romethium, Caulon, and Narycia; navigated the straits of Messina; went past the Sicilian promontory of Pelorus; sailed by the home of King Aeolus, son of Hippotes; and headed toward Temese and its mines, Leucosia, and the rose gardens of ever-mild Paestum. From there he passed by Capri and Minerva's promontory; past the hills of Sorrentum, with their choice vineyards; past Herculaneum, Stabiae, and Parthenope, built for leisure; and thence past the temple of the Cumaean sibyl. Sailing on, he approached the hot springs; Liternum, home of the mastic tree; the river Volturnus, which rolls sand in drifts along its bottom; Sinuessa, where doves flock; oppressive Minturnae; Caieta, named for Aeneas' old nurse, who is buried there; Formiae, the home of Antiphates;† Trachas, surrounded by a marsh; Circe's land; and Antium with its hard-packed beach.

When the crew steered the ship into this harbor (for the sea had now become rough), the god uncoiled himself and glided with great rolling curves into his father's temple, built near the golden sands. After enjoying the hospitality of the divinity whose son he was, the Epidaurian left his father's altars, now that the sea was calm again, and, with his clicking scales furrowing the sand, slithered up the ship's rudder and rested his head on the lofty stern until they reached Castrum, the sacred abode of Lavinium, and the mouth of the Tiber. Hither thronged the entire population, mothers and fathers and the virgins who preserve your fire, Roman Vesta, rushing to meet the god and greeting him with happy shouts. As the ship was towed upstream, burning incense crackled on altars that lined the riverbanks, perfuming the air with its smoke, and animals for sacrifice warmed the knives that were plunged into their throats.

The ship now entered the capital of the world, the city of Rome. The serpent, upright, leaned its head against the top of the mast and looked around for a suitable place to dwell. The river divides into two parts at a place called "the Island" and flows with equal streams past both sides of the land between them. Here the son of Apollo again brought himself down from the Latin ship and, again assuming his form as a god, entered Rome as bringer of health to the city and put an end to the plague.[63]

Now, Aesculapius arrived at our temples as a foreign god, but Caesar is a

---

*At 15.702 I read *nobilitata* (sc. *Lacinia,* 701: "the Lacinian promontory, known for . . .") with Anderson (1982a), Bömer, Haupt-Ehwald, and LaFaye, rather than *nobilitate* with Miller-Goold. The goddess referred to is Juno (Bömer at 15.702, 7.439).

†15.717: Antiphates was the king of the Laestrygonians (Homer, *Odyssey* 10.105–111) and is mentioned by Macareus at 14.233ff.

god in his own city.* Preeminent as he was in war and peace, neither his campaigns, crowned with triumphs, nor his accomplishments at home, nor his fame, acquired so quickly, did more to make him a new star in the sky, a comet streaming through the heavens, than his own offspring.† For of all Caesar's achievements none was greater than being the father of this son. Was subduing the seagoing Britons greater? Or sailing his victorious fleet up the papyrus-lined Nile, the river with seven mouths? Or adding the rebellious Numidians to the Roman Empire, and African Juba, and Pontus, swelling with the fame of Mithridates? Or celebrating many triumphs, and deserving many more? Are any of these greater than being the father of such a great man? And by making Caesar's son ruler of the empire, O gods, you mightily blessed the human race! Lest he be born from mortal seed, therefore, his father had to be made a god.

When Aeneas' mother, the golden goddess, saw this, and saw, too, the bitter death prepared for the pontifex,‡ saw the conspirators arming themselves, she turned pale, and then she said to all the gods, accosting each in turn: "See what a massive effort has gone into plotting against me! See what treachery seeks to take the one life left to me from the line of Trojan Iulus! Will I be the only goddess forever racked by cares, cares that are all too justified?—I who was recently wounded by Diomedes' Calydonian spear,§ I who am now overcome by Troy's fall, poor defenseless city; and I who now see my son driven by years of wandering, tossed on the sea, entering the realms of the silent dead, and waging war with Turnus, or, rather—to tell the truth—with Juno.

"But why do I now recall the ancient losses of my line? The fear that grips me keeps me from remembering all that is past. Look! Do you see that criminal daggers are now being sharpened? Stop them, I beg you! Repel this crime! Don't let the murder of the pontifex put out the fires of Vesta!"‖

Such words did an anxious Venus fling out to all of heaven, but in vain. Yet she did move the gods to pity, for though they could not break the iron decrees of the ancient sisters, they sent sure signs of the coming sorrows just the same. For they say that the sound of arms clashing amid dark clouds and the terrifying blasts of horns and trumpets heard in the sky gave warnings of the crime. A dark and grieving sun cast a ghastly light upon an alarmed world. Fiery meteors were often seen below the stars, and drops of blood often fell, mixed with rain. The somber face of the morning star was splotched with black corro-

---

*15.746: "Caesar is a god": Ovid refers to Julius Caesar, assassinated in 44 B.C.

†15.750: "than his own offspring": Julius Caesar's great-nephew and adopted son Octavian, who in 27 B.C. adopted the name Augustus, by which he was known thereafter.

‡15.763: Julius Caesar was *pontifex maximus* when he was assassinated. The *pontifex maximus* was the head of the college of *pontifices,* one of "the four major colleges of the Roman priesthood," with "general oversight of the state cult" and other duties. See *OCD* (3d edition) s.v. *pontifex/pontifices* 1219–20.

§15.769: "I who was recently wounded": Diomedes mentions wounding Venus at 14.477–478. The incident occurs at *Iliad* 5.330–342. It was hardly "recent."

‖15.777–778: The extinguishing of the fire always burning in the temple of Vesta would presage the fall of Rome (Bömer at 15.777–778, 7.461–462).

sion; the chariot of the moon was drenched in gore. The Stygian owl gave sinister omens in a thousand places; in a thousand places ivory statues wept, and they say that chanting voices and threatening words were heard in sacred groves. No animals showed favorable signs when sacrificed. Their livers warned that great upheavals were at hand, and lobes cut from them were found among the entrails. They say that in the Forum and around men's houses and the temples of the gods dogs howled all night long and ghosts of the dead wandered, while tremors shook the city.

Yet the warnings of the gods could not conquer the treachery fated to come, and naked swords were carried into the temple. For no place in the city seemed so favorable for the crime, for this terrible murder, as the Curia.* Then indeed did Venus beat her breast with both hands and struggle to hide Aeneas' descendant in the cloud in which Paris was spirited away from Menelaus, who was threatening him with death, and which concealed Aeneas, too, when he escaped the sword of Diomedes.

Her father then said to her: "Are you trying to move immovable fate on your own, my dear daughter? You can, if you wish, enter the house of the three sisters yourself. There you will see a massive work of bronze and solid iron, the record of all that has ever happened in the world and that ever will happen, an archive indestructible and eternal, that fears neither collisions in heaven, nor raging thunderbolts, nor ruin of any kind. And there you will find engraved on imperishable steel the destiny of your race. I myself have read it and fixed it in my memory, and I shall tell it to you so that you will no longer be ignorant of the future.

"The one for whom you labor, Venus, has finished his time on earth and completed the years he owed to the world. He will ascend to heaven as a god and be worshipped in temples everywhere, thanks to you and to his son, who, as heir of his name, will alone bear the burden placed upon him; and in the war he wages as the courageous avenger of his murdered father he will have us for an ally.† Under his command the walls of besieged Mutina will come down, and the city will sue for peace. Pharsalia will feel his power, Emathian Philippi will once again be soaked in blood, and the bearer of a great name will be conquered in Sicilian waters. The Egyptian wife of a Roman general, trusting too much in her marriage, will also fall, her threats to enslave our Capitol to her Canopus made in vain.‡

---

*15.801–802: The Curia was the building where the Roman Senate met; it had earlier been consecrated as a temple. (See Bömer at 15.800–802, 7.469.)

†15.819: "his son": Julius Caesar's great-nephew and adopted son Octavian, later known as Augustus.

‡15.823–828: 15.823–824: "Pharsalia will feel his power": "In a poetic fiction Ovid shifts Pharsalus in Thessaly, where Julius Caesar defeated Pompey on August 9, 48 B.C., and Philippi in Macedonia, where Cassius and Brutus succumbed to the Triumvirs in late autumn of 42 B.C., into the same vicinity as towns of Emathia [hence "Emathian Philippi" at 15.824], which here incorporates Macedonia and Thessaly but was originally a term for a part of Macedonia" (Haupt-Ehwald at 15.823f., 2.485–486). 15.825: "the bearer of a great name": In 36 B.C. Sextus Pom-

"Why name for you the barbarian nations that lie near oceans east and west? All lands on earth where people dwell will be his. The sea, too, will submit to him. And when he has brought peace to the world, he will turn his mind to the rights of his countrymen, and out of his high regard for justice, he will establish laws and by his own example serve as his people's moral guide. Looking ahead to a future age and the coming generations, he will require the son of his virtuous wife to assume his name and burdens, and not until he is old and his years equal his achievements will he reach his celestial home and his kindred among the stars. Until that time, take up this soul from its murdered body* and make it a brilliant star, so that divine Julius can always behold our Capitol and our Forum from his lofty dwelling place!"

The moment Jupiter finished speaking, caring Venus arrived at the house of the Senate and, visible to no one, caught up the soul of her own dear Caesar as it left his body, lest it vanish in air, and bore it to the stars. As she carried it, she felt it gather light and begin to burn; and she released it from her arms, and it flew above the moon, streaming fire on its way down the sky. And now a star itself, it shone in heaven. Seeing his son's great deeds, Caesar acknowledges that they are greater than his own and rejoices that his son surpasses him.

Though the son forbids his own actions to be placed above his father's, fame obeys no commands and goes where it will, and it carries him, unwilling, beyond his parent, opposes him in this alone. Thus did lordly Atreus yield to the fame of Agamemnon; thus did Theseus outshine Aegeus; thus did Achilles surpass Peleus. Finally, if I may use an example appropriate for Caesar and his son, thus, too, is Saturn less than Jupiter. Jupiter rules the heavens and the three kingdoms of the universe, the earth is under Augustus: Each is father and sovereign lord.

Gods, companions of Aeneas, you before whom fire and sword gave way; gods of our native Italy; Quirinus, father of our city; Gradivus, father of invincible Quirinus; Vesta, worshipped among Caesar's household gods; and you, Apollo, a part of Caesar's household, along with Vesta; and you, Jupiter, who hold the Tarpeian citadel on high; and all you other deities whom a poet has a sacred right to call upon: May that hour be slow in coming, may my life be over long before it comes, the hour that dear Augustus leaves the world he rules and enters heaven and, absent from us, hears our prayers!

I have now completed a work that neither Jupiter's wrath, nor fire, nor sword, nor time's corruption can ever destroy. Let that day that has dominion

---

peius, the youngest son of Pompey the Great, was defeated by Octavian's admiral, M. Agrippa, in a naval battle off the coast of Sicily between Mylae and Naulochus (Haupt-Ehwald at 15.825, 2.486). 15.826: Ovid calls Cleopatra, Marc Antony's lover, his "Egyptian wife." 15.828: Canopus, a city in lower Egypt, was notorious for its opulence (Haupt-Ehwald at 15.828, 2.486).

*15.836–840: 15.836: The "son of his virtuous wife" is Tiberius, son of Augustus' wife, Livia, by Tiberius Claudius Nero, her former husband. 15.840: The "soul" referred to is that of Julius Caesar.

over nothing but this body end my life on earth whenever it may choose to. The better part of me will be carried up and fixed beyond the stars forever, and my name will never die. Wherever Roman might extends, in all the lands beneath its rule, I shall be the one whom people hear and read. And if poets truly can foretell, in all centuries to come, I shall live.[64]

NOTES

Introduction

1. Almost all our information on Ovid's life comes from *Tristia* 4.10, an autobiographical poem, which, like all autobiographies, gives the poet's life the shape he wanted it to have and presents him as he wanted to be seen.

2. *Tristia* 1.2.77–78 and *Epistulae ex Ponto* 2.10.21–29.

3. Ovid says at *Tristia* 4.10.33–34 that he accepted the first appointment in government available for young men, a position on the board of three (*tresviri capitales*), which had oversight over the police and also over prisons and executions. (See *Der Kleine Pauly* 5.938–939, s.v. *Tresviri* b.) He indicates at *Fasti* 4.383–384 that he was also "one of the board of ten *stlitibus iudicandis,* presiding over lawsuits." These positions "were usually alternatives," Fantham says, that is, one held one or the other, not both. "But shortage of candidates may have enabled O[vid] to hold successive offices" (Fantham [1998] at *Fasti* 4.384, 166).

4. When his beard had been cut only once or twice, he says (*Tristia* 4.10.57–58).

5. *Tristia* 4.10.69.

6. Publication of *Amores*, McKeown 87; see the chapter titled "Chronology," 74–89. Recognition gained from the *Amores*, Kenney (1982) 420.

7. *Ex Ponto* 4.9.3–4.

8. He pleads his case, Kenney says, "ostensibly to Augustus, really before the bar of public opinion, to which he can be seen repeatedly appealing over Augustus' head" ([1992] xi).

9. Ovid refers to his *Medea* at *Tristia* 2.553–554, and it is mentioned by Quintilian (*Institutio Oratoria* 8.5.6) and by the Elder Seneca (*Suasoriae* 3.7).

10. *Tristia* 1.7.13–14; 27–30; 2.555–556; and 3.14.19–24.

11. Private meeting with an angry Augustus, *Tristia* 2.131–134 and *Ex Ponto* 2.7.56; Ovid must leave Italy by a certain date, *Tristia* 1.3.5–6; his poems removed from Rome's libraries, *Tristia* 3.1.59–80 and *Ex Ponto* 1.1.5–10.

12. Augustus used the milder form of exile known as relegation, which allowed Ovid to keep his property and civic rights but enabled the emperor to designate the place where Ovid must live. The poet indicates that he was "relegated" at *Tristia* 2.135–138, 5.2.61–62, and 5.11.21–22.

13. Ovid uses the polarity of heaven and hell for Rome and Tomis at *Ex Ponto* 3.5.55–56. Although Tomis, Claassen notes, was only about twenty days by sea from Brundisium, the port of departure from Italy by ship to places east, longer overland, the poet deliberately creates "the impression of a vast gulf between the two worlds" (68, 69). At *Ex Ponto* 1.8.33–38 Ovid lovingly recalls favorite places in Rome. Kenney on Ovid's relegation to Tomis, (1982) 442.

14. *Tristia* 2.207.

15. Ovid identifies the *Ars Amatoria* as the poem that provoked Augustus' wrath at *Tristia* 1.9.59–62; and 2.5–9, 303–316, 539–542, and 545–546; and at *Ex Ponto* 2.9.72–74; 2.10.12 and 15–16; 2.11.2; and 3.3.37–40.

16. However important the role played by the *Ars Amatoria* in Augustus' decision to banish Ovid (in comparison to Ovid's "mistake"), from exile the poet insists that his own morals were not like those implicitly advocated in the *Ars Amatoria,* which was written in his youth as an amusement, he says, and, though not praiseworthy, was meant to be funny (*Tristia* 1.9.59–62; see also 2.353–356).

17. He must not reveal his "mistake," *Tristia* 4.10.93–100; see also *Ex Ponto* 1.6.21–22, 2.2.57–59, and 3.3.72–74. Quotation, Kenney (1992) x.

18. Ovid pleads for a change of place for his exile at *Tristia* 2.183–186 and 4.4.49–52. In *Ex Ponto* he is more insistent (or more fervid), hoping or praying that the emperor (Augustus or his successor, Tiberius) will lessen his wrath, e.g., 1.9.27–30, 1.10.40–44, 2.7.79–80, and 4.6.19–20; will recall him from exile, e.g., 1.4.47–58, 1.7.47–48, 3.6.37–38, and 4.9.71–74 (?); or will allow him to change his place of exile, e.g., 1.1.77–80; 1.2.63–64, 103–104, 127–128, 147–150; 1.6.27–48; 2.2.65–66, 107–110; 2.8.71–76; 3.1; 3.3.59–64; 3.6.37–38; cf. 3.7.29–32; 3.9.1–3, 27–28, 37–38; 4.8.83–88; 4.13.43–50; and 4.14.5–14.

19. *Ex Ponto* 4.16.1, 3–4, 45–52.

20. Solodow makes a sharp, but to my mind false, distinction between metamorphosis and change: "[T]he subject of [Pythagoras'] speech [15.75–478] is not really metamorphosis at all, but rather mere change." And while he acknowledges "the poem's strong sense that the world is variable, complex, chaotic, incomprehensible," he insists that "this is only the background against which the poem's central phenomenon is to be seen. The theme of the poem is not mutability, but metamorphosis, which is very different" (167). The difference for Solodow is that change is "directionless" (167) and also "reversible," while metamorphosis is directed and fixed, and he uses Lycaon in book 1 as an example: "[T]he change in Lycaon is permanent. Having become a wolf, he will remain one through all time . . . This is what distinguishes Ovidian metamorphoses from the mere changes catalologued in Pythagoras' speech [in book 15], which were

endless and often reversible" (176). But the "unceasing flux and movement" that, Solo-dow says, govern the world of the *Metamorphoses* (176) are not to be characterized as "only the background" for metamorphosis but rather serve as the dynamic context necessary for it, and they powerfully reinforce the idea, so important for metamorphosis to be thinkable, that boundaries—of person, of self, of objects—are permeable. Some metamorphoses in the poem, moreover, are reversible: Tiresias was "metamorphosed" into a woman and then back into the man he originally was (3.324–331). Circe changes Ulysses' companions into animals and then, when Ulysses threatens her, back into their human selves (14.276–305). The world itself is created by the metamorphosis of Chaos (1.5–88); through Jupiter's flood it undergoes metamorphosis back into a watery chaos; and it is then re-created through what I would call a second metamorphosis (1.89–451). If some metamorphoses are reversible, why not all?

And Pythagoras does not assert (nor does Ovid imply) that change is "directionless," only that it exists. It may appear to be directionless because it is slow. Indeed, change in the world of the *Metamorphoses* may be called metamorphosis in slow motion, a point Ovid may be said to make in the story of the sybil, whose metamorphosis from a vibrant and attractive girl into nothing but a voice takes a thousand years and so would appear to be a slow change (14.129–153). In the world of the poem, metamorphosis happens and is real and believable *because* the world is governed by "unceasing flux and movement."

21. Galinsky (1975) 62.

22. Hellenistic poetry about metamorphosis, Galinsky (1975) 2; the poem's "modern" style, Kenney (1973) 118; the narrator's "genial tone," Galinsky (1975) 159.

23. The poem as an epic of love, Wilkinson (1955) 206; Galinsky (1975) 31, 43, 97; Conte 354; and Barkan 91; as an epic of rape, Segal (1969a) 93; as a "microcosm of human psychology," Kenney (1986) xviii; nothing larger than personal experience recognized, Solodow 156.

24. Solodow 37.

25. Conte 353; Solodow 34.

26. Kenney (1982) 457.

27. Kenney (1973) 126, 127.

Metamorphoses

BOOK ONE

1. In the opening lines of the *Metamorphoses* (1.1–88) Ovid presents his plan for the poem in a prologue (1.1–4) and follows it with a cosmogony, a description of the creation of the universe (1.5–88). The creation of the universe is the first part of the first section of the poem (following the prologue) according to Wilkinson's division of the poem, which he adapted from Crump 274–278 (and which I accept):

Prologue: 1.1–4
Introduction: The Creation and the Flood, 1.5–451
Part 1:   Gods, 1.452–6.420
Part 2:   Heroes and Heroines, 6.421–11.193
Part 3:   "Historical" Personages, 11.194–15.870
Epilogue: 15.871–879

See Wilkinson (1955) 148n.; Galinsky also accepts Crump's division, with a minor variation (1975) 85; Nagle (1989b) 29–31 surveys "structural studies" of the *Metamorphoses*.

In the first line ("My mind leads me to something new, to tell of forms changed") Ovid emphasizes three things (in addition to his subject, "forms changed"): that he is doing something "new"; that "the primary force behind his poem is his own active rational intelligence" (Anderson [1997] at 1.1, 150), his "mind"; and that he will "tell" of metamorphoses, not "sing," as Virgil says he will do in the first line of the *Aeneid* ("Arms and the man I sing," 1.1), indicating to us that he "does not take up Virgil's attitude as a prophet whose song is inspired by divine power and obeys laws beyond his own choice" (Due 94).

For an undertaking as vast and complex as he proposes, Ovid invokes not just one god (as do Homer's *Iliad* and *Odyssey,* Lucretius' *De Rerum Natura,* and Virgil's *Aeneid*), but all gods, this "highly unusual" invocation "the first of its kind" (Bömer at 1.2, 1.12). Of course, invoking a host of unnamed gods may be like invoking none at all.

In the prologue, Ovid proposes a continuous ("unbroken," 1.4), i.e., "epic," poem about change that will run from the beginning of the universe to his own time and that will be "'fine-spun,' unpretending—in a word, *unepic*" (Kenney [1986] xv). These lines present the "generic paradox" on which the poem is "founded" (Hinds [1987] 132) and "establish two paths that continue throughout the work: constant change and a unified eternal poem" (Barkan 20).

In his account of the creation of the universe from chaos which follows the prologue (1.5–88)—this cosmogony is the poem's first metamorphosis—Ovid has produced "a quite acceptable synopsis of the most widespread theory of the creation" (Due 98). As Lee notes, Ovid's cosmogony

> seems to owe most to Stoic teaching. . . . The four elements can be traced back to Empedocles of Agrigentum. Anaxagoras had held that Reason . . . created the world by imposing order on Chaos. Plato regarded the stars as divine beings. . . . Socrates had seen in man's erect posture a symbol of his superiority over the other animals. . . . The Pythagoreans originated the doctrines of the Five Zones. . . . The Stoics included all these points in their system, which had as a fundamental tenet the identification of God with Nature. (at 1.5–88, 70)

Barkan notes a "cosmology of layers" in 1.5–20 (earth, sea, and sky, with repeated references; hot, cold, wet, and dry; soft, hard, heavy, and light), "the precondition," he says, "for a metamorphic universe because it establishes the orders among which the flow of transformations will take place" (28).

At 1.32–88 Ovid describes "the Creation proper" (Lee at 1.32–88, 74), beginning with the formation of the earth ("molded . . . into the shape of a great ball," 1.34) and culminating in the birth of the human race ("The earth . . . was dressed in human figures," 1.87–88), "the crown of creation" (Due 99). The human race and the cosmos, Myers says, "are intimately related because of their identical constituents," that is, the four elements. "This close relationship may suggest," she continues, "why in the *Metamorphoses* the transitions between human, animal, and natural phenomena seem to be so frighteningly fluid and easy" ([1994a] 42–43). It may also suggest, as Feeney says, that "a human's transformation into a rock or a tree is a reversion to origins." Moreover, "since there may have been divine elements at man's creation, and since the celestial element may have been lingering in the primeval mud . . . , a human's elevation to deity may also be seen as a return to something cognate" (194). Ovid's cosmogony shows metamorphosis as the founding principle to which all that has been created owes its existence.

While the poet's account of creation borrows heavily from Stoicism, as indicated earlier, it is modeled, Wheeler suggests, on Homer's ecphrasis of the shield of Achilles (created by Hephaestus) at *Iliad* 18.478–608. This ecphrasis, Wheeler says, "[a]ncient critics of Homer . . . interpreted . . . as a philosophically conceived allegory of the creation of the universe by a demiurge" (97–98). In calling chaos a "rough, disordered mass" (*rudis indigestaque moles*, 1.7), Ovid "hints that chaos is a raw material that awaits refinement in the hands of an artist" (Wheeler 105). He makes the Stoics' "god, a superior kind of nature" (1.21), the demiurge who, by the process of creation, shapes this "raw material" into the world. The poet "explicitly identifies the creator's artistic status" (Wheeler 106) by referring to him as "maker of the world" (*mundi fabricator*, 1.57), as "the creator of all things, the source of a better world" (*ille opifex rerum, mundi melioris origo*, 1.79). "These terms," Wheeler says, "bear witness to the especially Ovidian idea that art lies behind the order of nature" (106).

In his discussion, Wheeler maps points of similarity between Homer's ecphrasis of the shield of Achilles and Ovid's ecphrastic cosmogony, noticing that "both poets depict an object as it is made. . . . [I]n each case, the creative artist plays the same role of establishing the point of view from which we see what is created" (106–107). In lines 1.21–31, Ovid "explicitly defines the borders of the universe and the relative position of its elements and regions, and so establishes a visual framework for the developments that follow." In lines 1.32–68, the "central part of the cosmogony . . . elaborates and embellishes this framework." Ovid's cosmogony is thus "structured in the way that other ecphrases are in the *Metamorphoses*" (Wheeler 109), namely, Vulcan's artwork on the door of the palace of the sun in book 2.5–18, which the cosmogony "prefigures," and Minerva's tapestry in book 6.70–102, for which the cosmogony "sets an example" (Wheeler 112, 113). Wheeler reads the demiurge of the cosmogony ("god, a superior kind of nature," 1.21) as "a figure for the poet" and "the ordering of the universe as a metaphor for the creation of the poem," making the "'real' subject of Ovid's cosmogony . . . the literary creation of *Metamorphoses*" (117).

Ovid gives the human race an equivocal origin: lest any region be without its own creatures (*animalibus*, 1.72), the demiurge (at 1.73–75) created the stars and the gods (for heaven), fish (for the seas), beasts (for the earth), and birds (for the air). But an *animal* more holy than these and able to dominate the rest was lacking (1.76–77), and so the human race was made, in one or the other of two ways: *either* the demiurge of the cosmogony made it from divine seed (*divino semine*, 1.78), *or* Prometheus (a god of mythology, as opposed to Stoic cosmogony) mixed some of the newly made earth with rainwater and fashioned an *effigies* (1.83), a "likeness," of the gods. Thus the ambiguous position of the human race as belonging to the "perfect" universe of the cosmogony or to the radically imperfect world (as we shall see) or earth of the gods, themselves created, and of metamorphoses.

After the quasi–philosophical–scientific cosmogony, the demiurge disappears and is not referred to again, and the universe in which all the metamorphoses occur is now in the hands of the gods of mythology: Jupiter, Juno, Apollo, Minerva, and so on. Yet the poet, for whom the demiurge is a "figure," "like the God of the creation, remains within or behind or beyond or above his handiwork, invisible, refined out of existence, indifferent, paring his fingernails" (Joyce 215)—except for his frequent apostrophes, addressing characters in the poem, that make him not so invisible after all.

2. The formation of the world from chaos, crowned by the birth of the human race—metamorphosis as creation—is followed (1.89–150) by four ages, gold, silver, bronze, and iron (an adaptation of Hesiod's five generations in his *Works and Days* 109–201)—metamorphosis as decline. When change is the governing reality, an ideal time (the age of gold) that corresponds to the apparent perfection of the created world cannot last: paradise is temporary. The moral degeneracy of the iron age (which won't last either, but will be swept away by the flood: 1.262–312), in which "every kind of forbidden crime was soon committed" (1.128–129), leads with seeming inevitability to the Giants' attempt to invade the kingdom of the gods (1.151–153). Ovid's brief adversion here to the battle of gods and Giants, "a popular epic topic" (Due 101), enables him to introduce the gods, who played no role in the creation and have been absent until now (except for the brief mention of Prometheus as the creator of the human race: 1.82–86). Jupiter, the chief deity, defeats the Giants by shattering the mountains they have piled up to climb to heaven and crushes them beneath the debris. Their blood, soaking into the earth, produces a second human race, as bad as the first in the degenerate state to which it has fallen.

It is now clear that divine action is needed: "[S]ome measures have to be taken against all this wickedness" (Due 102), epitomized by "the foul banquet at Lycaon's table" (1.165). And so the stage is set for Jupiter to call a council of the gods, an epic device for setting a plot in motion, in which, typically, "the opening human situation is taken under consideration" (Anderson [1997] at 1.163–252, 168). Ovid's council of the gods, however, is not typical, for the poet "avails himself of a tactic from epic parodies . . . that describes the Council as a rowdy meeting of the Roman Senate. It becomes clear that Jupiter plays the role of Augustus and that the gods are . . . obsequious senators" (Anderson [1997] loc. cit.). Furthermore, Jupiter, "[c]onsumed by . . . terrible rage, rage worthy of himself" (1.166), is concerned not for humans but for himself and "irrationally concludes from the violence of Lycaon that all human beings must be exterminated" (Anderson [1997] loc. cit.). He wants to make the world safe for lesser divinities, he says, who are not yet allowed to live in heaven, including "nymphs, fauns, satyrs, and mountain-dwelling deities" (1.192–195), although the biggest threat—to the nymphs, at any rate—is the gods themselves, Jupiter chief among them, as we shall see in the stories of Daphne and Io, soon to come (Due 74; see also Anderson [1989a] 99).

Ovid compares the gods' response to Jupiter's speech to the Romans' devotion to Augustus "when a godless band was raging to wash away the name of Rome with Caesar's blood" (1.199–205). It is not clear whether Ovid is referring to the assassination in 44 B.C. of Julius Caesar (Augustus' great-uncle, who had adopted Augustus as his son before he himself was murdered) or to failed attempts to assassinate Augustus. (See Bömer at 1.200, 1.87, who thinks the latter more likely.)

As an example of human wickedness that justifies his decision to destroy the world, Jupiter tells the assembled gods the story of Lycaon, who, the god says, served him human flesh and planned to murder him as well (1.211–239). This is the first of many "embedded" tales in the *Metamorphoses*, stories told by characters in the poem. A major feature of Ovid's narrative technique, these embedded tales demonstrate the poem's "premise" that "story-telling" (which Solodow calls "the most popular activity in the poem") "is a fundamental means of comprehending the world" (Solodow 34). Ovid at one place in the poem embeds a story within already embedded stories to create four levels of narration. This occurs in book 5, where the narrator tells of an unnamed Muse, in the course of a story she is telling Minerva, singing to the goddess the song that another Muse, Calliope, sang as an entry in a contest and that included Arethusa's telling Ceres, mother of Proserpina (whose abduction by Pluto is the subject of Calliope's song), how she was pursued by the river Alpheus (5.337–678). "[T]his complication of the narrative syntax," Conte says, "by multiplying the narrative levels and voices, produces an effect of giddiness, of a labyrinthine fugue: the account seems to be sprouting continually from itself and moving away in an infinitely receding perspective" (353; see also Nagle [1989a]).

Lycaon seeks to pervert the basis for the relation between humans and gods, created by sacrifice, by turning it into an act of cannibalism: "Lycaon is by implication defying the gods by imputing cannibalistic motives to the sacrificial act" (Barkan 27). In book 15, Pythagoras will claim a connection between eating flesh (an integral part of sacrifice) and cannibalism (15.456–478), and in urging human beings to avoid eating meat, which to him is cannibalism, he is, in effect, urging them not to sacrifice. Not to sacrifice is not to worship the gods. By urging that humans abstain from flesh, Pythagoras is urging them to sever their connection with the gods.

Bloodthirsty Lycaon is changed into a bloodthirsty wolf, although not by Jupiter, and his transformation "freezes in physical form the spirit that has all along animated [him]" (Barkan 25), for Lycaon, "notorious for his viciousness" (*notus feritate*, 1.198), as a wolf possesses "the same vicious look" (*eadem feritatis imago*, 1.239).

Jupiter first thinks of destroying the world by fire but rejects that idea, fearing that heaven would be "ignited accidentally" (1.254–255), and decides "to drown the human race" by flooding the world (1.260–261). The god first sends torrential rains and then enlists the aid of his brother, the sea god Neptune, who orders all rivers to flood the earth (1.262–290). While the universe was created by the "elevated but rather vague demiurgus," Due says, the "operating forces" that now destroy it are "individual and personal gods of a different rank and order[,] . . . science transformed into mythology" (108–109).

Solodow describes Ovid's narrative of the flood and its consequences as "affective" rather than "linear"; that is, the "snapshots" composing the narrative "do not so much tell an unfolding story as evoke a series of feelings," with the "emotional climax," the death of the human race by drowning or starvation (1.311–312), "reserved for the end." The flood is thus "articulated as a tricolon crescendo," Jupiter, who initiates the flood, receiving the fewest lines (twelve: 1.262–273); Neptune, who helps him, almost half again as many lines as Jupiter (seventeen: 1.274–290); and "the effects of the flood" the most lines (twenty-two: 1.291–312; see Solodow 125).

Deucalion and Pyrrha, the human couple who survive the flood, ask the goddess Themis how the human race can be restored (1.377–380) and are given instructions. Thus Ovid, "who has been emphasizing Jupiter's role as destructive deity, allows the 'Father' god no part in the re-creation of humanity" (Anderson [1997] at 1.313–415, 181).

Fire and water are the most basic of the four primary elements that constitute the universe, and they occupy places at its opposite boundaries, fire the highest place, water the lowest (1.26–31). Each element causes the destruction of the world, water in the flood in book 1, fire in the conflagration caused by Phaethon in book 2.1–400. In 1.416–433 fire and water work together to re-create the non-human world, operating as a *discors concordia* (1.433), or "harmony of discord."

At the beginning of the *Metamorphoses*, in the metamorphoses from chaos to creation, back to chaos, then re-creation, with water and fire as the agents of both destruction and re-creation (1.5–2.400), Ovid shows change as both the cause and nature of existence. This representation of change as the governing principle of the physical and material world corresponds to the subject of Pythagoras' sermon at 15.75–478.

This section of the poem, "introduction: creation and the flood," which began at 1.5, ends at 1.451.

3. The first part of the poem, "gods," begins at 1.452 and continues to 6.420 (see n. 1).

Ovid makes the transition from the flood and its aftermath to the story of Apollo and Daphne (1.452–567, the first story in part one) by means of the "stepping-stone method," viz.: monsters born spontaneously after the flood included the Python, killed by Apollo, who commemorated the deed by establishing the Pythian games, for which a crown of oak leaves was the prize, inasmuch as the laurel (the meaning of Daphne's name in Greek), a crown of which later replaced the oak leaf crown, did not yet exist— and this story tells us how it came to exist (see Frank J. Miller 471–472).

The tale of Daphne and Apollo introduces "the love motif" (Due 112) and is the first of ten love stories in the *Metamorphoses* in which either the lover or the beloved "is pictured as a hunter" (Davis [1983] 15–16). Apollo is obviously the hunter here, and he leaves off pursuit of wild animals and his enemies "in favor of a new victim, the virgin Daphne," in what is an "erotic hunt": "[T]he literal hunt turns easily into a sexual hunt" (Parry 270).

Apollo (the patron god of the emperor Augustus) is made to fall in love by Cupid, the god of love, who demonstrates to the arrogant, boastful archer-god his (Cupid's) superiority over him at archery (1.452–473). Cupid's (love's) importance is emphasized at the beginning of the poem and again in book 5 (the rape of Proserpina) and in book 10 (the story of Venus and Adonis). And Cupid's teacher was Ovid, as the poet tells us in his *Ars Amatoria* (1.17).

The target of love-struck Apollo's predatory lust is Daphne, who is beautiful but rejects her beauty and prefers to live as a virgin-huntress, devoted to the virgin goddess, Diana, "'unmarried, forever!'" as she says (1.486–487). Cupid's blunt arrow of lead (which strikes Daphne, causing her actively *not* to love Apollo) "introduces a secondary theme," Barnard says, that has to do with "questions of Daphne's identity, a split between her alluring body, which attracts Apollo, and her virgin self." Her transformation into the laurel tree "mends the scission and enables the nymph to preserve her identity as a virgin" (35), but "only by sacrificing her humanity" (Parry 274).

Apollo tries to persuade Daphne of his worthiness as a lover even as he pursues her, an inherently comical situation made more so by what he says and by the fact that it is august, Olympian Apollo, "once the god of light and reason" (Barnard 26), who says it. "'[W]ait'" he cries "'I'm not your enemy!'" (1.504). But he is. He touts his qualifications: son of Jupiter, god of prophecy, god of poetry, god of archery, god of medicine (1.517–524), but his prophecy, poetry, and medicine don't work, and his boasts about his archery are what got him into the fix he's in.

In a vivid simile in which he portrays the pursuing Apollo as a hungry hunting hound, the fleeing Daphne as a terrified wild rabbit (1.533–539), Ovid mingles human and animal qualities, Barnard says (Apollo, she adds, "is for all purposes 'human'"), to make the god "a hybrid in our imagination, existing in that grotesque interval in which he is neither fully human nor fully dog but both at the same time. . . . The grotesque in its distortion . . . reveals the true nature of the lover" (25–26).

Daphne's metamorphosis into the laurel, which, Barnard says, "enables [her] to leave a body split by opposing forces of beauty and chastity," also has elements of the grotesque (1.549–550: "a fine layer of bark covered her soft breasts; her hair turned to leaves; her arms became tree branches"), and "its [the grotesque's] ominous presence, as the human slips away, blends with the foolishness of Apollo [at 1.553–556 Apollo takes physical liberties with the caught Daphne, now an immobile tree] to produce a scene that is both disturbing and humorous." Apollo's last words to Daphne (1.557–565), an "overstated paean, too grandiose, too eloquent," give him away. "The laurel of victory becomes . . . a symbol of his amorous defeat" (36, 40, 42).

4. Ovid begins the transition from the story of Apollo and Daphne to that of Jupiter and Io (1.568–746)—which includes the tale of Syrinx that Mercury tells Argus to lull him to sleep (1.689–712)—with a figure called ecphrasis (the rhetorical term for a formal description in poetry of a natural setting or a work of art. In the ecphrasis here the poet describes the valley of Tempe in northern Greece cut by the Peneus River between Mount Olympus and Mount Ossa as the river flows to the Thermaic Gulf. Tempe was famous in antiquity for its natural beauty, and in Roman times, as Bömer notes, it was the "prototype" of the magnificent classic wooded valley (at 1.568–582, 1.179).

The words in an ecphrasis "make the still work of art move," Barkan says (9), and in that sense the *Metamorphoses* is itself a kind of great ecphrasis, a description of a constantly changing physical, emotional, and psychological world, a world whose fluidity is presented in words, words that remain forever the same.

The transition is made through a formula, "all save only X" (Kenney [1986] 384; to my knowledge first identified by Frank J. Miller 472; see also Solodow 43–44). Local rivers gather to console—or congratulate—Peneus on the transformation of his daughter Daphne into a laurel tree. "Inachus alone was absent" (1.583), hiding in his cave and grieving for his missing daughter Io, raped by Jupiter and then changed by the god into a heifer to conceal his extramarital activity from his wife, Juno.

The situation at the beginning of the story of Jupiter and Io is similar to that at the beginning of the tale of Apollo and Daphne, for "Jupiter woos Io very much as Apollo wooed Daphne." Moreover, just as in Apollo's pursuit of Daphne the god's "divine majesty . . . is deflated at the first touch of love," there is a similar comical incongruity in Ovid's portrayal of Jupiter, who is bullying, insensitive, pompous, and violent in his approach to Io, but then acts like a "henpecked husband" when confronted by Juno (Otis 104, 105), exhibiting a "kind of pusillanimity in extra-marital love-affairs [that one would] hardly . . . expect to meet with at a heroic—let alone divine—level" (Due 115).

Daphne retains her human identity after she becomes a laurel (shrinking from Apollo's kisses, 1.556; and nodding as if in agreement with the god, 1.566–567), and Ovid carries this aspect of metamorphosis further in the story of Io, describing the girl turned heifer as conscious of the fact—as a heifer would obviously not be—that she is eating bitter grass, sleeping on the bare ground, and drinking muddy water. In addition, when she tries to hold out her arms to beg for mercy, she realizes that she doesn't have arms; when she tries to cry out, she can only moo; and when she sees her reflection in the water, she is terrified. Worst of all, as a cow Io cannot speak, cannot identify herself to her father or beg for help or tell what happened to her (1.632–641). "The failure of speech," Altieri notes, "constitutes the most touching and depressing aspect of many metamorphoses. It exemplifies the fact that the person transformed can no longer create either his own identity or his present reality but becomes captured in the materiality of natural force" (259; other metamorphoses that emphasize the inability to speak are those of Lycaon [1.163–252], Callisto [2.401–530], Actaeon [3.138–252], and Philomela [6.421–674).

Io's anguish forces her to an action impossible for a cow: she traces the letters of her name in the dust with her hoof. In "spelling out her name and her sad change" (1.650; the information "her sad change" is provided by a "sign," an *I*-and-*O*-tracing cow), Io creates a story worthy of Samuel Beckett.

The myth of Syrinx (*syrinx* is the Greek word for "reed pipe") which Mercury tells Io's guard, Argus, and which has "the odd goal of putting its audience to sleep," is both a tale of "erotic pursuit, for which Daphne and Apollo is the prototype" and an embedded narrative (Nagle [1989a] 102). It repeats the pattern of the story of Daphne and Apollo, as Galinsky notes: both girls worship Diana; each has a god as would-be lover and is unwilling to accept his advances; each is changed by a river god into a plant that "becomes the emblem of the god" who pursued her ([1975] 174).

There is also, Coleman says, "a close thematic relation," in this case, of contrast, between the story of Syrinx and that of Io, within which it occurs: "Jove is successful, Pan is not; Io's change into an animal is temporary, Syrinx's change into a plant is permanent; Io's change is a torment to her, Syrinx's a release" (465).

Embedded narratives, Keith says, are one of the ways by which the poet "draws attention to his own act of story-telling in a poem in which story-telling is such a prominent feature" (3). The attention Ovid draws to his own storytelling here is accentuated by the way in which the story is told: The twenty-four–line tale is narrated in two nearly equal parts of eleven and a half and twelve and a half lines, the first in direct discourse by Mercury (1.689–700a), the second in indirect discourse by the narrator (or Ovid), who tells us what Mercury would have said if Argus had remained awake (1.700b–712). "Ovid reappropriates his fictional narrator's tale in the middle, thus calling attention to the two different narrative levels" (Nagle [1989a] 102).

Switching from direct to indirect discourse in the middle of the tale also calls attention to the two audiences for it, Argus, and us, its readers, one of whom (we, the readers) Ovid assumes—correctly, I would say—wants to follow the story to its conclusion, the other of whom (Argus) the story "bores . . . to death" (Konstan 16). Ovid underscores the soporific effect of the story on Argus by having Mercury bring with him (and use as part of his disguise) the wand he habitually carries "that induces sleep" (1.671–672); but he uses it not to put Argus to sleep but only to deepen the sleep (1.715) once the tale has him on his way (Fredericks 245).

Asking why Mercury's story has "opposite effects" on its two audiences, Konstan notes that Argus "tunes out" and falls asleep "at just the moment when Pan is set to present his arguments" (to Syrinx, at 1.700), for what interests Argus from the beginning is not "the living nymph and her struggle with the god" but "the inarticulate tones into which her voice has been transformed." He is thus a "detached, rather than involved, narratee"—as Mercury correctly assumed he would be—in contrast to us, Ovid's readers, who have "an ability [and a desire] to participate both in the passion of the god and the fear of the nymph" (18–19). As befits the creature set to guard the pitiful Io, Argus is "insensitive to the emotional appeal of Mercury's narrative" (Konstan 21).

After Mercury strikes off Argus' head, Juno removes the creature's hundred eyes and places them in the feathers of the tail of her bird, the peacock.

5. Io as a cow wanders to Egypt, is restored to human form there, and gives birth to a son, Epaphus, her child by Jupiter. Reverse metamorphoses (Io's is described at 1.738–

746) are rare in the *Metamorphoses*. Only Tiresias (3.324–331) and Macareus and his companions (14.299–305), in addition to Io, are turned back into human form after undergoing transformations. I am excluding here the "shape-shifters" Proteus (8.730–737), Mestra (8.738–878), Achelous (9.1–88), Thetis (11.221–265), Periclymenus (12.556–572), and Vertumnus (14.641–771), and the "higher" or Olympian gods, who can change themselves at will (see Arachne's tapestry at 6.103–128 for examples).

Epaphus has a playmate, Phaethon, whose claim to descent from the Sun Epaphus doubts, driving Phaethon to seek out his father so as to prove his (Phaethon's) identity. Again, Ovid uses the "stepping-stone method" (see n. 3) to move from one episode (Io) to the next (Phaethon). In this case the quarrel between the two boys about Phaethon's paternity "is almost certainly a pure invention of Ovid to link the story of Io with that of Phaëthon" (Wilkinson [1958] 238). That story, which is introduced at 1.750, will occupy the last thirty lines of book 1 and will continue through the first four hundred lines of book 2. It is the first instance in the poem of Ovid's frequent practice of introducing a new story at the end of a book and continuing it in the next book (Solodow 13–14).

The story of Phaethon, together with that of Deucalion and Pyrrha, Barkan observes, "completes Ovid's basic description of our world and the world of the poem. In many respects," he says,

> the two episodes complement each other: the first deals with the formation of human beings, the second with the formation of heaven and earth; the first proceeds from chaos to order, the second . . . from order to chaos; the first is a flood, the second a fire; the first treats human values in an abstract and universal way, the second is concerned with human responses in a very specific case. Yet parallels underlie these differences. Both episodes are based upon the inextricability of violence and creation, and both have at their core that peculiarly Ovidian cosmology by which human values are literally infused into the nature of things. (32–33)

BOOK TWO

6. Ovid's account of the boy Phaethon's attempt to drive the chariot of his father the Sun (1.750–2.400) is, as Otis notes, the "longest single episode of the poem [and] one of the most epically conceived" (108). Otis goes on to observe that the "underlying theme [of the episode] is the incongruity of the cause with the result" (113), by which he means that in the version of the story Ovid tells, the suffering of the world, indeed, the near-destruction of the entire universe, is brought about by "a typically boyish quarrel, a weak mother's embarrassment, and a weak father's unthinking attempt to allay a child's incredulity" (109).

Although Phaethon himself does not undergo metamorphosis in the course of his ride, except for experiencing "considerable psychological change, from doubt to pride to terror, from youthful ambition to vain desire of escaping his proud wish" (Anderson [1997] at 2.1–366, 227), "the story does concern the stepwise transformation of the world" (Barkan 33). The first stage of this transformation occurs within Ovid's description of the palace of the Sun (2.1ff.), where Phaethon has gone in search of his father.

The artwork Vulcan has carved on the silver doors of the Sun's palace is presented as an ecphrasis (see n. 4), one of three ecphrases of this type in the poem. (The other two are the tapestries of Minerva and Arachne at 6.70–128 and the scene engraved on the bowl for mixing wine that Anius, king of Delos, gives to his departing guest Aeneas at 13.685–699.)

Vulcan, Barkan says, has engraved "a highly symmetrical and ordered representation of the universe, balancing sea, earth, and sky, along with their respective inhabitants," thereby joining "aesthetics with cosmic values: a supremely orderly work of art [that] depicts a peacefully layered cosmos" (33). In the next stage of the world's transformation, a move "from art to life," the Sun describes "a far more disorderly cosmos" in his effort to dissuade Phaethon from driving the chariot (2.63–87). "The third stage in the transformation [of the world]," Barkan says, "is Phaethon's ride itself" (2.150ff.). The chaos that he creates "goes beyond the mere confusion among the categories or layers of the cosmos," for "Phaethon's ride threatens the very existence of the categories." The final stage in this transformation is "the world that results from Phaethon's ride," that is, our present world, "full of irreparable asymmetries of all kinds" (2.210ff.). Barkan concludes, "So we have taken a path from extreme idealization [the depiction of the world on the doors of the palace of the Sun] to a state of tension and danger [the Sun's preview of what Phaethon will face on his ride] to a condition of absolute chaos [Phaethon's actual ride] to a quiescent form of irregularity" (33–35).

The contrast between Vulcan's "highly symmetrical and ordered representation of the universe" carved on the doors of the Sun's palace and the real world "full of irreparable asymmetries of all kinds" created by the failed artist Phaethon (as Wise sees him [52]) suggests a parallel with the second ecphrasis mentioned earlier, the two tapestries, one highly ordered, the other with "no apparent structure" (Anderson [1968] 103), woven by the divine and human artists, Minerva and Arachne, in their competition at 6.1–145. This parallel shows Ovid's preoccupation with art in the *Metamorphoses,* or, more precisely, with two competing aesthetics, one classical and formal (the "divine" art of Vulcan and Minerva), the other "realistic" and non-formal (the "human" art of Phaethon and Arachne).

Phaethon, Wise notes, is "inattentive, if not oblivious to the palace doors" and "does not consider the meaning of the artifact" (46). Nor, Wise says, does he even know the names of the horses of the Sun (2.192, the names are given at 2.153–154), and so he is unable to control them. "This particular ignorance, the ignorance of a verbal expression of the identity of a living thing, is integrally related to the origins of the flight: it is Phaethon's disbelief in the spoken assertion of his own identity that motivates his voyage" (Wise 50).

Galinsky comments that Phaethon "has no conception of the social and beneficent function of the Sun and his chariot," and compared to his father is "a lightweight, not in the least because he has failed to establish any identity of his own" ([1975] 51).

Phaethon's friend (and distant relative) Cycnus, who, because of his grieving for Phaethon, turns into a swan (2.367–380), is the first of three Cycnuses in the *Metamorphoses,* all of different parentage, all changed into swans. The other two are referred to at 7.371–379 and 12.72–145.

7. Ovid's transition to the story of Callisto (2.401–530) is made by means of what Solodow calls a "narrative link" (15): Jupiter sees Callisto in Arcadia when he makes a tour of the walls of heaven to inspect them for possible damage from the fire caused by Phaethon's ride. Ovid never actually mentions Callisto by name, according to Haupt-Ehwald, because the story was quite well known (at 2.401–530, 1.111). The poet also treats the story at *Fasti* 2.153–192.

In making Callisto the daughter of Lycaon (2.495), Ovid forgets that except for Deucalion and Pyrrha the entire human race, including Lycaon and his offspring, had perished in the flood brought about by the crimes of Lycaon and his contemporaries (Haupt-Ehwald at 2.401–530, 1.112). Another incongruity: the constellations of the

Bears which Callisto and her son Arcas are changed into are said never to set in the ocean at 2.171–172 before the sea gods agree with Juno never to let that happen (at 2.530–531; see Solodow 29).

In the council of the gods in book 1, Jupiter had told the assembled deities that he must destroy the human race to make the world safe for nymphs (and other lesser divinities: 1.186–195). Shortly after the world is destroyed by a flood and the human race is re-created by Deucalion and Pyrrha, we see that the world has indeed been made safe, not for nymphs, however, but for their divine rapists: Apollo (who fails in his attempt to rape Daphne) and Jupiter (who successfully rapes Io). Now the world has been nearly destroyed by fire, has been restored (2.406–408), and is safe once again— for divine rapists. And now it is noon and time for Jupiter to seek another diversion. (Io was also raped at noon: "Mid-day heat . . . introduces tales of lust," says Segal [1969a] 4.)

In order to approach Callisto without frightening her, the god disguises himself as the virgin goddess Diana, Callisto's patron (2.425–427), "lust disguised as the very sym-bol of chastity" (Reinhold 326). Callisto fights Jupiter with all her strength, and after he rapes her and returns to "the lofty heights of the gods," she hates the place "that shared her guilty secret," and, as she stumbles away, disoriented, almost forgets to pick up her quiver and arrows from the ground and take her bow down from the tree on which she had hung it (4.434–440). Curran notes Ovid's "understanding of the sheer horror of the experience [of rape] for the woman and his ability . . . to portray her terror" ([1978] 232).

When Callisto rejoins Diana and her attendant nymphs, the goddess, a virgin, does not sense the nymph's "guilt." The other nymphs, however, do notice the difference (2.451–452; Bömer comments: "Nymphs . . . are . . . not virgins like Diana, with the exception, naturally, of those who belong to Diana's band . . . , [who] at least were supposed to be virgins. But in fact they are not, Ovid says, for they have indeed noticed what only an experienced woman can notice, but not a virgin; they have marked the change that has taken place in Callisto" [at 2.452, 1.352–353]).

Callisto's condition becomes clear, when she is nine months pregnant, even to Diana, and the goddess summarily casts the girl out of her company, lest she pollute a sacred stream the goddess and her attendants are preparing to swim in (2.460–465). O'Bryhim notes that Callisto would defile the water because she was pregnant, and particularly because she was nine months pregnant: "Women [in Ovid's Rome] who were about to give birth . . . were considered to be ritually unclean" (77). Moreover, O'Bryhim says, immediately after giving birth, mothers and newborn infants in Rome "were required to purify themselves in a ritual bath with water drawn from a special source" (79). By casting Callisto out, therefore, Diana "has also denied her the only means of purifying herself after Arcas' impending birth" (78).

Rejected by Diana, Callisto gives birth alone and unattended and, being "ritually un-clean," "is cut off from society until she is purified" (O'Bryhim 79). It is at this moment that Juno decides to get her revenge by changing the girl into a bear—violently: "And grabbing Callisto by the hair, she sent her sprawling to the ground" (2.476–477). Ovid emphasizes Callisto's loss of human speech (2.482–484), like Io's in book 1 (see n. 4), although her mind, also like Io's, "remained the same . . . after she became a bear" (2.485). She lives a life of degradation, misery, terror, and excruciating frustration. "[B]ecause she is raped," W. R. Johnson says,

> she is punished by the world. First she is expelled from her sisterhood by her sister/mother, who thus makes herself complicit with the rapist. . . . [S]he suffers childbirth and then she

further suffers the loss of her child. She is punished by yet another mother figure [Juno], and in this punishment her inability to communicate the wrong she has suffered becomes literal and physical. She is now excluded from all human society, has become an animal, she who had been used as if she were an animal; she is transformed into an animal by the wife of the male who treated her as an animal. ([1996] 20–21)

After fifteen years Callisto encounters her son Arcas out hunting and recognizes him, although he sees only a bear apparently threatening him. Just as Arcas is about to kill Callisto with his spear, Jupiter intervenes—"the rapist as *deus ex machina*," W. R. Johnson says ([1996] 14)—and transforms mother and son into the constellations the Great Bear (Ursa Major) and the Guardian of the Bear (Arcturus). Juno, still vengeful, travels to the realm of the sea divinities Tethys and Ocean and appeals to them to prevent these constellations from touching the sea (as Homer knew they did not: *Iliad* 18.487–489 and *Odyssey* 5.273–275). Callisto's second transformation "is no honor or consolation," says Anderson ([1997] at 2.496–507, 291), and Juno's success in keeping the nymph, who was never purified after giving birth to Arcas, from following "the other constellations into their bath [in] the sea, a prime source of purification," means that Callisto "must now remain throughout all eternity a polluted outcast among the stars" (O'Bryhim 80).

8. Leaving the realm of Tethys and Ocean, Juno travels through the air in a light chariot drawn by her peacocks, Ovid says, whose bright colors came from Argus (that is, from the eyes of Argus, when Mercury killed him: 1.717–723) at the time when the raven changed from white to black (2.531–535). This coincidence in time that Ovid contrives for changes in the plumage of two birds, the peacock and the raven, serves as his "stepping-stone" (see n. 3) to the next series of tales: the raven, Apollo and Coronis, the crow, and Erichthonius and the daughters of Cecrops (2.531–632). This transition may seem "abrupt and forced" (Kenney [1986] 387) or "patently artificial" (Galinsky [1975] 94), but, so seeming, it calls attention to itself, as Altieri says Ovid's transitions do, "because Ovid wants to make us reflect on the importance of man's being able to progress from one story to another" (257).

Kenney calls this series of tales an example of "'Chinese box' technique ([1986] 387–388): the tales begin with a reference to the raven's metamorphosis from white to black (2.534–541), which introduces the story of Apollo and Coronis (2.542–547), which, in turn, leads to and frames the crow's tale of Erichthonius and the daughters of Cecrops and the crow's story of her own metamorphosis (2.547–595). In addition to the crow's account, there are five additional first-person narratives of transformation in the *Metamorphoses*: those of Arethusa (5.577–641); Glaucus (13.917–965); the sibyl (14.130–153); Macareus (14.276–286), who also relates (at 14.299–305) his change back into human form; and Hippolytus-Virbius (15.492–546: Nagle [1989a] 120, who omits the sibyl's and Hippolytus-Virbius' stories of their change; I exclude here the river-god Achelous' account of his voluntary shape-shifting in the story he tells of his combat with Hercules for the hand of Deanira at 9.4–88). Ovid completes the frame by returning to the raven and its flight to Apollo to report Coronis' infidelity, the effect of this report on the god, and his punishment of the raven by changing it from white to black (2.596–632). Keith discusses these "embedding" and "embedded" narratives in detail (9–61) to illuminate the complexity of Ovid's storytelling, particularly some of the ways the poet "draws attention to his own act of story-telling in a poem in which story-telling is such a prominent feature" (3; see also Nagle [1989a] 102–103).

The raven and the crow are connected by the unfortunate consequences they suffer for officious talking. The raven's "tongue was his undoing" (2.540), while the crow's "punishment," she says, "can serve as a warning to other birds not to run risks by talking" (2.564–565). In the event, however, the warning does no good. There may or may not be some topical reference that we know nothing about.

The raven has no real story. He is determined to inform Apollo about Coronis' infidelity and will not be deterred by the crow and her cautionary tale of losing to the owl her place as Minerva's bird because she reported to the goddess the disobedience of Cecrops' daughters. The raven rejects the crow's advice and continues on his way. Apollo, distraught after he rashly kills Coronis upon learning from the raven of her infidelity, changes the bird's feathers from white to black. The interest here is in Apollo and Coronis, not the raven, who, although now a "disgraced informer" (Anderson [1997] at 2.596–632, 305), is simply the instrument for the tale. The crow, however, is of interest for her autobiography (the crow was born a princess: 2.570). Since she was the victim of "erotic pursuit ('god chases nymph')" that was "foiled by metamorphosis," as Nagle says ([1989a] 102–103), she is closely linked to Daphne and Syrinx in book 1, who also avoided rape through metamorphosis. There is an additional, inverse link to the Io-Mercury-Argus-Pan-Syrinx complex in that the tale Mercury tells Argus has its intended effect, to Argus' harm, while the crow's story of her own experience which she tells the raven fails in its intended effect, to the raven's harm.

Apollo's killing of Coronis is the first of a series of regretted, avoidable, or accidental deaths in the *Metamorphoses*. Others are Jupiter's killing of Semele (3.297–309), Cephalus' unintended killing of Procris (7.835–862), the avoidable death of Icarus (8.220–235), Deianira's unintended killing of Hercules (9.134–272), Eurydice's presumably avoidable second death (10.50–63), the accidental death of Hyacinthus (10.178–219), and the avoidable death of Adonis (10.708–716). Jupiter's deliberate killing of Phaethon can possibly be included as regretted (2.304–328), and Ceyx's death by shipwreck as avoidable (11.478–569). Theseus is almost killed by poisoned wine given to him by his father, Aegeus (at the instigation of Medea), who takes his son for a stranger: a near-miss (7.404–423).

The death of Coronis represents Apollo's second failure in as many books. He is his own worst enemy. His rash and arrogant boasting led Cupid to afflict him with a passion for Daphne, and Daphne with an antipathy (or powerful indifference) toward Apollo. Here, the god's knee-jerk rage leads him to kill Coronis, an action he immediately regrets. His medical skill fails him in his attempt to revive Coronis (2.617–618), even as it failed to cure him of his passion for Daphne (1.521–524). He does one thing right, however: he snatches his son Aesculapius, the baby with which Coronis was pregnant when she died, from the girl's womb as she burns on her funeral pyre, gives him to the centaur Chiron to rear, and so saves Aesculapius so he can in turn save Rome from plague in book 15. Chiron's daughter Ocyrhoe will prophesy this in the next episode, when she calls Aesculapius "bringer of health to the whole world" (2.642: *toto . . . salutifer orbi;* cf. 15.744, where Aesculapius, having come to Rome to stay, is called "bringer of health to the city": *salutifer urbi*).

9. Chiron's delight in having Aesculapius to rear (2.633–634) serves as a somewhat offhand transition to the next tale, that of Ocyrhoe, Chiron's daughter and a prophetess, who is also introduced in an offhand way: "And now here comes the centaur's daughter" (2.635–636).

Ocyrhoe's ability to prophesy seems to be not a divine gift but something she has learned to do: "Not content simply to master her father's arts, the girl also made predictions about the future" (2.638–639). Nevertheless, she begins to prophesy here because she is "gripped by the prophesying madness and . . . burn[s] with the god" (2.640–641). She first gives a prophecy about Aesculapius and then about her father's death. As indicated in n. 8, Ocyrhoe predicts Aesculapius' role in saving Rome from a future plague (2.642–644). She also foretells his resurrection of the hero Hippolytus (2.645–646). This prophecy will be validated by Hippolytus himself, known as Virbius in his revivified form, in book 15, where he describes his death and then his resurrection, thanks to Aesculapius (15.497–535). Aesculapius will himself be struck down by Jupiter, Ocyrhoe says, but then brought back to life, and so he will "twice make [his] fate new" (2.645–648).

She next foretells her father's future suffering (2.649–654): Chiron was (or, here, will be) accidentally but incurably wounded by an arrow poisoned with the blood of the Hydra shot by Hercules at someone else. Since the centaur is a god, he cannot die and so be released from his pain until Prometheus changes places with him and becomes immortal. (See Apollodorus 2.5.4.)

Ocyrhoe's prophecy is interrupted by her own metamorphosis. Perhaps she would have foretold Chiron's translation into a constellation or, with 2.655 rendered as referring to her instead of to Chiron ("Part of the future remained" instead of "Part of his future"), perhaps her own transformation into a mare, now beginning. (See Haupt-Ehwald at 2.655, 1.130 for consideration of both possibilities.)

Why do the fates interrupt her? Why is she forbidden to say more, stopped from using her voice (2.657–658)? Why has the art of prophecy brought the anger of the god down on her (2.659–660)? Why would she prefer not to have known the future (2.660)? Whose future? Aesculapius'? Chiron's? Her own? The last seems unlikely, since she is experiencing her future right now, and the statement "I would prefer not to have known the future" (2.660) does not seem to me to mean "I would prefer not to be undergoing transformation into a mare."

I do not think that, as Keith says, the story of Ocyrhoe and the two narratives that precede it (about the raven and the crow) reveal "a recurrent concern with the issue of an 'appropriate' use of the voice," while the two tales about Battus and Aglauros that follow it (2.676–832) have to do with "'careless use of the language'" (135). As for the raven and the crow, these messengers who bring a god bad news are unjustly punished. Battus and Aglauros, by contrast, represent foolish attempts to deceive a god or renege on an agreement with a god. (Aglauros is a two-time offender.) Nor does Ovid seem to me to make it "clear [in Ocyrhoe's case] that prophecy is tantamount to tiresome loquacity," that is, "tantamount to [the] tiresome loquacity" of the raven and the crow, "unfeeling, garrulous truthtellers" (Barkan 296 n. 8). The Ocyrhoe episode remains puzzling to me. Perhaps it and the other four as well have reference to what Keith calls "the historical context," by which she means the emperor Augustus' restrictions on free speech (135–136). Or perhaps Ocyrhoe—with her gift of prophecy—"has brought down the anger of the god," that is, Jupiter (2.659–660), upon herself by prophesying his killing and then restoring Aesculapius to life, for what deity wants to hear about his mistakes before he makes them?

Ovid's emphasis on Ocyrhoe's loss of human speech while she is speaking (2.665–669) reminds us of Io and Callisto, similarly afflicted, although in Ocyrhoe's case the loss is particularly acute, since she was a prophetess. Ocyrhoe's new name is Hippô or Hippê (Haupt-Ehwald at 2.675, 1.131), both meaning "mare."

Ovid uses the "stepping-stone method" (n. 3) again in the transition from the story of Ocyrhoe to that of Battus: Chiron is distraught at the loss—or metamorphosis—of his daughter and asks Apollo for help, but the god, even if he could have aided Chiron, was far away, tending cattle in Messenia, or, rather, not tending cattle, which wandered away and were stolen by Mercury, the theft observed by Battus alone (2.676–688). The story of Mercury's theft of Apollo's cattle first appears in the Homeric *Hymn to Hermes,* in which the infant Hermes steals the animals in the evening of the day he is born. The focus in Ovid's version is on Battus, the old rustic who observes the theft, his betrayal of Mercury, and (not in the *Hymn to Hermes*) the god's outsmarting his betrayer and then punishing him by turning him to stone. Battus, accepting a cow from Mercury in exchange for his silence about the theft, had said (pointing to the stone), "That stone will talk before I do" (2.696–697). When he later reveals Mercury's theft to the god himself in disguise, Mercury simply turns him into the stone ("the paradigm of inanimate silence," says Anderson [1997] at 2.676–707, 314) that Battus had said would talk before he did. This story itself, as Anderson indicates ([1997] at 2.676–707, 314), is a transition to the next one, that of Mercury and Aglauros, daughter of Cecrops, king of Athens, to which Ovid passes (2.708–710) by having Mercury simply fly on his winged feet from Messenia in southwestern Peloponnesus to Athens.

Passing over the city, Mercury sees young girls in procession to the Parthenon, the temple of Athens on the Acropolis, in the festival known as the Panathenaia, and is captivated by the beauty of Herse, a daughter of Cecrops (2.711ff.).

Curran notes the "bravura writing" in Ovid's succession of three similes in lines 2.716–729, describing Mercury as kite, Herse as morning star and moon, and Mercury (again) as lead missile from a Balearic sling: "Between the . . . *circular* motion of the first simile (male lust restrained by caution) and the *rectilinear* thrust of the third (male lust let loose), stands the static, serene, two-part simile" that compares Herse's beauty first to the morning star and then to the moon ([1978] 236; for an analysis of the entire passage describing Mercury's passion for Herse [2.708–736] as an example of Ovid's humor, see Galinsky [1975] 164–168).

The story takes an unexpected turn when Aglauros attempts to extort gold from Mercury in return for helping him satisfy his lust for her sister. Minerva then punishes Aglauros by afflicting her with Envy, an abstraction that Ovid personifies and gives a striking physical reality. (Minerva thereby also takes revenge on Aglauros for disobeying her orders in opening the basket containing the infant Erichthonius which the goddess asked Aglauros and her sisters to guard: 2.552–561.)

Ovid's description of Envy (2.760–796) is the first of four vivid personifications of abstract entities in the *Metamorphoses.* (The other three are Hunger, 8.784ff.; Sleep, 11.592ff.; and Rumor, 12.39ff. Tisiphone, the Fury who drives Athamas and Ino mad, could perhaps be considered a fifth: 4.473–511.) Ovid's Envy, Feeney says, is the "most complex" of these personifications, "for here we are dealing with a human emotion which issues from human interaction and manifests itself in human events" (243). Feeney notes that Invidia, Envy's name in Latin, "refers to a flawed act of vision," that is, *in-videre,* "'to look at askance,'" which Ovid emphasizes throughout the passage: Envy "could never look straight at anyone" (2.776), the poet says, and as Minerva departed, Envy "watched the goddess . . . out of the corner of her eye" (2.787; Feeney 245). Envy's "difficulty in looking at Minerva . . . is the quintessence of her own affliction: she must look, she cannot bear to look." Nor can Minerva bear to look at Envy, for when the door to Envy's house swung open, the goddess "saw Envy . . . and . . . averted her eyes" (2.768–770). (See Feeney 246.)

Aglauros is a "ready victim" for Envy, Feeney says, for "she is someone who has trouble controlling her vision": she *looked* into the basket Minerva gave her and her sisters to guard, although explicitly ordered not to (2.552–561), and she is "the first to see Mercury coming" when he is looking for Herse (2.740–741). Ovid connects these "two dangerous acts of sight" when he says that "Aglauros regarded him [Mercury] with the same glint in her eye that she had when she looked on golden-haired Minerva's hidden secret" (2.748–749; Feeney 245). Envy "works through [Aglauros'] flawed sight," Feeney observes (247), for she "put[s] before her eyes a vision of her sister, her sister's happy marriage, and the handsome god" (2.803–804), and Aglauros "often wanted to die so as not to have to see such happiness" (2.812).

Solodow notes that one can "readily visualize" Ovid's description of Envy "as a movie":

> The scene opens with a view of first the setting of Envy's house, then (as the camera moves in, so to speak) the house itself, as they appeared to Minerva. Next Minerva arrives and knocks on the door, which flies open. Through the door she then catches sight of Envy, and Envy in turn sees her. Finally, Ovid describes Envy's actions as she approaches Minerva and then her appearance. Though this last marks the climax of the scene, everything that has preceded is turned to good effect: not one detail fails to impart something about Envy. (201)

When Mercury reenters (he departs at 2.751 and returns at 2.815–816), Aglauros, now livid, sits in the doorway of the palace and blocks the god's way, declaring, "I'm not going to move until I force you to leave" (2.817). She is "[n]o longer interested in gold, [but] merely wants to spoil things" (Anderson [1997] at 2.708–732, 318). Mercury opens the door with his wand, and Aglauros, whose mental state (pathological envy) becomes a physical condition, finds she cannot rise, and now she turns to stone (2.818–832). Fränkel notes that Envy was described as "cold, pallid, sluggish, stiff, and hardly able to rise," and Aglauros "in the moment of petrifaction is pictured as cold, pallid, sluggish, stiff, and unable to rise" (209 n. 9). Mercury leaves abruptly when the metamorphosis is complete without satisfying his lust for Herse.

This story and the preceding tale of Battus "finish in inconsequentiality," Galinsky says, as their "original raison d'être . . . is simply abandoned," along with the role of Mercury, which is merely "transitional" to the next story, that of Europa (2.833–875); that story, in turn, serves as a transition to the stories of Cadmus and his family in book 3 ([1975] 94–95). Kenney comments on that "inconsequentiality," noting that the *Metamorphoses'* "fluid and often elusive texture faithfully reflects that of life itself and the ever-changing universe, in which individuals, families, peoples, cities, empires, territories come and go without apparent reason or order" ([1986] xxvii).

10. Ovid begins the Europa episode near the end of book 2 (2.833–875), following his frequent practice of linking books in the poem by introducing a story at the end of one book and continuing it in the next (see n. 5). In the first two lines of book 3, Ovid concludes the story of Jupiter's rape of Europa, which itself introduces the story of Cadmus, Europa's brother, whom their father sends in search of the lost girl.

Jupiter locates Sidon, where he sends Mercury, as "the land that looks up from the left at your mother among the Pleiades" (2.839–840). That is, to Jupiter facing south from Mount Olympus, Sidon is on the left; it is also almost directly under the constellation of the Pleiades, one star of which is Mercury's mother, Maia. (See Haupt-Ehwald at 2.839f, 1.143.)

Otis (121) notes that Ovid introduces "the most startling of all the metamorphoses of [the first two books], that of Jupiter into a handsome bull," with lines that "express the *leitmotiv*" of these books: "Two things never fit together well, can never abide in one and the same place: majesty and infatuation" (*non bene conveniunt nec in una sede morantur / maiestas et amor,* 2.846–847). These lines neatly encapsulate the deliberate incongruity in Ovid's representations of Jupiter (and Apollo) in the first two books. (See Otis' excellent comments on *maiestas* and *amor,* 122–127.)

Jupiter turns himself into no ordinary bull but "a bull who, in his way, has just as much to show as the god" (Galinsky [1975] 162), for he "creates a perfect form by infusing his own divinity into the humble object that he chooses to imitate" (Barkan 71). The "humorous tone" in Jupiter's metamorphosis "changes to overt ridiculousness as Jupiter the bull, in order to overcome Europa's hesitation, even playfully leaps on the grass and lies down on his side on the sand—something no real, love-stricken bull would do" (Galinsky [1975] 163).

Ovid's image of the frightened (but surely excited) Europa sitting on the bull's back, holding onto one of his horns as he swims away with her through the sea, her robe fluttering in the wind, has served as the inspiration for later art and was itself perhaps influenced by ancient paintings of this subject (Solodow 224 with n. 40 [255]). His poetic source was likely the second-century B.C. Greek pastoral poet Moschus' *Europa* (see Otis 395–396), and Ovid himself also described the scene in his long elegiac poem *Fasti* 5.603–620.

Commenting on Ovid's description of the bull's horns, "clearer than fine crystal, and you could argue that they were made by hand" (2.855–856), Solodow observes that Ovid here "embraces . . . a doctrine that is astonishing for its utter novelty and unexpectedness—namely, that nature imitates art" (210; see 210–212 for other examples). It is equally astonishing when an artist in the *Metamorphoses* imitates Ovid, as Arachne surely does when she renders the bull's abduction of Europa in the tapestry she weaves in her competition with Minerva in book 6. "Now Arachne depicts Europa, deceived by the semblance of a bull: You would think it was a real bull swimming in a real sea. Europa herself seems to look back at the land she has left and to cry out for her friends and, fearing the touch of the lightly splashing waves, to draw up her nervous feet" (6.103–107). Ovid's description of the rape of Europa in book 2 is word-painting of the highest order. His character, the artist Arachne, however, outdoes her creator in *her* rape of Europa, for it is an even more brilliant rendition of the famous scene that she depicts in her tapestry, which is, we must not forget, her creator's ecphrasis.

BOOK THREE

11. Ovid concludes the story of the rape of Europa, begun at the end of book 2, in the first two lines of book 3, thus linking the two books (n. 5). Europa's father, Agenor (named at 2.858), is introduced (at 3.3–5) "to provide a causal link between tales" (Henderson at 3.1–95, 41), that is, between the rape of Europa and the story of Cadmus and his house (3.3–4.603). That story begins with the exile of Cadmus from Tyre in Phoenicia because he cannot find his sister Europa. He then founds Thebes in Boeotia, after slaying a huge serpent that, once slain, "becomes a mirror, since Cadmus is now directed [at 3.95–98] to look upon it as a reflection of himself" (Barkan 43). The teeth of the serpent, when planted in the ground, produce the future population of Thebes. The story ends with the metamorphosis of Cadmus into a serpent (4.569–589) that is "seen as a parallel to the beast that Cadmus destroyed" and that bears "a strong resemblance to the serpents" that Tiresias will observe at 3.324–331 (Barkan 42).

The lengthy tale about Cadmus and his family, which Hardie calls "a self-contained unit within the flux" of the *Metamorphoses,* "tells of a *ktisis* ["founding," that is, of

Thebes] that goes wrong." The exile (Cadmus) who founds a city "is driven into a second exile." According to Hardie, this long episode was "constructed with constant reference" to Virgil's *Aeneid* (the epic of the founding of Rome) and "is in fact the first example of an '*anti-Aeneid*'" ([1990] 224–226). A recurring theme, "the intervention of a vengeful god to punish a mortal who errs," Hardie comments, connects all the stories in this episode. This structure is the means for Ovid's "close and intricate imitation of the *Aeneid*." The poet's version of the myth of the house of Cadmus, "[l]ike the *Aeneid*, . . . contains two large-scale interventions by Juno in pursuance of her hatred and anger," viz., her schemes to destroy Bacchus' mother, Semele (2.256ff.), and Bacchus' aunt Ino (4.420ff.) Whereas Virgil's Juno "conducts a one-woman feud with Aeneas," Juno here is only one of three gods who take vengeance on Cadmus and his house. (The other two are Diana and Bacchus.) Nevertheless, Ovid "heighten[s]" Juno's importance in the story. First, the goddess has "particular grounds for hostility," an "earlier reason," and a "fresh reason" (3.259–260), that is, Europa and Semele. "[T]his distinction between old and new causes for Juno's wrath is Virgilian." (See *Aeneid* 1.23ff.) Second, the two accounts of Juno's vengeance "mark the beginning and the end of the important sub-plot of the birth and nursing of Bacchus," and the second one (Juno's vengeance against Ino) "functions as the climax to the whole sequence of divine vengeances that runs through the story of Cadmus' race" ([1990] 231–232).

At the site of Thebes (chosen by the heifer that Apollo instructs Cadmus to follow: 3.10–13), the Tyrian hero encounters a serpent guarding a spring in a "virginal" grove, that is, a grove "untouched by the blade of an axe" (3.28), and the serpent kills several of Cadmus' servants before Cadmus himself attacks and kills it in a violent battle (3.46–94). Parry notes the interweaving of "sanctity, virginity, and death" in this segment of the myth, in which "a sacred spring in a virginal forest is the setting for bloody slaughter" (278).

Ovid's description of Cadmus' battle with the serpent is the first of several action scenes in the poem that display the poet's great narrative genius. (Others are Perseus and the dragon, 4.706–752; Achelous and Hercules, 9.31–88; and the battle of Lapiths and centaurs, 12.210–535). "[L]ike a good film director," Henderson notes, "[Ovid] has a very exact, lucid and detailed mental picture of each successive phase of the struggle" (at 3.72ff., 50).

The poet's simile describing the warriors rising out of the ground from the sown serpent's teeth is drawn from the Roman theater, the curtain of which was not split vertically, as in the modern theater, so as to be opened by the halves being drawn to the right and the left. Rather, the curtain was raised or lowered from the floor, like a window shade, but in reverse. It was down "at the beginning of the play, so that the stage was visible, [and] was drawn up at the end, in order to cover it. As it was being drawn up figures inwoven or painted on it would [gradually] become visible, first their heads, finally their feet" (Haupt-Ehwald at 3.111ff., 1.153).

Ovid's statement about Cadmus as he ends the first part of the Cadmus cycle, that "no one ought to be called happy until he dies" (3.136–137), expresses a commonplace sentiment in antiquity, the locus classicus of which occurs at Herodotus 1.32.7–8, Solon's words to Croesus: "Hold off until someone is dead, and do not ever call him blessed, merely lucky." The relevance of this sentence to Cadmus is seen first in the story of Cadmus' grandson Actaeon (3.138–252).

12. The story of the hunter Actaeon (3.138–252), destroyed by the virgin goddess Diana, who is also goddess of the hunt, portrays Diana "as the symbol both of outraged

virginity, and of the violence [that is] inseparable from the hunt itself" (Parry 272). The violence of the hunt here includes the "typical nightmare of the hunted that he might become the game and be hunted in turn" (Fränkel 98–99). Ovid suggests a parallel between Actaeon and Diana as hunters by having them encounter each other at midday after a morning each has spent hunting (3.143–185; Preussner 97). There is more than a parallel between them, however, for Diana is in fact a "numinous version" of the young hunter, Barkan says, and when Actaeon "looks directly" at her "unshielded brightness," he "shatters his identity and multiplies it." This "equation . . . of Actaeon with the holy form of himself as hunter . . . inexorably brings about the complementary equation, of Actaeon with the beastly form of himself as hunter, the stag whom he has been hunting. Yet the most powerful change is neither on the sublime nor on the beastly level but rather inside Actaeon's psyche" (45).

As happens with Io, Callisto, and Ocyrhoe in books 1 and 2, Actaeon's speech fails, his effort to speak is blocked, in a circumstance in which the hunter becomes the hunted through metamorphosis into an inarticulate stag. The effect of his loss of speech is particularly acute, for he "retains his human consciousness and thus feels the double pain of wanting to express his condition and seeing himself in a condition where human action is impossible" (Altieri 259). Unlike Io, who identifies herself to her father and sisters by scratching her name in the dust with her cow's hoof, Actaeon as a stag has no way whatsoever to communicate with his companions. His every effort to do so only confirms him as a stag, terrified and about to die. At this point his consciousness "has been acutely distanced from his shape [and] exists as a separate entity . . . , helpless as it oversees his miserable fate" (Barkan 46).

Diana's vengeance reveals the dark side of *maiestas,* now divorced from *amor* (2.846–847, not that it has been particularly bright), in the intensity and violence of the goddess' rage and also in the human qualities with which Ovid characterizes her and by the specifically Roman coloration he gives to the theme of the mortal surprising the goddess at her bath. For Diana as an example of "outraged female propriety" has "obviously Roman characteristics. Her bath reminds us of the toilet of a wealthy Roman virgin or matron" (Otis 134), "surrounded by *ancillae*" (Henderson at 3.166, 62; see also Solodow 86–87).

The darkness of *maiestas* is further stressed by Actaeon's innocence ("the fault was fortune's; . . . for how can a simple mistake be called a crime?" 3.141, 142; and, further, Actaeon "stumbled into the grove. That is where the fates were leading him," 3.175–176) and by his "gruesome death," which is a "penalty that is out of all proportion to his innocent trespass" (Galinsky [1975] 66).

13. Ovid's transition from Actaeon to the story of Semele (3.253–315) by means of a discussion of the young man's fate includes a variation of the formula "all save only X," used in the transition from Daphne to Io (see n. 4): "Jove's wife alone neither praised nor blamed Diana" (3.256–259). As for the discussion itself, Galinsky notes that "[i]t is . . . in keeping with Ovid's desire to avoid involvement in moral issues, let alone resolutions, that here as elsewhere he restricts them to the most superficial and general level" ([1975] 102).

The vengeance theme, begun in the story of Actaeon, continues in the Semele episode, with Juno as the aggrieved deity. (See the comments in n. 11 on Juno's vengeance.)

Juno attacks Semele for getting pregnant by Jupiter (yet another instance in the *Metamorphoses* of blaming the victim), and her revenge is as calculated and devious as Diana's revenge on Actaeon was impulsive and direct. The goddess adopts the guise of

Semele's old nurse Beroë (3.273–278), a particularly invidious move, since "the nurse serves as a trusted intimate" in classical literature (for example, Eurykleia in the *Odyssey*, the nurse in Euripides' *Hippolytus*), as Anderson notes ([1997] at 3.276–278, 365).

Incited by Juno-Beroë, Semele asks Jupiter for a gift without being specific, and, like Apollo to his son Phaethon at 2.42–46, the god promises foolishly but irreversibly to give her whatever she names. She then asks him (3.292–295) to come to her the way he comes to Juno, that is, in his full godhead, the force of which a mortal cannot withstand. The results are predictable (and as Juno intended), and after Semele dies, Jupiter snatches the infant Bacchus from her womb (just as Apollo snatched his son Aesculapius from the womb of his dead mother, Coronis, at 2.629–630), sews it up in his thigh, and so brings it to term (3.310–312). The newborn Bacchus' aunt, Semele's sister Ino, rears the baby at first, thus incurring the hatred of Juno, who will later punish her (at 4.416–542), and then gives it to nymphs on Mount Nysa (3.313–315). The Nysa of Dionysian myth, according to Haupt-Ehwald, was originally in Thrace (*Iliad* 6.133) but was shifted to many other locations of Dionysian cult and vine growing, lastly to India (at 3.314, 1.166).

14. Ovid's transition to the brief story about Tiresias (3.316–338) is "abrupt [and] in epic style" (Kenney [1986] 392): "While all this was taking place on earth . . . , it happened that Jove . . . began to tease Juno" (3.316–320). The story prepares for and introduces the Narcissus episode, which has no connection with the house of Cadmus. (Tiresias himself is descended from Udaeus, one of the warriors who sprang up from the dragon's teeth sown by Cadmus: Apollodorus 3.6.7). Ovid here tells how Tiresias became blind (the result of Juno's vengeance) and then a seer (Jupiter's compensation for Juno's cruelty). Narcissus' mother, Liriopé, consults Tiresias at the beginning of the story of Narcissus and Echo about the fate of her newborn baby. Tiresias reappears at the beginning of the story of Pentheus, the grandson of Cadmus, and makes a prophecy about Pentheus' destiny (3.511–527).

Barkan calls Tiresias' change of sex (his qualification for judging the dispute between Jupiter and Juno) a "mirror metamorphosis": the copulating serpents, one male, one female, "form a perfect representation of a mirror-image relationship, where gender distinguishes the images on either side of the mirror. Tiresias is turned into his own reflection by the same laws of sexual optics." But he is able "to control the metamorphic power that has overtaken him. By reconfronting the serpents and effecting the return change himself, he succeeds in coming back from the world of the looking-glass. He becomes the reflection of his own reflection—which is to say, himself again," although he is not quite the same, for his self has been "irrevocably expanded" by the experience (41–42). The blindness (from Juno) and the gift of prophecy (from Jupiter) follow from the original metamorphoses (though otherwise caused in the narrative), for on the one hand he has seen too much, and on the other hand his experience has given him special insight.

15. The Tiresias episode, just preceding, introduces Ovid's story of Echo and Narcissus, and the transition from the one to the other is brief and simple: Narcissus' mother, Liriopé, was the first to receive a prophecy from Tiresias after he became a seer (3.339–342).

Asked if Narcissus will "live to see a ripe old age," Tiresias replies, "'If he never knows himself'" (3.346–348), alluding to the maxim of the oracle of Apollo at Delphi, "Know thyself." Tiresias' prophecy, is, of course, paradoxical, but Narcissus' frustrated self-love, with his initial lack of awareness of the identity of the beloved, is also paradoxical (Galinsky [1975] 52). Tiresias, with the expanded sexual consciousness that results from his experience of both sexes (a "mirror" experience: see n. 14), is uniquely fitted to make this prophecy about Narcissus.

Ovid was possibly the first to combine the tale of Narcissus with that of the nymph Echo (Fränkel 84 and 214 n. 38), who, by the time she falls in love with Narcissus, already bears the eponymous affliction, the result of Juno's vengeance (3.359–369; the theme of vengeance continues here and in Nemesis' punishment of Narcissus in answer to the prayer of one too many potential lovers: 3.404–406).

Since Echo had used her voice in conversation with Juno as a means to thwart the goddess' perennial effort to catch her philandering husband in his extramarital love-making, Juno cripples the nymph's capacity to talk and thus to engage in the conversations necessary for two would-be lovers to begin and carry on an affair. The cruelty of Juno's punishment becomes clear when Echo falls in love with the cold and unresponsive Narcissus "and yet must vainly try to pursue her love in terms of his loveless words" (Anderson [1997] at 3.339–510, 372).

Where Echo fails in joining herself to Narcissus, Ovid succeeds, linking the two by what Vinge calls the "motif of reflection," auditory for Echo, visual for Narcissus (11). The poet links them further with a striking verbal parallel: at 3.385 he says Narcissus is "puzzled by what seemed to be a voice answering his own" (*alternae deceptus imagine vocis*)—Echo's voice—and at 3.416 he is "caught by his image in the water" (*visae conreptus imagine formae*). *Imago* is thus used of Echo's voice (*imagine vocis*) and Narcissus' reflection (*imagine formae*), the word in the same case (ablative) and the same metrical position in the line in both instances (Vinge 12). Nuttall, moreover, notes "a symmetry in the way Narcissus is reduced to something resembling Echo's strangely restricted mode of courtship" (145). As Narcissus' life ebbs, Echo finally unites herself with him, at least linguistically. For when they spoke earlier, Nuttall says, "the joke was that [Narcissus'] very rejection ended with words which, on her lips, proffered love." Now at the end, when Narcissus says, "Alas, dear boy, . . . the place [i.e., Echo] gave back the words," and when he says "Good-bye!" Echo says "Good-bye!" too (3.500–501): "Now the words of Echo and Narcissus merely coalesce, they are the same and utter nothing but sadness" (145).

The setting for Narcissus' tragedy is a *locus amoenus* (an idyllic pastoral locale), where Narcissus, "virginal hunter," as Parry calls him, relaxes after hunting (3.407ff.) and which contains a pool, Parry says, "itself clear and virginal [that] attracts the boy, reflecting a virginal face in its virginal waters" (276). Except for the description of the pool as "silvery, sparkling" (*argenteus*, 3.407), Ovid, Anderson says, "characterizes the pool and its location entirely in negatives: no mud, leaf, animal, human being, or even sunray has 'touched' it," and so "the pool [is] an appropriate symbol of Narcissus' personal negativity" ([1997] at 3.407–410, 379).

This virginal pool is "the final barrier to lust," Parry says (3.450: "It's only the surface of this pool that keeps us apart!"), but the same pool, "represented here as the guardian of [Narcissus'] virginity[,] is, by this very token, ultimately responsible for his death" (279–280).

Narcissus' beauty is not described but "is only implicit in the reactions of those around him," Vinge says (13), until he himself sees his reflection in the pool. Stupefied, he becomes still, "like a statue carved from Parian marble," Ovid says (3.419). What he sees must thus be "like a statue" too (Barolsky 256), a statue contemplating a statue! ("The simile implies the lifeless beauty that Ovid sees in this whole story": Anderson

[1997] at 3.418–419, 380.) Here, a warm, living boy "becomes" (in the simile) a cold statue. Compare him with Pygmalion's sculpture, a cold statue that becomes a warm, living girl (10.243–297).

Narcissus' lament to the trees above him and to his image in the water (3.442–462) changes to exclamation when he recognizes himself: "Why, you're me!" (3.463), in Latin, *iste ego sum. Iste,* a demonstrative of the second person, is "a mixture of 'that' and 'your,'" as Nuttall says: "Here it expresses very directly the frustration of the whole endeavour: it is as if Ovid can no longer say *tu,* 'you,' because there is no clear Other to address; at the same time, however, there is certainly an object, of a kind, associated with an apparent Other Person: the image, after all, is manifestly there, hence *iste.* But— finally—even that is identical with the observer: *iste ego sum,* 'I am that you,'" (144).

Vinge draws attention to what she calls "the hunger and thirst motif": when Narcissus was quenching his thirst in the pool, he saw his image, and "another thirst began to grow" (3.415). Hunger could not pull him away from the pool (3.437–438). The only food he takes is for his "wretched passion" (3.479). The simile of "edible fruits," ripening apples and grapes (3.482–485), to describe his skin reddening under his blows continues the motif (17–18). In the end, Narcissus dies of "physical . . . and mental starvation" (Fränkel 84).

Ovid describes the hopeless paradox of self-love in which Narcissus is caught in his lament, "What I want, I've got; what I've got, I want" (*quod cupio, mecum est: inopem me copia fecit,* 3.466, the word *copia,* "plenty," ironically repeated from the exchange between Narcissus and Echo at 3.391–392: Narcissus: "I'd die before I'd give myself to you!" [*ante . . . emoriar quam sit tibi copia nostri*], Echo: "I'd give myself to you!" [*sit tibi copia nostri*]). The oxymoron at 3.466 (*inopem me copia fecit*), more literally translated as "plenty makes me poor," recalls Love's parents Poverty and Plenty (Penia and Poros) in Plato's *Symposium* (203b1–c6).

Narcissus' tears splash into the water and break up his reflection (3.475–476); when it is recomposed, and he can no longer endure looking at his image, "as yellow wax over a small flame runs, or as frost fades in the warm morning sun, so he slowly melted away" (3.486–490). "The loss of form through the boy's tears on the water, the melting wax, and the melting frost," Barkan says,

> remind us of Narcissus' error at the same time as they stand for an important metaphoric truth in Ovid's world: the mutability of matter. All these types of dissolution finally suggest that the real transformation in the story is that of Narcissus into his reflection. Even if, in one sense, the two figures are identical, in another way the "real" Narcissus through his love drains all the life out of himself and into his unsubstantial mirror image. When Echo repeats his *Eheu* [Alas] and his *vale* [Farewell], she is paralleling his reflection in the water. What was a full-blooded young man has now become a reflected image and an echoed sound. (52)

The flower Narcissus turns into is not "significantly lovely . . . , [but] merely pretty. . . . [His] metamorphosis is an anticlimax" (Anderson [1997] at 3.508–510, 388).

16. Tiresias reenters the narrative in the transition from the story of Narcissus to the Pentheus episode (3.511–733)—a transition of the "all save only X" type (see n. 4): Tiresias' reputation grew; only Pentheus rejected him (3.512–514)—introducing it with a prophecy (3.516–525), as in the preceding tale (3.346–350). A caricature of fatal arrogance, Pentheus mocks and taunts Tiresias—for the disastrous event that caused his blindness and for the blindness as well (3.515–516)—*before* the seer makes his prophecy, and by so doing provokes him into making it as a retort: Pentheus would be better

off, Tiresias says, if he, too, were blind, so he would never see the rites of Bacchus (3.517–518). This prophecy thus parallels the one given to Narcissus, who, Tiresias had said, would live long if he should never know himself. Here in the final episode of book 3 Ovid sounds what Anderson calls its "overriding theme" ([1997] at 3.516–518, 390). Each major character in the book sees or experiences something and as a result suffers fateful (or fatal) consequences: so Cadmus (3.95–98), Actaeon (3.173–193), Semele (3.283–309), Tiresias himself (3.324–331), Narcissus (3.413–505), and Pentheus (3.701–733). The story of Pentheus also continues the equally important theme of divine vengeance and, in fact, "raises [this theme] to a tragic height and works, by suggestion," Otis says, "to produce the horrendous Juno" of the story of Athamas and Ino at 4.416–562 (138).

Ovid uses the myth of Pentheus and Dionysus, dramatized by Euripides in his play the *Bacchae,* as the basic frame for his story—with significant alterations—with which he blends an adaptation of the Homeric *Hymn to Dionysus,* that is, the story that Acoetes, the ship captain and devotee of Bacchus who is captured and brought to Pentheus, tells the young king of Thebes (3.582–691). Ovid's Acoetes (the name is possibly taken from the *Pentheus* of Pacuvius, a second-century B.C. Roman playwright: Otis 400–401) fills both the role of the Stranger (= Dionysus) in the *Bacchae* and the helmsman of the ship in the *Hymn to Dionysus* (who is not the captain and not named) and so serves to meld the two adaptations.

In the first part of the episode (3.511–576; see Anderson [1997] at 3.511–576, 389), Pentheus "harangues" his people as they rush out to accept the rites of Bacchus (3.531–563), not on "tragic issues," however, but on "the more familiar ones of Augustan propaganda and Vergilian epic [we remember that we are in the midst of Ovid's "anti-*Aeneid*": see n. 11] as [he] speaks for native Roman values of manliness and martial preparedness against the alien vices of effeminacy and religious fakery that he attributes to Bacchus and his corrupt followers" (Anderson [1997] at 3.511–576, 389).

Pentheus exhorts his subjects: "Remember . . . the stock you come from and put on the courage of [the] Serpent" (3.543–545). "By turning the serpent into the Founding Father of Thebes," Anderson says, "Pentheus patently abuses current Augustan rhetoric" ([1997] at 3.543–546, 392–393). He does more than that, however. When he invokes the serpent as a model for his people, Pentheus gives an unconventional interpretation of Theban "history," to say the least. It was Cadmus who, in fighting the serpent, showed courage, not the monstrous creature, who attacked the men Cadmus sent to get water from the spring the serpent guarded (3.35–49). Pentheus is, of course, descended from the serpent: his father, Echion (3.526), was the only peacemaker among the Sown Men (3.126–128). The young king passes over Echion and his role, however, in his rush to recommend the serpent as a model for his people. Pentheus thus feels more loyalty to the indigenous serpent than to Cadmus, to whom, as a foreign invader, he may here implicitly compare Bacchus, the foreign invader he is fighting against. Anderson ([1997] at 3.513–516, 390) sees Pentheus as a parallel to Mezentius, the exiled Etruscan (hence native) king fighting on the side of Turnus and against Aeneas, whom Aeneas kills at the end of book 10 of the *Aeneid,* because of the Theban king's contempt for the gods (3.514), the distinguishing characteristic of Mezentius (cf. *Aeneid* 7.648). Pentheus and his invoking of the serpent, the indigenous foe defeated by the founder of Thebes, should resonate uncomfortably in this "anti-*Aeneid*" with Ovid's Augustan-age hearers and readers.

In the second part of the episode (3.577–700: Anderson [1997] at 3.577–700, 396), Pentheus confronts Acoetes, the Tyrrhenian ship captain, who tells him how he became a devotee of Bacchus. Ovid here merges the characters of the Stranger in Euripides' *Bacchae* and the unnamed helmsman in the Homeric *Hymn to Dionysus*, for Acoetes is captured in Thebes, brought face-to-face with Pentheus (3.572–576), and bears the brunt of his murderous rage (3.577–581), as happens with the Stranger in the *Bacchae*. Acoetes gives Pentheus an account of his own life, including his encounter as a ship captain with the god Bacchus, whom his mutinous, piratical crew try to kidnap, incurring their own metamorphosis as a result (3.582–691)—this encounter adapted from the Homeric *Hymn to Dionysus*, the unnamed helmsman in which is the source for Acoetes' role as ship captain here.

Acoetes before Pentheus is not Bacchus in disguise, as is the Stranger before Pentheus in Euripides' *Bacchae* (*contra* Haupt-Ehwald at 3.575f., 1.183, who say Ovid "hints" at 3.658 that Acoetes is Bacchus; Kenney [1986] 394, who says, "Ovid does not identify Acoetes with the god, but clearly expects his readers to do so"; Nagle [1989a] 103 n. 14, who mistakenly says that Bömer takes Acoetes as Bacchus, though he does not; see Bömer at 3.511–733, 1.571; and perhaps others). He narrates his autobiography to Pentheus, at the climax of which the god Bacchus reacts to the attempt by the ship's crew members to kidnap him over the objections of Acoetes after they had promised to take him to Naxos by turning the sea into a bed of ivy, immobilizing Acoetes' ship, and changing the crew into dolphins. These metamorphoses demonstrate the god's power to Acoetes and make a believer out of him (3.691).

If Acoetes when he is before Pentheus were Bacchus in disguise, he would play two roles in his autobiography, that of the boy as Bacchus in disguise and the ship captain Acoetes, and the narrative would be a "fabrication," a "lying" tale rather than a "true" account, a "witnessing" that led to conversion. It might be said that Bacchus "inhabits" Acoetes as he stands before Pentheus, as Juno, earlier in book 3, "inhabits" Semele's nurse Beroë, as Jupiter "inhabits" Diana, in the story of Callisto in book 2, and as Athena "inhabits" Mentes in book 1 of the *Odyssey* and Mentor in books 2 and 3. But in each of these instances we are told that the gods are thus disguising themselves.

Acoetes is "another warner" (Anderson [1997] at 3.574–576, 395) after Tiresias, and aims, in his embedded narrative (Nagle [1989a] 103), to deter Pentheus from the deadly folly of opposing Bacchus (as the crow aims, in narrating his autobiography to the raven in book 2, to deter him from his foolish mission to Apollo). He fails, however (as the crow fails), and fades away (unlike Dionysus in the *Bacchae*, who leads Pentheus to Mount Cithaeron and to his death there).

Acoetes represents himself in his narrative as in a situation parallel with Pentheus' (and, therefore, potentially on common ground with him) in that he stood alone in opposition to his violent crew when they sought to kidnap Bacchus, just as Pentheus has stood alone in opposition to his frenzied people when they have sought to join the rites of Bacchus. The parallel, though, is obviously an inverse one, for Acoetes is "right" to oppose his crew, Pentheus "wrong" to oppose his people. Acoetes' story, however, only inflames Pentheus' rage, and the king instantly orders him to be tortured and killed. But he is miraculously freed from prison, and we hear no more of him.

In the third and final part of the episode (3.701–733), Pentheus, acting on the same violent impulse that led him to drive out Tiresias while the old man was still speaking (3.526) and to condemn Acoetes, goes on his own to Mount Cithaeron (3.701–703). Bacchus does not entice him to go or appear at the place to exult in Pentheus' death (as in Euripides' *Bacchae*). "We can . . . regard the grotesque killing as an exclusively human act" (Anderson [1997] at 3.701–733, 407). Attacked by the frenzied women, his mother in the lead (3.710–715), Pentheus appeals to his aunt Autonoe, invoking the shade of her son Actaeon. This allusion by a character in one story to a character in an earlier story is an unusual instance of self-reference (and perhaps "Ovid's own invention": Otis 141). But Autonoe "had no idea who Actaeon was and pulled off Pentheus' right arm" (3.719–722). Actaeon, dying, had knelt on forelegs that had once been arms and "turned his mute and pleading face like a pair of outstretched arms" toward his companions (3.240–241). Pentheus, though, his arms torn out of their sockets, "had no arms . . . to reach out to his mother with and, showing the gaping holes where his arms had been, . . . said, 'Look, Mother!'" (3.723–725). "[T]his," says Anderson with forbearing understatement, "is an even worse kind of 'hunt'" ([1997] at 3.715–718, 407).

The story of Pentheus has no proper metamorphosis (apart from those in the embedded narrative of Acoetes), although his mother and the other women who attack him think he is an animal (Otis 140). We might, however, consider his being torn apart as a kind of metamorphosis of destruction, like the flooded world in book 1 or the world on fire in book 2, only that Pentheus, unlike the twice-destroyed world, is never restored, his corpse not even reassembled from its scattered parts, as a grief-stricken Cadmus in Euripides' *Bacchae* laboriously gathers up the remains of his grandson and reassembles them, except for the head, which Pentheus' mother, Agave, has impaled on her thyrsus.

Pentheus had intended to make a "lesson" (*documenta,* 3.579) of Acoetes by killing him. Now he himself has become an "example" (*exemplis,* 3.732) for the women of Thebes (Anderson [1997] at 3.732–733, 409). With this reference in the final two lines of book 3, Ovid begins the transition to the next story, that of the daughters of Minyas, with which book 4 begins, for the Theban women "performed the new rites, offered incense, and worshipped Bacchus at his sacred altars" (3.732–733), "[b]ut Minyas' daughter Alcithoe did not think the god's rites had to be accepted" (4.1–2).

BOOK FOUR

17. The account of Bacchus' arrival in Thebes, which began in book 3 with the narrative of the Theban king Pentheus' opposition to the god (511ff.), continues in book 4 in the tale of the three daughters of Minyas, called Minyades, who also opposed the god (4.1–415), and thus bridges the two books (n. 5).

The Minyades, unlike the other women of Thebes (3.732–733), deny Bacchus' divinity and refuse to celebrate the god's festival, electing to stay indoors and do "Minerva's work," but at an inappropriate time (4.32–35), defying the command of the priest of Bacchus to the people of Thebes to put their tasks aside and join in the god's rites. He warns them that "if the god [is] insulted, his wrath [will] be savage" (4.8–9). The Minyades are turned into bats for refusing to honor Bacchus (4.389–415).

Before giving us his account of what the Minyades do in their unbelief, Ovid narrates the hymn the Theban women sing to invoke Bacchus (4.11–31), reciting it in his own voice, "seemingly inspired by the Theban reverence" (Anderson [1997] at 4.16–17, 413); or, perhaps, since he knows the outcome of the Minyades' blasphemy, which takes the form of working and telling stories, Ovid, also a storyteller, dissociates himself from it by, as it were, singing the god's hymn, too, directly quoting the last four words of the women singing the hymn in the last line (4.31).

Bacchus is summoned under many names: as "Bromius" (4.11), alluding to "the noisy celebrations of Bacchic rites" (Anderson [1997] at 4.9–12, 412); as "Lyaeus" (4.11), referring to the "relaxing effect of wine" (Anderson [1997] at 4.9–12, 412; from

Greek, *luô*, "I loosen"); as "Nyseus" (4.13), a reference to Mount Nysa, where the god
was born or reared (see 3.314–315); as "Thyoneus" (4.13), a reference to his mother
under the name Thyône, or to his nurse (Gantz 2.474, 475); as "Lenaeus" (4.14), referring to (1) the winepress and (2) a yearly Attic dramatic festival (the Lenaea) in honor
of Dionysus (*LSJ* s.v. *lênaios*); as "Nyctelius" (4.15), "supposedly a compound of two
Greek words (*nykto-*and *teleios*) that refer to the nocturnal rites of the god" (Anderson
[1997] at 4.13–15, 413); as "Eleleus" (4.15), which "connotes the wild cry with which
[worshippers] called on the deity" (Anderson [1997] at 4.13–15, 413); as "Iacchus"
(4.15), "a name especially associated with Dionysus at Eleusis" (Anderson [1997] at
4.13–15, 413); as "Euhan" (4.15), deriving "from one of the standard outcries in Bacchic rites, *euhoe* or *euae*" (Anderson [1997] at 4.13–15, 413); and as "Liber" (4.17),
Bacchus' standard Latin epithet (Anderson [1997] at 4.16–17, 413), originally referring
to an old Italian agricultural deity, from Greek *leibô*, "I pour"; Greek *loibê*, "drink offering"; Latin *libare*, in its meaning "to pour out" as a drink offering (Lewis and Short, s.v.
Liber 3); sometimes punned with Latin *liber*, "free."

The reference to Bacchus "without horns" (4.19) differentiates him from representations of him *with* horns as a result of confusing him with the Phrygian god Sabazius
(Haupt-Ehwald at 4.19, 1.197).

In the hymn Ovid refers to Bacchus' rejection by Pentheus and the Tyrrhenian sailors
(recalling book 3) and by Lycurgus, king of Thrace, whom Dionysus drove insane and
who then killed his son with an axe, thinking, in his madness, that he was chopping a
branch from a grapevine; hence Ovid's reference to him as the one "who once wielded
the axe with double blade" (4.22; see Apollodorus 3.5.1 and, additionally, Homer, *Iliad*
6.130–140). "[O]ld, drunken Silenus" (4.26, called literally "the old drunken one" in
the Latin text) refers to the archetypal figure of the elderly satyr who is a follower of
Dionysus/Bacchus (Grimal 419 s.v. *Silenus*; see Gantz 1.138). He will reappear at book
11.85–99, introducing the story of King Midas.

The Minyades, spurning the outdoor rites of Bacchus, remain indoors "doing Minerva's work," that is, drawing out wool, spinning it into thread, and weaving it into cloth
(4.32–35), and decide to tell stories "'to make the time go by and to have something to
listen to'" (4.40–41). This is the setting for the embedded narratives of Pyramus and
Thisbe, the loves of the Sun (which begins with the tale of Mars and Venus), and Salmacis and Hermaphroditus. With this setting Ovid connects weaving and storytelling.
"Greeks and Romans posited a relationship between weaving and poetry," Anderson
says, and "the poet 'weaves' and 'spins' his imaginative fabric of words. Here the girls
are parallel to the poet himself" ([1997] at 4.36–39, 415). In book 6, in the weaving
contest between Minerva and Arachne (1–145), stories (ecphrases by definition) are
woven into the tapestries created by the two rival weavers. Both the Minyades and
Arachne, in their weaving and storytelling, "defy a god and pay for it with their own
metamorphosis" (Barkan 57), the daughters of Minyas becoming bats, Arachne a spider.
Both episodes (and others besides) share an "emphasis upon the personality of the artist, the reasons for his performance and his ultimate fate" (Leach 106). Also in book 6,
the raped, mutilated, and thoroughly brutalized Philomela weaves an account of what
has happened to her into a tapestry (574–580) that she sends to her sister Procne, the
wife of the perpetrator of the crimes against her.

The stories told by the Minyades, who are not from Thebes but from Orchomenos (in
Boeotia) and whom Ovid "juxtaposes . . . to the reverent female population of Thebes"
(Anderson [1997] at 4.1–415, 410), suspend the narration of the Cadmus cycle (Ovid's
"anti-*Aeneid*"), which will resume with the episode of Athamas and Ino at 4.416ff.

Taken together, these stories are "the first of several groups of embedded tales in the

Metamorphoses . . . narrated by a series of different narrators . . . , or a series of tales told by the same narrator" (Nagle [1989a] 103; other narrators are a Muse [incorporating Calliope's song] at book 5.269–678; Achelous and Lelex at book 8.577–884 and [Achelous continuing] at book 9.4–88; Orpheus in book 10; and the sibyl, Achaemenides, and Macareus at book 14.129–440).

In the sequence of tales told by the Minyades, which have passion and its conse-quences as their subject, Due notes the following "type[s] of pairs . . . : boy and girl [Pyramus and Thisbe], man and woman [Mars and Venus], man and girl [the Sun and Leucothoe—and Clytie], and woman and boy [Salmacis and Hermaphoditus]." In addi-tion, with regard to their "status," Due observes (in the same order) "two human be-ings, two gods, god and human being, and . . . a pair representing the intermediate level between god and man: a nymph and a son of gods" (130). Due also discerns patterns in the metamorphoses that characters undergo in these tales: Pyramus and Thisbe are "separated in life" yet "buried together in one tomb." The Sun and Leucothoe "have been united in life but are separated by her death. . . . Leucothoe comes from death to a vegetative half-life because the Sun will not leave her." As for Clytie, "as the Sun leaves her, her life fades away until finally she is but a flower." Salmacis and Her-maphroditus "become for ever [sic] united in life," a state that "seems to reverse" the outcome of Pyramus and Thisbe, whose "common tomb" immortalizes "a mutual but unfulfilled love," while the "coalescence" of Salmacis and Hermaphroditus "is exactly the opposite," that is, a one-sided but fulfilled love. Thus we have this pattern: "[T]he two metamorphoses in the central story [Leucothoe and Clytie] go from death to plant and from life to plant." Those in the first and last story (Pyramus and Thisbe, and Salmacis and Hermaphroditus) are "memorial transformations accompanied by unifi-cation in death and unification in life respectively" (131).

The unnamed daughter of Minyas who tells the first story, that of Pyramus and Thisbe (storytelling was her idea: 4.37–41), first goes through three others in her mind (4.43–51), rejecting them in favor of the tale of Pyramus and Thisbe, which she intro-duces with the metamorphosis that it explains (4.51–52), since this story was not "com-monly known" (4.53). "[F]rom what we know of the three rejected tales," Anderson says, this daughter of Minyas "chose the narrative with the greatest pathos and amatory appeal" ([1997] at 4.51–54, 416–417). It is also the first story in the poem "that focuses exclusively on human love" (Anderson [1997] at 4.55–166, 417), although it is "the love of children" (Due 127). As such, it contrasts sharply with the preceding tales in books 1, 2, and 3 of lust and rape by the gods (and the mutual lust of Mars and Venus in the story that follows), in the feelings the lovers share, in their innocence, their naïveté, their failure to consummate their love, their sharing of tragedy. With Pyramus and Thisbe, Anderson notes, Ovid begins "a progressive exploration" of human love ([1997] at 4.55–166, 417).

The setting of the story is Babylon, "the exotic and romantic East," Due says, and notes that its ingredients—the father who forbids the marriage of Pyramus and Thisbe, "their ensuing decision to run away together, dramatic action [in] deserted graveyards, drama of error and suicide"—are all part of "the stock-in-trade of romances" (125, 126).

Barkan comments on the "world of perceptual confusion" that the two lovers are "thrown into," "barely seeing each other through the chink in the wall, then scarcely seeing any more clearly in the dark once they escape to Ninny's tomb, and finally mak-ing fatal perceptual mistakes concerning the question of who is alive and who is dead" (57).

Pyramus, late for his rendezvous with Thisbe (4.105, 110–112), discovers her bloody shawl on the way, leaps to the wrong conclusion, and, after he has "wept all over the familiar article and covered it with kisses" (4.117), drives his sword into his belly, draws it out, and then, as he lies on the ground, "the blood spurt[s] upward in an arc, like water that shoots from a hole in a pipe where the lead's worn through and jets into the air in a hissing stream" (4.121–124). Ovid needs to get the white berries on the mulberry tree spattered with blood so they can change color—this is the metamorphosis the story "explains," mentioned at the beginning (4.51–52)—and this is how he does it, although the exaggeration and the homely simile, demonstrating Ovid's "penchant for visual over-explicitness" (Galinsky [1975] 179), makes Pyramus' self-inflicted mortal wound grotesquely comic.

The water pipe, Ovid says, "ejaculates" the water (*fistula . . . / eiaculatur aquas,* 4.122–124). For Newlands, this ("Pyramus' manner of dying") "suggests a gigantic orgasm" (143). Anderson notes, however, that this (or possibly *Fasti* 1.270) is the "first appearance of the verb" *eiaculor* in Latin, "the noun *eiaculatio* did not exist in ancient Latin," and thus "any sexual inferences drawn from the word [i.e., *eiaculatur,* 4.124] must be regarded as anachronistic" ([1997] at 4.122–124, 425).

From the innocent but secret, unconsummated but tragic love of children in the dark of night, Ovid, in the next tale about "the loves of the Sun" (4.170), told by Leuconoe (4.168), the second Minyad to speak, turns to adultery, exposure, and revenge (the story of Mars and Venus) and thence to lust, treachery, rape, and now exposure *as* revenge (the Sun, Leucothoe, and Clytie), and, as Barkan indicates, also turns from dark to light (57). Leuconoe uses the well-known story of Mars and Venus (Homer, *Odyssey* 8.266–366; also *Ars Amatoria* 2.561–592) to introduce the less familiar one of the Sun, Leucothoe, and Clytie (Anderson [1997] at 4.167–270, 430).

The poet exploits the dual nature of the sun as natural phenomenon and anthropomorphic deity here (as he will exploit Salmacis' dual nature as pool and nymph: Fränkel 88), for as source of light he "constitutes a general threat to all lovers, since his telescopic gaze is always likely to expose" them (Parry 277), and as human-like god he can be made to fall in love, as he is here by Venus, for revealing her affair with Mars.

Vulcan, the craftsman-god (creator of the artwork on the doors of the Sun's palace: 2.1–18), after hearing from the Sun about his wife's adultery and recovering from the shock, "fashioned from tiny links of bronze a net invisible to the eye to use as a snare, handiwork finer than the finest thread" (4.176–179). His "lovingly woven trap," Janan says, "becomes . . . a quintessential metaphor for artistic excellence" ([1994] 437). After the net fell, Vulcan "threw open the ivory doors of the bedroom and let in the gods" (4.185–186)—the flashbulb of the camera, so to speak, catching the couple *in flagrante delicto*—to see the lovers caught in the artful trap "body bound to body" (4.186), an image that foreshadows Salmacis and Hermaphroditus, fused into a single body at the end of that tale (4.373–379).

To retaliate for the Sun's exposing her love affair with Mars, Venus causes him to fall in love with Leucothoe, and, unlike other deities in love with mortal women, the Sun pines, pales, goes into eclipse, forgets all his other girlfriends, actually suffers because of his love for Leucothoe (4.192–208). Finally, he assumes the form of her mother so he can gain entrance to her bedroom and be alone with her (4.217ff.). So Jupiter took on the form of Diana to disarm Callisto and keep her from running away (2.425ff.). But there are differences: Jupiter as "Diana" kisses Callisto, but his kiss is "not a chaste kiss, not the way a girl should kiss another girl" (2.430–431). The Sun, as Leucothoe's mother, by contrast kisses her "like a mother kissing her dear daughter" (4.222). Jupiter interrupts Callisto in mid-sentence and identifies himself to her by raping her (2.432–

433). Having conquered her, he abruptly returns to the sky (2.437–438), leaving her filled with loathing for the virgin forest where she was raped (2.438; cf. 2.418) and so disoriented that she almost forgets to retrieve her quiver and her bow from the tree limb she had hung it on (2.439–440). The Sun, by contrast, identifies himself to Leucothoe before he reassumes his divine form. Frightened, she drops her distaff and spindle and, Ovid says, "[e]ven her fear became her" (4.225–230). Unable to wait longer, the Sun "resumed his true form, his natural splendor, and the girl, though terrified by the unexpected sight, was overwhelmed by this splendor and submitted without complaint as he forced himself upon her" (4.230–233; "[t]he sentence implies *both* seduction *and* rape" [Janan (1994) 441]).

The spurned Clytie, adopting the roles of both the Sun and Venus in the Mars-Venus episode, avenges herself by exposing the affair and making sure that Leucothoe's brutal father knows about it (4.234–237). "'He forced me to, against my will,'" Leucothoe tells her father (4.238–239)—she "retrospectively constructs the act as rape" (Janan [1994] 442)—even as he buries her alive (4.239–240), "a punishment," Segal says, "doubtless chosen for the sake of the antithesis between light and darkness, earth and sky" ([1969a] 51).

Leucothoe, "the victim of violence," and Clytie, its "(indirect) instigator," one "cherished by the Sun," the other "rejected by him," turn into plants (frankincense and heliotrope) "whose focus is ex-centric, away from themselves and on their ex-lover, either turning towards him in his daily round, or rising towards him as incense" (Janan [1994] 443).

Alcithoe, the third daughter of Minyas (named at 4.274), narrates the final tale in the series, the story of Salmacis and Hermaphroditus (4.274–388). She begins (4.276–284) by mentioning a series of possible tales, only to reject them (or at least the first, about Daphnis) as "too well known" (4.276) in favor of the one she tells, selected because it is "charming and novel" (4.284). The only story familiar to us, however, is that of Daphnis (Theocritus, *Idyll* 1.64–142, and Virgil, *Eclogue* 5.20–80; see also Grimal 128 and 481 s.v. *Daphnis*).

In Salmacis and Hermaphroditus we have not two innocents (like Pyramus and Thisbe), nor two experienced adults (like Mars and Venus), nor mature god and young girl (like the Sun and Leucothoe), but a virgin boy who disdains females and an older woman who is "entirely open to love, sex, and marriage" (Anderson [1997] at 4.302–304, 445). What brings them together is the clear, clean pool, which, like the pool that Narcissus discovers, "attracts a virginal youth through its suggestions of innocence and purity" (Segal [1969a] 52). This pool, however, comes with a nymph, indeed, *is* a nymph ("Ovid plays upon the double nature" of Salmacis, who "both is and is not identical with the pool she inhabits": Fränkel 88).

Salmacis, the only nymph "not known to fleet-footed Diana" (4.304), has no interest in the hunting life. Instead, she prefers to bathe in her pool, wash herself, comb her hair, and look at her reflection in the water (4.308–312). She "lives the life of a very expensive Roman *demimonde*" (Due 129). Critics note parallels between this tale and the story of Echo and Narcissus in book 3 (for example, Segal [1969a] 52–53, Nugent 161–162 and 182 n. 5). Hermaphroditus is like Narcissus in his touch-me-not virginity. A pristine pool is his undoing, as it is Narcissus'. But Salmacis is both Echo and Narcissus rolled into one: She desires, powerfully, like Echo, but is embodied and takes the initiative (as Echo, only a passive responder, cannot). Like Narcissus, Salmacis loves to look at herself in her waters, but her autoerotic pool-gazing serves only to stimulate her predatory effort to catch Hermaphroditus.

The pool is the (literal) point of contact between Salmacis and Hermaphroditus. He is at first drawn to it because it is clear and clean (4.297–300), as noted earlier. After Salmacis retreats (or appears to retreat) from her aggressive—and, to Hermaphroditus, offensive—overture (4.317–340; Salmacis' address to the youth at 4.320–328 is adapted, hilariously, from naked, brine-soaked Odysseus' speech to the proper, well-brought-up Nausicaa at *Odyssey* 6.149ff.), Hermaphroditus, "thinking he was all alone" (4.340–341), cavorts around the pool, dips his toes in it, then his feet—virginal all the way—and, finally, "[t]aken with the mild and inviting" water (4.344: *temperie blandarum captus aquarum*), jumps in. The pool is "inviting" (*blandarum*) because it is neither hot nor cold but "mild" (*temperie*), just what this fastidious, sex-threatened boy likes. Nugent thinks it "problematic" that Hermaphroditus finds the pool (which, to repeat, is Salmacis) "irresistible to enter" but "eschew[s] any sexual desire for" Salmacis (165). In my view, however, it is a fine but seeming paradox that expresses a psychological truth about Hermaphroditus. He wants to play with female sexuality on his own fastidious, virginal terms—that is, one-sided foreplay only—rather than engage with Salmacis' sexuality in a reciprocating way in all its robust vitality. The only "problem" for him, however, is that his "play" in the pool so stimulates Salmacis that she jumps in after him and displays that robust vitality by kissing him, caressing him, and wrapping herself around him (4.340–372).

The similes Ovid uses to describe Salmacis enveloping Hermaphroditus at 4.361–367 (a snake coiling itself around the eagle carrying it off, ivy twining around a tree, an octopus underwater sliding its tentacles around its prey) represent Hermaphroditus' reaction to full and energetic sex.

Salmacis prays to the gods to "'let no day take him away from me or me away from him'" (4.371–372), an articulation of her innermost desire, and she gets what she prays for—Hermaphroditus' body fused to hers in permanent union—but not exactly what she wants, for Hermaphroditus is made soft in the pool, becomes "half the man he was" (4.380–382). *He* prays that any other male who enters the pool "'turn suddenly soft when its water touches him and emerge from it half a man!'" (4.385–386: *exeat inde / semivir*), a mean prayer that is also answered, although it merely expresses the effect of Salmacis' demanding sexuality upon Hermaphroditus, for he could "stand firm" (*perstat,* 4.368) only when he "denied" (*denegat,* 4.369) pleasure to Salmacis. When they become fused into one, their "single visible form makes the mutuality of love and marriage impossible" (Anderson [1997] at 4.373–375, 453).

As two lovers who are so fused, Salmacis and Hermaphroditus "are balanced by the inevitable Ovidian parallel of Narcissus, one being who becomes two lovers" (Barkan 273).

When this last tale is finished, Bacchus takes his revenge on the daughters of Minyas for refusing to worship him, announcing it with the sound of drums and flutes and the odor of myrrh and saffron in the air (4.391–393). First the god transforms the spun yarn and cloth the sisters have spent the day weaving, a product of culture (and of their defiance) sponsored by Minerva, Bacchus' opposite, into ivy, grapevines, and clusters of grapes (4.394–398) and so "into the fabric of nature herself" (Barkan 40). The Minyades themselves he changes into bats, which hate daylight and "take their name from the evening" (4.414–415; *vespertilio,* Latin for "bat," is derived from *vesper,* "evening").

As in the stories of Io, Callisto, and Actaeon, Ovid emphasizes the sisters' loss of human speech (4.412–413). In their case, however, it is a greater loss, for they were storytellers—artists (and their story introduces the theme of "artistic failure": Leach 111). In this respect, their fate is similar to that of other artists in the poem who also "fail": the Pierides (book 5); Arachne and Marsyas (book 6); Daedalus, perhaps (book 8), whose artwork kills his son Icarus; and Orpheus (books 10 and 11).

18. With the story of Athamas and Ino (4.416–562), Ovid returns to his narration of the house of Cadmus (and to his "anti-*Aeneid*": see n. 11). After Pentheus is punished for refusing to accept Bacchus and his rites, only the daughters of Minyas fail to honor the god. When they are turned into bats, "the public honor [given to Bacchus] is unanimous" (Anderson [1997] at 4.416–419, 459). All of Cadmus' children and grandchildren have been killed or ruined (Autonoe and her son Actaeon, Agave and her son Pentheus, and Semele) except for Semele's son by Jupiter, the god Bacchus, and Cadmus' daughter Ino and her two children. Ino's pride in and devotion to Bacchus incite Juno's murderous wrath (4.417–431). She hates Bacchus, who, as her husband's bastard son, is a living insult to herself; she hates Ino for her devotion to Bacchus; and she is jealous of Bacchus' power to avenge himself upon his enemies.

She can learn, however, even from an enemy, for Bacchus "has made the power of madness very clear indeed" (4.429–430). So Juno goes to the underworld and asks the Furies to drive Ino's husband, Athamas, mad, knowing that will lead to the destruction of Ino and her children.

The tale is divided into three parts, as Anderson notes ([1997] at 4.416–542, 459), followed by a kind of concluding epilogue: (1) Juno and her rage: 4.416–431 (sixteen lines); (2) Juno in the underworld, Tisiphone, and the Furies: 4.432–511 (eighty lines); (3) the madness of Athamas and the destruction of Ino and her children: 4.512–530 (nineteen lines); epilogue (in two parts): Venus' intervention to save Ino and Melicertes through metamorphosis (4.531–542), and Juno's vengeful transformation of Ino's mourning friends (4.543–562; thirty-two lines, total).

In his representation of the underworld, Anderson says, Ovid "has in mind Vergil's description of Aeneas' visit" there at *Aeneid* 6.268ff. ([1997] at 4.436–438, 461). If this section of the *Metamorphoses* is an "anti-*Aeneid*" (n. 11), then this is an anti-(Virgilian) underworld—a real hell—a vast city, which, Anderson says, Ovid "Romanizes" ([1997] at 4.443–446, 461–462), and in which disembodied spirits wander, endlessly going through the motions of their former lives.

Arriving at the place the Furies inhabit, Juno sees the great sinners of antiquity: Tityos, Tantalos, Sisyphus, Ixion, and the daughters of Danaüs (4.457–463). Tityos tried to rape Latona, the mother of Apollo and Artemis, was killed by Apollo, and has his *viscera* (4.457) eaten daily by vultures in the underworld (see Homer, *Odyssey* 11.576–581; Virgil, *Aeneid* 6.595–600; and Apollodorus 1.4.1). Tantalos is "tantalized" forever—unable to eat and drink, for the water and fruit close at hand perpetually withdraw when he reaches for them—for being "unable to digest great blessedness," as Pindar says, when he was honored by the gods (Pindar, *Olympian* 1.54–64; see also Homer, *Odyssey* 11.582–592, and Apollodorus, Epitome 2.1). Sisyphus is punished, according to Apollodorus (1.9.3), for betraying Zeus' rape of Aegina to her father, Aesopus. Ixion is bound to an eternally spinning wheel for trying to rape Juno (Apollodorus 3.16.20 and Pindar, *Pythian* 2.31–33, who also names him as the first mortal to commit murder). Juno, the target of Ixion's attempted rape, stares long and hard at him here (4.464–465). The daughters of Danaüs, forced into marriage with their cousins, murdered their husbands on their wedding night (Hypermnestra was the exception) and are punished by having perpetually to draw water in leaky vessels (Apollodorus 2.1.5 and Horace, *Odes* 3.11.25–32). Ovid, in his reference to the "Seat of Crime" (4.456) and his description of the great "sinners," borrows from Tibullus 1.3.67–80, changing, however, the "Seat of Crime" from "the place of punishment for evil" in Tibullus to "the actual seat from which the Furies rise to greet the goddess," as Anderson notes ([1997] at 4.455–456, 463; for the great "sinners," see Anderson [1997] at 4.457–459, 460–461; and 462–463, 463–464).

Ovid's description of Tisiphone in the underworld and inflicting madness on Athamas and Ino (4.481–511) is similar to the poet's personifications of Envy, already encountered at book 2.760–796; and of Hunger, Sleep, and Rumor, still to come (see n. 9).

Athamas, maddened by Tisiphone, "hunts" his wife, Ino, and their two children, thinking she is a lioness with two cubs (4.512ff.). Autonoe's son Actaeon was the victim of a "hunt" at book 3.138–252, and Autonoe and Agave, deluded like Athamas here (but by Bacchus), "hunted" Pentheus at book 3.511–733.

Ovid, "poetic and vague," as Anderson says ([1997] at 4.534–535, 471), has Ino (in Thebes) jump with her son Melicertes into the Ionian Sea (4.519–530), a geographical impossibility, for this body of water extends between Greece and southern Italy.

The transformation of Ino's grieving friends into stone—or seabirds—by an angry Juno combines two motifs, Anderson says: "terminal comment on events from contemporary onlookers" (as, for example, people's comments on the rightness of Diana's metamorphosis of Actaeon at 3.253ff.) and "sympathy for a victim" leading to metamorphosis of the victim's friends (as happens to Phaethon's sisters at 2.340ff.: Anderson [1997] at 4.543–562, 473).

Cadmus is "overcome by grief" (4.564–565) because of all that has happened and, with his wife, Harmonia, leaves Thebes and wanders (4.565–568), "once again . . . like Aeneas" (Anderson [1997] at 4.563–568, 476). Arriving in Illyria and reflecting on the past, he asks himself if the serpent he killed long ago at the site of what was to become Thebes was "'sacred'"—if that is "'what the gods are avenging'"—and prays to turn into a serpent himself (4.568–575). This is a change that, as Barkan notes, "does not come as a punishment from without but as the result of a prayer by Cadmus himself" (44). His metamorphosis was prophesied right after he killed the serpent on the site of the future city of Thebes: "Why, son of Agenor, are you staring at the serpent you have slain? Someday you will be a serpent at whom someone else will stare" (3.97–98), a serpent, Barkan also notes, "who is seen as parallel to the beast that Cadmus destroyed" (42).

Ovid describes Cadmus' transformation with what Anderson calls "grotesque realism" ([1997] at 4.581–585, 477): after he is partway changed, he falls onto his (snake's) belly and, his legs extending themselves and fusing into a tapering tail, stretches out his (obviously human) arms to his wife and asks her to touch him, to "take my hand, while it's still a hand, before I become all snake" (4.579–585). Anderson comments "We are invited to picture this strange creature, stretched out prone on the ground, its legs just now grown together, oddly waving its arms and talking!" ([1997] at 4.581–585, 476–477). Cadmus would have continued speaking, Ovid says, but his tongue became forked, and when he tried to say something, he could only hiss like a snake (4.586–589). Again, Ovid emphasizes the loss of speech, the characteristic that defines the human, which metamorphosis causes.

Harmonia, beginning to grieve as her husband before her eyes turns slowly into a snake, prays to become a snake also and is changed, but in the twinkling of an eye, not gradually like her husband (4.590–600). These two are one of the few happy couples in the poem, although, as Barkan says, "The occasional happy loves are also tangles," for the two are now "entwining serpents" (91). So ends the long section on Cadmus and Thebes that began at 3.1.

19. Cadmus and Harmonia, Ovid says, consoled themselves with thoughts of their grandson Bacchus. Acrisius, however (who is also related to Bacchus), rejected his grandson Perseus (4.604–611). "This is enough of a connection to provide the transition which Ovid requires" (Kenney [1986] 401), a transition that displays, according to Solodow, a kind of casualness and cleverness designed to call attention to the narrator (41–43).

As for Acrisius' and Bacchus' shared origin (4.607–608), Acrisius was descended from Belus (Belus-Danaüs-Hypermnestra-Abas-Acrisius), and Bacchus was descended from Belus' brother Agenor (Agenor-Cadmus-Semele-Bacchus). Belus and Agenor, in turn, were sons of Libye and Poseidon (see Bömer at 4.611, 2.188).

The Perseus episode, which occupies the final two hundred lines of book 4 (604–803), will continue in book 5 (1–249), and so it links the two books (see n. 5). It is the "first full-scale heroic episode" in the *Metamorphoses* (Mack [1988] 121) and thus appropriately begins a transition (at 4.604) from the first part of the *Metamorphoses*, on the gods (1.452–6.420), to the second part, on heroes and heroines (6.421–11.193). This transition will continue through 6.420. (See n. 1 for the organization and structure of the poem.) Otis calls this episode both a "little *Aeneid*" (following the just concluded "anti-*Aeneid*") and a "true parody of epic" (159 and 346).

We meet Perseus in midair, flying back to Argos with the head of Medusa. The sun is setting and it is getting dark, so Perseus, "afraid to entrust himself to the night," decides to stop in Atlas' kingdom in the west (4.627–630)—"a sensible man, . . . but what kind of hero can we expect if he is so timid about night flying?" (Mack [1988] 121). Atlas opposes Perseus, mistakenly thinking he is the son of Jove whom a prophecy mentioned as coming to steal his golden apples (that was to be Hercules, performing his eleventh labor; Apollodorus 2.5.11), and Perseus turns Atlas to stone with the head of Medusa (4.642–662).

Flying over Ethiopia after leaving Atlas, Perseus sees Andromeda, daughter of the Ethiopian king Cepheus and his wife, Cassiope, chained to a rock below as an offering to a sea monster, in compliance with an oracle that "had unjustly ordered Andromeda to pay for the sins of her mother's tongue" (4.670–671). Cassiope, Apollodorus tells us, had claimed that she was more beautiful than the sea divinities known as Nereids. Enraged, they (apparently) complained to the sea god Poseidon (= Neptune), who sent both a flood and a sea monster to ravage Ethiopia. The oracle Ammon prophesied that the Ethiopians would be freed from these calamities if they offered the king's daughter Andromeda to the monster (2.4.3).

The absurdity of Perseus as an epic hero, broached with Ovid's depicting him as afraid of flying at night, begins to be developed. Seeing Andromeda, Perseus is so struck by her beauty, Ovid says, "that he almost forgot to flap his wings as he flew" (4.676–677), a detail that gives us "a comic glimpse of [a] lovesick admirer [and] invites us to speculate momentarily on what would have happened if [Perseus] had indeed forgotten" (Mack [1988] 122).

When Perseus descends to the earth and speaks, the "comedy builds," Mack says ([1988] 122). The instant he alights on the ground he addresses Andromeda, chained to the rock and presumably naked: "'O' he said, 'O Girl-so-undeserving-of-*these*-chains-but-rather-those-that-bind-eager-lovers-to-each-other'" (4.678–679: *ut stetit "O," dixit, "non istis digna catenis, / sed quibus"*). The interjection "O" that, in a vocative phrase, usually precedes the name (as in "*O Caesar!*") is here placed between "The instant he landed" (*ut stetit*: an onomatopoetically bumpy landing by the overeager Perseus) and "he said" (*dixit*) and is thus separated from the "long periphrasis . . . standing at the point where in ordinary Latin discourse we expect a personal name" (Mack [1988] 123). Perseus' "O" can be both an involuntary exclamation at the moment of his impact with the ground and the "O" used before a name in the vocative (only here, as Mack notes, there is Perseus' long, flowing phrase in place of the proper name). Moreover, we have "the Homeric motif in reverse (for it is usually the newcomer who is asked to identify himself)," and "the fetters treated as if they were bracelets" ("Tell me . . . why you are wearing these chains," 4.680–681), which, together with the address to Andromeda, "are so out of place under the circumstances that we can hardly avoid laughter" (Mack [1988] 123).

The absurdity continues: Andromeda (a "virgin girl," 4.682) "would have covered her face with her hands out of modesty" if they "hadn't been bound to the rock" (4.682–683; does she tug at the chains involuntarily?). But wait: she can cry! And she does (4.684). But she won't talk—until it occurs to her that Perseus will think *she* is guilty of something, and so she begins to speak, but is interrupted by the sea monster, heading right toward her (4.684–690). Her parents appear, helpless and in the way, weeping, beating their breasts, clinging to their daughter, who is bound to the rock. Whatever else may be wrong with Perseus, he ever has his eye on the main chance and knows the right moment to cut a deal: I'm Perseus, the son of, etc., Perseus, who, etc., and if I save her, I get her, OK? (4.697–703; "exacting a promise from people already in *extremis*," Otis says [347]).

Then the action begins: The monster comes like a speeding ship; when it was as far "as a Balearic sling can hurl a lead bullet," Perseus attacks like an eagle seizing a snake; he buries his sword in the monster's back, and it reacts like a cornered boar (4.706–723). "If one epic simile is good, Ovid implies, four must be better. . . . In fact, there is almost as much simile as there is narrative" (Mack [1988] 124), that is, almost nine of the eighteen lines encompassing the first to the last simile (4.706–723) or the twenty-nine lines describing the battle (4.706–734).

The combat finally ended, Perseus victorious, Andromeda freed at last from the rock and reunited with her parents, who are singing Perseus' praises and welcoming him as their son-in-law—the hero decides to wash his hands ("pays no attention to his lovely prize," says Anderson [1997] at 4.740–743, 490) and fusses with the head of Medusa, putting it on a bed of leaves and seaweed (where was it all this time?), which promptly hardens into coral (4.735–746). Why does Ovid do this? Probably to reassert the absurdity with which this part of the episode began and "[p]ossibly to remind us that Perseus was never in any danger at all, that the greatest contest was, in fact, a farce, since Perseus had his ace in the hole all the time" (Mack [1988] 124).

The narration continues with the irrelevant: sea nymphs, having observed the seaweed on which Medusa's head rested turn to coral, experiment with other seaweed, successfully (4.747–752)—as Perseus watches, still ignoring his hard-won bride.

The hero then sets up three altars (4.753–756), to Jupiter, Mercury, and Minerva, that is, his father and the two divine benefactors who helped him indirectly here and directly in his successful mission to obtain the head of Medusa, about which we are soon to hear. In that effort, Mercury and Minerva aided Perseus by leading him to the daughters of Phorcys (known as Graiai), whose single shared eye and tooth he stole to compel them to tell him the way to nymphs who give him winged sandals, a leather pouch, and a helmet rendering the wearer invisible, all necessary for flying to Medusa, beheading her, carrying back her severed head, successfully evading her sister Gorgons, and flying away again. Mercury also gave Perseus his hooked sword, and Minerva guided his hand when he cut off Medusa's head (see Apollodorus 2.4.1–3).

Next comes the wedding of Perseus and Andromeda, followed by a wedding banquet (4.758–764), which is followed, in turn, by obligatory autobiographical storytelling, the models for which are *Odyssey* 9–12 and *Aeneid* 2–3. Cepheus initiates it by asking Perseus how he was able to behead Medusa (4.769–771). After Perseus answers Cepheus (4.772–789), an Ethiopian prince asks the hero why Medusa alone of her sisters had snakes growing from her head (4.790–792). Perseus' response to these two questions, an embedded narrative (see Nagle [1989a] 104–105), is unusual in several ways. First, as Mack notes, Perseus' answer to Cepheus' question is brief, 18 lines (4.772–789), compared to Odysseus' 2,180 lines in the *Odyssey* and Aeneas' 1,517 lines in the *Aeneid* (Mack's count). Second, "against all epic convention," Mack says, "[Perseus'] words are not quoted directly but reported by the narrator." Third, Perseus' severing of Medusa's head: "[T]he deed itself is seen to be unheroic. Only craft and stealth, not valor, were needed" ([1988] 124). Fourth, Perseus answers the Ethiopian prince's question (4.793–803) with "the first-person speech that epic convention leads us to expect" (Mack [1988] 125), but he reports not what he himself saw or experienced but what he heard secondhand: "This [that Medusa's original hair was her most striking feature: 4.796–797] I learned from someone who . . ." (4.797). As to how Medusa's hair was changed, "Neptune . . . is said . . ." (4.798–799). What Perseus narrates directly is something he "knows only by hearsay" (Mack [1988] 125; and it turns out to be "a quite Ovidian aetiological tale of divine rape" [Nagle (1989a) 105]).

In the tale of the rape of Medusa, "the deity," Anderson observes, "punishes the innocent victim of rape, and the rapist goes unscathed" ([1997] at 4.798–801, 496).

BOOK FIVE

20. The story of Perseus, begun at 4.604 and occupying the final 200 lines of that book, continues in book 5 for 249 lines and so links the two books (see n. 5). At the climax in book 5 of this "first full-scale heroic episode" in the *Metamorphoses* (Mack [1988] 121), an epic battle is fought during a wedding banquet between the forces of Perseus, the new husband of Andromeda, and Phineus, to whom she was betrothed before Perseus entered the picture. This battle draws on Odysseus' combat with the suitors in his palace in book 22 of the *Odyssey* but "takes its motivations and vocabulary more patently from the rivalry between Turnus and Aeneas for the hand of Lavinia" in the *Aeneid* (Anderson [1997], introduction to his notes to book 5, 497). The poet's "pentad," Perseus-Andromeda-Phineus-Cepheus-Cassiope, moreover, is to be compared, Bömer says, to the "well-known Virgilian pentad" of Aeneas-Lavinia-Turnus-Latinus-Amata, and the entire episode serves as a "parody" of the *Aeneid* (at 5.1–249, 2.230). Bömer goes on to observe that Virgil has "covered up" the fact (in the *Aeneid*) that King Latinus' daughter Lavinia was betrothed to the native Italian prince Turnus before Aeneas appears on the scene by having the king "attribute his change of mind to an oracle." In the *Metamorphoses* the situation is "demythicized" (*entmythisiert*) and "returned to the original facts of the case": "Ovid represents Cepheus as the father-in-law . . . who promises the bride to the new, attractive son-in-law, Perseus, without mentioning the fact that he has already betrothed her to another, and who cannot in his confused hesitation blame it on the gods." With "sophistic over-subtlety," Cepheus proposes that "one acts rightly when one does not keep a clearly given promise" (at 5.1–249, 2.230). But none of these characters possess "ennobling virtues" (Mack [1988] 126). If Cepheus is a transparent Sophist, Phineus is a "heel" (*Schuft*: Bömer at 5.1–249, 2.230) for whom Ovid "has rigged sympathy," but who "rapidly fritters it away" (Anderson [1997] at

5.30–33, 501). Perseus, moreover, is unbelievably vindictive and cruel in his treatment of Phineus—as vicious as any god in the poem.

Perseus and his men are colossally outnumbered—after "many had been killed [and] many more remained" (5.149), the hero is surrounded by Phineus and a thousand followers (5.157–158)—but battles on like the cowboy hero in a grade B Western whose six-shooter never needs reloading. After this thousand has been whittled down to a couple of hundred, Perseus, growing tired, turns to his secret weapon, the head of Medusa (5.177–180). "[F]rom this point," Anderson says, "[his] enemies will be halted in the moment of action, transformed into striking statue poses": Thescelus becomes "the 'javelin-thrower'" (5.181–183); Ampyx, "a 'swordsman'" (5.184–186). "Each of these 'statues' reminds one of Hellenistic art and its emphasis on unbalanced, twisted bodies" ([1997] at 5.181–183, 184–186, 515; and at 5.198–199, 516). And so, confronting with the head of Medusa the two hundred who survived the hand-to-hand combat, Perseus turns them all to stone (5.208–209).

Finally, the two antagonists, Perseus and Phineus, face each other: Phineus, aghast to see his men—and so many of them—frozen in stone, gives up and begs for mercy (5.210ff.). Perseus, however, forces the head of Medusa in his face even as Phineus tries desperately to avert his eyes, and turns him to stone, too: "and the quivering lip, the pleading look on his face, the praying hands, the cowering body—all were caught in marble" (5.234–235), a "'monument,'" Perseus says, "'that will last for ages, and . . . always be on display'" in Cepheus' house "'so my wife can console herself with the image of her former fiancé'" (5.227–229). As Barkan comments: "The hapless Phineus is rendered manifestly impotent without being granted the solace of removal from the scene of his defeat. To extend his life as a piece of decoration is the worst possible insult" (55).

Perseus' treatment of Phineus contravenes the heroic code's prescribed way of dealing with fallen enemies (*Iliad* 24, Sophocles' *Ajax*) in so brutal a fashion as to impart the utmost savagery to Ovid's parody of the *Aeneid,* in particular, the confrontation of Aeneas and Turnus in book 12. As Bömer says, in the circles of true believers and loyalists at Rome, this could only appear "as infamy and pure mockery of the patriotism sanctioned by Virgil and Augustus" (at 5.1–249, 2.230). If there is such a thing as literary treason, Ovid's parody of Virgil's *Aeneid* in his "*Perseid*" would seem to be it.

Ovid completes the story of Perseus with his return to Argos (bringing Andromeda with him), where he restores his grandfather Acrisius to the throne that Acrisius' brother Proetus had wrested from him, whence he goes to Seriphos to settle an old score with Polydectes (5.236–249). Earlier, Acrisius was characterized as the only individual in Greece to remain opposed to Bacchus, denying that he was the son of Jupiter and denying as well that his own grandson Perseus was also the son of the god—something he came to regret, Ovid says (4.607–614). Now Ovid calls Acrisius Perseus' "wronged grandfather" (5.237), and the poet's comments here "completely change our earlier impression of the man" (Anderson [1997] at 5.236–238, 520).

In a portion of the tale that Ovid does not tell, Polydectes, ruler of Seriphos, had through a ruse sent Perseus off to fetch Medusa's head in order to get him out of the way so Polydectes could marry Perseus' mother, Danaë. When Perseus returns to Seriphos, he finds his mother and Polydectes' brother Dictys suppliants at unspecified altars, fearing violence from Polydectes. Perseus promptly turns Polydectes and his cronies to stone (Apollodorus 2.4.2–3). In Ovid, Polydectes "insisted that the slaying of Medusa was a fiction" (5.246–247). Perseus flashes the Gorgon's head at Polydectes and turns him to stone (5.247–249), punishing him "for the same kind of disrespect that has characterized all his [Perseus'] enemies, from Atlas to Phineus: belittlement of his heroism" (Anderson [1997] at 5.236–293, 519).

Perseus is the only human character in the poem with the power of metamorphosis (which possession of Medusa's head gives him). He is also, as Barkan notes, "a master of motion, as we see in each of his battles." The hero's "mastery of motion," Barkan continues, "which enables him to elude Atlas, to escape the dragon [in book 4], and to be everywhere at once in the battle with Phineus's men [in book 5], is, in a sense, the first prerequisite for the magical powers of metamorphosis that he is granted" (53).

21. A casual transition introduces the next set of tales: Minerva, Perseus' helper during his battle with Phineus, flies from Seriphos, Perseus' last stop (in Ovid's account), to Mount Helicon in Boeotia, home of the Muses, to see the spring created there by Pegasus, the winged horse born from Medusa's neck when Perseus beheaded her (5.250–259). Minerva is welcomed by the Muse Urania, who shows her the spring. After surveying the locale, the goddess calls the Muses "happy in work and home alike" (5.267–268). This comment elicits a reply from an unnamed Muse ("[o]ne of the sisters," 5.268), who qualifies Minerva's assessment with the story of Pyreneus (5.269–293), an embedded narrative that is the first in a series of three such narratives, each with a deeper degree of embedding than the one preceding. The Muse is interrupted by the sudden arrival of a flock of noisy birds with human voices (5.294–295), and to explain their conduct to Minerva—the outcome, essentially, of a contest between the Muses and the birds in their original, human form, when they were Pierides, daughters of Pieros—the Muse continues the series of embedded narratives that will occupy the rest of book 5 (5.300–678).

The story of Pyreneus (5.269–293), told by the unnamed Muse, is embedded at one level ("Ovid" and the unnamed Muse). The Pierides' entry in their contest with the Muses, a song about the monster Typhoeus' attack on the gods (5.318–331), retailed to Minerva by the unnamed Muse, is embedded at two levels ("Ovid," the unnamed Muse, and the Pierid singer). The Muses' entry, the story of the rape of Proserpina and its aftermath, originally sung by the Muse Calliope, her song now re-sung by the unnamed Muse (5.341–661), is also embedded at two levels ("Ovid," the unnamed Muse, and Calliope), but it contains Arethusa's autobiographical account of her near-rape, which she relates to Ceres (5.577–641), and which is thus embedded at the third level ("Ovid," the unnamed Muse, Calliope, and Arethusa). Nagle notes that by means of embedding here Ovid creates "a tripartite analogy between three pairs of audience and narrator: As Ceres is to Arethusa, and as Minerva is to the Muse reporting Calliope's song, so too is the reader to Ovid." This analogy provides "divine sanction for Ovid's role as narrator and his reader's role as attentive audience." The "similarity in the tales told" reinforces this analogy: Arethusa's story parallels Calliope's about the rape of Proserpina, "which in turn parallels the divine rape tales, such as the Apollo and Daphne, which Ovid has told *in propria persona*" ([1988a] 110–111).

These embedded tales occur toward the end of part one of the poem, "gods" (1.452–6.420), in a section that, beginning with the Perseus episode at 4.604 and continuing to 6.420, serves as a transition to part two, "heroes and heroines" (6.421–11.193). Part two has a similar transition to part three, "'historical' personages" (11.194–15.870), composed entirely of the Orpheus episode, which runs from 10.1 to 11.84, that is, almost to the end of part two (which continues to 11.193), and that transition, too, contains a long embedded narrative, Orpheus' song at 10.148–739. These two long transitions (1,298 and 823 lines, respectively) correspond in several ways, in addition to containing lengthy embedded narratives. First, these narratives, Nagle says ([1988a] 101), have "prominent and symmetrical location[s]," Calliope's being "roughly the same distance from the beginning of the Metamorphoses [sic] as Orpheus' cycle is from its conclusion." Second, these narratives, Nagle continues, "reflect Ovidian content, themes, and techniques to such an extent that they can be regarded as 'miniatures' of the larger poem." Third, Nagle says, they "contain the instances of deepest embedding in the Metamorphoses [sic]" ([1988a] 101): Arethusa's account of her near-rape, embedded within Calliope's song of the rape of Proserpina (5.577–641), and Venus' tale of Atalanta and Hippomenes (10.560–707), embedded in Orpheus' story of Venus and Adonis (10.503–739). Additionally, "the competing claims of love and death" (Nagle [1988a] 123) figure prominently in the song of Calliope, that is, the rape of Proserpina, and in the experience of her son Orpheus: Calliope sings of a mother who loses her daughter to the lord of the underworld, while Orpheus actually loses his wife, Eurydice, to death and appears before the lord of the underworld and his new bride, Proserpina, to plead for Eurydice's return to the upper world. (In his appeal he alludes [at 10.28–29] to his mother's song of Proserpina's rape in book 5.) Proserpina can return to heaven, Jupiter tells Ceres, "on the strict condition" (*lege . . . certa,* 5.531) that she has eaten nothing in the underworld, while Orpheus' wife, Eurydice, can return to life "on this condition" (*hanc . . . legem,* 10.50), that Orpheus not look at her until they emerge from the underworld (this parallel noted by Nagle [1988a] 123–124).

The unnamed Muse who narrates the embedded tales in book 5 seeks from the beginning to establish a sympathetic connection between Minerva and herself and her sisters: "O Minerva," she says, "if only your excellence had not led you to greater achievements, you would have been part of our chorus" (5.269–270). Her first embedded tale, the Pyreneus episode (5.269–293), which she tells Minerva in order to qualify the goddess' admiration of the Muses' happy state (5.264–268), establishes the Muses' virginity, Patricia Johnson says, and so "links them closely with Minerva . . . in her role as a sympathetic fellow virgin" (140). The Muse-narrator also, Nagle notes, seeks to influence Minerva's reaction by calling Pyreneus "savage" (5.274) and by claiming (a bid for sympathy), "I'm still not quite myself again" (5.275), that is, after Pyreneus' attempted rape. Her parenthetical comment "for no crime is forbidden here" (5.273) is "typical" of her "desire to guide [Minerva's] response" (Nagle [1989a] 105).

The story of Pyreneus is oddly told. There is a gap in the narration, Nagle notes, between 5.284, when the Muses enter Pyreneus' house to get out of the rain, and 5.285–287, when the rain stops and the Muses prepare to leave (precisely the period of time when one would expect Pyreneus to make his move). "The audience is given no hint," Nagle says, about what transpired *during* the visit ([1989a] 106): nothing, perhaps. But the unnamed Muse has represented herself and her sisters to Minerva as terrified virgins (5.273–274), seeking a kind of alliance of sympathy with the virgin goddess. At any rate, the Muses seem never to have been in any real danger, since at the first sign of aggression from Pyreneus they sprouted wings and fled (5.287–288): "The swift and facile escape indicates that the Muses had no real cause for fear" (Leach 113). Pyreneus, moreover, is so deranged ("madman that he was," 5.291) that he thinks he can fly off in pursuit of the Muses. In the attempt, however, he falls from his palace tower and is killed (5.289–293).

The noisy arrival of the flock of nine talking birds (5.294–295; called magpies, although "jays are perhaps more likely," according to Kenney [(1986) 404]), introduces the next set of embedded tales, which are told (or sung, rather) to Minerva by the unnamed Muse to explain the birds' recent transformation from human girls known as

Pierides, or daughters of Pieros, into the magpies they now are (5.300ff.). These tales are actually entries in a contest proposed by the Pierides for possession of territory: should the Muses lose, they would give up the Hippocrene spring (5.311–312; called here the spring of Medusa), which Minerva had come to Mount Helicon to see (5.256–259), and the spring of Aganippe. Calliope with her song defends, Hinds says, "nothing less than her own and her sisters' right to control the fountain of poetry, the Hippocrene" ([1987] 126). Haupt-Ehwald observe that the Pierides are only a "Hypostase" (principle or essence = incarnation) of the Muses, who were also called Pierides (at 5.294–678, 1.270). This observation leads me to suggest that Ovid gives us here two sets of Muses, so to speak, one human, the other divine, and presents a contest in art (that is, poetry) between these human and divine "specialists" in poetry. "This is the first contest in the poem," Nagle notes, "to be followed immediately by another," the contest in weaving between the goddess Minerva and the human girl Arachne at book 6.1–145 ([1989a] 106). The tapestries they produce, described in ecphrases, correspond (that is, in their ecphrastic embeddedness and as contest entries) to the embedded tales the unnamed Muse narrates here.

Both entries in the present contest are "emphatically narratives of narratives," Nagle says, for Minerva "does not witness the contest directly, but listens to an anonymous Muse's report" ([1989a] 107). The song of the Pierides, as the Muse presents it, is short (thirteen lines, 5.319–331) and anonymous (the Pierid sister who sang it is not identified by name), with eight of its thirteen lines given indirectly (5.319–326), "abridged [we assume] by a presumably biased reporter," and just five in direct speech (5.327–331), and those lines only "a bare catalogue of the disguises of the Olympians in retreat" (Nagle [1989a] 107). All of the Muses' entry, by contrast, is given in direct speech, we (and Minerva) hear it in its entirety (321 lines, 5.341–661), and its singer, Calliope, is not only identified by name but also introduced (5.338–340). As Anderson reminds us, Calliope "is traditionally the principal Muse, goddess especially of epic poetry, but also of other genres for Roman poets" ([1997] at 5.337–340, 532). The unnamed Muse's audience, Minerva (and we, the readers), is "at the mercy of another authority," that is, "the presiding nymphs' verdict" (Nagle [1989a] 107), with regard to the respective merits of the two songs, particularly the Pierid sister's song, since we hear only an abbreviated, mostly indirect, version if it. As we shall see, Calliope's song caters to the presumptive concerns of the nymph judges.

The daughter of Pieros selected to represent the sisters in the contest begins badly, for she plunges into her song without waiting for a decision by lot to determine who will go first (5.318). She sings of the battle between Jupiter and the monster Typhoeus (an "outworn subject": Hofmann 227), and in her version, incomplete and abbreviated by the narrating Muse, Typhoeus emerges from the earth and drives the gods in terror to Egypt, where they ignominiously change themselves into animal shapes in order to hide from him (5.319–331). She ends her song here, with Jupiter as a ram cowering in Egypt along with the other gods, a contemptuous representation of the Olympians, rather than proceeding on to the true end of the tale, Jupiter's victory over Typhoeus when the god pins him beneath Mount Etna. (See Apollodorus 1.6.3 and Gantz 1.48–51.) Calliope, however, at the beginning of her song (5.346ff.), "slyly 'finishes' the story of Typhoeus and demolishes the Pierid blasphemy" (Anderson [1997] at 5.346–348, 533; see also Hinds [1987] 128–129). Arachne, the Pierid sister's counterpart in the contest with Minerva in book 6 (which she, like the Pierid singer, loses), also represents the gods using animal disguises when they rape a variety of human and divine females (6.103–128), a depiction that resonates with the Pierid sister's image of the gods here.

Leach notes another connection between the Pierid's song and Arachne's (as well as the embedded narratives of the Minyades in book 4 and Orpheus in book 10). All, she says, "have one common element . . . and that is their emphasis upon the personality of the artist, the reasons for his performance and his ultimate fate. In all four cases, the fate of the human artist, regardless of his talents, is disastrous" (106).

When the narrating Muse completes her version of the Pierid's entry in the contest, she defers to Minerva in a rhetorical gesture: "but perhaps you're in a hurry and don't have time to listen to our song" (5.333–334). Minerva urges her to continue (5.335–336): she had come to Mount Helicon in the first place out of "curiosity about another *fama,* concerning the spring Hippocrene" (this curiosity expressed at 5.256–259), and is thus "a goddess interested in stories" (Nagle [1988a] 110). Her interest in the contest "is not purely aesthetic; she gets its message and applies it in her own contest with Arachne. The connection between the two [contests] is prominent and explicit," as the opening lines of book 6 make clear (6.1–7; Nagle [1988a] 110). The Muse's pause demarcates the Pierid sister's song from Calliope's to come, and enables the Muse to introduce her sister Muse with a preamble that can only serve to arouse expectations in the audience (5.337–340).

Calliope takes the rape of Proserpina as the subject of her song and begins with a standard invocation for a hymn to a god or goddess, in this case Ceres, Proserpina's mother (5.341–345: "Ceres was the first, . . . of her I must sing . . ."), but then continues with what is anything but a standard hymn to a deity and gives a version of this myth like no other that we know of. (See Hinds [1987] 52–57 and 72–98 and Anderson [1997] at 5.356–437, 534–535. Ovid gives another version of the rape of Proserpina at *Fasti* 4.417–618. See the commentary on these lines by Fantham [1998] 173–209, with comparisons to Ovid's account here.)

Calliope's next lines, describing Typhoeus pinned beneath the island of Sicily (5.346ff.), "correct" the Pierid sister's incomplete account with its representation of Typhoeus on the loose and the gods cowering in Egypt in their animal disguises.

The earthquakes caused by the monster as he struggles against the weight of the island leads Dis, "the king of the silent dead," who fears light leaks in the roof of the underworld, to inspect Sicily's foundation (3.356ff.; cf. 2.401ff., where Jupiter, following his inspection of the "mighty walls of heaven" after the conflagration caused by Phaethon has been extinguished, spies Callisto). The inspection completed, Dis is driving about in Sicily when Venus sees him and urges her son Cupid to afflict the god with love and so extend their "empire" to the underworld, and he obeys (5.363–384).

As noted earlier, Ovid introduces Cupid and Venus at key points in the *Metamorphoses*: at the beginning (book 1, the story of Daphne and Apollo, Cupid alone), here in book 5, and in book 10 (Orpheus' story of Venus and Adonis: 10.503–739; for this general point, see Stephens [1957–58] 178). The latter two places where Venus appears are "turning points" in the poem, that is, transitions from one major section to the next (as mentioned earlier in this note).

According to Patricia Johnson, Calliope makes a "highly significant digression" from all other versions of the rape of Proserpina when she attributes it "to the sole agency of Venus and Cupid" (125): Rome in general, and the Julian family in particular (including Augustus), Patricia Johnson reminds us, were closely identified with Venus through her son Aeneas, whom the Julians thought of as the founder of their line (128–129). Since Venus "plays a crucial role in . . . Augustan ideology," reference to her in art or literature will inevitably "reflect . . . upon . . . the Julians, and particularly Augustus" (130). Venus' role in the rape of Proserpina (in order to extend the goddess' empire), Johnson thinks, is completely at odds with "the goals, if not the letter, of Augustus' moral program" (132). It is difficult, though, to assess Ovid's tone. He is, it seems to me, more glancing parodist than straightforward and serious critic of Augustan politics or ideology or anything else. The *Aeneid,* too (the "official" epic of Augustan Rome), is a target for the poet's wicked style, for Venus' opening words to her son here echo *Aeneid* 1.664f, where Venus appeals to Cupid to make Dido, queen of Carthage, fall in love with Aeneas. There she begins, "*nate, meae vires, mea magna potentia, solus, / nate . . .*" ("My son, my only strength, sole agent of my powers, / My son . . ."; Day Lewis, trans.)." Here, echoing Venus in the Aeneid, the goddess addresses her son Cupid, "*arma manusque meae, mea, nate, potentia*" (5.365: "My son—my weapons, my hands, my power—"); this line also echoes the famous beginning of the *Aeneid: arma virumque cano . . .* (1.1, "Arms and the man I sing . . ."). Patricia Johnson also sees *Metamorphoses* 5.365ff. as a "commentary on the Aeneid's patriotic and maternal Venus," for she is presented here as "a sexual imperialist who lacks even the excuse of the glory of Rome to fall back upon for her behavior" (135), while the echo of *Aeneid* 1.1 is surely tongue in- cheek parody.

Calliope could hardly have designed a cannier strategy for a singing contest before judges who are nymphs than her song of Venus, Dis, and the rape of Proserpina, the story of the rape including a nymph threatened for defending Proserpina (that is, Cyane) and an account of the near-rape of another nymph, Arethusa (told by herself), since "most targets of Olympian rape or seduction were nymphs," and Calliope's song can only arouse "her audience's [that is, the judging nymphs'] sympathy on behalf of the victims of and protesters against sexual aggression" (Patricia Johnson 141, 144).

The rape of Proserpina takes up one line: "in a single instant, almost, she was seen, loved, and raped by Dis" (5.395). "The speed . . . is breathtaking" (Curran [1978] 218), so fast, in fact, that Cahoon calls the rape of Proserpina "the absence at the center of [the] story, for what is missing from this 'Rape of Proserpina' is precisely the rape of Proserpina" (61). Later, when Ceres appeals to Jupiter to have Proserpina released from the underworld, the god will deny that Proserpina was ever raped: "But if we can just call it by its right name, what happened was not a violation; it is, in fact, love" (5.524–526).

Arethusa's extensive first-person account of her own near-rape (5.577–641) makes up somewhat for the crucial missing element in Calliope's rendition of the rape of Proserpina. But if more violence by the powerful Dis against a helpless female is needed, that god's savage treatment of the nymph Cyane, who tries to stop him in his hurtling chariot as he returns with Proserpina to the underworld, will supply it. Cyane lives in (but is not identical to) the pool that bears her name, and after Dis violently flings his scepter into her pool to open a way to the underworld, in grief both for Proserpina and for the violation of her pool, these together an "inconsolable wound" (5.426), she is consumed by tears and dissolves into this pool (5.409–437). Her wound, Segal says, "symbolically parallels the rape [of Proserpina] itself " ([1969a] 54).

After a futile search for her daughter, Ceres learns from the nymph Arethusa that Proserpina was carried off by Dis and now lives with him as queen of the underworld (5.487ff.). Wilkinson says that these lines, Arethusa's account to Ceres (5.489–508), "must rank among Ovid's most beautiful imaginings, culminating in two unforgettable lines" ([1955] 201–202): "but she was a queen, even so, ruling now in the world of darkness, the powerful consort now of the king of hell." These lines are indeed as poignant, as bittersweet, as any in the *Metamorphoses,* but they would surely have reminded Ovid's first readers, if not us, of the dead Achilles' scathing comment to the living Odysseus when they meet in the underworld in book 11 of the *Odyssey:* "I would rather follow the plow as thrall to another man, one with no land allotted him and not much to live on, than be a king over all the perished dead" (11.489–491; Lattimore, trans.).

Sensing that Ceres will not want to hear her own story just now (why she, a nymph from Elis in western Greece, now lives in Sicily; how she was almost raped; and how she was transformed into a spring), Arethusa volunteers to postpone it to "another, more suitable time, when you're not so worried, don't appear so downcast" (5.498–501), thereby demonstrating such "a good sense of timing and propriety" and "so effectively . . . arous[ing] that goddess' interest," that Ceres "returns immediately for the rest of the story" (Nagle [1989a] 108).

A first-person account of a metamorphosis, such as Arethusa tells (5.577–641), is somewhat rare in the *Metamorphoses*. (Arethusa's is the second of six; see n. 8.) An autobiographical narration of sexual assault by a victim of such an assault is rarer still. Arethusa's account of her own near-rape is the only tale of its kind in the poem, and it gives us "a first-person female perspective" for other similar tales of rape that we've heard so far (Nagle [1988a] 108), capping these tales at this point of transition from one section of the poem to the next. (The insertion of Arethusa into the narrative of the rape of Proserpina is an Ovidian invention, according to Haupt-Ehwald at 5.474ff., 1.287, with Bömer's apparent agreement at 5.487–508, 2.351.)

Their own adversity and suffering create no compassion in the gods: lèse-majesté must be punished, no matter what. Thus Ceres viciously transforms the boy who laughs at her, as she greedily drinks, into a lizard as his mother looks on and weeps (5.451–461): "A mother is deprived of her child pitilessly by a god who seeks hers" (Anderson [1997] at 5.459–461, 545). Proserpina, too, the victim of rape, "suddenly reveals her own power to victimize others," Cahoon says, "as she follows her mother's example and transforms [the boy] Ascalaphus . . . into a bird of evil omen" (57), a screech owl, for revealing that she had eaten pomegranate seeds in the underworld (5.543–550). After narrating that transformation, Calliope tells of the "sympathetic" change of the Sirens, Proserpina's companions when she was raped, who, after looking everywhere for her throughout the world, were granted the bodies of birds by the gods so the girls could fly over water in their continuing search. In an unusual metamorphosis, the Sirens, whom Calliope calls "learnéd" (*doctae*, 5.555; the term was applied to the poets of Ovid's time who imitated the tradition of learnéd poets in the Hellenistic period, Callimachus, for example, Ovid's source and model for much of the *Metamorphoses*), retained, instead of losing, their human faces, especially and in particular their human voices, "lest their song, made to soothe all who heard it—such a great gift—lose the tongues it needs for singing" (5.552–563). Nagle notes another "unique" quality of that digression, the fact that most of it (8.5 lines out of 11.5) is told in an apostrophe by Calliope to the girls ([1988a] 106–107)—girls who, Anderson comments, may be her own daughters, since "their mother is usually named as one of the Muses" ([1997] at 5.554–555, 555).

At the end of Arethusa's story, Ceres flies in her serpent-drawn chariot to Athens, gives the chariot to one Triptolemus, along with some seeds, and orders him to sow the seeds in certain parts of the earth (5.642–647). In his version of the rape of Proserpina at *Fasti* 4.417ff., Ovid names Triptolemus (at *Fasti* 4.550) as the infant son of Metanira and Celeus, king of Eleusis (a few miles northwest of ancient Athens and the place where the Eleusinian mysteries, sacred to Demeter and Persephone [= Ceres and Proserpina] were practiced), whom Ceres, disguised as an old woman, attempts to make immortal by means of fire until she is thwarted by the baby's terrified mother. Traditionally, that child is named Demophon; Apollodorus 1.5.1–2 makes Triptolemus Demophon's older brother. In the Homeric *Hymn to Demeter,* the name is given as Demophoön (234, 238), and Triptolemus is represented as one of the leading men of Eleusis (149–155) and one of the four individuals whom Demeter showed how to conduct her rites and to whom she taught her mysteries (473–479). At *Fasti* 4.559–560, Ceres predicts that Triptolemus will be the first to till the soil. (See Gantz 1.64–66 and 69–70 for extended discussion of Triptolemus.)

Triptolemus' role in Calliope's song, as Anderson notes, "was traditional in cult, myth and art long before Ovid" ([1997] at 5.645–647, 565). At 5.648ff. Triptolemus goes to Scythia, "a nonagricultural region" (Anderson [1997] at 5.648–650, 565), where the king, Lyncus, out of envy for the gift Triptolemus has to bestow, tries to murder him while he is "sound asleep" (*somno . . . gravatum,* 5.658), recalling Lycaon in book 1, who similarly tried to murder Jupiter when he was "sound asleep" (*gravem somno,* 1.224), as Anderson observes ([1997] at 6.657–659, 565). Calliope ends her tale with Ceres rescuing Triptolemus by turning Lyncus into a lynx and ordering Triptolemus to return to Athens (6.659–661). The unnamed Muse then tells Minerva about the outcome of the contest and about the Muses' metamorphosis of the Pierides, who became abusive when they learned they had lost, into magpies, and this completes the explanation she had begun at 5.300ff.

BOOK SIX

22. Books 5 and 6 are bridged by the goddess Minerva in her role as audience for the unnamed Muse's account of the singing contest between the Muses and the Pierides in book 5 (250–678) and as artist-participant in a weaving contest with the mortal Arachne at 6.1–145 (the next episode), which, as Nagle notes, is the second contest between divine and human artists in the poem and its first instance of "*nonverbal* embedding" ([1989a] 108; Nagle's emphasis). Minerva herself, or rather her thought process, serves as the transition to the episode. She had heard the Muse's story of the contest and had approved of their song and their anger, which she thought was justified (6.1–2). She then says to herself, "'There's not enough praise here'" (*laudare parum est,* 6.3; "because she had praised the Muses": Haupt-Ehwald at 6.3, 1.302), echoing the unnamed Muse at the end of book 5 who had lashed out at the Pierides for refusing to accept defeat: "'Since it is apparently not enough for you to deserve punishment'" (*quoniam . . . vobis / supplicium meruisse parum est,* 5.665–666). Thus we get at the very beginning of the tale, von Albrecht says, the anger of the gods as a motif, not in response to a particular instance of hybris, but owing, rather, to the goddess's desire to emulate the Muses. Whereas they punish Pyreneus and the Pierides out of necessity, reacting, not acting, Minerva, by contrast, is represented here as having a general desire to punish and then seeks an opportunity for herself. As 6.5–7 make clear ("she began to think about how to punish Arachne of Lydia, who, she had heard"), it has already been determined that Arachne will perish before the encounter with Minerva occurs (von Albrecht [1984] 460–461). In line 6.6, translated "[Arachne,] who . . . saw no reason . . . to yield to the goddess" (*quam sibi . . . non cedere laudibus*), the verb *cedere,* "yield," von Albrecht observes, here means "give way to" (*nachgeben*) in the sense of "take second place to" (*nachstehen*). That is, Arachne sees no reason to consider herself an inferior artist in comparison with Minerva. Although Arachne's inflexibility will later be her undoing, von Albrecht says, here, provocation of Minerva is not at issue. It is simply Arachne's success and fame that Minerva feels herself challenged by ([1984]) 461).

Ovid emphasizes Arachne's undistinguished background: ordinary parents, a small house in a small town (6.7–13). Her fame, the poet says, "lay in the art of weaving" (6.7–8). According to von Albrecht, Ovid thus motivates her conduct and her pride in her art through her social origin. She has worked her way up by her artistic talent and is thus understandably proud of it. She is therefore not prepared to recognize superiority in another without putting it to the test. In her eyes, her proposal to have a contest in weaving with Minerva (6.25) is not blasphemy. On the contrary, she offers Minerva what she herself considers a fair chance, and her way of thinking is fully understandable when one considers the course of her life ([1984] 461).

From Minerva's side, however, Arachne is the opportunity the goddess has been looking for to vent her wrath. She initiates the tragic drama, the *Arachne*, so to speak, which she "writes" and "stars" in, by playing the role of an old woman who warns the girl to "yield to the goddess" (6.32, *cede deae*, the same word used at 6.6, where Arachne is said not "to yield [*cedere*] to the goddess"; see above), offering her motherly advice but expressing it in such a way as to provoke the girl (von Albrecht [1984] 458). Arachne rises to the bait: "'Why doesn't your goddess come here herself'" (6.42: *venit*, present tense), and Minerva springs the trap. "'She *has* come,'" then "taking off her disguise and revealing herself as the goddess" (6.43: *venit*, perfect tense). Arachne's present-tense *venit* is immediately outdated, von Albrecht says, by Minerva's perfect-tense *venit*, which he calls the shortest and most impressive speech in all of Ovid ([1984] 458). Minerva's "speech" also provides an incomplete tragic Recognition, "incomplete" because, although Arachne recognizes Minerva as goddess (but only blushing briefly and involuntarily, like the sky at dawn, rather than prostrating herself before the goddess, as the nymphs and Mygdonian women do: 6.44–49), she is not afraid (6.45), as she should be, and "persists in her plan and rushes into ruin" (6.50–51). It is the incomplete nature of Arachne's Recognition that guarantees her Fall.

As the contest begins, Ovid describes in detail the looms being set up for weaving (6.53–60). He earlier described, also in detail, Arachne alone at this process, beginning at the beginning: working the fleece into balls, pulling wool out from them to spin into thread, spinning it, and weaving with the threads spun (6.17–23). Von Albrecht makes the interesting comment that Ovid is a poet of human work ([1984] 461).

The poet then shifts our gaze with lightning speed from the loom and the specifics of the process of weaving to a rainbow forming in the sky and the brilliant delicacy of its multiple hues in a simile describing the radiant colors goddess and mortal girl are using, and thus conveys the aesthetic awe a viewer (or reader) feels when watching two expert artists at work (6.61–67). Although the rainbow simile refers to the colors used by both weavers, it seems to anticipate (and give approval to) Arachne's tapestry and its aesthetic rather than to Minerva's: The "reference to the metamorphic arts of nature [in the simile] establishes a norm. The art of continuous changes, radiant with multiplicity but confounding clear definition, reflects a reality in the universe that is similarly fluid. In both subject and method Arachne's tapestry fulfills this aesthetic" (Barkan 3).

Although the two artists work simultaneously, Minerva's tapestry is fittingly described first, since she is a goddess. She weaves a representation of the contest between herself and Neptune to name (and be the patron deity of) Athens (6.70ff.). A contestant in the weaving competition thus describes in her entry an earlier contest in which she competed against a far more powerful opponent to decide which of the two is the better creator—thus, one may say, a contest about creativity itself. Perhaps her choice of subject ("self-praise and self-vindication," Feeney calls it [191]) is meant to intimidate or demoralize Arachne, if she steals a glance at Minerva's tapestry as she herself works. (Minerva's tapestry is clearly intended to deliver a lesson: 6.83ff.)

Minerva renders the twelve Olympians (*bis sex,* 6.72: Ovid's mistake or Minerva's, since for their competition Minerva and Neptune, two of the twelve, stand in front of the—now ten—seated divinities?), who serve as judges of the contest, with "[a]n exact rendering [that] identifies each one like a signature" (*sua quemque deorum / inscribit facies,* 6.73–74). Each deity is thus represented as he should be, von Albrecht says: Minerva's art is hieratic, official, and polis-related ([1984] 459). Minerva herself is "[t]he only figure described in any detail" in the central panel, as Hardy observes, adding, "The impression is that of an artist absorbed with herself" (143).

The contest between Minerva and Neptune to become the patron deity of Athens was also the subject of the group of sculptures on the west pediment of the Parthenon, the temple dedicated to Athena at Athens created by the fifth-century B.C. sculptor Phidias. The temple and its sculptures were the ultimate representation of classical Greece in visual art.

Minerva's central panel in her tapestry is supplemented by the depiction of four additional contests in the four corners (but of a totally different kind), "[s]o that Arachne . . . may understand by examples the price she can expect to pay for her reckless daring" (6.83–85). These are contests that mortals lost to gods, undergoing metamorphosis as punishment for defeat. (Little or nothing is known about the myths referred to, and nothing is known about them as contests. See Anderson [1972] at 6.87–98, 163–164; and Bömer at 6.87–100, 3.32–35.) A theocentric perspective prevails in Minerva's tapestry, von Albrecht says, and the fact that mortals, not gods, are subject to transformation is an indication of that ([1984] 459). The narrator, however, undercuts Minerva's warning message, Hardy notes, for he "increasingly elicits pity for the punished mortals, instead of outrage at their daring" (144): in the fourth corner all we see is the grieving father Cinyras "lying on temple steps made from the bodies of his own daughters, hugging the stones and weeping" (6.99–100).

Minerva frames her work "with a border of olive branches, the emblem of peace, and so ends with the image of her own tree" (6.101–102), a reassertion of her victory over Neptune (and reinforcing the figure of Victory at 6.82). Barkan sums up Minerva's tapestry thus: "[T]he gods sit all-powerful in the middle (of the universe or of the work of art), whence they deal out punishing metamorphoses to mortals . . . The whole picture is highly moralistic[,] . . . and bound up with that moralism is an aesthetic of sharp definition and finality" (3). The form, content, and moral purpose of the tapestry are "'classical' and Augustan," in Curran's words ([1972] 84), and, indeed, the ecphrasis describing it contains a reference to Augustus himself: the gods sit, Ovid says, "in august majesty" (*augusta gravitate,* 6.73), using the adjective that Octavian adopted as his official title in 27 B.C. "Once Octavian became Augustus," Anderson says, the adjective's "natural religious associations became complicated with political ones. Thus, here we might imagine Jupiter and the panel of gods as Augustus and his Senate" ([1972] at 6.73, 161).

Arachne's tapestry (6.103ff.) has no order ("no center, no corners to be filled," Vincent 369), but it does have a central theme: gods raping females, changing themselves into animals to perpetrate their violations. And so by contrast with Minerva's tapestry, it is gods, not humans, who undergo (self-)metamorphosis, in order to have unions with mortal women, and the perspective is purely an earthly one, von Albrecht observes ([1984] 459). These vignettes are enclosed in a border of intertwining flowers and ivy, the latter of which evokes the Dionysian and the erotic (von Albrecht [1984] 459).

Of the twenty-one rapes (in twenty-four lines: 6.103–126), Jupiter is responsible for nine, Neptune for six, Apollo for four, and Bacchus and Saturn for one each. There is little violence in these scenes; it is, rather, the "element of deception" that is emphasized (Hardy 145). Europa is "deceived" (*elusam,* 6.103) by Jupiter. Asterie, it is true, is "in the grip" of Jupiter as an eagle (*teneri,* 6.108), but the eagle "struggles" with her (*luctante,* 6.108). Leda is simply "lying beneath" (*recubare,* 6.109) the swan. Jupiter "made . . . Antiope pregnant" (*inplerit,* 6.111, literally, "filled") with twin offspring. He "took" Alcmena (*cepit,* 6.112; glossed by Bömer "erotice per vim, dolum," that is, "erotically, by force, trickery," at 6.112, 3.39). He "fooled" (*luserit,* 6.113) Danaë, Aegina, Memory, and Proserpina. Neptune is "changed" (*mutatum,* 6.115) into a bull "for the maiden Canace" (*virgine in Aeolia,* 6.116, translated "for love of . . . Canace," from sense: see Bömer's gloss "'sie stellte auch dich . . . dar, verliebt in die Tochter des Aeolus,'" "'she [Arachne] also represented you [Neptune], in love with Aeolus' daughter,'" at 6.116, 3.40).

Neptune "engender[s]" (*gignis,* 6.117) Otus and Ephialtes, who are named in Latin only as Aloidae (6.117), that is, sons of Aloeus, whose wife, Iphimedeia, bore Otus and Ephialtes to Poseidon/Neptune (Bömer at 6.117, 3.41) but is not mentioned as Neptune's victim. He "deceive[s]" (*fallis,* 6.117) Theophane. Ceres "felt" (*sensit,* 6.119) Neptune as a horse; Medusa "felt" (*sensit* again, 6.119) him as a bird; Melantho "felt" (*sensit,* 6.120) him as a dolphin.

For the first three of Apollo's four rapes there is neither verb nor victim (if indeed they are rapes: "[M]odern scholars . . . cannot fix the episodes to which the tapestry refers": Anderson [1972] at 6.122, 167); he is simply "there" (*illic,* 6.122; that is, on the tapestry) as a farmer and then "wearing" (*gesserit,* 6.124) the feathers of a hawk and then a lion's skin. For the fourth, he "fooled" (*luserit,* 6.124) Isse. Bacchus "deceived" (*deceperit,* 6.125) Erigone, and Saturn "created" (*crearit,* 6.126) the centaur Chiron; no victim-mother is named. The ecphrasis, Hardy says, "increasingly focuses the audience's attention away from the act of violence and onto the element of guile," and "near the end [the victims] start to disappear . . . altogether" (145). Halfway through Jupiter's list the narrator simply says that the god impregnated Antiope (6.111). Then Neptune engenders Otus and Ephialtes (6.117). When we reach Saturn, who "created" Chiron (6.126), the focus is on "the generative power of the gods, both in changing their shapes and in fathering new life," and it has indeed become "more difficult to see the description as an attempt to provoke sympathy for the women so routinely victimized by the gods" (Hardy 146).

After the description of Jupiter as a bull seducing Europa (6.103–107: five of the twenty-four lines), there is a compressed quality to the ecphrasis—twenty transformations of gods, if not twenty rapes, in nineteen lines—that may remind us of the way the unnamed Muse distorts the song of the Pierides, compressing it into thirteen lines, eight of which she gives in indirect statement (see 5.319–331 and n. 21). The focus on the metamorphoses of the gods here may also remind us of the Pierid singer's blasphemous representation of the gods cowering as animals in Egypt in an attempt to hide from Typhoeus. Arachne, however, doesn't demean the gods. Her defiant attitude about her ability as an artist *vis-à-vis* Minerva has led critics and scholars to assume that her art is defiant, too. But unless it is ridiculing the gods to represent them transformed into various shapes, and I don't know that it is, Arachne honors Jupiter as the most versatile shape-changer with nine transformations; to Neptune, defeated by Minerva in *her* tapestry, Arachne gives six. There is no shame for the male gods in rape, more's the pity. That being so, why should a god (Jupiter) be ashamed that as a swan he seduced Leda, as golden rain Danaë, as fire Aegina? (As Feeney says, "Arachne depicts nothing about the gods that was not already present, however faintly, in epic tradition" [193]).

Minerva's anger at Arachne's success—and we remember that the goddess came away from the Muses angry and spoiling for a fight, as von Albrecht has emphasized—is fueled not only by the girl's talent ("Minerva could not fault the work," the narrator says: 6.129–130) but also, perhaps, by the attention Arachne gives to defeated Neptune as well as by the subject of the tapestry. This is a virgin goddess who has recently come from (and been part of) a conclave of prudish virgins, where she had heard (in Calliope's song) herself singled out by Venus as a deity opposed to love and sex. Urging her son Cupid to afflict Dis with passion, Venus had said, "Have you not noticed that Minerva and . . . Diana have no use for me?" (5.375–376). Minerva has many reasons to be a hostile, even hateful, critic (and she is both contestant and judge). And the narrator's designation of Arachne's woven tales as "crimes of the gods" (6.131), which occurs between Minerva's wrecking the tapestry and beating Arachne with her shuttle, can be taken as reflecting the goddess' reaction to those tales. Venus would have rejoiced. (And we never hear the opinions of Jupiter, Neptune, Apollo, Bacchus, and Saturn.)

Arachne's tapestry shares with Minerva's "one element of visual formalism," Curran says, its border of flowers interwoven with ivy (6.127–128), although "the way in which Ovid chooses to characterize Arachne's border constitutes an allusion to the fluid nature of his and Arachne's methods of composition" ([1972] 84). It shares another element as well, the precisely mimetic—even photographic—realization of her images. This is emphasized at the beginning of the ecphrasis: Arachne "depicts Europa, deceived by the semblance of a bull: You would think it was a real bull swimming in a real sea" (6.103–104). The paradoxical contrast—the bull and the sea Arachne depicts are not really a bull and a sea (and the bull is really Jupiter, so it is doubly unreal), but you would think (*putares*, 6.104) from her representation that it was a real bull, a real sea (*verum taurum, freta vera,* 6.104)—emphasizes what I called earlier Arachne's precisely mimetic realization.

A brief critique of the tapestry, which separates Jupiter and Neptune from the other gods rendered by Arachne, directly states this aspect of Arachne's aesthetic, which she shares with Minerva. "All these," that is, the two gods and the fifteen rapes and metamorphoses described in the preceding lines, "Arachne rendered, each with its own likeness [*faciem . . . suam,* 6.121], and the places, exactly [*faciem . . . locorum,* 6.121]" (6.121–122). These lines echo an earlier statement by the narrator about Minerva's tapestry ("An exact rendering identifies each one [sc. each god] like a signature," 6.73–74: *sua quemque deorum / inscribit facies*) and suggest that Arachne's precisely mimetic realization matches Minerva's. Earlier, I quoted Barkan's comment on the rainbow simile that the narrator employs to describe the colors the two artists use (6.63–67): "[T]he metamorphic [art] of nature establishes a norm. The art of continuous changes, radiant with multiplicity but confounding clear definition, reflects a reality in the universe that is similarly fluid. In both subject and method Arachne's tapestry fulfills this aesthetic" (3). Arachne's art, however, unlike the rainbow's colors, subtly grading from one to the next, does not "[confound] clear definition," as I've indicated. Otherwise, Minerva would have faulted it.

Curran, as I have noted, calls Minerva's tapestry "'classical' and Augustan," adding, "in its order and symmetry," while Arachne's "has virtually no discernible visual order" ([1972] 84). This echoes an earlier comment by Anderson: "The goddess produced a perfect piece of Classicistic art, structurally balanced and thematically grandiose. . . . Arachne on the other hand wove a swirl of divine figures. . . . There is no apparent structure to the tapestry" ([1968] 103). These critics (and others), as they differentiate sharply between Minerva's and Arachne's art, identify Arachne's aesthetic as Ovid's.

(Curran: Arachne's border of flowers and ivy alludes to "the fluid nature of his [Ovid's] and Arachne's methods of composition" [(1972) 84]; Anderson: "Symmetry is no prerequisite to Ovidian art; a set of loosely ordered tales can form a masterpiece" [(1968) 103]; see also Galinsky [1975] 82–83 and Barkan 4.) Leach seems to me to be closer to the truth, however, when she observes that Ovid draws from both aesthetics, the classicistic and idealizing and the "modernistic": while the "vision of Arachne's tapestry is perfectly in keeping with the world vision of the *Metamorphoses*," she says, and while "Minerva's and Arachne's versions of mythology and metamorphosis assert the power of the gods: the one as a force of order, the other as a force participating in the flux of nature," yet Ovid himself "maintains a vision embracing both points of view," thus making it "impossible to identify Ovid's perspective entirely with Arachne's" (103, 104). Moreover, "the poem itself contains principles and perspectives that simultaneously complement and contradict one another . . . , visions of order and chaos intermingled. Only in the tapestries are these perspectives drawn apart as if for momentary clarification" (118).

Arachne cannot endure Minerva's violent attack. Still defiant (*animosa*, 6.134), she hangs herself. Mercurial Minerva pities her (*miserata*, 6.135) and, lifting her up, arrests her suicide, but then says, "Live on, shameless girl, but hang forever, even so" (6.136), and decrees "the same punishment" (6.137) for all her descendants. This is obviously not a favor, and Arachne would be better off dead, for Minerva's transformation of the girl is a vicious reduction that compels her to produce works—spiderwebs—that are minimalist in content, and in their form, simplicity, and symmetry "classicistic," and so like Minerva's art in a grotesque way. But "[w]orst of all," Feeney says, citing Seneca (*Epistulae Morales* 121.23), "a spider's work is not art. All spiders produce the same, none is more skilled than the next. . . . At the end, it really is true that you would know she was taught by Minerva" (as Ovid had said at 6.23; Feeney 193–194).

23. Ovid's transition from the Arachne story to the story of Niobe is "based on theme," Anderson says, "not on the superficial connection that is established in [lines 6.146–147]" ([1972] at 6.146–147, 172). "The thematic link" between the stories, Anderson continues, "is here defined in such a way as to suggest the dominant notes of this story, Niobe's unyielding attitude and haughty words" ([1972] at 6.150–151, 172). The Arachne story, however, belongs to a category of themes that the Niobe story does not belong to—artists and their condition in the world—and Arachne's "hybris," if that is what her attitude is to be defined as, is qualitatively different from that of Niobe. Moreover, the Niobe episode develops "from a quite clear-cut and simple vengeance tale into a truly remarkable study of human suffering" (Otis 147).

Niobe's husband, Amphion, to whose "art" Ovid refers at 6.152, was an accomplished lyre player who with his brother Zethus built the wall around Thebes, "the stones following the sound of Amphion's lyre" (Apollodorus 3.5.5).

Niobe's reference to her father, Tantalus, at 6.172–173 is ominous, for he invited the gods to a banquet and sought to serve them his own son Pelops, whom he had killed and cooked (see Pindar, *Olympian* 1.36–66, who, however, rejects the story). "Any Roman audience," Anderson says, "would have recalled [Tantalus'] notorious end in the Underworld as an archetypal figure of sin" ([1972] at 6.172–176, 176).

Jupiter is both Niobe's grandfather and father-in-law, because he was the father of Tantalus as well as the father of her husband, Amphion.

The Niobe episode, Otis observes, "falls into three distinct parts," the first being the "[h]aughty [m]other" (6.146–203), the second, the "[k]illing of the [s]ons" (6.204–

266), and the third, the "[k]illing of the [d]aughters and Niobe's [m]etamorphosis" (6.267–312). "The first shows the crime or *hybris*," Otis continues, "the second, the punishment, the third, the *pathos* of Niobe" (147). Her metamorphosis, Otis goes on to say, "is not punishment at all, not even an act of divine pity, but the very image of Niobe's final condition. . . . Her petrifaction is only the consequence of a calamity that had already stunned her to the point of absolute insensibility. . . . The *Niobe* thus marks the transition . . . from metamorphosis as an act of divine punishment to metamorphosis as a natural phenomenon" (151).

Niobe, Ovid says, sinks down amid the corpses of her sons, daughters, and husband, "rigid with grief," and then the poet describes her turning to stone, virtually body part by body part. "She was weeping, though," he continues, and then she was magically transported to her native land, where she was set on a mountain peak and "dissolved into tears" (6.301–312).

While Ovid used tragedies by Aeschylus and Sophocles as sources (among others) for the Niobe episode (Otis 404), it is something other than a tragedy. The poet stresses Niobe's suffering, her *pathos*, but there appears to be no *mathos*, that is, no learning, no recognition, that accompanies or follows her fall. Her metamorphosis, perhaps, substitutes (or serves as an objective correlative) for her learning, her recognition, for, "despite the hardening of her form," Anderson says, "something continues to live in Niobe and to comment eternally on her life. What interpretation we are to place on her weeping—remorse for her words, sorrow for her children, shock at her disaster—Ovid does not prescribe. One thing is clear though: her tears are a permanent denial of that once foolishly asserted felicity" ([1972] at 6.310–312, 194).

24. "When a god or goddess has punished a mortal in the *Metamorphoses*," Anderson notes, "Ovid frequently makes his transition by registering the popular impression of the event, to which he attaches a new story" ([1972] at 6.313–316, 195), as here, in the transition from the story of Niobe to the tales of the Lycian farmers (6.317–381) and Marsyas (6.382–400): "Then indeed all the people, men and women alike, feared Latona's wrath" (6.313–316). Both stories are embedded narratives, the former doubly embedded. An unnamed narrator begins the episode of the Lycian farmers at 6.317 ("and one of the men said: 'Long ago in Lycia, too . . . ,'" 6.317) and begins quoting the guide who conducted him to Lycia and who is the source of the story. Nagle notes that the anonymous narrator, "one of the men" (6.317: *e quibus unus*), parallels the anonymous Minyad sister (4.36: "one of them," *e quibus una*) who tells the first of the sisters' tales (Nagle [1989a] 109). In this last section of part one ("gods": 1.452–6.420), Ovid's embedded narratives give a final emphasis to storytelling itself.

The tale of the Lycian farmers softens the harsh image of Latona given in the Niobe episode, for it "portrays [her] in the role first of a victim and, only after ample provocation . . . , as a punishing goddess. . . . Here the goddess is appealing, the human beings nasty; here justice resides with the power that metamorphoses the humans" (Anderson [1972] at 6.313–381, 194–195). The Lycian farmers' transformation into frogs fits their crime. They "have acted like brutes," Anderson says, and "they become such. They have shown a perverse delight in wallowing in water and mud; that is now their eternal fate" ([1972] at 6.370–374, 200). Ovid shows, Anderson continues, "an intimate causal relation between the rude voices of the men and of the frogs, between the very desire to utter [insults] and the deformation of the human mouth into the gross wide amphibian's jaws" ([1972] at 6.377–381, 200–201).

One story leads to another: "after whoever it was" (6.382) relates the account of the

Lycian farmers, "someone else" (6.383) remembers Marsyas, a studiedly casual transition that makes us "reflect," as Altieri says Ovid's transitions generally do, "on the importance of man's being able to progress from one story to another" (257). The Marsyas episode (6.382–400), another embedded narrative (told indirectly), and also another account of a contest between a divine and a human artist, serves "as a pendant to the sequence of Arachne, Niobe, and the Lycian farmers" (Nagle [1989a] 110). It is the last in Ovid's series of narrations of divine vengeance (Otis 129) as well as the last story in part one of the *Metamorphoses*.

Marsyas' penalty for losing a flute contest to Apollo is to be flayed alive. As the flaying begins, Marsyas cries out, "'Why are you tearing me from myself'" (6.385: *quid me mihi detrahis*), a "witty observation," as Anderson calls it, that is rhetorical and totally unrealistic: "Marsyas is talking with most unlikely sophistication" ([1972] at 6.385–386, 202). Embedding creates a distancing effect, it is true, but even so one asks why a poet so intelligent, urbane, and sensitive to violence and the pain and suffering it causes would describe scenes that can compete with any modern-day splatter film. Galinsky suggests that Ovid's description of the flayed Marsyas ("Blood ran everywhere, his muscles were totally exposed, his naked arteries throbbing," 6.388–390) "was a sight that was not uncommon in the amphitheater, where the dismemberment of gladiators or criminals by wild animals thrilled the spectators for its sheer gore." Ovid displays little interest, Galinsky continues, in Marsyas' suffering: "[I]t is only the gory details that are brought closer to us, and not the agony of Marsyas" ([1975] 134).

For Leach, the satyr Marsyas provides yet another example of human "artistic failure" (127; her consideration of this theme begins at 107) in a series of such failures that extends from the Minyades in book 4 to the Pierides in book 5 and Arachne earlier in this book. Marsyas' metamorphosis, however, mitigates for Barkan the shocking and grotesque suffering of this artist in Ovid's description of "the birth of the immortal organism [the river Marsyas] generating itself from a literal flowing of the dying man's blood." Barkan continues, "Soon the flow of blood gives way to the equally organic flow of tears, as country people, forest gods, fauns, nymphs, and shepherdesses all lament his demise [6.392–400]. [T]he vengeance of the god has been transformed into the pity of nature and all nature's immanent deities" (79). In the *Metamorphoses*, we remember, the natural world was created separately from and exists before the gods. Like humans, the natural world suffers the gods' violence: aside from the seemingly endless stream of nymphs, creatures of nature, raped by the gods, there is (on a grand scale) the destruction of the world by the flood, caused by Jupiter in book 1, and Phaethon's conflagration in book 2, caused by his father, Apollo's, foolish indulgence. And so, having suffered itself, the natural world is capable of mute sympathy for the suffering of another.

25. Ovid makes a long, complex, and elaborate two-part (or "hinged") transition at 6.401–420 (complete with its own metamorphosis-vignette) from the story of Marsyas to the tale of Tereus, Procne, and Philomela (6.421–674), a transition that also moves us from (or connects) part one of the poem ("gods") to part two ("heroes and heroines," 6.421–11.193), hence its length, complexity, and elaborateness (and perhaps its two-part or "hinged" quality): a closing flourish and/or an opening fanfare. The poet begins (6.401–411, the first part of the transition) with the formula that Kenney calls "all save only X" (see n. 4): all Thebes mourned Amphion and his children and hated Niobe for causing their deaths, except her brother Pelops, who, tearing open his robe to beat his breast (likewise mourning for his sister, presumably), reveals his ivory shoulder, which he was given at the time the gods restored him after his (and Niobe's) father, Tantalus,

carved him up and served him to the gods at a dinner Tantalus had invited them to. As a result of this gross violation of the meal (more than usually sacred because its guests were gods), Tantalus is "tantalized" in the underworld with food and water he can never quite reach, as well as threatened by the imminent fall of a stone (Apollodorus, *Epitome* 2.1, 2.3; Homer, *Odyssey* 11.582–592; Pindar, *Olympian* 1.36–66). This vignette of Pelops looks back to Lycaon at book 1.163–252 (who sought to serve human flesh to Jupiter) and forward to Procne's and Philomela's killing, cooking, and serving Procne's son Itys to his father, Tereus, in the next episode.

The second part of this transition takes us to that episode. All the princes of the neighboring cities go to Thebes to offer their consolation (6.412–420): all, that is, except the princes of Athens (the "all save only X" formula again), for this city was just now concluding a war that Tereus of Thrace had helped it win (6.421ff.). Ovid thus introduces the story of Tereus, Procne, and Philomela (6.421–674), with which he begins part two of the poem.

This episode is one of Ovid's most grotesquely violent and bloody tales. (The poet ended part one, we remember, with the grotesquely violent account of the flaying of Marsyas.) Humans, it seems, are no different in this department from the gods. It has often been said that the *Metamorphoses* is an epic of love. It is, of course, "about" many things, but one must surely add power, abuse of power, or power and the powerless to the list, one or more of which we could designate as the theme of the story of Tereus, Procne, and Philomela.

When Tereus, king of Thrace, defeats an army besieging Athens, Pandion, king of Athens, makes him an ally by giving his daughter Procne in marriage to him (6.424–428). But the marriage is doomed from the start, as circumstances and certain events of the wedding ceremony show (6.428–434). The screech owl, the bird of ill omen that perches on the roof of the newlyweds' bedroom and under which Tereus and Procne are married and have a son Itys (6.431–434), we met earlier as Ascalaphus, the boy who tattled on Proserpina for eating the pomegranate seeds that require her to live half the year in the underworld, thus transformed by Proserpina as punishment (5.534–550). All the things that are wrong about the wedding are presumably known only to the narrator and to us, the readers, and not to Pandion and Procne, and presumably not to the Thracian, Tereus, himself, otherwise Pandion presumably would have called the wedding off. The narrator's aim is to create foreboding in the readers.

Five years after his marriage, Tereus returns to Athens to fetch Procne's sister Philomela to take her back to Thrace for a visit with Procne, and when he sees her he is "inflamed . . . like a field of dry straw someone puts a match to" (6.455–457): His "inborn lust . . . aroused him" (*innata libido / exstimulat*, 6.458–459), for "the people in his land are prone to sexual passion" (6.459–460).

"Inborn lust"—a "proclivity for sexual passion," as Bömer calls it (*proclivitas in Venerem*)—as a "national characteristic," Bömer says, is in general more a reproach that northern peoples make against southern peoples than, as here, one that southern people make against a people of the north (like the people of Thrace). Thracians were, in fact, Bömer continues, characterized in antiquity as cruel, cunning, crude, oath-breaking, and above all alcoholic. There is little indication that they were "prone to sexual passion" (Bömer at 6.458, 3.131).

An important motif in this tale is the confusing of things that emphatically do not go together: Tereus' lust is fueled by his watching Philomela embrace her father (6.478–482), a description that, Barkan says, "is based upon the forcible union of things which ought to be kept separate: the girl's filial piety, her sexuality, Tereus's role as brother-in-law, his *innata libido*" (60). When Procne avenges herself and her sister, Ovid says that, "[c]onfusing right and wrong, she plunge[s] ahead, obsessed with the revenge she imagine[s] for Tereus" (6.585–586). This vengeance, Barkan notes, "represents the nadir in the drama of conflation and confusion. . . . The banquet that concludes the tale," for which Procne and Philomela have killed Procne's own son and served him as food to his father, Tereus—a most horrible "confusing"—"climaxes the confusions among discrete categories and identities" (62).

Segal notes four "temporal markers" in the episode. The first ("The Titan sun had led the season of the year through five autumns when Procne . . . ," 6.438–440) "sets the disaster in motion"; the second ("And now the sun had but a little labor left to do, and his horses' hooves were pounding on the downward path of heaven," 6.486–487) "introduces the success of Tereus' scheme"; the third ("The sun-god had traveled through the twelve signs of the zodiac, and a whole year had passed," 6.571) "indicates the duration of Philomela's imprisonment"; the fourth ("It was the time appointed for the young women of Thrace to perform the rites of Bacchus, celebrated every other year," 6.587–588) "leads [Philomela] to freedom and revenge." These markers, "sacred time," Segal calls them, "could suggest a larger world-order framing these events" and thus the possibility of cosmic justice. Yet their "remoteness . . . sets off the moral isolation of the human world and the absence of the gods" ([1992] 286).

Segal also notes "spatial contrasts" in the episode: Tereus lures Philomela "from the civilized city of Athens . . . to the desolate forest in the wild land." He continues, "The violence implicit in the shift from Athens to Thrace is also symmetrical with an abrupt spatial shift within Thrace," as Procne and Philomela "move from enclosure to dangerous wilderness and then back to a domestic interior" ([1992] 287–288).

Finally, Segal comments on several animal images spaced throughout the tale (6.516–518: "[Tereus] like an eagle . . . when it drops a hare from its hooked talons into its lofty nest"; 6.527–530: "[Philomela] was shaking, like a frightened, wounded lamb dropped from the jaws of a gray wolf . . . , or like a dove, its feathers all bloody, . . . in terror of the powerful talons that had gripped it"; 6.559–560: Philomela's tongue wriggles "as the tail of a snake . . . twists and turns"; and 6.636–637: "[Procne,] like a Bengal tiger dragging a doe's suckling fawn, . . . dragged Itys"). The first image describes Philomela (and Tereus) on Tereus' ship sailing to Thrace as he anticipates satisfying his lust. The "animal imagery . . . recur[s] for the horrors of his crime [the second, third, and fourth images] . . . and for Procne's revenge [the fifth image], . . . until it becomes reality, in the metamorphosis in the end" (at 6.667–674; Segal [1992] 285).

Focus on the animal imagery in the episode leads naturally to consideration of the violence Ovid so graphically represents:

> But Tereus seized her tongue with a pair of tongs and, as it resisted, as it called "Father!" again and again and struggled to speak, hacked at it hard, hacked it out of her mouth with his sword. The stump remaining quivered [in pain and terror], while the tongue itself lay trembling on the bloody ground, whimpering, and . . . wriggled its way to the feet of its mistress, and there it died.
> After this bestial act Tereus is said—though I can hardly believe it—to have gratified his lust upon the girl's mutilated body again and again. (6.555–562)

Tereus is a brutal and unfeeling animal; Philomela is in shock, her distress grotesquely displaced to her severed tongue, dying on the ground; the only "feeling" individual is the narrator.

How can Ovid create such savagery? Why did he create it? According to Galinsky, the poet "revelled in bloodthirsty and repulsive descriptions of human agony simply because he liked cruelty" ([1975] 129). Ovid's "delight in grotesque cruelty," Galinsky continues, "is a concession to the taste of the Roman public and a concession that does not seem to have been grudgingly granted." He quotes Arthur Darby Nock: "'[C]ruelty and pleasure in exercising and witnessing cruelty existed in the amphitheater and in the household,'" and adds, "Their appeal, at Ovid's time, was nothing short of monumental, as is indicated by the truly staggering number of beasts alone which the Emperor provided for the arena. And a premium was put . . . on killing these animals *crudeliter* [cruelly], and the humans fared no better." An additional factor was "the great popularity at this time of the untragic presentation of tragic myths in the form of the pantomime," an important aspect of which was "the tendency toward sensationalism" ([1975] 138–139).

Yet Ovid and the Romans were not more bloodthirsty nor did they take more delight in cruelty than Shakespeare and the Elizabethans, Barkan contends, for "[w]hat is horrible in Ovid's Tereus story Shakespeare makes twice as horrible in *Titus Andronicus* [which uses Ovid's version of the myth]. Not one rapist but two, not one murdered child but five, not one or two mutilated organs but six, not a one-course meal but a two" (244).

Philomela, imprisoned, isolated, mute ("her mouth, made tongueless, had no way to tell the deed," 6.574), shares the condition of blocked utterance with Io, Callisto, and Actaeon, but here this motif modulates into a larger theme, communication itself, with which, Barkan observes, the story is "centrally concerned" (245). As Barkan explains: "Many of the great figures of [the] poem define themselves by their struggle to invent new languages. That is clearest in the case of metamorphic victims like Actaeon or Io, who must labor to use human language fitting their consciousness once their shape has turned beastly. . . . Philomela's is merely the most extended of all these struggles. Her mutilation is another language-denying metamorphosis [that] requires her to create a new medium, a composite of words and pictures" (247), that is, the "red signs" (*purpureas . . . notas*, 6.577) she weaves "across [the cloth's] white threads, spelling out the crime" (6.577–578), creating the "account of her sister's pitiful fate" (6.582) read by Procne. "[M]ad Ireland hurt you into poetry," Auden says in his obituary poem, "In Memory of W. B. Yeats." Tereus' inhuman savagery, or (if Galinsky is correct) all-too-human, that is to say, all-too-Roman, savagery, has *forced* Philomela to become an "artist." But unlike earlier human artists in the poem (the Minyades, the Pierides, Arachne, Marsyas), she does not fail: in fact, she does not succeed until she becomes an artist; her artwork saves her. But it does more, as Segal notes: "Philomela's weaving is both the art-work of the tale and the agency of revenge within the tale" ([1992] 283).

Those "red signs" reappear at the end of the story, after the sisters are transformed into birds, in the *notae* (6.670), the "signs of the murder on their breasts, their plumage streaked with blood" (6.669–670). Segal comments, "[T]he signifying marks of the artwork . . . return at the end . . . as the marks of blood that remain stamped upon the face of nature in perpetual witness of the savage deed" ([1992] 283).

Ovid's transition to the next tale, the brief story of Boreas and Orithyia (6.675–682), flows naturally from the episode of Tereus, Procne, and Philomela: Pandion, king of Athens and father of the two sisters, dies from grief, and Erechtheus becomes king. Two of Erechtheus' four daughters, Procris (whose story, told by her widowed husband, Cephalus, we shall encounter at 7.686–862) and Orithyia, "were equal in beauty" (6.680). Boreas (the north wind) is enamored of Orithyia (another Athenian princess, another Thracian). "But the reputation of Tereus and his fellow Thracians hurt Boreas, and for a long time the god had no success with Orithyia . . . , as long, that is, as he was content to court her politely" (6.682–684). Ovid thus modulates the sad theme of Tereus, Procne, and Philomela into a happier variation. But when politeness and charm fail to work, Boreas, after a soliloquy (6.687–701) in which he rationalizes reverting to type (and to his nature), abducts Orithyia (the sad theme momentarily reappears), but marries her, and has twin sons, Calais and Zetes, winged at birth, or, as some say, becoming winged later (6.702–718). The happier variation, momentarily threatened, is firmly reestablished.

This brief tale serves as a transition to the story of Jason, Medea, the quest for the golden fleece, and the aftermath, which will occupy almost half of the next book (7.1–424). Calais and Zetes as young men set sail with the Minyans "in search of the sheep's skin with the bright, shining fleece" (6.719–721). Then as book 7 begins, the Minyans are on the open sea (with Calais and Zetes on board their ship). Thus Ovid bridges books 6 and 7 by beginning the next episode at the very end of book 6.

BOOK SEVEN

26. The transition to the story of Jason, Medea, the quest for the golden fleece, and the aftermath begins at the end of book 6, through the myth of Boreas and Orithyia, whose twin sons, Calais and Zetes, joined the expedition. That myth bridges books 6 and 7 (see n. 25), for, as book 7 begins, Jason's ship, the *Argo* (referred to simply as "their Thessalian ship" in line 1), with Calais and Zetes on board (7.3–4), is sailing through the sea to the land of Colchis, through which the "swift waters of the muddy Phasis" flowed (7.6).

The quest for the golden fleece (9.1–158) is the first part of a five-part narrative that centers on Medea and occupies more than half of book 7 (extending to 7.452). The second part (7.159–296) describes Medea's rejuvenation of Jason's father, Aeson; the third (7.297–349) narrates the tale of the elaborate vengeance Medea exacts from Pelias, king of Iolcus, on Jason's behalf; the fourth (7.350–403) describes Medea's flight to Corinth and from there to Athens, where Aegeus, king of Athens, receives her; and the last part, the shortest of the five (7.404–452), tells of Medea's failed attempt to poison Theseus, Aegeus' long-lost son, when he comes to Athens for the first time.

Medea's soliloquy (7.11–71), in the first part of the episode, gives us the first "true account of the genesis of love," Otis says: "It is with Medea," he continues, "that the famous duel of [love and shame] enters the *Metamorphoses* . . . and points the way for Scylla [8.44–80], Byblis [9.487–516], Myrrha [10.320–355], and Atalanta [10.611–635]" (172–173; book and line numbers indicate their soliloquies). Wilkinson, who sees Medea's soliloquy as the first of five "expressing a conflict in the soul of a woman about to commit a crime," omits Atalanta from this list and adds Althaea (her soliloquy at 8.481–511; see Wilkinson [1955] 205, with note).

We have seen Thracian Tereus in the grip of overpowering passion; now "the *libido* shifts from the man to the woman" (Otis 216), and we have a parallel female figure, also a barbarian, also in the grip of an overpowering passion. But the similarities simply enable us to emphasize the great differences: Tereus never exhibits a divided mind, neither before, during, nor after his first rape, his mutilation, and his successive rapes of Philomela. He never expresses moral conflict. Instead, he lies in bed, "smoldering with passion for Philomela, recalling her face, her hands, the way she moved, imagining the parts of her body he hadn't yet seen, feeding his lust" (6.490–493). Medea, by contrast, in a long soliloquy describes her moral conflict with such clarity of mind that we wonder how she can give in to her passion.

She begins by identifying her condition (7.11–21): "'I wonder if this . . . is what is called being in love'" (7.12–13). She acknowledges the conflict: "'Desire pulls me one way, my mind another way'" (7.19–20). This is immediately followed by what are among the best-known lines in the *Metamorphoses*: "'I see clearly which [way] is better, and I know it is right, yet I follow the way that is worse'" (7.20–21: *video meliora proboque, / deteriora sequor*). Medea's insight into her dilemma is Ovid's version of Phaedra's famous statement in Euripides' *Hippolytus*, "We know what is right, we recognize it, but we do not do it" (380–381).

As the soliloquy progresses, the more questions Medea raises and the more doubt she expresses, the more intense her passion becomes. Toward the end of the soliloquy, the question "'Shall I therefore leave my sister, brother, father, gods, my native land, and be gone with the wind?'" (7.51–52) is answered, "'Oh yes! Yes! For my father is a savage, my country is barbaric . . .'" ("*nempe pater saevus, nempe est mea barbara tellus . . . ,*" 7.53–55). And the questions "'[W]hat about the clashing rocks . . . ? What about Charybdis . . . ? What about Scylla . . . ?'" (7.62–65) are answered, "'No matter, for holding Jason, clinging to my love, I can sail anywhere'" (7.66–67).

The "opposition" rouses itself for one last attack on her passion: "'But do you consider this marriage, Medea? Aren't you concealing your guilt under a false name? Look what a terrible wrong you're about to do!'" (7.69–71)—and wins! The soliloquy ends, moral abstractions—Righteousness, Duty (to her parents), and (woman's) Virtue—appear, and Desire is defeated and flees (7.72–73). Or so it would seem. But moral abstractions cannot overcome insistent, burning passion for the present, living object of that passion. Medea, although she thinks she has subdued her passion, then sees Jason, "the flame she had managed to put out blaze[s] up again" (7.77), and her fate is sealed. But she is aware of what she is doing; she does not delude herself: "'I see what I am going to do; it won't be ignorance of the truth that deceives me, but love'" (7.92–93). For Tereus (as Ovid portrays him), this kind of clear-eyed, rational assessment was never an option.

The return of Jason, Medea, and the Argonauts provides the transition to the second part of the tale, the rejuvenation of Aeson (7.159–296). The entire population of Iolcus turns out to welcome the Argonauts and to give thanks for their safe return, except for Jason's father, Aeson, "absent from the rites . . . worn out with old age" (7.162–163). Jason asks Medea to restore Aeson's lost years, that is, to make him young again (7.164–168). "The Medea we see" in this part, Anderson says, "has very little to do with the love-torn girl we have watched earlier. Now she is an accomplished witch, delighting in her powers and rather amusing us by her skill" ([1972] at 7.159–293, 262), and (in the details Ovid lavishes on her work as a sorceress) providing us almost with a "how-to" manual for restoring lost youth. Testimonial to the effectiveness of Medea's magic comes from Bacchus, who wants to use it to restore the youth of his nurses (7.294–296).

In the next part of the story, Medea's revenge on Pelias (7.297–349), "the lurid is added to the fantastic," Galinsky says, and "[t]he emphasis once more is on the graphic narrative and details" ([1975] 65). Like the best kind of snake-oil salesman, Medea tricks Pelias' daughters (who want to make their father young again) in an Ovidian version of "bait and switch." She lures their interest by telling them how she had taken away Aeson's old age and then closes the "sale" by giving a demonstration of her "product": she turns an aged ram into a frisky lamb. Three days later, Medea boils a worthless mixture of "plain water and strengthless herbs" (7.327). In a twist both diabolical and funny, Medea enlists the girls to help her, that is, to help her kill their father Pelias. She tells them to drain Pelias' blood, and the old man's daughters, all naïveté and dumb obedience, take knives and commence stabbing their father blindly (they cannot bear to look) until, bleeding profusely, the old man manages to rise partway from his bed and cry out: "What are you doing, daughters? Who gave you knives to kill your father?" (7.346–347). Medea cuts his throat to stop him from talking and stuffs him into the vat of boiling water—gratuitously, it would seem, for he would have died anyway—and makes her getaway in her serpent-drawn chariot.

In the fourth part of the story, Medea's escape from Iolcus to Corinth and from there to Athens, where she marries Aegeus, king of Athens (7.350—403), Ovid refers to a number of metamorphoses that occurred in the regions Medea flies over. Here, Anderson says: "we are not interested in Medea as a dramatic character at all. She merely serves as a vehicle for the amusing display of [the poet's] erudition" ([1972] at 7.350–403, 281). Ovid reduces to four lines (7.394–397) the narration of Jason's betrayal of Medea and her revenge—the murder of the king and princess of Corinth and of her own children (the basis for Euripides' *Medea*). The poet compresses this episode in Medea's career perhaps because he himself had written a tragedy, now lost, on this subject, a play that was highly regarded in antiquity, for example, by Tacitus (*Dialogus* 12) and Quintilian (10.1.98).

The fifth and final part of this episode (7.404–452) introduces Aegeus' son Theseus (whom Medea attempts to kill), provides Medea's exit, and leads to the transition to the next set of tales, which have Aegina as their setting (Minos and Aeacus, 7.453–489; the plague at Aegina and the creation of the Myrmidons, 7.490–660; and Cephalus and Procris, 7.661–862). Narrating a familiar episode in the myth of Theseus, Ovid perhaps felt no need to motivate Medea in her attempt to poison the hero. (Bömer simply says, "In Athens, Medea recognizes the danger that the new arrival [Theseus] can pose to her" [at 7.404–424, 3.300].) In any case, the poet gives most of his attention to the poison, aconite, that Medea puts into Theseus' wine, that is, its source and the derivation of its name: the saliva of the three-headed dog, Cerberus, which, when the monstrous creature was dragged from the underworld by Hercules, fell on the ground, hardened, and became poisonous. "And because it was formed and grows on hard stones, farmers call it 'aconite'" (7.418–419: *aconita,* 7.419, plural of *aconitum,* from Greek *akonē,* "whetstone," LaFaye says, calling it a suspect etymology [2.43 n. 2]). When Medea's attempt fails, she escapes, concealed in a cloud, and we hear no more of her.

A celebration in thanksgiving for Theseus' life, which includes a hymn to the hero that recounts his achievements before he came to Athens, ends the episode (7.425–452). These lines lead to the transition to the next set of tales, as indicated earlier. Although there is general rejoicing, "Nevertheless," the transition begins, "Aegeus did not enjoy perfect happiness" (7.453–455).

27. As indicated at the end of n. 26, Ovid makes the transition from the tale of Medea at Athens (the fifth and last part of the long episode on Jason, Medea, the golden fleece, and the aftermath) to the next two stories with lines that qualify the general rejoicing at Athens after Theseus arrives there and is saved from poisoning: "Nevertheless . . . , Aegeus did not enjoy perfect happiness after he found his son" (7.453–455), a variation, it would seem, of the "all save only X" formula (see n. 4).

What mars Aegeus' happiness are the preparations for war against Athens being made by Minos, king of Crete, to avenge the death of his son Androgeos (7.456–458). Ovid apparently accepts the version of the myth in which Aegeus is responsible for Androgeos' death (see Apollodorus 3.15.7). These preparations bring Minos to Aegina to seek an alliance with Aeacus that Aeacus declines (7.459–489). They also bring Cephalus to Aegina (after Minos departs) as Aegeus' emissary, also to seek an alliance, between Athens and Aegina for the coming war with Minos, an alliance that Aeacus agrees to (7.490–511).

Cephalus' mission to Aegina provides the occasion for a pair of embedded narratives, the first told by Aeacus, the second by Cephalus. Cephalus has observed to Aeacus that many familiar faces from his last visit are missing (7.512–516). Responding to the implied query, Aeacus tells Cephalus (and those with him) the story of the devastating plague at Aegina and the subsequent repopulation of his city with Myrmidons, or "ant-men" (7.517–660). The next day, Cephalus replies to a query from Aeacus' son Phocus about his unusual spear, which Phocus has admired (7.672–680), by telling him how he acquired both a magical hunting dog and the spear, and how he came to kill his wife with it accidentally (7.690–862).

Cephalus, Kenney notes, "has no special connection with Aeacus in the mythological tradition: Ovid juxtaposes them because their stories complement and contrast with each other" ([1986] 418; the ways in which they do this will be discussed below). Both characters, as Ovid presents them, "are aged heroes who have each undergone a great sorrow" (Otis 175).

Aeacus' tale falls into two parts, in the first of which he recounts the destruction of his city by a plague (7.517–613), in the second its miraculous repopulation with Myrmidons (7.614–660).

Ovid's plague narrative stands in a tradition of such narratives, beginning with the fifth-century B.C historian Thucydides, who, in his history of the Peloponnesian War, gives an eyewitness report of a historical plague at Athens in 430 B.C. as a survivor of that epidemic and describes it and its social effects with clinical detachment (2.47–54). Next in the tradition comes the first-century B.C. Roman poet Lucretius (there are no known poetical descriptions of the plague in the Hellenistic period: Bömer at 7.523–613, 3.333), whose plague narrative (*De Rerum Natura* 6.1138–1286), Bömer says, goes straight back to Thucydides (and Theophrastus). Virgil, Ovid's other great Roman predecessor, gives an account of a plague in Noricum (a district corresponding to present- day Austria) and along the Timavus River (which flows into the Gulf of Trieste) in his third *Georgic* (3.478–566), a plague that affects animals only.

Next after Thucydides, says Bömer (whom I am paraphrasing here), Lucretius and Virgil are both important for Ovid (Virgil less so). Because of their literary status and because of the fact that this literary theme was newly established in Roman literature, Ovid could not evade the poetic obligation of *aemulatio* and so took the opportunity to enter the lists with a plague description of his own. In order to do this, he changed Aegina's mythological tradition, introducing a plague narrative of his own invention at this point in his poem, with Lucretius, Virgil, and Thucydides as his models. Thucydides offers the only eyewitness account of a historical plague (as noted earlier), Lucretius confronts events with the observing eye of the scientist interested in causes and phenomena, whereas Virgil's plague description is confined to the animal world (Bömer at 7.523–613, 3.333).

With typical originality, Ovid on the one hand presents his descriptions of a plague as an embedded narrative, thus at one remove from actuality ("emphasizing its status as narrative rather than as event": Nagle [1989a] 110), but told, on the other hand, as a first-person eyewitness account (by Aeacus) and thus made immediate, vivid, and personal. Its origin is attributed not to a natural (and so scientifically determinable) cause but to Juno, and that distinction is emphasized: "'A deadly plague fell upon my people because of Juno's wrath,'" Aeacus begins. "'As long as we thought the pestilence had natural causes, . . . we battled it with all our medical knowledge'" (7.523–526; Aeacus doesn't say how he learned that Juno caused the plague). In any case, since the approach to the description is not scientific (and/or sociological), the narrator can devote himself to pure description (without analysis) of the physical and emotional effects of the epidemic and the suffering and despair of those afflicted, humans and animals, all of which the narrator emphasizes by relating how they affected him: "'What was I feeling then? Just what you would expect me to feel: I hated life and wanted to share my people's fate. Everywhere I looked the ground was strewn with bodies'" (7.582–583).

Anderson has noted that "the whole epidemic is one fascinating metamorphosis" ([1972] at 7.558–560, 303), a comment that leads to the observation that the destruction of the Aeginetan population by plague and its re-creation by miraculous metamorphosis present in microcosm events parallel to the destruction of the world by flood in book 1 and by fire in book 2, followed by the world's re-creation in the former case and its restoration in the latter, these being the most spectacular events in a world in which ceaseless change is the eternal drama.

The plague at Aegina and the city's miraculous repopulation through the metamorphosis into human beings of ants, which in their industry and discipline are human-like (7.624–626; and particularly Roman-like), a story, essentially, of death and resurrection, also brings to mind (and was perhaps intended to resonate with) Virgil's juxtaposition of a plague narrative (in which only animals are affected) at the end of the third *Georgic* (3.478–566) with a treatise on bees (also human-like, Roman-like, too: *Georgics* 4.67–85), which can be "miraculously" re-created by anyone from the carcasses of bullocks, if he or she knows how to do it, in the fourth *Georgic* (4.1–314, especially 281–314; and 530–558), likewise a story of death and resurrection or, more accurately, life from death, confined, however, to the animal kingdom.

28. The story of Cephalus and Procris, the second of two embedded narratives told during the Athenian Cephalus' mission to Aegina, is set off in several ways from the first, the Aeginetan king Aeacus' tale about the plague at Aegina and the repopulation of his city with Myrmidons or ant-men. First, Aeacus' tale is punctuated by the end of a day, and the two tales are thus separated by the demarcation of an intervening night (7.661–663). Second, Cephalus tells his story the next morning to a different audience, Aeacus' son Phocus alone (Aeacus is still asleep), while the two other sons, Telamon and Peleus, are recruiting men to accompany Cephalus back to Athens as allies in Athens' impending war with Minos (7.665–669). Moreover, Aeacus, Segal says, "belongs to the heroic part of the frame. His absence leaves Cephalus an audience of younger men . . . , naturally more sympathetic and appropriate to a tale of love" ([1978] 185). Third, Cephalus tells his tale in a different location, a location "inside," that is, the interior of the palace, in a "beautifully furnished apartment" (7.670–671). The change of scene is highly significant, for "an atmosphere of intimacy is created," Pöschl says, that is noticeably different from the earlier atmosphere. With this move inside the palace, "an area of interiority is opened that is intentionally contrasted with what was expressed before [in Minos' threat and Aeacus' story], that is, the danger of war, the reality of war, extensive disaster, miraculous salvation: From the open area we step into an area of stillness, as Cephalus and his companions enter the inner part of the palace" ([1959] 328). With this change of scene there also comes a corresponding "shift from the political themes centered upon Aeacus to the personal and erotic themes centered upon Cephalus" (Segal [1978] 186).

Cephalus' story is elicited by Phocus' admiring comments and questions about the Athenian's spear (7.672—680), which is thus centered in our attention before the tale begins. Ovid intensifies the implicit demand for an account of the spear by having one of the two sons of Pallas who are attending Cephalus jump into the conversation with a description of the spear, a rhetorical move on the narrator's part that heightens Phocus' (and our) interest still more, both by the description itself and by delaying Cephalus' entry into the conversation (7.681–684). Now Phocus, his curiosity concerning this spear whetted still more, asks about it directly, in questions that are, however, reported indirectly: "Then Phocus . . . wanted to know all about the spear, who gave it, and why—where such a fine gift came from" (7.685–686). Cephalus' lengthy silence (7.687–688: two corrupt lines replaced in the translation by Tarrant's suggested line; see the footnote at 7.687–688) following Phocus' questions heightens dramatic interest still more, until, "moved by grief for the wife he had lost," he begins the story "with tears in his eyes" (7.687/8 [Tarrant]–689). Although we know that Cephalus' tears are started by an onrush of grief for his lost wife, Phocus does not, only that his questions about the spear have somehow moved Cephalus to tears—and all we know is that the spear, Cephalus' sudden grief and tears, and his lost wife are somehow connected. But by this preliminary buildup our attention has been focused on the spear, and it has been freighted with great significance, as yet potential. If we pause for a moment, however, and think about this focus on Cephalus' spear (having read the story to the end), we quickly come to Bömer's recognition that "[a]ccording to all the laws of psychology and logic a man does not carry continually with himself the weapon with which he has killed his beloved wife, the sight of which reduces him to weeping without let-up, particularly in this case, since he [Cephalus] certainly knows that he doesn't need it anyway." Bömer continues, "Cephalus carries it in spite of that for a 'purely poetic reason' . . . , namely, so that Phocus can ask him about it and Ovid can establish a connection between the narratives of Aeacus and Cephalus" (at 7.672–865, 3.367), presumably the personal loss and grief common to both stories.

The narrative falls into three parts, or into two parallel parts divided by a briefer tale that is different from but related to the other two. In the first part, Cephalus tells of his interlude with Aurora (not an affair) and his subsequent testing of his wife, Procris (7.690–758 = sixty-nine lines); in the third, he tells of Procris' jealous suspicion of him and her accidental death at his hands by the spear she had given to him, the spear he carries now that Phocus wondered about (7.795–862 = sixty-eight lines). These two parallel parts of almost equal length are separated by the story of the wondrous dog, Hurricane (also a gift to Cephalus from Procris) and the Theban fox that it pursued unto their simultaneous metamorphoses into marble, "one about to escape, the other poised to seize" (7.759–794 = thirty-six lines, quotation at 7.791). Because of this insertion, Pöschl says, "the symmetry of both outer parts stands out even more strongly" ([1959] 334). This middle story also "continue[s] our suspense," Anderson says, "by concentrating on the second gift." By the end of this second part, "[i]t has been a hundred lines since Ovid introduced this motif [of the spear] and began our suspense" ([1990] 133).

Hunting locales serve as the setting for the first half of the first part, all of the setting for the second part, and much of the setting for the third part; and the hunt itself provides a motif important for the first and, of course, dominating the third. In the first part, shortly after his marriage, Cephalus encounters (and is carried off by) Aurora, "goddess of the golden dawn," while hunting on Mount Hymettus (7.700–704). Enraged because Cephalus, deeply in love with Procris and not shy about expressing it, refuses to become involved with her, Aurora sends Cephalus back to his wife with an insidious prediction that sows doubt in his mind about Procris' fidelity and so becomes self-fulfilling (7.711–713). Cephalus decides to put his wife's fidelity to the test when he returns to Athens and his home (7.714–725). The hunting motif comes into play in the disguised Cephalus' attempt to seduce his wife, in what Davis calls "the entrapment episode." In this episode, Davis says, "Cephalus approaches his wife with the stealth of a hunter seeking access to his prey. . . . [H]e has begun to treat his wife as a 'prey,'" and he "perverts the domestic scene by 'ambushing' his wife" ([1983] 134).

The second or middle part of the tale, the magical dog Hurricane's pursuit of the Theban fox (7.759–794), which ends in a dead heat "recorded," so to speak, in marble, "holds the violence of the hunt ominously in the background while we wait for the main thread of the story to resume" (Segal [1978] 184). In the third part of Cephalus' tale, the account of how his wife's suspicions led ultimately to her accidental death from his spearcast (7.795–862), "Procris' attempt to spy on her husband is, on the structural level, an inversion of the roles played in the earlier episode in which Cephalus, made unrecognizable by Aurora, tries to entrap his wife. . . . The slaughter of Procris completes that systematic (and reciprocal) perversion of *venatio* [hunting] and *amor* [love] which the entire fable exemplifies in Ovid's version. . . . The *venator* [hunter] . . . ends by 'hunting' his spouse in the most literal sense possible" (Davis [1983] 145–146).

Pöschl observes that the outer, or first and third, narratives exhibit from the outset correspondences and parallels. Both narratives begin with the recollection of happy love (7.698: "love bound her to me, too"; and 7.800: "We shared an affection that was mutual, a bond of love that held us both"). The strength of that love is clearly indicated through comparison with the gods' kind of love, in the first narrative, by the actual appearance of the goddess Aurora (7.700ff.), and in the second by the imagined comparison of Jupiter and Venus (7.801–803: "She would not have preferred the bed of Jove to my love, and there was no one who could have captivated me the way she had, not even Venus herself, if she had come to me").

In the first narrative, Pöschl continues, Cephalus, as though possessed by a demon, persists in his effort to make Procris betray herself (7.737–740), while in the third narrative, as an intentional contrasting parallel Procris shows herself to be so deeply affected by the news of Cephalus' faithlessness that she collapses in helplessness, but does not give up hope that it is all a mistake (7.826–834). That is, Pöschl says, while Cephalus holds fast to his suspicion, although there is every indication that he deceives himself, Procris *refuses* to suspect her beloved, although there is every indication that he really is unfaithful. When the other's faithlessness seems to be conclusively confirmed, their respective reactions, Pöschl notes, are totally contrary: Cephalus attacks Procris in cruel triumph at the first sign of weakness (7.741–742), whereas Procris, dying from the wound Cephalus has given her and convinced that he was unfaithful to her, yet recognizes, in what Pöschl calls this moment of her physical and spiritual destruction, her unshakeable love (7.854–855). Just before she dies, however, Procris realizes that Cephalus was faithful after all, and is reconciled, with what Pöschl terms a farewell gesture of her inner love (7.860–862). This observation leads Pöschl to remark on the forgiveness and reconciliation that make a true rather than a contrasting parallel at the end of the two narratives, for in the first Cephalus finally comes to realize, all too late, that in the same circumstances as Procris (that is, is tested to the limit) he would have acted no differently (7.747–750), that it is inhuman to demand of another person (even more so of one's wife) what goes beyond his or her powers.

As Pöschl puts it, the contrast between the brutality of a husband who, in a blind rage of jealousy, humiliates his beloved and violates and destroys their mutual happiness, and the gentle goodness and nobility of a wife whose love expresses itself in limitless forgiveness—this contrast has found convincing and touching expression in the conflict of the two characters and the two narratives. This contrast is really between two natures, both filled with deep love, between Cephalus' hurtful cruelty, which is a sick form of his passionate love, and Procris' magnanimous and loving forgiveness, which comes from the goodness and nobility of her being. Procris' loving nature is enhanced, rather than diminished, by her small weakness (that is, her hesitation: 7.739–740), which only makes her seem more human. The couple's reconciliation, which enables them to renew the happiness of their love and unites them even more after Cephalus admits he has wronged Procris and begs for forgiveness, comes about only because Procris, the one who was injured, forgives.

Pöschl notes that the spear Procris gives Cephalus when she gives him her love (again) she receives back again as a death weapon that pierces her breast. The spear thus becomes a symbol of love and death, the forgiving love she grants and the death she receives, a symbol of the disaster that grows from an unusual love and from the demonism and weakness that are inherent in human nature. (The magical spear fails to return to Cephalus, as it is supposed to do [7.684], a lapse on Ovid's part [Anderson (1990) 133], although had it done so, the drama of Cephalus' horror at the discovery of what he has done [7.842–850] would have been considerably lessened.)

It is Cephalus, unless we have forgotten, who narrates this tale about his own brutality and his wife's forgiving love, and the manner in which he tells it, Pöschl concludes, shows "the purification through sorrow" that he has undergone. (For the foregoing, see Pöschl [1959] 338–342.)

Cephalus manages to tell Procris the truth about "Breeze" just before she dies. In her last moment, "[w]hile she could still look at anything at all," Cephalus says, "she looked at me and breathed on me her last unhappy breath . . . , and then, with a little smile, she seemed to die content" (7.860–862). The look Procris gives Cephalus just before she dies and they are separated forever will be paralleled by the split second in which the eyes of Orpheus and Eurydice meet in a glance that dooms her return to earth and forbids them a life together (10.56–59). In the one instance, it is the look that saves the couple, especially Cephalus, from unbearable sorrow. In the other instance, the look condemns the couple, especially Orpheus, to unbearable sorrow.

As Cephalus concludes his story, both he and his listeners are weeping (7.863). "Then Aeacus entered," Ovid says, "with his two sons and the newly formed and well-equipped army, of which Cephalus now took command" (8.863–865). Aeacus, his story, and Cephalus' original mission, with which the episode on Aegina began, thus frame Cephalus' tale: "The private world of the Procris-Cephalus story is surrounded by a public, heroic world," Segal notes ([1978] 183), and thus the contrast between the two worlds is amplified. Aeacus' entry also ends the book and begins the transition to book 8.

Ovid treats the story of Cephalus and Procris differently in his *Ars Amatoria* (3.687–746). Anderson (1990) makes a detailed analysis of the two versions to support his contention, contrary to the traditional view, that the version in the *Metamorphoses* was written before that in the *Ars Amatoria,* in the process illuminating both versions with rich insights.

BOOK EIGHT

29. In the opening lines of book 8 (1–5) Ovid completes the transition begun at the end of book 7 (Cephalus' return to Athens with soldiers from Aeacus: 7.863ff.) and begins a series of stories centering on Minos and Crete, in the first of which (8.6–151)

he narrates the tale of Scylla, daughter of Nisus, king of Megara, who betrays her father and his kingdom, under siege by Minos, king of Crete.

As Bömer notes in his introduction to this episode (4.11), while Scylla, daughter of King Nisus of Megara, is for Ovid at times identical to the Sicilian sea monster, also named Scylla and stationed opposite the whirlpool Charybdis (Homer, *Odyssey* 12.222–259), the poet gives the latter Scylla a history at *Metamorphoses* 13.730–737, 13.898–968, and 14.1–74 that cannot be reconciled with the Megarian Scylla here. (Ovid himself at *Amores* 3.12.21–22 notes that it is "we poets" who have conflated the two Scyllas.)

Primary emphasis in the story, with its "traditional theme" of "the traitress within the gates," is laid upon "the motif of forbidden/unnatural/thwarted passion, prominent in the Tereus-Procne and Medea episodes." Scylla's two soliloquies (8.44–80 and 8.108–142) "again recall Medea, and dominate the episode" (Kenney [1986] 420; see Anderson [1972] at 8.1–151, 333–334, for other versions of Scylla and Nisus and for references to other stories "of a girl who betrays her city for love of the attacking commander").

The narrative of Scylla is the second of five episodes in the *Metamorphoses* that deal with human passion and its consequences (see n. 26 for a list of these tales) and in which love and shame are in conflict, the first being Medea's at 7.11–71. With Scylla's speech, Otis says, "a new motif . . . —that of the frustrated female *libido*—is now introduced" (217). Scylla's address to herself, Otis observes, is "in the 'empathetic-sympathetic' style of narrative" and thus "is not sharply differentiated in point of view from the narrative proper: both the author's *description* of Scylla's emotions and her own account of them represent Scylla's psyche at work as Scylla herself sees it" (64).

Scylla's name does not occur in the story until she herself tells Minos who she is at 8.91. "Ovid has carefully avoided giving her name," Anderson says, "so that this occasion is all the more striking" ([1972] at 8.91, 342). At 8.93–94 Scylla tells Minos that she is giving him "not simply a lock of hair, but my father's life" (8.94: *patrium . . . caput*, literally "father's head," *caput* for the Romans by metonymy also meaning "life"). Scylla's choice of words, Anderson observes, "forces us to imagine the bleeding head of Nisus rather than the lock of hair" ([1972] at 8.94, 343). That is, it is as though Scylla has scalped her father and presented Minos with the scalp.

Scylla's metamorphosis into the bird *ciris* or "shearer," Barkan says, is "a definition of the extreme state into which [she has brought herself] and a relief from the agony of [that extreme state]." Moreover, Scylla's transformation "define[s] the disordering [drive] that lead[s]" to this change. "Minos," Barkan continues, "perceives Scylla's alienation from order, and his curse essentially creates the transformation: ["'May the gods drive you from the universe, infamy of our age; I pray that you have no place on land or sea!'" (8.97–98)]. Denied land and sea, she must become a bird" (65–66).

The episode ends (at 8.151) with the metamorphoses of Scylla and her father. At 8.152–154 Minos is back in Crete. "We are told nothing further of the Athenian war," Hollis says; "the poet almost suggests that Scylla's parricide drove Minos straight back in horror from Megara to Crete" (at 8.104–144, 47).

30. Ovid makes the transition from the Scylla and Nisus episode to the story of Daedalus and Icarus (8.183–262) by the simple process of following Minos back to Crete and reporting his actions there to deal with his "family's disgrace," evidenced by the Minotaur, "the monstrous hybrid offspring [that] made plain its mother's [Pasiphaë, Minos' wife] bestial adultery [with a bull]" (8.155–156). Determined to "remove this shame

from his household" (8.157), Minos decides to confine the Minotaur in an underground maze, the original labyrinth (Gk. *labyrinthos,* a pre-Greek word [Kirk (1962) 5; see Palmer 9]). Enter Daedalus, "known throughout the world for his genius in the art of building" (8.159), to design and build the labyrinth, where Minos then imprisons the Minotaur. Continuing the transition to the story of Daedalus and Icarus, Ovid takes us quickly through a brief "side-trip" narrative about Theseus, the Minotaur, and Ariadne (8.169–182; one can put the pieces of the myth together by consulting Apollodorus 3.1.3–4, 3.15.7–8, and Epitome 1.7–9), and then brings us back to Daedalus simply with the word "meanwhile" (*interea,* 8.183): "Daedalus, meanwhile . . ."

Like Arachne, as well as the Minyades, the Pierides, and Marsyas, Daedalus is an artist who suffers for his art, but unlike them, he does not suffer in his own person (through his artwork he loses his son Icarus), nor is his suffering caused by a god. We are moving mythwise, as it were, to Orpheus in book 10, who also suffers, but not because of his art (which actually gives him the opportunity to bring his beloved wife, Eurydice, back from the dead), but *in spite* of his art: it is the human Orpheus, not Orpheus the artist, who, though told not to, looks back at and instantly loses Eurydice as they return to earth from the underworld.

Hoefmans notes the "uniqueness" of this episode "in the whole of the *Metamorphoses,*" which she describes thus: "no gods, no magic" (148). The absence of gods, she goes on to say, gives the story "a certain philosophical atmosphere, derived from . . . Lucretius" (148), the first-century B.C. Roman poet whose philosophical or "scientific" epic *De Rerum Natura* (*On the Nature of Things*) uses the atomic, that is, materialist, theory of matter promoted by Epicureanism to explain the world and existence and so dispel the fear of death, the cause for Lucretius of all human evil, fear of death itself caused by belief in myths and the gods.

Daedalus hates Crete and his exile there and longs to go home (8.183–184; Ovid doesn't say why Minos kept him there). To an ancient Greek or Roman, separation from home and the longing to return are sufficient justification for just about any action. Daedalus analyzes his problem: there are three media for escape, three ways to travel— land, sea, and air. Land is impossible, since Crete is an island; sea is likewise impossible, since Daedalus has no ship, and Minos, the archetypal ruler of a "thalassocracy" (as Thucydides recognizes: 1.4, 8), controls the sea. That leaves only the sky, the air, which Minos does not (and cannot) block, since it is by definition an impossible medium for humans for traveling—for all, in fact, but gods and birds.

These three media of travel—land, sea, and sky (= earth, water, and air)—defining the world that confronts Daedalus in his dilemma, represent, Hoefmans notes, "the Epicurean [triad]" (150), that is, they are the basic elements of existence and inject the Lucretian "atmosphere"—Lucretius' great poem is grounded in (and expounds) Epicurean philosophy—at the beginning of the tale.

Daedalus' impasse—his powerful longing to go home totally blocked, totally frustrated—recalls the impasse that Io as heifer faces when she seeks so urgently to communicate her identity and story to her father, and her very desperation forces her to create a solution, drawing the letters *I* and *O* with her hoof in the dirt (1.643–650); and it also recalls the impasse of Philomela, raped, mutilated, tongueless, imprisoned, and isolated, when she, also urgently seeking to communicate what has happened to her, in her frustration hits upon a solution, the tapestry she weaves for her sister with signs telling the story of her abduction and rape (6.511–579). Likewise for Daedalus, out of his desperate situation the creative solution is forced: "[T]he sky at least lies open. That's the way we'll go!" (8.186). And so, as Ovid says, "He now turns his mind to arts unknown' (*ignotas animum dimittit in artes*, 8.188) "and makes nature anew" (*naturamque novat*, 8.189). By contrast, Arachne, the "suffering artist" who precedes Daedalus in the *Metamorphoses*, weaves a tapestry in a kind of reactive counterpoint to Minerva's. Orpheus, however, who follows Daedalus in the poem, like him begins to practice his art—begins to sing so wonderfully—only when he is in deepest despair, after the second loss of Eurydice, and at the nadir of his experience.

Ovid now describes the process of Daedalus' art-making step by step. We are not told what his is creating, as if there is no blueprint, as if Daedalus is improvising step by step: he "places feathers in a row, beginning with the smallest" (8.189–190). The phrase "in a row" translates *in ordine* (1.189), which also means "in order." This is a seeming (but only seeming) paradox of creation: Daedalus "renews nature,"Hoefmans says, "*because he creates an ordo*. That is the way in which things have been created, by perpetual change of order in nature" (151). It is only at the end of the description that we know for sure what Daedalus is fashioning: "to make them [the row of feathers] like a real bird's wings" (*ut veras imitetur aves*, 8.195).

The poet next contrasts the concentration of Daedalus, who is intensely engaged in the concrete *work* of wing-making, with the lighthearted, unengaged *play* of his son Icarus (8.195–200), holding in his hands the same materials (feathers and wax) his father is using but "unaware he [is] handling something that would be deadly for him" (8.196) and "getting in the way of his father's amazing work as he himself play[s]" (8.199–200). In addition to presenting a contrast between Daedalus and Icarus, this passage also foreshadows Icarus' death, the result of his foolish ignorance.

The narrator now returns to the intense concentration of Daedalus, whom he calls "creator," *opifex* (8.201), as he puts the finishing touches on the wings, tries out his own pair, and gives Icarus instructions (8.200–208). The word *opifex* is used only one other time in the *Metamorphoses*, in the section in book 1 describing the creation of the universe (1.5–88): "the creator of all things, the source of a better world" (1.79: *ille opifex rerum, mundi melioris origo*). Ovid thus links Daedalus as wing-maker for freedom to creator of the universe, seeming "to suggest that his creation of a tool with which a human being can fly is of the same order as the creation and the start of a better world" (Hoefmans 143). This "better world" in book 1 was made without gods in a "pre-gods" time (see nn. 1 and 2), just as Daedalus creates his wings without help from the gods in an atmosphere or context free of gods.

Next, the narrator again foreshadows the coming death of Icarus when he describes Daedalus fitting the boy's wings on his shoulders, weeping, his hands trembling as he does so, and then their taking off, with Daedalus in the lead but looking back anxiously at Icarus (8.208-216).

Three observers on the ground watch father and son as they pass overhead, a fisherman, a shepherd, and a ploughman (8.217–220), "the prototypes," Hoefmans notes (144), "of the Silver Age people (users of tools allowed by Jupiter)." This scene graphically portrays what Hoefmans calls the Roman "compromise" in the *homo faber* (= man the maker) controversy, according to which Romans (or Latin literature) accepted only those tools that Jupiter allowed humans to use in the silver age—tools for farming and raising cattle (142; see *Metamorphoses* 1.123–124).

In this scene, Ovid "concisely presents the old *homo faber* controversy," as these onlookers, "users of allowed tools," gape at Daedalus and Icarus, "the *homo faber*" (and his son), who, by contrast, have "ventur[ed] into the realm of the gods" (144, see 8.219–220: "They [the observers] believed they [Daedalus and Icarus] were gods because they could fly through the air"). Hoefmans likens the onlookers to Lucretius' credulous "wretches who are ignorant of what is possible and what is not possible" (*De

Rerum Natura 6.64–65). "The flight of Daedalus," Hoefmans says, "presented as a matter of fact, is one of those possible things" (150). In a Lucretian universe, which is the setting, Hoefmans claims, for the episode of Daedalus and Icarus, "the wings are a natural consequence of progress. Daedalus' *mind* conceived them and created them according to nature" (156).

Icarus first appears in the story when Daedalus is well along if not already finished making the two pairs of wings: he stands at his father's side and, "unaware [*ignarus*, 8.196] he was handling something that would be deadly for him," plays (*lusu . . . suo*, 8.199) with feathers and wax (8.195–200), the material involved in his fall to his death in the sea, and hinders his father's work. If Daedalus is *homo faber*, Icarus is *homo* (or *puer*) *ludens*, a deadly role to have in this context. Just as Daedalus' instruction and his tears and trembling hands foreshadow the disaster that befalls Icarus, so the boy's play here foreshadows his later play when he begins "to delight in flying" (8.223), the prelude to and cause of that disaster.

Daedalus' ability to direct his mind to arts unknown and make nature anew, that is, to invent the means for humans to fly, includes precise technical knowledge of the limitations of his invention's capacity to perform under certain specific adverse conditions (too much heat, too much sun: 8.204–205). Therefore, he tells Icarus, "be sure to take a middle course" (8.203–204), "[f]ly in between" (8.206, that is, between sun and sea). This *homo faber* is very much a father, and so he weeps as he fits the wings on Icarus' shoulders, his hands tremble, he is anxious for his son, like a mother bird teaching its fledgling to fly, teaching Icarus "the destructive art" (*damnosas . . . artes*, 8.215; *damnosas* in whose judgment? Daedalus' or the narrator's?), looking back at him as they fly (8.210–216).

Icarus' fall is predictable, expected. The boy is characterized as "daring," as "delight[ing] in flying" (8.223), and he abandons his father, that is, abandons the middle course, "lured on by desire for the open sky" (8.224), that is, for the limitless. He goes too high, comes too close to the sun, and subjects his wings to the stress of heat they were not (could not be) designed to withstand; the wax melts, the wings come apart; and Icarus falls into the sea and drowns (8.224–230).

Daedalus finds his drowned son in the sea, "curse[s] his art" (*devovit . . . suas artes*, 8.234), and buries the boy's body in a tomb on land (8.233–235). As Hoefmans emphasizes, Icarus' death is not—"cannot be seen . . . as"—punishment of Daedalus. There are no gods, no "punishing agent" (147). No matter how Daedalus feels about his art at the moment he recovers Icarus' body from the sea, he did fly, and he got free from Crete. Despite Icarus' death, the wings are a marvelous invention; the flight frees Daedalus from exile. Is the loss of his son Icarus too high a price for Daedalus to pay? William Faulkner once said in an interview that the artist's "only responsibility is to his art. He will be completely ruthless if he is a good one. He has a dream. It anguishes him so much he must get rid of it. He has no peace until then. Everything goes by the board: honor, pride, decency, security, happiness, all . . . [T]he 'Ode on a Grecian Urn' is worth any number of old ladies" (Meriwether and Millgate 239). Although Daedalus "curse[s] his art," Ovid never says that he gave it up, that he regretted making the wings, that he wishes, in retrospect, that he had remained on Crete. Virgil's Daedalus, by contrast, carving the myth of the Minotaur, including his own role in the story, on temple doors in Cumae after he escapes from Crete, is unable to include Icarus' fall in the relief: "Icarus too would have had a prominent place, if his father's / Grief had allowed: but twice, trying to work the boy's fall / In gold, did Daedalus' hands fail him" (*Aeneid* 6.20–33a; quotation from 30b–33a; Day Lewis, trans.).

Daedalus' former nephew Perdix, now a partridge, shows up at the interment of

Icarus, expressing glee at Daedalus' loss (8.236–238). He was Daedalus' pupil, outshone his teacher by inventing the saw and the compass, and Daedalus, envious, threw the boy from the Athenian Acropolis, intending to kill him. Minerva, however, intervened and changed Perdix into a partridge in midair (8.236–259; thus the origin of that partic-ular bird, the Latin word for which is *perdix*). Now Perdix rejoices, in a spectacular but understandable display of *Schadenfreude*. Ovid juxtaposes but does not comment. The story ends with Daedalus "exhausted" (*fatigatum*, 8.260) and finding refuge with Coca-lus, king of Sicily (8.260–262; Ovid also tells the myth of Daedalus and Icarus at *Ars Amatoria* 2.21–96).

31. Ovid's transition at 8.262–271 from the narrative of Daedalus and Icarus to the next episode, the story of Meleager and the Calydonian boar hunt (8.271–546), resumes and completes the tale of Theseus, the Minotaur, and Ariadne, which the poet narrated briefly in the transition from Scylla and Nisus to Daedalus and Icarus at 8.169–182. The tribute sent to Minos ends, and the city of Athens rejoices (8.262–266). Ovid ig-nores the story of Theseus' father, Aegeus,' suicide after he saw the black sail on Thes-eus' ship returning from Crete, the prearranged signal for Theseus' death in Crete and which he forgot to change to a white sail indicating victory over the Minotaur. (See Apollodorus, Epitome 1.7–11).

As a result of Theseus' success in Crete, his fame has spread throughout Greece, and people in its various cities ask for his help in dealing with dangers they face, including the inhabitants of Calydon, plagued by a wild boar (8.267–271).

This episode comes at the midpoint of the *Metamorphoses* (book 8 straddles the middle, the midpoint occurring about 8.544), and as much as any other story in the poem reflects Ovid's penchant not only for mixing genres, in this case, epic and tragedy, but for parodying them as well.

In his version of Meleager and the Calydonian boar hunt, the poet narrates a myth familiar to his readers, for "[t]he story of Meleager was one of the most celebrated Greek myths, treated by poets of all ages, from early epic-writers down to Hellenistic times" (Hollis at 8.260–546, 66). Ovid's sources were "some sort of Hellenistic *epos*" (Otis 194) and a lost play of Euripides, the *Meleager*, together with a Latinized version of it by the second-century B.C. Roman poet Accius. (See Otis 194–196 and Hollis at 8.260–546, 66–69.)

Ovid's description of the actual hunt (8.329–444) is "the most strictly formal piece of epic writing" in the *Metamorphoses* (Hollis at 8.329–444, 77): the poet's representa-tion of the boar and the destruction it causes (8.284–297) "is an embroidery of stock epic material" (Hollis at 8.284–286, 72). Ovid introduces this epically famous boar hunt in a decidedly unepic way, prefiguring what is to come: "The reason for their mission was a hog" (8.271–272: *causa petendi / sus erat*). "[W]e should have expected a more dignified word for the boar this first time," Anderson says, "if Ovid's intention were serious" ([1972] at 8.272, 359). As for the poet's depiction of the boar, Horsfall comments, "it is the great length of Ovid's description that is immediately striking: first, five lines . . . on [the boar's] physique, then eight . . . on the havoc he wreaks. . . . Ovid passes nothing by: eyes, neck, bristles, forequarters, foam, squeals, tusks compared to an elephant's and breath which acts like a flame-thrower. . . . The damage wrought by this super-boar of course matches his astounding physique" (320–321).

Then comes the catalogue of hunters (8.298–328), "a traditional element of unmis-takeably epic origin" (Horsfall 319); but with thirty-eight hunters listed in twenty-six lines (8.301–326), Ovid's catalogue, Horsfall says, is "jejeune [sic] and static" (322), except for the description of the "Tegean girl," Atalanta, "the glory of the Arcadian forest" (8.317; she is not to be confused with the Boeotian Atalanta at 10.560ff.), who "stands as the climax of the Catalogue" (Horsfall 322), and to whom and to whose effect on Meleager Ovid gives eleven lines (8.318–328).

Ovid turns Meleager (and the narrative) from admiring Atalanta's beauty back to the hunt with a biting allusion to Virgil's *Aeneid* (considering the "burlesque" he makes of the hunt): "But it was not the moment to say more (and his [Meleager's] modesty would not allow him to). The more pressing task, the great contest, was now upon him" (8.327–328). *[M]aius opus* (8.328), the phrase translated as "[t]he more pressing task," serves as Ovid's "most heavily loaded and significant Virgilian echo to date," alluding to *Aeneid* 7.44, *maius opus moveo*, "A grander theme I open" (Day Lewis, trans.), the words Virgil uses to introduce with great solemnity the second or Iliadic half of his epic, "which is a *maius opus* because the *Aeneid* is now no longer an epic of Aeneas and his men but narrates the affairs of all Italy" (Horsfall 323). Ovid, too, is at the halfway point of his work, and since "hunting was an activity on a par with war," the boar hunt is "an authentically heroic enterprise, undertaken by some of the greatest names of myth" (Horsfall 322).

When the boar emerges from its reedy marsh (8.338ff.), the "burlesque" begins: "Portrayed in grand epic language," Horsfall says, "[the boar] charges . . . the huntsmen . . . like the bolt of lightning which serves as the dominant image of his rage . . . ; in his path the forest is crushed and the hounds are scattered as he lives up to our fullest expectations of his performance. . . . The heroes . . . open fire in language of exceptional grandeur, with a neatly varied triad of failures" (324), as Echion wounds a maple tree; Jason overshoots his target; the head of Mopsus' spear falls off as the weapon flies toward the boar (8.345–354). The boar in turn lays low three hunters, wounding two and killing one (8.355–364). "Worse follows, as the hunters are revealed as ever more incompetent" (Horsfall 325). Nestor pole-vaults into a tree to escape the boar—a "send-up" of the Iliadic Nestor, "eternally reminiscing about what a devil of a fellow he was in his prime" (Kenney [1986] 422). The boar wounds yet another hunter, and the Dioscuri, "in their most martial guise" (Horsfall 326), throw their spears and miss. Telamon pursues the boar into the dark underbrush, trips over a root, and falls flat on his face. At this point, it is the boar 11, the hunters 0. Then, while Achilles' father, Peleus, helps his brother Telamon to his feet (Peleus' "only achievement," Horsfall says [327]), Atalanta shoots an arrow—the first to hit the boar—and wounds it, but only slightly (8.365–383). The hunters overreact; Meleager overpraises her: "You deserve the prize for valor!" (8.387: *virtutis honorem*), thus inserting "the key ironic term of the whole episode: *virtutis*. The girl is to be honored for ability befitting a man: *vir-tus*" (Anderson [1972] at 8.387, 368). "To heighten the paradox," Horsfall comments (327), "the men now react in a conventionally feminine way, by blushing": "The men grew red in the face," Ovid says, "and flung their spears all at once and in disorder" (8.388–389).

In this context, Ancaeus' epic vaunt and his physically exaggerated preparation for his blow (he raises himself on his toes, 8.398) seem not only arrogant but fatally silly. When the boar buries its tusks in Ancaeus' abdomen (8.400), "his bowels slithered out in a wet and bloody heap on the ground" (8.401–402), "Ovid's one gruesome piece of realism in this episode" (Hollis at 8.402, 85).

Having just witnessed the outcome of Ancaeus' "[r]eckless courage" (8.407), Theseus warns his friend Pirithous, "Back, O heart of my heart . . . A little distance is the better part of valor" (8.405–407), making "explicit for the first time the anti-heroic character of this whole narrative" (Horsfall 329). The burlesque continues as the hunt moves to its climax. Theseus hurls his spear, which, hitting the branch of an oak tree, is deflected from its target (8.408–410); the great Jason, procurer of the golden fleece

(7.1–158), throws a second time and now succeeds in killing "an innocent hound," for his spear, "passing through its belly, stuck in the ground" (8.411–413). Finally, Meleager fatally wounds the boar (8.414–419), "[t]he decisive blow . . . recounted very quietly, without a climax" (Hollis at 8.414, 86).

I have used the word "burlesque" to describe Ovid's presentation of the boar hunt, taking the term from Horsfall, who calls the hunt an "extended heroic burlesque in epic form" (331), his hunters "great heroes whose heroism and whose competence as hunters are regularly and ludicrously deficient" (330). But then we are confronted with an abrupt change of mood and genre, from burlesque of epic to a narration at 8.445–525 of Althaea's revenge and Meleager's death, which is "clearly inspired by Tragedy" (Hollis, introduction to 8.445–525, 89).

Althaea's dilemma—she must kill her son to avenge her brothers' deaths—"permits [Ovid] to analyze the sensitive conscience of a woman at the mercy of a passion" that resembles Procne's in the story of Tereus, Procne, and Philomela at 6.401–674 (Anderson [1972] at 8.445–525, 371). Wilkinson considers Althaea's speech at 8.478–511 similar to those by Medea, Scylla, Byblis, and Myrrha, that is, as "expressing a conflict in the soul of a woman about to commit a crime" ([1955] 205; see n. 26 above). The poet "narrates the tale with considerable sympathy, and the delineation of Althaea's dilemma, by narrative and soliloquy, is one of his masterpieces" (Anderson [1972] at 8.445–525, 372; Hollis, *contra*, sees Althaea's soliloquy as overly rhetorical [at 8.445–525, 89]).

There is no other act of revenge—or killing—in the *Metamorphoses* like Althaea's: she sets fire to a log that by burning somehow saps the life of her son, two metamorphoses involving "the secret intimacies of different things," one (the burning of the log) causing the other (Meleager's death), both showing "that human experience is a series of contagions" (Barkan 91). Ovid describes Meleager's death with an exquisitely tender sadness: "The fire, far away, and his pain flared up together, together they died down, together they went out; and his spirit gently entered the soft, still air, as white ash slowly covered the fading ember" (8.522–525).

But then Ovid's description of Meleager's sisters mourning their late brother returns us to something like the burlesque of the boar hunt: they beat their bodies black and blue, embrace Meleager's corpse again and again, smother it with kisses, smother the bier on which it lies with kisses, and, after the body is burned, gather the ashes and hug them to their breasts, throw themselves on Meleager's grave, try to embrace his name cut in the stone, and fill the letters incised there with the water of their tears (8.533–541), making the "mourning degenerate into a totally unepic near-necrophilia" (Galinsky [1975] 136), that is, making a parody of the mourning.

A straightforward, tightly constructed plot line underlies these moves from genre to genre and from burlesque to tragic anguish to tender sadness to parody-by-exaggeration: Meleager falls in love with the huntress Atalanta and so awards her the prize for killing the boar (which she alone of the hunters, except for Meleager, succeeds in wounding); the oafish hunters object, chief among them Meleager's uncles, threatening Atalanta with physical harm; Meleager then attacks and kills his uncles; Althaea, to avenge them, burns the log, and Meleager dies; his sisters mourn him. The well-known story becomes, in Ovid's hands, a brilliant and original tour de force occupying a place of honor at the center of the *Metamorphoses*.

32. Ovid, Kenney says, has "heavily contrived" the transition (at 8.547–550) from the episode of Meleager and the Calydonian boar hunt to the tales that end book 8 (and continue into book 9), the setting for which is the home of the river-god Achelous, for

the Achelous River is not on the way from Calydon to Athens (of which Erechtheus is king and Minerva the patron deity) but, rather, lies west of Calydon and flows into the Ionian Sea on the west coast of northern Greece ([1986] 423). Theseus would travel east to reach Athens from Calydon.

These tales, embedded narratives, are told by two different narrators. The River Achelous, acting as host to Theseus and his companions because his stream is swollen with rain and thus impossible for them to cross (8.550–559), initiates the storytelling with tales that explain how the Echinades islands became islands (8.577–589) and also how the nymph Perimele became an island (8.590–610). After a brief interlude at 8.611–620 (with significance for the poem as a whole), Lelex tells the story of Baucis and Philemon, which is followed by a second brief interlude that extends the first and is also significant for the poem as a whole (8.725–737). Achelous then narrates the tale of Erysichthon and Mestra (8.738–878). A third brief interlude now ends the book (8.879–884) and continues in the opening lines of book 9—lines 1–3—introducing the final embedded narrative in the series, Achelous' account of his defeat by Hercules in a wrestling match in which they contended for the hand of Deianira (9.4–88).

As a series, these narratives (which call attention to the poem's "premise," that "storytelling is a fundamental means of comprehending the world" [Solodow 34]) recall earlier series of stories in the poem, that narrated by the Minyades in book 4, by the unnamed Muse in book 5, and particularly the two tales told by Aeacus and Cephalus in book 7, in which host and guest exchange stories, as they do here. The episodes related by Achelous and Lelex also occur just after the midpoint of the poem (8.577–9.88; the midpoint is about 8.544), thus balancing the stories of Daedalus and Icarus and Meleager and the Calydonian boar hunt, which appear just before the midpoint (8.183–546). Around these two sets of centrally located stories cluster Ovidian themes, practices, or issues that have significance for the entire *Metamorphoses*. Ovid's interest in art and artists—in creativity—manifests itself in the story of Daedalus and Icarus. The poet's delight in mixing styles and genres (and parodying them) is exhibited in the Calydonian boar hunt: epic, burlesqued in the hunt itself; tragedy, enacted in Althaea's dilemma and its resolution; and tragedy then parodied in the description of Meleager's sisters mourning their dead brother.

Here, the interludes that follow the initial "ice-breaking" tales told by Achelous and the next one, told by Lelex, identify poem-wide issues of credibility of narratives and types of metamorphoses.

Inviting Theseus and his companions into his house, Achelous advises the hero not to expose himself "to these violent waters of mine that often sweep away huge tree trunks and tumble boulders so thunderously down my stream" (8.551–553). Achelous' implicit reference to his forms as anthropomorphic god and river will be continued and developed in the first stories he tells and expanded further in his comments (the second interlude mentioned earlier) preceding the narrative of Erysichthon and Mestra.

The setting for these stories, the cave of Achelous, "its floor covered with damp moss, its ceiling studded with rows of conch and murex shells" (8.563–564), where Achelous and his guests recline on couches around tables while barefoot nymphs heap those tables with food and then serve the guests wine in jeweled goblets (8.565–573), is "nothing other than a first-century grotto-nympheum," Solodow says, "each one of its features finding close parallels in contemporary construction" (78–79), and "might remind [Ovid's] audience of some of their own ornate grottoes by the sea along the Campanian coast, where they too might dine in luxury" (Anderson [1972] at 8.562, 383).

Achelous tells his guests the stories of the Echinades islands and of Perimele in response to a question from Theseus ("'What place is that? It seems to be an island'" [8.573ff.]). There are actually six islands in the sea, opposite the mouth of the Achelous, he learns, five of which, the Echinades, lying nearer the river's mouth, were nymphs who forgot to invite Achelous to a banquet: "'I swelled with wrath and rain, grew as huge as I become in full spate, uprooted trees from the forest, tore a piece of earth from the fields, and swept it and the nymphs together into the sea,'" where the piece of land was broken up into five islands, one for each nymph (8.583–589). The sixth island, beyond the Echinades, was formerly the nymph Perimele, raped by Achelous and then rescued by his intervention with Neptune, who turns her into an island to "save" her, when the girl's father, enraged by her rape, pitches her into the sea (8.590–610).

Now swollen with rain and hence impossible to cross, Achelous invites Theseus and his friends to stay with him until his waters abate. But when the Echinades nymphs forget to invite Achelous to their banquet, he "swells with water and with anthropomorphic rage," Feeney says:

> The more Achelous concentrates on the harmony between his personality and his element, . . . the more difficult it becomes for the reader to overlook the split. . . . If the water and the person are presented as one and the same, how can the woods or the fields be separated from themselves? And if these material objects are separated from their material embodiments, what of the nymphs, who find themselves swept into the sea together with the physical environments which are their habitation, and simultaneously their "selves"? (235)

This focus on the play between a deity's anthropomorphic embodiment and his or her natural element recalls the description of the river Peneus, father of Daphne, at 1.568–576; more significantly, the river Inachus at 1.583–587, who, lamenting the loss of his daughter Io, augments his water with his tears; and, more significantly still, the pool Salmacis at 4.297–379, "who both is and is not identical with the pool she inhabits" (Fränkel 88) and whose dual nature Ovid exploits to the fullest. Here, the river and god Achelous, swollen with rain or rage, and the nymphs who inhabit the islands they are, lead up to issues of metamorphosis (and its connection to storytelling) and the power of the gods, now explicitly articulated by a disbelieving Pirithous: "You made that story up" (*ficta refers,* 8.614), he says to Achelous, "and you allow the gods too much power if you think they give bodies their forms and take those forms away" (8.614–615). Lelex, another of Theseus' companions, objects: "The gods' power is immense and has no limit; whatever they want is done" (8.618–619). Case in point: the oak and linden trees he once saw in Phrygia (an eyewitness: "I've seen the place myself," 8.622: *ipse locum vidi*), the metamorphosed forms of the dear old peasants Baucis and Philemon, who entertained gods unawares and whose story Lelex tells to counter Pirithous' contemptuous disbelief (8.622ff.). "[T]he gods," Feeney says, "are the hardest case for epic fiction, the sharp edge of the problem of how to represent and authenticate anything in the world of the narrative." Here, "[i]n the very centre of his poem," Feeney continues, "Ovid removes the cover, to reveal the complicity between poet and audience which underpins his enterprise, as well as the fragile limits to that complicity" (229).

When Pirithous expresses his disbelief in Achelous' tale, and Lelex objects to that disbelief, "[t]wo possible audience reactions to the divine stories of the *Metamorphoses* are acted out for us," Feeney comments. For everyone except Pirithous, "Achelous' account becomes a *factum,* an event, however amazing" (230). We (the audience or readers), Feeney says, will agree with Pirithous in part, but not wholly, for we need "some suspension of disbelief . . . for the narrative to proceed at all." Ovid does not want to destroy "our ability to give . . . credence to his fictions," nor does he wish to let "us forget that fictions are indeed his subject." By presenting us with "these two polarized alternatives [Ovid] is making us realize that to swim successfully in the sea of the *Metamorphoses* we must be both Lelex and Pirithous" (230).

Pirithous and Lelex are ostensibly discussing the power of the gods, but their real subject is "the power of the poets," according to Feeney. For when Pirithous tells Achelous that he allows "the gods too much power" if he thinks "they give bodies their forms and take those forms away" (8.614–615), he is raising "the possibility that we will not follow the poet in his bestowal and removal of forms." And when Lelex replies, "The gods' power is immense" (8.618–619), "we may," Feeney continues, "substitute the poet's own quasi-divine craft" and so rephrase Lelex's statement: "The *poet's* power is immense and has no limit; whatever *he* wants is done." The poet's power consists in part in "the ability to make us 'believe' in the teeth of [his] continual reminders of his poetic world's fictional status" (231–232).

Lelex tells the story of the pious couple Baucis and Philemon (8.620–724) to support his contention about the power of the gods. The theme of the tale, "the reception of the great at a humble peasant dwelling" (Hollis at 8.611–724, 106), goes back to Homer's *Odyssey* and the swineherd Eumaeus' reception of Odysseus in disguise at book 14.1–81. (See Hollis at 8.611–724, 106–112, who identifies possible antecedents to or sources for the story, traces it forward to Ovid, and discusses its various aspects.) Philemon, Hollis says, "is a type of the traditional Italian peasant, with a cottage he has lived in all his life . . . his ideal marriage . . . and the Italian meal which he lays before his guests" (Hollis at 8.611–724, 111), which was "one such as a poor man might eat in the Italian countryside" (Hollis at 8.664ff., 119). Philemon and Baucis are thus a "model for the good old days," and the story has special significance for the Rome of Augustus (and of Ovid): "There it was official policy to glorify the simple life of Italy's past" (Hollis at 8.611–724, 111).

What strikes the modern reader is Ovid's emphasis on the thoroughgoing mutuality of Philemon and Baucis, who are equals utterly: they are the same age (8.631: *parili . . . aetate*), and "[t]hey gave the orders, and they obeyed them" (8.636: *idem parentque iubentque*). When Jupiter and Mercury arrive at the couple's cottage, Philemon draws up a bench and invites the gods to sit, and Baucis throws a coarse blanket over it. Baucis stirs up the fire and pulls down from the rafters kindling and branches (for feeding the fire), which she puts under a bronze pot; she then strips the outer leaves from a cabbage she intends to boil, a cabbage picked by Philemon. Philemon takes down a side of bacon from a roof beam, cuts a slice from it, and puts it into the pot to boil. They both attempt conversation as they shake out a mattress covering a willow couch (on which the gods will recline for their meal) and cover the mattress with a spread. Baucis brings out a three-legged table with one leg shorter than the other two, makes the table level by wedging a pottery shard under the short leg, wipes the table, sets food out on it, and gets out a wine bowl and cups (8.637–670). This last series of actions is the only one performed by one member of the couple that is not balanced by an action of the other. They both notice the wine bowl filling up of its own accord, they both pray for forgiveness for the simple meal, they both chase (and are worn out by) their one goose, they both struggle up the mountain the gods have ordered them to ascend, they both weep for their countrymen when they see the area flooded. When Jupiter asks them both together what they would like, they confer and (Philemon reporting their "joint decision": 8.706) essentially ask for the continuation of their mutuality unto death: They would like to be priests of the temple their cottage has been turned into and to die at the same instant: "'Let me never see my wife's grave,'" Philemon says, "'nor let her ever have to bury me.'" The gods grant the couple's prayer, and one day when they are quite old, "Baucis saw leaves growing from Philemon, and . . . Philemon, in turn, saw leaves growing from Baucis, too." They speak together as long as they are able to, and, just before the trees they are changing into cover their mouths, cry out, "'Farewell, beloved,' at the same moment, and at the same moment leaves grew over their mouths and covered them" (8.679–719). The "tree trunks standing side by side that were once their two bodies" can be seen "[e]ven today," Lelex says (8.719–720), their mutuality made permanent by their metamorphosis, one into an oak, the other into a linden tree (8.620–621): though different, they are still equal.

Pirithous might also call this story *fictum*, "made up," but Lelex accepts it as *factum*, an actual event, a "fact," justifying his belief with the assertion, "The old men who told me this story were not simpleminded, nor was there any reason they should want to lie to me" (8.721–722). If we as readers are to be both Pirithous and Lelex, as Feeney says we must be, "to swim successfully in the sea of the *Metamorphoses*" (see above), then we "believe" the story of Baucis and Philemon by allowing it to engage us, to command our attention; we "believe" it by appreciating its artfulness, its arrangement of detail, its coherence of plot, its verisimilitude—all those elements that make a story a story. Lelex believes the tale not because the old men told him it was true (they did not), but simply because they told it. It is not that it is a true story, but that it is "true" as a story. What *is* true, what is "fact," are the trees. "Indeed, I saw garlands hanging from the branches," Lelex says (*equidem pendentia vidi / serta super ramos*, 8.722–723), referring to branches of literal trees, literally rooted in the world of *facta*. We retrace Lelex's steps back to the trees. There he began, and there we, too, begin, with the literal trees. Out of the natural world come stories, created by poets—or by old men who told a story well, as well as Ovid—with gods and transformations and all the rest. Out of *facta* come *ficta*: this is the essential metamorphosis, creating stories where there were (or are) only *facta*, events, phenomena, the natural and human world. We know the difference, and we also remember the original sequence of their coming into being: First, the natural world and the human race are created (1.5–88) by an *opifex* (1.79), then come the gods (1.89–451), to do what they do, good and bad, and to "people" the stories the poets create. Ovid slyly gives Jupiter pride of place by letting him tell the first story in the work, that is, the first embedded narrative, his encounter with the murderous Lycaon (1.163–243; its affinity with the tale of Baucis and Philemon was noted earlier), a tale he himself is a character in, a fact that subtly reinforces this "characterhood" in the *Metamorphoses*: Jupiter lives (only) in the world of *ficta*, not the world of *facta*.

Lelex's audience was moved, both by the story and by its teller (8.725; "even Pirithous is impressed," says Hollis at 8.725, 128). Theseus now wants to hear about "the wondrous things done by the gods" (*facta . . . / mira deum*, 8.726–727). If we are still able to substitute "the poet" for "the gods," as Feeney suggests for 8.618–619 ("The gods' [now read: "poet's"] power is immense"), then what Theseus wants to hear, we might say, are the *facta mira*, "wondrous things done," by the poets, in a word, their *ficta*, fictions, fashioned from the facts of the world.

Achelous responds to Theseus with a recapitulation of the first words of the poem: "There are some . . . whose forms were once changed and then remained in their new bodies: *sunt . . . quorum / forma semel mota est et in hoc renovamine mansit* (8.728–729; cf. 1.1–2: *In nova fert animus mutatas dicere formas / corpora*, "My mind leads me to something new, to tell of forms changed to other bodies"). Here, Achelous' *forma semel mota est et in hoc renovamine mansit* repeats 1.1–2, *in nova . . . mutatas . . . formas / corpora*. He then expands his statement: "There are others who have the power [*ius*, lit., "right"] to change into many forms" (*sunt, quibus in plures ius est transire figuras*,

8.730). "Achelous," Fantham says, "marks a new phase in the epic by laying down . . . a formal distinction between those who undergo a single metamorphosis without further change . . . and the privileged beings who have the right to pass through a number of shapes" ([1993] 22). Most of the stories told in the first half of the poem, Fantham adds, have to do with transformations of humans—"offenders or victims"—by the gods, with "quite a few instances" of gods changing their forms (for example, Jupiter into the goddess Diana for Callisto or into a bull for Europa in book 2, Apollo into Leucothoe's mother in book 4, Minerva into an old woman for Arachne in book 6). "Now, as Book 8 draws to a close," Fantham says, "Ovid is about to pass from his simpler routines into more elaborate tales varying the metamorphosis of men by gods [the first part of Achelous' statement: 8.728–729] with magical stories of multiple change [the second part of Achelous' statement: 8.730]" ([1993] 22). Achelous adduces Proteus as an example of those "who have the power to change into many forms," listing nine transformations the god of change had undergone—the range of possibilities, as it were—that together make up almost all the categories of created existence: human, animal (warm- and cold-blooded), mineral, vegetable or plant, water, and fire (8.731–737; only earth and air are missing).

Achelous' description of the possibilities of metamorphosis recapitulates, in the middle of the poem, the opening statement of its theme and expands it from a single kind of change that we might call "simple" by adding a second kind that we might call "complex" ("magical stories of multiple change," in Fantham's words). This description of kinds of metamorphosis, recapitulating and expanding the poem's stated theme in a setting of embedded narratives (two already related, two yet to come), reinforces the connection between metamorphosis and storytelling and the notion of storytelling as metamorphosis. Achelous' illustrative *fictum* is on the way, the tale of Erysichthon and his daughter Mestra (instead of a story about Proteus, as we might have expected, "because Vergil had told the tale of Proteus too well," in the fourth *Georgic*: Fantham [1993] 23).

Mestra, capable of changing herself into a variety of shapes at will, and the subject of and reason for Achelous' story (Ovid does not give her name; it is known from Hesiod's *Ehoiai* [Gantz 1.68]), does not appear after she is briefly introduced (8.738–739) until almost the end of the 141-line tale (8.738–878), and takes up only 28 lines (8.847–874). It is her father, Erysichthon, and his crime and punishment that occupy most of the narrative and the narrator's attention.

Erysichthon is characterized solely as the ultimate sinner, "a man who scorned the gods and refused to burn incense on their altars" (8.739–740). To illustrate this, Ovid refers to Erysichthon's desecration of a grove sacred to Ceres, introducing his statement, "He is even said . . ." (*ille etiam . . . / dicitur*, 8.741–742), not so much to distance himself from it as to express incredulity, as if to say: "Can you believe it? He is even said. . . ." Ovid—or Achelous—next proceeds to describe in detail Erysichthon's chopping down an ancient oak sacred to Ceres and killing the nymph who both lives in and is the tree, as well as a servant who objects to his brutal violence (8.743–776). Erysichthon's only motive is "a dominating impiety" (Hollis at 8.738–878, 133). He is shortly afflicted by Ceres with a "ravening hunger," as Feeney notes, a punishment that "mirrors the blind voraciousness of [his] moral character" (243) and that comes by way of a visitation of Hunger herself, whom Ovid describes in one of his great personifications of abstract entities (8.784–822; see n. 9 for the others). In Ovid's personification of Hunger, "the very image of a hungry person," Solodow says, "[e]ssence lies on the surface" (198).

As constant, insatiable hunger works its devastating effect upon Erysichthon, he consumes all his substance and is reduced to his only daughter, Mestra, whom he sells into slavery in order to have enough money for more food (8.823–848). She refuses to accept slavery, however, and prays to Neptune for deliverance (she is at the seashore, as we shortly learn), since, she says, "'you possessed the prize of my stolen virginity,'" a statement that Ovid quickly validates with a comical aside, "—for it was Neptune who had stolen that prize" (8.848–851), as if we needed the confirmation. Mestra is instantly changed into a fisherman, complete with fishing pole, line, hook, and bait, before the eyes of her new master, who has been chasing her and who now, dumbfounded, asks her where the girl went. Mestra, instantly in her new role and "enjoying it, that she was asked about herself" (*a se / se quaeri gaudens*, 8.862–863), swears that "'[a]s the god of the sea aids my arts . . . there has been no one on the shore except me for quite a while—and certainly no woman'" (8.866–868), a statement with a double entendre (Hollis at 8.866–867, 146), since he/she invokes Neptune as aiding her "arts" (*has . . . artes*, 8.866), both the art of fishing and her newly acquired, Neptune-given art of metamorphosis. The man believes her (*credidit*, 8.869) and walks away "completely fooled," and Mestra regains her original form (8.869–870). This is metamorphosis, supplemented by quick wit and a ready tongue, as delightful deliverance, something new in the poem.

Achelous quickly ends the tale, running through the shapes Mestra adopts to escape the masters her father sells her to and then abruptly telling us that Erysichthon, with nothing else to eat, "began to bite off mouthfuls of his flesh, and the poor wretch ate himself to feed himself" (8.871–878). "[H]aving devised a perpetual solution to Erysichthon's needs," Fantham notes, "Ovid can only end the narrative by violating the logic of Mestra's talent," since her father's "final downfall" is inconsistent with that talent ([1993] 31).

The stories of Philemon and Baucis and Erysichthon are linked by theme, that is, piety rewarded versus impiety punished ("*impietas* punished": Anderson [1972], at 8.725–878, 400) and by Ovid's "use of a recurrent landscape" that provides "a contrast between the sacred trees into which the pious Baucis and Philemon are transformed . . . and the sacred grove . . . which the impious Erysichthon violates" (Segal [1969a] 57).

Solodow expands on these observations by noting that Philemon and Baucis, "[t]hough very poor, . . . serve the gods an appetizing banquet" and "at the end of their lives" are "rewarded by being changed into sacred trees," while Erysichthon, who "dared to cut down a grove of sacred trees[,] is punished with insatiable desire for food. The themes of food, hunger, and sacred trees, strangely combined, run between the two stories" (16).

Achelous now remembers (in the final lines of the book: 8.879–884) that he, too, can change himself "'into a certain number of shapes,'" including a bull, which in turn reminds him of his horns and then of his lost horn. These lines serve as a transition to the next tale (Achelous' contest with Hercules), and this transition, continuing in the opening lines of book 9, bridges the two books.

BOOK NINE

33. At the end of book 8, Achelous had mentioned to his audience that he, too, like Mestra (in the story he has just told), can change into various shapes. That statement triggers the memory of the time when as a bull he lost a horn and was left with only one, as he now is, in his form as an anthropomorphic river-god (8.879–884). These lines, ending book 8, begin the transition to the next episode (in book 9). Achelous'

groans (*gemitus*, 8.884) as he remembers his lost horn arouse Theseus' curiosity, and as the transition continues in book 9, he asks Achelous why he groaned (*gemitus*, 9.1) and how he lost his horn (9.1–2; the transition thus bridges the two books). In answering Theseus' question, Achelous narrates an account of his wrestling match with Hercules for the hand of Deianira (9.4–88), the final embedded narrative in the series the river-god initiated in book 8 with his story of the origin of the Echinades islands (8.577ff.).

Following Achelous' tale here, Ovid continues with the myth of Hercules, narrating stories of Hercules' killing Nessus for the centaur's attempted rape of Deianira; the hero's death, brought about by Nessus (with Deianira as unwitting accomplice); and his apotheosis (9.101–272).

Thus the lengthy Hercules episode (9.4–272) begins with Achelous' embedded narrative, the last of a series of such narratives (as noted) delivered in the river-god's cave that, except for this tale, has nothing to do with Hercules. Then, with a rather abrupt "stepping-stone" transition (see n. 3; Achelous lost his horn, "[b]ut you, Nessus, were destroyed by your fierce lust": 9.98–102), the poet switches to an omniscient narrator for the remainder of the section on Hercules. This change of narrator within the episode is a factor that makes the tone of the whole, from wrestling match to deification of the hero, "not altogether easy to define" (Kenney [1986] 425), and critics differ in their interpretation of Ovid's representation of Hercules, a hero who was "particularly dear" to the Stoics of ancient Rome (Kenney [1986] 425) and whose "behavior and attitudes were held up for imitation" (Stephens [1958a] 274).

As Achelous tells the story, the wrestling match was not a planned contest. A fight between Achelous and Hercules simply broke out. After the girl's other suitors yielded to Achelous and Hercules (9.13), they presented their qualifications to Deianira's father, Oeneus. Achelous reports Hercules' "presentation" of his credentials indirectly in two lines: his father, Jupiter, as Deianira's father-in-law, his renown for his labors, and his triumph over his stepmother's commands (9.14–15; commands are usually "done" or "carried out," Bömer notes; when Hercules speaks of his "triumph over" [*superata*, 9.15] them, we detect Hercules the braggart, he says [at 9.15, 4.281]), if, that is, Achelous is reporting accurately. This brief, indirect, none too flattering account from a biased reporter reminds us of the unnamed Muse's retelling of the Pierid's song in the singing contest with the Muses (in book 5).

Achelous then repeats directly at greater length (eleven lines: 9.16–26) his own speech to Oeneus. He is a god, while Hercules is mortal; he is a native of Calydon, not a foreigner; the absence of a god's wrath or of labors as punishment ought not to count against him. In the last four lines, Achelous addresses Hercules, not Oeneus, taunting him in a deliberate provocation: either Hercules' boast that Jupiter is his father is a lie, or else Hercules is illegitimate, "'born in shame'" (9.23–26).

He then gives Hercules' reaction: "While I was speaking, Hercules had been staring at me with a fierce look on his face, seething, barely able to control his rage" (9.27–28). "The philosophers' model of self-control," Feeney comments, "is dismissed at a stroke as Achelous reports Hercules' response to his taunts" (206). Now Hercules wants to fight (Achelous says). "'My fists are more powerful than my tongue. Go on, win the debate—as long as I win the fight'"; he moves toward Achelous in a menacing way; and the combat begins (9.29ff.). Barkan characterizes it as "a confrontation between the magnificent bodily strength of the great hero and the self-transforming powers of his adversary." Since Achelous is "much more verbose," it is "as if rhetoric itself is a protean talent" (72), or, to put it another way, "self-transforming powers" and rhetoric are the same, the one exercised in the domain of the physical, the other in that of the verbal.

This contest recalls the earlier one between Minerva and Arachne (in book 6) in that it was Minerva's sheer power that defeated Arachne's equal talent. It also anticipates the debate between Ajax and Ulysses (in book 13), archetypes, respectively, of brawn and brains, although their contest is between competing speeches, inferior and superior rhetoric.

According to Galinsky, Ovid here and throughout the Hercules episode parodies the conflict between Aeneas and Turnus in Virgil's *Aeneid* as well as the *Aeneid's* Augustan themes ([1972] 98, 116). The contest between Hercules and Achelous suggests, Galinsky says, that "the conflict between Turnus and Aeneas [in the *Aeneid*] was no more than a quarrel over a girl" ([1975] 30; the earlier contest between Perseus and Phineus over Andromeda in book 5 was a more extended parody of the Aeneas-Turnus conflict: see n. 20).

Achelous ends the account of his combat with Hercules with the loss of his horn and its transformation into the Cornucopia or Horn of Plenty (9.85–88). As if on cue, a servant nymph enters with the horn, "filled to overflowing with luscious fruit . . . as their dessert" (9.89–92).

Barkan observes that in breaking off Achelous' horn, Hercules makes "a solid substance of what was a shifting, protean form," that is, the Cornucopia, which "embodies a transforming power in the real world" (78–79).

Continuing with Hercules (but shifting from embedded narrative to an omniscient narrator), Ovid makes a "stepping-stone" transition (at 9.98–102, as noted earlier) from Hercules and Achelous to the next story, the centaur Nessus' attempted rape of the hero's bride, Deianira, while ferrying her on his back across the river Evenus (9.103–133). The swollen Evenus does not stop Hercules: "'I've just defeated one river [Achelous], and I might as well conquer another,'" he says, making the crossing a second contest (9.115; see Bömer at 9.115, 4.307, for interpretation of this line) and heading for the river's rougher waters (9.116–117). While Hercules is thus occupied—"[a]ll too intent on proving his heroism" (Anderson [1972] at 9.93–133, 424)—Nessus attempts to rape Deianira, whose scream alerts the hero. Now on the opposite bank of the river, he shoots the centaur with a poisoned arrow. Dying, Nessus smears his tunic with his poisoned blood and gives the garment to Deianira, telling her it is a love charm (9.119–133).

From the Nessus episode, which serves as the transition to the next part of Ovid's story of Hercules, the hero's death and apotheosis (9.134–272; Anderson [1972] at 9.93–133, 424), and also furnishes the means for that death, the poisoned garment–"love potion" that Deianira sends to him, Ovid "hastens on," Feeney says, to the end of the hero's life, "his apotheosis so dominating that the deeds which justify it are crowded out," filling only two lines (206): "During the long interval that followed, Hercules' great deeds filled the earth and satisfied his stepmother's hatred" (9.134–135).

Deianira, like Procris earlier (7.824–825), hears "scurrilous gossip" (*fama loquax*, 9.137) "that Hercules was gripped by a passion for the princess Iole" (9.140). In this case the gossip is true, although Ovid indicates that it might not be, or may only be exaggerated ("gossip—which likes to mix the false with the true and from the tiniest grain of fact swells through its own lies," 9.137–139). Again, like Procris, Deianira believes the gossip, and she goes to pieces, recovers (9.141–143), and plans a course of action in a brief soliloquy (9.143–151).

After surveying the possibilities, from hysterics, to going home to her family, to murdering Iole, Deianira decides to send Hercules through the servant Lichas "the tunic stained with Nessus' poisoned blood, hoping it would revive his dying love for her" (9.153–157).

Ovid describes the effect of the poisoned garment on Hercules in all its gory detail (9.159–175) and with the same gusto we saw in his description of Apollo's torture of Marsyas and Tereus' rape and mutilation of Philomela in book 6 (see nn. 24 and 25), giving us, Galinsky says, "an overdone technical description of the externals of the man's pain without even hinting at the spiritual dimension of the hero and of his suffering" ([1972] 99–100).

Hercules, in his agony, gives a speech (9.176–204), addressing Juno at the beginning, then listing many of his deeds ("Was it for this that I . . . ?" [9.182]), including all of the canonical Twelve Labors (9.184–197; his battle with the centaurs is inserted into the list at 9.191: see Nilsson 213–214). As unlikely, that is, nonnaturalistic, as his soliloquy is, it becomes more so toward the end: "The savage wife of Jove grew weary of giving me orders; I never grew wearing of carrying them out" (9.198–199), recalling Marsyas' equally unlikely statement while being flayed alive (6.385: "Why are you tearing me from myself?" see n. 24). Hercules concludes his speech, "Can anyone still believe the gods exist?" (9.203–204; cf. the famous passage in Euripides' *Heracles Mainomenos*, 1340–46), his denial undercutting his own soon-to-come deification: "The hero who is about to be a god," Galinsky says, "denies the existence of gods" ([1972] 101).

Ovid now leads us through Hercules' final moments before he mounts his funeral pyre, as the hero "stagger[s] along the heights of Mount Oeta, ravaged with pain" (9.204–205), ending with a description of Hercules' brutal slaughter of the hapless Lichas (9.204–229).

Finally, wrecked as he is, Hercules cuts down trees and makes his pyre (he is, after all, Hercules), gives Philoctetes (as in Sophocles, *Philoctetes* 799–803), not Philoctetes' father, Poeas (as traditionally: see Apollodorus 2.7.7), his bow and arrows and orders him to light the fire, spreads out his lion's skin, and lies upon it, with his head resting on his club, "looking for all the world," Ovid says, addressing him, "as though you were reclining at a dinner among cups full of wine with a garland on your head" (9.229–238; "the key image of feasting," Feeney says [206]). The fire envelops the pyre and begins "to lick at the limbs of Hercules, who lay composed, contemptuous of the flames" (9.239–241).

And now the scene changes to heaven, where Jupiter addresses the gods, who are already worried about Hercules, announces the hero's apotheosis, and mildly threatens Juno (9.241–261). This "second divine council," Feeney says, recapitulates "the poem's first analogy" (that is, the divine council at 1.177ff.), and "[t]he new senatorial procedure of Augustan times surfaces once more, as Jupiter commends his son to the gathering, utilizing the jargon of imperial apotheosis" (206–207): "Gods and goddesses, I am pleased to see that you are afraid for Hercules, and I am also pleased to be called the father and guide of a remembering people and for my offspring to be the beneficiary of your favor. For though your concern stems from his great achievements, since I'm his father I am in your debt, nevertheless" (9.243–248).

Meanwhile, Hercules, the mortal part of him, has burned away, leaving "only the signs of his father, Jove" (9.262–265). Ovid compares the deified Hercules to a snake that sheds its skin and "is young again and revels in its new and glistening body— so Hercules, when he lost his mortal flesh, grew strong in the better part of himself" (9.266–269). Although snakes in classical antiquity have "revered associations," they also "connote destruction and treachery," Anderson observes, and so the simile is "ambiguous" ([1972] at 9.266–267, 435). The phrase in italics, "grew strong *in the better part of himself*" (*parte sui meliore,* 9.269), will be repeated virtually verbatim in Ovid's prediction at 15.875 of his own future apotheosis through poetry "*The better part of me (parte . . . meliore mei)* will be carried up and fixed beyond the stars forever" (Kenney

[1986] 428). Hercules, now a god, Ovid says, becomes "an awesome, august, weighty figure" (9.270), the phrase *augusta . . . gravitate,* sc. *verendus,* repeated from the narrator's description of the gods as Minerva represents them in her tapestry at 6.73: there the deities "sit in august majesty" (*augusta gravitate sedent;* see n. 22). Hercules, Feeney says, "is moving into the sphere of Minerva's gods. . . . The divine-human analogies of both divine councils allow the adjective's [that is, *augusta's*] force to spill over from the gods to Augustus, and back again" (207, moreover, Augustus "was often thought of as another Hercules": Fränkel 212 n. 24).

Hercules' apotheosis is the first of four in the *Metamorphoses,* followed by those of Aeneas and Romulus in book 14 and Julius Caesar in book 15, a progression of mounting importance to Ovid's Rome. (The poet's own predicted metamorphosis at 15.871–879 may be a fifth.) Barkan notes that apotheosis in the poem "is a metamorphosis that denies metamorphosis, producing a transfigured form of the individual that is and is not the human self." In all four apotheoses, "the destination . . . is the removal of all the physicality and particularity that makes metamorphosis possible," and the figures apotheosized "become their own distilled essence when they enter the realm of the gods" (82). Ovid likewise in "a metamorphosis that denies metamorphosis" at the end of the work becomes his "own distilled essence," becomes his poem.

34. After his account of Hercules' death and apotheosis, Ovid narrates a series of shorter tales (9.273–453) on his way to the Byblis episode (9.454–665), the "major story" of the book (Anderson [1972], at 9.450–665, 449), and that of Iphis (9.666–797). These brief tales (three of which are embedded narratives), "assembled with attention-grabbing ingenuity" (Solodow 43), are for the most part an intertwined sequence about parents and children (Anderson [1972] at 9.394–417, 445) and function as a lengthy transition of larger than usual "stepping stones" (n. 3). Now that Hercules' widow, Iole, is married to the hero's son Hyllus, Hercules' grieving mother, Alcmena, has someone to talk to, and she tells Iole about the birth of her famous son, which Juno tried to prevent, and about the helping role played by Alcmena's servant Galanthis, whom Juno turned into a weasel as punishment for tricking the goddess of childbirth into letting the birth take place (9.273–323; this is the first embedded narrative).

Kenney notes the close juxtapositions of Hercules' death with his birth and his transformation into a god with Galanthis' metamorphosis into a weasel: "The hero's parting role . . . is thus to provide an anticlimactic transition to the short episodes which preface the story of Byblis" ([1986] 428).

Alcmena's "difficult labor," Nagle observes, "is the unique case of a first-person account by a victim of the combination of Jupiter's *amor* and Juno's consequent *ira;* victims like Callisto, who are transformed into animals [2.401–530], are unable to tell their own story; the conclusion of Alcmena's tale includes a displaced version of that pattern, in the primitive transformation of her loyal maidservant Galanthis" ([1989a] 112–113). Juno considers Galanthis' crimes to be "(1) verbal deceit, (2) allowing a hated birth to occur, and (3) laughing at the thwarted godhead. The invention of the weasel's freakish habit, perpetuated through an eternity of weasels, captures all these crimes at once by uniting the organs of speech and parturition and through that union by producing what is in some respects a ludicrous freakish creature" (Barkan 67).

Iole responds with a tale that she says is even sadder (Nagle refers to Iole's "transitional gambit of one-upmanship": [1989a] 113) about her half-sister Dryope, who was turned into a lotus tree (9.325–393; this is the second embedded narrative). This is a richer and more complex story than the one told by Alcmena. Lotis, the nymph changed into a lotus tree to escape the lust of Priapus (9.346–348), is "a 'doublet' of Daphne . . . and Syrinx" (Kenney [1986] 428). Daphne's fate is likewise verbally echoed in Dryope's (Segal [1969a] 36): at 1.556 Ovid says of Daphne, "[the tree] shrank from [Apollo's] kisses, even though it was a tree" (*refugit tamen oscula lignum*); at 9.365 Dryope's family "kissed the trunk, still warm" (*tepido dant oscula ligno*). The "sexual violence" that "affects . . . Priapus' immediate victim, the nymph Lotis, . . . lives on," Segal notes, "to reach indirectly those . . . free from such attacks." When Dryope plucks the flower, although her intent is "innocent and . . . maternal," she "symbolically reenacts that earlier violence, and so . . . herself suffers the vengeance which the defenceless Lotis could not exact from the lustful powers which pursued her" ([1969a] 37–38). It is as if the lotus possesses the stored-up energy of metamorphosis, born of the nymph Lotis' rage, and that energy infects Dryope when she plucks the flower and turns her into a lotus, too.

As Dryope is changed, her mouth, Ovid tells us, "ceased to exist at the moment she ceased to speak" (9.392). Ovid has here equated talking with living and calls attention to the linkage by saying *when* Dryope ceased speaking, her mouth ceased to exist. As Solodow notes, for Ovid, "[l]ife, or at least the life of an individual self, is practically coextensive with talk. In Ovid's rhetorical view of life, discourse creates identity" (190).

Just as Iole concludes her story, a rejuvenated Iolaus suddenly materializes in the doorway, his appearance termed "something very strange" (*res nova,* 9.397), a phrase that provides a tenuous link to Iole's "wondrous tale" (*factum mirabile,* 9.394). The now deified Hercules, Ovid explains (9.400–401), had persuaded his new goddess wife, Hebe (whose name in Greek means "youth"), thus to reward his former charioteer (Iolaus as Hercules' charioteer: Apollodorus 2.5.2; Iolaus also participated in the Calydonian boar hunt: 8.310). This mini-episode thus serves as a transition to the next tale, for Hebe is about to swear that she will never make anyone else young again, when Themis intervenes (9.401–403) and, to explain her intervention, gives a lengthy and complicated prophecy to the reader (9.403–417; this is the third embedded narrative in the series, a "*future tense* narrative," Nagle notes [her emphasis], like that of Ocyrhoe at 2.642–654, both being prophecies [(1989a) 113]).

The narrative goal, lest we forget, is the story of Byblis, yet to come; the narrative thread, introduced by the appearance of Iolaus, is rejuvenation, but the way to the goal is complicated. Themis' prophecy begins with reference to the war of the Seven Against Thebes and some of its principals (9.403ff.), including the two sons of ruined Oedipus, Polynices, attacking Thebes as a member of the expedition of the Seven, and Eteocles, defending Thebes. Their conflict for the throne vacated by their father creates the "civil war" Themis refers to at 9.403–404. Themis also mentions Capaneus and Amphiaraus, also members of the Seven, and Amphiaraus' son Alcmaeon, who kills his mother, Eriphyle, to avenge her earlier betrayal of his father (and her husband), Amphiaraus, and because she intended to kill him. Alcmaeon is eventually killed himself on the order of his former father-in-law, Phegeus. Alcmaeon's two sons by his second wife, Callirhoe, avenge their father's murder after the years "taken" from Iolaus to rejuvenate him are added to theirs and they instantly mature. (See Apollodorus 3.6.2, 3.6.8, and 3.7.5–7, for a clearer telling of the story of Amphiaraus, Alcmaeon, and Alcmaeon's sons which Themis refers to so elliptically.)

In the episode that continues from Themis' prophecy (9.418–453), various gods, having heard Themis, demand the same gift (rejuvenation, not instant aging) for their favorites, until Jupiter quells their clamor by telling the gods that it is all done by fate, that both they and he are ruled by fate, and that thus his sons, Aeacus, Rhadamanthus, and Minos, have had to grow old. They are now (as the gods see) "weary with age, Minos especially" (9.440–441).

We have now nearly reached our narrative goal, for Minos (who, readers remember, is king of Crete), "old and feeble," fears an insurrection against himself led by his subject Miletus, but Miletus voluntarily exiles himself from Crete, founds a city on the coast of Asia Minor (southeast of the island of Samos) that he names for himself, and soon has twin children by Cyanee, the daughter of the river Meander, named Byblis and Caunus (9.443–453), the subjects of the next (and our long-awaited) story.

35. Ovid makes the transition to the story of Byblis and her incestuous passion for her twin brother, Caunus (9.454–665), through a series of links: from Jupiter and Minos (father and son), thence to Minos and Miletus (king and subject), and then to Miletus and Byblis and Caunus (father and children: 9.434–453). This is the third of a series of five stories about women struggling with powerful passions that wreck their lives. (See n. 26.)

The Byblis episode is often discussed in tandem with the last in the series, the story of Myrrha, also the victim of an incestuous passion, for her father, Cinyras (10.298–502). They are both of nearly equal length, as Nagle observes, the earlier having 212 lines, the later 205 lines ([1983] 304). Byblis' incestuous desire for her brother is never consummated, however, whereas Myrrha's for her father is consummated, and they make love many times. "The darkest shades, the worst horrors, of incest are reserved for the *Myrrha* episode to come," Otis says (225). Anderson ([1972] at 9.630–632, 461) notes a precise verbal link between the two tales. At 9.630 Ovid speaks of Byblis thus *incertae tanta est dicordia mentis* ("So great is the conflict in a confused heart"), and at 10.445 he says of Myrrha *tanta est discordia mentis* ("so great was the conflict in her mind"; variations in translations are due to differences in context). In both stories, Galinsky observes, "the inner conflict of the heroines" is expressed "in monologues . . . that have many motifs in common." Both heroines, moreover, act similarly: they "leave their homeland . . . , wander through exotic lands . . . , and sink down exhausted prior to their metamorphosis." Yet the two narratives have many differences, as Galinsky notes: (1) Myrrha is fully aware of her impious love when she begins her monologue, while Byblis is not; (2) Byblis' monologue ends with a decision, but Myrrha's does not; (3) Byblis is the single protagonist in her story, while there are at least three central characters in the Myrrha episode (Myrrha's father, Cinyras, and the Nurse, in addition to Myrrha); (4) the Byblis story lacks a confrontation between two persons, whereas the Myrrha story has several; (5) external events (in contrast to inner conflict) are given more space in the Myrrha episode than in the Byblis episode; and (6) the descriptions of the two girls' metamorphoses are totally different ([1975] 88–89).

A certain moralizing tone has crept into critics' reading of the Byblis episode. Nagle, for example, contends that Byblis "does not seem to deserve the sympathy Ovid shows her" ([1983] 309). Otis is more fulsome and stringent in his criticism of Byblis: she overcomes her shame (*pudor*) through "fluid sophistry," for in her monologue (9.474–516), he says, "[a] . . . question of morality has quickly become only a question of strategy" (219). Kenney, however, notes—correctly, in my view—that while Ovid does indeed seem "overtly to declare the moral" of the story at the beginning, when he says, "Now, Byblis is a warning to girls to fall in love in the way that's allowed, the normal way" (9.454), here "his tongue is firmly in his cheek" ([1986] 429–430).

What is striking about Byblis, to me, at least, is her ordinariness, particularly in comparison with the heroines of the first two episodes in the set of five, Medea, a sorceress with magical powers; and Scylla, a princess who falls in love with the commanding general of an army besieging her father the king's city and steals her father's magical lock of hair, which enables him to remain powerful, to give it to the general to win his love. Neither Byblis nor the context of her story has any such exotic characteristic: she could be the girl next door.

Ovid describes her passion for her brother as a thing that grows inside her without her knowledge: to her, her affection for Caunus seems totally innocent at first (9.457–465). Then her love for him, continuing to grow within her like, one is tempted to say, a cancer, begins to take possession of her, again without her full awareness of it—at least when she is awake (9.466–469). Her passion enters her dreams, where she makes love to her brother and even seems to have orgasms (9.469–484). It then crosses into her conscious, waking mind by the bridge of memory ("How delicious to remember!—though the pleasure was too brief and the night went by too swiftly" 9.485–486). Next, Byblis, fully conscious of her passion, enlists her mind, which Ovid earlier described as "divided and confused" (9.473: *dubia . . . mente*), to achieve her passion's goal, its fulfillment. This "outer" process, by which her passion works to control her (in contrast to the "inner" process, which used her dreams), is one of rationalization and is expressed, appropriately enough, in a spoken-aloud monologue (9.487–516): "If only I could change my name and marry you [that is, Caunus]!'" Byblis begins (9.487). "'What stops us is the one thing we shall always share'" (4.494), that is, their brother-sister relationship. The first rationalization, the "biblical" precedent (and authorization), so to speak, deals with that: "'But the gods have certainly made love to *their* sisters'" (9.497–499, with examples). This is, however, a back-and-forth, binary, or *men / de* process. "'Why am I trying to make human ways correspond to the gods' ways, which are different?'" (9.500–501). Little by little, three steps forward, two steps back, her passion for her brother advances through her conscious mind. She has imagined—dreamed of—making love to him. Now she must think about it from *his* side, must think about his making love to her: "'Yet *this* is something two must want to do! Suppose I'm eager to do it. It will seem wicked to him'" (9.505–506). Then the two steps back. "'Where did this example [the sons of Aeolus sleeping with their sisters: 9.507] come from? . . . What is wrong with me? Leave me alone, obscene passion'" (9.508–510). But again, three steps forward: if he had fallen in love with her first, she could give herself to her passion for him (9.511–512). But then, by twisted logic that isn't three steps forward but fancy footwork, she says: "'Shall I, then—since I wouldn't have rejected him had he made advances to me—shall I myself, then, make advances to him? . . . Will you be able to confess your love?'" (9.513–514). The engine of her passion drives her over this last obstacle, thrown up by her mind, to the next step: "'Love will force me to! . . . a secret letter will confess my hidden passion'" (9.515–516). To emphasize her passion's triumph, in the first line after Byblis' monologue Ovid says, "She liked this idea, it overcame *her divided and confused mind*" (9.517), using the same phrase (*dubiam . . . mentem*) that he had used shortly before the monologue began in describing Byblis' reaction to her sexual dreams: "trying to dream her dream again and, *divided and confused in her mind,* [she] would cry out" (9.472–473; *dubia . . . mente,* 9.473).

Byblis' passion, having seized her mind, advances to the next front, that is, out of her conscious mind, itself "external" to her sleeping and dreaming mind, to what, *mutatis mutandis,* we might call "hard, cold print," a letter. The final "campaign" of her passion at first meets resistance: "She starts, then stops; she writes, then rejects what she has written. . . . She doesn't know what she wants to say" (9.523–526). Then, after writing "'Your sister'" but erasing it—it is obviously a wrong way to begin (9.528–529)—she, or rather her passion, is off and running (9.530ff.), initially referring to herself anonymously as "'a lover'" (*amans,* 9.531).

Her passion's final campaign, though crucial to victory, is doomed. Emboldened by early success, it has overreached, and total and disastrous defeat is in the offing.

Byblis' statement in her letter, "'Leave questions of morality to old men; let them investigate what's allowed, what's right and what's wrong, let them uphold the fine points of the law'" (9.551–552), repeats a theme, Kenney says, that Ovid had "handled as a boy in one of his practice declamations" ([1986] 430), as we know from Seneca, *Controversiae* 2.2.10, and that readers of Catullus will recognize: "Let us estimate the talk of disapproving old men, all of it, as worth but a single *as*" (5.2–3).

A servant delivers the letter to Caunus, and he begins to read it but (predictably), "instantly enraged, hurl[s] it from himself" (9.574–575). He barely restrains himself from killing the servant, who reports Caunus' reaction to Byblis (9.576–581). Shocked at first, Byblis recovers, her passion intact and strong (9.581–584), and then in a final soliloquy (9.585–629) replays her actions and in an almost lawyerly way plans her next step. With perfect hindsight she now sees that the letter was a mistake: "'I should at least have spoken myself instead of confiding my feelings in a letter,'" she says (9.601–602); but, as Kenney notes ([1986] 430), this is an "ironical" statement, for Byblis "had followed Ovid's own advice to the lover to plead his cause first by a letter" (at *Ars Amatoria* 1.435ff.). She should have given some hints beforehand, in order to test Caunus' reaction. She now recognizes that dropping the tablet as she handed it to the servant was a "clear omen" (9.595–597, see 9.571–572). She should have approached Caunus directly, person to person. Perhaps it was the servant's fault. In any event, she must try again—Caunus "'wasn't born from a tigress; he doesn't have a heart made of stone'" (9.613–615). Moreover (her keenest lawyerly insight), though it would have been better never to have told Caunus of her passion for him, she cannot now undo what she has done, and since Caunus will never be able to forget this, there is no point in repudiating her feelings for him, for in doing so she will make it seem (to Caunus) that she "'wanted him in a casual way'" (9.622) or was testing him or even trying to entrap him. She ends with a clear, cold, realistic, and accurate appraisal: "'I cannot avoid the fact that I did a wicked thing: I made advances to him in a letter. My passion stands revealed, and though I go no further, I cannot be called innocent. And so I may as well go after what I want; I have nothing left to lose'" (9.626–629; the final line is a marvel: *quod superest, multum est in vota, in crimina parvum*).

Byblis embraces her passion and openly and literally pursues Caunus until, in Lycia, on the southern coast of Asia Minor (and a long, long way from her home in Miletus), "you fell," Ovid says in an apostrophe, "exhausted from pursuing Caunus, and there you lay" (9.630–651; quotation at 9.649–651). With the apostrophe, Anderson says, the poet "draws us into the scene and extracts sympathy for the dying girl" ([1972] at 9.649–651, 462). As she lies there, she soaks the grass "with a river of tears," and beneath it water nymphs create a spring (9.656–658), into which she is transformed. "[W]ater," Parry observes, "is the last refuge of virginity," that is, "[s]ometimes metamorphosis into water provides asylum for the preservation of virginity" (279), a highly ironical outcome in the case of Byblis, for the last thing she wanted to do was to preserve her virginity.

The place where Byblis collapses, Segal says, is "a typical *locus amoenus*" and in her metamorphosis "Byblis herself *becomes* [his emphasis] one of those mysterious, latently violent settings which usually frame tales of disastrous passion: a flowing spring under a tree, a removed and tranquil spot" ([1969a] 32).

36. Ovid "affects . . . a casual transition" (at 9.666–668) from the story of Byblis to that of Iphis (9.666–797), "as if nothing connected [them] except the vague possibility that news might have spread from Miletus to Crete" (Anderson [1972] at 9.666–668, 465). What does connect them, of course, is that this episode is, like the story of Byblis, another tale of "aberrant sexual impulse," as Feeney says (195), along with the Myrrha narrative in book 10. (More on parallels between Byblis and Iphis below.)

Ovid with a few strokes of his pen creates the setting in Phaestus where Telethusa, wife of the commoner Ligdus, is about to give birth. Ligdus decrees, sadly and reluctantly, that if his wife bears a girl, the baby must be put to death; he cannot afford to rear a girl (9.675–679). Thus Telethusa is certain to bear a girl. Ligdus' decision, Anderson says, "constitutes one of the stock motifs of New Comedy" ([1972] at 9.673–674, 466). Thus we can also know that everything will turn out all right in the end. That it will is reinforced by Telethusa's dream just before she gives birth, in which the Egyptian goddess Isis (referred to as Io at 9.687; Isis is often identified with Io, as Anderson notes [(1972) at 9.684–688, 466]) tells her to ignore Ligdus' command and keep her baby, whatever its sex. "I am a helping goddess," she says, "and I bring aid when asked" (9.699–700). Kenney comments that the cult of Isis "flourished at Rome in Ovid's day [and] women were under her special protection" ([1986] 430). The gods attending Io, or Isis (named at 9.690–694), in Telethusa's dream-vision were depicted variously, Anubis as having a human figure and a dog's or jackal's head; Bubastis, the daughter of Isis and Osiris, as a cat or as a woman with a cat's head; Horus (also known as Harpocrates), the son of Isis and Osiris, as the "ideal child"; and Apis as a bull with a multicolored hide. Osiris, Isis' husband, was murdered by his brother Seth and torn into pieces, which were scattered throughout Egypt, until Isis found them and resurrected him. In the annual ritual commemorating the god's resurrection, Osiris is, as Ovid says, "ceaselessly sought" (9.693) by worshippers in the cult of Isis. (This information about the Isis myth and cult is taken from Anderson [1972] at 9.690–694, 467; Bömer at 9.692, 4.483–484; and Kenney [1986] 431.)

When Telethusa gives birth to a girl, she orders the infant's nurse to rear it as a boy. The nurse is the only person besides Telethusa (and eventually Iphis herself) who knows the baby's true sex. Fortunately, Ligdus chooses a name for the child (her grandfather's) that either sex can bear. The luck continues: Iphis' face "would have been attractive in either sex" (9.704–713; quotation at 9.713). When she turns thirteen, her father arranges for her to marry Ianthe. The two girls had known each other from the time they were small children. Ianthe happily anticipates her wedding day. "Iphis, though," Ovid says, "loved a girl she could never hope to possess" (9.714–725; quotation at 9.724). She laments her fate in a soliloquy (9.726–763) that offers a contrasting parallel to Byblis' monologue (9.487–516).

Unlike Byblis, Iphis does not in her soliloquy seek to rationalize her feeling for Ianthe, whom she has loved since they were both children. Instead, she deplores it as unnatural ("a strange, a monstrous passion," 9.727–728; see also 9.728–730). Whereas Byblis sought examples among the gods (beings at a level above humankind) to justify her love for her brother, Iphis, arguing from "nature," uses animals (beings at a level below humankind) to "prove" the unnaturalness of her love for Ianthe: "'Cows don't fall in love with cows, nor mares with mares,'" and so on (9.731–734). Continuing to stigmatize herself (to the point of absurdity), Iphis calls her passion for Ianthe "wilder," even, than Pasiphaë's for the bull, for the union of woman and bull (she says) was at least a heterosexual one (9.735–740).

Iphis hints at the eventual solution, although she states it as an impossibility: even

Daedalus could not turn her (or Ianthe) into a boy so they could love each other naturally (9.741–744). That is, even the quintessential artist, who "makes nature anew"
(*naturam . . . novat* 8.189), cannot perform a metamorphosis that will make *her* nature
anew. She therefore counsels herself to accept her condition, and while she flirts momentarily with the idea of approaching Ianthe—the "Byblis strategy" ("True, there is
no guard . . . that keeps you from embracing her. . . . She herself won't deny herself to
you," 9.750–752)—she immediately banishes the thought ("But even so, she is not to
be yours," 9.753–754). Although the gods have given her much, although her father,
Ianthe, and Ianthe's father all want this union, "nature does not want it" (*non vult natura,* 9.758), and nature is "[m]ore powerful than all those put together" (9.757–758).

The wedding day approaches; Telethusa postpones it and then postpones it yet again.
When she can delay it no longer, she takes Iphis with her to the temple of Isis, who,
we remember, had appeared to her in a dream just before Iphis was born (9.684–701),
and there prays in desperation to the goddess to help them (9.759–781). Isis changes
Iphis into a boy practically on the spot. What Daedalus could not do, the goddess Isis
can: if "nature does not want it," then Isis will simply change Iphis' nature. Iphis can
now marry Ianthe. They do so and live happily ever after, a literally fabulous ending.

The juxtaposition of the Byblis and Iphis episodes, connected, as Feeney notes, by
"aberrant sexual impulse" (see above), has led to a moralizing interpretation to the
effect, more or less, that Iphis is "rewarded" (gets her wish to have Ianthe) because she
resists "unnatural" desire, whereas Byblis is "punished" (with a metamorphosis downward) because she gives in to "unnatural" desire. Galinsky, for example, contends that

> [Ovid] designed the story of Iphis . . . as a counterpart to the story of Byblis' incestuous
> and doomed love for her brother Caunus . . . by inventing as its focal point Iphis' unnatural
> love for a girl, Ianthe. Besides thus establishing a basic similarity between the two episodes,
> Ovid also links them by working out a strong element of contrast. In the Byblis story,
> human pathology prevails from beginning to end, whereas an atmosphere of piety and
> beneficence reigns in the story of Iphis. Byblis comes to ruin; Iphis does not . . . Iphis' is
> an impossible love which is finally made possible by a god. ([1975] 86)

Barkan notes that Iphis deserves a beneficent (and wish-fulfilling) transformation in
part because of her "moral rigor" and her mother's "piety" (71).

But Byblis' passion for her brother comes upon her as an affliction and isn't recognized for what it is until she is in its grip. She considers this passion not so much
unnatural as socially unacceptable owing to the bad luck that has made Caunus her
brother. She does, in any case, try to resist her passion, for fear of breaking the incest
taboo, so deeply ingrained in her. Iphis herself, while acknowledging that Pasiphaë's
love for the bull was monstrous, says that "it was still a female loving a male" and
asserts that "[m]y passion is more insane than hers" (9.736–738). She, at least, would
hardly condemn Byblis. In fact, by the strict argument from "nature" with which Iphis
condemns her love for Ianthe, Byblis' passion for Caunus is perfectly natural. "Aberrant" (Feeney's term) is, ultimately, too broad-gauged a description to use to link the
two girls and their passion. Byblis could physically make love with Caunus: nature does
not oppose; only society does. Iphis cannot, in terms of her story, make love with Ianthe. For her, to say it isn't "natural" simply means the equipment is lacking. But that is
all that is missing. Ironically, Iphis' love for Ianthe is not only socially acceptable (because of Telethusa's deception), it is socially promoted (by the two girls' fathers).

Although she lacks the natural means to love Ianthe, Iphis has what Barkan calls
"a manifest destiny of masculinity" (71). Her unisex name (9.710), her unisex face
(9.712–713), the fact that she was reared, that is, dressed (9.712), as a boy, her "quite

masculine love for Ianthe," in Barkan's words, "[a]ll these signs of masculinity bespeak a deeper accuracy about Iphis' identity than the fact of her sexual anatomy" (71). All she needs, then, is a sex-change operation, which Isis performs, so to speak, with her metamorphosis. There is no possibility, alas, for Byblis to become "desiblingized" for Caunus by surgery or by metamorphosis. The two girls parallel each other inversely: Byblis faces social condemnation for her passion, although it can be "naturally" consummated; Ianthe has social approval for her passion, although that approval is based on a misapprehension (fathered, or, rather, "mothered," upon her society by Telethusa's deception), but her love cannot be "naturally" consummated. In their respective dilemmas, Byblis is unlucky, Iphis very lucky. Ovid makes no moral judgment. As the most rhetorical of Roman poets, this "prophet of the surface" (Lanham 48) is neither a moralist nor an immoralist. He is, rather, a poet of phenomena, and among the phenomena of life are passions like Byblis' and Iphis' (and those of many others in the poem), along with countless other wondrous happenings in the brilliant, shifting world.

BOOK TEN

37. All of book 10 and book 11.1–193, occurring at the end of part two of the poem, "heroes and heroines" (6.421–11.193), serve as a transition to part three, "'historical' personages" (11.194–15.870), and provide as well a "climax of the *Metamorphoses,* where Ovid is on the point of shifting his focus from the realm of myth [parts one and two of the poem] to the legendary past of the Trojan War and Rome's genesis [part three]" (Stephens [1958b] 293), and so "down to my [Ovid's] own time" (1.4).

This transition to part three is given to Orpheus (all but the last 109 lines, the story of Midas: 11.85–193), "the paradigmatic poet of myth," as Anderson calls him ([1989b] 2), and narrates an account of his life from his marriage to and double loss of Eurydice (10.1–85) to his own death and reunion with his wife in the underworld (11.1–84), these two events framing the song Orpheus sings to an audience composed of trees, beasts, birds (10.143–144), and even stones (11.2). This is "the longest song that, so far as we know, any ancient poet ever imagined for this archetypal poet" (Anderson [1989b] 2).

This transition also shares features with an earlier parallel transition at 4.604–6.420 that comes at the end of part one, "gods" (1.452–6.420). See n. 21 for discussion of the similarities between these two transitions.

Ovid's "local" transition—"local" in the sense of moving from tale to tale rather than from part to part—from the Iphis episode at the end of book 9 to the story of Orpheus and Eurydice at the beginning of book 10 (1–85), is one of his most casual: Hymenaeus attended the wedding of Iphis and Ianthe (9.795–797) and then "flew through the immense sky, making his way from Crete to the land of the Cicones, called by the voice of Orpheus" (10.1–3). The "thematic links" between the two tales, however, are "considerable," as Coleman notes. "The motifs of *pietas* and homosexuality (rejected by Iphis) already look forward not only to Orpheus' recital but to his own situation. Like Pygmalion [10.243–297], Iphis is rewarded by a miracle that converts the unnatural into the normal" (470).

In Virgil's *Aeneid,* the hero Aeneas' journey to the underworld in book 6 as a Trojan refugee concludes the first or Odyssean half of the poem (books 1–6). Following Aeneas' emergence from the underworld as the first Roman at the end of book 6, the second or Iliadic half of the *Aeneid* (books 7–12) begins, in which Aeneas will go to war to establish himself and his Trojan followers, the ancestors of Romans to come, on

Italian soil. So, too, in Ovid's less symmetrical but nevertheless carefully ordered poem, which in its own way comments on the *Aeneid,* Orpheus, the "archetypal poet" and "paradigmatic poet of myth," as Anderson calls him (see above), enters the underworld at the climax, the turning point, of the poem on a mission of love, to recover his wife, Eurydice, and emerges with his mission a failure, the miracle he performed in persuading the gods of the underworld to release his wife from the land of the dead undone by his all too human weakness as a lover when he proves unable to abide by the condition set for his wife to return to earth and turns around just before they reach the upper world to see if she is still there behind him.

Now doubly bereft (and the second bereavement is more difficult to bear), Orpheus retreats to the mountains of Thrace, withdraws, in his grief, from heterosexual love, and, alone at first, makes music now only for the natural world, which responds miraculously (like the inhabitants of the underworld), as trees uproot themselves and gather at the place where he sits playing his lyre to listen to his songs (which are embedded narratives) of "boys loved by gods and girls gone mad with forbidden desire and rightly punished for their lust" (10.152–154), as Ovid says, omitting any mention of Orpheus' most striking song, the tale of Pygmalion, the story of whom, in some ways an inverse parallel to Orpheus' own story (see n. 39), can stand as the singer's fantasy of the artist's success against all odds in the matter of love.

At the beginning of book 11, however, Thracian women who are devotees of Bacchus, raving mad as well as angered by Orpheus' rejection of the female sex, violently break into the *locus amoenus* his music has created (complete with its own shade: 10.90), interrupting his personal magical consolation; their Dionysian flutes and other instruments of jarring cacophony drown out the single Apollonian lyre; and the women literally tear the poet apart. His head and his lyre are tossed into the Hebrus River and float downstream, still making music together (11.52–53). Once again in the underworld, this time to stay (and the gods down there can now "[r]ejoice in the death of us both," 10.39), Orpheus finds his Eurydice and, though lyreless now, recovers his lost love.

The story of Orpheus, from his marriage to Eurydice through his death and return to the underworld (10.1–11.66), "provides a good illustration," Coleman says, of a "complex [elaboration] of the inset technique." By separating Orpheus' suffering from his death and inserting between them "a series of stories forming the singer's grief-stricken recital," Ovid indicates that he "intended the whole of this section to be seen as a single organic unit" (466).

Any commentary on Ovid's narration of the myth of Orpheus and Eurydice must mention Virgil's earlier version of the tale in the fourth book of the *Georgics* (453–527), a work of didactic poetry, ostensibly on farming (its title from the Greek word *geôrgica,* "things agricultural") and probably published in 29 B.C. (some thirty years before Ovid began writing the *Metamorphoses*), for, as Knox says, "Ovid's portrayal of Orpheus assumes the background of Vergil's representation" (49). Because of Virgil's earlier version, the later poet "can, as it were, fill in the blanks" (Knox 50), and he does so, for, as Hill observes, "[e]verything that Virgil omits, Ovid dwells upon and everything that Virgil concentrates on, Ovid changes or omits" (125). Thus, in his version of Orpheus and Eurydice, Ovid (but not Virgil) mentions the wedding (10.1–10), Orpheus' meeting with Proserpina and Pluto (10.15–17), his song to them (10.17–39), the effect of his song on the inhabitants of the underworld (10.40–48), Eurydice's dramatic entry (10.48–49), the condition of her return (10.50–52), and the journey back (10.53–55; Anderson [1982b] 37–39 outlines the two versions in parallel columns to illustrate the differences between them).

Ovid also emphasizes Orpheus' conscious decision to enter the underworld (10.11–13); Virgil's Orpheus seems to wander there while singing (*Georgics* 4.464–470).

Both Ovid and Virgil narrate Orpheus' turning around, but they give significantly different reasons for it. Virgil says that a "sudden madness seized the heedless lover" (*subita incautum dementia cepit amantem, Georgics* 4.488), but, as David West comments,

> Ovid makes better sense. In [10.]53 he stresses the steepness of the path . . . , the unbroken silence all about them all this long journey, the darkness, the impenetrable mist. And Eurydice was just a girl . . . , so all of these are not just atmospheric descriptions of landscape, but provide causes for the effects that follow, Orpheus' fear . . . that she might weaken and fail, his eagerness to see her. . . . All these are natural and particular human thoughts and they combine to produce a more particular, sensitive, sympathetic and consistent imagining of Orpheus' mentality than what we find in Virgil. And Ovid crowns it all with a point borrowed from Virgil's *subita . . . dementia cepit amantem . . .* , but transformed by an inexpressible exploitation of Latin word order, *flexit* amans *oculos* [10.57, "turned, loving her, to look," more literally, "turned, loving, his eyes"]. He was a lover. That explains all. (10)

While Virgil's Eurydice "rebukes her husband," Hill notes, "Ovid's is far more understanding" (125), adding, "Whereas Virgil gives a somewhat lofty account, Ovid tries to get inside his character" (127).

Ovid begins his narration with Hymenaeus, the god of marriage, called by Orpheus to his wedding with Eurydice, "though it was a futile summons" (10.1–3). Ovid thus makes it clear that Orpheus' musical genius "cannot secure the happiness of his private life" (Leach 119). The god comes, but brings with him nothing that portends good fortune. Moreover, the wedding torch he carries fills everyone's eyes with smoke and will not ignite (10.4–7). In the very next sentence, which begins, "What happened next was worse than this omen" (10.8), Eurydice is bitten by the snake and dies, the mood here one of "high pathos," intensified by "[t]he contrast with the happy marriage of Iphis and Ianthe, which provides the narrative link between tales and between books" (Segal [1989] 58).

The narrator tells us in the sentence that follows (the fifth, which begins at 10.11) that Orpheus had mourned Eurydice "long enough" (*satis,* 10.11) in the world of the living and "dared" (*est ausus,* 10.13) to descend to the underworld "to work on" (*ne non temptaret,* 10.12; see *OLD* s.v. *tempto* 6) "the shades in the world below." Orpheus' mourning "long enough" has occasioned some commentary, as has his daring to descend to the underworld "to work on" the shades there: "That adverb 'satis' is damning, no matter how one views it," Anderson says, and with it Ovid "scants Orpheus' grief when [Eurydice] first dies: Orpheus laments 'enough' to the upper air!" ([1982b] 40, 47). Segal thinks Ovid is responding to Virgil's version by suggesting "a human limit and measure lacking in the wild grief of Virgil's hero or even parodying Virgil ([1989] 59, 81). Orpheus' decision to go to the underworld is "stated in a self-consciously rhetorical *ne non temptaret* [lest he not work on]" and "sounds more like flamboyance than serious mourning" (Anderson [1972] at 10.1–85, 475), or suggests "timidity and despair," a "more human characterization" of Orpheus (Segal [1989] 59).

It seems to me, though, that Ovid and Orpheus are eager to get to where Eurydice is: the underworld. For Orpheus, Eurydice came and went in the blink of an eye. The first ten lines of book 10 are composed of four sentences of three, two, two, and three lines each. Hymenaeus is called to the wedding, though futilely (1–3). He is present, but brings nothing solemn, happy, or lucky (4–5). The wedding torch will not ignite (6–7). But what happens next is worse: a snake bites the new bride on the ankle as she walks along, and she dies (8–10). The next (fifth) sentence, by contrast, is six-plus lines long (11–17a, if we take the colon after "he said" as a full stop) and narrates the end of Orpheus' mourning in the upper world, his resolve to go down to the under-world and "work on" the shades, his arrival there, where he makes his way through the ghosts and comes before Proserpina and Pluto, the ruling gods there, and strikes introductory chords on his lyre and begins to sing. Orpheus has wept for Eurydice "long enough" in the world of the living, Ovid says, because the bard wants (1) to extend the range of his artful mourning by descending to and appearing in Hades and (2) to plead for Eurydice's return. His mourning among the living is cut short, and his song of grief among them (and reference thereto) is omitted in favor of the song in which he pleads for the return of his wife before the gods of death. The economy of narration in 10.1–17a also allows Ovid to give greater prominence to Orpheus' song in the underworld as a climax of this section of the myth (Primmer 127).

Orpheus' expression of grief—"the greatest song of the greatest mythical singer" (Primmer 129)—is, or begins as, a rhetorical performance, a speech as much as a song (*ait*, "he said" [10.17]; *loqui*, "'[if I may . . .] speak the simple truth'" [10.19–20]; *dicentem*, "as he spoke" [10.40]) and not a spontaneous outpouring: He has a (rhetori-cal) goal, unheard of, really, to win the release of his wife from death by his power of persuasion. It is the performance of his life. And so, what sort of performance is it? How does one go about persuading the gods of the dead? What makes him successful?

While, on the one hand, Orpheus' song (which could equally, perhaps, be called a speech) is formally organized, with the rhetorical characteristics of a courtroom plea (as analyzed by Primmer, clearly and in detail, 129ff., with an outline on 130), on the other hand, "Ovid portrays an Orpheus who wants to make his case with all the re-sources of rhetoric but who loses his skill in speaking when face to face with the powers of death and of love" (Primmer 130–131). That is, he is so overwhelmed by the reality of death that "he begins to deform his speech" (Primmer 131), becoming personal and confessional. "'I wanted to be able to bear it, I won't deny that I've tried to: Love de-feated me'" (10.25–26). As Primmer says, Orpheus stops addressing the judges and "loses himself in his love" (132). He wavers; he doubts that the god of love is known in the underworld, but maybe he is, if the old story (of Pluto's abduction of Proserpina) is not a lie (10.26–29). When he makes a formal supplication (the technical rhetorical term is *obsecratio*), he begins his plea not in the usual way, as Primmer notes, that is, "by all that's dear to you," but, rather, "by what I dread" (132), saying, "'I beg you by this place so full of fear, by this great void and the silence of your vast domain'" (10.29–30). He continues to express his overwhelming realization of death's power and ac-knowledges that death "owns" us all (including Eurydice): he simply "pleads with the 'owners' that they lend back to Eurydice her unfinished years" (Anderson [1972] at 10.37, 478). Orpheus concludes his song with a stubbornness born of despair (Primmer 135). "'And if the fates deny this favor to my wife, I know I do not want to go back up above. Rejoice in the death of us both'" (10.38–39). At this point he is speaking simply as a man, not as a great poet, a man who realizes that while love is the most powerful force in life, the reality of death is more powerful still (Primmer 135).

This interpretation of Orpheus' descent to the underworld runs counter to the views of those critics who would make it a kind of indentured parody of Virgil's narration in the *Georgics*, for example, Otis 184; Galinsky (1975) 250; Anderson (1982b) 36–40; or those who see it as a revolt against Augustan themes in Roman life and literature: Segal (1989) 55, 56, 71. Likewise, my reading of Orpheus' song to the gods of the under-world, derived from Primmer's, runs counter to those of Otis 184, Leach 120, and An-derson (1982b) 40–41; Segal (1989) 82–83, while finding "much to agree with" in

Primmer's reading, still asks whether "Orpheus' 'anti-rhetoric'" may not be "the trump card of a master player at rhetoric."

The abduction of Proserpina by Pluto, which Orpheus refers to in his song (10.27–29), was told by Orpheus' mother, Calliope, in book 5.341–571, and by referring to it "Orpheus in effect," Hinds says, "scrutinises for a moment, by the criteria of poetic truth and falsehood, an earlier portion of the very work of literature in which he himself stands" ([1987] 135).

Orpheus' song brings the underworld to a halt momentarily, or at least stops some of the celebrity sinners, busily carrying out their various eternal punishments (Tantalus; Ixion; Tityus, who is not named but whose liver is mentioned; the daughters of Danaus; and Sisyphus: 10.40–44). The poet is "offering a witty description," Hill says, of "an especially favourable reaction to poetry" (on the part of the sinners) that includes a "grotesque alliteration" in the description of Sisyphus' response (128): "and you, Sisyphus, sat down upon your now still stone" (*inque tuo sedisti, Sisyphe, saxo*, 10.44). The Furies weep, for the first time, "the strangeness of the scene" marked by Ovid's comment at 10.45: "They even say that . . ." (Segal [1989] 61).

Proserpina and Pluto relent and summon Eurydice, who, "[a]mong the recent dead, . . . came, walking slowly, limping from her wound" (10.46–49; "she was some distance from the throne room and had a sore foot," David West 9). They state the condition under which they will let her return with Orpheus to the upper world and the penalty for failure to observe the condition (10.50–52). And "suddenly," says Hill (128), "the mood changes and the young couple are in real earnest"; "the awesome nature of their situation comes home to them; [and] song gives way to *muta silentia*" (10.53: literally, "mute silences"). The story moves swiftly to its dénouement: five lines after Orpheus and Eurydice set out, she is falling back to the underworld (10.53–57, in contrast to the twenty-three lines given to Orpheus' song at 10.17–39; the point is suggested by Anderson [1982b] 47).

Orpheus looks back at Eurydice, "fearing [she] would fail and eager to see her" (10.56). She falls back, each struggles to grasp the other, and Eurydice dies a second time, but does not blame Orpheus (10.57–63; for he turned because he loved her; thus she "understands . . . that the very failure of her spouse is a proof . . . of his love": Segal [1989] 66). She utters a final "'Farewell'" (10.62; "the saddest word there is": David West 10), which her husband can barely hear.

"Orpheus was stunned," Ovid says "by the second death of his wife" (10.64), and the poet describes the bard's state by means of three recherché comparisons that refer to otherwise unknown metamorphoses of three humans into stone (10.64–71). The similes are odd and jarring.

Unable to reenter the underworld, Orpheus withdraws to the mountains of Thrace, where, after three years, he "fled the love of females," either "because it had ended sadly for him [that is, with Eurydice], or because he had vowed to be faithful" (10.79–81). Many women still "longed for unions" with him, the narrator says, "and many grieved when he rejected them" (10.81–82), here foreshadowing the motive for the Thracian women's fatal attack on Orpheus in the next book (11.6ff.).

Orpheus also changes his sexual orientation and, becoming a pederast, introduces pederasty to the Thracians (10.83–85), an aspect of the tradition of Orpheus that Bömer attributes to the Hellenistic writer Phanocles, a source for Ovid's myth of Orpheus (at 10.83, 5.37–38). Ovid implies, without precisely saying so, that this change is the result of Orpheus' grief at the loss of Eurydice, his pledge of fidelity, and his subsequent rejection of the love of women. He will change back, after his death, when he rejoins Eurydice in the underworld (11.61–66), a change that is anticipated in the progression of the stories he tells in his lengthy song, which occupies almost all of the rest of book 10 (148–739).

38. After narrating the death of Eurydice and Orpheus' first manifestation of grief, Ovid leads up to the story of Cyparissus, in which the next section (10.86–142) culminates, by naming the trees that miraculously uproot themselves and come to a treeless, shade-less field—for which they provide instant shade—to listen to Orpheus play his lyre and sing.

Orpheus by his art thus creates for himself a *locus amoenus* or ideal pastoral setting, which is also the locale favored for violence—frequently sexual assault, but not al-ways—in the *Metamorphoses* (Parry passim and Segal [1969a] 76f. and passim), a vic-tim of which Orpheus will become at the beginning of book 11: this poet not only "invites" his own violent death by spurning the love of women (10.79–82), but also reinforces the invitation by providing (by means of his art!) the setting in which (in this poem) a violent death is most likely to occur. In "a final tribute to [Orpheus'] power," however, Bacchus punishes the poet's murderers, the god's Thracian devotees, by turning them into trees (11.67–84), "a metamorphosis that Ovid seems to have in-vented" (Galinsky [1975] 90).

Readers may find the catalogue of twenty-five trees and two kinds of vine (ivy and grapevine) that Ovid recites at 10.90–108 dry and otiose, to say the least, but Pöschl's analysis of this passage shows that the poet has named the trees and arranged them in groups (while brilliantly using the Latin hexameter to mark the arrangement) in such a way as to reflect the situation of the grieving Orpheus. The first and last trees enumer-ated, the Chaonian oak and the cypress, correspond, Pöschl says, for both represent tragic deaths. Chaon was accidentally killed by his brother Helenus while hunting and was changed into a tree ([1968] 394), and Cyparissus accidentally kills the pet stag he loves, as Ovid tells us (10.109–142). These trees know about the deep sorrow one causes oneself, Pöschl continues, and so Orpheus, Chaon, and Cyparissus are bound by mythological references ([1968] 394).

The second type of tree mentioned, poplars (Heliades), and the next-to-last, the um-brella pine, likewise correspond, the former representing the daughters of Helios, who were changed into amber-producing poplars as a result of their endless lamentation for their dead brother Phaethon, as Ovid also tells us (2.340–366), and the latter represent-ing Attis, into which, mourning for Cybele, he was changed. Thus, Pöschl says, two trees bearing mythological references appear at the beginning of the catalogue and two at the end. The four trees framing the catalogue recall mythological events that are related to one another in similar ways: the pair composed of the first and last (the trees that Chaon and Cyparissus became) tragically killed or killing in hunting; the pair composed of the second and next-to-last (the trees that the Heliades and Attis became) grieving unto metamorphosis over loved ones. The guilt of the former pair and the grief of the latter pair reflect Orpheus' fate ([1968] 394–395).

The trees, moreover, are divided into two groups, and the first group is further di-vided into two subgroups (while a similar division in the second group is less clear): (1a) the Chaonian oak through the ilex (10.90–94; ten trees); (1b) the plane tree through the viburnum (10.95–98; eight trees); (2a) ivy, grapevine, and elm (10.99–100; two vines and one tree); and (2b) mountain ash through the umbrella pine (10.101–105; five trees), plus the cypress (10.106–142).

The trees in (1a), Pöschl says, are large and stately (up to the seventh, the "delicate" [*fragiles*, 10.93] hazel); those in (1b) are a quite different kind: they "love water and

create the image of an idyllic landscape," the "genial plane tree" (10.95) evoking the
locus amoenus that is the setting of Plato's *Phaedrus* (229a1–b2) and serving as the Greek
prototype of the famous beech under which Virgil's shepherd Tityrus sings of Amaryllis
at the beginning of the *Eclogues* (*Eclogue* 1.1–5). These "friendlier trees that belong to
the inviting pastoral world" now associate themselves "with the great trees that have a
noble character," but with them we move out of the realm of epic and into that of the
pastoral: the sphere of love is not far away. And, in fact, in (2a) we have "the tender,
affectionate" twining ivy, the symbol of love in Greek and Roman poetry. In (2b),
"stately, beautiful" trees again appear and conclude the list: the palm and the umbrella
pine (the latter the only tree in the catalogue proper to receive three lines: 10.103–105)
elevated through their respective associations, the palm significant as a victory prize
and the umbrella pine (through mythology) associated with the ceremonial and the
sublime. Also, (2a) and (2b) are linked by the ivy and the umbrella pine, which belong
to the sphere of love. Then, at the end, the catalogue returns to the epic sublimity of
the beginning, as the mythological allusions at the beginning are taken up in an elevated
further way, with the result that sublimity and love are joined in a kind of reprise
(Pöschl [1968] 395–398).

The pastoral trees in (1b) provide the bridge from the "more heroic sphere" of (1a)
to the sphere of love, which begins with the ivy in (2a) and is fully realized in Attis,
who has become the umbrella pine, in (2b) and in Cyparissus. The sound of the lines
changes from lyric lightness to darker, slower, serious lines, more pregnant with meaning, when the plants associated with love appear, this change mirroring Orpheus' grieving state. At the beginning the trees respond to the magical lyric beauty of Orpheus'
music by gathering around the bard, and the pastoral trees create a relaxed mood. As
soon as the trees symbolizing love appear, however, the movement becomes slow and
heavy: Orpheus' sorrow is displayed in rhythmical form and the trees share his grief
(Pöschl [1968] 403).

Nagle notes that the "catalogue of trees is also a catalogue of stories" (the laurel and
the lotus created in stories told by Ovid at books 1.452–567 and 9.346–348, respectively, in addition to the already mentioned poplars [formerly Heliades: book 2.340–
366], Chaonian oak, umbrella pine, and cypress), and since the audience was "gener-
ated" by Orpheus' singing, "[t]his audience *for* stories is an audience *of* stories"
([1988a] 119, 120; her emphasis).

Ovid relates the story of the metamorphosis of the boy Cyparissus into the cypress,
the last tree in his catalogue, at 10.106–142 as a transition to and link with the stories
Orpheus (and his character Venus) will tell (10.148–739). The narrative of Cyparissus,
Coleman says, "has particular relevance both to Orpheus' own situation and to one of
the major themes of his recital," that of a lover's causing the accidental death of someone "especially dear" to him (467). This is the "first appearance" of the story, Kenney
tells us, adding that Cyparissus is an "inverse anticipation" of Hyacinthus and Adonis,
"slaying not slain by accident"; that "the mistaken javelin-cast recalls the death of Procris" at 7.840ff.; and that "the motif of the mourning cypress inverts that of the triumphant laurel" at 1.560ff. ([1986] 432–433).

Cyparissus' metamorphosis into the cypress, Solodow says (183), "makes the situation clear in several ways: the boy's grief is manifested in the cypress's gloomy dark
green color (an emotion), Apollo's in the fact that he will weep over it himself (a relation), and it will also be a symbol of death and sorrow to mankind (an association)."

39. Ovid's transition from Cyparissus to Orpheus' song (10.148–739) takes the form
of a summary statement at the end of the catalogue of trees ("Such was the forest of

trees the seer had drawn to himself," 10.143–144), followed by a description of Orpheus tuning his lyre (10.145–147), after which he begins to sing (10.148ff.).

The bard's audience is composed of the aforementioned trees (which provide the necessary shade: 10.90), wild animals, and birds, and stones, too (11.2), that is, the vegetable, animal, and mineral world—all the non-human world (though some of the trees were once human beings) except for fish, who have to wait to hear Orpheus sing until after he is killed and his lyre and severed head float down the river Hebrus, into which his killers toss them. What the fish would hear, if there were any to listen (Ovid, of course, never mentions fish), would be only "some kind of tearful sound" from the lyre and "something tearful" from Orpheus' singing head (11.52–53).

It is an unusual audience, though no more so than the ghosts (including famous sinners) in the underworld and the gods ruling them who heard him there. Orpheus never sings before a living human audience in the poem. The nearest he comes to it is the maddened Thracian women intent on tearing him to pieces, whose ritual racket drowns out his quieter music (11.1–19).

Orpheus' song, an embedded narrative occurring within the long transition from part two of the *Metamorphoses,* "heroes and heroines," to part three, "'historical' personages," parallels the lengthy embedded narrative in the similar transition from part one, "gods," to part two, sung by his mother, the Muse Calliope, at 5.341–661 in a competition with the Pierides, as reported to Minerva by an unnamed Muse who actually re-sings the song Calliope sang, the subject of which was the rape of Proserpina. Orpheus referred to that song in his plea to Pluto and Proserpina for the release of Eurydice (10.27–29). Both embedded narratives contain stories embedded within themselves, Arethusa's autobiographical story in book 5 and Venus' cautionary tale to Adonis at 10.560–707. (See n. 21 for further parallels between these two transitions and the embedded narratives in them.)

Nagle, as stated earlier, notes the connection between the embedded narratives of Calliope in book 5 and Orpheus in book 10, both of which "reflect Ovidian content, themes, and techniques to such an extent that they can be regarded as 'miniatures' of the longer poem" ([1988a] 101; see n. 21). Each of these "miniatures," Nagle says, "is a reprise of the themes of the larger [poem], up to the point at which the miniature occurs. Since Orpheus' cycle occurs later, naturally it recapitulates more themes." In Calliope's song, Nagle continues, we can see "a reprise of divine rape and divine vengeance" (Otis' divisions of the *Metamorphoses,* as she notes; for Otis, see the bibliography). "[T]o these, amatory pathos is added in Orpheus' cycle" ([1988a] 121).

Nagle also notes "a movement in a consistent direction, from divinity [Calliope in book 5] to legendary bard [Orpheus in books 10 and 11] to historical human poet [Ovid himself in his versions of Homer's and Virgil's epics in books 12–14 and in the epilogue at the end of the poem (15.871–879)]." This movement "parallel[s] the chronological movement of the poem through mythical, legendary, and historical periods." Moreover, Nagle adds, "[l]ike his human counterpart [Ovid], Orpheus is mortal; in form and content, his miniature is a more obvious reflection of Ovid's [work]" ([1988a] 122). That is, "[l]ike Ovid, Orpheus uses geography and genealogy as organizing principles. . . . Orpheus' cycle begins, as the Metamorphoses [sic] itself does, with tales of divine *amores.* . . . Next come brief . . . tales of divine vengeance" ([1988a] 112–113). In addition, Knox says, "The sequence of tales [in Orpheus' song] incorporates all of the stylistic devices . . . characteristic of the *Metamorphoses.* The figure of Orpheus as a learned poet . . . is by this time [the conclusion of his song] virtually indistinguishable from Ovid himself" (61–62). Thus the embedded narratives in books 5 and 10 themselves, especially the latter, Orpheus' song, as well as the linkages between them, confirm an emphasis on poetry at these transitional and climactic moments at the end of parts one and two of the *Metamorphoses*.

Note that in quoting Orpheus' song (10.148–739), I shall treat Orpheus as the narrator and enclose in double quotation marks only those parts of his song that are in his voice. Dialogue by other characters within Orpheus' song I shall put in single quotation marks within double quotation marks. Dialogue within dialogue I shall mark with a further set of double quotation marks.

Orpheus commences his song by invoking his mother, the Muse Calliope, to inspire him and announces that he will begin with Jupiter (10.148–149), an "introductory formula" with an "overwheming literary tradition" (Galinsky [1975] 185). The formula is turned on its head, however, for it more appropriately introduces songs sung "in a more solemn key" (10.150), like the epic battle of gods and giants (10.150–151), and not songs with "a lighter melody" (10.152) that the poet will now sing in his new homosexual pose, about "boys loved by gods and girls gone mad with forbidden desire and rightly punished for their lust" (10.152–154), although he does begin with Jupiter (the god's abduction of Trojan Ganymede).

For Orpheus, a "lighter melody" includes a depiction of Jove as searching through the gods' costume shop of metamorphoses, so to speak, for a bird form to put on (so he can fly down to earth) that "wasn't beneath his dignity" (10.157–158) and finding the eagle, the form of which in the mythical tradition the god assumed to carry off Ganymede.

Juno's disapproval (10.161) recalls her suspicion of Jove in the Io episode at book 1.601ff. and "the god['s] amorous embarrassments" there (Segal [1989a] 93), and with the story of Jupiter and Ganymede and the following myth of Apollo and Hyacinthus we see that Orpheus' song, like the *Metamorphoses* itself, "begins . . . with tales of divine *amores*" (Nagle [1988a] 113). The mythical bard's presentation, Jupiter-Ganymede/Apollo-Hyacinthus, moreover, is a chiastic reprise of book 1's Apollo-Daphne/Jupiter-Io and is a sexual reversal as well. (Janan notes that though Daphne has "temporal primacy" ["Apollo's first love was Daphne," 1.452], Hyacinthus has "emotional primacy" ["My father, Apollo, loved you (Hyacinthus) above all others," 10.167]: [1988] 118.)

The connection between stories narrated by Ovid in book 1 and by Orpheus in book 10 implies a connection not only between two parts of the poem but also between their narrators. The linkage between the two poets is further emphasized by Orpheus' story of Apollo and Hyacinthus, which offers an immediate parallel to the just concluded story of Cyparissus, told by Ovid, a parallel inviting us, Nagle says, "to compare Ovid and Orpheus as narrators" ([1989a] 114).

In the story of Apollo's accidental killing of his beloved Hyacinthus, the god's superflung discus, after a long, high flight, falls back to earth and then, when Hyacinthus runs to pick it up, bounces up from the ground and strikes him in the face, a scene worthy of slapstick or a cartoon—except that the blow is fatal. Apollo is as frustrated here ("his medical skills were useless," 10.189; they were similarly useless when he killed Coronis and then repented his action: 2.618) as he was chasing Daphne in book 1; but in the pure Ovidian manner, as Galinsky notes, "seriousness and humor coexist and intermingle," for in Apollo's effort to save his dying beloved and the narrator's comparison of the boy's lolling head to a drooping violet or poppy blossom whose stem has been cut (10.185–195), Ovid presents "one of the most moving scenes of death and suffering in the poem" ([1975] 161, 162).

Unable to revive his dear, dead Hyacinthus, Apollo transforms the boy's blood that had spilled on the ground into the eponymous flower, on whose petals the god inscribes the letters AI AI (10.209–216), the Greek word for "alas" as well as the vocative case of the hero Ajax's name in its Greek spelling, which letters the ancient Greeks and the Romans saw on the petals of the hyacinth. (Orpheus alludes to Ajax at 10.207–208.) The notion of the hyacinth as inscribed with these letters leads Orpheus to extended references to writing (and "authorship"). At 10.198–199 Apollo says, "'My right hand will be *branded* forever with your death'" (emphasis added; *inscribenda . . . est,* lit, "will be inscribed"), adding, "'I'm the reason your life is ending'" (*ego sum tibi funeris auctor,* lit, "I am the author of your death"). At 10.210 Orpheus says, "Hyacinthus' blood had . . . streaked the grass" (*signaverat,* lit., "had marked with a sign")—which marking is the direct cause of the flower, as the sequence of Latin tenses shows: more literally, "[T]he blood that . . . had marked the grass with a sign ceases to be blood" (10.210–211). As Barkan notes, Hyacinthus' "death not only stains the earth but also signs it" (79–80). At 10.215–216 Orpheus says of Apollo, "He himself inscribed [*inscribit*] his lamentations on the petals, tracing the letters 'AI AI' [*AI AI / . . . inscriptum*], on them, spelling out his grief" (*funestaque littera ducta est*). Perhaps Ovid is reminding us, through Orpheus, that the archetypal poet's story, like the signs on the hyacinth, is being *written:* Hyacinthus and Apollo, and Orpheus, too, are Ovid's written creation. (In addition to Barkan, cited above, Janan [1988] 120ff. calls attention to the emphasis on writing here.)

Galinsky notes that the tales of Ganymede and Hyacinthus "provide links to Orpheus' own, homosexual love after the loss of Eurydice," while the stories of Hyacinthus and Adonis "focus attention on Orpheus' loss of his beloved and on his incurable grief" ([1975] 90). Finally, as Knox observes, the story of Apollo and Hyacinthus is balanced by the narration of Venus and Adonis at the end of Orpheus' song: Apollo "deserts his customary haunts in order to be with Hyacinthus" (10.167–170), Knox says, and Venus "abandons her traditional abodes for Adonis" (10.529–532). "[T]ogether these two sections represent" Orpheus' singing of "boys loved by gods" (10.152–153), which the bard announced as half his theme at the beginning of his song (51–52).

The transition from the story of Hyacinthus to the brief tales of the Cerastae and Propoetides is made by "sheer antithesis" (Anderson [1972] at 10.220–242, 493): "Sparta is proud to be the birthplace of Hyacinthus," but Amathus did not want "to give birth to the Propoetides . . . nor to the people" who come to be called Cerastae (10.217–223). With these stories, told in twenty-three lines (10.220–242), the narrator brings us to Cyprus, the "home" of Venus, and to Amathus, one of her cities there, where the story of Pygmalion (10.243–297), for which these stories "serve as foil and introduction" (Kenney [1986] 433), will unfold. The Cerastae (whose name is derived from *keras,* the Greek word for "horn," and thus means "horned," their ultimate condition after Venus turns them into bulls), however unrelated they may be to the theme Orpheus announced for his tales (10.152–154), nevertheless give Ovid the opportunity to specify a use for metamorphosis, for Venus decides to inflict on the Cerastae "'something between death and exile,'" that is, "'the punishment of a changed form'" (10.233–234; Solodow 168ff. maintains that the poem at large rejects metamorphosis as reward or punishment).

According to Ovid, Venus punishes the Propoetides for denying her divinity by turning them into the first prostitutes, the first stage in a metamorphosis that ends with their turning to stone (10.238–242). Ovid introduces the Propoetides as *obscenae* (10.238), which I've translated "whorish" (proleptically, for they aren't yet prostitutes), *contra* Bömer, who, while acknowledging uncertainty about Ovid's usage here, nevertheless prefers to gloss the word with *abominandus,* "to be despised," rather than with *impudicus,* "immoral," "unchaste" (at 10.238, 5.92).

The story of the Propoetides sets the stage for the tale of the sculptor Pygmalion and his creation of an ivory statue of a fabulously beautiful girl with which he falls in love and which eventually comes to life (10.243–297). Pygmalion creates his ivory statue in reaction to the "depraved lives" of the Propoetides and because he is "shocked by all the vices the female mind [is] naturally given to" (10.243–245). Elsner-Sharrock, interpreting Pygmalion's reaction to the Propoetides, comment that he "rejects the positive-aggressive sexuality" of these women and "creates a chaste alternative, yet one which is secretly the fulfilment of his own erotic dream" (170). Pygmalion thus recalls Hermaphroditus, who rejected Salmacis in the flesh, preferring a kind of dreamy sex with a fantasy of Salmacis (that is, her pool) to actually making love with her in person in all her robust sexuality (4.285–388; see n. 17).

The story of Pygmalion is neatly divided into two halves of twenty-seven lines each (10.243–269 and 10.271–297), with Venus standing in the center (10.270), "halving [the episode] into a before-and-after portrait of the artist," the "before" segment reflecting Pygmalion's contempt for women, the "after" section showing the artist's passion transforming cold ivory into warm human flesh (Bauer 12–13). In the first half, Pygmalion, repelled by the Propoetides but tired of living "as a wifeless bachelor" and "sleeping night after night alone, with no one to share his bed," carves from "snow-white ivory" a statue of a woman who is impossibly beautiful and falls in love with it (10.245–249).

The medium itself, "snow-white ivory" (*niveum . . . / . . . ebur,* 10.247–248), "is erotic even before it becomes female," Sharrock says (40), since "ivory" (the adjective, *eburneus*) has erotic associations in elegy and elsewhere, as does "snow-white" (*niveus*).

Another feature of ivory makes it additionally appropriate as the medium for Pygmalion's statue, which will, as a result of his devotion, cross the boundary that separates a cold, white inanimate object from the warm, living human flesh the ivory statue will become. This statue, Ovid (or Orpheus) says, looked like a real girl and wanted to move, "so artfully was the art concealed" (10.250–252; more on the statue's wanting to move below). It is the ivory itself that aids what Elsner-Sharrock call the "deceptivity of realism," for "[i]n Greek and Roman literary tradition, ivory had strong associations with deception," beginning with Penelope's "pun" at *Odyssey* 19.562–567, where, naming the two gates dreams issue from, she says the dreams that flow through the "sawn ivory" (*pristou elephantos,* 19.564) "deceive" (*elephairontai,* 19.565). The most significant example of ivory's association with deception, Elsner-Sharrock note, occurs at *Aeneid* 6.893–898, when Aeneas exits the underworld by means of the ivory gate, through which "[t]he Shades send up to earth false dreams," instead of passing through the gate of horn, which "affords the outlet for genuine apparitions" (Day Lewis, trans., both passages). "In this Homeric-Vergilian tradition," Elsner-Sharrock say, "ivory is liminal—the material for a gate between worlds—just as the *eburnea virgo* ["ivory girl," 10.275] . . . is a liminal woman, a woman who makes the transition from falsehood (*simulati corporis,* 'a simulated body,' 253; *simulacra . . . puellae,* 'the simulacrum of a girl,' 250) to real flesh (*corpus erat!* 'she was flesh!' 289)." A "more corporeal . . . theme" that the Greek and Roman tradition of myth "offered . . . to the deceptivity of ivory" is found in Pelops' ivory shoulder (Pindar, *Olympian* 1.26ff.). Elsner-Sharrock observe that "the ivory shoulder [of Pelops] is not merely an artificial substitute for the real thing: it is also, in the complex context of Pindar's narrative, a symbol for the problematics of true and false stories. Again the theme of ivory as the material of artifice . . . plays upon and points to the poetics of deception" (162–163).

If it weren't for the ivory statue's "modesty" (*reverentia,* 10.251), Orpheus says, "you could believe she . . . would like to move" (10.250–251). Elsner-Sharrock note an "association of prostitutes and sexual movement," that is, responsive movement in intercourse. It is *reverentia,* they say, that "stops the statue behaving like a whore" (172, 173), that is, like the Propoetides (who lacked *reverentia*). But it is Pygmalion who has both given the statue its *reverentia* and made one—a viewer, or us, the readers—"believe" (*credas,* 10.250) that it "would like to move" (*velle moveri,* 10.251). It is Pygmalion, that is, who wants ultimate control over any female's sexuality, who is put off by sexual forwardness or aggression in a female (just as Hermaphroditus is), who wants to be the sole actor ("doer," initiator) in the act of sex.

A parallel to his creator Orpheus in many ways, as various commentators have observed (Viarre 240–242; Galinsky [1975] 87; Segal [1989] 27, 70, 85ff.; Anderson [1989b] 5), Pygmalion marks a kind of progress from his creator's stance: although like Orpheus he rejects women (Viarre 240; Segal [1989] 27, 70; Galinsky [1975] 87), he does not turn to boys because of the Propoetides but simply lives unmarried and sleeps alone. He wants a better kind of woman. His need (or his desire) leads him to new heights of inspiration, and with "wondrous artistry" (*mira . . . arte,* 10.247) he carves an ivory statue and gives it a beauty that, Orpheus says, "no woman could ever be born with" (10.248–249). With this statement Orpheus has now become an art critic and says, in effect, that the statue is the consummate union of art and reality, conforming to the idea of "*l'art-vérité*" in antiquity, as Viarre says (242), a mimesis made in heaven. Pygmalion gazes spellbound (*miratur,* 10.252, echoing *mira,* "wondrous," sc. *arte,* at 10.247) at his work and his passion grows hotter.

Orpheus' creation, Pygmalion, thus responds differently to his provocation (the Propoetides) than Orpheus himself to his own, which was not dissimilar to Pygmalion's, and the bard can learn from his character's response. Because it was but the third year after Eurydice's death, Orpheus had fled, sought refuge from (*refugerat,* 10.79), the love of women, whose *ardor* drove them to seek unions with the bard (10.78–82). Orpheus' experience with Eurydice alive and dead was likewise not dissimilar to Pygmalion's with his ivory statue for the twenty-seven lines before Venus' involvement (at 10.270). In only seven lines (10.4–10) Orpheus is married and widowed. In the underworld, after her husband's song to Proserpina and Pluto, Eurydice, when the gods call her, comes slowly (10.48–49). Orpheus watches her for at least part of that painfully slow approach. But she is a shade, not the flesh-and-blood girl he married. He is in her presence now for perhaps nine lines (10.49–57), two lines longer than it took to marry and to lose her. Viarre describes the parallel between Orpheus and Pygmalion in their respective relations with their beloveds thus: "The first stage of their [Orpheus' and Pygmalion's] journey is a failure [*échec*]: Orpheus turns around; Pygmalion touches his statue, embraces it, is afraid of harming it, and finally, when it doesn't come to life, adorns it like a statue of a goddess" (241). As Anderson says, "[W]hen the artist [Pygmalion] succumbs to the beauty [of the statue] and desires to animate it and possess it in marriage . . . it is as though [he] relives the earlier career of Orpheus, when he desperately loved his dead Eurydice and was ready to risk everything to restore her life" ([1989b] 5).

Later (in book 11), Orpheus is successful with Eurydice, Viarre says, like Pygmalion with his statue-now-become-flesh, although the bard has to die to achieve his success. "One could say that Orpheus is saved by his death—which has something of ritual about it—as Pygmalion [is saved] by his prayer to Aphrodite" (241–242).

In animating his beloved statue in the second half of the tale (10.271–297), Pygmalion realizes the dream of Orpheus, his creator, who wanted to revive Eurydice (Viarre 244; as Sharrock says, "Orpheus makes his creation, Pygmalion, do that which he himself tries to do but fails: bring the beloved to life" [38]). Hence Orpheus' Pygmalion may be said to lead his creator out of the woods figuratively and out of the woods of Thrace literally (it happens at the beginning of book 11), away from his love of boys, which he turned to in his despair, to successful reunion with Eurydice, although his death at the hands of the maddened Thracian women must intervene, for it is the means to that reunion and thus to his success.

About midway through the first half of the episode, Pygmalion begins to kiss his statue and he thinks it kisses him back and believes his fingers sink into real flesh when he touches the statue's limbs (10.256–258). "The very sensuality of the scene," Sharrock tells us, "reminds us, by contrast, that the ivory is hard and cold" (43). Pygmalion gives gifts to the statue, "seashells, smooth stones, small birds, flowers . . . , lilies, gaily decorated balls," and amber (10.259–263). All of these gifts (except for the amber), Sharrock says, are "erotic" (44–45). At the end of this section of the tale, after dressing and undressing the statue (10.263–266), Pygmalion lays it on a bed covered with deep purple sheets and puts soft down pillows under its head, "as though she could feel them" (10.267–269). "An atmosphere of contrasting sensuality and non-sensation is evoked by the flash of purple in the bed-coverings set against the pale ivory woman," Sharrock says, "and the soft feather cushions which she cannot feel" (45).

In the second half of the episode (10.271–297), Pygmalion makes a sacrifice at a festal day for Venus and prays to the gods "—he didn't dare say 'let my wife be the ivory girl,'" but, rather, asks, "'let my wife be *like* the ivory girl'"—and Venus "understood," sensed (*sensit,* 10.277) what he was asking for and gave him a favorable sign (10.273–279). This is Venus' second appearance in the story. In the first, she turns the Propoetides into prostitutes and then into stone (10.238–242). After her first appearance, Pygmalion carves his ivory statue; after her second, he caresses the statue to life, reversing "[t]he fate and the texture, as well as the moral position, of the Propoetides" (Barkan 77).

Pygmalion returns home, lies down on his bed with "the statue of his girl" (*simulacra suae . . . puellae,* 10.280), and begins to kiss it and to caress it, something he has never quite done before (10.280–281). "A change has already begun," Sharrock notes, "for now it is not a statue, or a girl, but a statue of a girl (*his* girl, this time). . . . Although in the 'reality' of our story there is no original for the *simulacrum* to be an image of, the text seduces the reader (and his own love seduces Pygmalion) into thinking, for a moment, that there is" (46).

Pygmalion's caresses (he "felt her breasts with his hands. As he touched them . . . ," 10.282–283), Sharrock says, are "an image of the original 'caress' of the sculptor's tool which first marked out the breast. . . . There are two parallel metamorphoses in this story: one from raw material into statue, the other from statue into woman" (47). The statue softens and turns into flesh, a live, human girl.

The statue's "[v]ivification," Sharrock comments, "is synonymous with sexual arousal." That is, the clause "She seemed to grow warm" (10.281: *visa* [sc. *puella,* 10.280] *tepere est*) "answers" the earlier description of Pygmalion's arousal when, Orpheus says, "liquid fire for the body of the girl that seemed so real poured into his heart" (10.252–253: *haurit / pectore . . . simulati corporis ignes*). When he felt (10.282: *temptat;* also 10.283: *temptatum . . . ebur*) the ivory girl's breasts, they "softened" (10.283: *mollescit*), and their "hardness no longer resisted but yielded to his fingers" (10.283–284: *positoque rigore / subsidit digitis ceditque*). "The touched ivory is seduced ivory," Sharrock says, "which becomes *mollis* [soft], sexually attractive and compliant. . . . The statue ceases to resist Pygmalion's love and is shaped to his erotic art" (47).

Orpheus describes the statue's softening and yielding with a figure that likens the ivory to "beeswax from Hymettus," which, he says, "turns soft in the sun and is worked by the hand and formed into many shapes" (10.284–286). This second metamorphosis (from cold, inert ivory statue into warm, living human girl) is thus "expressed through a simile taken from . . . almost exactly the same means used to effect the first metamorphosis," and the simile's melding of Pygmalion's "erotic and artistic touch . . . connects the two creations," that is, the two metamorphoses (Sharrock 47). At last, "[s]he was real, and alive!" (10.289: *corpus erat!*), and now "the sculpting is complete and the work of art takes on its final shape," Sharrock says; but the action of Pygmalion that makes her come alive also "kindles sexuality" and "arouses her" (48). The statue's metamorphosis, its "vivification," as noted above, "is synonymous with sexual arousal."

The price to be paid for the miraculous metamorphosis, the sexual arousal and all the future lovemaking it promises, is irreversible entry into the world of constant change. "Art is generally used to transform human, transient loveliness into eternal beauty," Jane Miller says, but in this story "the sequence is reversed. The eternal beauty of the statue, once brought to life, must undergo decay and destruction" (213; cf. Helen's weeping when she sees her old woman's wrinkled face in a mirror in Pythagoras' discourse at 15.232–233).

Pygmalion thanks Venus effusively for the statue's coming to life and promptly marries the girl, with the goddess in attendance at the wedding (10.290–295).

One of the parallels between Orpheus and Pygmalion is their ability, through the magical power of their art, to cross boundaries, whether "the boundaries between inert matter and living consciousness" (Segal [1989] 27) that both cross, Orpheus when he moves trees, beasts, birds, and stones with his art, Pygmalion when he animates ivory with his; or Orpheus in his power to cross the divide between life and death as when he enters Hades, still living, moves the denizens there, and persuades the underworld gods with his singing.

Orpheus' creation Pygmalion, who through the metamorphic power of his art creates the ideally beautiful woman in ivory and with the same metamorphic power, now compounded by his passion, brings that ivory statue to life, re-creates his creator's love of women and, through his success in uniting himself with the one he loves, augurs future success for his creator in reuniting with his wife, a reunion that, ironically, is brought about by a group of maddened women in the (now) mistaken belief that Orpheus despises them. Orpheus, we may say, is restored by his own art, which, like Pygmalion's, has taken on a life of its own. (The Pygmalion episode takes on a life of its own because it in no way corresponds to Orpheus' announced themes, but, as it were, goes off in its own direction.)

40. Paphos, the daughter of Pygmalion and his former statue, now flesh-and-blood wife, bears Cinyras ("[t]raditionally the first king to rule in Cyprus": Grimal 103 s.v. *Cinyras*), "who could have been counted among life's lucky ones," Orpheus says, "if only he had been childless" (10.298–299). But he was not; he had a daughter, Myrrha. Ovid thus makes the transition from Pygmalion to the story of his great-granddaughter and her incest with her father, Cinyras, through genealogy (Galinsky [1975] 92), that is, family connectedness (the essence of the episode) and also through a contrary-to-fact condition (Solodow 45) that enables Orpheus to move smoothly into his rhetorical "warning"—"It's a dreadful story I'm about to tell. It's not for you, daughters; and it's

not for you, either, fathers" (10.300)—"rhetorical" because the bard's audience is composed of trees, birds, beasts, and stones, and because the warning repeats the one Ovid issues at the beginning of the story of Byblis at 9.454f. At both places the poet's "tongue is firmly in his cheek" (Kenney [1986] 430, 434). The warning here, however, is much longer, and it is balanced in an "on-the-one-hand-this-but-on-the-other-hand-that" way: "or, if my song is too seductive," Orpheus continues, "don't put any faith in this part of it, don't believe it happened; or if you *do* believe it, then believe the punishment that followed" (10.301–303). Orpheus' warning is thus "finely poised," as Hopkins says. That is, "the narrator register[s] that he is about to tell of events which might ordinarily be thought of as loathsomely sinful, and simultaneously alert[s] his reader to the possibility that this is not the only legitimate way in which they might be envisaged" (789; more on this below).

The story of Myrrha is "the centerpiece of Orpheus' song" (Knox 54) and, at 205 lines (10.298–502), the longest tale Orpheus tells. (For comparison, the next longest, at 148 lines, is the episode of Atalanta and Hippomenes, told by Venus to Adonis at 10.560–707.) This episode is the only one of Orpheus' stories that corresponds to his announced theme of "girls gone mad with forbidden desire and rightly punished for their lust" (10.153–154; see Bömer at 10.154, 5.63).

Ovid marks the climactic moment of the Myrrha narrative in two ways. First, this moment lies athwart the center of Orpheus' song proper (10.447, counting from 10.155, where the story of Ganymede begins, to 10.739, the end of book 10 and Orpheus' song). Next, at 10.446ff. Orpheus begins, "It was the time of night when all is silent, and Boötes has guided his wagon between the two Bears and onto the downward slope. The girl made her way in the dark to her evil deed." The climax of the tale, when Myrrha sets out in the dark, thus coincides with the moment when "[t]he Wagon reaches its highest point, around midnight, and from there turns downward toward its setting" (Haupt-Ehwald at 10.446f., 2.159) and Boötes heads for home. Myrrha also is heading for "home," her father's bed. At that same moment, Orpheus continues, Icarus (known also as Icarius, as in Apollodorus [see below]; he is not the Icarus who was Daedalus' son) hides his face, and his daughter Erigone, "made holy by her pure love for her father," hides hers, too (10.450–451). An "ideal father-daughter pair," Anderson says, after their unjust and unfortunate deaths (Apollodorus 3.14.7), Icarus and Erigone were "honored with places among the stars, Icarus as Bootes or Arctophylax, Erigone as Virgo" ([1972] at 10.448–451, 513).

Orpheus' song itself has been placed in a frame consisting of two sections of about equal length, the account of Orpheus and Eurydice (10.1–85) and the death of Orpheus (11.1–84). Moreover, the entire Orpheus myth (10.1–11.84) serves as the transition from part two to part three of the poem and at a key juncture that one can arguably call the climax of the *Metamorphoses,* as Ovid turns his *carmen perpetuum* and begins his poetical journey "home" toward Rome and his own time (see n. 37).

This ordering of the narrative, both the Orpheus episode and the story of Myrrha within that episode (along with the astronomical coincidence within the tale of Myrrha), tells us that we are at the heart of the work and, with Myrrha, at the heart of the heart of the poem. The story of Myrrha thus has a serious claim to our attention, no less so than the narrative of Pygmalion.

Two additional features of the Myrrha tale deserve to be noticed. They are, first, its multiple linkages with stories outside the song of Orpheus, with Orpheus himself, and within his song; and, second, its emphasis on language, that is, on the meaning and use of words and their power.

As for linkages with stories outside the song of Orpheus, Otis connects Myrrha to Medea, Scylla, Byblis, and Atalanta, all of whom exhibit an inner conflict (expressed in soliloquies) between love and shame (172–173; see n. 26 and also Coleman 468). Otis also includes the story of Myrrha among the narratives of Tereus-Procne-Philomela (6.421–674), Scylla, Byblis, and Ceyx-Alcyone (11.410–748), all of which share the theme of "amatory *pathos*" and have other common characteristics (205–206).

Galinsky links the stories of Byblis and Myrrha through their common subject, incestuous passion, and observes that these two tales are further connected by the warnings that preface them (as Kenney has also noticed; see above), by the fact that the two girls' "inner conflict is set forth in monologues . . . that have many motifs in common," and by the similar settings for their metamorphosis: both characters "leave their homeland . . . , wander through exotic lands . . . , and sink down exhausted prior to their metamorphosis" ([1975] 88; Anderson calls attention to the echo of *incertae tanta est discordia mentis*, "[s]o great is the conflict in a confused heart" [9.630], referring to Byblis, in *tanta est discordia mentis*, "so great was the conflict in her mind" [10.445], which refers to Myrrha: [1972] at 10.440–445, 512–513). Galinsky also sees the Myrrha episode as linked with the story of Pygmalion, "by contrast" (I agree that they are linked, but rather by similarity: see below), and with the story of Venus and Adonis through coincidence "between narrative continuity and thematic connection." Finally, Galinsky observes that "the nature of Myrrha's love is related by contrast to the character of Orpheus' love. . . . By means of this foil, Orpheus' own pure, strong love for Eurydice is idealized even more" ([1975] 89–90).

For Barkan, the Myrrha episode "has much in common with that of Tereus," in that "[c]ategories of human experience are blurred and as a result the individual is left completely unprotected" (63; Anderson [1972] at 10.452–453, 513, notes the screech owl, a bird of ill omen that, as he says, "haunted the wedding of Procne and Tereus" [6.431–432] and now "utter[s] its mournful cry" [10.452–453] as Myrrha stumbles through the dark to her father's bed). Barkan contends, in fact, that "the whole career of love in the middle books of [the] poem revolves around versions of endogamy. To love oneself, one's close family relations, one's own sex, one's own creation: these are the themes that Ovid concentrates on, and he balances them against such examples of exogamy as Scylla and Medea" (91).

These linkages between the Myrrha episode and other tales outside Orpheus' song demonstrate that episode's centrality as well as the interlocking nature of the *Metamorphoses*, a closely woven work. But the Myrrha story resonates more with its local environment and even with "the plight of Orpheus himself," as Coleman notes, through "the excesses of suffering that love can cause [and] the final hovering between life and death," that is, of Eurydice, and also of Myrrha at the time of her metamorphosis (469).

Within the song of Orpheus we find a connection between the Myrrha episode and the other major tales Orpheus narrates, those of Hyacinthus, Pygmalion, Venus and Adonis, and, to a lesser degree, Atalanta, the connection that of one character's obsessive love for another. And between the Pygmalion and Myrrha episodes we find linkage through a particular kind of obsession, incest, and through a particular kind of incest, the passionate love of creator for creation (Pygmalion's case) or creation for creator (Myrrha's case): Pygmalion, Fränkel observes, was "allowed to marry his spiritual daughter, so to speak, [and] Myrrha . . . was gripped by an incestuous passion for her real father" (96, see also 219 n. 68). As Leach, speaking of Myrrha, notes, "The incestuous love of child for father is only a reversal of Pygmalion's passion for the woman he has created by his art" (123). The connection is made specific: Myrrha's prayer at

10.483–487 "for suitable punishment, scrupulously worded," Nagle says, "is comparable, in its own way, to her great-grandfather Pygmalion's carefully worded prayer" at 10.274–276 ([1983] 314). And when Myrrha expresses to her father her wish for a husband "'just like you'" (*similem tibi*, 10.364), she "speaks like her ancestor Pygmalion," who prayed to the gods for a wife "'*like* the ivory girl'" (*similis . . . eburnae*, sc. *virgini*, 10.276), as Viarre notes (239; see also Anderson [1972] at 10.363–367, 507; and especially Elsner-Sharrock 180–181).

As we look back at the story of Pygmalion, now refracted through its thematically related and inverse twin, the Myrrha episode, we may come to realize that after that episode things were not left, as Barkan says, "in such an affirmative condition," for Myrrha's falling in love with her father "leads to an undoing of all the certainties celebrated by the story of Pygmalion" (78). And with the Myrrha narrative as a kind of commentary on the tale of Pygmalion, we may perhaps affirm Pygmalion differently, may at least cease to glorify him at the expense of his great-granddaughter (as Otis 421 and Galinsky [1975] 89 do), and, with more compassion for and less condemnation of Myrrha, see her in a better light. And if metamorphosis is "clarification," "a change which preserves," as Solodow claims (174, 176–183), then Myrrha's transformation into heavenly sweetness, the source thereof, should tell us something in retrospect about Ovid's attitude toward her passion for her father, for I don't think the poet condemns her. Hopkins, moreover, considers it "significant" that Adonis, "the child of her incestuous union, though 'male conceptus' [sic; 10.503: "so unfortunately conceived"], turns out on birth to be 'formosissimus' [sic; 10.522: "most beautiful"]," and he notes "that although the myrrh tree into which Myrrha is transformed is twisted and weeping it is also beautiful and fragrantly-perfumed, part of the fabled sumptuous opulence of Arabia" (789). Adonis is anointed with his mother's sweetness, the myrrh tree's tears (10.513–514), and so is prepared to become the lover of Venus, the goddess of love, as the incest link is extended to the very heart of love itself. For Adonis, Orpheus says, in the most stunning compression of time in the poem, "the son of his own sister and grandfather, enclosed in a tree till recently, a newborn infant a moment ago, just now a most beautiful baby, already a boy, now a young man, now even more beautiful than himself . . . now . . . delights the eye even of Venus, and avenges his mother's passion" (10.520–524; Venus' son Cupid denied that Myrrha's passion was his doing [10.311–312]). Adonis looks just like Cupid, though (10.515–518), and "[w]hen Venus falls in love with him [as the result of Cupid's kissing her, for one of Cupid's arrows grazed her breast (10.525–526)] she continues the pattern of incest" (Galinsky [1975] 102).

A second noteworthy feature of the Myrrha episode is the theme of language, that is, the meaning, use, and power of words. This theme extends through the tale. It manifests itself in word-plays; in linguistic paradox; in the truth, falsity, or double meaning of words; and in the striking recurrence of the word *nomen* ("name," that is, what a word signifies), used to focus on key words—"father" and "daughter," for example.

Toward the end of her monologue (10.320–355), Myrrha asks herself, "'Don't you realize . . . how many names [*nomina*, 10.346] you're confusing? Will you become your mother's rival and your father's mistress? Will you be called the sister of your son and the mother of your brother?'" (10.346–348). Commenting on *nomina* here, Anderson says Myrrha "has longed to deny the reality of these absolute words [that indicate relations, such as "father," "daughter"] and produce a new, changed reality" ([1972] at 10.345–346, 506).

At 10.363–367 Cinyras fails to understand Myrrha's double entendre, "'Someone just like you,'" when he asks her what kind of man she wants to marry, and says, "'I hope you will always be such a loving daughter!' At the words 'loving daughter,' Myrrha dropped her eyes" (*pietatis nomine dicto,* 10.366, lit., "the *nomen* '*pietas*' having been said"). Myrrha's words, "'Someone just like you,'" alter the conventional meaning of *pietas,* but only because in this particular context they evince a kind of excessive *pietas.*

At 10.401–403 the nurse, trying to comfort Myrrha, tells her, "'Both your mother and father are still alive. . . .' At the word 'father' Myrrha heaved a deep sigh" (*patre audito,* 10.402, lit., "father having been heard," the equivalent of *nomine patris audito,* lit., "the name 'father' having been heard"). At 10.438–439 the nurse tells Cinyras that "he was someone's true love—and gave a false name" (*nomine mentito,* 10.439, lit., "with the name fabricated"). At 10.467–468, after Myrrha, fearful, has entered her father's bed, Cinyras tries to reassure her: "Perhaps, too," Orpheus says, "since she was so young [*aetatis . . . nomine,* 10.467, lit., "because of the name of her age"], he called her 'daughter' [*filia*], and she called him 'father' [*pater*]—lest their sin lack names" (*sceleri ne nomina desint,* 10.468, lit., "lest names be lacking to their crime"), the "names" indicating that their "sin" or crime is incest. But more is at issue here than incest: Ovid's Roman hearers and readers would have shuddered at this use of "daughter" and "father" in these lines because, as Hopkins points out, "the festival of Ceres, at which Cinyras' wife [and Myrrha's mother] is officiating" while father and daughter consummate their union, "was . . . dedicated to the celebration of the intimacy of the bond between mother and daughter. On this occasion it was specifically forbidden for fathers to be mentioned: the very words 'pater' and 'filia' . . . were under interdict" (794).

Finally (for the repetition of *nomen*), at the end of the episode, after Myrrha has been changed into the myrrh tree, Orpheus says, "But there is honor even for tears, and now from the bark myrrh drips—and keeps its mistress' name" (10.502, *nomen erile tenet*), an ordinary enough comment, but in a context stressing *nomina,* "a key to the essences" (Barkan 64), the "distillation," of Myrrha, all she is and has done, is myrrh, the precious, divinely fragrant substance.

In addition to the multiple uses of *nomen* throughout the story, linguistic paradoxes and plays on words abound. "It's a sin to hate one's father," Orpheus as narrator says, "but love like this is a greater sin than hatred" (10.314–315): thus, love = sin. A host of suitors arrives to vie for Myrrha's hand. "Choose one man from all these to be your husband, Myrrha," Orpheus says, "provided that one man is not among all these" (10.317–318).

Myrrha wrestles with *pietas* (difficult to translate, but here rendered as "family ties"): "'But it's not true that family ties condemn this kind of love,'" she exclaims at 10.323–324 (*sed enim damnare negatur / hanc Venerem pietas*), that is, she would like to change the meaning of the word.

Myrrha struggles with the intractability of language, its refractory nature, the refusal of words to mean what you want them to mean, their sticking as signifier to some basic signified (to create meaning, signification). This feature of language leads her in her monologue to invoke "natural law" when she notes that the parent-child relation does not constrain animals from copulating (10.324–331). In the great debate about natural law in fifth-century B.C. Athens, there was, in fact, as Hopkins notes, an "alternative tradition" that "appealed to the precedent of animal behaviour for the 'natural laws' which would govern human conduct" (791; see also Guthrie 104: "The bestial criterion of natural behaviour [taking animals as models] was also known in the fifth century"). "[B]y revealing in [Myrrha, in this section of her soliloquy] the workings of the conflicting claims of Natural Law," Hopkins observes, "Ovid creates sympathy for [her] predicament" (791). The poet also, Hopkins continues, by "[t]he witty poise of his treatment" (at 10.323–333), alerts us "to the reality of the problem encapsulated in Myrrha's predicament," enabling us "to maintain a complex attitude to the girl [and] never laps[e] into a position of simple approval or disapproval" (791).

In her discussion with herself, that is, in her soliloquy, Myrrha also notes (10.331–333) that in some countries parents and children of the opposite sex mate without compunction, "'and family ties [*pietas*] are strengthened by this doubled love'" (*geminato . . . amore,* 10.333; Ovid, Hopkins says, "would certainly have known about the reality of the incestuous unions of Persia and Egypt" [792]). For her, the names of things are the problem, the cause of what is wrong, even including, in one example, their inflected endings: "'And so, if I were not the daughter *of* great Cinyras, Cinyras I could sleep *with,*'" she says (10.337–338), playing upon Latin's use of the suffix *-ae* to form both the genitive and dative singular of first-declension nouns (*Cinyrae, Cinyrae,* 10.338), the juxtaposition suggesting that her problem would be solved if only the genitive and dative cases of her father's name had different suffixes.

At 10.463–464 the nurse says to Cinyras, as she offers Myrrha to him in the dark, "'Take her, Cinyras, she's all yours'" (*accipe,* . . . */ ista tua est*). "Here," Janan says, "*tua* means *both* daughter *and* lover—the linguistic realization of incest. *Ista* further underlines the doubleness; its etymological meaning is 'that one of yours,' so that the nurse ends up saying redundantly, 'Take her, Cinyras, that one of yours is yours'—as Myrrha redundantly is" ([1988] 128).

At 10.471, when Myrrha returns to her father's bed for the second time, the narrator comments, literally, "the next night twins the evil deed" (*postera nox facinus geminat*), the "twinning" of "twinned love" (*geminato . . . amore,* 10.333) thus raising love to the second power, *amor quadratus,* love squared. But *pietas,* said at 10.333 to be "strengthened by this ['twinned'] love," is not correspondingly increased but halved—or subtracted altogether. It is *pietas,* family ties, that in fact creates the ultimate paradox and points up the intractable nature of language: "'Now, though, because he's already mine, he isn't mine,'" Myrrha says, "'and our close tie dooms me'" (10.339–340). At the end of her monologue Myrrha untwists the artificial opposition between nature and convention that she herself has created and realizes that they are not at odds, that it is she who has confounded and confused laws and names, *et iura et nomina* (10.346). In the first four of a series of five rapid-fire questions (10.345–348) Myrrha asks herself: "'But do you really expect anything more, you guilty girl?'" (*inpia virgo,* 10.345, a contradiction in terms, the equivalent of "guilty innocent"). "'Don't you realize how many laws you're confounding, how many names you're confusing?'" she continues. "'Will you become your mother's rival and your father's mistress? Will you be called the sister of your son and the mother of your brother?'" The last two questions also point to contradictions in terms, and Myrrha knows it. "'Since you haven't let this unspeakable union happen in fact, don't imagine it in your mind. Don't foul great nature's compact with this forbidden sex!'" (10.351–353). And she hammers the subject: "'You think you want to? The act itself forbids it!'" (*res ipsa vetat,* 10.354). Myrrha has attempted to mold language to her desire, but unlike Pygmalion's ivory statue, language will not soften under her efforts. There is a bedrock reality that some words or terms express, *pietas,* for example, which does not increase when love is "twinned." Nor is a father a lover for his daughter, nor can a daughter be the rival of her mother or the mother of her brother. Myrrha is eager to twist, bend, and shape language to her own ends—to justify her passion—but she ultimately realizes that a certain reality asserts itself, which, while it can be expressed in language, does not, in fact, require the mediation of language: *res ipsa vetat.*

After Myrrha is discovered by her father and flees (10.472ff.), she wanders, pregnant, for nine months until, exhausted and barely able to move, she "compose[s] this prayer: 'If any gods hear sinners when they confess: I deserve a bitter punishment, and I do not shun it, but let me not by living violate the living nor by dying defile the dead. Banish me from both realms! Change me! And so deny me life and death.' There is indeed a god who hears a sinner's prayer, and last requests do have their own divinities" (10.483–489).

The change is too slow for Myrrha, and she goes to meet (*obvia*, 10.497) and sinks into the tree that she is turning into and that is growing upward over her body and buries her face in its bark. As Bömer says, "[S]he does something quite unusual, she surrenders herself . . . to her fate, . . . indeed, she even hastens her own transformation" (at 10.497–498, 5.164). She loses all feeling as her corporeal self disappears, although she continues to weep, "her hot tears [run] down the trunk of the tree" (10.497–500), "and her metamorphosis robs . . . her of all senses save that of sorrow" (Coleman 468–469). But Orpheus speaks of the "honor" due her tears (*honor,* 10.501), for they are now fragrant myrrh that drips from the bark of the tree she has become, preserves the name (*nomen,* 10.502) of its mistress, "and will spread it far and wide in time to come" (10.502). The storied fragrance of myrrh offers the final judgment on Myrrha and may even, despite her self-condemnation, confirm her earlier assertion that *pietas* "'[is] strengthened by this doubled love'" (10.333).

41. The final tale in Orpheus' song, the story of Venus and Adonis, is related in two parts (10.503–559 and 708–739) that frame the narrative of Atalanta and Hippomenes (10.560–707), told by Venus as lover to her beloved Adonis. This latter story is thus embedded in another embedded narrative and is thus nearly as deeply embedded as Arethusa's tale about her rape by the river Alpheus at 5.577–641 (see n. 21).

Nagle calls Arethusa's story "the most deeply embedded tale in the poem" ([1989a] 108), as technically it is, since, to match its depth of embedding, Venus, who is here on the same level of narration as Calliope in book 5, would have to represent Atalanta or Hippomenes telling their story herself or himself. In book 5, a nameless, unstoried Muse, who is at the second level of narration there, as Orpheus is in book 10, repeats to Minerva her sister Muse Calliope's winning entry in a singing contest with the Pierides. There is no framing story there about the anonymous Muse as there is here about Orpheus at the beginning of books 10 and 11. Nor is there a story about Calliope, Venus' narrating counterpart, other than that she competed in a contest and won, as there is here about Venus. In book 5, Calliope allows Arethusa to tell her tale to Ceres (whose story—the loss of her daughter Proserpina—Calliope told previous to Arethusa's); here, Venus herself tells the story of Atalanta and Hippomenes to Adonis, but the embedding is more complex and, I would say, more sophisticated than that in book 5, since the narrating characters (Orpheus and Venus) have their own stories and since there are linkages among the tales narrated (Atalanta and Hippomenes are linked to Venus and Adonis; Venus and Adonis to Orpheus, as well as to Orpheus' stories about Myrrha and Pygmalion).

This last part of Orpheus' song, 40 percent of the whole (237 of 592 lines), parallels the entire Orpheus section (10.1–11.84). That is, the Venus-Adonis narrative frames the story of Atalanta and Hippomenes that Venus tells Adonis just as Orpheus' personal story (Orpheus and Eurydice, 10.1–85; the death of Orpheus, 11.1–84) frames the story he has been telling his audience of trees, beasts, birds, and stones and is now concluding. In addition, the second part of the Venus-Adonis story ends with a death, just as the second part of Orpheus' myth will end in his death.

The birth of Adonis from Myrrha after she has been changed into the myrrh tree (10.503–518) serves as the transition from Myrrha to the Venus-Adonis episode (as well as that episode's beginning) and, like the transition from Pygmalion to Myrrha earlier, is genealogical (see n. 40), but more intensely so, because Adonis is the fruit of "doubled love" (*geminatus . . . amor,* 10.333) or incest (his mother being his sister and his father his grandfather 10.520–521). Adding to the intensity is the detailed description of Myrrha-the-myrrh-tree's birth agony, even more painful because a tree unequipped for birth is giving birth. Its labor pains have no words to cry out with (*neque habent sua verba dolores,* 10.506), nor does the mother have a voice with which to call upon Lucina, the birth goddess, for help (10.507). This mute state is in contrast to Myrrh's previous volubility not only in her monologue, but also in her pre-suicide, meant-to-be-last words, which come through a closed door to the nurse's ears (10.382–383) and so thwart the girl's suicide.

The two-part Venus-Adonis narrative covers Adonis' entire life, from birth to death, as well as the beginning of his perpetual hereafter as the anemone, the "wind flower."

After Lucina helps the myrrh tree to a cesarean fission and Adonis emerges, naiads lay the infant on a bed of soft grass and bathe it in its mother's tears, that is, in myrrh (10.512–514). This baby is so beautiful that even Envy would admire it, and it looks so much like the naked Cupids artists paint that only its lack of a Cupid's quiver distinguishes it from them (10.515–518): "Art . . . sets the standard by which to judge the looks of Adonis," Solodow comments (211). That is not surprising, since his great- (or great-great) grandmother was originally a beautiful ivory statue. Observing that "nothing is swifter than the passing years" (10.520), Orpheus in fewer than four lines (10.520b–523) traces Adonis' life from conception ("the son of his own sister and grandfather") onward to manhood, remarking on his beauty along the way, whereupon, "now even more beautiful than himself," he "delights the eye even of Venus and avenges his mother's passion" (10.523–524). Orpheus thus invites us to recall Myrrha's entry into her father Cinyras' "obscene bed," the "sin" they committed there, and, when she left it, the "guilty seed" she carried in her "monstrous womb," the "crime" conceived there (10.465–470), that is, Adonis.

Commentators have noted a possible allusion in the reference to Adonis as avenging his mother's passion to a version of the Myrrha story that Ovid did not accept in his adaptation of it, in which Venus afflicted Myrrha with her incestuous passion for her father, and Adonis now avenges that passion when his beauty causes Venus to fall in love with him, and her love causes her to suffer when he dies (Anderson [1972] at 10.520–524, 520; Knox 58–59). But as Orpheus makes clear (and Anderson [1972] at 10.313–315, 504 recognizes), Myrrha's passion for her father was caused by the Furies, not by Venus' son and agent Cupid (10.311–314). Bömer interprets Orpheus' saying that Adonis avenges his mother's passion (10.524) to mean that Adonis, unawares, inflamed Venus through his beauty, although neither of them at the time perceived as punishment that which, in the end, had that effect (because of Venus' grief; see Bömer at 10.524, 5.177–178).

But one can think of Myrrha's incestuous passion as being *vindicated* by Adonis' beauty (although one has to press the meaning of *ulciscitur* at 10.524 to do so) when Venus, love divinely embodied, falls in love with Adonis. The virtual juxtaposition of Adonis' conception and Venus' response to him supports such an interpretation. Since Adonis is indistinguishable from paintings of Venus' son Cupid (who is the efficient cause of his mother's love for Adonis when he pricks her with an arrow while kissing her: 10.525–526), the incest theme (originating in Pygmalion's love for his statue) is continued here. The message in the bottle, then, at the heart of the heart of the *Meta-morphoses,* whose theme has often been considered love (Wilkinson [1955] 206, Galinsky [1975] 97, Barkan 91), thus reads: Love loves Love, which is the distillation, or refinement (aided by Adonis' myrrh bath at birth), of the *geminatus amor* that produced Adonis and that, Myrrha suggested, strengthens *pietas* (10.333).

The story of Venus and Adonis balances the early tale of Hyacinthus and Apollo, as I noted in n. 39 (citing Knox), the two tales (along with the seven-line tale of Jupiter's abduction of Ganymede, 10.155–161) representing Orpheus' theme of "boys loved by gods" (10.152–153). Like Apollo, Venus abandons her usual haunts (Apollo: 10.167–170; Venus: 10.529–531), and also like Apollo, she tags along with her beloved when he goes hunting and even hunts small game herself (Apollo: 10.171–173; Venus: 10.535–541). As Apollo's lost beloved becomes a flower, the hyacinth, so Venus' beloved, when he dies, becomes the anemone. But there the parallels end. Venus, Orpheus says, not only ceased to frequent her usual places, "[s]he even stayed away from heaven—preferred Adonis to heaven" (10.532), that is, temporarily gives up her godhead, something Apollo isn't said to contemplate doing. Hyacinthus is killed by his lover, though accidentally; Adonis is killed by a boar, despite his lover's warning to leave ferocious animals alone. The most important difference between the two stories, however, lies in the fact that Venus and Adonis are a heterosexual, not a homosexual, couple. The reader assumes prospectively that when Orpheus says, at the beginning of his song, that he will sing of "boys loved by gods," he means male gods because, as the narrator told us earlier (10.79–85), the bard, who retreated to the mountains of Thrace after his second loss of Eurydice, has rejected the love of women and introduced pederasty to the people of Thrace. That assumption is confirmed by the first two stories Orpheus tells, about Ganymede and Hyacinthus. But Orpheus' intention undergoes a metamorphosis in the course of his song.

In representing Orpheus as changing his sexual orientation from hetero- to homosexual, Ovid follows (or dips into) the Hellenistic (or even earlier) tradition that characterizes Orpheus as homosexual. (See Bömer at 10.83–84, 5.37–38; and Makowski 27 nn. 7 and 8, and the references they cite.) But after Orpheus' minimal acknowledgment and his first two stories, nothing further is said on the subject, and by the end of Orpheus' song, "boys loved by gods" has turned into the heterosexual love between Venus and Adonis. While Anderson may go too far in claiming that "as the stories of boy-love unfold, Ovid's inescapable conclusion forces itself on us . . . that boy-love ranks far below heterosexual love in terms of affection, mutual concern, and chances for extensive happiness" ([1982b] 45), there does seem to be "a climactic progression in the order of the songs," as Segal says, "for the last one illustrates the power of love over the love-goddess herself" ([1989] 89).

Venus throws herself into the outdoor life in order to be with Adonis (10.533ff.), but has no taste for hunting, has no interest in becoming a real huntress, and avoids "big game," such as boars, wolves, bears, and lions. She also urges Adonis to follow her example, for her sake as much as for his ("'Your rashness can hurt *me*!'" 10.545). She hates lions most of all. Adonis asks her why—out of politeness, perhaps—and she seizes the opportunity Adonis' question gives to tell him the story of Atalanta and Hippomenes. She immediately interrupts herself, after she begins, to suggest they lie down on the grass in the shade of a poplar tree, and so they do, Venus with her head in Adonis' lap. She begins again, though she pauses often to kiss him.

The relation of the story Venus tells Adonis to its frame, the story of Venus and Adonis themselves, has occasioned much misinterpretation, it seems to me. According to Coleman (469), Anderson ([1972] at 10.503–739, 517–518), Nagle ([1988a] 116), and Segal ([1989a] 90), the tale of Atalanta and Hippomenes does not fit (or support) the goddess' warning to Adonis (at 10.542–552) to avoid animals of the fiercer sort, a warning that precedes (but doesn't specifically initiate) her story and that she makes more specific at its conclusion (10.705–707). That is obviously true, but we cannot stop there, for her warning has a relation to the story of Atalanta and Hippomenes as well as a meaning for Adonis (as her story itself does, too), and this warning, along with his disregard for it, is highly significant.

We need to start from the beginning: Venus' story is called forth in answer to Adonis' question to her. He asks her why, as she says, she "'hate[s] the entire breed of lions'" (10.552), and she answers, "'I'll tell you why,'" adding, "'and you'll marvel at the incredible thing that happened because of an ancient offense against me'" (10.552–553). An important motive for Venus' narration stems from her desire to stop running around in the woods with Adonis, that is, to stop Adonis from running around in the woods hunting, and, more particularly, it stems from her desire to lie down with him in an inviting place. (And who knows what may happen next?) His question gives her the opening she needs for that.

Before taking up Venus' warning to Adonis, we must consider the moral of the story she tells him vis-à-vis Atalanta, who, rather than Hippomenes, is the nearer example for Adonis. In commenting on Atalanta's beautiful body, Venus says it is like her own— or Adonis', should he become a woman (10.578–579), obviously a possibility in the world of the *Metamorphoses*, and here, as the present subjunctive instructs us in the clause, *si femina fias* (10.579), a politely put future-less-vivid possibility. But since it is the goddess Venus who is saying it to Adonis, it is very possible indeed: there is a hint of a threat in Venus' comparison of Atalanta's beauty to Adonis'.

An oracle tells Atalanta, "'"Run from the very idea of a husband—yet I predict you won't run from it"'" (*fuge . . . / nec tamen effugies*), adding, "'"and though still alive, you'll lose yourself"'" (10.565–566). There are thus two warnings in play here: Venus' own to Adonis (10.542–552) and the oracle's to Atalanta, the latter a warning of "[l]ove as a threat to personal identity," in Nagle's words ([1988a] 115). Atalanta heeds the oracle, or tries to, but she cannot resist Venus and so succumbs to love, and that is how she happens to lose her "self" through metamorphosis, although she is innocent. (Orpheus "fails to single out anything illicit in [Atalanta's] behaviour, and indeed it is Hippomenes who by his lust brings punishment on them both," Anderson says: [1982] 46.)

Venus' warning to Adonis is as clear as the oracle's to Atalanta, and she repeats it at the end of her story: "'And so, my dearest, run from these and every other kind of beast that offers its chest to battle but not its back to flight, lest your fearlessness hurt us both!'" (*effuge, ne virtus tua sit damnosa duobus,* 10.705–707). In addition to being similar in their beauty, Atalanta and Adonis have an additional connection: they are warned to "run from" (*fugere, effugere*) specific dangers.

Defeated in her race with Hippomenes because she could not resist Venus' golden apples, symbols of love (Anderson [1972] at 10.661–662, 529), and so succumbing to love, Atalanta ultimately loses her "self" in metamorphosis.

Adonis loses his life because he doesn't heed Venus' warning to avoid large and dangerous animals when he hunts, and the narrator tells us why he doesn't heed her warning. Immediately after Venus tells Adonis that his *virtus* will hurt them both (10.707), she flies away in her swan-drawn chariot, and Adonis resumes hunting, for, the narrator says, "his fearlessness stood opposed to such a warning" (*stat monitis contraria virtus,* 10.709). Predictably, before she's out of earshot he is fatally gored by a wild boar, an animal she warned him not to hunt. Adonis ignores Venus' explicit warning to him, however, in order to heed another warning, the warning the oracle gave to Atalanta. The consequences of the failure to obey that warning are graphically described in Atalanta's story, which Adonis understands perfectly (as well as one of Venus' motives for telling it, love; and its moral, love as a threat to personal identity, as Nagle says). Adonis would rather die hunting, exercising his *virtus*, than, like Atalanta, lose his "self" through love, which loss already may have begun to happen when Venus persuades him to stop hunting and lie down with her, and then tells him that Atalanta is as beautiful as he is, *should he become a woman,* which I interpret as an oblique assertion of her power and thus a subtle threat. As every Homeric hero knows, it is better to die for *virtus* than lose one's self in love—or become a woman. Toward the end of book 2, Ovid prefaces his description of lovesick Jupiter absurdly turning himself into a beautiful white bull in order to seduce Europa by observing, "Two things never fit together well, can never abide in one and the same place: majesty and infatuation" (*maiestas et amor,* 2.846–847). We can now add a gloss to that: *virtus* and *amor* don't fit together well, either. It seems clear to me that Adonis knows that if he heeds Venus' warning, he will fail to heed the warning in the story Venus tells him. And so, like Achilles before him, Adonis chooses *virtus* and a short but glorious life.

But what of the message in these deeply embedded stories at the heart of the heart of the *Metamorphoses*, that Love loves Love, the message in the bottle, as I called it earlier? Love loves Love is the first part of that message. The rest of it is Love loses Love: "[T]he goddess of love is as helpless as her victims in coping with the power of love," as Coleman says (469). The moral of both tales together ("examples of Venus' power and impotence": Coleman 469), as well as commentary on Adonis' preference of *virtus* to *amor,* is given by what I might call their objective correlative (and Adonis' semiotic epitaph), the anemone (from Greek *anemos,* "wind") that Venus creates from the courageous blood of the dying hunter: "Our delight in this flower is brief . . . , for the wind that gives it its name soon tears off the light and lightly clinging, easily falling petals" (10.737–739). There is breath-catching poignancy in this symbol that Ovid, Orpheus, and Venus create from blood for *amor,* for *virtus,* and for the war between them.

Stephens (1958b) reminds us of Venus' importance throughout the *Metamorphoses*. In book 5, at the first "turning point" of the poem, the embedded tale that is a "miniature" *carmen perpetuum* and a twin to Orpheus' song, as Nagle (1988a) has shown, Venus urges Cupid to afflict Hades with love so that love will rule in all three realms of the world (5.365ff.). Venus is obviously present in the long myth of Orpheus (10.1–11.84), within which the second "miniature" *carmen perpetuum* occurs and which is the second turning point, if not climax, of the poem, as Ovid ends the second part of his work and moves toward Rome and his own time. In the third part of the poem, in which Aeneas, the son of Venus, is introduced (in book 13), the *Aeneadum genetrix,* "mother of the sons of Aeneas" (that is, Romans), as Lucretius calls Venus (*De Rerum Natura* 1.1), "is seen more and more as the ancestress of the Roman people," Stephens ([1958b] 299) says, taking the initiative in Aeneas' deification (14.585–608), saving Rome at the time of the Sabine invasion (14.772–804) and, in the final book of the poem, carrying Julius Caesar's soul to heaven (15.843–848; see Stephens [1958b] 290–291, 295–300).

BOOK ELEVEN

42. The end of Orpheus' song coincides with the end of book 10, and book 11 resumes (and concludes) the story of Orpheus himself with a narration of his death and reunion with Eurydice in the underworld and Bacchus' punishment of the maddened Thracian

women who killed the bard (11.1–84), these lines forming the second part of the frame for his song. Ovid makes a connection to the first part of that frame (10.1–85) by referring at 11.1–24 to Orpheus' audience of trees, beasts, birds (described at 10.86–106 and 143–144), and stones (11.2), to which snakes are added at 11.21, and to the women who attack him, presumably the same ones Orpheus earlier rejected (10.81–82), "still angry at being rebuffed by . . . the mourning widower" (Hill 134), appearing now as maddened followers of the god Bacchus (ritual worship of whom led to temporary insanity, as Ovid indicates here, saying that they were "possessed by an insane Fury," *insana . . . regnat Erinys,* 11.14), one of whom is "seen [at 11.6–8] in an isolated pose," in the way the devotee of Bacchus "was depicted in ancient art, with wind-tossed hair, animal skin . . . and the ritual thyrsus or wand" (Murphy at 11.6, 44), with which she strikes Orpheus in the mouth. The wooded *locus amoenus* (pleasant locale) which Orpheus created with his song (10.86ff.), where he sang and played the lyre, and which was normally the site for love and song, has again become a place for savage violence (Parry, passim; Segal [1969a] 15).

At first the stones the women heave at Orpheus are "overcome by the sweet harmony of his voice and lyre" (11.11) and fall harmlessly at his feet like suppliants "seeking forgiveness for such a mad attack" (11.12–13). But then, in a graphic clash of the Dionysian (= Bacchic) and Apollonian aesthetic (Orpheus is called "Apollo's poet" at 11.8), the noise of the women—their instruments, their clapping hands and their wailing, howling voices—drowns out Orpheus' music, and the stones no longer hear him and are now reddened with his blood (11.15–19): Orpheus' "civilizing art" has been overcome by "the insanity and wild chaos of his murderers" (Segal [1989a] 68).

Before they turn to Orpheus for the kill, the maddened women (now called "maenads," *maenades,* 11.22, from Gk. *mainomai,* "to be mad") attack and tear apart "his adoring audience . . . enchanted still by the sound of his voice, still singing" (11.20–22), and "the spell of his art becomes fatal to the charmed circle he has created" (Leach 126).

As the women rush at Orpheus, he is "like a stag in the arena in the morning, about to be killed by dogs" (11.25–27), a reference to contemporary entertainment in amphitheaters at Rome, for, as Murphy notes, "the Roman shows which ended with gladiatorial contests began in the morning with the hunting . . . of wild animals" (at 11.26, 45). Ovid has just referred to Orpheus' listeners as his "adoring audience" (11.22, as noted above), implying a theater and a performance, and now, "when . . . the imagery of performance recurs, it has been contaminated by the violence: the theatre has become an amphitheatre . . . and Orpheus, again on stage, is not now a singer, but a doomed stag about to be torn apart by dogs" (Hinds [1987] 35).

Some of the women attacking Orpheus seize the hoes, rakes, and mattocks thrown down by farmers working nearby as they fled the scene in horror to use as weapons on him. And now the bard whose singing moved the shades of the dead, persuaded the gods of the underworld to release his wife from death, and brought animate and inanimate nature into his presence to listen to him, "for the first time ever spoke in vain and moved nothing with the sound of his voice" (11.39–40), and so "[t]he poet dies unheard" (Segal [1969a] 76).

In saying who (or rather what) wept for Orpheus, Ovid addresses him with a fivefold "you" (*te*): "birds wept for you . . . , wild beasts wept for you, stones wept for you, and forests . . . wept for you. . . . Trees shed their leaves in mourning for you" (11.44–47). In his use of the second-person pronoun here, Ovid, as Kenney notes ([1986] 437), "echoes and recalls Virgil's description of Orpheus' lament for Eurydice" (her first death) at *Georgics* 4.465–466 (lines that David West calls "the most plangently musical . . . in Latin poetry" [9]). He also out-*te*'s Virgil five to four, while neatly reversing the application of the older poet's *te*'s: Ovid's narrator addresses Orpheus with them, Virgil's, Eurydice. Note that just as Orpheus never sings before a live human audience—no audience is mentioned at 10.11–12a, where Orpheus mourns Eurydice, presumably in song, before descending to the underworld—no human mourns for him when he dies, although there are plenty of human mourners in the *Metamorphoses*.

Ovid glances again at Virgil's tale of Orpheus and Eurydice in his description of the bard's severed head and lyre floating downstream in the Hebrus River: in Virgil, the head of Orpheus, which the river "rolls" downstream (*volveret, Georgics* 4.525), twice cries "'Eurydice,'" "and all along the stream the banks echo 'Eurydice'" (*Georgics* 4.525–527). In Ovid, though, Orpheus' lyre, as it "floats" along (*labitur,* 11.51), "[makes] some kind of tearful sound," and "the lifeless mouth" of the bard (also floating) "[murmurs] something tearful, and from the banks of the river a tearful echo [comes]" (11.51–53: *flebile nescio quid . . . flebile . . . / . . . flebile*), that inarticulate gurgling making a comment on Orpheus' head in Virgil, "as if to say 'Who could pretend to hear distinctly the words uttered by a floating and lifeless head?'" (Solodow 104).

After it floats out to sea, the lifeless head washes up on the shore of Lesbos, where a snake, in a gruesome scene perhaps invented by Ovid and "attested only here" (Kenney [1986] 437), with "wide-open mouth" and "gaping jaws" is about to sink its fangs into it when Apollo appears at the last moment and turns the snake to stone—with mouth still wide-open and jaws still gaping (11.54–60). Rather than accept the snake as an indication that "no vestige of [Orpheus'] enchanting power remains" (Leach 126), I prefer to see Apollo's sudden appearance, which recalls the earlier reference to the god (when one of the maddened women hurled her thyrsus "at the mouth of Apollo's poet" but didn't hurt him: 11.7–9), as a sign that some aura of Orpheus' power, externalized as a theophany of the bard's patron, lingers and now turns the snake to stone.

Ovid makes no further reference to Orpheus' head, which, according to the Hellenistic poet Phanocles, on whom, Murphy says, Ovid draws "[f]or many of the closing details of the story," continued to sing even after it was buried. (See Murphy at 11.54ff., 47; for mythic variations of the fate of Orpheus' head, see Segal [1989a] 159.)

Orpheus returns to the underworld, recognizing the places he had seen on his earlier visit, finds Eurydice, and is reunited with her (11.61–63), "this happy ending . . . Ovid's invention" (Kenney [1986] 438; Viarre 246 suggests a parallel between Pygmalion's success in bringing his ivory statue to life and Orpheus' reunion with his beloved). Orpheus, Ovid says, "clasped [Eurydice] tightly in his loving arms" (11.63), although, when the living Aeneas meets his father, Anchises, or, rather, his shade, in the underworld in book 6 of Virgil's *Aeneid,* he tries to embrace him three times and embraces only air (6.700–702; Viarre 242 notes the contrast), as does Odysseus, when he tries to embrace the shade of his mother, Anticleia, in the underworld (*Odyssey* 11.204–222), and Achilles, when he tries to embrace the shade of Patroclus, when Patroclus appears to him in a dream (*Iliad* 23.97–101). Apparently the dead can embrace the dead, but the living cannot.

Now the lovers can stroll as they wish, with first one, then the other, leading the way, "[b]ut now Orpheus can safely look back at his dear Eurydice" (11.64–66). Is it really a happy ending? It seems to be a matter of a glass half full or half empty. For Leach, "Orpheus becomes nothing more than an ordinary human lover. . . . The picture [Leach means the reunion between Orpheus and Eurydice] is charming, but hardly representative of a successful union of love and art. . . . Personal satisfaction for the artist seems only to be obtained in a withdrawal from art into love" (127). For Segal, though, the conclusion "is the triumph of [Orpheus'] love," and Ovid ends his story of Orpheus "with the happy glances of lovers" ([1989] 69). Elsewhere, however, Segal notes that "when Ovid and Eurydice are reunited . . . , they exchange only looks, not words," and he then asks if Ovid has a reason for "giving the most famous of all poets nothing to say at this great moment" ([1989] 84). Master rhetorician that he is, though, Ovid knows that a description of silent actions and gestures—the rapturous embrace, the playful strolling, the almost mischievous looking back—all these are much more expressive than any words Orpheus could possibly speak.

Art is prominent throughout the long Orpheus episode, but it is always functional, it always has a purpose, it is not created for sheer aesthetic pleasure ("art for art's sake"). Thus Orpheus in book 10 seeks to gain the release of Eurydice from the underworld through his art. When he fails for human reasons, he consoles himself with his art. His character Pygmalion, finding no human females acceptable, carves an ivory statue in order to have a female likeness to lavish his love upon. Venus' story to Adonis, if it is to be considered art, has a specific purpose: to control Adonis. In the underworld, however, the dead Orpheus does not sing. Yet, as Hill notes, Orpheus' art and his love "have indeed triumphed there, together they have achieved that most ancient and most primitive ambition, the conquest of death, though not, perhaps, precisely as they had hoped" (135). Within the world of Ovid's story, Orpheus and Eurydice have no further need for art.

Bacchus, angry that his devotees murdered Orpheus, turns them into trees (11.67–84), "an ironical note for those who had refused to succumb to the musical charms that had moved the . . . [Chaonian oak tree] and other trees of Thrace" (Coleman 470).

43. Ovid ends part two of the *Metamorphoses* ("heroes and heroines") and so the "mythical" sections of the poem with the story of King Midas (11.85–193). Part three, "'historical' personages," begins at 11.194 with the tale of the twice-lying Laomedon, ruler of Troy.

The poet moves from the death of Orpheus to the Midas episode by means of what Solodow calls the "transition through absence" (43–44). After punishing the Thracian women who killed Orpheus, Bacchus travels to Asia Minor, where his devotees gather around him, except for the satyr Silenus, who is "absent" (11.90), for in his drunken state he has lagged behind and been seized by Phrygian peasants, who bring him to Midas, their king (11.90–92). Midas, who was instructed in the rites of Bacchus by Orpheus (11.92–93; along with "Eumolpus of Athens," the mythical origin of the priestly line of the Eulmopidae at Eleusis and regarded as the founder of the Eleusinian mysteries or as one of the first to be deemed worthy of instruction in these mysteries: Bömer at 11.92–93, 5.264), returns Silenus, Bacchus' "foster father" (*altor,* 11.101), to the god and is offered as a reward whatever he wishes ("the age-old theme of the Binding Promise and the Foolish Wish," as occurs with Phaethon at 2.44–46, Semele at 3.287–291, and the sybil at 14.130–142: Kenney [1986] 438). Midas is thus specifically linked to Orpheus, and his story has, as Leach says (131), a "deliberate thematic relevance to its context," that is, to the long section on Orpheus, for which it might be thought to serve as a kind of coda at this pivotal and transitional moment in the poem.

Midas is not motivated by greed in desiring a golden touch, as Coleman thinks (470; both Coleman and Otis [193] see the story of Midas as the reverse of the Pygmalion episode). Rather, the king exhibits, Leach says, "as much of an aesthetic as a pecuniary craving for gold," and when "with child-like joy" he seeks to turn everything in sight to gold, he "seems to see his new power as a form of art capable of transforming the entire universe" (131). Thus, when Midas asks Bacchus for the power of metamorphosis, which the golden touch obviously is, he is asking the god to make him an artist, for, as Solodow comments, "metamorphosis is a kind of art," and "the processes of metamorphosis and artistic creation are alike" (203, 204). But this artist seeks merely to gild by his touch everything under the sun indiscriminately, rather than, by applying a craftsman's artistry, to transform the natural and thereby make something new (as Daedalus had done: see 8.188f.). His art is characterized by a magical mimesis that is both simplistic and mad. Leach says that the Midas episode offers as its theme "the artist as the recreator of a lost golden age" (132), but I would revise that and call the episode's theme the artist's attempt to create a golden age in the present, which is by definition impossible to do: golden ages are always in the past and so always "lost."

The parable-like quality of the Midas story and its linkages to the Orpheus myth lead one to ask if the tale was meant to confirm that complex story, counter an objection to it, or answer a question that it raises. Is Ovid saying, then, through the Midas tale, that, "[u]nlike his predecessor Vergil [he] has no bright visions of the way in which the lost ideal might be recaptured" (Leach 132)? Using another approach, one can say that Orpheus—to return momentarily to his death—is killed when, by a manifestation of Gresham's law in art, bad, Dionysian music of the Thracian maenads drowns out the good, Apollonian music of Orpheus (11.15–19), and the missiles hurled at him, no longer affected by his music, do the work they are intended to do. With that notion as a premise, one can say that the story of Midas would seem to suggest that the false and mindlessly mimetic art of Midas is the best we can hope for in a post-Orpheus world.

Yet Midas' era of "gilt art" passes quickly, and in the next tale, chapter two of the Midas story, Apollo manifests his power, specifically, his power as an artist (Apollonian art, we learn, still reigns), while the episode confirms (if we doubted it) that Midas has no aesthetic judgment whatsoever. Forgiven for his foolishness and relieved of his golden touch, Midas, "[d]espising his wealth, . . . took to the fields and forests, where he worshipped Pan. . . . But he was as thickheaded as ever, and, as before, his foolish notions were going to get him into trouble again" (11.146–149). And if we missed the point before, we can surely get it now: the rustic god Pan challenges the sophisticated poet-god Apollo to a poetry contest, which is to be judged by another god, Mount Tmolus (who, as both mountain and anthropomorphic deity, provides another example of what Solodow calls a "split divinity" [94–96]).

Midas is "charmed" by the "crude tune" Pan plays as his entry in the contest (11.161–163). Then Tmolus gives the nod to Apollo. Ovid describes the god before he begins to play: he "was wearing a laurel crown . . . on his golden head, and his rich purple cloak swept the ground. In his left hand he held his lyre, inlaid with ivory and studded with precious stones; and in his right he held his plectrum: the very image of an artist" (11.165–169). The poet's portrait of Apollo, Murphy says, "may have been modelled on the statue of Apollo by Scopas set up in the temple [to Apollo] which Augustus built on the Palatine" (at 11.165–169, 54). The Latin clause I've translated "the very image of an artist" (11.169: *artificis status ipse fuit*) "may mean," Solodow observes, that "'the very pose is that struck by a master performer' or 'that created by a sculptor.' The play on words draws attention to the source of the pose" (225).

Apollo's playing matches his appearance, and when his "accomplished fingers plucked the strings," Ovid says, Tmolus was "charmed by the sweetness of his melody" and "ordered Pan to lower his pipes in defeat before the lyre" (11.169–171). Midas speaks out against the decision, calling it unjust, and is punished by Apollo, who causes a pair of donkey's ears to grow on his head (11.172–179). Ovid earlier told us that the king "was as thickheaded as ever" when he retreated to fields and forests—*pingue sed ingenium mansit* (11.148)—and that explains why he preferred Pan's music to Apollo's. "Midas' disastrous foray into literary criticism," Kenney says, "is characterized in the technical language of Augustan and Alexandrian poetics. . . . Latin *pinguis* epitomized all that the taste of those bred up on Callimachus [as Ovid was] agreed to reject in poetry. . . . Midas . . . clearly had never been instructed in the hierarchy of genres, in which bucolic was outranked by the lyric" ([1986] xxvii). In growing the ears of a donkey, Midas is "made the living embodiment of the Greek proverb describing the unmusical as *onos lyras*, a donkey (listening to) the lyre" (Kenney [1986] 438).

Unlike other competitions in art in the *Metamorphoses* (those between the Muses and the daughters of Pieros in book 5, between Minerva and Arachne and between Apollo and Marsyas in book 6), in this one the loser (Pan) hardly suffers at all, and Midas, an untalented schlock artist and accidental critic with no taste, is mildly metamorphosed. This episode seems an odd way to conclude parts one and two of the *Metamorphoses*, the "mythical" sections, which culminate in the long, rich, and often moving story of Orpheus (10.1–11.84) just preceding the tale of Midas. It seems odder still for Ovid to end the mythical sections of the poem with this particular story just prior to beginning part three, the historical section on Troy and Rome, which will continue to the end of the poem. Can the two-part Midas story, then, be taken as an introduction to part three? I agree with Gordon Williams that Ovid's poetry "seems, to a degree most unusual in Roman poetry, to have been created basically for its own sake, with no ulterior purpose, no message," and that "Ovid was a poet deeply out of tune with what hindsight can identify as the main stream, the whole political trend, of his time. . . . He was a genius who struggled to keep poetry to itself and out of politics" (53, 100). Nevertheless, I wonder if Ovid separates the mythical and historical parts of the *Metamorphoses* with the story of Midas as an anticipatory editorial comment, so to speak, on what comes next: his "*Iliad*" (12.1–13.622); his "*Aeneid*" (13.623–14.608), which his "*Iliad*" "introduces"; Romulus; and Rome (14.609–15.870).

44. Apollo leaves Mount Tmolus in Lydia, flies north and west to Troy, and comes "to land just this side of Helle's narrow sea" (11.194–196) from the perspective of Mount Tmolus, which is south and east of the strait.

With Apollo's flight, Ovid moves from parts one and two of the poem (1.452–11.193) to part three, "'historical' personages" (11.194–15.870). The poet makes this transition from part to part "seem less arbitrary than it 'actually' is," Due says, because Apollo's flight "expresses an acceptable progression and variation of motif." That is, just prior to the Midas episode, Bacchus, after punishing the maenads who killed Orpheus, "leaves the scene of the crime" (at 11.85–87). Apollo now, after punishing Midas, "leaves both his victim and his country." The reader is thus "taken from one vengeance-episode to another: Both King Midas and King Laomedon have to pay for their greediness and stupidity" (141; although in n. 43 I agreed with the view that Midas is not motivated by greed in seeking his golden touch). As for the timing of Apollo's arrival in Troy, "Ovid contrives," Murphy says, "that Apollo should fly over Troy just at that moment when Laomedon is building the walls, rather as an historical novelist manoeuvres his characters on to the scene of famous events" (at 11.199, 56). The brief tale of the founding and first sack of Troy (11.194–220) itself serves as a transition to the narrative of Peleus and Thetis (11.221–265), whose story leads to Peleus at the court of Ceyx, king of Trachis (11.266–409), and on to the long tale of Ceyx and Alcyone (11.410–748) as well as to the stories of Peleus' son Achilles, the Trojan War, and the war's aftermath narrated in books 12–14.

Kenney notes that "[f]or the ancients, in so far as a distinction was made between history and myth, the Trojan War tended to mark the dividing line" ([1986] 439). The Romans considered the Trojans their ancestors, for as myth would have it, the Trojan prince Aeneas, son of Venus and Trojan Anchises, escaped from Troy when the Greeks defeated it, traveled as a refugee with a small band of followers to Italy, and there established himself and the Trojans accompanying him in a city called Lavinium, which he founded, north of which his descendants eventually founded Rome.

Troy itself was founded in perfidy, since Laomedon cheated Neptune and Apollo out of the gold he had promised them for building walls around his city and even denied making a promise to them (11.199–206). When Neptune retaliated by flooding the plains of Troy and forcing Laomedon to offer his daughter Hesione to a sea monster, Hercules rescued her, and Laomedon cheated him as well, refusing to give him the horses he had promised as the reward for saving Hesione. Hercules attacked and defeated Troy and gave Hesione to Telamon, a fellow warrior, who, Murphy says, is mentioned only to introduce his brother Peleus (at 11.217, 56).

"Ovid's readers," Kenney notes, "would remember the familiar passages of Horace [*Odes* 3.3.21–24] and Virgil [*Georgics* 1.501–502 and *Aeneid* 4.541–542] in which the fall of Troy and the tribulations of the Trojans and their descendants are traced back to Laomedon's treachery" ([1986] 439). Current readers may notice that Hercules rescues Hesione and, denied his reward, conquers Troy, "though he has been dead for two books" (Solodow 29; Hercules dies, or, rather, is apotheosized, at 9.262–272). Whether Hercules' disappearance is truly a discrepancy or is due to a deliberate "sense of time-lessness" (Solodow 29, who gives additional examples) is difficult to say. Wilkinson notes that in parts one and two of the work, the mythical sections (1.452–11.193), "there is really no chronological progress," and "[a]s we pass from one saga-group to another the tide of time flows and ebbs beyond the horizon of history" ([1958] 234).

The poet passes, via Telamon, to Peleus, as noted: Hercules gives Laomedon's daughter Hesione to Telamon rather than to Telamon's brother Peleus, for Peleus was already married to the goddess Thetis, mention of whom leads to an account of Peleus' violent capture of the goddess who would become his bride. ("Peleus was the only mortal to obtain a goddess as his *formally wedded* wife": Murphy at 11.220, 56).

Ovid tells the story of Peleus and Thetis, already married, according to the poet (11.217–218), as Peleus' "erotic quest," to use Fantham's term for his bride ([1993] 25)—or, more accurately, his victim. The tale, as Fantham notes ([1993] 25), is divided into five parts of nearly equal length: (1) "prologue" (11.221–228); (2) "the stage setting" (11.229–237); (3) "the first round" (11.238–246); an "interlude" for "recovery and prayer" (11.247–248); (4) "renewed preparations" (11.249–256); and (5) "the final round" (11.257–265).

In the "prologue," Jupiter, enamored of Thetis himself, in order "to prevent the world from having anything greater than himself" (2.224), directs Peleus to marry Thetis. Traditionally it was Themis who warned Zeus away from Thetis lest she bear him a son greater than himself (Fantham [1993] 25 n. 17). Here, Ovid, departing from tradition, has the sea god Proteus give this information to Thetis, although he "had no role in earlier versions of the story of Thetis" and traditionally "would never give any of his secret knowledge except under duress" (Fantham [1993] 25).

In "the stage setting," Ovid describes a secluded cove in Thessaly with a hard-packed beach and a cave, the origin of which is hard to determine: "formed by nature or made by the hand of an artist? . . . More likely an artist made it" (11.235–236). This place offers a variation of the *locus amoenus* or "pleasant locale" that is the scene of so much sexual violence in the *Metamorphoses* (Parry and Segal [1969a] passim). The scene is particularly exotic (as befits the place where Achilles will be conceived) in that, first, the cave seems to have been made as much by an artist as by nature: "The hesitation between nature and art contributes to the unreality of the atmosphere, the sense that . . . one is stepping . . . into a world where shapes are indeed less fixed, reality more fluid" (Segal [1969a 22); and, second, the sea goddess Thetis rides to it daily, nude upon a dolphin, to sleep.

With Thetis thus disposed—naked and asleep—Peleus in "the first round" throws himself upon the sleeping goddess and, when she resists, tries to rape her. Continuing an apostrophe begun at the end of the previous section, Ovid "intensifies the excitement by seeing the event through Thetis' startled eyes as she is roused from sleep" (Fantham [1993] 26). The goddess succeeds in preventing Peleus' success by a series of shape changes, from freely moving bird to stationary tree trunk, neither of which works, to tigress, "a new sensation in Augustan Rome and a paradigm of savagery in Augustan poetry" (Fantham [1993] 27), which does work (Peleus "let go . . . in a hurry," 11.245–246), but only because Peleus "does not know that these shapeshifters of mythology never use their shapes offensively: it is rather as if the shapes were a hallucination that succeeded by terrifying the adversary" (Fantham [1993] 27).

In the "interlude" Peleus retreats for "recovery and prayer" (Fantham's term; see above), and the sea god Proteus (in the fourth part, "renewed preparations") encourages him to try again, but this time (1) to take a rope and tie Thetis up and (2) not to be deceived by "the hundred or so forms she will pretend to be" (11.253), this latter piece of advice "show[ing] that Thetis' transformations are mere illusions and giv[ing] Peleus a guarantee that she must return to her basic shape" (Fantham [1993] 28).

In "the final round" Peleus, following Proteus' advice, ties Thetis down, with her arms stretched out, so she is open and especially vulnerable to rape. Although she changes "into one form after another" (11.261; Thetis, like Daedalus with nature [8.189], literally "makes her forms anew": *illa novat formas*), she finally gives up, becomes herself, and yields. Ovid leaves the forms she changes into "unspecified," Fantham says, "so that he can stress instead the physical hold of man over woman" ([1993] 28). Peleus now "embrace[s] her, satisfie[s] his desire, and fill[s] her womb with mighty Achilles" (11.264–265).

The reference to Troy at the beginning of the preceding short tale (11.199), together with the mention of Achilles at the literal end of this one (11.265: *Achille* ends the line), "would arouse in readers," Due says, "the expectation that now comes the Trojan war" (143). But (Due continues) in order to give Achilles "time to grow up," Ovid reverses the two main events in Peleus' career, his murder of his brother Phocus (and his purification for it) and his union with Thetis, here put first but traditionally preceded by that murder (143–144), to which the poet gives less than a line (11.267; at 7.668ff. Phocus serves as Cephalus' host and audience for Cephalus' account of his wife, Procris', tragic death, while his father, Aeacus, slept). That reversal, Due notes, enables Ovid to bring Peleus as a refugee to the court of Ceyx, king of Trachis (11.266–270), where he will hear the story of Ceyx's brother Daedalion and Daedalion's daughter Chione, the next tale (143–144).

45. Ovid places Peleus' murder of his half-brother Phocus (son of Aeacus and the sea goddess Psamathe) after his marriage to Thetis, reversing the traditional order of these events in the hero's career (as noted in n. 44) and thereby provides the transition (at 11.266–270) to the next tale, the story of Daedalion and Chione (11.291–345), which

Peleus hears from Daedalion's brother Ceyx, king of Trachis. Peleus has come to Trachis as an exile from Aegina after killing Phocus, whose mother, Psamathe, is the sister of Peleus' wife, Thetis. This section (11.266–409) falls into three parts, as Murphy notes (introduction to 11.266–409, 58): (1) Peleus' arrival at the court of Ceyx (11.266–290); (2) the story of Daedalion and Chione, which Ceyx tells to Peleus (11.291–345); and (3) the account of the monstrous wolf sent by Psamathe to avenge the murder of Phocus, together with Peleus' eventual cleansing from blood guilt (11.346–409).

Happy in wife and son, Ovid says, Peleus was fortunate in every way, "if you overlook the crime of cutting his brother Phocus' throat" (11.267), a statement that Solodow calls a "transition through the absent thing," that is, Phocus' murder must be excepted for Peleus' happiness to be perfect. This is a variation of the "transition through absence" (43–44; Murphy [at 11.267, 58] also refers to Ovid's use here of "the *exception* as a linking device").

The violent Peleus, who twice raped, or tried to rape, his wife-to-be while she slept, succeeding the second time (11.238–246; 260–265), and who has now been exiled for fratricide, provides a strong contrast to peaceable, kindly Ceyx. The king rules Trachis "without violence or bloodshed" (11.270), he is generous even with the "ordinary folk" who come to his kingdom (11.283–284), and he is the object of his wife, Alcyone's, "nervous and clinging devotion," in Murphy's words (at 11.384, 63). Alcyone is thus contrasted with Thetis, who, after her marriage to Peleus, has left her husband and returned to her father, Nereus', kingdom in the sea (11.400–401), as Kenney observes ([1986] 440)—not that one can blame her. Moreover, when Peleus arrives in Trachis, Ceyx is mourning the loss of his brother Daedalion; the king's grief for him (along with other details) indicates a powerful love for his brother that can be contrasted with Peleus' violence toward his half-brother.

The story of Daedalion and his daughter Chione (11.291–345), told to Peleus by Ceyx, "first occurs here" (Kenney [1986] 440), and its attribution to Ceyx, Otis says, is Ovid's invention (232). This tale is the first embedded narrative in part three of the *Metamorphoses,* and, as Nagle notes, it serves "as a reprise of many themes of the larger poem," in Apollo's and Mercury's begetting of sons by Chione, in "her ensuing hubris and resulting punishment, and [in] her father's reaction and metamorphosis" ([1989] 115). But earlier themes are varied, extended, and combined in such a way as to give this story its own individual character. For example, Chione is raped not by one god but by two, the first rape (by Mercury, who couldn't wait) that of a "sleeping victim" (Curran [1978] 218). The only other such rape, which happens to be narrated in the episode that precedes this one, is that of Thetis by Peleus (as Curran notes), for whose benefit Ceyx is telling the story. Chione is the only character raped successively by two different rapists. (Peleus tries twice to rape the sleeping Thetis but succeeds only in a second, later attempt.) What makes Mercury's rape of Chione even more odious than Peleus' rape of Thetis is that the god puts Chione to sleep in order to rape her, instead of discovering her asleep, as happens in the case of Peleus and Thetis. Apollo defers his pleasure until nightfall, when, disguised as an old woman (11.309–310; presumably to gain entry to Chione's room), he rapes Chione using a modus operandi similar to the Sun's when he disguised himself as Leucothoe's mother to enter that girl's bedroom (4.217–233).

Chione asserts that she is more beautiful than Diana and even finds fault with the goddess' beauty (11.321–322), behavior that is a variation of Niobe's (6.165–202) and Lethaea's (10.69–71) and that Ovid "explains" with the truism "Glory itself harms many, does it not?" (11.320). Diana shoots Chione in the tongue with an arrow, a particularly cruel attack that, in addition to proving fatal, renders the girl unable to speak, but without metamorphosis, the usual way a character is made mute (e.g., Daphne, Io, Callisto, Actaeon, Dryope). Diana's direct attack on Chione's organ of speech recalls Tereus' cutting out of Philomela's tongue to prevent her from exposing him as the rapist of his wife's sister (6.549–557).

The intensity of Daedalion's "angry grief" (Solodow's phrase) propels him into figurative metamorphosis as a bull (that is, in his frenzy he is compared to a bull stung by hornets: 11.332–336), and then into literal metamorphosis as a hawk, Apollo's alternative to Daedalion's suicide (out of pity for him: 11.339), aspects of this change recalling those of Perdix, Tereus, and Nisus and foreshadowing that of Aesacus, whose story follows Ceyx and Alcyone's. In his changed form, Solodow says, Daedalion "reveals himself plainly. The hawk encapsulates the man" (177).

Ceyx's story is essentially finished at 11.345, but Ovid represents it as broken off by the breathless arrival of Peleus' herdsman Onetor with news of the marauding, monstrous wolf that emerged from a marsh beside a temple sacred to Nereus and his daughters (11.359–368). One of these is Psamathe, who Peleus assumes has sent the wolf to devastate his herds and so to punish him for the murder of her son Phocus (as well as to provide a funeral offering to Phocus' ghost: 11.380–381).

Onetor's speech "reads like a parody of the traditional messenger-speech of tragedy" (Murphy at 11.349ff., 61), and Peleus' calm response (11.397–399; he had instantly perceived the origin and purpose of the attack) contrasts with Onetor's overexcitement. The incident serves as an introduction to the next episode (Ceyx and Alcyone, 11.410–748) in two ways. First, it provides a characterization of Ceyx's wife, Alcyone, who "leap[s] out" (11.385) of the palace distraught, falls upon her husband's neck, and begs him not to accompany the party he wants to send out to hunt down the monstrous wolf and so "preserve two lives in one" (11.383–388): "Alcyone's loving concern . . . foreshadow[s] the story to which these events are a prelude," Kenney says ([1986] 440), while Otis observes that "[h]er affection is from the start coloured by a sense of impending tragedy" (234). Second, the incident of the wolf, and especially its metamorphosis into marble in mid-slaughter of a heifer (11.403–406), provides the reason (in addition to his brother's metamorphosis) for Ceyx to undertake his fatal journey by sea to Claros to consult the god Apollo at his temple there, the subject of the next episode.

46. The story of Ceyx and Alcyone, Otis says, "represents a decisive point in Ovid's *carmen perpetuum* ["continuous song," 1.4] of metamorphoses" (261). At 339 lines (11.410–748), the episode is the second longest tale in the *Metamorphoses* (after the myth of Phaethon, 433 lines long: 1.747–779 and 2.1–400; Pythagoras' sermon at 15.75–478 is longer but is not a myth) and the first long narrative in the final or "historical" part of the poem, occurring early therein. (The just-preceding stories of Laomedon, Peleus and Thetis, and Daedalion and Chione are ascending steps that lead up to it.) Kenney calls this episode "perhaps the most moving" tale in the poem ([1986] 440).

Otis, who gives a masterly reading of the story, terms it "essentially an epic," though without gods as agents (233), representing, along with the stories of Pyramus and Thisbe and Cephalus and Procris, "the Ovidian ideal," (270), which is "conjugal love— the love of husband and wife" (266)—but these examples of "conjugal love" are hardly an "ideal" one wants to pursue, for the stories of these lovers end tragically.

Otis divides the narrative into four parts: (1) the departure of Ceyx (11.410–473), (2) the storm (11.474–572), (3) Alcyone's dream (11.573–709), and (4) the return of Ceyx and the metamorphosis of Ceyx and Alcyone (11.710–748). "The principle of balance," Otis notes, "is very clear: the *Departure* balances the *Return;* the long *storm* (Ceyx) passage balances the long *sleep-dream* (Alcyone) *ekphrasis*" (234).

The winds and waves (seen as a single entity) in the storm function like a character, serving, after Ceyx and Alcyone, as "the real third party—the main opposition—in their drama" (Otis 238), and for almost half of the storm section (11.474–572), that is, from 11.492 to 11.534 (forty-three lines), "there is no mention of anything but waves, winds and sky" (Otis 239).

There is a long tradition of literary storms, from Homer to Virgil, Galinsky notes, and "[b]y Ovid's time, storms . . . had become literary conventions or even set pieces." Using his storm "to write *about* this tradition," Galinsky says (his emphasis), Ovid "unleash[es] The Compleat Storm, the longest ever in Latin literature before Lucan," and surpassing all of Ovid's predecessors "in thunder, lightning, waves, rain, darkness and disaster" ([1975] 145).

To describe the action of the storm Ovid uses the simile of a siege, drawn from epic, that begins, "[T]he winds attacked fiercely from all directions" (11.490–491: *omnique e parte feroces / bella gerunt venti*). But the poet has reversed the usual application of the epic simile, Otis observes: "[I]nstead of comparing men to waves and winds he compares waves and winds to men. In fact the waves and winds are themselves the besiegers" (240). Ovid's description of the storm can be divided into three parts (after a beginning section at 11.474–481 that introduces the crew of the ship and the waves and wind): (1) an "antiphonal trilogy" focusing on the crew (11.482–489), then the waves and wind ("the war declared . . .") (11.489–491), and then the crew again (11.492–494); (2) "two doublets," the first at 11.495–506 (storm) and 11.507–513 (waves-wind), the second, at 11.514–523 (storm) and 11.524–536 (waves-wind), "accentuating and heightening the first"; and (3) a second "antiphonal trilogy" that again focuses on the crew (11.537–550), then the waves and the wind ("victory") (11.551–557), and then the crew again, as well as Ceyx (11.557–569). "The action and emotion rise throughout to a climax in the last line": "Suddenly, a black wave crested high above the swells, then broke and buried [Ceyx] beneath its flood" (11.568–569; see Otis, quoted above, 243–244).

And so Ceyx, drowning, "is forsaken by the gods and abandoned to nature itself," which Ovid represents (in the winds) "as inanimate forces . . . that take on, as it were, malevolent personal purpose" (Otis 245–246).

Meanwhile, Alcyone (from 11.573ff.) busies herself as she waits by preparing for Ceyx's return, going "again and again to the temple of Juno, approaching the altar of the goddess on behalf of her dear husband, who was no more, praying that he would be safe" (11.578–580; Alcyone prays to Juno, Murphy [at 11.578, 72] reminds us, because she is the goddess of marriage). Juno, however, wishes "to rid her altar of these beseeching hands to which death clung" (11.584)—as Kenney says, "Alcyone, though she does not know it, is in mourning and therefore until the funeral rites are duly performed her touch pollutes the altar" ([1986] 441)—and sends Iris to the cave of the god Sleep to instruct him to send in turn a false ghost to Alcyone to tell her Ceyx is dead. In this third section, centered on Alcyone's dream (11.573–709), there is, Otis says, "a definite movement from anxious ignorance . . . to tragic knowledge" that is "beautifully balanced around the central Somnus [Sleep] scene." The method of action is indirect ("both Juno and Somnus act by intermediaries: they meet neither each other nor Alcyone herself") and "serves to isolate and give remoteness to the pivotal figure of Somnus as well as to separate Alcyone and her woe from the world of Juno and Somnus" (Otis 246–247), although, as Feeney notes, there is another reason for what Otis calls Sleep's remoteness.

The scene in the cave of Sleep is "the exact opposite of the Storm or of the anguished and vocal farewell of Alcyone," Otis says. "To the boisterous rage of the tempest [11.495–496] there is counterset the soporific murmur of Lethe [11.603–604] and Iris' exquisite invocation of Sleep [11.623]. . . . To the ominous night on the ocean [11.521 and 11.549–550] there is opposed the soothing darkness of the House of Sleep [11.595–596]" (248–249). Moreover, while "Ovid's humour is in abeyance" during the storm, in the cave of Sleep "a light and muted . . . humour plays over the whole scene" (Otis 250).

The figure of Sleep is the third of four great personifications in the poem (see n. 9). Feeney observes that the personification of sleep (along with those of envy and hunger) "involve[s] us in what it is like to feel something," and since sleep is "a self-contained state, . . . the House of Sleep is a self-contained unit of narrative, with Sleep himself uninvolved in any direct engagement with the characters of the narrative; such action as he partakes in is indirect, mediated via his agent, Morpheus" (243).

Sleep chooses Morpheus to appear to Alcyone in a dream in the guise of her husband's ghost. Morpheus, whose name (like the *morph-* in metamorphosis) comes from the Greek word *morphê,* "form," is "a specialist," Fantham says, "skilled in conveying the gait, expression and even intonation of men, in fact Metamorphosis personified" ([1979] 338). "[L]ike a good confidence trickster," she notes ([1979] 338), "he forestalls challenge" with his first words to Alcyone: "Do you recognize your Ceyx, my poor darling? Or has my death so changed my appearance?" (11.658–659).

But why, Fantham asks, "is the trusting wife fobbed off with a false ghost when true friends and lovers since Homer had been granted the comfort and protection of their beloved dead?" ([1979] 339). In answer, she says that Ovid creates Morpheus in order "to avoid the traditional encounter, and deny the return of Ceyx's spirit." This is "the consequence of the physical return, the restoration of Ceyx's body and ensuing metamorphosis" (all soon to come). Ovid does not want to "detract from the climactic value of the return by any hint of how it will take place, so he must not allow Ceyx to address Alcyone before this reunion of bodies." And so Ovid rewrites "the original separation tragedy of shipwreck, loss and eternal mourning, bringing Ceyx's body back to the shores of Trachis and sending Alcyone to the shore to find him. This excluded the return of the ghost, for which Ovid substituted the perfect impersonator, motivating his coming by the distaste of Juno for contamination from the vows of the bereaved" ([1979] 344). By this means, Ovid "was able to represent Alcyone's grief and love in the last phase of the narrative with a pathos that matched and even surpassed her love and foreboding at the outset" ([1979] 345).

There is in the episode overall, Otis notes, a "rise and fall of . . . tension, [a] rhythmic succession of violence and quiet." Moreover, Ovid contrasts "the real and the unreal, the demythologized storm and the mythologized sleep." The storm lacks "the usual divine machinery . . . [,] and the inanimate forces of nature" are given a "malevolent personality." Finally, "the most personal and subjective of events—the lover's dream—is . . . objectified and clothed in the garments of epic fantasy and myth." Alcyone's speech, after her dream (11.684–707), "corresponds . . . to the last thoughts and words of Ceyx in the storm" (11.544–569): "Ceyx implores the waves to carry his body back to Alcyone; Alcyone laments her inability to join Ceyx in his death and burial." An "impasse" has now been reached "from which the metamorphosis can logically issue" (Otis 251).

Ceyx's return parallels his departure. At 11.463–471 Alcyone stands at the water's edge and watches Ceyx, then the ship, then the sails gradually disappear from sight. At 11.714–728 Alcyone, again on the shore, catches sight of "something far out that seemed like a body floating in the water" (11.715–716); then, as it is washed closer to shore, she sees that it is a body, and as it is carried by the action of the waves closer still, she realizes that it is indeed Ceyx. "It's him!" (11.725; Otis makes this extended observation [252]).

Ovid varies the amount of time that elapses as a human being undergoes metamorphosis, sometimes making a change sudden, sometimes drawing it out, as he chooses. The duration of the process naturally coincides with and is a function of the poet's description of it (since a metamorphosis exists only in the poet's words), and that description is sometimes lengthy and detailed, sometimes not, also as he chooses—but only to some extent, since naturalistic expectations play a role in Ovid's determining the length of his description of a metamorphosis: Perdix, thrown from the Acropolis at Athens by Daedalus, has to be changed into a bird before he hits the ground if he is to be saved. The process (that is, Ovid's description of it), from throw to change, takes five and a half lines (8.250b–255). Metamorphosis into a tree can and does vary (for the trees aren't going anywhere), from Daphne's (nine lines: 1.548–556) to Dryope's (forty-four lines 9.349–392). Changes into birds can vary, too, but within a much shorter time, hence line, frame: Nisus becomes an osprey in a line and a half (8.145b–146). Ovid offers that metamorphosis in parentheses almost as a detail he forgot and now adds as an afterthought. Daedalion, like Perdix, has to be changed in midair to avoid dying in a fall, and turns into a hawk in six and a half lines (11.339b–345).

The foregoing remarks obviously do not reflect a systematic study and are intended only to give some indication of the variations in length of time and number of lines that Ovid makes in describing metamorphoses. The examples, chosen somewhat at random, can provide background for Alcyone's change into a bird and Otis' observation about it. At 11.731 Ovid says, "Alcyone leaped up on [the jetty] and—a miracle—she was flying!" and continues at 11.732: "Beating the air with newborn wings . . ." (The change occupies a single line). "The moment of [Alcyone's] metamorphosis," Otis says, "defies observation: the wonder of the bystanders is really a belated perception of the fact. The transition is so smooth, the movement from anguished attempt to completed act is so natural, so emotionally inevitable, that there can be no exact demarcation of before and after" (254).

Ceyx, likewise, is quickly changed, though Ovid draws out the process slightly with two questions (two indirect questions in the Latin) to dramatize the change from dead man to living bird: "[O]r did Ceyx feel her kissing him? Was it merely the motion of the waves that made him seem to lift his head? It was hard for people there to say, but surely he did feel it, and, at last . . . they were both turned into birds" (11.739–742). "[T]here is no resuscitation like Ceyx's in ancient literature, outside Ovid himself," Fantham observes ([1979] 344). Otis comments: "[W]hen Alcyone reaches his body and kisses him with her beak . . . the moment of change is lost in the swift sequence of emotions and events. That love should so dare, that love should so respond to love, is the almost necessary climax of a passion that will not be thwarted" (254). "Such a metamorphosis never was," Fantham concludes ([1979] 342).

There is an additional metamorphosis in the story, to which Otis draws attention: Ceyx, struggling in the water, had "longed for the waves to wash his lifeless body home" to Alcyone (11.564), and, as Otis says, his "request . . . has been in fact fulfilled, . . . the malice of the storm has been transformed into sympathetic obedience to his desire" (254).

Commenting on the "symphonic balance of the whole episode," Otis notes that

[t]he harsh introduction . . . is countered and transformed by the irenic close. . . . The violence of the storm is offset by the quiet in the Cave of Sleep, the malice of the storm-

waves by the humanity of the waves that waft Ceyx back to Alcyone; above all the terrible separation of the lovers by their blessed reunion. . . . The change of the lovers into halcyon-birds has a truly cosmic significance: the hostility of man and nature transformed by love; death made into new life; human tragedy converted to cosmic beneficence (256).

The gods are conspicuously absent, as Otis observes: "The winds and the waves . . . do in fact fulfil both Alcyone's and Ceyx's desire while the gods do nothing. . . . The metamorphosis is therefore a true expression or symbol of what we might call the natural victory of love, or . . . the beneficent identity of man and nature" (366).

Ovid's description of Alcyone and Ceyx as halcyons and of the "halcyon days" ("for seven tranquil days in winter Alcyone broods on her nest floating on the water. At that time of year the sea is calm": 11.745–747) "faithfully reflects ancient scientific teaching," Kenney says, adding, "the *aition* is [Ovid's] own" ([1986] 442).

For Ovid's sources for the story of Ceyx and Alcyone, see Otis 421–423. Griffin thinks that the "general drift and tone of the Hellenistic dialogue [the pseudo-Lucianic *Halcyon*] are very similar to what we find in Ovid and prevent us from accepting . . . Otis' view that [quoting Otis, 233] 'Ovid deliberately changed a more or less typical legend of divine vengeance into a quite different tale of human bereavement and sorrow'" (323).

Since, for Ovid's story to unfold, Ceyx must take a journey by sea in order to be shipwrecked, the poet motivates his character to consult an oracle of Apollo, but makes the logical (and closer) choice, Delphi, the site of the premier shrine of Apollo in ancient Greece, impossible to reach, by having a character named Phorbas, and his Phlegyan "bandits" (Murphy at 11.413, 65), block the road to Delphi (11.410–414). The second most important temple of Apollo was at Claros (Kenney [1986] 440), more than two hundred miles across the Aegean Sea from Trachis (Fantham [1979] 341 n. 47), near Colophon, which was on (or near) the coast of Asia Minor (northwest of ancient Ephesus, northeast of the island of Samos). Ceyx's ship "had sailed perhaps halfway to its destined port, no more than that," Ovid says (11.478–479), when the storm comes on. That is, they are about one hundred miles out to sea.

At 11.429 Alcyone says, "I've often read the names [of those shipwrecked at sea] on empty tombs," referring to cenotaphs, which were "empty tombs set up in memory of those lost at sea," as Murphy notes. "The horror of death by drowning at sea," he continues, "is a common theme of Greek and Latin literature. . . . [I]t is not death which is to be feared, but the loss of funeral rites" (at 11.429, 65).

At 11.475–477 Ovid says, "The sailors brought their oars to the side, then raised the yards to the top of the mast and unfurled the sails to catch the stiffening wind." As for the first action, according to Murphy, "the oars are turned alongside the ship. It is only later when the storm breaks that they are taken inside the ship . . . and the oarholes are stopped up" (at 11.475, 68). The second action is described in a straightforward way, as Haupt-Ehwald note: the sailors draw the yards at the mast upward (they hoist the yards) and then lower the sails reefed on the yards (at 11.476, 2.213; but at 11.470 Alcyone is said to watch the sails fluttering at the top of the mast).

At 11.705–706 Alcyone says, "[A]nd one inscription on our tombstone will unite us, if not one urn," the one inscription, as Murphy notes, juxtaposing their names. "*Alcyone Ceycis coniunx*" (at 11.706, 77), which scans as the first half of a hexameter line, ending at the hephthemimeral (seventh half-foot) caesura.

47. Ovid's transition from the story of Ceyx and Alcyone to that of Aesacus and Hesperia (11.749–795), with which book 11 ends, has the casual manner the poet so often employs to go from one tale to the next. An old man watches Ceyx and Alcyone

flying together (11.749–750). "Then someone nearby—or perhaps it was the same old man—said, 'The bird you see there with the slender legs, gliding over the water . . .'" (11.751ff., referring to the now changed Aesacus). This story, which "makes its first appearance here" (Kenney [1986] 442), "is yet another embedded narrative of erotic pursuit," Nagle says, "with the differences that the suitor is mortal, and remorseful after unintentionally causing his victim's death" ([1989a] 116).

Otis sees this episode and that of Peleus and Thetis as "a pair of end-pieces that are meant to set off the mighty epic [of Ceyx and Alcyone] that lies between them" (231). The story also has affinities with those of Ceyx and Alcyone and Daedalion and Chione (11.291–345), since Aesacus, like Ceyx and Alcyone (11.741–742) and Daedalion (11.339–343), is changed into a bird through "divine pity" (11.784–786), as Murphy observes (at 11.784, 80).

The narrative of Aesacus and Hesperia also recalls the story of Orpheus and Eurydice at 10.1–85 in that (as Solodow observes) "at the moment of union (Eurydice's marriage, the rape of Hesperia) the woman is bitten by a snake and dies; the man renounces the world; and the gods take pity on the bereaved lover" (17; Hesperia's death by snakebite ultimately looks back to Virgil's story of Eurydice's death [on the point of being raped] at *Georgics* 4.457—459, as Segal [(1969a) 25 n. 55] and Murphy [at 11.775–776, 80] note).

With this tale Ovid arrives at the time of the Trojan War: "Peleus, the father of Achilles, has already made his appearance in the Ceyx story, and now, in Aesacus, we are introduced to the brother of Hector," Achilles' great Trojan opponent in that war (Murphy, introduction to 11.749–795, 79). The unnamed narrator mentions Aesacus' ancestry (11.754–758), omitting Tros, founder of the line, however, and beginning with his children, Ilus, Assaracus, and Ganymede. The line of descent is: Tros; Ilus; Laomedon; Priam; Aesacus, Hector, and others. The episode, looking back to earlier stories while bringing us to the Trojan War, ends the long approach (that started with Laomedon at 11.194ff.) to the event that marks the beginning of "history" and that introduces the increasingly "Roman" books of the *Metamorphoses,* books 12 through 15. "The preparation . . . has been so careful that few readers would have realized that they were passing from one world to another, from myth to history" (Due 148).

BOOK TWELVE

48. Ovid's brief reference in the opening lines of book 12 to the funeral of Aesacus links book 11, at the end of which the story of Aesacus occurs, to book 12 (as often; see n. 5), and the funeral itself provides the opportunity for the familiar "transition through absence" (Solodow 43–44) from Aesacus to the Trojan War: "Paris . . . failed to appear for his sad duty. He soon returned, however, bringing to his country the wife he had stolen—and a lengthy war" (12.4–6).

After forward-pointing references in book 11—the building of Troy and Laomedon's treachery (11.194ff.) and the marriage of Peleus and Thetis (11.221ff.), with Achilles' birth soon after (11.264–265)—the third part of the poem ("'historical' personages") now gets under way in earnest with Ovid's version of the Trojan War and its aftermath, at least that aspect of the aftermath that formed the Romans' foundation myth: the Trojan prince Aeneas' flight from Troy, his wanderings, and his arrival in Italy, where he establishes himself and his Trojan followers (the subject of Virgil's *Aeneid*), where his son Ascanius will found Alba Longa, and where his (and Ascanius') descendants will found Rome (Virgil, *Aeneid* 1.267–277 and 8.42–48; and Livy, *Ab Urbe Condita* 1.3.3).

Books 12.1–13.622 of the *Metamorphoses* are referred to as Ovid's "*Iliad*," books 13.623–14.608 as his "*Aeneid*," these parts of the *Metamorphoses* thus named for the famous works of Ovid's two great predecessors. Ovid plays variations on the subjects of those works that would raise their authors' eyebrows considerably, for these variations serve also as a commentary, devastating at times, on the "originals" they are derived from. In his "*Iliad*" and his "*Aeneid*" Ovid also makes considerable geographical and chronological progress toward the Rome of his own time, the goal for his work that he announced in the opening lines ("from the first origin of the world . . . down to my own time," 1.3–4).

Ovid's "*Iliad*," at 1,250 lines (12.1–628, 13.1–622), constitutes slightly more than 10 percent of the poem's 11,995 lines. His "*Aeneid*," at 954 lines (13.623–968, 14.1–608), about 8 percent. Their combined total of slightly more than 18 percent represents a considerable portion of a work to devote to "imitation" of two earlier epics with which the *Metamorphoses* has virtually nothing in common except length and the dactylic hexameter in which it was written.

Earlier critics have seen a falling-off in quality in the last four books of the *Metamorphoses* in comparison with the first eleven (for example, Fränkel 101–111, 221–222 n. 79; Wilkinson [1955] 221–226; Otis 278ff., especially 282–305). Galinsky, however, believes that Ovid retains the "tone and spirit" of the earlier books of the *Metamorphoses* in the narrative of books 12 through 15 ([1975] 217), and most recent critics would probably agree with him.

Homer had established the history of Troy "once and for all," as Due says, and Virgil, "the new classic and Homer's peer," firmly linked Troy to Rome "as the background and source of . . . her greatness" (140–141). Ovid in his "*Iliad*" and "*Aeneid*" removes the substance of these works, except for bits and pieces, and uses what is left in each as a kind of sketchy framework for substance of his own that "deflate[s] the whole heroic ideal, as set forth in the Homeric tradition and recently restated by Virgil in close and complex symbolic relation with the Augustan myth" (Coleman 475; he is referring specifically to the episodes in book 12 of Caeneus and the battle of Lapiths and centaurs and, in book 13, to the Judgment of Arms, as the debate between Ulysses and Ajax for the arms of Achilles is called).

Ovid gathered the material for his "*Iliad*" (12.1–13.622) from various sources and little from the *Iliad* itself—bits and pieces, as I have said. The account of the Greeks at Aulis (12.1–38), with the omen of the serpent that devours the nine birds, the seer Calchas' interpretation of this omen, and the serpent's metamorphosis into stone (12.11–23), appeared in the *Cypria,* one of several no longer surviving poems in the collection known as the Epic Cycle (for which see Evelyn-White), which was probably produced not long after the *Iliad* and the *Odyssey* were created and which fleshes out the story of the Trojan War from the Judgment of Paris to the death of Odysseus. (*Iliad* 2.299–330 also narrates, in flashback, the omen of the serpent and the birds and Calchas' interpretation of it.)

The story of Agamemnon's sacrifice of his daughter Iphigenia, with the last-minute substitution of a deer for the girl (12.24–34), was also told in the *Cypria.* Ovid's predecessors, Aeschylus, at *Agamemnon* 228ff., and Lucretius, at *De Rerum Natura* 1.84ff., describe the sacrifice of Iphigenia—she is killed—as does Euripides in the *Iphigenia at Aulis,* where she is saved by the miraculous intervention at the last moment of Artemis, who substitutes a hind on the altar for the girl, if the concluding section of the play (from 1570, especially 1578, to the end) is authentic, although, as Lesky says, it "shows signs of disrupted transmission and arouses the suspicion of Byzantine interpolation"

(362). Kenney notes that "[b]y accepting the version in which an animal was substituted for the girl [Ovid] is able to treat the story unemotionally in a passage of fast-moving 'bridging' narrative" ([1986] 443). Ovid has, in fact, conflated the Greeks' two departures from Aulis into a single departure, omitting a great deal in between, all of which he condenses into one line: "after enduring much hardship they [the ships] arrived at the Phrygian shore" (12.38; see Due 148).

The *Aithiopis*, another poem in the Epic Cycle, narrated the deaths of Achilles and Memnon and the Judgment of Arms (recounted by Ovid at 12.580–628, 13.576–622, and 13.1–398, respectively). The *Little Iliad*, also in the Epic Cycle, also set forth the contest for Achilles' arms. In Ovid's version of the Judgment of Arms, Solodow notes, "[a]ll the familiar incidents [that occur in the *Iliad*] come up exclusively" (32).

At 13.399–575 Ovid touches briefly on the Greek hero Philoctetes' return to Troy (the *Little Iliad*, as well as lost plays by Aeschylus and Euripides and Sophocles' *Philoctetes*: see Jebb, *Sophocles: Philoctetes* xiii–xxxi); the death of Priam (the *Little Iliad*, and described dramatically in book 2 of Virgil's *Aeneid*); the rape of Cassandra (the *Sack of Ilium*, another lost work from the Epic Cycle; and Euripides' *Trojan Women*); the murder of Astyanax, the infant son of Hector and Andromache (the *Little Iliad*; also in the *Trojan Women*, with a brief mention at Euripides' *Andromache* 9–111); and the slaughter of Priam's and Hecuba's son Polydorus by Polymestor, king of Thrace (Euripides' *Hecuba*), before narrating lengthier accounts of the sacrifice of Priam's and Hecuba's daughter Polyxena (the *Sack of Ilium* and Euripides' *Hecuba*), Hecuba's grief, her discovery of her son Polydorus' body, the revenge she takes on Polymestor, and her metamorphosis into a dog (variants of or references to these found in the *Hecuba*).

Ovid ends his "*Iliad*" with the death of Memnon (13.576–622), which is out of place, since that hero was killed by Achilles, and Achilles' death has already been described (12.580–628). Ovid refers to Memnon's death, however, only in connection with the successful effort of Aurora to secure her son's immortality from Jupiter.

I have omitted from this brief sketch of events in the Trojan War mentioned in Ovid's "*Iliad*" the non–Trojan War stories he includes, that is, the episodes of Caeneus and the battle of Lapiths and centaurs (12.146–535; Nestor refers to the battle of Lapiths and centaurs at *Iliad* 1.262–272, mentioning Caeneus by name at 1.264) and that of Periclymenus (12.536–576; Periclymenus is one of Nestor's eleven brothers, all killed by Hercules, whose slaughter of them is mentioned at *Iliad* 11.690–693). Ellsworth notes that these stories are "[i]nserted" in the pause in battle that occurs after the death of Cycnus and before the death of Achilles, while the ten-year period between Achilles' battle with Cycnus and his own death "are summed up in [a] single line" at 12.584: "With the war drawn out for almost ten years now . . ." ([1980] 24–25). As for Ovid's "relation to the *Iliad*, near yet utterly removed," this, Solodow says, "is most aptly expressed in his mention of the confrontation between Hector and Achilles" at 12.75–77: "Searching through the line for either Cycnus or Hector, he came upon Cycnus and engaged him in battle. (Hector's death was delayed until the tenth year.)" Solodow comments, "The climactic event of the *Iliad* is relegated to nothing more than a casual parenthesis" (32).

Although Achilles, the major character of the *Iliad*, appears directly in only one story in Ovid's "*Iliad*," that of Cycnus at 12.70–145, his presence is felt throughout, since his actions, both in killing Cycnus and in inviting the chieftains to a celebratory dinner during the truce that follows, bring about the stories of Caeneus, the battle of Lapiths and centaurs, and Periclymenus (12.146–579); and after he is killed by Paris and Apollo at the instigation of Neptune, who retaliates for the loss of his son Cycnus (12.580–

628), his arms are the subject of the contest between Ulysses and Ajax (13.1–398); his ghost demands the sacrifice of Polyxena (13.439–480); and before his own death he had killed Memnon, with whose funeral and metamorphosis Ovid ends his "*Iliad*" (13.576–622). (See Ellsworth [1980] 28).

The arrival of the Greek ships at the Phrygian shore (12.37–38) comes as no surprise to the Trojans, who are there to meet them, because they have been informed by Rumor, whose "global centre for the dissemination of hearsay" (Kenney [1986] 443) Ovid describes at 12.39–63 in the last of four great personifications, three of abstract states, the fourth an abstract phenomenon (see n. 9).

Ovid's Rumor, who brings the news to the Trojans that the Greek fleet is approaching, recalls Virgil's description of the figure at *Aeneid* 4.173–190. (Virgil's Rumor goes to inform Dido's suitor, Iarbas, of the Carthaginian queen's affair with the interloper Aeneas: 4.191–197.) Ovid, however, instead of describing Rumor herself, "catalogues her minions and allies and conducts the reader on a tour of her house" (Solodow 251 n. 60).

The poet uses his representation of Rumor, Feeney says, "[a]s a condensation of ancient attitudes towards the plasticity of tradition and the variable nature of poetic truth" and then proceeds "to demonstrate what he means with his own comprehensive rewriting of Homer, and with the portrayal of Nestor's partial and misleading paradigmatic act of epic narrative, which itself supplants the Trojan war as it smothers the mighty Hercules [later in this book: 12.169–541]" (248).

In the first engagement of Greek and Trojan forces, after Hector has slain Protesilaus and Cycnus his thousand (12.67–69, 72–73), Achilles goes "[s]earching through the line for either Cycnus or Hector" and comes upon Cycnus (12.75–76). Their hand-to-hand combat represents "the culminating duel of the *Iliad* between Achilles and Hector, which is virtually ignored by Ovid" (Ellsworth [1980] 27).

Achilles bears down on Cycnus in his chariot, "brandishing his spear with his powerful arm" (12.79) and shouting, "Whoever you are, young man, console yourself as you die with the thought that you were slaughtered by Achilles from Thessaly!" (12.80–81). The word for "slaughtered," *iugulatus* (12.81; *iugulo* means "to cut the throat of"), makes Achilles "seem like a butcher or a brigand," for it "stresse[s] the brutal and bloody aspects of killing" (Glenn 161).

Not in the least intimidated, Cycnus counters that he wears his armor "for show" (12.90), the truth of which Achilles soon learns, for in a comical scene (12.98ff.), the Greek hero, his frustration mounting, hurls a second and then a third spear without effect at Cycnus, who stands exposed before him, not defending himself. Then Achilles "raged like a bull in the arena" when it "lunges at the red cloak driving it mad" (12.102–104). No doubt the simile drawn from Roman bullfighting (introduced into Rome by Julius Caesar, according to Pliny, *Natural History* 8.182) suggests the poet's "intense modernity" (Solodow 239–240 n. 2), but it suggests even more the "wrath of Achilles," the *Iliad*'s great theme, announced in the first line of that poem ("Sing, goddess, the wrath of Achilles, son of Peleus") and the cause of its tragedy. Here, Achilles' wrath moves, as his frustration mounts, to depths of ridiculousness, not heights of tragedy. Unable even to scratch Cycnus' skin after repeated attempts, Achilles jumps down from his chariot "roaring in his fury" (*fremebundus*, 12.128), beats Cycnus with his weapons, throws him on the ground, and strangles him with the chin strap of the Trojan's helmet (12.128–143; this recalls Menelaus' similar near-strangling of Paris at *Iliad* 3.369–376). When Achilles prepares to strip Cycnus' body of its armor, he finds the armor empty, the body gone: the warrior's father, Neptune, has changed him into a swan (12.143–145; Cycnus is the third of that name in the *Metamorphoses* to be changed into a swan, the meaning of the Latin word *cycnus* [from the Greek word *kugnos*], all unrelated. The other two are at 2.367–380 and 7.371–379). Ovid has reproduced the *Iliad*'s Wrath of Achilles in a grim burlesque of the heroic in the Cycnus episode, caricaturing that wrath and, by extension, deriding the Homeric poem's warrior ethos. In what comes next, Nestor's stories of Caeneus and the battle of Lapiths and centaurs, this derision is even more evident.

49. The transition at 12.146–181 from the Cycnus episode to the stories of Caeneus, the battle of the Lapiths and centaurs, and Periclymenus (12.182–576; with a brief interruption by Tlepolemus at 12.536–541, which provides a bridge to the story of Periclymenus), all narrated by Nestor, is composed of events that follow naturally from Achilles' defeat of Cycnus: Cycnus' death leads to a truce, during which a feast day occurs; Achilles uses that occasion to host a dinner for Greek chieftains (none of whom is named, except for Nestor and Tlepolemus); the dinner is followed by stories, notably those told by Nestor and thus embedded narratives.

We have just seen in direct narrative—in "actuality"—Ovid's version of the heroic age in Achilles' combat with Cycnus. There will be no more direct narration of fighting and warfare in Ovid's "*Iliad*" except for Achilles' death, instigated by Neptune to avenge Cycnus and carried out by Apollo, using the hand and bow of Trojan Paris (12.580–606). Now, in Nestor's tales, we see the heroic age indirectly, in stories told about it, as recollected. But a distinction needs to be made, for these heroes divert themselves, Ovid says, "not with the music of the lyre, nor with songs, nor by listening to the boxwood flute" (12.157–158), that is, not in the way Achilles in the *Iliad* diverts Patroclus and himself in his tent after he withdraws from the fighting, accompanying himself on the lyre as he sings *klea andrôn*, "men's deeds of renown" (9. 189), the august subject of epic poetry. Rather, Nestor and companions here engage in "conversation" (*sermone*, 12.159) about "courage" (*virtus*, 12.159), somewhat less refined, less elevated, than music of the flute or Achilles' songs, as they recall "past battles, their own and their enemies', ... telling and retelling ... stories about dangers met and overcome" (12.160–162; see Due 149–150). Ovid used the word for "conversation" (*sermo*) earlier to describe the "tales" that "rumors pour ... into idle ears" (*sermonibus*, 12.56), and the word's appearance here hints that Nestor's indirect narrative is unreliable (with more evidence for its unreliability soon to come).

Another contrast to Achilles' banquet and Nestor's stories, a contrast nearer in time and closer in culture than the *Iliad*, is Dido's banquet for Aeneas and his companions at the end of book 1 of the *Aeneid*, to which, Mack (1988) notes, Ovid alludes here. At that banquet, the Carthaginian court bard Iopas sings about a subject that Achilles, Nestor, and company implicitly reject at 12.157–158 (quoted earlier):

> He sang [Virgil says] of the travelling moon and the sun's manifold labours;
> He sang the creation of man and beast, of fire and water;
> Arcturus he sang and the rainy Hyades and the twin Bears;
> The reason why winter suns race on to dip in the ocean
> And what slows down the long nights.
> (*Aeneid* 1.742–746; Day Lewis, trans.)

After Iopas' song, Dido attempts (successfully) to "prolong the evening in conversation" (1.748: *noctem sermone trahebat*) by having Aeneas tell about his adventures, a clause Ovid echoes directly at 12.159, "they prolonged the evening in conversation" (*noctem sermone trahunt*). "Vergil's banqueters," Mack says, "enjoyed music and song; Ovid's Greeks, in contrast, have no taste for culture: they do not want to listen to a song about the nature of the universe like [Iopas'], nor do they want to listen to heroic song like that of Aeneas [in *Aeneid* 2]. What they want to do is talk—about themselves, of course" ([1988] 129). Although the announced topic is "courage" (*virtus*, 12.159), "we search in vain," Mack notes, "for any indications of valor in the gory account of slaughter that follows" ([1988] 129), that is, in Nestor's stories.

Achilles, the great warrior and doer of deeds—as we've just seen—passes the heroic-age baton unwittingly to Nestor, the "arch-reminiscer," as Kenney calls him ([1986] 443), for "[t]here are clearly heroic speakers as well as fighters" (Glenn 163). That is to say, the invulnerable Cycnus reminds Nestor of Caeneus, also invulnerable, and with his story about Caeneus, Nestor "seeks to cap the preceding *Cycnus*" (Coleman 474; similarly Glenn 163), for as Ovid, that is, Nestor says, "what is even more amazing about [Caeneus; that is, more amazing than his Cycnus-like invulnerability] is that he was born a girl" (12.174–175). If there is a competition here between Achilles, the doer of deeds ("in the unconventional role of audience," as Nagle puts it [1989] 116), and Nestor, the speaker of words (Glenn 163–165 hints at the idea), the old talker wins it, and Achilles cooperates in his own defeat, for he asks Nestor questions (12.179–181: Who was Caeneus? Why was his sex changed? How do you know him? Who killed him?) that give him an opening of more than 350 lines, not only for the story of Caeneus but also for the long account of the battle of Lapiths and centaurs. And in answering, Nestor makes Achilles look foolish: Who was Caeneus? She was from your hometown, and your father, Peleus, might well have married her, had it not been for Thetis (12.189–195). How do I know Caeneus and how did he die? From (and in) the battle of Lapiths and centaurs, in which your father (as we learn) played a prominent role, killing six centaurs (a point made by Glenn 164). Later, in a passage that retroactively underscores the oddness of Achilles' ignorance, Tlepolemus, Hercules' son, takes Nestor to task for leaving out *his* father, who had told him "many, many times," he says, "that he had defeated the cloud-born centaurs" (12.536–541). Could Peleus have been so silent about a battle he played a prominent role in that his son Achilles knows nothing of it?

Even though Nestor is more than two hundred years old (12.187–188), what is "most noticeable" about his account, Nagle says, is his "extreme precision" in recounting warriors, weapons, blows, and wounds ([1989a] 116). Nestor has "an extraordinary memory for trifles," Mack comments, adding, "[W]ounds are what interest him most" ([1988] 130]). Moreover, his embedded tales, because of where they are told—by the battlefield, a scene of ultimate action—and because of their audience of heroic warriors, doers of ultimate deeds, make the point that speaking words about deeds, that is, telling stories, is equivalent to doing deeds.

The subject of Nestor's narrative about Neptune's rape of Caenis (Caeneus' name as a girl), her sex change, and acquisition, as a male, of physical invulnerability, may seem out of place in its setting, a battlefield encampment in which, *après combat*, warriors eat, drink, and swap war stories. Yet, in his version of a famous epic about wrath caused by woman-stealing set at the end of a war caused by woman-stealing, in which the humanity of the women stolen (Helen, Chryseis, Briseis) gets little or no consideration, Ovid offers a story about rape that is different from all the many other such narratives in the *Metamorphoses* and that puts the *Iliad's* background rapes in perspective because of its particular "awareness of the implications of the physical vulnerability of women," as Curran says. Curran notes that

[t]he story shows that the only totally sure way for a woman to avoid rape is to give up her own sex and become a man. . . . The crime just committed against [Caenis] determines her greatest desire, that she lose her womanhood ["I don't ever want this to happen to me again: I don't want to be female anymore. Give me that, and you'll give me all I'll ever

want": 12.201–203]. Ovid makes clear the aggressive nature of rape and its intention to harm or hurt by having Caenis call it an *injuria* [12.201] and, much more explicitly a few lines later, by identifying sexual penetration with a wound: changed from woman to man, Caeneus is now to be immune from any kind of penetration. ([1978] 228)

For, as Ovid says, "[Neptune] had . . . made it impossible for *him* ever to be wounded or to be killed by the sword" (12.206–207). The theme of "the physical inferiority and timidity of women" in Caenis' wish (12.201–203) is sounded again, Curran says ([1978] 229), when the centaur Latreus taunts Caeneus for having once been a woman (12.470ff.).

Nestor follows the story of Caeneus' change of sex (which ends at 12.209) with a narrative of the battle of Lapiths and centaurs in which Caeneus took part (12.210–535), a well-known story; Nestor himself refers to it in the *Iliad* (1.262–273), mentioning Caeneus by name (1.264). "Frequently celebrated in art and literature," Coleman says (474), the myth is represented in the sculpture at the west end of the temple of Zeus at Olympia as well as in the metopes of the Parthenon at Athens, where, Galinsky observes, "it symbolizes the struggle of civilization against barbarism" ([1975] 126). But there was ambivalence about the myth. Homer (*Odyssey* 21.293ff.) and Horace (*Odes* 1.18.7–9) refer to it "as a warning of the dangers of excessive drinking" (Coleman 474 n. 4).

Ovid uses Nestor's stories, which occupy almost four hundred lines of text (12.182–535 and 12.542–576), "to play a trick with chronology," Kenney says, for "when the main narrative resumes [at 12.580], the war is in its tenth year" ([1986] 443). The episode of Lapiths and centaurs in particular "acts as a substitute for the extensive fighting around Troy" (Solodow 32) or as a "'surrogate' for the *Iliad*" (Nagle [1989a] 117; Due 150, Ellsworth [1980] 26, and Mack [1988] 128 make similar points). This episode, then, is the heart of Ovid's representation of the *Iliad*. But things are off center, for the heart of Ovid's "*Iliad*" is an embedded narrative, a story told, not a direct narrative of events. The setting for the battle of Lapiths and centaurs, Ovid's "substitute" or "surrogate" for the events of the *Iliad,* is a domestic one, a wedding feast, and the fighting thus occurs not on a battlefield but at a place where, as Due puts it, "fighting is normally out of place" (76). The weapons used for the most part—a wine bowl, goblets, wine jars, cauldrons, a candelabra, a table leg, an altar with a fire burning on it, antlers affixed to a pine tree (a votive offering), a lit torch, a stone threshold, a fire-hardened stake, a boulder, a tree trunk, a treetop, a crowbar, and a massive pile of uprooted trees (these last used against Caeneus)—are "freakish" and the wounds they make are "ghastly" (Fränkel 102). Finally, the battle of Lapiths and centaurs has no connection whatsoever with Homer's *Iliad*, unless one links the violent impulse to woman-stealing that starts the battle to the woman-stealing that lies behind the *Iliad.*

Galinsky thinks Ovid's "main concern" in his version of the battle of Lapiths and centaurs "is to display a *variatio* of more and more grotesque ways for men and half-men to die" and adds that the poet "revels in ever new ways of imagining how bodies can be mangled, maimed, and disintegrated," all of which Galinsky considers a "concession," for the most part, "to the taste of the Roman public" and due to "the great popularity at this time of the untragic presentation of tragic myths in the form of the pantomime" with its "tendency toward sensationalism" ([1975] 126, 138–139). For Anderson, by contrast, Ovid's "grotesque combats" in this tale "are travesties of the original myth," and "[t]hey take unmistakable aim at the glib assumption . . . that Theseus and Lapiths heroically upheld the values of Greek and indeed human civilization" ([1995b] 8).

Amid the grotesque descriptions of weapons, wounds, and death, there occurs a scene highly incongruous with its setting, Ovid's thirty-six–line vignette of Cyllarus and Hylonome, a young centaur couple who are deeply in love (12.393–428). About two thirds of this digression are given in equal parts to a description of each centaur. The final third brings them to the wedding as a loving pair and describes how they died together.

Cyllarus is, naturally enough, the most handsome centaur one could imagine: he has long blond hair, a blond beard, and the part of him that is human "seemed like a beautiful sculpture" (12.395–399). Cyllarus loves only Hylonome, who is, also naturally enough, "the loveliest of the lady centaurs" (12.405–406). Ovid narrates in detail the attention Hylonome gives to enhancing her beauty, that is, to her *cultus* (12.408; adding, "to the degree a centauress can make herself attractive" [12.408–409] and so calling attention to "the incongruity of a centaur whose toilet is so careful" [Solodow 88]), describing her hair, the flowers she adorns it with, her face-washing, her bathing, the quality of the animal skins she wears, and the way she wears them (12.409–415).

Cyllarus and Hylonome seem out of place here (in the postnuptial brawl), although Ovid describes them as "fighting fiercely, side by side" (12.418). A spear comes out of nowhere and strikes Cyllarus: a small wound, Ovid says, but in the heart. The spear is pulled out (by whom Ovid does not say), and Cyllarus lies dying. Hylonome rushes to him, takes him in her arms, and presses her lips to his to keep his soul from escaping. When she sees that Cyllarus is already dead, she says something that, the detail-obsessed Nestor reports, "the uproar kept me from hearing," a comment out of Samuel Beckett, throws herself on the spear that killed her beloved, and dies with her arms around him (12.419–428), "a standard pattern" for lovers' deaths that Ovid "has used several times before," Galinsky notes, those of Hyacinthus and Pyramus and Thisbe, for example ([1975] 127–128).

Solodow comments that in the *Iliad* "bloody battle scenes are interspersed with others that remind us of peace and domestic tenderness" (giving as examples *Iliad* 6.237–529 and 11.221–230). Here, though, he says, "the tender is tinged with the grotesque" (88). Galinsky, however, characterizes "the story of the two loving centaurs" as one of "cliché-ridden triteness" ([1975] 128). These observations seem accurate: the interlude of Cyllarus and Hylonome is incongruous in its context (the battle of Lapiths and centaurs), a tale that is itself incongruous with its setting (Ovid's "*Iliad*"), that setting incongruous with what it represents (Homer's *Iliad*); and the interlude is "tender" and "grotesque" with "cliché-ridden triteness." But Ovid uses this "triteness" creatively, just as James Joyce uses the clichés of romantic pulp fiction in his depiction of Gerty MacDowell in the thirteenth or "Nausicaa" episode in *Ulysses,* a scene that may serve as a modern analogue for Ovid's tale of Cyllarus and Hylonome.

The episode ends with Caeneus (12.459–535), who kills Latreus, the biggest centaur, after enduring taunts and insults from him ("*Girl!* Remember what you were born as, what happened to you, *girl!* and go . . .": 12.474ff.), as well as attacks—though they are harmless—with a Macedonian pike and sword. Then all the centaurs assault the invulnerable Caeneus together, and since they cannot wound him, bury him beneath a heap of tree trunks and smother him to death, or nearly so, for before dying he changes into a rare bird and flies away.

So ends Ovid's version of the battle of Lapiths and centaurs. In selecting this tale "as his sole representative of heroic warfare," Coleman says, "expounding it as the mere exhibition of brute force and senseless slaughter that it was and associating it with the fantastic story of Caeneus, [Ovid] is in reality pouring scorn upon the whole epic tradition of the aggrandizement of war. The epic tone is therefore parodic" (474).

At the end of Nestor's account of the battle of Lapiths and centaurs, Hercules' son

Tlepolemus, one of the Greek chieftains listening to Nestor, objects that his father wasn't even mentioned in Nestor's story of the battle, yet, Tlepolemus says, "he certainly told me many, many times that he had defeated the cloud-born centaurs" (12.540–541). Thus it is an objection to Nestor's story, made by a member of his audience, that provides the transition to the narrative of Periclymenus (12.542–576), which Nestor then launches into in order to explain why he hates Hercules and why he "would have left Hercules out of his account of the battle if Hercules had, in fact, been present" (Mack [1988] 131). (With this story Ovid again elaborates on a reference from the *Iliad*, as he has done in the preceding two stories, for at *Iliad* 11.689–693 Nestor, speaking to Patroclus, says that Hercules attacked Pylos and killed his eleven brothers–all his father's sons except himself.)

Nestor responds to Tlepolemus carefully. He neither affirms nor denies the truth of his questioner's objection, that is, his omission of Hercules from the preceding tale. Rather, he asks Tlepolemus why (by mentioning his father, Hercules) he thus compels him "to lay bare sorrows buried by time, and to mention my hatred for your father and the harm he did to me" (12.542–544). He quickly acknowledges, however, that Hercules "accomplished things that are beyond belief, and the world is full of his benefactions" (12.545–546). But then he notes that "we" are not singing the praise of enemies (*nec . . . laudamus*, 12.547–548)—for who would want to? (12.547–548)—and tells the story of Periclymenus to explain why Hercules is his enemy. In doing so he praises Hercules somewhat: the death of his brother Periclymenus was "astonishing" (*mira*, 12.556) because Hercules' arrow wounded him—he was now an eagle and in flight— and made him fall to earth, and the impact drove the arrow through his body and killed him. At the end of his account, Nestor addresses Tlepolemus. "Do you *still* think I am obliged to proclaim the exploits of your father, Hercules, O handsome admiral of the fleet from Rhodes?" (12.573–574), while insisting that he seeks no revenge for his brothers and that his friendship with Tlepolemus is "firm" (*solida*, 12.576).

Nestor is both circumspect and courageous in responding to Tlepolemus, as those who remember their Homer will recognize from the way Nestor addresses him: as "handsome admiral of the fleet from Rhodes." For in the Catalogue of Ships in *Iliad* 2, Homer, naming Tlepolemus and mentioning the nine ships he brought to Troy from Rhodes, explains how the hero came to Rhodes: as a grown man at home Tlepolemus struck and killed Likymnios, a beloved elderly uncle of his father (2.653–670), and fled thence to Rhodes. So Tlepolemus has a reputation as a hothead even among Homeric warriors, hotheads by definition, and as no respecter of age. The reference to Nestor as "old sir" (*senior*, 12.540) is thus somewhat chilling. This "heroic speaker" cannot respond to Tlepolemus without some concern for his own safety. That he stands his ground, that he does not revise his tale of Lapiths and centaurs by adding Hercules to it (and there is no evidence that Hercules was present: see Gantz 1.277–281), while being careful to acknowledge Hercules' achievements in other areas in general and in killing his brothers in particular, testifies to his courage. Finally, the *Iliad* supplies an element of poignancy to Nestor's exchange with Tlepolemus and his story of Periclymenus. In book 5 Hercules' son encounters the Trojan warrior Sarpedon, insults him, brags about his father, Hercules', earlier sack of Troy (as he implicitly brags about Hercules to Nestor here), and asserts that he is about to kill Sarpedon. The Trojan warrior, in turn, acknowledges Hercules' sack of Troy (as Nestor acknowledges Hercules' achievements here), and then kills Tlepolemus, although Tlepolemus wounds him in the thigh (*Iliad* 5. 628–662). Readers of Ovid's narrative here who remember the *Iliad* will know that the death of the rash Tlepolemus cannot be long in coming.

The story of Periclymenus ends Nestor's long recitation, which takes the place of the events of the *Iliad,* as noted earlier. Ovid's account of the Trojan War is all but over, lacking only the death of Achilles (with which book 12 ends) and the debate over his arms (in the first part of book 13: lines 1–398). Due notes that this tale "resumes . . . a number of themes" from earlier parts of the poem. Like Thetis (in book 11), Periclymenus can transform himself into any shape he wishes (12.556–558), a gift from Neptune, giver of special gifts also to Cycnus and Caeneus. The battle between Periclymenus and Hercules recalls the stories of Peleus and Thetis and Cycnus in that "the superhero [Hercules, Peleus, Achilles] has difficulties with an unusual foe." Periclymenus becomes a bird, like Daedalion, Ceyx and Alcyone, Aesacus, Cycnus, and Caeneus, whose "transformation[s] in a way saved them from death, while that of Periclymenus proves fatal to him." Lastly, "the detailed description of his death echoes the *Lapiths and Centaurs*" (151).

Nagle observes that the "preamble" to the story of Periclymenus (12.542–548) and its "conclusion" (12.573–576) "justify explicitly the neglect of Hercules, framing the account of the event which motivated the exclusion." When Nestor says that his "vengeance for [his] brothers" is "keeping silent about [Hercules'] mighty deeds" (12.575–576), the old warrior reverses the goal of epic, to preserve *klea andrôn* (men's deeds of renown), justifying this by the "values of the heroic code of epic itself," to "harm enemies" and "avenge kin." Finally, Nagle comments that the exchange between Nestor and Tlepolemus "retroactively undermines the reliability of the account of Lapiths and centaurs, and it does so in the context of epic poetry," the goal of which (as noted) is to preserve *klea andrôn.* Nestor is thus an unreliable narrator. ("A story is what its narrator makes it," as Mack says [(1988) 131].) And if he is unreliable, why should any of the other narrators of embedded stories in the *Metamorphoses* be considered reliable? Why should the ultimate narrator of the poem be considered reliable? "Ovid raises the issue of possible distortion," Nagle says, "first within the personification of [Rumor]" at 12.53–61, lines describing the false, garbled, inflated, erroneous, and so on small-r rumors that inhabit the house of Rumor. He continues with this issue "in Nestor's neglect of Hercules, and then immediately and with greatest clarity" in the soon-to-come debate over the arms of Achilles at the beginning of book 13 ([1989a] 117).

If narrators of embedded narratives in the *Metamorphoses* are unreliable, this is not a good time to find out, since more than three quarters of the poem have gone by (77.5 percent: 9,297 lines [books 1–12] out of 11,995), much of it in embedded narratives (31 percent: 2,885 lines out of 9,297). But (with the same supposition) what lies ahead is worse, for 57 percent of the remaining three books (13–15) consists of embedded narratives (1,537 lines out of 2,698; I am using Nagle's line counts for all the embedded stories in the *Metamorphoses,* but not adding on the number of lines of multiply embedded stories: [1989a] 101–124), and this is the "historical" section of the poem. Even if Nestor is the only unreliable narrator in the work, Ovid may be suggesting that nothing in the epic tradition is stable, from Homer to his Roman successor, Virgil, a highly idiosyncratic version of whose *Aeneid* Ovid will soon present (13.623–4.608).

50. Nestor's long storytelling session, which he concludes with the account of his brother Periclymenus' death at the hands of Hercules, the father of one of his listeners, is punctuated by the end of Achilles' dinner, the end of the scene, and the end of the day: The chieftains chez Achilles rise from their couches and go off to bed (12.577–579). The following scene, which begins with Neptune and Apollo looking down upon Troy and plotting the death of Achilles (the next episode: 12.580–628), implies a new

day and requires no special transition. Achilles' death was related in the *Aithiopis,* a lost poem from the Epic Cycle, as noted in n. 48.

When Ovid's Neptune, in seeking Apollo's aid, says that he himself cannot fight Achilles hand to hand (12.586–596), he is following the tradition according to which Achilles is killed by the Trojan Paris, with the help of Apollo. But the role Neptune does play here in Achilles' death is "peculiar to Ovid," as Kenney says ([1986] 445), for in the *Iliad,* Poseidon (that is, Neptune), along with Athena (that is, Minerva), gives Achilles moral support when he is nearly overwhelmed by the river Scamander, which he attacks in his rampage after the death of Patroclus (21.284–297).

Apollo, Ovid says, "in order to carry out his uncle's intentions—and his own" (12.597–598), goes down to the battlefield, finds Paris, urges him to kill Achilles, aims his bow for him, and guides the arrow to its mark (12.598–606). In an apostrophe to Achilles, the poet says to the hero (12. 610–611), "But if you had to die in battle with a woman, you would prefer to have fallen under the axe of Penthesilea," that is, rather than at the hand of Paris, since the Trojan prince was considered womanish (Haupt-Ehwald at 12.610, 2.276). According to the *Aithiopis,* Penthesilea, the Amazon queen who came to Troy and fought on the side of the Trojans, was killed by Achilles (Evelyn-White 506).

In his eulogy for the hero, Ovid uses a metaphor of measurement in which he contrasts the volume of Achilles' ashes, so to speak, to that of his fame: although these ashes are "hardly enough to fill an urn," his fame "fills the entire world." It is this fame that gives "the true measure of the man," and by means of that measure Achilles "remains what he was," that is, in life: he does not become his low-in-volume ashes (12.615–619). Ovid's assertion that Achilles lives on, in effect, in his fame, the man's true measure, is undercut by Nestor's demonstration a few lines before that the tradition preserving fame is uncertain and unstable, for it is dependent not on a "true record" of some kind but on the prejudices and biases of individuals. (See n. 49.)

When Ovid says that since Achilles' fame gives the true measure of the man, the hero "does not feel the emptiness of Hades" (*nec . . . sentit,* 12.619), the poet, Kenney comments, "follows the (un-Homeric) version in which Achilles was translated to Elysium or the Islands of the Blessed" ([1986] 445). Or, in another bit of Ovidian-Homeric intertextuality, Ovid may be alluding to Odysseus' famous address to Achilles in the underworld in book 11 of the *Odyssey,* in which the living hero says to the dead one: "But you, Achilles, there's not a man in the world more blest than you—/ . . . and now down here, I see, / you lord it over the dead in all your power / So grieve no more at dying, great Achilles" (11.482–486; Fagles, trans.). Achilles replies angrily to Odysseus, "By god, I'd rather slave on earth for another man— . . . than rule down here over all the breathless dead" (11.489–491; Fagles, trans.). If Ovid is alluding to Achilles' words to Odysseus in *Odyssey* 11, the poet's blithe comment that Achilles "does not feel the emptiness of Hades" contains a subtle irony, because while the exchange between the two heroes in *Odyssey* 11 informs that comment, the comment ignores the exchange.

The death of Achilles motivates the next long section of the poem, the debate between Ajax and Ulysses for the dead hero's weapons and armor (traditionally called the Judgment of Arms) at book 13.1–398, which Ovid introduces at the close of book 12: "Even his [Achilles'] shield itself . . . started a war, and men took up arms over his arms" (12.620–621). By introducing the Judgment of Arms at the end of book 12, Ovid links this book with the next, a practice he follows with many other books in the *Metamorphoses.* (See n. 5.)

BOOK THIRTEEN

51. Ovid begins book 13 precisely where he left off at the end of book 12: the chieftains, whom Agamemnon there ordered to take seats and serve as judges in the dispute between Ajax and Ulysses over the arms of Achilles (12.626–628), now do as they were bidden and, with the ordinary soldiers standing in a circle behind them (13.1), listen as first Ajax and then Ulysses present their arguments for being awarded the arms. This long episode (13.1–398) all but concludes Ovid's account of the Trojan War within his *"Iliad,"* for immediately after the decision is rendered by the chieftains (as a result of which Ajax commits suicide), Ulysses goes to Lemnos to fetch Philoctetes and his arrows, necessary for Troy's fall (13.399–401), and the capture of the city occurs shortly after they return (13.402–404).

Homer does not narrate the story of the contest for Achilles' arms. That story was told in the *Aithiopis* and the *Little Iliad,* lost works of the Epic Cycle, in the latter of which Ajax goes mad and kills livestock of the Achaeans and then himself (Evelyn-White 508). In Ovid's version of this debate, "[a]ll the familiar incidents [of the *Iliad*] come up" in the arguments of Ajax and Ulysses, "who refer to them while conducting their suit for the arms" (Solodow 32), their versions of the same events often at odds with each other. "Homer's epic exists as ammunition to be used in an oratorical duel" (Solodow 32).

At the end of Nestor's account of the battle of Lapiths and centaurs in book 12, Tlepolemus, a member of his audience, objects to the old warrior's failure to mention Tlepolemus' father, Hercules, who, he claims, played an important role in the defeat of the centaurs. Nestor, without admitting Tlepolemus' claim, tells him that Hercules was his enemy and explains why: Hercules sacked Nestor's city, Pylos, and killed his eleven brothers. Tlepolemus' challenge raises the issue of the reliability of the narrator and, by extension, the credibility of the epic tradition (Nestor's account stands for the events of the *Iliad*: see n. 49), which preserves *klea andrôn,* "men's deeds of renown."

These issues—the reliability of the narrator and the credibility of traditional accounts—reappear in the debate between Ajax and Ulysses here, for, as Nagle says, in juxtaposing "two quite different accounts of the same events," the debate highlights "even more effectively than can a single narrator's story . . . the effect of a speaker's . . . selection, arrangement, and interpretation of details" ([1989a] 117).

This debate was the kind of "promising . . . subject" that "[t]he rhetoricians of Rome [in Ovid's time] did not overlook" (Wilkinson [1955] 230). In fact, according to Seneca, Ovid borrowed the last two lines of Ajax's speech, "Heave that brave man's arms into the midst of the enemy, order us to go get them" (13.121–122), from his rhetoric teacher Porcius Latro (Seneca, *Controversiae* 2.2.8). It may be that just as Ovid caters to the Romans' taste for violence in episodes of grotesque brutality such as the battle of Lapiths and centaurs (as Galinsky claims; see n. 49), so here, inasmuch as "the *declamatores* [public orators] played a most prominent part in the intellectual climate [of Rome] and . . . exerted a profound influence on the taste of their audience" (Due 152), the poet seeks to entertain his Roman readers with a set piece of rhetorical declamation in what Solodow calls "a brilliant example of forensic oratory" (19).

But Ovid's Judgment of Arms is more than "an exhibition of Roman rhetoric in a mythological setting" served to his readers by a virtuoso of rhetoric, showing them (and us) what he can do (Stanford 141–142), although it certainly is that, too. The *Metamorphoses* itself is a work "about" many things: ceaseless change and the implications of that, love—and rape—and the violent use of power, "a poem largely about victims," Segal says ([1969a] 93). But it is also, perhaps more than anything else, about narrative itself, as Solodow says: "The premise of the poem is that story-telling is a fundamental means of comprehending the world," (34), and its "point of focus" is "the narrator himself," the teller of stories, who "alone unifies the poem" (37).

Ovid examines this premise, "that story-telling is a fundamental means of comprehending the world," and its corollary, that it is "a fundamental means" of ruling the world, in the debate between Ajax and Ulysses for the arms of Achilles as nowhere else in the *Metamorphoses*. For each speech is a narrative about the speaker that he presents in order to prevail in the world in the way he sees himself. At its simplest (although it is not simple), the Judgment of Arms (or Ovid) aims "to illustrate the recurrent conflict between men of action and men of counsel, a literary commonplace as old as Homer" (Stanford 139). As expressed here, the conflict both modulates and articulates into higher relief the poet's expression of that conflict in book 12, where (as indicated in n. 49) Nestor, the "heroic speaker" (and teller of slaughters), is engaged by means of his stories—of Caeneus, the battle of Lapiths and centaurs, and Periclymenus—in a contest with Achilles, the heroic doer of deeds (and recent slayer of Cycnus) for the attention and approval of the Greek chieftains (Nestor's listeners and Achilles' dinner guests) and of Ovid's readers, who, collectively, represent "reality" for Ovid and for his only living heir, the poem itself in the moment it is read. Nestor, I believe, wins the contest there.

The present contest is between two speakers, or, rather, between two speeches, one by a heroic doer of deeds (like Achilles) who "[f]rom the beginning . . . declares himself a man of action. . . . And as he finishes speaking, he wishes to appeal to action, not words" (Anderson [1963] 21), the other by a truly heroic speaker of words who, by comparison, makes Nestor seem archaic, old-fashioned.

Altieri calls Ajax "the basic exemplum of the man of permanence" and "the perfect antithesis of Ovidian man" (259). His opponent, Ulysses, can by contrast be termed the basic exemplum of the man of change, of "Ovidian man," and so "the perfect antithesis" of "the man of permanence," Ajax, or, as I would call him, "the man of myth." For myth seeks to arrest change, to make permanent an established status quo: myth "transforms history into nature," as Barthes says (129), to give (seeming) permanence and universal significance to what is particular and ad hoc. Metamorphosis, however, seen as the law of constant change, is "the perfect antithesis" of myth (to continue with Altieri's term) and, for Ovid, the law that underlies nature, that has given rise to all that is, and that governs the future history of all that is.

As a kind of proto-Barthes, Ovid understands myth's aim, to transform history into nature, that is, to make the particular and the ad hoc seem permanent and universal, the way things are, and he attacks myth from within, so to speak, by binding it to its archenemy, change. For by linking nature, myth, and history, which is the raw material of myth (those three representing, in order, the divisions of the *Metamorphoses*), in a seamless epic about metamorphosis "from the first origin of the world . . . down to my own time" (book 1.3–4), he can (or change will) destroy myth, which actually rests on an illusion (mistaking nature as permanence rather than as change), and so undermine that which myth protects with its illusion of permanence, that is, power. For the powerful seek to establish and make permanent their power through myth, not realizing that constant change is the law that underlies nature, and that nature therefore ceaselessly opposes—and, over time, successfully erodes—the ostensibly permanent structures of power human beings just as ceaselessly strive to build (and fortify with myth). Ovid, whether or not by conscious design I cannot say, begins his "demonstration" of metamorphosis' opposition to (and eventual victory over) myth seemingly far from his goal, with the formation of the world out of chaos, but he does so at least partly in order to establish the primacy of nature and its law, which is change. He makes his way to his goal, "to my own time," that is, to the time and place where Augustus (as it happens) with the help of myth has set up his structure (as it happens) of Roman power.

But how will the master of metamorphosis himself survive change, the destroyer he has tied so tightly to myth, which is the archdefender of the structures of power, and to history? The answer to that question, implicit in the emphasis in the *Metamorphoses* on storytelling, embedded narrative, and narrators, becomes clearer in the Judgment of Arms, where, Lanham says, "[t]he speeches are the point, not the armor"; "[t]he ultimate lesson the debate teaches is . . . that the best talker wins" (11, 12). At the end of Ulysses' speech, "[t]he chieftains were moved," Ovid says, "and their decision made it clear what eloquence could do, for a skillful speaker carried off a brave man's arms" (13.382–383). The "real winner," though, Lanham says, "is not so much Ulysses as *Eloquence*" (12), Ovid's "*Eloquence*," and it is that quicksilver eloquence "that frees [Ovid] from his submission to the forces of natural flux and enables him to remain detached and capable of manipulating them" (Altieri 260), and capable as well of chronicling (and causing by chronicling) the undoing of myth, which he nimbly feeds to the maw of insatiable change.

How does eloquence win the debate between Ajax and Ulysses? The first step toward victory is taken (by Ovid) when Ajax leaps up in anger to make the first speech, "unwisely," Wilkinson says ([1955] 230), but Ovid presents his character as unable to restrain himself: "trembling with rage and scowling fiercely" (13.3–4), he rises to speak. Ajax, however, is acting in character. (And his speech will represent his character, as will Ulysses' his: this is *ethopoeia* [character delineation]; see Otis 284.) By following Ajax, Ulysses automatically gains the upper hand rhetorically, for he is able not only to rebut his opponent charge for charge, but also to make points against Ajax that Ajax will not have the opportunity to reply to. The sheer length of Ulysses' speech (254 lines: 13.128–381) in comparison to Ajax's (118 lines: 13.5–122) represents a second step toward victory: to some extent he overcomes Ajax by sheer verbiage. The length of Ulysses' speech also demonstrates his character just as Ajax's brevity demonstrates his: Ulysses is silky and at ease in the world of words.

As in earlier parts of Ovid's "*Iliad*," Homer's poem (or events in it) stands in the background as the point of reference for both speeches.

Ajax's speech, as Bömer notes, follows the classical convention for organization and is divided into *exordium*, or introduction (13.5–6); a combined *probatio/refutatio* (13.7–119), or establishing of proof (in this case, of his own merit) and refutation (of his adversary's claims to merit); and *peroratio* (for which Bömer uses the alternative term "Epilogus"; 13.120–122), a highly rhetorical recapitulation (or demand, claim, or appeal) with which a speech ended. The *exordium* and *peroratio* are "disproportionately short," while the body of the speech shows Ovid's intentional representation of the speaker as a man who is possessed, particularly, of a soldier's integrity and characterized more by a straight-ahead warrior mentality than by an urbane adroitness (Bömer at 13.5–122, 6.206).

Ajax begins (*exordium*, 13.5–6) by gesturing toward the Greek fleet drawn up on shore nearby and noting, ironically, that he is making his case in front of the ships— "and to think that Ulysses contends with me!" His reference to the ships recalls Hector's attempt to burn them, until he is stopped by Ajax (*Iliad* 15.674ff.). In the second section (*probatio/refutatio*), in which he seeks to establish himself as deserving Achilles' arms (*probatio*) while refuting Ulysses' claim to them (*refutatio*), Ajax picks up his opening reference to Ulysses in an adverse comparison of his opponent to himself (13.7–20; Bömer at 13.5–122, 6.206), as he elaborates on his earlier remark about the ships ("He certainly wasn't slow to fall back before Hector . . . , but I faced Hector's flames," 13.7ff.): it is easier to wage war with words than to fight; speaking doesn't come naturally to him, nor action to Ulysses; and so on. Ajax's disqualification of himself as a speaker, a standard feature in an *exordium* (Plato, *Apology* 17c6–18a6, for example; see Burnet 66–67), would seem to gain additional rhetorical value in this particular context, for he stresses that his métier is action, not words, while Ulysses' is speech making, and it is war, after all, the theater of action par excellence, that they are in the midst of, and the contest is for the armor of war. The trouble, however, is that one should use the "unaccustomed-as-I-am-to-speaking" conceit as rhetorical *eirôneia* only when one doesn't really mean it, and here there is no irony: Ajax says it straight.

Whatever Ulysses may have done, Ajax continues, he did at night, without witnesses (13.14–15; a reference to *Iliad* 10, which narrates the night patrol of Ulysses and Diomedes into enemy territory).

Ajax next alludes to his own family line (13.21–33; his father, Telamon, sacker of Troy; his grandfather Aeacus, a judge in the underworld; and Jupiter) and his kinship with Achilles as qualifications for the armor, while denigrating Ulysses as descended from Sisyphus, one of the great sinners punished in the underworld (see book 10.44). Ajax's reference to his aristocratic ancestry, while true, will be easily trumped by Ulysses at 13.140–141 with a "statement of meritocratic principle" that, Kenney says, would have special resonance for Romans ([1986] 447).

At 13.34–42 Ajax mentions his renown for individual courage—he joined the army early and readily—and makes a transition to an assault on the character of Ulysses by noting that his opponent tried to avoid service by feigning madness until exposed by Palamedes ("We cannot let him wear the finest armor there is, can we, when he wanted to wear none at all?" 13.40; see Bömer at 13.5–122, 6.206–207).

Ajax now launches his attack on Ulysses (13.43–119) in the place, Bömer says, of a *refutatio,* portraying him as a vicious betrayer of comrades: if only he had been truly mad, or had been believed to be mad, and had not come to Troy (13.43–44), then Philoctetes would not now be languishing on the island of Lemnos, where, Ajax implies, Ulysses marooned him, although Philoctetes is at least still alive because he did not come to Troy with Ulysses (13.45–55; Bömer at 13.5–122, 6.207). On the way to Troy, Philoctetes was bitten on the foot by a snake at an altar on the island of Tenedos (according to the lost epic *Cypria:* see Evelyn-White 494), or Chrysé (according to Sophocles, *Philoctetes* 260–270). The wound festered and would not heal, and Philoctetes' cries of pain made sacrifice impossible and him unbearable to his fellow chieftains. Odysseus, on orders from his "chiefs," Agamemnon and Menelaus, took him to the island of Lemnos and left him there, with only his bow and arrows to sustain him (Sophocles, *Philoctetes* 1–11, 260–270; cf. Homer, *Iliad* 2.716–725; and see Gantz 2.589–590).

Next (13.56–62), Ajax mentions Ulysses' great crime of falsely accusing Palamedes of treason (while framing him by planting gold in his tent which he claimed Priam gave Palamedes for betraying the Greeks). Palamedes was "convicted" and executed: if only Palamedes had been marooned (like Philoctetes), he would still be alive. (The story of Palamedes was told in the *Cypria:* see Evelyn-White 492, 494, and 504; see also Apollodorus, *Epitome* 3.7–8.) While not denying these charges, in his speech to the chieftains Ulysses easily and cunningly defends himself against them.

Ajax is now halfway through his speech and has yet to make a decisive case either for himself or against Ulysses. He next turns (13.63–81) to what Bömer calls "Ulysses' disloyalty" (at 13.5–122, 6.207), his desertion of a helpless Nestor on the battlefield (narrated at *Iliad* 8.78ff.), and goes on to describe his own later rescue of Ulysses when he was wounded and crying out for help (a reference to *Iliad* 11.434ff.): "trembling, ashen with fear, and terrified that he was going to die," as Ajax describes him (13.73–74). Ajax distorts both situations considerably, for in the former scene in the *Iliad*, Agamemnon, Idomeneus, both Ajaxes, and Odysseus all abandon Nestor. He is rescued by Diomedes. In the latter scene, Ulysses kills the Trojan warrior (Sokos) who wounded him and then battles the Trojans surrounding him as Ajax and Menelaus come to his rescue. While Ajax now takes on the Trojans pressing to kill Ulysses, Menelaus leads him from the battlefield. There is no mention of Ulysses' running despite his wound.

Reverting to the *probatio,* Ajax speaks again about his own courage (13.82–97) and then (13.98–119) describes Ulysses' cowardice and unfitness for Achilles' arms (Bömer at 13.5–122, 6.207). He conflates and rearranges events from the *Iliad.* When he describes Hector's appearance in battle, "bringing his gods . . . with him" (13.82–84), he is referring to the Trojan prince's successful advance to the Greek ships at *Iliad* 15.306ff. He then says that he knocked an exulting Hector on his back with a stone, and when Hector demanded that someone fight him hand to hand, he (Ajax) alone dared to face him and was, in answer to the Greeks' prayers, chosen by lot and was not defeated (13.85–90). Here Ajax reverses the order of events and again distorts the "Iliadic record": when at *Iliad* 7.73ff. Hector challenges any and all Greeks to a duel, nine warriors volunteer, including Ajax and Ulysses, and Ajax is chosen by lot from among the nine; in the course of their duel Ajax does indeed knock Hector down with a stone, although Apollo quickly stands him up (*Iliad* 7.268–272). Ajax now returns (in his speech in Ovid: 13.91ff.) to Hector's attack on the ships (*Iliad* 15.306ff.) and recalls how he (not Ulysses) "took my stand in front of a thousand ships" (13.93). To the alert reader or listener (who can recall precisely the events of the *Iliad*), Ajax's conflation, distortions, and confusing of these events bespeak inaccuracy and lack of control (as well as a casual attitude toward the truth). Ajax ends this section of his speech with a rhetorical flourish ("the arms are seeking Ajax, not Ajax the arms!" 13.97) that was "especially popular with rhetoricians and their pupils" (Haupt-Ehwald at 13.97, 2.287) but seems clumsily and unconvincingly applied here.

Having set up his own achievements on the battlefield as a foil, Ajax now attacks Ulysses' cowardice and unfitness (13.98–119; as noted earlier). Ulysses, he says, operates only by stealth and never without help—"nothing done in daylight, nothing without Diomedes" (13.100)—and makes a second and fuller reference to *Iliad* 10 (the first was at 13.14–15), the account of the night patrol by Ulysses and Diomedes into enemy territory, which yielded the Trojan spy Dolon (and his information about the Trojan plans) and the horses of Rhesus, king of Thrace and a newly arrived Trojan ally (killed, with twelve of his soldiers, by Diomedes, who also kills Dolon). Ajax also alludes to Ulysses' kidnapping of the Trojan seer Helenus (who knew the conditions necessary for Troy's capture: Apollodorus, Epitome 5.9–10) and his theft of the Palladium, an image of Minerva possessed by the Trojans, acquisition of which was one of the special conditions revealed to the Greeks by Helenus. (The *Little Iliad,* a lost poem in the Epic Cycle, narrated Ulysses' kidnapping of Helenus and his theft of the Palladium, with the help of Diomedes: Evelyn–White 508, 510). Ajax caps this section of his speech with two rhetorical points leading to an antithesis that contrasts the two contenders, extends his argument, and prepares for his three-line peroration: (1) the brightness of Achilles' helmet would give away Ulysses, hiding in ambush (13.105–106); (2) moreover, Ulysses is too much of a weakling to bear the weight of Achilles' helmet or carry his spear (13.107–109). Ajax now veers from his point as he thinks of Achilles' shield (described at *Iliad* 18.478ff.), which "has the whole world in its vastness engraved upon it" and thus "does not suit a coward's hand, made for stealing" (13.110–111; Ulysses will make a telling rejoinder to this at 13.286–295). And if the Greeks give Ulysses Achilles' armor, Ajax says (now veering back to his point), in armor too heavy for him he will only run more slowly from the battlefield and will be caught and stripped of that armor (13.112–116). In an antithesis contrasting himself and Ulysses, Ajax says that Ulysses' present armor is pristine, that is, untried; hence he needs no new armor, while his own is full of holes, that is, much used in battle, hence in need of replacement (13.117–119).

In his *peroratio* (13.120–122), Ajax returns to the *exordium* (let our actions, not our words, decide, 13.120) and concludes with a version of a conceit used by Ovid's teacher Porcius Latro (as reported by Seneca and mentioned earlier): "Heave that brave man's arms into the midst of the enemy, order us to go get them" (13.121–122).

The ordinary (and non-voting) soldiers murmur their approval of Ajax (13.123–124). Haupt-Ehwald quote F. H. Bothe's comment that Ajax's speech is like that of a Roman tribune of the people, not pleasing except for a kind of naturalness, while Ulysses' noble words, adorned with all the brilliance of artifice, are like those of a senator delivered to patricians, "whereby it happens that the *plebs* [people] approve the former . . . [13.123], the *optimates* [nobles] vote for the latter [13.382]" (at 13.123, 2.289).

Although it may be true that Ajax, as Stanford says, "makes as strong a case as can be made against Ulysses" (139), there is nevertheless an artlessness to his speech at its best and an unprofessionalism at its worst that make him seem amateurish rather than credible (although Due defends Ajax: "He is not not a trained rhetorician" [153]).

Ulysses now rises (13.124) and, instead of launching immediately into his speech, studies the ground for a moment as if lost in thought—an indication of great self-possession. He then "look[s] up at the chieftains," Ovid says (13.125–126), and so "displays his own solidarity with his audience" (Due 154). This representation of Ulysses comes from *Iliad* 3.216ff., the Trojan elder Antenor's description of Ulysses as a speaker, and conforms to the rules laid down by the teachers of rhetoric (Haupt-Ehwald at 13.125f., 2.289). Ulysses' "studied pause," Due says, "arouses the expectations of his audience" (153) and thereby freights his opening words with an emotional gravity that is hard to resist.

Ulysses' speech, which, Haupt-Ehwald note, has been constructed in strict accordance with the rules of rhetoric, yet not obviously so (at 13.128ff., 2.290), follows a pattern similar to Ajax's: *exordium* (13.128–139), *probatio* (13.140–267), *refutatio* (13.268–338), and *peroratio* (13.339–381; Bömer's analysis at 13.128–381, 6.237–238).

Ulysses begins brilliantly (and now we feel the full effect of his pause), not by attacking Ajax (as Ajax began his speech by attacking Ulysses), but by addressing the entire audience (Bömer at 13.128–381, 6.237–238) and saying (in the first sentence of what is a two-sentence *exordium* in Latin), if only Achilles were alive, there would be no doubt about who should possess his legacy, "and you would have your arms, Achilles, and we would have you." But since Achilles is gone—and Ulysses now wipes imaginary tears from his eyes, a brilliant rhetorical gesture—"who better should get the arms of great Achilles than the one who got great Achilles for the Greeks?" (13.128–134). This, as noted, is all one sentence in Latin, and in it Ulysses adroitly seeks to disarm his audience and gain its goodwill ("a deft *captatio benevolentiae*," as Stanford says [140]). In the second sentence, Ulysses neutralizes Ajax's opening sally against him as a speaker and nothing else (13.9–12) by asking the chieftains not to begrudge his talents, which have always served them well—and not to resent his eloquence, now used on his own behalf, but often on theirs (13.135–139; Wilkinson sees a *captatio benevolentiae* also in Ulysses' reference here to his eloquence: [1955] 232).

At the beginning of the *probatio,* Ulysses rebuts Ajax on the issue of ancestry (13.140–158; Ajax raised the issue at 13.21ff.) and more or less wipes up the ground with him on this subject: (1) ancestry should not count, but mine is better than his; (2) I claim the arms on the basis of merit (the "famous statement of meritocratic principle" [Kenney (1986) 447] referred to earlier), not on the basis of my father's innocence in shedding kindred blood, a dig at Ajax's father, Telamon, and uncle Peleus, who killed their half-brother Phocus (see *Metamorphoses* 11.266ff.); (3) nor should kinship count (Ajax and Achilles were first cousins); (4) or, if it does count, Achilles' father, Peleus, or his son Pyrrhus ought to get the arms, or his cousin Teucer (Ajax's half-brother), who isn't claiming them and wouldn't get them if he were.

In the rest of the *probatio* (13.159–267), Ulysses enumerates, often brilliantly, his achievements on behalf of the Greeks, "guided by the order they occurred in" (13.161), as evidence for his claim to the arms on the basis of merit: he brought Achilles to Troy from Scyrus, where his mother, Thetis, had sent him, disguised as a girl (fooling everyone, "including Ajax," 13.163–164; invented by Ulysses: Kenney [1986] 447), to keep him out of the war she knew would cause his death (13.162– 170; the Epic Cycle does not mention this story, for which see Apollodorus 3.13.8; Homer refers to Thetis' knowledge of Achilles' short life at *Iliad* 1.415–418 and her foreknowledge of his death at *Iliad* 18.94–96).

Since he brought Achilles to Troy, Ulysses says, "[t]he things he's done . . . belong to me" (13.171). Ulysses' phrase, *opera illius,* "the things he's done," repeats *operum* at 159, "a contest about things we've done," Ulysses' assertion that merit should be the criterion for awarding Achilles' arms. Thus, Ulysses says, it was he who "brought down Telephus with a spear," and he goes on to lay claim to a host of deeds performed by Achilles, including the slaying of Hector (13.171–180). Turning to events at Aulis (13.181–195; see 12.8ff.), Ulysses recalls how, after "[a] grim prophecy" (13.184, about the necessity of sacrificing Agamemnon's daughter Iphigenia; see 12.27ff.), he "talked to" Agamemnon and "managed to change his tender feelings" for Iphigenia (13.187– 188). He did not—not that we know of—but in claiming that he did, Ulysses "conciliates Agamemnon by palliating and sharing the odium of this terrible decision" (Kenney [1986] 448). And he went to Mycenae to fetch Iphigenia from her mother, a task for which deceit was required and at which Ajax would have failed miserably.

Ulysses now alludes (13.196–204) to his "daring mission" to Troy, along with Menelaus, to seek the return of Helen (referred to in the *Iliad* at 3.205ff. and 11.138ff.; described at Apollodorus, Epitome 3.28–29), an exploit demanding a combination of eloquence (see *Iliad* 3.216ff.) and courage.

Ulysses begins the final section of the *probatio* (13.205–267) with a summary of actions he claims he performed during nearly ten years of inaction, while the Trojans remained inside their city walls (13.211–215), a summary that is "an acute stroke of Ovid's invention," Kenney says, for, as readers of the *Iliad* are aware, that poem "knows nothing of [Ulysses] in these capacities" ([1986] 448; it is Nestor who advises the Greeks to surround their camp with a trench: *Iliad* 7.336ff.). Where there is no "Iliadic record," Ulysses can say what he wants; where there is, he distorts it, as did Ajax.

And Ulysses blatantly distorts the record of the *Iliad* in this part of his speech. He faults Ajax for not opposing Agamemnon when, in an irrational and inexplicable reaction to a dream, all of which he glosses over with the phrase, "[Agamemnon] deceived by a dream" (13.216–217; see *Iliad* 2.1–210), the king ordered the Greek soldiers to run to their ships, board them, and sail home. Ajax should have resisted this, Ulysses asserts, should have rallied the men and fought—but instead he ran away. Homer says nothing of this, in fact mentions neither Ajax nor any other chieftain by name except Agamemnon and Ulysses in his description of the scene in which the men all ran to the ships. But Homer's silence becomes a kind of proof of Ajax's inaction. In what he says next, Ulysses makes as if to correct the *Iliad*'s omissions: "I saw you, Ajax, . . . when you cut and ran" (13.223–224). But *he* (Ulysses) stemmed the flight (the *Iliad* agrees), and Agamemnon assembled the troops (Ulysses is being diplomatic; he himself took the scepter, the sign of the king's authority, from the hand of Agamemnon, apparently dazed, and used it to rally the chieftains and assemble the troops: *Iliad* 2.185–210). Recalling the famous scene at *Iliad* 2.212ff. in which Thersites, an angry common soldier, in "uppity" fashion rebukes Agamemnon—a rebuke he deserves—Ulysses blames Ajax for Thersites' outburst because Ajax "did not dare to open his mouth. But Thersites dared" (13.231–233).

In a statement calculated to enrage the angry Ajax further, Ulysses claims credit for whatever Ajax accomplished thereafter, "since I dragged him back when he took to his heels" (13.236–237), just as he earlier took credit for Achilles' deeds (13.162ff.). Altieri comments, "[T]he man of fictions is the master of fact . . . , and thus he can claim credit for actions he makes possible, not just for his specific deeds" (259).

Ulysses next cites Diomedes as a kind of character reference (13.238–242), while "correcting" Ajax's sneering remarks about Dolon and Rhesus (13.98–100). But Ajax was wrong there to attribute the deaths of Dolon and Rhesus to Ulysses, and Ulysses is likewise wrong here to claim credit for killing them and Rhesus' soldiers (13.243–250): all the killing in this episode in the *Iliad* is done by Diomedes (*Iliad* 10.454–497). He names the many warriors under Sarpedon whom he claims to have killed, proof of which can be seen in his wounds, and he ends the *probatio* with another rhetorical gesture, tearing open his tunic and exposing his chest (with scars, presumably), while noting that Ajax has never lost one drop of blood. What is otherwise proof of Ajax's excellence as a warrior is cited now as a sign of his inaction or cowardice (13.255–267).

Ulysses has not spared Ajax in the *probatio,* the part of his speech (as typically) devoted to proving his own merit. In the *refutatio* (13.268–338), however, he attacks Ajax without letup, rebutting that warrior's argument point for point. As for the battle around the Greek ships (13.268ff., rebutting Ajax at 13.7f. and 91ff.), Ulysses dilutes Ajax's claim in a way calculated to be most effective with the chieftains, who will judge the issue: "Let him give you some credit, too" (13.272), and now stands on the "Iliadic record," naming Patroclus as the warrior chiefly responsible for saving the ships. In fact, at *Iliad* 16.101ff. Ajax is forced by Hector to retreat, and a Greek ship is set on fire (the ship of Protesilaus, now dead: *Iliad* 15.704–706; *Metamorphoses* 12.67–68). Achilles' friend Patroclus, wearing Achilles' (original) armor, leads a contingent of Myrmidons (troops of Achilles) into battle and drives Hector and the Trojans back from the Greek ships and puts out the fire on Protesilaus' ship (*Iliad* 16.257ff.). Ulysses, as Kenney notes, thus "continues his tactics of isolating Ajax" ([1986] 448).

Next (13.275ff.), Ulysses refutes Ajax's account of his hand-to-hand combat with Hector (13.87ff.), distorting the record as he does so, calling Ajax the "ninth to volunteer" (13.277), while in fact the two Ajaxes (ours here, the son of Telamon; and Ajax the son of Oileus) are the third and fourth to volunteer, and it is Ulysses who is the ninth (*Iliad* 7.161–168). Nor is it true that Hector "left the field without a mark on him," as Ulysses claims (13.279), for in their duel Ajax wounds Hector in the neck with his spear (*Iliad* 7.260–262) and later knocks him flat on his back with a stone he hurls at him (*Iliad* 7.268–272).

To refute Ajax's charge (13.103ff.) that (1) the brilliance of Achilles' armor would give Odysseus away, since he operates only by stealth, from ambush; and that (2) he isn't physically able to bear the weight of the armor, Ulysses (at 13.280ff.) injects a note of personal grief (as at the beginning of his speech) before reminding his audience that when Achilles was killed, it was he who carried the hero's body, still in its armor, from the battlefield. According to the lost Epic Cycle poem, the *Aithiopis*, it was Ajax who carried Achilles from the battlefield while Ulysses followed behind him, holding the Trojans at bay (Evelyn-White 508; at Sophocles, *Philoctetes* 373, Neoptolemus quotes Ulysses as saying he saved Achilles and his arms). Ulysses continues: not only does he have the strength to wear Achilles' armor, but also he is aesthetically sensitive enough to appreciate the artistry of Achilles' shield (described at *Iliad* 18.478ff.), in contrast to Ajax, who "demands that he be given a set of arms he cannot even begin to under-stand!" (12.295): "Finally," says Altieri, "the opposition centers on Achilles' Shield: Ajax sees its physical weight as something that would limit Odysseus' skill at running away, but Odysseus retorts that the shield is more than an object, it is a text which must be interpreted, which must be a source for imaginative creation. . . . Only the man of imagination is worthy of [Achilles'] heritage" (260).

Ulysses (at 13.296ff.) rebuts Ajax's charge (made at 13.34ff.) that he sought to avoid joining the Greek expeditionary force going to Troy by asserting that with such an accu-sation Ajax maligns Achilles, whose mother tried to keep him out of the Trojan War and who thus came to Troy late. Achilles, he says, was detained by a loving mother, while he himself was detained by a loving wife: "The first days of the war we gave to them, the rest to you" (13.302). It is as much Ovid as Ulysses speaking here, Bömer observes, for the argument for not coming to Troy is too frivolous not to be seen through at once and would have gotten a laugh in the Homeric assembly at the "histori-cal" time of the Judgment of Arms. It is only later (in the *Odyssey*), through his tarrying with Circe and Calypso, that Ulysses becomes characterized as "a woman's man," a characterization he flirts with here (at 13.301–302, 6.275–276). Bömer goes on to say that Ulysses cuts it very fine indeed in his statement that Achilles was found out by the wit of Ulysses, but not Ulysses by Ajax (13.304–305), a statement that in any case cannot refute the charge he seeks to rebut here (at 13.304–305, 6.276).

At 13.37ff. Ajax had mentioned Palamedes' exposure of Ulysses in the latter's attempt to avoid service in the army and, at 13.56ff., Ulysses' revenge on Palamedes. Ulysses answers this (at 13.306ff.) by noting that Ajax insults the chieftains as well as himself ("again Ajax is isolated": Kenney [1986] 449), since, if it was wrong for him (Ulysses) to accuse Palamedes, it could not have been right for them to condemn him—but Pa-lamedes could not prove his innocence, and the evidence against him (the gold Ulysses had planted in his tent) was there for all to see. The flimsy sophistry we've heard in the just concluded rebuttal of the charge of attempted draft dodging continues, with an even flimsier argument, Bömer says, though it is not so obvious at first glance: Ulysses *knew* his charge against Palamedes was false, but the Greeks did not, and they acted in good faith. But Ulysses insinuates that they were in collusion with him and seeks to make them accessories (at 13.308–309, 6.277).

Next, Philoctetes (13.313ff.), mentioned by Ajax at 13.45ff. Here, Bömer comments, Ovid strains his hearers' knowledge of myth—told "straight" in Sophocles' *Philoc-tetes*—since they knew "the case of Philoctetes." For Ulysses baldly to maintain that

Philoctetes' "obedience" saved him borders on cynicism. And in the following lines ("let Ajax go," that is, go get Philoctetes, 13.321ff.) "irony gets the upper hand" (at 13.318–319, 6.279–280).

Ulysses now brings his *refutatio* to a climactic end (13.333–338) by predicting the success of a future undertaking necessary to Troy's fall which he links to (and guarantees by) two past successful undertakings that were also necessary for Troy's fall: he will possess Philoctetes' arrows, just as he kidnapped Helenus (and learned his vital secrets), and just as he stole from Troy the image of Minerva called the Palladium. These undertakings are all similar in that, in order to be accomplished, they required or will require intelligence and stealth. In his final statement, "And Ajax contends with me?" (13.338b, *et se mihi conferat Aiax*?), Ulysses hurls back at Ajax his words at the beginning of his speech, "[A]nd to think that Ulysses contends with me!" (13.6b, *et mecum confertur Ulixes*!), his rhetorical question (in the subjunctive mood) demonstrating his finesse in comparison with the heavy-handedness of Ajax's exclamation (in the indicative mood).

The momentum Ulysses achieves in the climax at the end of the *refutatio*—his reference to future and past thefts (13.333–338, made vivid by an apostrophe to the absent Philoctetes), including the theft of the Palladium—carries him into his peroration (13.339–381), in which he indicates the Palladium's significance, taunts Ajax for being unable to steal it, and briefly describes his foray into Troy to get it. His assertion "and I conquered Troy then, when I made it possible for Troy to be conquered" (13.349) becomes the foundation for his claim that his merit—which resides in his intelligence—is superior to Ajax's and entitles him to the arms. Ajax interrupts, pointing to Diomedes and whispering, as Ulysses' response makes clear, that Diomedes, too, deserves credit for the theft of the Palladium (13.350–351). Ulysses not only takes the interruption in stride but also uses it to make a point that further discredits Ajax's claim to the arms: Diomedes *does not* seek the arms of Achilles *because* he knows "that a warrior eager to fight is less valuable than a thinking warrior" (13.354–356a). He elaborates this point for another thirteen and a half lines (13.356b–369), isolating Ajax even more by naming six chieftains, in addition to Diomedes, who are *not* seeking the arms, using the negative to "prove" that they know Ulysses deserves them, because "[b]rains are more powerful than brawn; true strength lies in the mind" (13.368–369): Q.E.D.

In the final eleven and a fraction lines (13.370 through the first dactyl of 381), Ulysses addresses the chieftains directly now for the first time, commanding in two imperatives that the arms be awarded to him ("award," 13.370; "confer," 13.372). He immediately softens these imperatives by beseeching the chieftains: "And so I beg you . . ." (13.376), and cites four bases for his request ("by our now common hopes, by the walls of Troy soon to fall," plus two more, 13.375–379), ending with another imperative, "[R]emember me" (13.380). His final stroke is as dramatic as his pause and apostrophe (as he pretends to weep) to Achilles at the beginning: "Or if you will not give the arms to me—give them to her!" as he points to the Palladium (13.380–381), a more dramatic "demand" than Ajax's (to heave the arms into the midst of the enemy and then order the contenders to go after them: 13.121–122), and more effective for its appearance of selfless honesty.

The chieftains were "moved," Ovid says, "and their decision made it clear what eloquence could do, for a skillful speaker carried off a brave man's arms" (13.382–383).

The words "a brave man's arms" (*fortisque viri . . . arma*, 13.383) repeat Ajax's phrase at the end of his speech ("Heave that *brave man's arms*," *arma viri fortis*, that is, Achilles' arms, "into the midst of the enemy," 13.121), the repetition seeming to indicate that the "brave man" at 13.383 is Achilles, not Ajax. If, however, one takes the phrase as referring to Ajax (they were "a brave man's arms," that is, Ajax's, because he deserved to have them, because he was brave), then he and Achilles are yoked by the phrase and stand opposed to Ulysses, the "skillful speaker" (*disertus*, 13.383)—and they are also linked by rage (Ajax, Ovid says, having withstood all else, "could not withstand" one thing, "his own anger," 13.385; Achilles was said earlier to have "raged like a bull" [12.102] and to have jumped down from his chariot "roaring in his fury," [12.128]).

Whether or not Ajax and Achilles are thus paired, Bömer seems right to insist (against Stanford's view that Ovid makes his "preference" clear [139] and Due's that he "remains neutral" [154]) that Ovid is objective: Ovid "has presented the bases and grounds [*Gründe und Begründungen*, that is, for the decision] as objectively as possible; objectivity operates more powerfully here than expressions of sympathy or antipathy" (at 13.382–383, 6.294). And objectively speaking, it is this Ulysses who deserves this Achilles' arms, not this Ajax. In book 12, an implicit contest between a "heroic doer of deeds" (Achilles, slaying Cycnus) and a "heroic speaker of words" (Nestor, narrating the episodes of Caeneus, the battle of Lapiths and centaurs, and Periclymenus) comes out in favor of the heroic speaker of words. Here, the contest is in the same arena, but now between two speeches, one by a heroic doer of deeds, the other by a heroic speaker of words, and the latter wins the prize. The heroic doer of deeds is out of his element.

It is not a moral issue, *pace* Anderson ([1963] 21–23), Due (implicitly, 153–154), Otis (284), and Kenney ([1986], 449–450); nor is the heroic "deflated" (Coleman 474–475), at least not intentionally, any more than the Elizabethan age is deflated when Shakespeare is presented in modern dress and adapted to modern concerns. We may want to believe (as Ajax does) that accouterments of physical action such as the arms of Achilles should go to the one who best exemplifies physical action (and so would best wear them). But it is not a contest in words about who is best in deeds; it is a contest in words about who is best in words. Ajax tries to be as slippery, as "rhetorical," as Ulysses and does his share of distorting and falsifying the "Iliadic record." He doesn't lose because the effort to become a skillful speaker goes against the grain of his more moral nature, which thus inhibits him. He's just not as good as Ulysses in the arena he's chosen to enter. As Lanham says, "The ultimate lesson the debate teaches is . . . that the best talker wins" (12).

In the context of the *Metamorphoses*, Ulysses also deserves the arms more than Ajax. It is not ordinary armor. It has an aesthetic value that neither Ovid's Ajax nor his Achilles, for that matter (the Achilles of book 12), can truly appreciate. This armor is a magnificent work of art. Who can imagine the shield of Achilles, with the entire world engraved upon it by Vulcan, the original ecphrasis in Western literature, battered and full of holes, as Ajax's present shield is (13.118–119), and as Achilles' shield would surely become if Ajax owned it? Ulysses' speech, Otis says, "is in essence a defence of art and *ingenium* [talent], even of aesthetic sensitivity (Ulysses knows a work of art when he sees it)" (359). It is all to the good, that is, to the preservation of art, that Ulysses will not be using Achilles' shield very much as he continues to operate by stealth. And even as Ovid's "objectivity operates more powerfully . . . than expressions of sympathy or antipathy" (Bömer, see above), the poet "leaves no doubt where his sympathies lie" (Wilkinson [1955] 234–235).

Ajax is consumed with outrage at the decision (13.384–386) and commits suicide by falling on his sword (13.391–392).

Hyacinths spring up from the blood of Ajax that falls on the ground, bearing the letters of his name in the Greek vocative case marked on the petals: *AIAI* (making an eternal apostrophe to the dead warrior: "[Thou] Ajax!"). For Hyacinth, the petals show *AI AI* (Greek for "Alas! Alas!": see 10.215–216). "The grafting of Ajax on to the Hyacinth tradition may be Ovid's own invention," Kenney says ([1986] 450). It is an odd metamorphosis for Ajax, first, because the flower is already occupied, so to speak (and Hyacinth must now share *AIAI*, letters that no longer spell out his lament exclusively), and second, because one would expect something more robust, more expressive of Ajax's nature, if, as Solodow says, metamorphosis is "clarification" (174). For the hyacinth does not seem to express some recognizable "essential or incidental" characteristic of Ajax (Solodow 174), and it is unlikely that it reveals something about his nature hidden until now.

52.   Both Ajax and Ulysses had mentioned Philoctetes, the Greek warrior marooned on the island of Lemnos, in their respective speeches during the Judgment of Arms (Ajax, 13.45–55; Ulysses, 13.313–338). As Ulysses said then, Philoctetes' presence at Troy (or, rather, his bow and arrows) was required for the Greeks to defeat the Trojans (13.320), and he expressed his willingness to go to Lemnos and bring the wounded warrior and his weapon to Troy (13.333–334). Reference to Ulysses' mission, following the Judgment of Arms, and to the victory over Troy that mission makes possible (13.399–403), thus serves as a natural transition to the next two episodes, the stories of Hecuba and Memnon's funeral, with which Ovid ends his "*Iliad*" (13.404–622).

In calling Lemnos "a place infamous for the murder of men long ago" (13.399–400), Ovid refers to the slaughter of the men of Lemnos by the women of the island for refusing to sleep with them. Hypsipyle, daughter of Thoas, king of Lemnos, alone saved her father by hiding him (Apollodorus 1.9.17; cf. Herodotus 6.138).

Ovid gives the Trojan defeat hardly more than a line and a half (13.403–404: "[A] final effort was made to end this war at last. And now Troy fell, Priam fell"; some scholars think that 13.404–407 are not authentic, for example, Kenney, "probably not Ovid's": [1986] 450; Bömer at 13.404–407, 6.299, however, accepts the lines as genuine: "a . . . brief, anticipatory synopsis") and then moves on to the story of Hecuba, which "starts with an epic tableau in Vergil's manner" (Due 155) that describes the aftermath of the defeat: Ilium burned; the aged King Priam killed at the altar of Jupiter; Cassandra violated; the Trojan women dragged from the temples of Troy; the boy Astyanax, son of Hector and Andromache, thrown to his death from the tower of Troy; Hecuba pulled away from Hector's grave by Ulysses (13.408–428), compressing into twenty-one lines what Virgil gives more than five hundred lines to (*Aeneid* 2.298–804). Moreover, "[b]y turning the fall of Troy into a background for the metamorphosis of Hecuba," Solodow says, "[Ovid] places private suffering above national catastrophe" (141), reversing Virgil's general priority in the *Aeneid*.

For the episode proper (13.429–575), Ovid draws upon Euripides' *Hecuba* ("a smooth abbreviation of Euripides," says Otis 286), but he "handles his material freely for rhetorical and pathetic effect" (Kenney [1986] 450).

The story of Hecuba has as its subject the deaths of Hecuba's last two children, Polyxena and Polydorus, and her quite different reactions to these deaths, in response to the latter of which she goes mad from grief and rage and is changed into a barking dog— the objective correlative of her madness.

Before beginning the narrative about Polyxena, Ovid gives ten lines of background to the section on Polydorus (13.429–438: the boy's murder by Polymestor, king of Thrace, and Polymestor's motive) so that he can maintain the tale's momentum by making a smooth and fast transition from Polyxena to Polydorus (at 13.533–535).

A personal appearance by Achilles, or rather his ghost (13.441–448), about whom we may have forgotten in the intensity of the debate between Ajax and Ulysses over his arms, appropriately reminds us at the end of Ovid's "*Iliad*" of its supposedly central character, "supposedly," for ever since Achilles' slaughter of Cycnus early in Ovid's "*Iliad*" (12.70–145), the focus has been on words—Nestor's long narrative in book 12 and the debate between Ajax and Ulysses in book 13. Achilles now returns briefly as a kind of hand from the grave or the dead killer who keeps on killing to demand that Polyxena, the young daughter of Priam and Hecuba, be sacrificed as an offering to his shade. Note the symmetry: the Greek king's daughter Iphigenia was sacrificed at the beginning of Ovid's version of the Trojan War; a daughter of the Trojan king and queen is sacrificed at the end of it.

Polyxena gives a noble speech and then is brutally killed, preserving her royal demeanor and virginal modesty to the very end (13.477–480). Her death evokes a long speech from Hecuba (13.494–532), at thirty-nine lines nearly as long as the account of the girl's death itself (forty-two lines: 13.439–480), which includes her death speech. But Hecuba's expression of her grief at the death of Polyxena—"she remains powerful, articulate, and self-possessed," her speech "full of grace and fine cadence" (Barkan 22)—serves as a powerful contrast to her reaction to the death of her son Polydorus, whose body she discovers washed ashore on the coast of Thrace at the spot where she goes to get water to bathe the dead Polyxena: the other Trojan women "screamed" (*exclamant,* 13.538), but Hecuba "was mute with grief" (*obmutuit illa dolore,* 13.538), and "grief . . . choked her voice and swallowed the tears that welled up in her" (13.539–540: *devorat ipse dolor*). This is the point at which her metamorphosis begins, as Barkan says: "The repeated *dolor* is the real cause of metamorphosis, and it produces changes that amount to the destruction—literally, consumption [*devorat ipse dolor,* 13.540]—of her personality. Her voice, which has been her essential quality, is now silenced; indeed, Ovid never quotes her again" (Barkan 22).

In the first stage of her metamorphosis, Hecuba freezes, "hard and still as stone" (13.540–541, recalling Niobe at 6.301–309, Due says [156]), and then "arm[s] herself with rage, put[s] on rage like armor" (13.544), "resolved to get revenge," and becomes "the living image of punishment" (13.546). The last phrase, *poenaeque in imagine tota est,* repeats verbatim Ovid's description of Procne at 6.586, at the moment when she learns from Philomela's tapestry what has happened to her sister and prepares to free her and then avenge both her sister and herself. The phrase, Barkan says, "suggests an aesthetic reduction: her [Hecuba's] emotional state is on the verge of being so extreme that she is almost nothing but a poetic image of that state" (23). For Solodow, the phrase "points to the likeness between metamorphosis and the clarity won by art" and "invite[s] us to view" changed figures "as *imagines,* 'clear pictures,' of their former characters, relations, or activities" (206–207).

At the moment of her revenge, Hecuba, not content with plucking out Polymestor's eyes, "plunged her hands . . . into the sockets and gouged out . . . the place where [his eyes] had been" (13.563–564). The Thracians attack Hecuba with spears and stones, "but she, with a low growl, tried to bite the rocks they threw at her and then, opening her mouth to speak, tried to speak, but barked instead" (13.567–569). Barkan comments: "The dog biting at stones is a sign of complete futility, an individual attacking its own violence and its own metamorphic stoniness. . . . [Hecuba] is both the dog and the stones. . . . Violence and inarticulateness have coalesced in the course of Hecuba's human transformations" (23), and he notes the stages of these transformations as "she moves from a human mother [after Polyxena's death] to an image of punishment . . . to an image of futility to the literal shape of a futilely punishing animal" (67).

Ovid moves to the next episode, the story of Memnon, by means of the familiar "transition through the absent person," as Solodow calls it (43–44): Trojans, Greeks, even gods were moved by Hecuba's fate—all but Aurora, mother of Memnon (13.572–577). (Speaking of the transition here, however, Solodow 26–27 says only that a "recherché contrast joins Memnon to Hecuba.")

The account of Memnon's funeral (13.578–622), the final event in Ovid's "*Iliad*," is chronologically out of place, since Memnon's slayer, Achilles, died at the end of book 12 (580–628). This is the last of four "deliberate exceptions" to chronology, in Galinsky's words; the other three are the story of Callisto at 2.401–530, "presupposed in the story of Phaethon" at 2.171–172; the reference to Atlas at 2.296–297 (also in the myth of Phaethon), whose story is not told until 4.631–662; and, "most strikingly, the reappearance of Hercules" at 11.211–215 and 15.12–18, after his death at 9.159–272 (Galinsky [1975] 85, although the last instance is not strictly a reappearance of Hercules but a recollection about him by someone else; Hercules appears in a dream in the same recollection [15.21–25] in his deified form). Solodow (29) adds a fifth: Medea at 7.357–358 flies over the serpent turned to stone by Apollo as it prepares to strike the severed head of Orpheus at 11.56–60. Yet this story fittingly ends Ovid's "*Iliad*," for Memnon, "a Trojan hero turned into a bird, can be seen as a complement to Cycnus . . . , rounding off the Trojan section of the poem . . . as [Cycnus] introduced it" (Kenney [1986] 450–451). In addition, as Due observes, the story of Memnon, in which Aurora seeks honor from Jupiter for her dead son, itself an endpiece for Ovid's "*Iliad*," "leads up to the endpiece of the following long complex of stories [Ovid's "*Aeneid*," 13.623–14.608]," that is, "[t]he scene between Venus and Jupiter" (14.581ff.), which is thus parallel to the story of Memnon (157). Finally, in ending his "*Iliad*" with the funeral of Memnon, Ovid nods to Homer's *Iliad*, which concludes with the funeral of Hector (Ellsworth [1980] 27; as Ellsworth notes, Hector, Cycnus, and Memnon were "the three most famous victims of Achilles": see Pindar, *Olympian* 2.79–83, and *Isthmian* 5.38–41).

Memnon himself, already dead, is lost in this episode. His mother, Aurora, "completely blind to Hecuba's tragedy" (Due 157), appears before Jupiter to ask the god to give her son "honor of some kind as solace for his death" (13.598), but (as Due 157 notes) for the first eight lines of her thirteen-line speech (13.587–599) she complains about the lack of respect shown to her on earth (manifested by the low numbers of temples, feasts, and altars dedicated to her) and asks Jupiter to honor Memnon in order to "heal a mother's wounds" (13.599), showing, Due says, that "what she really cares for is her own prestige" (157). Whereas Hecuba, Due continues, "destroyed as a human being by her sorrows . . . [,] seems to have been only a subject of conversation among the gods" (at 13.573–575), Aurora is solaced by Jupiter "because her sorrow is not real or serious, when compared to that of Hecuba" (157), that is, Hecuba's sorrow is too "real" and too "serious" for Jupiter to deal with.

Jupiter answers Aurora's prayer, and the scene shifts immediately (within the same line: 13.600) to Memnon's blazing pyre, from the ashes of which, swirling upward after it collapses, a flock of birds called Memnonides is born. These birds form two groups and fight to the death, reappearing on the anniversary of this event to battle again and die (13.600–619). "The image and the vocabulary throughout the description," Kenney observes, "are appropriate to Roman funeral games" ([1986] 451). The birds, born from black smoke (13.601) and black ashes (13.604), are a kind of black goshawk (*accipiter gentilis*) according to Haupt-Ehwald, and can be observed in the Troad in the autumn (at 13.618f., 2.326). The black color of the birds, Kenney says, is "doubly appropriate" to Memnon, who as king of the Aethiopians was black, and to "the mourning context" ([1986] 451).

Ovid ends the episode by returning to its beginning, where he had noted the contrast between the response made by humans and other gods to Hecuba's sad fate and Aurora's response, or, rather, her non-response. Now (13.620–622) he says that while others found Hecuba's misfortune "especially sad," Aurora "was lost in her own sorrow" and, still weeping for Memnon, "bathes the entire world in the dew of her tears" (thus giving the origin of dew). And so the tale ends with a contrast between true suffering, which reduces the human sufferer to a crazed animal, and "aesthetic" suffering, which lightly leads a pained goddess to "artful" performance: "Hecuba howls; . . . Aurora daily covers the world with dew" (Glenn 175).

Ovid's "*Iliad,*" his version of the Trojan War, leaves us with the notion that the "reality" of it is nasty and brutish (although not short), while the heroic tradition that preserves *klea andrôn,* "men's deeds of renown," is unreliable and unstable. To paraphrase Lanham (63), if Homer fashioned a heroic myth for the Trojan War, Ovid saw the Trojan War in need of mythologizing—and announces a warning of realism in play just as he embarks on his "*Aeneid,*" which comes next (13.623–14.608).

53. Ovid's "*Aeneid*" (13.623–14.608) follows immediately upon the poet's "*Iliad*" and narrates the journey of the Trojan prince Aeneas with a band of followers from Troy to Italy, where, according to Roman legend, he established his Trojan followers and where his descendants founded Rome. The story was given its canonical form by Virgil in his *Aeneid,* published a little more than twenty-five years before the *Metamorphoses* and an instant classic. For Virgil's *Aeneid,* with its account of Aeneas' migration from a razed Troy to Italy, immediately became the national epic of Rome, offering a justification, in the development of its hero, Aeneas, who is felt to embody the national Roman experience, for Rome's *imperium,* or empire, presented by Virgil as a divinely ordained "manifest destiny."

Virgil concludes his epic with the death of Turnus, an Italian nobleman who challenges Aeneas' marriage to Lavinia, daughter of Latinus, king of Latium (the part of Italy where Aeneas and his Trojan followers arrive), and opposes the Trojans' settlement there. Turnus was engaged to be married to Lavinia before Aeneas appeared on the scene. Aeneas kills Turnus in a battle between the latter's forces and the Trojans. Ovid, by contrast, ends his "*Aeneid*" with Aeneas' death (presumably of old age) and his subsequent apotheosis.

Ovid's "*Aeneid*" is presented as a "counterclassical" (to borrow W. R. Johnson's term [1970]), alternative version that can best (and perhaps only) be understood against the backdrop of Virgil's epic, which Ovid "dismantle[s]" (Tissol 183). At 954 lines (13.623–14.608), Ovid's "*Aeneid*" is about one tenth as long as Virgil's (and constitutes a little under one twelfth of the *Metamorphoses*). Of these 954 lines, only 190 actually focus on Aeneas, the Trojans, and their journey from Troy to Rome, up through the hero's death and apotheosis. In the remaining lines many stories are narrated, the longest of which are connected through shared characters, several of which are embedded narratives, two of which are stories within embedded narratives, and none of which bear directly on Aeneas. In the outline below, the sections of Ovid's "*Aeneid*" in which Aeneas and the Trojans appear are marked "A & T."

1. A & T 13.623–729: Aeneas and the Trojans travel from Troy to Zancle in Sicily with several intermediate stops; narration of the stories of the daughters of Anius (13.643–674) and Orion of Thebes (engraved on a wine bowl given by Anius to Aeneas: 13.681–701), both of which are embedded narratives.
2. 13.730–968: Scylla, Galatea-Acis-Polyphemus (an embedded narrative [13.750–897], with Polyphemus' song, "sung" by Galatea [13.789–869], the equivalent of a story within

an embedded narrative), and Scylla-Glaucus, with an embedded narrative at 13.917–965 that describes Glaucus' metamorphosis.

3. 14.1–74: Scylla-Glaucus-Circe.
4. A & T 14.75–100: Aeneas and the Trojans journey from Sicily to Libya and back to Sicily, thence past various islands off the Italian coast, including Pithecusae; this section includes the story of the metamorphosis of the Cercopes (inhabitants of Pithecusae) into apes (14.91–100).
5. A & T 14.101–157: Aeneas and the Trojans arrive at Cumae in Italy, and Aeneas and the sybil journey to the underworld; this section includes the story the sybil narrates to Aeneas, an embedded narrative (14.130–153).
6. 14.158–222: Achaemenides tells his story to Macareus, an embedded narrative (14.167–222).
7. 14.223–440: Macareus in turn tells his story to Achaemenides, an embedded narrative that begins in indirect and then switches (at 14.233) to direct discourse and that contains within it the story narrated by a servant of Circe's to Macareus (14.318–434).
8. A & T 14.441–464: Aeneas and the Trojans journey from Caieta (on the coast of Italy) to the estuary of the Tiber River and are received by Latinus, king of Latium; Aeneas' successful mission to Evander to seek aid against Turnus; Venulus' unsuccessful mission to Diomedes to seek aid against Aeneas and the Trojans.
9. 14.464–511: Diomedes' story, told to Venulus (including the metamorphosis of Acmon), an embedded narrative.
10. 14.512–526: Venulus; the metamorphosis of the Apulian shepherd.
11. A & T 14.527–608: war between the Trojans and the Rutulians; metamorphosis of the Trojan ships; Venus' intercession with Jupiter on behalf of Aeneas; and the apotheosis of Aeneas

This outline, brief though it is, makes it clear that Ovid launches Aeneas and the Trojans in about 56 lines within the 107–line segment (1), the remaining 51 lines or so being devoted to the stories of the daughters of Anius and Orion, and then departs for other narrative climes, returning occasionally to touch base with the narrative framework and nudge his characters onward, and ends his "*Aeneid*" by sending Aeneas to heaven in 28 lines (14.581–608) within the final 82-line segment (11).

The outline also clearly shows how Ovid, in Mack's words, "incorporates Roman history in a framework of Greek myth and makes Vergil's *Aeneid* only a fragment in a much larger whole." While Aeneas "trudges gloomily ever onward toward Rome, Ovid carries his readers into other worlds where sea nymphs comb each other's hair and tell stories of their love affairs" ([1988] 128). And while Ovid scatters bits and pieces of Virgil's "historical" account of Aeneas among his own mythical narratives in his "*Aeneid*," he "foreground[s]," Hinds says, "*Virgilian stories of metamorphosis*" (his emphasis) and shows us that "[t]here is a *Metamorphoses* latent in the *Aeneid*, . . . in Circe, and in the biform Scylla, . . . in the transformation of Aeneas' ships into nymphs and in the transformation of Diomedes' companions into birds." In Virgil's *Aeneid*, Hinds continues, "these myths are fragmented, scattered, unresolved: not until Ovid's own poem are they gathered into perfection and system" ([1998] 105, 106), as Ovid reverses the relationship between Virgil and himself and instead of becoming an "epigonal reader of the *Aeneid*" makes Virgil "a hesitant precursor of the *Metamorphoses*" ([1998] 106). Moreover, in addition to scattering parts of Virgil's "historical" account of Aeneas among his own mythical narratives, Ovid also severely reduces elements of Aeneas' experience that Virgil, dwelling upon at length, made profoundly meaningful in the development of his hero. For example, the poet treats the story of Dido, queen of Carthage, and Aeneas' love affair with her, which he must sacrifice to the call of duty, in four lines (14.78–81); Virgil devoted all of book 4 of the *Aeneid,* 705 lines, to Dido and Aeneas. Ovid thus makes it "difficult," Altieri says, "for the reader not to realize that Vergil's epic is like all the stories in the *Metamorphoses*—not reality but a creation of reality dependent on the imagination of a single storyteller" (just as Nestor's account of the battle of Lapiths and centaurs in book 12, which, Tlepolemus claimed, omitted the important role of his father, Hercules, was "dependent on the imagination of a single storyteller"). "Vergil tries to convince us," Altieri continues, "that the primary story for his culture was the destiny of Rome and . . . the virtues required to realize that destiny, while Ovid makes the story one of a series of stories, many of which contradict the Vergilian virtues" (261–262).

Ovid employs two strategies to "dismantle" the *Aeneid*. First, as Tissol says, he "empt[ies] the story of Aeneas of its Vergilian themes but only to replace them with others" (178). In particular, Ovid "rework[s] the subject matter" of books 3 and 6 of the *Aeneid*, in the former of which the Trojan seer Helenus, newly established in a second Troy at Buthrotum, offers Aeneas hope for (and an important prophecy about) his future, and in the latter of which Aeneas has a profoundly significant encounter in the underworld with his father, Anchises, who gives him a vision of Rome's divinely ordained future greatness that will sustain him through the trials of the second half of the poem. These are "the prophetic books," Tissol comments, "in which the *Aeneid* becomes most explicitly a providential history. In Ovid's version, the hand of providence is conspicuously lacking, as is any connection between plot and cosmic order. . . . In its place Ovid offers an answer to the *Aeneid*, subsuming its plot and characters to illustrate the universal prevalence of flux" (178–179).

With his second strategy (which is dovetailed with the first), Ovid, Solodow says, "frustrates attempts to attach Virgilian meanings to the story Virgil had told; he transforms it from a national into a personal history . . . , into a subjective rendering of the history of individuals" (136). Thus Ovid "converts" the parts of Aeneas' story that he keeps "to the record of scattered personal experiences lacking lofty motivation and significance and illustrating instead the private nature of human existence, which is shaped not by the gods or fate or history or nationality or virtue, but rather by ordinary motives and psychology, by circumstance and chance" (143). Ovid's insistence on the primacy of individual personal experience extends to storytelling, and he reminds readers "that no single version of a story can claim to be canonical." Because of "the nature of story-telling, which is to say, of story-tellers," there will always be variations among different versions of the same stories, inasmuch as narrators differ from one another and have their "own desires and interests and fears" (Solodow 154–155).

Aeneas appears at the very beginning of Ovid's "*Aeneid*" (13.623ff.), where he is described as carrying his sacred gods and his father on his back when he leaves Troy, and is called *pius* ("devoted," 13.626), his trademark epithet in Virgil's *Aeneid*, for the first and only time in Ovid's version. (In the epitaph he composes for his nurse Caieta, who dies shortly after the Trojan refugees reach Italy, Aeneas refers to himself—the epitaph is in Caieta's voice—as "[t]he boy I reared, known for his devotion": *notae pietatis alumnus*, 14.443). Aeneas does not speak in this section (13.623–729), nor is he referred to again in it after Anius, king of Delos, shows him the sights of the city (13.634–635; it is Aeneas' father, Anchises, also called *pius* [at 13.640], who addresses Anius [at 13.640ff.]). More than four hundred lines go by before Aeneas is mentioned again, at 14.78, where he is the object of a verb, the subject of which is Dido (Ovid's four-line version of *Aeneid* 4 at 14.78–81). This is the midpoint of Ovid's "*Aeneid*" (14.81 is line 427 of 954), and Aeneas has yet to open his mouth. The narrator reports that Aeneas asked the sybil to allow him to enter the underworld (14.105–106). She replies in direct discourse (14.108–113), and in eight and a half lines (14.113–121) Ovid covers the mighty (and long: 901 lines) sixth book of Virgil's *Aeneid*, Aeneas' trip to the underworld. It is only as he and the sybil are trudging back to the upper world that Aeneas (finally) says something: thinking the sybil may be a goddess, he thanks her for the trip and promises to honor her as a divinity once he has returned to the upper world (14.123–128). Aeneas' six-line speech provides the sybil an opening—the speech's purpose, apparently—to tell him her story (14.130–153), and Aeneas does not speak again in Ovid's "*Aeneid*," although many others do (Achaemenides, Macareus, Circe's servant, Diomedes, etc.) He soon disappears again (after 14.154–157) for nearly three hundred lines (Macareus addresses him in a two-and-a-half-line apostrophe at 14.245–247, but Aeneas does not reply to him) and reappears at 14.441ff. to deposit the ashes of his old nurse Caieta in a marble urn and to inscribe an epitaph on her tomb.

From Caieta (the place where Aeneas' nurse died, now named for her; see 14.157) the Trojans sail to the mouth of the Tiber, and in three lines (14.449–451) Aeneas is received by King Latinus, marries the king's daughter, and finds himself at war with Turnus, his new wife's abandoned fiancé. After one line (14.456) on the success of Aeneas' effort to obtain aid from Evander (Virgil's *Aeneid* 8), Aeneas disappears yet again as the narrator turns to the Rutulian Venulus' unsuccessful effort to obtain aid from Diomedes (a Greek warrior, transplanted, like the Trojan prophet Helenus, from the *Iliad*). Toward the end of the final section of Ovid's "*Aeneid*" (14.527–608), Aeneas reappears in time to kill Turnus—Venus sees him defeat the Rutulian prince, but we do not (14.572–573)—put an end to the gods' wrath (13.581–582), and benefit from his mother's successful campaign among the gods to have him made divine (14.585–596), the process of his apotheosis a kind of baptism in the river Numicius that washes away his mortality (described in the closing lines of section [11], 14.600–608).

Aeneas is hardly more than a stick figure and even so is seldom seen. As Solodow says:

> Aeneas has . . . no set of personal qualities which give him an identity and distinguish him from others. . . . His homeland is never said or shown to be of any importance. . . . [He] is nowhere at all represented as founding the Roman nation. Nationality is not a defining trait—a very unRoman thought. . . . [H]is actions do not lead to anything outside his own life. Absent is a notion of quest or mission, of destiny, of a promised land. . . . Aeneas is not a specially important figure; he is not central either in Ovid's narrative or in the history of the world. He is not conspicuous for any virtue, or for any vice either. (155)

Moreover, Ovid's Aeneas, denied both the warrior and "other-directed" heroism of Virgil's Aeneas, denied existence as a public figure dedicated to the common good and symbolic of Roman Man (which Virgil's Aeneas seeks to become), is virtually denied as well the "personal experience" so important for Ovid, according to Solodow (see above).

Ovid's "*Aeneid*" brings the *Metamorphoses* from Troy, the boundary between the Greek "mythical" and the Roman "historical" realms (and parts of the poem) to Italy. Perhaps to emphasize the bridge-like quality of this section, Ovid fills his "*Aeneid*" with many interconnections among its parts. As Wilkinson says, Ovid "interweaves Greek and Roman legends cunningly, so that we never feel there is a complete break in the texture and continuity of the poem." Aeneas' arrival in the Straits of Messina (13.728–729; these straits run between Sicily and the Italian mainland), Wilkinson continues, leads to Galatea, Polyphemus, and Acis, as told to Scylla; to the story of Scylla, Glaucus, and Circe (connecting books 13 and 14); and thence to the episode of Picus, Canens, and Circe (in book 14). "Circe brings us very near to Rome," Wilkinson concludes, "her island, now a rugged mountain-peak joined to the mainland by the drained Pontine Marshes, is visible from the neighbourhood of the Campagna," while Picus (in Macareus' story) is "the mythological king of Italy. . . . By such easy stages does the Greek world melt into the Italian" ([1955] 219–220).

Otis notes additional connections in Ovid's "*Aeneid.*" Of the four major episodes—
(1) Galatea-Acis-Polyphemus (13.719–897; the line numbers here and for the other
three episodes are Otis'), (2) Scylla-Glaucus-Circe (13.898–14.74), (3) the adventures
of Ulysses' men (14.75–319), and (4) Circus-Picus-Canens (14.320–440)—"[t]he first
two are basically Sicilian," he says; "the transition from Sicily to Italy occurs when
Glaucus . . . swims across the Tuscan sea to Circe's home in Italian Circeii [14.1ff.]"
(which lies between Caieta and the mouth of the Tiber). The last two are Italian. "There
is also an obvious correspondence," Otis says, "between (1) and (3) and between (2)
and (4). The first episode . . . describes the Cyclops . . . before the visit of Ulysses; the
third . . . describes the visit and its effect." As for correspondences between (2) and (4),
"in both," Otis says, "Circe is balked of her desire (for Glaucus and Picus) and, in both,
exercises her vengeance on the woman preferred to her (Scylla, Canens)." The last story
"advances the movement of the poem by bringing in a Roman site at its close: Canens
becomes a Roman spring, the famous Camenae near the Porta Capena" (288–289).

Segal considers the "unifying function of landscape" as "especially clear in [books 13
and 14], where it brings together the tales of Acis and Galatea, Glaucus and Scylla,
Circe and Picus, and Pomona and Vertumnus [outside Ovid's "*Aeneid*" at 14.623–771].
All of these tales unfold against a more or less homogeneous background of mysterious
shore or remote woods" ([1969a] 58).

Aeneas, Ovid says, carried out of Troy on his shoulders his "sacred gods" and "something else sacred," his father Anchises: "From all the wealth of Troy the devoted son
selected these as his share of the spoils" (13.624–626; *praeda* [626], here translated
"share of the spoils," is usually taken to mean "prize," "booty," or "spoils"). While Virgil
also describes Aeneas as carrying his father and his gods out of burning Troy on his
back, he by no means refers to Anchises as Aeneas' "share of the spoils" (see *Aeneid*
2.707–723). "To speak of choosing Anchises" from all Troy's wealth, Solodow comments, "is to place Aeneas' father . . . on a level with material goods" (144).

Aeneas and his band of followers, departing from Antandros, sail past "the guilt-
stained dwellings of Thrace" (13.628), the site of Hecuba's revenge for the murder of
her son Polydorus and of her metamorphosis (13.533–575), and head south and west
to the island of Delos. Antandros was an ancient city on the northeastern shore of the
Gulf of Adramyttium in the area of Aeneas' origin. The timber trade was concentrated
there because of the town's proximity to the forests of Mount Ida (see Bömer at 13.627–
628, 6.369), and Aeneas and his band of Trojans go there to build the fleet of ships they
sail to Italy (as Virgil tells us: *Aeneid* 3.5–6).

On Delos, their first stop, Aeneas as a tourist is shown the sights of the city (Solodow
144), including its famous landmark, the two trees Latona held on to when she gave
birth to Apollo and Diana (13.634–635), by its king, Anius, in total contrast to Virgilian
Aeneas, who, within six lines of disembarking (*Aeneid* 3.79), prays to Apollo for a second Troy (3.85–89), and immediately receives back an answer from the god's oracle
(3.94–98). "By eliminating prophecy from his version of *Aeneid* 3," Tissol says, "Ovid
eliminates the most obvious manifestations of divine purpose and the corresponding
structural comprehensibility of events granted by Vergil to his reader" (184).

At a state dinner, Anchises' query to Anius about his absent children elicits from the
king a story (13.643–674; the first of several embedded narratives in Ovid's "*Aeneid*"),
which, "though touching, remains unconnected to Aeneas' mission" (Solodow 144),
while providing an oblique commentary on Aeneas, or the Virgilian enterprise: "[S]o
much uncertainty buffets the affairs of humankind," says Anius (13.646), that he has
lost nearly all of his children. This uncertainty, Tissol observes, "reflects Ovid's great
theme of universal flux, here set in contrast to Vergilian providence" (184). Nor are the

Trojans, we learn, the only ones to have suffered terribly at the hands of Agamemnon and the Greeks. Finally, Anius, without blaming his son Andros, ascribes the loss of his daughters to Andros' weakness: "Fear conquered [his] devotion [*pietas*] to his sisters, and he surrendered them to the Greeks for punishment" (16.663–664). Having begun with "uncertainty" in "the affairs of humankind," at the end of Anius' story "Ovid introduces that familiar Vergilian theme, *pietas*," Tissol comments (184), "to show its utter defeat in this context," mentioning Aeneas specifically (13.665–666). Tissol concludes: "The arbitrary exercise of brute force by Agamemnon, the weak timidity of the son, the helplessness of the daughters—such aspects of human character and experience Ovid presents in a deliberately inappropriate context. . . . The reader is now left to ponder which version of the Trojans' visit to Delos may have the greater ring of truth" (184).

On the day of their departure from Delos, the Trojans finally consult the oracle of Apollo, "who ordered them to seek their ancient mother and their ancestral shores" (13.678–679). The phrase "seek their ancient mother," Kenney says ([1986] 451), is "an unmistakable allusion" to *Aeneid* 3.96 (*antiquam exquirite matrem*). There the oracle speaks directly, and its prophecy leads to rejoicing. Anchises identifies the place as Crete in a fifteen-line speech (*Aeneid* 3.103–117), and the Trojans sacrifice to various gods and then happily depart from Delos. Ovid, by contrast, simply says, "The king sent them on their way" (13.679), and names the gifts Anius gives to Anchises (a scepter), Ascanius (a cape and quiver), and Aeneas (a wine bowl). The story engraved on Aeneas' gift (another embedded narrative; see Nagle [1989a] 119) he then "reads" to us in an ecphrasis (13.685–701; see Solodow 229–230 for detailed exegesis of this passage). Ovid gives the wine bowl an antiquarian (and simultaneously anachronistic) authenticity. Its creator, Alcon, was the name of a famous relief sculptor in the Hellenistic period—an antiquarian reference for Ovid's time, an anachronistic one for the Trojans' time. Alcon's birthplace is Hyle, also the origin of Tychias, who made the shield of Ajax (*Iliad* 7.220–221; Due 23). The story of the daughters of Orion serves as a pendant to the story of the daughters of Anius, Bömer says (citing Ludwig), and he notes the unique instance of an ecphrasis combined with a metamorphosis (at 13.685–701, 6.384). Kenney sees "thematic similarities both with the daughters of Anius and with Polyxena" ([1986] 451).

"Remembering their origin from the line of Teucer," Ovid says, "the Trojans set sail for Crete" (13.705–706). Having inserted the gift-giving and the ecphrasis of the relief carved on the wine bowl between the oracle (13.678–79) and the interpretation of it here, Ovid now compresses into two lines Virgil's twenty-four-and-a-half-line account (*Aeneid* 3.99–123) of the Trojans' excited wonderment at the meaning of the oracle, Anchises' interpretation of it as signifying Crete, the sacrifices offered to various gods for a successful journey, and the Trojans' happy expectations before departure.

But they quickly leave Crete, "unable," Ovid says, "to endure the island's climate for long" (13.706–707), and now the poet has reduced to less than a line Virgil's sixty-line narrative of the Trojans' plague-ridden sojourn on that island (*Aeneid* 3.132–191), almost half of which (3.147–171) the earlier poet devotes to a dream Aeneas has, in which Troy's gods command him to leave Crete and sail to Italy, the Trojans' new homeland in actuality. (Anchises was mistaken in thinking it was Crete.) Noting that in Virgil "the cause of [the Trojans'] departure is supernatural," Solodow says, in Ovid's version, "the departure seems a casual affair. . . . By setting the motivation in the sphere of physical comfort, Ovid has radically altered the significance of the episode. Aeneas' subsequent wanderings appear to lack motivation altogether" (145).

From Crete, on their way to Italy via Buthrotum (13.707–721), the Trojans sail north and west to the Strophades Islands (south of the island of Zacynthos, which is itself west and slightly north of Olympia on the mainland), from there past the islands of Ulysses' kingdom (including Neritos, represented here as an island, otherwise the name of a mountain on Ithaca: Haupt-Ehwald at 13.771, 2.335), and on to Ambracia, where they take in the sights, including the stone the shepherd Cragaleus was turned into by Apollo after Cragaleus judged a dispute among Apollo, Artemis, and Hercules as to which of them should rule over Ambracia and decided in favor of Hercules (Grimal 112 s.v. *Cragaleus*). Ovid erroneously associates Ambracia with the temple of Apollo at Actium, a short distance south and west of Ambracia, on the southern shore of the Ambracian Gulf near the Ionian Sea. (Ambracia is north of the Gulf of Ambracia.) From Ambracia the Trojans travel to Dodona, opposite the southern part of modern Corfu (its Latin name in antiquity was Corcyra) and considerably inland, which, with its talking oak, was a famous oracular site, and to the Chaonian Gulf (north of Corfu; Dodona and the Chaonian Gulf belong together literarily, if not geographically: Bömer at 13.716–718, 6.396–397, with references). Ovid alludes to the story of the Molossian king Munichus: he, with his wife, three sons, and daughter, were attacked by robbers, who set fire to the building they were in; they were saved by Jupiter, who changed them into birds (in Ovid, only the sons: 13.717–718; see Bömer at 13.716–718, 6.396, who cites Antoninus Liberalis, the ancient source of the story). The Trojans next sail toward the land of the Phaeacians, identified in Ovid's time with Corfu (Bömer at 13.719, 6.397), and thence to Buthrotum, "a second Troy" (13.721), on the mainland opposite the northern part of Corfu. From there, "[c]ertain of their future after Helenus, the son of Priam, foretold it, they sailed . . . to . . . Sicily" (13.722–724). In Ovid, Aeneas and the Trojans are in and out of Buthrotum in four lines (13.720b–724a), compared to Virgil's 206-line narration of the Trojans' stay there (*Aeneid* 3.300–505). In Virgil, Aeneas receives a new prophecy from Helenus (*Aeneid* 3.374–462) which Solodow calls "the climax" of *Aeneid* 3: "[T]hough indicating the many dangers which lie ahead, it assures Aeneas of his ultimate success and informs him by what signs he will know that he has reached the appointed place in Italy" (145). Ovid makes Helenus' prophecy quite brief (a line and a half: 13.722b–723) and turns it, Solodow says, "into a very general, perfunctory account . . . , [and] [b]y breaking the connection between divine guidance and the movements of the Trojans, . . . converts them from pioneers and founders to wanderers, and converts their destiny from what had to occur to what happened to occur" (145–146).

The Trojans land on Sicily at Zancle, just south and west of the Straits of Messina, where Scylla and Charybdis (13.730–731), the monster and the whirlpool, lurk, between whom or which ships pass at their peril when they sail through the straits. Here the account of the Trojans' journey stops and remains suspended for 309 lines (13.731–14.71) while Ovid narrates the connected episodes of Galatea, Acis, and Polyphemus, and Scylla, Glaucus, and Circe, before resuming where he left off at 14.72.

54. Ovid introduces Scylla at 13.730–731 ("The coast on the right is plagued by Scylla"), turns away from her momentarily to describe Charybdis, her companion danger (13.730–731), and returns to her at 13.732–734: "Now, Scylla, her belly disfigured by a girdle of fierce dogs growing from it, has the face of a girl and actually was a girl at one time, if the tradition the poets have left us is not entirely false." He thus describes Scylla's first metamorphosis only to leave it (and the story connected with it) for an earlier time in the girl's life that is blissful in comparison with what comes later but is now (in Ovid's telling) suffused with a special poignancy created by our knowledge of

the disfiguring change to come. (The story leading up to it is narrated at 14.1–74.) In qualifying his assertion that Scylla was once a girl—if the poetic tradition is not false— Ovid once again reminds us, in his "alternative account" of Aeneas' journey from Troy to Rome, of the instability of poetic tradition (a theme very much in play since Nestor's narration of the battle of Lapiths and centaurs in book 12).

Before her metamorphoses, Scylla entertained Galatea and her sister sea nymphs from time to time with stories "about all the young would-be lovers she had eluded" (13.737). On one such occasion, presumably, one of her stories elicits a tale from Gala-tea, who tearfully tells Scylla of her own unwanted would-be lover Polyphemus and his murder of her beloved, whose name is Acis. Scylla, who disappears from view during Galatea's tale, is thus the subject of a narrative (Ovid's in the *Metamorphoses* and those of other poets), is a narrator herself (13.737; Ovid, Nagle says, "creates the impression that she customarily hurried off to convert the events of her life directly into narrative for a highly appreciative audience"), and is a "narratee" for or listener to Galatea's story (Nagle [1988b] 79). She will later hear Glaucus' narrative about his transformation (13.917ff.).

The story of Galatea, Acis, and Polyphemus (13.750–897), an embedded narrative told by Galatea herself (for comment on which see Nagle [1989a] 119), presents the first of three love triangles in Ovid's "*Aeneid*" (Nagle [1988b]) that are linked to one another by the characters they share: Scylla elicits (13.747–748) and listens to Galatea's story; she then becomes a member of the love triangle Scylla-Glaucus-Circe (14.1–74); and Circe then serves as the link to the third love triangle, Picus-Canens-Circe (14.318–434), in which she repeats her role in the second as spurned would-be lover.

Galatea's story falls into three parts. In the first (13.750–788) she describes the tri-angle composed of herself, Acis, and Polyphemus and makes a comment that impels us to question her reliability as a narrator: "And if you asked me, I really could not say which consumed me more, hatred of the Cyclops or love of Acis. My feelings were evenly balanced" (13.756–758; see Nagle [1989] 119). In this part she both character-izes and introduces Polyphemus. In the second part (13.789–869) she "sings" (or re-sings) his song; and in the third part (13.870–897) she describes Polyphemus' attack upon Acis and her lover's metamorphosis into a river.

In creating his Polyphemus, Ovid adds the savagery of Homer's Cyclops (in *Odyssey* 9) to what Segal calls the "amusing country bumpkin" ([1969a] 60) that is the Poly-phemus of the Hellenistic pastoral poet Theocritus in his sixth and eleventh *Idylls,* the result a grotesque, gargantuan Cyclops as well as "burlesque of a high order" (Kenney [1986] 452; see Ellsworth [1986] 28 and n. 8, 28f., and [1988] 337 and n. 11 for refer-ences to the *Odyssey* in Ovid's story of Acis, Galatea, and Polyphemus; see Farrell for a discussion of this episode as a "dialogue of genres," that is, of pastoral, elegiac, and epic poetry).

Ovid makes a significant departure from Theocritus' eleventh *Idyll* by turning the poet's central conceit upside down. In Theocritus, the lovesick Polyphemus cures him-self of his unrequited love for Galatea with song: "There is no remedy for love at all . . . , neither salve nor powder, . . . other than the Muses" (1–3; see also 80–81). Ovid's Polyphemus by contrast is momentarily tamed by love ("Your lust for killing, your brutish nature, your mighty thirst for blood all subside, and ships now safely come and go": 13.768–769), but his song to Galatea ultimately transmutes his unrequited passion into murderous rage, directed at Acis, and leads him to attack and kill the boy (13.860–884; see Leach 130).

Ovid in this episode also creates a glancing parody of Virgil's second *Eclogue* (which imitates Theocritus, *Idyll* 11) and his seventh *Eclogue* (in which Virgil adapts Theocritus' four positive comparisons at *Idyll* 11.20–21 to his own positive and negative ones—three of each—at 37–38 and 41–42).

Polyphemus' song, Bömer notes, at 81 lines (13.789–869; the length happens to coincide with that of Theocritus' eleventh *Idyll*) takes up more than half of the episode (148 lines: 13.750–897; Bömer at 13.789–869, 6.420). Line counts, usually of limited value, can sometimes provide the basis for insights, nevertheless. Although Polyphemus begins with Galatea, he devotes more than half of his song to himself: his property, his gifts, and his features (13.810–837 and 840–855a, 43.5 lines); a significant number of lines to threats against Acis (13.860b–869, 9.5 lines); and less than a third to Galatea (13.789–809, 838–839, and 855b–860a, 28 lines).

The Cyclops lovingly describes his own features: he is huge, hairy, and has a single eye in the middle of his forehead (13.840–855), yet cannot understand why Galatea rejects him and loves Acis and wants him rather than Polyphemus to hold her in his arms (13.860b–861). His passion for Galatea suddenly changes to rage toward Acis as he recognizes that his own love for her is hopelessly unrequited (13.863b–869). Spying the couple (13.874ff.), Polyphemus goes running after them, bellowing threats; Galatea dives into the sea, leaving Acis, helpless and terrified, to his fate; but she is still able to record and say what happens next: Polyphemus crushes Acis beneath a fragment of mountain he hurls at him. But Galatea and Acis' mother, Symaethis (Bömer at 13.885, 6.448; Galatea at 13.885 simply says "we"), transform him into a river and river god: "[A]nd from the cleft in the rock [the mountain fragment, now split in two] came the sound of gushing water. Then . . . a young man suddenly appeared, standing waist-deep in a stream, . . . and . . . it was Acis, but Acis now become a river" (13.892–897a). Mack, without using the word, implicitly notes the *ethopoeia* in Galatea's tale. While observing that Acis (whom she calls "[t]he might-have-been hero") speaks only once in the episode, when he "ask[s] for help just before he is killed" (13.880–881), she observes that "[i]n contrast to her silent lover, Galatea is very talkative, but she doesn't talk about Acis; she talks about the Cyclops. She actually addresses the absent Polyphemus in the second person . . . [13.764–769]; she never speaks to Acis." Mack also remarks on the small number of lines Galatea devotes to Acis: a few at the beginning, describing him; a few at the end, describing his death and transformation. Yet she "remembers every word of Polyphemus' song. Why *does* she remember his song anyway?" She answers her question by saying, in effect, that the song is not half bad, while Acis, though handsome, is stupid ([1999] 54–55).

Commenting on Acis' metamorphosis, Barkan says that the boy "is reborn as a divinity, and at the same time he is reborn in his own person. . . . [M]etamorphosis leads to apotheosis and to a transfigured version of the original self. We are witnessing at once the birth of a divinity and the turning away from fluidity toward a stable identity" (81).

55. Book 13, the longest book in the *Metamorphoses* (968 lines), ends with the first part of the Scylla-Glaucus episode (13.904–968), and the second part (now Scylla-Glaucus-Circe) will begin book 14 (1–74). And so this story links the two books, as often in the poem (see n. 5). Ovid does not say precisely where Scylla goes after Galatea finishes her story and the group of listeners breaks up (as Bömer notes), only that she "returned" (13.900), and so it is impossible to deduce, Bömer says, where Glaucus sees her. The assumption, however, is that the meeting between Scylla and Galatea takes place on the coast of Sicily, somewhere between Naxus and Catina. Scylla then swims "home" to the Italian coast, her traditional locale (at the northern end of the Strait of

Messina), and that is where Glaucus encounters her, as he tells Circe (14.17–18). Circe herself goes to Rhegium, on the coast of Italy in the vicinity of Scylla's home, to find her (14.47–48).

At 14.1–10 Ovid says that Glaucus (after being rejected by Scylla) swam across the Tyrrhenian Sea to Circe's house, traditionally located just off the Italian coast on the island of Aeaea—later joined to the mainland as the promontory Circeii—between Caieta and the mouth of the Tiber, but closer to the former, leaving behind Mount Aetna, Zancle, Rhegium, and the Strait of Messina, that is (I assume), the general vicinity of the place where Scylla lives. For discussion of these geographical details, see Bömer at 13.735–737, 6.403–404.

There is no transition from the Scylla-Galatea story to the Scylla-Glaucus episode other than Scylla herself, who bridges the two tales, serving as a participant (or character) and audience in both. Glaucus simply catches sight of her on the shore as he swims by and, overcome with desire, tries to seduce her by saying "everything he could think of to keep her from running away" (13.907–908). He does not ease her fears, however, and she runs to the top of a mountain, "where the sea-god presumably cannot follow" (Segal [1969a] 17). Once Scylla feels safe, she stops and, "unsure whether Glaucus was monster or god, looked in awe at his sea-blue color, at the hair covering his shoulders and falling down his back, and at the lower part of his body, with the smooth and sinuous form of a fish" (13.913–915). Scylla was in the habit, we remember, of dropping in on the nymphs of the sea and telling them stories "about all the young would-be lovers she had eluded" (13.737), that is, she was in the habit of converting her experience—experience of a certain kind—into narratives for an audience (Nagle [1988b] 79). But how inventive can you be when it comes to making up stories about running away from love affairs that never happen? The substance of her tales must lie in her descriptions of her pursuers. So she flees to a place where she feels it's safe to take Glaucus in—and he is indeed something to look at—stops and, "in awe," appraises him from top to bottom. But it's a mistake, for Glaucus is no "young lover." He's perceptive ("Glaucus sensed what she was thinking," 13.916); he's persistent (unfortunately for Scylla, as we shall learn in the second part of the story); he's just been translated from human being to sea god; and, not least, he's a former fisherman, skilled at catching elusive prey. The story of his transformation, the third of six first-person accounts of a metamorphosis in the poem (see n. 8; it is also another embedded narrative), will be his bait. In good storyteller fashion—in good Ovidian fashion—Glaucus sets the scene, describing a truly virginal place, untouched by animals or scythe-wielding humans. And then, he says, "[a]s for what happened next—it sounds like something I might have made up, but why make up a story like this?" (13.935), using a standard rhetorical strategy, intended to hook a credulous hearer ("it sounds like something I might have made up"), which he then customizes by adding a question that hints at an ulterior motive in order to deny it ("but why make up a story like this?"), and, of course, his story is true (we think).

Glaucus then gives a near-clinical description of his metamorphosis, in which he "carefully distinguishes between what he remembers from his actual experience of apotheosis, and what he discovered after he regained consciousness" (Nagle [1989a] 120), telling how he saw fish that he had caught and laid on the grass quickened by contact with it and escaping back into the water; how he ate a handful of the grass, with its "mysterious juice" (13.944); how he felt his heart beat wildly; and how he was seized by an irresistible "longing for a different nature" (13.946). At a certain stage in the process he loses consciousness, and when he recovers his senses he finds himself changed in body and mind. His new body he describes; his mind he does not—perhaps as a god he's (now) given to chasing girls; he didn't chase them before; he cared only about fishing and the sea.

Glaucus ends his story by returning to and elaborating his earlier rhetorical ploy at 13.935 ("but why make up a story like this?"), saying to Scylla, What good is this new form, what good is it to be attractive to the gods of the sea, even to be a god, "if you are not moved by this?" (13.964–965)—and he seems sincere. But Scylla now has her new story of another lover she has eluded, and she's taking no chances: this would-be lover is not a boy but a god, and she's gone before he finishes speaking. His mind is indeed not the same: he is a god, he is furious at being rejected, and he turns to another god, Circe, for help.

This story has obvious similarities with Galatea's: they are both embedded narratives; they are linked by Scylla, an auditor in both; they are both love triangles. (Scylla and Glaucus will soon add Circe.) The rejected lover wreaks vengeance in both. (Circe's is yet to come.) In an odd parallel, the victim of the rejected lover's wrath in the former tale (Acis) is resurrected as a river god after being murdered (and as a river joins the element of his beloved), while the rejected lover here has just been changed into a sea god.

BOOK FOURTEEN

56. At the end of book 13, Glaucus, furious at being rejected by Scylla, departs for the house of Circe to ask her to use her magic on the girl in his behalf. Book 14 begins with Glaucus well on his way: he has left behind Mount Aetna, "hurled down, once, upon the giant's head" (14.1), that is, upon the giant Typho or Typhoeus, by Jupiter, thus ending a titanic struggle between them (see book 5.346–358; Hesiod, *Theogony* 820–868; and Apollodorus 1.6.3); and "the fields of the Cyclopes," that is, the locale around Mount Aetna, Vulcan's forge, where the Cyclopes worked, which, because of the "proverbial harshness of the landscape" (Bömer at 14.1–4, 7.9), was "untouched by hoe or plow" (14.2–3).

Ovid says, or seems to say, that Glaucus travels from Sicily to Italy. (For comment on the geography involved, see n. 55.) If so, he precedes (and anticipates) Aeneas, whom we left at Zancle at 13.729 and will return to at 14.72–76, where he and his fleet negotiate the Strait of Messina (which runs between the eastern corner of Sicily and Italy at the toe of the boot) and its twin hazards, Scylla and Charybdis. When Glaucus approaches Circe, Nagle says, "the pattern of the tale alters as his role changes, from unsuccessful suitor to unresponsive beloved. Now Circe, not Glaucus, is the unwelcome suitor, like Polyphemus in the preceding triangle. . . . Scylla is now recast in the role of Acis. . . . Ovid here has recounted two successive instances of one narrative paradigm . . . in order to establish it in his reader's mind" ([1988b] 82–83). Not only to establish it in his reader's mind but also to superimpose it on another paradigm already there. For these two stories (Acis-Galatea-Polyphemus [13.730–968] and Scylla-Glaucus-Circe [14.1–74]) follow Ovid's version of *Aeneid* 3 (13.627–729) and thus fill the place of *Aeneid* 4, which Virgil devotes in its entirety to the tragic love affair between Aeneas and Dido (whom Aeneas abandons). That story itself Ovid crowds into four lines (14.78–81) shortly after the conclusion of the Scylla-Glaucus-Circe episode. The story of Dido and Aeneas is, of course, not a triangle (Dido's husband, Sychaeus, is dead; and the queen has rejected a suitor, the Libyan prince Iarbas, before Aeneas arrives in Carthage), unless one makes duty, *pietas,* the virtue that summons Aeneas away from Dido, the third party. Thus Aeneas departs from Carthage, with *pietas,* and Dido is left behind and kills herself. (Ellsworth sees "a remarkable similarity" between the Scylla-

Glaucus-Circe episode and the story of Dido and Aeneas, the former of which Ovid "uses . . . to anticipate and reflect the situation of Aeneas," but draws no specific conclusions from this similarity other than to note that "triangle tales" "are characteristic of the post–Trojan War period, the best known being the Agamemnon/Clytemnestra/Aesgisthus": [1986] 30–31, 32.)

These two triangles also anticipate the triangle to come of Aeneas-Lavinia-Turnus (*Aeneid* 7–12; *Metamorphoses* 14.449–574). Solodow notes that "the Scylla episode, with others inserted within it [i.e., Galatea and Glaucus, 13.738–14.74], interrupts the story of Rome's creation," overwhelms "the frame narrative through size and thematic irrelevance," and so "undermines the importance of that narrative" (139). In addition, it seems to me that Ovid, in a bit of intertextual maneuvering, uses these narrative paradigms (the love triangles) to shift the emphasis of Virgil's canonic version of Aeneas-Dido (and Aeneas-Lavinia to come) away from an Aeneas who is *pietas*-driven and suffers as much as those he causes suffering to, to an Aeneas who (the paradigms imply) is a destructive force, like Polyphemus and Circe ("the quintessence of violent desire and overmastering sexual appetite," Segal [1969a] 62), and shatters innocent lives.

At 14.25–27 the narrator attributes Circe's susceptibility to love as possibly due to Venus' retaliation for Circe's father the Sun's disclosure of Venus' affair with Mars to her husband, Vulcan, who, after trapping the adulterous couple in bed together, exposed them in their hapless state to the teasing and mockery of the other gods (Homer, *Odyssey* 8.266–366). Ovid tells the story at 4.167–189 and at 4.190ff. says that Venus took revenge on the Sun by making him fall hopelessly in love with Leucothoe.

The cycle of vengeance that began with Venus now continues as Circe uses her magic (as Glaucus asked her to, but not for the purpose for which he sought it) to inflict horrible and grotesque "punishment" on the innocent Scylla. This magic, Segal says, "is a manifestation of that arbitrary violence which pervades the entire work" ([1968] 442). Scylla, in turn, "out of hatred for Circe," devoured several of Ulysses' companions when his ship passed between her and Charybdis (14.70–71; cf. *Odyssey* 12.223–259).

Ovid now brings the narration back to its ostensible subject and frame, Aeneas and his journey to Italy, by saying that Scylla would have sunk the Trojan fleet had she not been changed into a stone crag before the ships arrived at the Strait of Messina (14.72–74). And so this long digression, which began at 13.730, ends, Nagle says, "with a sudden, unexpected, change" (that of Scylla), a change that is "just in the nick of time" ([1988b] 78).

Aeneas and the Trojans depart from Zancle, near the entrance to the Strait of Messina, row through the strait, and "had almost reached the Italian coast" when they were "driven by winds to the shores of Libya" (14.75–77). This is a nautical feat, geographically speaking, of some magnitude (if they were driven in a straight line), since Aeneas could only have been a mile or two from the Italian shore when caught by the contrary winds and driven to Dido's kingdom in Libya, roughly 350 miles southwest, as the crow flies, with Sicily squarely in the way.

There (in Libya) Aeneas meets, loves, and leaves Dido in a short four lines (14.78–81, as noted earlier; Virgil devotes the 705 lines of *Aeneid* 4 to this love affair and its outcome). Dido, says Ovid, who refers to her not by name but by place of origin ("the Sidonian woman," 14.80), "took Aeneas in—into her home and into her heart" (14.78–80), describing her double captivation with the rhetorical figure of zeugma, which further compresses this already abbreviated narrative and which also, Solodow says, places "the inner event ["into her heart"] and the outer ["into her home"] . . . on the same level, an equation that undermines the meaning of Virgil's version" (147).

In another small but telling change, Ovid calls Aeneas Dido's "husband" (*mariti*, 14.79), thus agreeing with Virgil's Dido, who referred to her "marriage" (*coniugium*) with Aeneas, and so "refuting" Virgil, who accused Dido of "cloaking [*praetexit*] her sin with this name" (*Aeneid* 4.172).

Ovid's version of the affair, Solodow further observes, "lacks the abundant significance which it had in the *Aeneid*," and he asks, "What has happened to Aeneas' cruel and characteristic dilemma, whether he should follow his own human longings and remain with Dido or carry out the historical mission entrusted to him, which dictates that he leave? Why do we hear nothing of Dido's love for Aeneas, nothing of the hate that comes to take its place . . . ? To introduce these elements would be to invest the story with wide moral and historical significance" (147).

As a substitute for Virgil's account of Dido and Aeneas, Ovid has for 311 lines (13.732–968; 14.1–74) narrated two "mythological" love triangles that are linked by the figure of Scylla, in which innocent lives are ruined (Galatea's and Scylla's, the latter's horribly) by powerful interlopers (Polyphemus, Glaucus, and Circe). He has then attached to these linked triangles, as a kind of appendix and, perhaps, as a third triangle, the love affair of Dido and Aeneas, but an affair radically compressed from its canonical version, with every drop of its Virgilian significance squeezed out and now ready to be filled with the Ovidian significance that its neighboring triangles suggest.

57. In this section of Ovid's "*Aeneid*" (14.82–157), Aeneas and the Trojans travel from Dido's "sandy kingdom" (14.82) to Sicily and thence to Italy, where they land at Cumae and where Aeneas meets the prophetess known as the sybil, descends to the underworld with her as his guide, sees the shade of his father, Anchises, and returns with the sybil to the upper world. These seventy six lines thus cover that portion of Aeneas' and the Trojans' long journey to Italy described by Virgil in books 5 and 6 of the *Aeneid* (1,772 lines). The major events of *Aeneid* 5 are the elaborate funeral games for Anchises (whose death was reported at the end of *Aeneid* 3) and Juno's attempt to scuttle Aeneas' mission to found Rome by instigating the Trojan women to burn the Trojan ships while Aeneas and his men are engaged in these games. The high point of *Aeneid* 6 (itself "the focal point of the *Aeneid*": R. D. Williams 457) is Aeneas' encounter in the underworld with the shade of Anchises, who reveals to his son the metaphysical reality that underlies life on earth, including the nature of the afterlife, and then unfolds for him Rome's great future.

The major event of Ovid's "*Aeneid* 5" (14.82–100), by contrast, is the story of Jupiter's metamorphosis of the Cercopians, inhabitants of the island of Pithecusae (which the Trojans sail past), into apes as punishment for unspecified "fraud, deceit, and other crimes" (14.89–100). The high point of his "*Aeneid* 6" (14.101–157) is the sybil's wrenchingly sad personal story about the thousand-year-long metamorphosis into an increasingly old, old age that she is presently undergoing (14.130–153) as punishment for rejecting Apollo's advances.

At 14.82–84 Ovid says that Aeneas "came back" to the land of Eryx in western Sicily and there performed a sacrifice at his father's grave, despite the fact that, in Ovid's version, Aeneas hasn't been there before and Anchises hasn't died. (Anchises hasn't been mentioned since leaving Delos, alive and well, at 13.679–680.) Now, Ovid and his readers knew very well that in Virgil's *Aeneid* Anchises died in western Sicily at Drepanum, near Mount Eryx (*Aeneid* 3.707–711), whither Virgil's Aeneas truly returns (after departing thence for Italy at *Aeneid* 1.34–35 and being blown to Libya by a storm) at the beginning of *Aeneid* 5. It is hard to believe that a poet steeped, like Ovid, in the learned works of

Hellenistic scholar-poets and capable of displaying such learning himself was suddenly inattentive to detail and so unaware of his lapse here. I thus assume that the lapse is deliberate, a studied casualness as to details that signals unconcern. Moreover, Ovid devotes but one line to the honor Aeneas pays to his father at his grave (14.84), thus compressing out of existence—just as he made Anchises' death nonexistent—the elaborate funeral games that Virgil's Aeneas stages for Anchises in the *Aeneid* (5.104–603), games that "were in effect moral tales," as Solodow says, in which "each victory showed the power of some virtue" (147–148). Similarly, Ovid only glances briefly at the attempt made on the Trojan ships, saying, "[Aeneas] then weighed anchor in ships that Iris, at Juno's command, had nearly destroyed by fire" (14.85–86), "the near burning of the ships . . . but a preliminary to sailing onward" (Solodow 148). In Virgil, the burning of the ships turns into an opportunity to revive Aeneas' mission, so nearly destroyed by the fires, and to strengthen it and give it new purposefulness through divine confirmation (*Aeneid* 5.604–826). By passing over an important detail of Aeneas' journey and the death of Anchises, by ignoring the funeral games for Anchises, and by making only a brief and casual reference to the ship burning, Ovid offers an alternate account that seems dismissive of Virgil's canonical one, with its tone of high seriousness.

Ovid next describes the movement of Aeneas and the Trojans from Sicily past the kingdom of Aeolus (14.86–87; these are generally agreed to be the Liparaean Islands, a few miles north of the coast of northeastern Sicily), not mentioned by Virgil, and past the islands of the Sirens (14.87–88; these are located near Sorrento: see Bömer at 14.86–88, 7.35–36). Aeneas now loses his helmsman Palinurus, the loss described in half a line (14.88b; Virgil narrates the loss of Palinurus at some length at *Aeneid* 5.838–861, before the ships of Aeneas pass by the Sirens' islands). The Trojans next sail past the islands of Inarime, Procyta, and Pithecusae (14.89–90; Virgil does not name them at this point in his poem; Inarime and Pithecusae are two names for the same island: see Bömer at 14.88–90, 7.36–37).

Ovid now halts the journey to tell the story of the thoroughly unattractive Cercopians, inhabitants of Pithecusae, and their ugly metamorphosis into apes (14.91–100), perhaps as an alternative to Virgil's portentous, solemnly mythologized narration of the death of Palinurus, who, in a plain account, simply goes to sleep at the helm of Aeneas' ship, falls overboard, and drowns. In any case, this metamorphosis is the first of four in book 14, Myers says, that "involve the motif of speech" (the other three being those of the sybil [14.130–153], Diomedes' men [14.483–511], and the Apulian shepherd [14.514–526]) and reflect "a pattern of a concern with language and storytelling that . . . seems especially relevant here as Italian myths are first being broached and Augustan themes are poised to follow." Moreover, these stories "diffuse the Augustan implications of Vergil's poem [and] uncover . . . issues that have been attributed to the 'other voices' of the *Aeneid*" ([1994a] 102–103).

At 14.101–103, Ovid lands Aeneas on the Italian shore in the Gulf of Cumae, between "the walls of Parthenope on the right" (= Neapolis [modern Naples], where the Siren Parthenope was said to have been buried and which may originally have borne her name: see Bömer at 14.101–102, 7.43–44) and "the burial mound of musical Misenus . . . on the left" (Misenus was buried at the base of the promontory that projects into the gulf on its northern and western edge and that bears his name). At *Aeneid* 6.149–235 Virgil tells of Misenus, Aeneas' trumpeter, who, near the end of the voyage, challenged the gods to a musical contest, lost, and was pitched overboard by the sea god Triton, without Aeneas' knowledge. His body washes ashore at Cumae, and the sybil tells Aeneas he must find Misenus and give him a proper burial before he himself can descend to the underworld. Aeneas locates the body, burns it on a pyre, and buries the bones in a grave at the base of a promontory he then names for Misenus. Austin comments on the significance of Misenus for Virgil's narrative:

> With subtle art Virgil has interwoven this episode with the need to find the Golden Bough: the discovery of Misenus' body, and the preparations for his pyre, lead almost imperceptibly to the finding of the Bough, in the very forest where the trees are even now being felled. It is only when the Bough has been plucked that the burning of the body is described with ritual detail: so that death and burial encompass and accentuate the miracle by which a living man can descend to the underworld. (86–87)

Ovid's Aeneas lands at Cumae with Misenus' grave *already there* and serving as a landmark (along with the walls of Parthenope) for the reader in identifying the locale where the Trojans come to shore.

Continuing his no-nonsense approach, Ovid says that Aeneas "entered the cave of the ancient sybil and asked her to let him go down through Avernus and visit his father's spirit" (14.104–106). The sybil's response is short and to the point (14.108–113). She shows him the golden bough, and he gets it "almost as a ticket" (Due 38): "[A]ll trace has been removed of those details which in the *Aeneid* had imparted solemnity, mystery, and awe to the scenes that pave the way for Aeneas' descent" (Solodow 148).

Aeneas' trip to the underworld is an in-and-out affair: he spends four lines there (14.116–119), learns "the laws that govern this place and the dangers he must face in new wars" (14.118–119), and then heads back to the upper world. The descent is thus told in the starkest possible contrast to Virgil's 637-line version (*Aeneid* 6.263–899), in which Aeneas, in Solodow's words, "both reviews his past and has a vision of the future Romans whom he is to establish as a nation" (148). As the climax of Aeneas' visit in the *Aeneid,* Anchises shows his son illustrious Romans waiting to be born and the glorious Roman future. "Inspired by this," Solodow says, "[Aeneas] at last has some sense of what his mission is and what its fulfillment will be, and from this point on his determination is unwavering." Ovid, by contrast, "has little interest in Aeneas' mission and its alleged importance for world history, and no interest at all . . . in Virgil's metaphysical speculations" (149). What he is interested in here is the sybil's own story, "the private and personal" (Solodow 141).

As a sort of introductory flourish (which serves to elicit the sybil's narration), Ovid has his character Aeneas speak for the first and only time in the poet's "*Aeneid*" when he says to the sybil (14.123–128), "'Whether you're actually a goddess, or someone dear to the gods,'" he will always think of her "'as godlike,'" will always be grateful to her for letting him go to and return from the underworld, and will honor her as a deity in the future. "'I am not a goddess,'" she replies, and tells him the story, all too familiar in the *Metamorphoses,* of a young girl (herself) whom a god took a fancy to, tried to seduce, then punished for rejecting him (14.130–153).

In this more subtle variation, Apollo, the god in question, offers the sybil whatever she wants if she will give herself to him. She asks for eternal life. Apollo grants her wish and then, in the brilliant move of a practiced seducer, dangles before her the vitally necessary complement, eternal youth, if she will let him make love to her. She won't, and the god then withholds this gift, knowing that she has trapped herself in an increasingly bleak future—and she now knows it, too. "'And then a happy life for me was gone, [and] bitter old age with its halting step came in its place'" (14.130–143). She has lived seven hundred years and must live three hundred more in this slow metamorphosis that, relentlessly grinding on, wears her away with age until, she says—a perception all sentient people must have as they age—it will seem impossible that she was ever loved by Apollo, and he, should he recognize her, will deny that he ever did. Finally, she will have diminished to the point of invisibility and will be known only by her voice, which alone the fates will leave her (14.144–153; see the reference above to Myers [1994a] for the "motif of speech" in the sybil's metamorphosis). This is the fourth first-person account of a transformation in the poem (of six; see n. 8) and the only such account in which the change is still in progress.

The sybil's story, which takes the place of *Aeneid* 6, "is a wholly personal tale, without larger significance," Solodow says, "and the Sybil's resigned prophesying of her own disintegration seems designed as the very opposite of Virgil's confident prediction that Aeneas' descendants will one day rule the world" (150). Galinsky notes that the thousand years of the sybil's slow aging to old beyond old is "the precise amount of time that the souls in *Aeneid* 6 . . . spend in Hades before returning to the earth" (*Aeneid* 6.748; Galinsky [1975] 229). With the sybil's tale, Tissol observes, Ovid is suggesting "that Vergil's story is not the whole story, that arbitrary power and unintelligible suffering are more deeply embedded in the nature of things than are providential order and the working out of beneficent fate" (186). Once again, Nagle notes, Virgil's *Aeneid* has become "the frame for typically Ovidian content" ([1989a] 120).

From Cumae, Aeneas and the Trojans sail up the Italian coast to "the shore that was yet to be named for his [Aeneas'] agéd nurse" (14.157), that is, for Caieta, who died there (see 14.441–444). "Because his listeners knew Vergil," Bömer says, "Ovid does not need to mention a name" (at 14.157, 7.63). But Ovid is also "correcting" Virgil, Hinds tells us, for at the end of book 6 of the *Aeneid,* the older poet refers to the "port of Caieta" (*Caietae . . . portum, Aeneid* 6.900) before it is so named and then at *Aeneid* 7.1–4 tells of its naming in honor of Aeneas' nurse Caieta, who dies at this place. Ovid's "mock-pedantic correction is . . . designed . . . to show his enjoyment of a very . . . Ovidian moment in his predecessor." That is, for the first and only time in the *Aeneid,* Virgil bridges two books (something Ovid does repeatedly in the *Metamorphoses*), books that happen to be the last of the first or Odyssean half of the *Aeneid* and the first of the second or Iliadic half. He is thus bridging the two distinctive halves of the poem (Hinds [1998] 107–109; the quotation is from 109).

What Ovid begins here at 14.154–157 with his reference to the shore not yet named for Caieta he abandons for almost three hundred lines, not returning to it until 14.441–444, when Ovid says Caieta's ashes were placed in an urn and gives the epitaph inscribed on her gravestone. "Where Virgil had sought to close the *Aeneid's* most obvious structural break with a virtuoso narrative bridge," Hinds comments, "Ovid, with equal virtuosity, forces back open the gap between *Aeneid* 6 and 7, and inserts almost 300 lines of poetry into it" ([1998] 110–111).

58. At Caieta, Aeneas and the Trojans encounter the Greek Macareus, a member of Ulysses' crew who (he says) jumped ship at the first opportunity after Ulysses and his fellow Greeks sailed from Circe's island (14.440). Caieta was not a stop for Homer's Odysseus, though Virgil's Aeneas puts in there (*Aeneid* 6.900–901, 7.1–4, as noted in n. 57), and Macareus appears in neither the *Odyssey* nor the *Aeneid.* He is, in fact, Ovid's invention, the counterpart of Virgil's Achaemenides, likewise an invention (*Aeneid* 3.588–683), whom, in Ovid's narrative, Macareus recognizes among the Trojans, having last seen him in the land of the Cyclopes near Mount Aetna in Sicily (14.160–161).

The two Greeks exchange stories, which are thus embedded narratives (Achaemenides, 14.167–222; Macareus, 14.223–440). Achaemenides' tale plays off both the *Aeneid* and the *Odyssey* ("Within the Virgilian frame Ovid inserts a second Homeric frame": Kenney [1986] 455), for he offers Macareus what Hinds calls "a remake-with-sequel of the post-Homeric remake-with-sequel of the Cyclops episode which he . . . had already offered in Virgil's *Aeneid,* repeating some parts of the story and adding others (many of them Homeric) not covered before" ([1998] 111). Macareus responds with a story that plays off the *Odyssey* only, an "embellished remake," Hinds calls it ([1998] 112), of Odysseus' and his crew's encounter with Aeolus and the Laestrygonians and their year-long sojourn with Circe (*Odyssey* 10.135–574, 12.1–141), the "embellishment" including the episode of Picus, Canens, and Circe, a story within a story. "Macareus, then, is an Ovidian mythic double of Virgil's Achaemenides," Hinds says ([1998] 112). Hinds describes the intertextual complexity here: "Ovid thematizes his intertextual dialogue with his epic predecessor [Virgil] . . . by putting an Odyssean stray of his own into conversation with the Odyssean stray through whom Virgil had thematized *his* intertextual dialogue with *his* epic predecessor" ([1998] 112; see 114–115 for Hinds' description of further Ovidian intertextual complexity). It is only at the end of Achaemenides' narrative that we learn of his rescue from the Cyclops by Aeneas (14.218–220).

The differences between Virgil's and Ovid's Achaemenides are considerable, as one might expect (and as Bömer notes at 14.158–444, 7.66). In the *Aeneid,* it is Aeneas who narrates the Trojans' encounter with Achaemenides to Dido and others in Carthage. Also in the *Aeneid,* the Trojans see Achaemenides after they are already ashore, and it is Anchises who gives him refuge. Here it is Ovid who, by contrast, narrates the story of Achaemenides in the *Metamorphoses,* and here Aeneas is at sea and puts in to shore to rescue the Greek, who is frantically signaling to them. "No wonder Achaemenides praises [Aeneas] from the bottom of his heart," Galinsky says; the refugee's "paean on Aeneas' selflessness forms the beginning . . . and the end . . . of [his] account" (14.170–176, 213–220; Galinsky [1975] 232).

Virgil describes Achaemenides' appearance thus: "'in rags and a state of extreme / Emaciation, [he] stretched imploring hands to us / On the shore. We looked round. Appallingly dirty, his beard overgrown, / His rags held together with thorns'" (*Aeneid* 3.590–594; Day Lewis, trans.). Ovid's Achaemenides is "[n]o longer wearing animal skins held together with thorns and [has been] restored to his old self" (14.165–166). "In Vergil," Due comments, "Achaemenides is in the middle of his horrors and misery, squalid and desperate, and accordingly his address to the Trojans is high pathos. In Ovid Achaemenides is clean, safe, and far from the terrible dangers when he tells his story to Macareus . . . ; his story has now become a sailor's tale, and he tells it with considerable relish" (84).

Ovid's Achaemenides also rearranges the Virgilian Achaemenides' narrative, as Bömer also notes. That is, in Achaemenides' narration in the *Aeneid,* Polyphemus' killing and eating of Greeks comes first, and the blinding of Polyphemus comes next (the order in the *Odyssey*), and then the Cyclops himself appears and the Trojans (and Achaemenides) flee. In Ovid, the details are related "backwards," so to speak: first comes the hurling of the stones at Ulysses' ship (14.180–187, not mentioned by Virgil; Ovid goes back to *Odyssey* 9.481ff. for this), and only then does Achaemenides reveal the death of his companions (14.204ff.), which is skillfully placed at the end of his account as its climax (Bömer at 14.158–444, 7.66).

Ovid also "corrects" two "errors" in the Virgilian Achaemenides' narration, as Solodow observes. In the *Aeneid,* the Greek refugee tells the Trojans that his companions, forgetting about him, left him behind in the Cyclops' cave (3.616–618). This, as Solodow says, seems "very improbable," and if they did leave him behind, it is likewise improbable that "he managed to escape." Ovid more reasonably says that Achaemenides was "abandoned . . . among the rocks of Aetna" (14.160). As for the second "error," Virgil's Achaemenides sees Polyphemus eat "two" of his companions (*duo, Aeneid* 3.623), while Ovid's Achaemenides "correctly" recalls Polyphemus' eating "two at a time" (*bina,* 14.205), as happens in the *Odyssey* (for a total of six: 9.288–293, 311–312, 344). "These details . . . remind the reader," Solodow comments, "that no single version of a story can claim to be canonical" (154; Galinsky [1975] 231 also notes the first "correction").

In an account that (together with Macareus') exhibits what Otis calls "the plebeian, the man-in-the-street's view" (289), Achaemenides comments on the folly of Ulysses' taunting shouts, hurled back at the blind Cyclops and serving as a direction-finder for him to aim huge rocks at the departing Greek ship: "'Ulysses' shouting nearly sank your ship,'" he says to Macareus (14.180–181; cf. *Odyssey* 9.473–505: Odysseus' companions object in vain to the taunts their leader shouts back to Polyphemus).

Virgil's Polyphemus is "an uncanny monster," Otis says, who does not speak but, instead, lets out "a stupendous bellow, shivering the whole / Expanse of the sea, shaking Italy to its core / With fright, and reverberating through Aetna's anfractuous caves" (*Aeneid* 3.672–674; Day Lewis, trans.). Ovid's Cyclops, by contrast, is "a most articulate cannibal" (Otis 74), who rises to something like his old Galatea-wooing self in enumerating the ways he would (if he could) consume various parts of Ulysses' body (14.192–197; Hinds notes the "*intra*textual 'doubling' of the Cyclops and Circe, whose roles in the Achaemenides-Macareus complex ask to be read against their roles in the Galatea-Circe complex earlier in Ovid's *Aeneid*": [1998] 112 n. 20).

Ovid's Achaemenides and his story of the Cyclops lead directly to Macareus' account of the Greeks' encounter with Aeolus and the Laestrygonians (briefly told) and their sojourn with Circe (*Odyssey* 10) and so "from Virgilian subject matter [to] a Homeric one" (Due 84), that is, to Ulysses and Circe (14.223–440). Within that "Homeric subject matter," however, the tale of Picus, Canens, and Circe occurs as a story within a story (14.318–434), with which "we are now firmly on Italian soil" (Kenney [1986] 455).

Achaemenides, relating his story in direct discourse, says to Macareus at the end of it, "'[T]ell me what happened to you and your leader and to that collection of Greeks who entrusted their lives to the sea with you'" (14.221–222). Macareus then begins his narrative, but in indirect discourse, relayed to us by Ovid, who, Nagle observes, "intrudes briefly for 10 lines [14.223–232, Ulysses' and the Greeks' experience with Aeolus, god of winds] . . . , as a subtle reminder, before an even longer direct account [i.e., the rest of Macareus' story, 14.233–440, a longer account than Achaemenides' 56-line narration], which itself will contain an embedded tale . . . , that he himself is not the narrator. . . . [It is] the shift from direct [discourse,] and back to it, which most emphasizes the act of narration" ([1988b] 85 n. 14). Nagle also reminds us that Macareus is the "narratee" of Achaemenides' story as well as the narrator of his own, in which, moreover, he describes himself as the narratee of the story of Picus, Canens, and Circe, told to him by one of Circe's servants ([1988b] 86–87), a still further emphasis on the act of narration. Macareus' shifting role is like Scylla's in book 13.

Direct discourse begins as Macareus describes the Greeks' encounter with the cannibalistic Laestrygonians (14.233ff.), who destroy all but one of their ships, that of Ulysses, on which Macareus served as a crew member. As Ovid follows the *Odyssey*, Macareus next narrates his version of the Greeks' adventure with Circe, whom we've already met as the rejected lover of Glaucus and destroyer of Scylla (14.1–74). Linking that story to the tale of Picus and Canens, she serves in both as the third member of a love triangle and also, Segal notes, as "the destructive, sexual power which destroys innocence" (Segal [1969a] 65). In fact, as Segal also says, Circe unifies book 14 of the *Metamorphoses*, aided in that by her identity as "so eminently a goddess of metamorphosis." Her "elemental sexuality," moreover, "occupies the foreground," and her magic, which she uses to destroy those who thwart her desire, "is a manifestation of that arbitrary violence which pervades the entire work" ([1968] 441, 442).

In the *Aeneid*, the seer Helenus warns Aeneas about Circe's island as a place he must pass by before he can establish his city in a safe land (3.384–387), and, later, as the Trojans approach it, passing close enough inshore to smell the smoke of cedarwood burning on Circe's hearth and to hear her singing, hear the rattle of the shuttle on the loom as she weaves and the roaring and howling of the animals she holds captive that were once men, until she changed them—all this, of course, piquing the Trojans' curiosity, one imagines—Neptune on his own initiative sends a wind to blow the Trojans safely past the island (*Aeneid* 7.10–24). That is, Aeneas does nothing, prophecy and divine help do it all. Ovid's Aeneas, by contrast, in a more realistic situation, free of prophecy and a helping god, is urged by Macareus, the voice of experience, to "'stay away from Circe's shores'" (14.247)—a warning Aeneas heeds—and also receives, as an illustration of why he should stay away, not unmediated smells and sounds, like Virgil's Aeneas, but a full, eyewitness, though mediated, account (14.248ff.), including Macareus' description of his own double metamorphosis into an animal and back into his human form as well as a more ominous second story involving Circe and Picus, a great-grandfather of Aeneas' bride-to-be, Lavinia. This account makes it clear that Italy, far from being an Eden-like haven of tranquil harmony, lies under the incubus of the "avenging gods" and the "pathos of love" (to use Otis' terms) which we might suppose were left behind when we moved from the "mythical" to the "historical" section of the *Metamorphoses*.

As he and twenty-one other crew members approached Circe's house, Macareus says, they were confronted by a thousand tame wolves, she-bears, and lionesses, and then servants welcomed them into the atrium (14.254ff.), this detail emphasizing, Solodow says, "the homey quality of the scene" (31). "Homey" the scene may be, but as Macareus describes the roomful of Nereids and nymphs busily sorting out magic flowers and herbs under the supervision of a brilliantly cloaked Circe, we realize that her atrium is, as Bömer says, a "laboratory" (at 14.242ff., 7.89), a place where her change-causing "pharmaceuticals" (*medicamina*, 14.285) are compounded. Circe laces a mixture of roasted barley grains, honey, wine, and cheese (Ovid's expression for "cheese," *lac coagula passum*, 14.274, more literally, "milk having reacted to rennet," that is, made to curdle, avoids *caseus*, the prosaic word for cheese, Bömer says [at 14.273–274, 7.99]), with some of these drugs (just as Homer's Circe does at *Odyssey* 10.234ff.) and offers it to her visitors, and the effect of the drugs (combined with a light tap on their heads with her magic wand) is soon felt, for Macareus and his fellow Greeks begin to turn into pigs, all except for Eurylochus, who had abstained from the drink. He now goes to tell Ulysses, who returns with him and compels Circe to change the men back into their original forms (14.273–307).

Macareus gives the fifth first-person account of a transformation in the *Metamorphoses* (14.277–286; see n. 8). Reverse transformations such as the one Macareus describes for himself and his comrades (14.299–307) are rare (for humans, that is). Only Io (1.738–746) and Tiresias (3.324–331), in addition to Macareus, undergo them (Mnestra [8.738–739, 843–874], as Nagle notes, "is a rather different case" [(1988b) 85 n.

15]). Macareus, however, is in a class by himself, since he describes both his own meta-morphosis and his change back into human form. (See Nagle [1988b] 85–86.)

Macareus' narrative of his, his companions', and Ulysses' experiences in the house of Circe introduces the tale of Picus, Canens, and Circe (14.318–434), which, as noted earlier, Macareus heard from one of Circe's servants and now retells to Achaemenides, Aeneas, and the other Trojans. A story within a story, this episode takes up more than half of Macareus' narration (117 of 218 lines) and is the heart of it.

The kernel of the story is given at book 7.170–193 of Virgil's *Aeneid*: Latinus, king of Latium and father of Lavinia, whom Aeneas will soon marry, receives Aeneas in what was once the palace of Picus, Latinus' grandfather (*Aeneid* 7.45–48) and an early Italian deity and king (see *Metamorphoses* 14.320–321), and is now a temple. Near Latinus' throne stand cedarwood statues of the Latin "forefathers," including one of Picus, whom, Virgil says, Circe, frustrated in her desire, turned into a woodpecker (*Aeneid* 7.189–191; *picus* is the Latin word for "woodpecker"; the bird "was held sacred in the indigenous Italian tradition," Fränkel notes [104]).

Picus himself was a son of Saturn (Virgil *Aeneid* 7.48–49), who, in Virgil's account, when another son, Jupiter, exiled him from heaven, fled to Latium, which he named and civilized, his reign there a "golden age" (*Aeneid* 8.319–325). Picus is thus "a wholly Italian figure," Kenney says, and Ovid's references to the mountains and rivers of Lat-ium (the latter by name), as well as the Palatine hill, where Picus' beloved Canens was born (14.326–334), make it clear that (to repeat Kenney's comment, quoted earlier) "we are now firmly on Italian soil" ([1986] 455). But Circe, a Greek divinity who "per-sonifies two of the main themes of the poem, sexual passion and metamorphosis" (Galin-sky [1975] 234), is there with us. This is a different Circe from the one we meet in the *Odyssey*, who "can still span lust and lovely song, still unite brutalizing and ar-tistic capacities," as Segal says. For Ovid, Segal continues, "Circe is essentially one-dimensional: she is *only* sensuality and elemental sexuality" ([1969a] 66; his emphasis). Ovid's Circe, in other words, has separated lust and art, like Pygmalion, but from the opposite direction.

According to Greek legend, which Virgil does not follow, Circe was Latinus' mother (by Odysseus: Hesiod, *Theogony* 1011–1013; Apollodorus, Epitome 7.24, says Calypso bore Latinus to Odysseus), and Ovid describes her gathering herbs in Latium (*herbae*, 14.350; "magical plants," says Segal [1969a] 67) when she first sees Picus, entraps him through magic spells, and attempts to seduce him (14.349ff.). Here, "magic and [Ital-ian] landscape are fused," and "magic and erotic passion go together" (Segal [1969a] 68). The "taint" of Circe thus awaits Aeneas in Italy, and the stories about Circe—this is the point—"create an atmosphere far from the Augustan and Roman order which are supposedly Ovid's main themes here. Occurring in the very middle of Aeneas' journey, they raise doubts about how seriously we are to take the upward movement from chaos to order, from Greek myth to Roman *imperium*" (Segal [1969b] 273).

The story of Picus, Canens, and Circe which Circe's servant tells Macareus ("in se-cret," 14.310) is initiated by a white marble statue of a handsome boy with a wood-pecker on his head which Macareus sees in a shrine in Circe's house and asks the servant about (14.312–317; a "clandestine" narrative thus parallels the "erotic" play between Circe and Ulysses: Nagle [1989a] 122; the marble statue is an "undisguised anachronism": Solodow 79). After we learn the story of Circe's thwarted lust and her cruel metamorphosis of Picus, we see the statue of him that she keeps in her house in a different light. It calls to mind the statue of another lover in a love triangle, that of Phineus in Ovid's "anti-*Aeneid*," who loses his Andromeda to Perseus and is subse-quently turned to stone by Perseus with the head of Medusa. His stone image is then kept in the house of Andromeda's father (5.227–235). No longer able to gaze on the extremely handsome Picus, since she has turned him into a woodpecker, Circe, a kind of reverse Pygmalion here, keeps this memorial of the boy who once was but is no more, the boy who "looked just like that statue of him there," as the servant says. "Observe how handsome it is, and in the carved image see the true one of the boy" (14.322–323).

Nagle ([1988b] 87–91) notes the play of "illusion and [often untrustworthy] reality" that extends through this episode, not only in the servant's description of the statue of Picus, in which, she says, one sees the "real" boy, but also in the phantom boar Circe fashions to lure Picus to a secluded spot and in the goddess' demonstration of her power to Picus' companions and her metamorphosis of them (14.358–415).

Picus rejects Circe because he loves the nymph Canens, who enhances the Italian flavor of the story: she is the daughter of the Italian god Janus and the nymph Venilia and was born on the Palatine hill (14.332–334; the emperor Augustus lived there). Canens provides yet another connection to Aeneas' future, for through her mother, Venilia, she is the half-sister of Turnus (Virgil, *Aeneid* 10.75–76), the Italian prince betrothed to Latinus' daughter Lavinia before the Trojans arrive in Italy and thus the loser in the Turnus-Lavinia-Aeneas love triangle. Canens, whose name means "singer" (from *cano,* "I sing"), and who is distinguished, Ovid says, by her "gift as a singer" (*ars canendi,* 14.337), is a female Orpheus, and with her "Orpheus-like melodies" (Fantazzi 287) she is able to ""move woods and rocks with her songs, . . . soothe wild beasts, stop rivers from flowing, and make birds pause in their flight overhead"" (14.338–340). These "sweet, spellbinding melodies . . . were meant to contrast with Circe's weird incantations" (Fränkel 105), and she is the goddess' counterpart, but her "power is the result of the far less ominous *ars canendi,*" Segal says, for "[s]he possesses the harmless 'white' magic of art and poetry as opposed to Circe's 'black' magic of passion" ([1969a] 65; see also Myers [1994a] 109).

Distraught when Picus does not return from the hunt, Canens moves aimlessly through Latium until, ""worn out with loss and wandering,"" she flings herself down on the banks of the Tiber and, singing ""in a high quavering voice, the voice of grief itself,"" one final song, she literally dissolves into tears and vanishes ""like a vapor on a gentle breeze"" (14.421–432), "knowing nothing in her innocence of the powerful counterforce that has overwhelmed her own magic and broken the order of her world" (Leach 128). That "counterforce" is Circe, the "anti-artist," who is "far more powerful than the true artist Canens" and leads us to view Italy as "a country where natural and supernatural forces are wholly hostile to the fragile strivings of art" (Leach 141 n. 45). Circe, destroying the innocent love of Picus and Canens, is a harbinger of the soon-to-arrive Aeneas, who, "like Circe, a figure from the older world of Greek mythology, intrudes," and destroys the peaceful harmony of Turnus and Lavinia (Ellsworth [1986] 31–32).

At the conclusion of Macareus' tale, Ovid closes the circle of this section of his "*Aeneid*" with the funeral rites for Aeneas' nurse Caieta, who now gives her name to the place that was "yet to be named" for her (14.157) when the Trojans arrived and met Macareus. Who composed her epitaph (in her voice) Ovid does not say, but if it was Aeneas, as seems likely, the self-reference ("[t]he boy I reared, known for his devotion," *pietas,* 14.443), particularly to his defining characteristic in Virgil's *Aeneid,* is striking (14.441–444).

59. Ovid now brings his "*Aeneid*" swiftly to a close, compressing the events narrated by Virgil in books 7 through 12 of his *Aeneid,* which ends with the death of Turnus at

the hands of Aeneas, into 130 lines (14.445–574; Ovid's Turnus dies in two metrical feet within line 14.573). More than half of those lines (70: 14.457–526) are devoted to the embassy undertaken by the Latins, under the command of Venulus, to the Greek ex-warrior Diomedes, now living in exile in Italy in a town called Arpi (northeast of Naples, in Apulia), to seek his help against Aeneas and the Trojans; the story Diomedes tells Venulus to explain why he cannot help Turnus and the Rutulians, an embedded narrative (14.464–511); and the narrator's account of the metamorphosis of an Apulian shepherd, the account occasioned by a cave Venulus happens to pass on his return from the embassy to Diomedes. Ovid's "*Aeneid*" continues beyond Virgil's, ending (at 14.608) with the death and apotheosis of Aeneas.

Ovid's Aeneas and Trojans avoid Circe, of whom no mention is made (or needs to be made, after Macareus' story), and sail directly from Caieta up the coast of Italy to the mouth of the river Tiber, where they go ashore, having reached at last the goal of their long journey from Troy, but without fanfare from Ovid (14.445–448). Now landed, Ovid's Aeneas is simultaneously welcomed by Latinus, king of the Latins, and given Lavinia, the king's daughter, in marriage (expressed by zeugma at 14.449); he immediately finds himself at war with Turnus, the local prince to whom Lavinia has been engaged, and secures allies for this war, including the Etruscans, thanks to Arcadian Evander, king of Pallanteum, an inland city on the Tiber at the site of what will be Rome (14.450–456)—although the Latin Venulus' effort to obtain for Turnus the help of Diomedes fails (14.457–458, as noted earlier).

"Ovid's Aeneas," Solodow says, "does not arrive at a promised land" (150). Virgil's Aeneas, by contrast, does, and that poet invests the Trojans' landing at the mouth of the Tiber with a new invocation to the Muses "[t]o mark further the importance of this occasion" (Solodow 150; see *Aeneid* 7.37–45; the invocation ends with the famous lines "A grander train of events is now before me, / A grander theme I open": 7.44–45; Day Lewis, trans.), and, proceeding at a slow pace, does not narrate the embassy to Diomedes until *Aeneid* 8.9–17, nor its unsuccessful outcome until book 11.225–295.

Virgil's Diomedes views all the sufferings of the Greeks after their return from Troy to Greece (or beyond), including his own, as just punishment for their guilty actions (*Aeneid* 11.252–293). His speech, Solodow says, "demonstrates the moral superiority of the Trojans to the Greeks." Virgil, he adds, wants "to show the virtue of the Trojans, the Romans-to-be" (151, 152). Ovid's Diomedes, by contrast, "explicitly denies the general guilt of the Greeks" (152). On the contrary, according to Diomedes, it was Locrian Ajax who "'had seized a virgin from the care of a virgin and [so] brought down on us all the punishment he alone deserved'" (14.468–469). Moreover, Diomedes continues, "'Venus, remembering how I wounded her long ago, punished me for it now'" (14.477–478; Diomedes wounds Aphrodite at *Iliad* 5.330–342), making her actions sound "like a personal vendetta" (Solodow 152).

At the same time that he sharply differentiates his Diomedes from Virgil's, Ovid makes startling references to the *Aeneid* in Diomedes' speech to Venulus at 14.464–511, references that connect that hero not to his Virgilian counterpart but to Virgil's Aeneas. In both the *Aeneid* and the *Metamorphoses,* Hinds says, "Diomedes begins with an account of his and his fellow-Greeks' voyage home from Troy, culminating in the disastrous sea-storm off the Euboean promontory of Caphareus." But Ovid's Diomedes, Hinds continues, "goes on to describe a *further* period of wandering when he is driven out of his homeland . . . [,] and at this point . . . his story starts to sound distinctly like the story . . . of Virgil's Aeneas." Diomedes tells Venulus: "'But again I was driven from my father's lands, and nurturing Venus, remembering how I wounded her long ago, punished me for it now. I endured so much in trials at sea and so much in battles on land'" (14.476–479). "Substitute Juno's mindful anger for Venus'," Hinds says, "and what we have here is a near-double of the opening five lines of Virgil's *Aeneid*": "the hero who first from Troy's frontier, / Displaced by destiny, came to the Lavinian shores, / To Italy—a man much travailed on sea and land / By the powers above, because of the brooding anger of Juno, / Suffering much in war until he could found a city" (*Aeneid* 1.1–5; Day Lewis, trans.). As Diomedes continues (14.480–482), he now "shadows Aeneas' own first speech" in the *Aeneid*, when, for example, he says, "'I have often called those happy whose ship a storm and fatal Caphareus wrecked, and I wish that I had been with them then.'" Virgil's Aeneas: "Oh, thrice and four times blessed you / Whose luck it was to fall before your fathers' eyes / Under Troy's battlements! O Diomed, the bravest / Of the Greek kind, why could not I have fallen to death / On Ilium's plains and shed my soul upon your sword?" (*Aeneid* 1.94–98; Day Lewis, trans.) "Diomedes' death-wish," Hinds comments, "both repeats and caps Aeneas'. Aeneas, in the middle of a post-Trojan shipwreck, envies those of his compatriots who had died at Troy; Diomedes, in the middle of a further phase of wandering, envies those of his compatriots who had died in the middle of a post-Trojan shipwreck." Diomedes' next lines, "'After suffering the worst that war and the ocean's waves can do, my comrades lost their courage and begged for an end to their wandering'" (14.483–484), "pick up the opening of Aeneas' *second* speech in Virgil" at *Aeneid* 1.198–199: "Comrades, we're well acquainted with evils, then and now / Worse than this you have suffered. God will end all this too" (Day Lewis, trans.). "[A] closer inspection of the two death-wishes" (Diomedes' in the *Metamorphoses* and Aeneas' in the *Aeneid*) shows us that Ovid's Diomedes "reactivates" Aeneas' call ("an apostrophe spoken into the void") to himself—Aeneas had said, "O Diomed, the bravest / Of the Greek kind" (see above)—which now "elicits a 'response' from the Diomedes of the *Metamorphoses*, embarked on his own mini-*Aeneid*." Aeneas' calling out to Diomedes "become[s] a kind of allusive 'cue' for Diomedes' own death-wish" at 14.480–482. The effect, Hinds concludes, is to make "one of the most famous speeches of Virgil's *Aeneid* . . . for just a moment, *pre*-Ovidian" ([1998] 117–119). That is, Ovid makes a subtle shift in his and Virgil's relations to each other so that instead of Ovid's being Virgil's successor, Virgil becomes his "predecessor." By making this shift, Ovid establishes the authority of his own "*Aeneid*" over Virgil's and validates its commentary on the now no longer authoritative Aeneas legend as told by his "predecessor."

Diomedes tells Venulus that the metamorphosis of his comrades into birds, which has reduced the number of his men and so makes him unable to offer help to Venulus, was brought about chiefly by one man, Acmon of Pleuron. Acmon's arrogant challenge to Venus at the time, for which most of his friends, including Diomedes, rebuked him, "'revived [her] wrath and goaded her to fury'" (14.483–511; quotation 495). For Ovid's Diomedes, it is not a matter of collective guilt followed by collective—and deserved—punishment; rather, "an angered . . . goddess acts out of spite . . . on the spur of the moment" (Galinsky [1975] 237), punishing the many for the action of one, or, at most, a few.

The birds into which his men were changed, Diomedes tells Venulus, while not swans, were very like swans (14.508–509), thus "trying to specify to the Latin ambassadors, who might just possibly have ornithological interests, exactly what kinds of birds resulted from the metamorphosis" (Galinsky [1975] 237).

Returning from Arpi to Latium, Venulus passes a cave "which the half-goat god Pan now occupies, but which at one time belonged to a group of nymphs" (14.514–516). Ovid then tells us—but not Venulus—the story of the brutish Apulian shepherd who chased the nymphs and mocked them and insulted them with obscenities. He was changed into a wild olive (by the nymphs?), the bitter fruit of which "exhibit[s] the mark of his tongue" (14.517–526).

Fantazzi calls this narrative, which is unmotivated by and unconnected to anything that has gone before, "a brief native pendant to the tale of Diomedes" and suggests that Ovid "obviously intended to link up indigenous Italian legends with the more established tales of Greek mythology" (285). If the tale indicates a native Italian "hostility to art" (as Glenn 188 implies), it shows as well that the impulse to create and perform art is also native to Italy and can denature the crude and vulgar opposition to itself. (For the "motif of speech" in the metamorphoses of Diomedes' men and the Apulian shepherd, see n. 57 and the reference to Myers [1994a].)

Following Venulus' return from his unsuccessful mission to Diomedes, the conflict between Trojans and Rutulians intensifies, and Turnus sets fire to the Trojan ships (14.527–534). The goddess Cybele, whom Ovid refers to as "the sacred mother of the gods" (14.536), creates a rainstorm to douse the fires, breaks the ships' mooring cables with the force of one of the winds, and sinks the ships stem-first, a process that changes them into sea nymphs and that Ovid narrates in detail (14.535–555; metamorphosis of the ships, 549–555).

Describing the life of these new nymphs of the sea, Ovid plays with the paradox of "permanence amid change" (Galinsky [1975] 240). The nymphs are deep blue, as were the ships; they take delight in playing games in waters they once feared; "[t]hough born in hard and rugged mountains, they now live in calm and gentle waters" (14.557–558); remembering their own perils as ships at sea, they steady ships in trouble—unless the ships are Greek: they hate all Greeks, remembering the Trojan defeat, and were happy to see the wreckage of Ulysses' ship and the transformation of Alcinous' ship to stone (14.559–565). Ulysses' shipwreck is described (by Ulysses) at *Odyssey* 12.403–425, at the end of his long narration to Alcinous and the Phaeacians and so just prior to his departure from their island (though it happened years before). The metamorphosis of the Phaeacian ship that transports Ulysses to Ithaca occurs as the ship returns from Ithaca, that is, after Ulysses has arrived back on his native island (*Odyssey* 13.153–164).

Insofar as Ovid has at times followed the *Odyssey* in describing Aeneas' travels to Italy, his references to that work signal finality, the end of these travels—the conclusion of one chapter—and arrival, the beginning of another. They also hint at a contrast between a Greek ship wrecked and a Greek-bearing ship turned to stone and Trojan ships snatched from destruction and joyfully changed to fantastic creatures.

Virgil places the burning and metamorphosis of the Trojan ships at *Aeneid* 9.69–122, after Venulus goes to see Diomedes but before he returns (for Venulus' travel to and return from Diomedes in the *Aeneid,* see above). His version, naturally enough, is altogether different. He begins with the history of the ships (a flashback), and the time when Cybele, from whose sacred trees on Mount Ida the timbers for them were cut, receives from her son Jupiter the promise to change the ships into nymphs of the sea when their task is completed and they have reached their destination in Italy. Virgil thus presents the metamorphosis as ordained at the highest divine level before the ships are even built, and of his fifty-four–line passage, only four and a half lines are given to the actual metamorphosis (9.117b–122, omitting the spurious line, 121), in contrast to Ovid, who, in a thirty-six–line section (14.530–565), gives six and a half lines to a description of the ships' transformation (14.549–555a). Commenting on the two poets' versions of this event, Galinsky calls Ovid's version "a reminder of the fundamental differences between Vergil's view of myth and Ovid's. The gods exist in the *Meta-*

morphoses, but the supernatural does not" ([1975] 238; for a similar comment, see Solodow 131).

This prodigy—the metamorphosis of the Trojan ships—does not deter Turnus, and he keeps on fighting (14.566–568). Ovid now gives a clear-eyed statement of why men engage in warfare, a statement that is Thucydidean in its non-chauvinistic realism: "They no longer sought a kingdom promised as dowry," he says, "nor the scepter of a father-in-law, nor even you, Lavinia; they wanted simply to win, and they waged war because they were ashamed to lay down their arms" (14.569–572). This comment immediately precedes (and introduces and qualifies) the final section of Ovid's "*Aeneid*" (14.572–608): his very brief account of Trojan victory; the death of Turnus; the burning of his city, Ardea, and its metamorphosis into a heron (14.572–580); and his narration of the death and apotheosis of Aeneas, much later in "historical" time (14.581–608). It is true, as Solodow says, that Ovid, with these lines explaining why the Trojans and Rutulians fight, "explicitly rejects Virgil's account of what motivated the war," that is, "Virgil's combination of moral, divine, and historical causes," but it is hard to see how Ovid substitutes for these "a personal and psychological [cause]" (153), for "personal and psychological" can here refer only anonymously and impersonally to "[e]ach side" and a series of "they's" (14.568, *pars utraque;* and 14.569–572, subject-unspecific *habent, petunt,* and *gerunt*). It is Virgil, really, who brings the "combination of moral, divine, and historical causes" down to the "personal and psychological" at the end of *Aeneid* 12 in Aeneas' rage-inspired slaughter of a defeated Turnus to avenge the death of Aeneas' young charge Pallas, with which slaughter the poem, significantly, ends (12.938–952). Here Virgil has truly preempted Ovid, the poet whose signature is "the personal and psychological," and is truly "pre-Ovidian." Ovid himself, in fact, abandons "the personal and psychological" and substitutes for Virgil's "combination of moral, divine, and historical causes," all noble abstractions, one may say, the ignoble and destructive abstractions of fighting to win and waging war out of shame of quitting.

The end of Turnus, his city, and so the war is told in two lines (14.572b–574a), as Ovid, now perhaps taking his inspiration from Virgil (*Aeneid* 7.412–413, the introduction of Turnus: "and now the great name of Ardea lives on, but its glory is gone"; see Galinsky [1975] 243), moves on quickly to another metamorphosis, that of Turnus' burned-down city, Ardea, into a heron (*ardea* in Latin), which "flew up from the smoking ruins" (14.576–577; recalling the birds, Memnonides, that fly up from the ashes of Memnon's pyre at 13.604–619) and whose cries, ravaged form, and pallor represent the ruined city. With the metamorphosis of Ardea, "a great stroke of imagination," Solodow says, Ovid seeks "to encapsulate the city's destruction in the appearance of the heron: history is manifested as form" (182).

Ovid leaps from Ardea's transformation to Aeneas' apotheosis. The gods end their wrath, compelled to do so by Aeneas' "valor" (*virtus,* 14.581); Aeneas' son Iulus grows up; and Aeneas himself is "ready" for heaven (*tempestivus,* 14.584: Aeneas has arrived at the proper moment of his life, as Bömer says [at 14.583–584, 7.189]; or, as Due says, "he is 'ripe' for it" [85]).

But Aeneas' "valor," his "readiness," and Iulus' ascension to manhood notwithstanding, apotheosis, like everything else, is politics, personal politics, and Aeneas' mother has to campaign for her son. Soliciting votes, she "had paid a call on each of the divinities" (15.585; Venus *ambierat,* from *ambio,* "campaign," "lobby"; as Galinsky says, she "set the proceedings in motion like a Roman politician" [1975] 244). Nothing Aeneas has done is advanced as a reason for deifying him. In her seductive appeal to her father, Jupiter, Venus says, simply, he's your grandson, and he's already been to the underworld.

You can at least make him a minor divinity (14.588–591). Aeneas' deification is a favor sought and given; it "does not betoken any virtue in him" (Solodow 156).

The apotheosis of Aeneas is the second of four in the *Metamorphoses,* preceded by that of Hercules (9.229–272) and followed by those of Romulus, shortly to come (14.818–828), and Julius Caesar (15.843–851). All four apotheoses involve "the removal of all the physicality and particularity that [make] metamorphosis possible," and the four deified men "become their own distilled essence when they enter the realm of the gods" (Barkan 82). Aeneas is purified by water: Venus orders the river Numicius ("a small stream some 10 miles south of the Tiber," Kenney says [1986] 457) "to scour away the parts of Aeneas marked for death and carry them down in its silent course to the waters of ocean" (14.600–601). The hero's purification by water "almost perfectly complements Hercules' end," that is, "purification by fire" (Barkan 83).

Aeneas' apotheosis also makes an "unequivocal assertion of Italian legend over Greek. . . . With this naturalization of a foreign prince in Italy, Ionia is translated to Ausonia" (Fantazzi 286). The "people of Quirinus" (= Romans; Quirinus was the ancient Italian god "of the oldest settlers" of the hill of Rome that took its name, Quirinal, from him: *Der Kleine Pauly* 4.1314 s.v. *Quirinus*), Ovid says, "call [the deified Aeneas] Indiges" (14.607–608). This is "a name of uncertain meaning and etymology applied to native gods. Aeneas was identified with *Iuppiter Indiges,* the local Jove" (Kenney [1986] 457). With this reference to "one of the most hallowed cults of Rome, that of Aeneas *Indiges* at Lavinium," Ovid ends his "*Aeneid*" "on a very dignified note indeed," Galinsky says ([1975] 244–245).

Galinsky claims that Ovid's treatment of the myth of Aeneas "cannot . . . be construed as a depreciation of the Vergilian version. Ovid simply tells this story, as he tells all others, in other ways than did some of his predecessors" ([1975] 219). When, however, Ovid says Trojans and Rutulians fought "simply to win" and "waged war because they were ashamed to lay down their arms" (14.571–572), he is not merely telling the story "differently."

The myth of Aeneas had a profound significance for Ovid and his Roman hearers and readers. It served as "the cornerstone of Roman historical mythology," and after the *Aeneid* was published, that story "had come to stand at the center of national mythology," as Solodow says. Ovid "cuts down and reshapes the meaning of the *Aeneid,*" Solodow continues, and the poet "frustrates attempts to attach Virgilian meanings to the story Virgil had told; he transforms it from a national into a personal history, . . . into a subjective rendering of the history of individuals" (136), although not in the war between Trojans and Rutulians (as noted above) and hardly in the history of Aeneas. We hear the "personal" stories of Galatea, Scylla, Glaucus, the sybil, Achaemenides, Macareus, Picus, Canens, and Diomedes, to name the most prominent, in fact, of almost everyone, it seems, but Aeneas, who appears seldom in Ovid's "*Aeneid*" and speaks only once, briefly, and says nothing particularly significant. Moreover, the poet's "*Aeneid*" contains eight embedded narratives and one story within a story (two, if we count Polyphemus' song to Galatea, which she sings). This multiplicity of stories and individuals (and narrators as well) overwhelms the story of Aeneas, which, told in a fragmentary way through this 954-line section, hardly sustains our interest. Ovid appropriates this "cornerstone of Roman historical mythology" and builds on it a structure with a multitude of tales that have nothing to do with Virgil's Rome and its founding. When Ovid turns his attention to Aeneas and touches on his story, as told by Virgil, on the Dido-Aeneas episode (14.78–81), for example, displaced by the tales of Galatea-Acis-Polyphemus and Scylla-Glaucus-Circe; or on Aeneas' visit to the underworld (14.116–

119), crowded out by the sybil's sad tale of protracted divine vengeance; or on the war between the forces of Aeneas and Turnus and Ovid's assertion about what motivated it (14.449–458a, 527–548, 566–580), he is, to be sure, telling it "differently." But the difference is so great and so pointed that it is difficult not to conclude that this "smiling destroyer," as Conte (257) calls him, is indeed depreciating the Virgilian version, or at the very least undermining the notion of a single authorized version by suggesting that Virgil's story of Aeneas is just that, one story among the many possible stories about Rome's founding, told in just one of many possible ways of telling it—or them.

60. After Aeneas' deification, his son Ascanius inherited the rule. In the next thirteen lines (14.610–622), Ovid lists in a dry catalogue the eleven kings who followed Ascanius, up to and including Proca. Then, following a transition "as abrupt and arbitrary as any in the poem" (Kenney [1986] 457), the poet turns to the story of Vertumnus and Pomona ("It was during Proca's reign that Pomona lived," 14.623), which occupies the next 149 lines (14.623–771) and contains as an embedded narrative the story of Iphis and Anaxarete that Vertumnus, disguised as an old woman, tells Pomona in a final effort to get her to yield to his advances (14.698–764). At the end of the Vertumnus-Pomona episode, Ovid returns to Proca and the Roman kings ("Next after Proca, the unjust Amulius ruled," 14.772) and continues to the end of book 14 with a brief sketch of early Roman history (14.772–851), a little more than half of which is devoted to the apotheosis of Romulus and his wife, Hersilia.

The story of Vertumnus and Pomona, Ovid's invention (Bömer, at 14.622–771, 7.199; and Fantham [1993] 34–35), is the last of many stories in the *Metamorphoses* of sexual pursuit that end in seduction or rape (unless metamorphosis intervenes), and its nature—it breaks the pattern—and its placement in the poem are highly significant. To take the latter first, as the last love story, a story that occurs near the end of the *Metamorphoses* and precedes a long "cosmogonic" passage (the section on Pythagoras at 15.60–478), the tale parallels the episode of Daphne and Apollo, the first love story, which occurs near the beginning of the work and follows the "cosmogonic" section in book 1 (creation, through flood and restoration, 1.5–451). The two episodes thus form an "amatory frame within the broader cosmic framework created by the cosmogonic passages in Books 1 and 15" (Myers [1994b] 226). In addition, the "erotic tone" of the tale of Vertumnus and Pomona contrasts with "the introduction of Roman and cosmogonic themes" in books 14 and 15, just as the story of Daphne and Apollo contrasts with the cosmogony that it follows (Myers [1994b] 228).

As for the story's position in book 14, Galinsky notes that the tale separates and overshadows the "Roman-Augustan topics" occurring between Ovid's "*Aeneid*" and the Pythagorean section (in book 15), that is, the list of early Roman kings at 14.609–622, "whom the Julian family claimed as their ancestors," and the apotheosis of Romulus and his wife, Hersilia, at 14.805–851 ([1975] 253). The story is "emphatically placed," Myers says, for the tale, "with its erotic content, relegates the surrounding apotheoses in Book 14 [that of Aeneas, preceding, and those of Romulus and Hersilia, following the story] to a nonhierarchical position in the poem and does not allow the patriotic Augustan themes to overwhelm the narration" ([1994a] 126).

Vertumnus, the story's leading character, was an old Etruscan god "who seems to have been well-known in Rome mainly because of a bronze statue of him that stood . . . in the Vicus Tuscus [Etruria Street] . . . [and] was a landmark of sorts in the city" (Myers [1994a] 117). This statue, Fantham says, "served as a sort of urban substitute for Priapus, and regularly received harvest offerings from farmers and market gardeners"

([1993] 32). Most of what is known about the god comes from a poem of Ovid's contemporary Propertius (4.2), who derives Vertumnus' name from the Latin verb *vertere*, "turn" (see Propertius, 4.2.47–48), because of the god's "protean capacity for transformation" (Bömer, at 14.622–771, 7.198), but gives additional interpretations of the name: because the flooding Tiber "turned" back near Vertumnus' statue in the Vicus Tuscus in Rome (4.2.7–10); or because, as god of autumn, that is, the time of harvest, he was associated with the "turning" year (4.2.11–12). Ovid takes Vertumnus' role as an "urban substitute for Priapus" who "received harvest offerings" and "uses it to make Vertumnus one of the suitors of Pomona in the ancient days of King Proca" (Fantham [1993] 32). Pomona herself, the other leading character in the story, was an ancient Roman deity, and her name is clearly connected to *pomus*, "fruit tree," and *pomum*, "fruit" (Bömer at 14.622–771, 7.198; see *Metamorphoses* 14.623–626).

Ovid introduces Pomona as a "hamadryad" (14.623–624), a Greek wood nymph, who may at first be taken for "one more determined virgin on the model of Daphne or Arethusa" (Otis 294), but she is a *Latin* nymph (14.623), and the poet immediately makes it clear that she cares nothing about the wild but, rather, loves (*amat*) her fruit-bearing trees (14.626–627), "a tree-nymph who cultivates trees," as Davis says. Moreover, Davis continues, "[b]y cultivating apples . . . , she is simply cultivating the external projection of her own nature which is coincident with her name" ([1983] 68). Indeed, instead of a javelin, the accouterment de rigueur for a young girl or nymph devoted to the virgin huntress Diana and spending her time hunting in the forest, Pomona carries a sickle for pruning her trees and grafting branches onto them (14.628–631; see Davis [1983] 68–69). And when she isn't using this implement, she is irrigating her orchard to keep her fruit trees well watered (14.632–633). Caring for them "was her passion, her only interest [*hic amor, hoc studium*]; she had no desire for romance" (14.634; see Fantazzi 290). Pomona thus "typifies," Barkan says, "the practical, hardworking, agricultural side of fertility, but her concern for fertility is too narrow, since she rejects any possibility of fruit-bearing herself" (81).

But she fears violence—*vim* (14.635), sexual violence—from "her crude country neighbors" (14.635), that is, from "the rough and erotically truculent [divinities] of the countryside," whose "crude aggressiveness" Ovid emphasizes (Davis [1983] 70), and so she encloses her orchards (*pomaria*, 14.635) and shuns the male sex (14.636). As Davis says, "[H]er inner self and her orchard (two aspects of the same phenomenon) take on a new meaning as refuge from the male world" ([1983] 69). While many of the woodland deities did anything they could to possess Pomona, Ovid says (14.637–641), Vertumnus outdoes them in his love for her, although at first he was no luckier than they.

The story of Vertumnus and Pomona parallels the earlier episode of Daphne and Apollo (as noted above) and appears to be, like so many other tales in the poem, a narration of sexual pursuit ending in seduction or rape, whose "weapons in the arsenal of desire," Littlefield notes, are "force and pursuit, deceptions of appearance, and the blandishments of well-wrought words or specially shaped or ordered elements of the natural world," that is, magic. In this "last tale of romantic-sexual love in the *Metamorphoses*," Littlefield goes on to say, "the modes and strategies of love characteristic of the poem's preceding tales of passion" either fail or prove to be irrelevant. "A rhythm of expectation is broken, an attitude is overthrown. The poem's view of the nature of love is redefined; it undergoes a metamorphosis. . . . [W]hat has been disavowed is perfectly clear: rape, fraud, and the arts—verbal, plastic, and occult—seem no longer to be effective agencies through which to win amorous assent" (470).

But none of this is evident at first.

In the poem of Propertius (4.2, alluded to above), Vertumnus (the narrator) describes many of the forms he takes (a compliant girl dressed in fine silk; a man in a toga; a hay maker; a soldier; a harvest worker; acting sober, as a lawyer in court; as a drunken reveler and wearing a turban, passing himself off as Bacchus; with a lyre in his hand, as Apollo; with a whip, as a charioteer; an acrobat, tumbling on horses; a hunter; with a bird-catcher's reed, the patron god of fowling; with a felt hat and a rod, a fisherman; a neatly dressed peddler; a shepherd with a crook; with a basket of roses, a roadside flower seller [21–40]) and also enumerates some of the offerings grateful farmers bring to him, that is, to his statue in the Vicus Tuscus (fruit of various kinds, grain, cucumbers, gourds, cabbage, flowers: 4.2.13–18, 43–46). Ovid plays upon Vertumnus' capacity for changing his form and upon his role as recipient of offerings of produce and has him pursue Pomona by adopting a series of disguises (14.643–652), almost all of which represent characters with whom Pomona shares a vocational affinity—harvest hand, hay maker, plowman, tree or vine pruner, apple picker, soldier, fisherman ("more costume changes than bodily transformations," Barkan says [82]). These get him so far— close enough to Pomona to enjoy gazing at her beauty (14.652–653)—but no further. "What he needs," Fantham says, "is a match-maker, or *conciliatrix,* and his skills enable him to provide one" ([1993] 32), for he now disguises himself as an old woman and gains entry to Pomona's garden (the Sun similarly gains access to Leucothoe's chamber by disguising himself as her mother: see 4.217ff.). He argues on behalf of marriage in general and marriage with Vertumnus in particular (14.654–694) in a "*suasoria* that . . . is typical of a procuress or a genuine matchmaker" (Fantham [1993] 33), and in a cautionary tale warns Pomona about the danger of rejecting a devoted lover (the embedded narrative of Iphis and Anaxarete, 14.695–764).

Since Pomona's name identifies her with *pomaria,* orchards, as well as *pomus,* fruit tree, and *pomum,* fruit (as noted above), and since the enclosed garden is "an old and familiar symbol of virginity," when Vertumnus enters it "in the innocuous form of an old woman, [he] performs a symbolic action which in itself foreshadows the end of the tale" (Segal [1969a] 69).

As an old woman who is a matchmaker, Vertumnus can (and does) praise Pomona's beauty with impunity, can kiss her, even, without meeting resistance. "She" can expect her down-home example of the necessity for and benefits of mating (the elm tree and the grapevine, right there in Pomona's garden) to be all the more persuasive for coming from Pomona's own vocation. "She" cites Homer, alluding to Helen and Penelope. "She" even refers to the *Metamorphoses* itself (Hippodame in the battle of Lapiths and centaurs, 12.210–535). Most important of all, "she" praises Vertumnus, his constancy— he's a one-woman man—his looks, and his brilliance as a shape-shifter (a hilarious touch). Both Vertumnus and Pomona, "she" says, share a passion for gardening. Last of all, Vertumnus is desperately in love with Pomona.

The old woman now switches (14.693ff.) to a kind of "bad cop" routine and warns Pomona about gods (Venus and Nemesis) made angry by hard hearts and given to vengeance, leading into a cautionary tale "that will enable you to soften your heart and more easily give in" (14.697), the story of Iphis and Anaxarete (14.698–764). The story's conceit, Iphis the lover outside the locked door of his beloved, Anaxarete's, house, makes it an example of a *paraclausithyron* (at the closed door), a subgenre of ancient love elegy in which the lover takes up residence outside the closed door of his mistress' house and begs to be admitted. As Myers notes, "Most of the elements of this traditional amatory genre are present: the suppliant . . . [14.702], the nurse . . . [14.703], the tablets, the tear-bedewed garlands, and the sleeping on the hard threshold [14.707–710]" ([1994a] 123).

Anaxarete is "hard" (Latin *durus*), and the adjective is "repeat[ed] like a leitmotiv," Solodow says (Anaxarete: 14.712–713, 749–750, 758; the nurse, 704; the stone threshold on which Iphis lies down, 709). Her metamorphosis into stone is thus "perfectly natural and allows her to be seen for what she is" (179). When Iphis hangs himself from the top of Anaxarete's locked door ("in the traditional lovers' manner of suicide," says Myers [1994b] 239), in his death spasm his "'jerking feet banged against the door, like someone demanding to be let in'" (14.739–740). Now, by the act of dying, Iphis ironically achieves what he was unable to accomplish while living, for the door opens (14.740–741; had he not banged forcefully on the door before?). Later his corpse, or the sight of it, as Anaxarete sees from her window the funeral procession pass her house, turns her to stone—a statue "that looks just like" her (14.759) and that now, the old woman says, graces the temple of Venus-Looking-Out in Salamis (14.760–761; so called, because Venus "seemed attentive to the spectacle that offered itself to her view, as Anaxarete had been to the funeral procession of Iphis," LaFaye says [3.115 n. 3]).

The only parallels between Vertumnus' story and the situation for which he adduces it as a cautionary tale is Pomona's unwillingness, like Anaxarete's, to respond to a would-be suitor. Even so, Pomona is "less cruel" than Anaxarete (Segal [1969a] 69) and never called "hard." (Vertumnus as the old woman warns Pomona that Venus hates hard hearts: 14.693–694.)

In fact, it is the contrasts between the two stories that are striking. Iphis begins with a direct approach—as himself—and never gets past the closed door. Vertumnus, although he "surpasse[s]" all Pomona's suitors in his "passion" for her (14.641–642), is far cooler and smarter (and "less desperate": Segal [1969a] 69) than the overheated Iphis, and, instead of the "conventional . . . bribing" of the mistress' nurse (Iphis works on the nurse: 14.703–704), "becomes her himself and crosses over the threshold of the garden" (Myers [1994b] 233), and his success in doing that foreshadows the story's outcome, as noted earlier. Although Vertumnus' initial approach is indirect, when he later takes the direct approach, he is likewise successful, and the contrasts continue, for Pomona then sees him like the sun appearing from behind clouds (14.767–769), while Anaxarete, looking out the window of her house, finally "sees" Iphis for the first time, but as a corpse on a bier (14.751–753).

Pomona resists Vertumnus in the guise of an old woman until the god, frustrated by the apparent failure of all his efforts, throws off his disguise and "became his youthful self again, and appeared to Pomona like the brightest image of the sun when it breaks through an overcast sky . . . and shines again. . . . He was about to take her by force, but there was no need of force, for the nymph was swept away by the god and his beauty" (14.765–771). It is an exquisite and complex—hence typical—Ovidian irony that Vertumnus, "whose name embodies the concept of transformation—the stated theme of the *Metamorphoses*—" wins Pomona over "only when he renounces deception" (Davis [1983] 71), and "the final triumph of love" comes as a result of "a piece of proteanism that celebrates [Vertumnus'] essential constancy. He becomes, in a word, himself" (Barkan 82).

Pomona, Littlefield notes, is "an emblematic figure of abundant fruitfulness, a force of immortal earth," while Vertumnus, "the turner, the changer, insures the orderly alternation of seasons which govern the processes of budding, blossoming, flowering, and fruition and is her perfect complement" (471). Although we may have thought we were heading to the usual outcome—seduction or rape—Ovid has indeed broken the pattern in his final tale of love, and he ends the story of the "Italian virgin nymph" and the "Etruscan god" "with the chaste union appropriate to a national deity" (Fantham [1993] 36).

After the story of Vertumnus and Pomona, Ovid returns at 14.772 ("Next after Proca . . .") to the list of early Roman kings that he left at 14.623 to tell that tale, touching briefly on Amulius' usurpation of the throne; Romulus' installation of Numitor, Amulius' elder brother, as the rightful king; the founding of Rome (for these events see also Livy 1.3.10–1.7.3); the conflict between Romans and the neighboring tribe, the Sabines (provoked by the Romans' abduction of the daughters of the Sabines and of other tribes to be wives for Roman men); and the Roman girl Tarpeia's betrayal of her city by letting Sabine soldiers into the Roman citadel and their slaughter of her by heaping their shields upon her (14.772–777; for the conflict of Sabines [and others] and the story of Tarpeia, see Livy 1.9–1.11 and also, for Tarpeia, Propertius 4.4).

Next, Ovid briefly narrates the final phase of the Romans' war with the Sabines, including the metamorphosis of an icy spring into a boiling hot one (at the behest of Venus) to block the Sabines' silent movement from the Capitoline hill to the Palatine hill (Haupt-Ehwald at 14.785, 2.416) over a bridge with a gate sacred to Janus, if I correctly understand Ovid here (Holland 26–28 and 103–107, and Richardson s.v. *Ianus Geminus,* 207–208). Cf. Ovid, *Fasti* 1.259–274, where the poet briefly describes the same event. Ovid may here be referring to a shrine or small temple of Janus by the spring and near the gate Juno opened. After a bloody battle, the conflict is settled peacefully by Romulus and Tatius, the king of the Sabines. According to the terms of the settlement, Romulus was to share power with Tatius (14.778–804). Haupt-Ehwald (at 14.778, 2.415) think that Ovid adapted this story from the earlier Roman poet Ennius.

The book concludes with the apotheosis of Romulus, the third of four deifications in the *Metamorphoses* (14.805–851; Hersilia's apotheosis is included "as a kind of appendix": Solodow 192). Mars, Romulus' father, intercedes with Jupiter on behalf of his son, quoting back to Jupiter an earlier promise he had made: "'"One man there will be, whom you will lift up to heaven's azure"'" (14.814). Ovid himself has taken the sentence from Ennius, omitting, however, Ennius' last word, *templa* (temples), which begins a new line (*unus erit quem tu tolles in caerula caeli / templa*), and so taking *caerula* (azure) as a noun rather than as Ennius intended it, as an adjective: "azure temples" (see Skutsch xxxiii, 205–206). Due notes the contrast between Mars' intercession with Jupiter (14.806–815) and Venus' earlier intercession on behalf of her son Aeneas (14.585–591): "In dignified heroic verses the military god, with his helmet under his arm, reminds the King of gods of his promise. . . . Jupiter does not grant the request by kind compliments as he did to Venus but by clouds and thunder [14.816–817]" (85; Ovid's description of the circumstances of Romulus' apotheosis coincides with Livy's [1.16.1–2]).

Ovid's "technological comparison" for the process of Romulus' apotheosis, as Mars carries him off ("His mortal body burned away in the air, just as a lead bullet, shot from a sling, melts as it hurtles through the sky": 14.824–826), which the poet takes from Lucretius 6.177–179, "considerably deflates the ostensive gravity of the whole passage" (Due 86; Ovid uses the same simile at 2.726–729 to describe Mercury consumed by passion when he flies over Athens and sees Herse). And as Feeney notes, "[T]here is the disconcerting eclipse of the actual deed which entitles the hero to divinity: Rome is founded in five words, in the passive, with no named agent" (208; see 14.774–775: "At the festival of . . . Pales the walls of Rome were built," *festisque Palilibus urbis / moenia conduntur*). Romulus deified takes on "a form like that of berobed Quirinus" (14.828), "a Sabine god worshiped on the Quirinal hill, later as here identified with Romulus" (Kenney [1986] 459).

Barkan observes that "Hercules, Aeneas, Romulus, and Julius Caesar [15.843–851] all become their own distilled essence when they enter the realm of the gods just as Vertumnus becomes himself to woo Pomona" (82; Vertumnus drops his disguise at 14.765–769). These apotheoses (and Vertumnus' return to his true self) seem to me to point to Ovid's "apotheosis" at the end of the poem when he says, "The better part of me [his "distilled essence"] will be carried up and fixed beyond the stars forever" (15.875–876).

Romulus changes the name of his wife, Hersilia, to Hora when she is deified (14.851). Hora was a goddess paired with Quirinus and so a natural name for Hersilia to take. (See Haupt-Ehwald at 14.850, 2.420.)

BOOK FIFTEEN

61. Book 15 begins with the Romans searching for a king to succeed Romulus, "someone to bear the weight of so great a task" (15.1–2), that is, the task of being king, following the apotheosis of Romulus (and his wife, Hersilia) at the end of book 14. (The phrase "so great a task," *tantae . . . molis* [15.1], echoes Virgil, *Aeneid* 1.33, "So great a task it was to found the Roman nation," *tantae molis erat Romanam condere gentem*). After a search, Numa Pompilius, a Sabine from the city of Cures, is selected.

The break between books 14 and 15 reflects the historical break between Romulus and his successor, Numa, marked, the historian Livy (59? B.C.–A.D. 17?) tells us, by a year-long interregnum (1.17.6–7), during which the Roman "Fathers," a kind of ur-Senate, shared power among themselves. The people, however, wanted a king and were given the right to nominate someone for the kingship (who had to be approved by the "Fathers"). The people ceded their right to the "Fathers" (whom Livy now calls the Senate [1.17.11]), and they chose Numa, "renowned for his sense of justice and for his piety" and "most learned . . . in all divine and human law" (Livy 1.17–18.2), whom Ovid characterizes as "conceiv[ing] for his capacious mind a far greater inquiry" (than knowledge of his people, the Sabines) and seeking "to learn the nature of the universe" (15.5–6). With this last phrase, "the nature of the universe" (*rerum natura*, 15.6), Ovid alludes to the Roman philosopher-poet Lucretius (ca. 97–55 or 51? B.C.), who called his great work *De Rerum Natura* (*On the Nature of Things*). For references to additional echoes of Lucretius in book 15 (and there are many), see n. 62.

In his quest for knowledge Numa travels to Croton, a city in the extreme south of Italy founded by Greeks, where the Greek philosopher Pythagoras had come to live as an exile from his native Samos. After learning about the founding of Croton (15.12–57), Numa hears the teaching of Pythagoras, presented in a long sermon (15.75–478), stores it up in his heart, returns to Rome, and assumes the kingship (15.479–481).

It is chronologically impossible for Numa, who lived in the second half of the eighth century B.C., to have met and heard Pythagoras, who taught in Croton in the second half of the sixth century B.C., two centuries after Numa's reign (Bömer at 15.7–8, 7.252). According to Skutsch, the "old tale that Numa was a pupil of Pythagoras" was "invented perhaps by Aristoxenus" (a fourth-century B.C. Greek writer and polymath from Tarentum in southern Italy) but "was rejected as chronologically impossible by Cicero . . . , Livy," and others (263: see also Crahay-Hubaux, 290–291 and n. 1). Since Ovid was no doubt aware of the anachronism, one wonders why he seems to accept it here. As Bömer notes, the poet carefully avoids actually saying that Numa and

Pythagoras personally met. He says only that Numa went to Croton, Pythagoras (never named: "[a] man . . . Samian by birth," 15.60) taught there, and now distancing himself (after Pythagoras' sermon) with the phrase "they say" (*ferunt*, 15.480), concludes, "They say that Numa stored these and other teachings in his heart [and] returned to his fatherland" (15.479–480; see Bömer at 15.7–8, 7.252–253). "If Ovid prefers a version that he knows is mythical to the established facts," Crahay-Hubaux say, "it is not that he expects . . . to deceive his reader but much rather that he deliberately attributes to the alleged meeting a symbolic and mystical value that is, in his eyes, preferable to the material truth of the facts" (291).

Pythagoras, "the most venerable representative of Greek thought" (Crahay-Hubaux 291–292), whom Romans were said to have traveled to Croton to hear after the philosopher came there to live (Diogenes Laertius 8.14) and whom they had selected, "sometime in the fourth century B.C., as 'the wisest Greek' to be honored with a statue in the Comitium" (Galinsky [1998] 316), thus "had a Roman affiliation which was particularly suitable for one of the main themes of the last book of the *Metamorphoses*, the transfer from Greece to Rome" (Galinsky [1998] 315). As for Numa, Roman tradition saw him as "renowned for his sense of justice and for his piety" and "most learned . . . in all divine and human law" (Livy 1.17–18.2, as noted above). He (thus) "presides" over Rome's "cultural beginnings" (Otis 297) as an "incarnation of the Roman state no less venerable [than Pythagoras]" (Crahay-Hubaux 292) and has, for Ovid, the requisite *gravitas* as the Roman participant in a meeting that is "emblematic of the encounter between Greece and Rome which forms one of the major themes of the last book of the *Metamorphoses*" (Hardie [1995] 206).

Kenney observes that book 15 of the *Metamorphoses* "moves in a thematic circle: at its end the deified Julius is succeeded by the wise and virtuous Octavian (Augustus) as at its beginning the deified Romulus is succeeded by Numa" ([1986] 459–460). This "thematic circle" suggests a parallel between Numa and Augustus, and, in fact, Ovid links the two in several ways, as Crahay-Hubaux point out. Fame (*fama*) designates Numa for the kingship (15.3–4) and will also raise Augustus above his adoptive father, Julius Caesar (15.852–854). Moreover, both Numa and Augustus follow rulers who are deified and known by different names (Romulus *Quirinus* [14.827–828]; Caesar: *divus* . . . *Julius* = divine or deified Julius [15.842]) after their immortal part has been carried to heaven by a god, that of Romulus by his father, Mars (14.818–828), that of Caesar by his mother, Venus (15.843–851), each time by the express consent of Jupiter. Numa turned a warlike people to peaceful activities (15.482–484); Augustus, after avenging the death of his adoptive father, brings peace to the world and gives himself to civil legislation (15.832–834). As Crahay-Hubaux (whom I've followed here) say, we see in the poet the intention of assimilating Augustus to Numa (294–296).

Pythagoras' sermon is a "fragmented outline of the course of human history from the Golden Age . . . [15.96–103] to the greatness of Rome and the deification of Augustus [15.431–449] [that] offers a miniature recapitulation of the whole of Ovid's *Metamorphoses*. . . . And Pythagoras' ecstatic fancy that he wanders through the stars [15.147–152] . . . is close to Ovid's prophecy of his own celestial destination . . . [15.871–879], as he is transformed into the immortal fame of his own poetry" (Hardie [1995] 213). Thus Ovid suggests a parallel between himself and Pythagoras (Crahay-Hubaux 299) and implies that as Numa is instructed by the teaching of Pythagoras, so Augustus, whom Numa prefigures (Crahay-Hubaux, see above), is—or ought to be—instructed by the "teaching" of Ovid, that is, by the *Metamorphoses*.

When Numa arrives at Croton, he asks who founded the city (15.9–10) and hears an account from "one of the older inhabitants, who knew the history of past ages" (15.10–11) and tells Numa (and so us) the story of Hercules' visit to Croton (for whom the city was named) on his return from Spain, where he had acquired the cattle of Geryon (one of Hercules' labors, to which Ovid alludes at 9.184–185), his prophecy to Croton, and its fulfillment later by Myscelus of Argos. Hercules commands Myscelus in a dream to leave his own city, travel to Italy, and found a city there (15.12–25).

Myscelus' emigration from Argos is not without drama, for by seeking to leave his city, he breaks a law that forbids migration and stipulates death for offenders. Found guilty at his trial ("conducted according to Roman procedure," Solodow says [242 n. 24], and so another anachronism), he is acquitted when all the black pebbles dropped into an urn (indicating a guilty verdict) are miraculously changed to white—a metamorphosis effected by Hercules—and Myscelus is free to leave Argos, travel to Italy, and found the city; and he does so, naming it Croton (15.26–57).

The old citizen's story is an embedded narrative, which, Nagle says, he "stresses is the product of tradition at the outset" (referring to "'They say'" at 15.14). Ovid himself "emphasizes the source" of the story's "authority" at the end: "Such, according to the well-known tradition, was the first beginning" (15.58–59; Nagle [1989a] 123).

The account of the founding of Croton (the constitution of which, Diogenes Laertius says [8.3], was created by Pythagoras) offers a "Greek parallel to Rome, for both cities are founded by immigrants . . . driven to Italy by superior powers," that is, Croton by Myscelus sent by Hercules, and Rome by Aeneas commissioned by Jupiter or fate (Glenn 194). This narrative also "adds to the evidence that the Greek presence in and influence on Italy is very old . . . and that it is a civilizing one" (Glenn 195).

62. The sermon of Pythagoras at 15.75–478, the second-longest single episode (404 lines) in the *Metamorphoses* (after the story of Phaethon at 1.750–2.400), is the last of three "internal narratives . . . significantly marking" each of the five-book segments of the poem, the other two being the songs of Calliope at 5.341–661 and of Orpheus at 10.148–739. Calliope, Orpheus, and Pythagoras are "important literary figures of inspiration" in earlier poetry, and their narratives in the *Metamorphoses* "function as authenticators of the 'truth' and inspiration of the poem as [a] whole" (Myers [1994a] 163).

The role of Pythagoras' sermon in the *Metamorphoses* is more difficult to assess than those of the other two long internal narratives. In fact, nearly every aspect of the speech has been the subject of debate among scholars and critics, from the reputation of Pythagoras and neo-Pythagoreanism at Rome in Ovid's time to the nature and purpose of the sermon and its relation to and significance for book 15 and for the work as a whole.

Pythagoras, who lived in the sixth century B.C., was perhaps the most venerable philosopher before Socrates and probably the most influential. He voluntarily exiled himself from his native Samos around 531 B.C. to escape the rule of Polycrates, tyrant of Samos (see *Metamorphoses* 15.60–62), and settled in Croton in Italy, where he founded a religious sect that flourished for several generations (see *Der Kleine Pauly* s.v. *Pythagoras* 4.1264ff.) His teaching embraced "the religious and ethical and the philosophical and scientific" (Kirk, Raven, and Schofield 214)—this makes him distinctive—and included the doctrine of metempsychosis, or transmigration of souls, and, as a corollary, advocacy of some form of dietary restriction, perhaps vegetarianism (Kirk, Raven, and Schofield 231). As a philosopher whose "contribution to Greek thought . . . was original, seductive and durable" (Kirk, Raven, and Schofield 238), Pythagoras can embody for Ovid the Greek "sage," that is, the figure who is an authoritative fount of wisdom (although Ovid's portrayal of Pythagoras' views more nearly reflects the neo-Pythagoreanism in Rome in his own day). Since Pythagoras stands, as it were, for Greek philosophy, and since he lived and worked in Italy, he is an ideal choice on Ovid's part to represent the meeting of east and west, of Greece and Rome, and to preside over the "thematically logical development of the entire poem [from myth to history, via philosophy] as it culminates in its closing book" (Segal [1969b] 288–289).

Ovid's encounter with neo-Pythagoreanism may have come about through a Greek philosopher named Sotion, who, Fränkel says, "about the time when Ovid was completing the *Metamorphoses* . . . was preaching in Rome doctrines derived from the Pythagorean tradition." Sotion urged his disciples to become vegetarians, arguing that nature provides enough food, killing animals leads to murder, and, since souls pass from humans to animals (through transmigration), eating flesh is cannibalism. Sotion had an impact on Seneca (the philosopher; ca. 4 B.C.–A.D. 65), who studied under him as a boy and, Fränkel says, "was gripped by 'a love for Pythagoras' and became a vegetarian." Fränkel concludes, "It is quite possible that Ovid, too, heard and admired Sotion" (108–109; see also Crahay-Hubaux 285).

For the view that Pythagoras, Pythagoreans, and neo-Pythagoreanism were ridiculed at Rome (and in Roman literature) and that Pythagoras' sermon is (as a result) seriously flawed (if it is to be taken as straight) or parody or burlesque, and that Pythagoras is an unreliable narrator, see Segal (1969b) 279–284, Solodow 163–166, Knox 73 (who notes, however, that "we cannot look upon Pythagoras' speech simply as parody"), John F. Miller 478–479, W. R. Johnson (1970) 138–145, and Mack (1988) 142–143. For a rebuttal, specifically to Segal, see Little (1974). For a more balanced (though brief) assessment of neo-Pythagoreanism at Rome, see Wilkinson (1955) 215–219. Due maintains that the speech of Pythagoras conveys "an illusion of a philosophical basis for the world of the *Metamorphoses*, but not enough to conceal that it is an illusion" (162).

Hardie notes that the sermon Ovid puts into the mouth of his Greek sage is "a highly eclectic exercise in writing philosophical poetry" ([1995] 205), in which one can see borrowings, above all, from the Greek philosopher Empedocles and from the Roman authors Ennius and Lucretius (in whose style Pythagoras presents un-Lucretian ideas: Due 31). As for borrowings from Empedocles, Hardie comments, "[T]he broad outline, as well as much of the detail [of Pythagoras' sermon], is paralleled in the . . . poetry of Empedocles," including "a passionate attack on meat-eating and sacrifice" with which the sermon begins and ends (15.75–142 and 453–478; Hardie ([1995] 205 and n. 7). Additional parallels with Empedocles are noted by Crahay-Hubaux, in particular "a direct line of causality between metempsychosis and the practice of vegetarianism" at 15.158–175 and 453–478, along with "the idea of an age of gold that respected the life of animals" at 15.96–103, and the theory of the four elements at 15.237–251 (284; see also Myers [1994a] 41–42). Heraclitus' theory of constant change is represented in the body of the sermon (15.177ff.), and Pythagoras' *cuncta fluunt* ("'All things are flowing,'" 178) translates Heraclitus' *panta rhei*.

With regard to Ovid's borrowing from his predecessor, the Roman poet Ennius, Knox notes that Ennius' "exposition of Pythagoreanism" at the beginning of his lost work the *Annales* "forms the basis for Ovid's Pythagoras" (72). Ennius himself drew upon the Hellenistic Greek poet Callimachus, for whom, Knox says, "Pythagorean doctrine supplied some of the most important imagery in the polemical introduction" to that poet's (lost) work, the *Aetia* (72). Myers observes that at the beginning of the *Annales*, "Homer appeared to Ennius and evidently explained the Pythagorean theory of metempsychosis and perhaps also embarked on broader cosmological themes" ([1994a] 160). Ennius thus provided Roman poets with a model for didactic poetry on "the nature of things" (Myers [1994a] 160; for further comment, with examples, of Ovid's use of Ennius, not only in book 15 but also in book 14, see Hofmann 224–226).

Much of Ovid's "philosophic style" comes from Lucretius (Otis 301), his nearer predecessor and the author of the long didactic philosophical poem *De Rerum Natura, On the Nature of Things*. (For specific echoes of Lucretius in the sermon of Pythagoras, see Bömer at 15.4–6, 7.251–252; Haupt-Ehwald at 15.67ff., 2.427; 15.150ff., 2.434; 15.244, 2.441; and 15.340ff. and 340, 2.449; and Crahay-Hubaux 285 n. 2.) Due (31) comments on Ovid's "somewhat ironical attitude" toward Lucretius, since "the gospel of [Ovid's] Pythagoras is exactly the opposite [of] that of Lucretius: not dissolution, but immortality of the soul," expressed "in a 'Lucretian' phrase": *omnia mutantur, nihil interit* (15.165: "'Everything changes; nothing dies'"; Lucretius held that the soul, composed of atoms, which were indestructible, was dissolved at death back into atoms and so perished as such; see also Myers [1994a] 139–147, 158; and Kenney [1986] 461).

These borrowings, echoes, and parallels, briefly indicated here, should make it clear that the sermon of Pythagoras is a distinctly Ovidian literary construct, and his Pythagoras, too, as Myers points out, is "as much a literary as a philosophical figure" ([1994a] 162).

An outline of the sermon (after Bömer, at 15.60–478, 7.272, with modifications) will give the reader an overview of it as well as provide the basis for further comment:

A¹ 15.75–164: "Pythagoras theme" (vegetarianism and metempsychosis)
    1. 75–95:   vegetarianism
    2. 96–103a: the Golden Age; then, however,
    3. 103b–142: killing of animals for food and in self-defense, sacrificing of animals to the gods
    4. 143–152:   Pythagoras' lyrical declaration of authority as a prophet and his intention to prophesy
    5. 153–164:   metempsychosis and immortality of souls (with personal illustration: Pythagoras was Trojan Euphorbus at the time of the Trojan War)

B 15.165–452: "Metamorphoses theme"
    1. 165–178:   "everything changes; nothing dies" (the soul is always the same: an injunction against killing animals); "all things flow"
    2. 179–236:   time
        a. 186–198: day and night, sun and moon
        b. 199–213: seasons of the year
        c. 214–236: human aging
    3. 237–251:   elements and their constant changing
    4. 252–261:   nothing stays the same, (but) nothing perishes; things change
    5. 262–306:   changes in land, sea, rivers, cities, and islands
    6. 307–336a: springs and rivers that change or cause change
    7. 336b–360: Delos; the Symplegades, Aetna, the lake of Minerva (causer of change)
    8. 361–417:   zoological changes, some marvels (bees, hornets, etc., the phoenix, coral)
    9. 418–452:   cities (including Rome; the prophecy of Helenus; apotheosis of Augustus)

A² 453–478: "Pythagoras theme" (metempsychosis and vegetarianism)

As the outline makes clear, the vegetarian-metempsychosis theme, opening and closing the speech (and at 116 lines [15.75–164, 453–478] constituting more than a fourth of the total), serves as a frame for it. Serious advocacy of vegetarianism on Ovid's part has seemed absurd to many critics, those mentioned earlier, for example, who stress the ridiculousness of Pythagoras and neo-Pythagoreanism and are variously inclined to view the speech of Pythagoras as flawed or else as parody or burlesque. But vegetarianism as Ovid's Pythagoras presents it "is not . . . the main point." The "emphasis . . . is not on the eating of vegetables, but on abstention from flesh" (Little [1974] 18). Although transmigration of souls between humans and animals is the conventional reason in Pythagoreanism for abstention from meat, and indeed is the reason given by Pythagoras, the slaughter of animals does not injure souls, for they are immortal; it simply inconveniences them (see 15.169–175 and 456–462). Ovid's Pythagoras emphasizes another reason for abstaining from flesh: to avoid violence. As Galinsky says, "[I]t is clearly the . . . killing of animals that agitates Ovid most" ([1975] 141). Killing animals also shows profound ingratitude to creatures—sheep and oxen, for instance—that are great benefactors of humankind (15.116–126). It is *impietas* (Little [1974] 18).

Vegetarianism is proposed as a way to check the savage slaughter of our fellow creatures that meat eating requires and that, since it is the murder of one creature by another (15.88–95, 103–110), results in a kind of cannibalism, the "ultimate crime" of metamorphosis, as Barkan says: "Pythagoras accuses meat-eaters of being cannibals and characterizes all of us as victims of cannibalism: *tempus edax rerum*" ("'O time devouring everything!'" 15.234; Barkan 92). The violence done to animals leads to human murder (15.463–469). Murder and cannibalism are linked in the very first story in the poem, that of Lycaon, the emblem of human wickedness, who killed, cooked, and served to Jupiter (visiting him in human form) a human hostage and who thus caused Jupiter to destroy the human race (1.163–252). Myers sees a connection between the story of Lycaon and Pythagoras' belief in "carnivorism" as "the original sin," "one of the many ways," she says, "in which the material of Pythagoras' speech is intimately related to the concerns of the rest of the epic" ([1994a] 138, 139). In sum, "vegetarianism to the poet is only a means to a goal, to propagate a higher and to him, in fact, appropriate ideal: a life without bloodshed and murder, a life of peace" (Buchheit 95).

The sermon of Pythagoras is linked to the rest of the *Metamorphoses* in two important ways. First, it alludes, directly or indirectly, to specific parts of the poem (e.g., the story of Lycaon, just mentioned) and points ahead to the conclusion of book 15 (itself the culmination of part three, the "historical" section, and of the poem as a whole). Second, Pythagoras' great theme of mutability, the subject of almost three fourths of the sermon (15.165–452), expresses explicitly in philosophical-scientific discourse what was implicit in the theme of metamorphosis, presented in the preceding books in the mode of literary-mythical narration. Many would cavil—have objected long since—to calling Pythagoras' sermon "philosophical-scientific discourse," and they are correct, for, strictly speaking, Pythagoras' speech is "by no means characterized as a 'rational scientific' discourse." Rather, Ovid "appropriates and assimilates [philosophy], as he does every genre, to his mythical-metamorphic world" (Myers [1994a] 157, 158). This is philosophy "Ovidian style," incorporated, Due says, to further the poet's "artistic aims," adding, "[N]either Ovid himself nor . . . his readers would have regarded the philosophical passages in the *Metamorphoses* as anything but poetry" (30).

As for linkages between the sermon of Pythagoras and specific parts of the poem, Myers comments that the sermon "reviews the entire sequence of the poem by recapitulating themes from earlier passages . . . , especially Book 1, as well as foreshadowing the [poem's] Augustan conclusion" ([1994a] 133). Specific examples: the Golden Age: 1.89ff. and 15.96ff., 259ff.; the four elements: 1.15ff. and 15.237ff.; thunder: 1.54–56 and 15.69–70; and generation from slime: 1.416ff. and 15.375ff. (Myers [1994a] 133 n. 2; see also Solodow 248 n. 7).

Swanson has noted the inverse parallel between references to the creation in books

1 and 15. In the creation sequence in book 1, he says, "the disposition of the four elements is followed by the evolution of living forms; this in turn is followed by the definition of time inherent in the four ages and the four seasons of the Silver Age [see 1.24–124]. The order of this presentation—elements, living forms, time—is reversed in the central panel of [Ovid's] Pythagoras essay in book 15: lines 176–213 have to do with time (night, day, and the seasons); 214–236 with living forms and the change wrought upon them by old age; and 237–251 with the elements (earth, air, fire and water)" (21; see also Davis [1980] 123–125, 127). Thus Pythagoras' sermon and the philosophical section of book 1 serve as "the two parts of a philosophical frame to the whole poem" (Hardie [1995] 210–211; see also Otis 302).

Additional linkages take the form of allusions by Pythagoras to earlier sections of the poem, as Myers has observed. The change from land to sea at 15.262–295 recalls the flood at 1.253–312; the reference to springs and rivers, especially the Lycus and the Erasinus at 15.270–286, recalls Arethusa at 5.635–641. The generation of frogs from slime at 15.375–378 recalls the metamorphosis of the Lycian peasants into frogs at 6.317–381 and the appearance of many forms of life from slime after the flood at 1.416–437. The birds Pythagoras refers to at 15.385–386, the peacock, the eagle, and the dove, have all been mentioned earlier in the poem (the peacock at 1.722–723; the eagle at 4.362–363, 10.155–161, and 12.560–592; and doves at 13.669–674). Cadmus and his wife were turned into snakes at 4.563–603. Pythagoras refers to snakes as evolving from the backbones of the dead at 15.389–390. Hyenas change their sex (15.408–410), Pythagoras says—as Caeneus (12.169–209) and Iphis (9.666–797) changed theirs. The urine of lynxes is said to turn to stone at 15.413–415; Lyncus was changed into a lynx at 5.650–661. Pythagoras mentions coral at 15.416–417, recalling Medusa's head turning seaweed to coral at 4.740–752 (these examples from Myers [1994a] 147 and 156 with n. 90). Galinsky calls attention to Pythagoras' reference to Lucifer (15.189–190), Phoebus (15.190–191), and Aurora (15.190–191), all of whom Ovid has mentioned earlier: Lucifer as father of Ceyx (11.270–272, 11.570–572), Aurora as "ravisher of Cephalus" (7.700–713), and Phoebus as father of Phaethon (2.1ff.). See Galinsky (1975) 104–105.

As for the sermon's pointing ahead to the conclusion of book 15, this can be seen in the reference to Rome rising (15.431–435), which leads to the prophecy of Helenus, foretelling Rome's great future (15.439–449).

The theme of mutability in Pythagoras' sermon recapitulates the soundings of the idea that change governs all implicit in the mythical narratives of metamorphosis, although this has been frequently disputed. Fränkel is clear and explicit: "[T]he Pythagoras speech is incongruous to the main theme of the long poem" (110). Solodow, likewise: "The theme of the poem is not mutability, but metamorphosis, which is very different" (167). Coleman finds that metempsychosis, "a highly idiosyncratic version of the doctrine of flux" that involves all (but only) humans and animals, "does not accord at all well with [Ovid's] fabulous transformations," which are often "from human to non-sentient modes of existence—to rocks, rivers, plants, etc.," and "reserved for particular persons in particular circumstances," with effects that are "permanent and immutable" (462–463). Little argues that "[t]he philosophic basis which the Pythagorean digression provides is not for the metamorphoses of the poets, but for the phenomena of change in the real world of nature" ([1970] 354), and he rightly notes that Pythagoras several times questions the "credibility of poets . . . who, like Ovid, have taken their material from myth," for example, at 15.153–155, 281–284, 356–359, 389–390 (Little [1970] 352–353; on the "gap between philosophy and mythology" generally and Ovid's attitude toward this gap, see 347–360).

Against these critics we can begin with Little himself in a later essay: "It is, in fact, only in the speech of Pythagoras that Ovid finally does justice to his theme" ([1974] 21). Pythagoras, in the words of Myers, is not "setting up a dichotomy between the mythical metamorphoses of the poem and natural philosophy." Rather, "his speech emphasizes their similarity . . . by combining . . . scientific and mythological explanations and by highlighting the marvelous in nature, thus drawing our attention to the similarity of natural phenomena and mythical metamorphoses: they are both *mirabilia*" ([1994a] 135; Little [1974] 20 similarly). Pythagoras' sermon thus "represents a different manner of accounting for the material of mythology" (Knox 73).

Mutability and metempsychosis of souls, Barkan comments, "are . . . extreme points that help to define Ovidian metamorphosis":

> [Pythagoras'] most powerful assertions are those that combine the continuity of transmigration with the concreteness of physical change. Side by side with his assertions that individuals and the world as a whole are deteriorating and dying come other suggestions that all is part of a great cycle. . . . The cycle exists because nature creates organisms from other organisms. . . . Pythagoras sees that all forms come from other forms. . . . If insects are bred out of a dead animal carcass, then Ovidian metamorphosis affirms the continuity of vital energy while negating the effects of destructive mutability. (86–87; see also Segal [1969b] 284–286)

Ovid (or Pythagoras) concludes the long section on mutability (15.165–452) by describing the rise and fall of great cities of the past (15.418–452). The section begins with the observation, "'So we see times changing and some nations growing strong while others decline'" (15.420b–422a). As examples Pythagoras mentions Troy, Sparta, Mycenae, Athens, and Thebes, once illustrious and flourishing, now fallen and nothing but names (15.422b–430), and then Rome: "'Now, too, I have heard, Trojan Rome is rising, her great task to lay the foundations of empire by the waters of Tiber.'" Rome, too, is an example of mutability in that "'she changes her form as she grows and will, one day, be the capital of the vast world!'" (15.431–435a). With Rome at the end of a list of once great, now fallen cities, all subject to the law of change, we expect—"the rhetorical structure of this passage requires" (Tissol 187)—Pythagoras to prophesy Rome's fall, for the "juxtaposition of rising Rome to the fallen cities of the past . . . indicates clearly what [Ovid] foresaw for his city" (Anderson [1963] 27). Instead, he (or Pythagoras) "abruptly inserts" (Tissol 187) a prophecy given to Aeneas by the Trojan seer Helenus when Troy was falling (the time is problematic, see below) that foretells a new homeland for Aeneas; the rise of its city, Rome, to unparalleled heights; and Rome's mastery of the world under Augustus, who, "'"after the earth has enjoyed his presence,"'" will be welcomed in heaven, where "'"his final resting place will be"'" (15.439–449). Pythagoras strongly implies that he heard Helenus' prophecy himself ("'and as I well recall, Priam's son Helenus said the same thing to Aeneas,'" 15.436b–438; and, "'I repeat his [Helenus'] words as I remember them,'" 450–451) in his earlier incarnation as the Trojan warrior Euphorbus, slain in the Trojan War, this former life referred to at 15.160–164 as a personal example of metempsychosis. Helenus' prophecy about Rome (attested to by Pythagoras, who heard it himself) thus confounds the expectation created by the series of cities named by Pythagoras (with Rome the last mentioned) as subject to mutability. Or so it would seem. Helenus' prophecy, embedded in Pythagoras' internal narrative, is already at three removes from actuality (Helenus, Euphorbus, Pythagoras, Ovid or the narrator), and the violent death and reincarnation that separate the second from the third are enough to shake up anyone's memory. And Pythagoras has, in fact, misremembered his life as Euphorbus or, rather, his death. For in *Iliad* 16 Euphorbus kills Patroclus, and is himself slain in *Iliad* 17 by Menelaus, who has sprung to the defense of Patroclus' corpse to prevent Euphorbus from stripping it of its armor. Menelaus fatally stabs him with a spear "in the pit of the gullet . . . and clean through the soft part of the neck the spearpoint was driven" (*Iliad* 17.47–49; Lattimore, trans.), a death wound that Pythagoras inaccurately recalls: "'I . . . was . . . Euphorbus . . . , in whose chest Menelaus once lodged his heavy spear'" (15.160–162). "The philosopher's much vaunted memory . . . is . . . imperfect," says John F. Miller (476).

It gets worse: Pythagoras, as noted, has said that as Euphorbus he remembers Hele-nus' words of encouragement to Aeneas when Troy was falling, words that took the form of prophecy about Rome and its glorious future. But (1) Euphorbus was long since dead by the time of Troy's defeat, and (2) Helenus in any case delivered this prophecy to Aeneas not amid the flames of sinking Troy but sometime later, in Buthrotum in western Greece, where the Trojan seer had established himself after Troy's defeat and was living with Andromache, Hector's widow, and where Aeneas stopped on his way to Italy. (See Virgil, *Aeneid* 3.374–462, for the prophecy, which Ovid refers to at 13.722–724.) These discrepancies—and it is difficult to believe they are due to oversight—make Pythagoras an unreliable narrator and compromise the very statement, Helenus' prophecy, presented as a kind of guarantee that Rome's rise will continue and a declara-tion that Rome will be exempt from the law of mutability governing the rise and fall of great cities of the past. In addition, the credibility of that part of the prophecy foretelling Augustus' apotheosis is undermined, and, by a ripple effect, Ovid's later expectation of that apotheosis (15.868–870) is called into question.

Pythagoras' return to the "Pythagoras theme" (metempsychosis and vegetarianism, Bömer's term, see above) at 15.453, with some emphasis now on the transmigration of souls as a reason for abstaining from flesh (15.456ff.), moves quickly to the murder and cannibalism that killing animals leads to: "'and let us not gorge ourselves on meat from Thyestes' table!'" (15.462; Thyestes, brother of Atreus, was served the flesh of his own children by his brother and unknowingly ate it: Apollodorus, *Epitome* 2.13–14, and remembered in Aeschylus' *Agamemnon,* 1090–97 and 1217–22). Now directly relating animal sacrifice to human murder (15.463–469), Pythagoras ends his sermon with an exhortation to nonviolence toward animals (15.470–478: "'[C]onsume only the food that is gained by gentle means,'" 15.478) that recalls his earlier description of the Golden Age (15.96–103).

Numa "stored these and other teachings in his heart" (15.479), Ovid tells us, using a distancing "[t]hey say" (15.480), and returned to Rome, where he became king, mar-ried the nymph Egeria, and, "guided by the Camenae, . . . taught his people the rites of sacrifice and . . . converted them to the arts of peace" (15.480–484). Egeria, tradi-tionally the consort of Numa, was closely connected to the Camenae (spring nymphs) at one of the two springs she was associated with (Bömer at 15.482–484, 7.381). The Camenae were identified with the Muses (Kenney [1986] 456).

After Pythagoras' impassioned pleas to his hearers not to kill animals for sacrifice, it is surprising to read that Numa "taught" the Romans "the rites of sacrifice" (*sacrificos docuit ritus,* 15.483), and contradictory as well, for Ovid adds (in the same sentence: 15.483–484) that Numa "converted them to the arts of peace." Haupt-Ehwald note the incongruity but seek to rationalize it, an effort that does not satisfy: "Even if the general expression ['the rites of sacrifice'] does not compel us to think of blood sacrifice, nev-ertheless, the statement, immediately following the admonition of Pythagoras, is indica-tive of a purely superficial connection of themes" (at 15.483, 2.460). It is difficult to assess the tone, which may (or may not be) ironic. The passage may be an example of what Barkan means when he says, "[T]he greatest force of the speech [of Pythagoras] is the contrast with the Roman direction of the poem," and an additional instance of what he calls "an uneasy balance between Rome and Pythagoras" (87; for Barkan, the "uneasy balance" is represented by "apotheosis" versus "metamorphosis," "perfectibility" versus constant change," "social and political improvement" versus "magical transformation": 87–88).

63. Ovid's brief account of Numa's return to Rome from Croton, his reign, his death, and his wife's inconsolable grief, which drives her to wander to the valley of Aricia (15.479–490), provides a bridge to the stories of Hippolytus-Virbius (15.492–546), Cipus (15.565–621), and Aesculapius (15.622–744), and these in turn lead up to (and prepare for) the final episodes of the poem, the apotheosis of Julius Caesar and Ovid's eulogy of Caesar's adopted son, Augustus Caesar, emperor of Rome (15.745–870).

Ovid makes a casual transition from Numa to Hippolytus-Virbius: Numa's widow, Egeria, encounters him when she stumbles into the sanctuary of Diana Nemorensis ("Diana-of-the-Woods"), in the valley of Aricia (a few miles southeast of Rome), "where her groans and lamentations halted [the goddess' rites], established by Orestes" (15.489–490). Hippolytus-Virbius lives in the grove there as a devotee of Diana, who provides him with protection. Orestes was said to have instituted the rites of Diana in Aricia when, to cure the madness caused by his killing his mother, Clytemnestra, he brought an image of Artemis (= Diana) that he had taken from the goddess' sanctuary in the land of the Taurians (in Asia Minor) to the valley of Aricia (see Haupt-Ehwald at 14.331f., 2.381). The priest of Diana Nemorensis in the valley of Aricia, as Kenney reminds us, was "'the slayer, who must himself be slain'—the starting point of Frazer's *Golden Bough*." ([1986] 463).

The story of the Greek tragic hero Hippolytus, who dies a violent and unjust death (the subject of Euripides' extant tragedy *Hippolytus*) but is resurrected by Aesculapius, son of Apollo and god of healing, and transported to the valley of Aricia, where, with his name changed to Virbius, he becomes a devotee of Diana (his patroness [as Artemis] in Euripides' play), is perhaps taken from the *Aetia* of Callimachus (Myers [1994a] 22 and 127–129) and is briefly told by Virgil at *Aeneid* 7.761–782. (Ovid also tells this story at *Fasti* 6.737–762.) Hippolytus-Virbius "has a double life split between Greece and Latium. . . . [A]nd he is double, the copy of a Euripidean hero brought to Rome" (Barchiesi 185). The episode thus demonstrates Ovid's effort to interweave "Greek and Roman legends cunningly, so that we never feel there is a complete break in the texture and continuity of the poem" (Wilkinson [1955] 219).

Hippolytus-Virbius seeks to lighten Egeria's grief by telling her his sad story (15.492–546), essentially a recapitulation of the messenger's speech in Euripides' *Hippolytus* (1173–1254), which describes Hippolytus' violent death as a result of his father, Theseus', curse while traveling into exile from Troezen (on the road to Argos and Epidauros; Ovid's Hippolytus-Virbius is traveling from Athens to Troezen [15.506], a detail taken from an earlier, no longer surviving play by Euripides, the so-called *Hippolytus Kaluptomenos* [*Hippolytus Veiled*]; see Haupt-Ehwald at 15.504, 2.462). Hippolytus goes to the underworld—Euripides does not use this part of the myth—whence, after Aesculapius revives him with special medicines, he is carried off by Diana to Aricia against the will of Hades. There she changes his appearance and his name ("'since my own [name] could remind me of horses'" [15.542–543]: "Hippo-lytus," "loosed [in the sense of killed] by horses"), renaming him "Virbius" (15.531–544). He now inhabits Diana's grove "'as one of the lesser gods'" (15.545). "The story was clearly invented," Myers says, "to explain the exclusion of horses from Diana's grove at Aricia, ... and hinges on Virbius' etymologically suggestive name" ([1994a] 129), which, as Haupt-Ehwald note, appears to be derived from Greek, "*hêrôbios*" (hero-life). Haupt-Ehwald quote the late writer Cassiodorus (ca. A.D. 490–ca. 585), who observes that some call Virbius *vir bis factus* (a "man made twice"); others interpret Virbius as *vir bonus* (a "good man"), still others as *herobius* (the Latinized form of *hêrôbios*), as though the name were Greek *hêrôs anabebiôkôs*, "the hero who has been restored to life," shortened to *hêrôbios* (see Haupt-Ehwald at 15.542, 2.464).

Hippolytus-Virbius' story is an embedded tale (discussed briefly by Nagle [1989a] 124), in which he tells of his own metamorphosis, the sixth and last first-person account of a transformation in the poem (see n. 8), but he extends the motif, Bömer notes, by narrating first his own death, then his revival by Aesculapius, and finally his transformation (at 15.492–546, 7.385).

Hippolytus-Virbius, in describing his restoration to life through the medicine of Apollo's son Aesculapius (15.533–534), substantiates, as Keith (68) notes, the prophecy about the newly born son of Apollo made by Ocyrhoe, Chiron's daughter, at 2.644–645: "'[Y]ou will even be given the power to bring souls back from the dead.'"

Hippolytus-Virbius died a violent and unjust death in Greece but was resurrected as a god and lives on in Italy. Similarly, Julius Caesar suffered violent assassination and undergoes apotheosis into *divus Julius*, "divine Julius," and lives on as a new star in the sky (15.761–850). Galinsky observes that one of the ways "Ovid makes light of the notion of being or becoming a god" is by applying to deities "the class distinctions found in Roman society." As an example, he cites Hippolytus-Virbius, who, he says, "is aware of his status as ["one of the lesser gods," 15.545]." Another example, Venus' effort to get her son Aeneas deified, "verges," Galinsky says, "on the overtly comical": "O best of fathers," the goddess says to Jupiter, "make him a god of some kind, even if it's only a little one" (14.589–590; Galinsky [1975] 170). The rough parallel between Hippolytus-Virbius and Julius Caesar (violent, unjust deaths, followed by resurrection, as a deity for the one, in apotheosis for the other), their near-proximity in book 15 (the two narratives are separated by about two hundred lines: 15.547–744), and the interlocking connection between them (the approximately two hundred lines between the two episodes contain the stories of Cipus [15.565–621] and Aesculapius [15.622–744], the former linked to Caesar, the latter to Hippolytus-Virbius)—these lead one to ask whether Ovid "makes light" (to use Galinsky's phrase, cited above) of Caesar's coming apotheosis by associating him and it with Hippolytus-Virbius.

The poet makes an odd transition to the next story, that of Cipus (15.565–621), using the "stepping-stone method" (see n. 3), in this case a series of drawn-out comparisons: Hippolytus-Virbius was astonished by Egeria's metamorphosis "like the Etruscan plowman who ... once saw ..." (15.553–554), and was also as astonished "as Romulus when he saw ..." (15.560–561), and "as Cipus when he saw ..." (15.565). What the Etruscan plowman saw (15.553–559) was the birth (or forming) of Tages, the legendary founder of Etruscan prophecy (he was "the first to teach the Etruscan race how to open the secrets of the future," 15.558–559) from a clod of earth, whose name is derived from the Greek phrase *apo tês gês*, "from the earth," or from *ta gês*, "the things of the earth" (Bömer at 15.552–559, 7.399).

As for Romulus' astonishment at his spear growing in the ground of the Palatine hill (15.560–564), Haupt-Ehwald note that up to the time of the Roman emperor Caligula (A.D. 12–41) a cornel cherry tree was pointed out on the Palatine, which, according to legend, had grown from the spear Romulus hurled from the Aventine hill (at 15.560, 2.466).

The story of Cipus (15.565–621), "an otherwise unknown *praetor* of an unknown date" (Bömer at 15.565–621, 7.403), "takes us at one bound," Wilkinson says, "into [Roman] Republican times, more than a century beyond Numa" ([1955] 221). This story, and the Aesculapius episode that follows, are the only stories "from the entire history of the Roman Republic" in the *Metamorphoses* (Feeney 208 with n. 73). Scholars connect Cipus to Julius Caesar (to whose apotheosis this story leads, as do the episodes of Hippolytus-Virbius, just preceding the story of Cipus, and Aesculapius, just following it), who habitually wore a laurel wreath on his head and who declined the kingship of Rome when it was offered to him (Fränkel 226 n. 104; Kenney calls the story of Cipus "a compliment to Julius Caesar on account of Cipus' refusal of the kingship" ([1986] 464). Galinsky, observing that the laurel wreath "was the well-known personal badge of honor of Augustus," sees the story of Cipus as an example of Ovid's "sophisticated playfulness" vis-à-vis Augustus and his regime ([1975] 258).

Ovid "punctuates strongly" (Kenney [1986] 464) between the story of Cipus and that of Aesculapius (15.622–744), introducing the latter episode with an invocation to the Muses (15.622–625), the only story in the *Metamorphoses* so introduced (as Galinsky [1975] 253 observes). Barchiesi comments that the Muses are appealed to "as witnesses who preside over the *spatiosa vetustas* ["ancient past"] precisely when, for once in the poem, there is no need for them; that is, when the theme is recent history, well documented in written sources" (188). But Ovid here "introduces not simply the narrative of Aesculapius' journey to Rome," Knox says, "but the entire concluding section of the book" (75), that is, the eulogy of the emperor Augustus, introduced by an account of the assassination and apotheosis of Julius Caesar (15.745–870), as well as the concluding epilogue (15.871–879), in which Ovid asserts his own apotheosis as a poet (see n. 64). The "entrance of Aesculapius" may indeed serve "as foil to the apotheosis of Julius Caesar," as Knox says (75), but this "tale of Republican forms for introducing new cults" is also, as Feeney notes, "the immediate precursor to the institution of the imperial ruler-cult" at 15.745–870, the two sections roughly equal in length, the former 123 lines long, the latter 126 lines long (208 with n. 74). "[T]he contrast between the two forms," Feeney continues (209), "is marked" by the poet at 15.743–746: Aesculapius, Ovid says, "entered Rome as bringer of health to the city and put an end to the plague. Now, [he] arrived at our temples as a foreign god, but Caesar is a god in his own city."

As Feeney notes, "[T]he differences are indeed instructive" (209). In fact, beginning with the embassy to the oracle of Apollo at Delphi, "[t]he Republican modes of operation emerge clearly": the embassy's actions are referred to only by verbs in the third-person plural without a specified subject (= "they": *cernunt*, 15.628; *petunt*, 15.630; *adeunt*, 15.631; and *orant*, 15.633). "[T]he communal nature of the decision [to send the embassy] and mission receives the highest stress" (Feeney 209). The actions of the envoys to Epidauros are also described, Feeney notes, with noun-less (or pronoun-less) third-person plural verbs (*tetigere*, 15.644; *adiere*, 16.645; *oravere*, 16.646). Aesculapius appears in a dream to the head of the delegation, Quintus Ogulnius Gallus, whom Ovid simply addresses (in an apostrophe) as "Roman" (15.654, his name is known from elsewhere; see Bömer, at 15.653–655, 7.428), "any of whose three names [would] fit into the hexameter, so that his anonymity is seen as part of a comprehensive strategy. From beginning to end, no individual is named" (Feeney 209).

When Aesculapius arrives in Rome, "the entire population . . . and the virgins who

preserve your fire, Roman Vesta, [rush] to meet the god," Ovid says (15.729–731).
"The collective nature of the idealized Roman Republic could hardly have been more
strenuously asserted" (Feeney 210). This "collectivity" is subsumed under the name of
Caesar in the next section (15.745–870) as the word *Aeneadae,* or "sons of Aeneas" (=
Romans), by which Ovid refers to the embassy to Epidaurus (15.682, 695), is brought
down from plural to singular at 15.804 (*Aeneaden*), where it refers to Julius Caesar (see
Feeney 211–212). Ovid in a subtle fashion thus contrasts the collective, community-
oriented nature of the "good old days" of the Roman Republic when Aesculapius came
to Rome to the current rule of Rome now by one man, the emperor Augustus.

In book 2, Ocyrhoe, the daughter of Chiron, in her prophecy about Aesculapius
(2.642–648; one part of this prophecy was noted above in the comment on Hippolytus-
Virbius), calls him "bringer of health to the whole world" (*toto . . . salutifer orbi,* 2.642).
When Aesculapius arrives at the island in the Tiber, Ovid says, the god "entered Rome
as bringer of health to the city" (*venit . . . salutifer urbi,* 15.744), echoing here Ocyrhoe's
prophecy, substituting "city" (*urbi*) for "world" (*orbi*). At the time Ocyrhoe gave her
prophecy in book 2, Rome was not yet the power it was in Ovid's time, Keith notes. But
in the last five hundred lines of the poem, "Ovid arrives at the period of Rome's recent
history. . . . The city has become the center of the world, *orbis terrarum,* and it is unchal-
lenged for supremacy within the Mediterranean: Rome is both *urbs* and *orbis*" (71, 72).

The introduction of the cult of Aesculapius is a historical event, occurring in 292
B.C., the year after the plague Ovid describes at 15.626–629 (Haupt-Ehwald at 15.622–
744, 2.470). The god's journey from Greece to Rome "is conceived as a geographical
crescendo—a climactic series of revered names and connotations—that reaches its high
point at the divine snake's entrance into the city" (Otis 296). The "underlying idea" in
Ovid's account of the voyage "is that Rome has become the center of the civilized world"
(Fränkel 108), and the arrival of the god, "the last importation from Greece," serves as
"a sign of completion for Roman culture" (Barchiesi 190).

64. With the Aesculapius episode, Ovid arrived at historical Rome (293/292 B.C.; see
n. 63), and he now leaps ahead almost 250 years to his own time, the goal promised in
the opening lines of the poem (1.4: *ad mea . . . tempora*), and to the final section of the
work, a eulogy of the emperor Augustus, introduced by (and intertwined with) an account of the assassination and apotheosis of Julius Caesar, Augustus' great-uncle and
adoptive father (15.745–870). The poet's transition to this final section ("Now, Aesculapius arrived at our temples as a foreign god, but Caesar is a god in his own city,"
15.745–746) minimizes the temporal leap and so links the present to the historical (but
also mythological) past at least partly in order to mark a contrast between Republican
and imperial ways of introducing new cults, as Feeney notes (see n. 63). In an epilogue
in the final nine lines of the poem (15.871–879), Ovid declares the immortality he—
or his "better part" (*parte . . . meliore mei,* 15.875)—will achieve through the *Metamorphoses.*

Since Ovid was exiled by Augustus in A.D. 8, the year he finished this poem, "the
nature of Ovid's evaluation of Augustus" (Knox 75) has often been questioned: Is the
poet slavishly pro- or cunningly anti-Augustan? Is his panegyric of Augustus sincere or
subversive? Knox, who considers the problem a literary one (75), notes that Ovid's
model was Callimachus' *Aetia,* which "utilized encomiastic references to a ruler as a
frame for narrative," and thus Augustus (or possibly Julius Caesar: see Bömer at 1.200,
1.87) appears at the beginning of the poem, in book 1 (1.200–205), and both Julius
Caesar and Augustus appear at the end of it in book 15 in references that are "an obvious structural device to impart the appearance of unity" to the work (Knox 76).

Yet the problem is a political one after all. Feeney (citing Bömer [at 15.746–750, 7.454]) notes how "striking" it is "to observe the degree to which Ovid is concentrating on 'facts'" when he claims that Julius Caesar "was made a god by his son rather than by his mighty deeds," at 15.746–750 (218). "[I]t was, indeed, his son who made him a god" (Feeney 210–211). But is it really true, Feeney asks, that nothing Julius Caesar did "was more important, more worthy of apotheosis" (211), than, as Ovid says, "being the father of such a great man" (*quam tantum genuisse virum*, 15.758)? Leaving aside the fact that *genuisse* ("a worrying word": Feeney 211) is technically untrue, since Julius Caesar became the father of his grandnephew Augustus by adopting him, great achievements should be the basis for deification, and "Ovid's account of how Caesar became a god is always, as it were, stumbling against the mechanics of his elevation—through his heir" (211).

Ovid also, Feeney notes, omits here any reference to the Senate and the Roman people in the apotheosis of Julius Caesar, that is, to "[t]he wave of popular enthusiasm after the Ides of March [the date in 44 B.C. when Caesar was assassinated], culminating in the response to the appearance of the comet in July 44; [and to] the debates in the Senate on 1 January 42, and the carrying of a law to institute the cult [of Caesar]" (212). The absence of these events from Ovid's account of Caesar's apotheosis is all the more noticeable, according to Feeney, since the poet begins his account "directly after the Republican institution" of the cult of Aesculapius (the preceding episode), "which serves as an introduction, and a foil" (212). The Senate and the Roman people are directly involved in the inauguration of Aesculapius' cult in Rome, but "Caesar's cult . . . is presented as the responsibility of his son and his 'mother,'" Venus (212), whom Ovid now introduces, just before the assassination of Julius Caesar, as she lobbies the gods in heaven in an effort to prevent it (15.761–778). Her "celestial politicking" (Feeney 219) replicates Roman politics and thereby recalls Ovid's earlier comparison of Jupiter's consulting the gods in heaven to Augustus' consulting the Senate (1.200–205).

The gods cannot help Venus; they can send signs, but they cannot reverse fate (15.779–798). And so, unsuccessful in heaven in her attempt to stop the murder of Caesar, Venus, Ovid says, then tries to save him on earth by carrying him off from the Roman Senate wrapped in the same cloud she used in the *Iliad* to spirit Paris away from Menelaus and Aeneas from Diomedes' sword (15.803–806). Aphrodite (Venus' Greek name) cloaks Paris in a cloud and removes him from the battlefield—and from certain death at the hands of Menelaus—at *Iliad* 3.380–382. At *Iliad* 5.302–318 she also rescues her son Aeneas after Diomedes strikes him with a huge stone, not his sword, by covering him with a fold of her robe, not a cloud, and carrying him from the fighting. Perhaps Ovid in his borrowing conflates the scene at *Iliad* 5 with that at *Aeneid* 1.411–414, in which Venus hides Aeneas and Achates in a cloud to allow them to enter Carthage unseen. In any case, by treating Julius Caesar like a character in the *Iliad* and (perhaps) the *Aeneid*, Ovid accepts Caesar's apotheosis "as poetic material of the same status as Greek myth so that it could accommodate his usual flashes of wit and lightness of touch as well as seriousness" (Gordon Williams 95).

Jupiter stops his daughter from rescuing Caesar and invites her to enter the house of the fates and view their "record [in bronze and iron] of all that has ever happened in the world and that ever will happen" (*rerum tabularia*, 15.810), whereon she "will find engraved . . . the destiny of your race," but then rushes on to say that he himself has read it and will repeat it to her (15.807–839; his speech is modeled on Jupiter's words of reassurance to Venus at *Aeneid* 1.257–296, as Kenney notes [(1986) 465]). Solodow observes the touch of "Romanization" in Ovid's allusion (at 15.810) to the Tabularium, Rome's office of records (82). Ovid's description of Jupiter "researching" his prophecies by consulting the archives, so to speak, "has an intriguing blend of the grandiose and the ridiculous," Due says (86).

But either the source is unreliable or the research is flawed, for some of the history is wrong. When Jupiter says, "Under his [Augustus'] command the walls of besieged Mutina will come down, and the city will sue for peace" (15.822–823), it sounds as if Octavian (that is, Augustus, before he adopted his new name in 27 B.C.), in avenging his father's murder, laid siege to and conquered Mutina in 43 B.C. (held by D. Brutus, one of the murderers), when it was actually Marc Antony whom Octavian conquered (with help from the senatorial armies of the consuls Hirtius and Pansa) when he (Antony) was besieging Mutina. The battle of Mutina, as Due comments, was one of Augustus' "skeletons in the cupboard," and the emperor "did not want it to be remembered . . . that one of his first allies was at the same time one of his father's murderers." Ovid's "distortion" is so patent "that it becomes its own corrective" (87).

When Jupiter declares that Augustus "out of his high regard for justice . . . will establish laws and by his own example serve as his people's moral guide" (15.833–834), Ovid is oddly but "unmistakably" praising the "moral legislation" that was "the real cause of all [the poet's] troubles" and doing so "in the terms that Augustus himself used of it" in his own account of his achievements at *Monumentum Ancyranum* 8.5 (Gordon Williams 95).

Concluding the prophecy with Augustus' death in old age and his subsequent apotheosis, Jupiter orders Venus to proceed with the deification of Julius Caesar ("take up this soul from its murdered body and make it a brilliant star," 15.840–841). Venus, obeying, goes to the Senate and there "[catches] up the soul of her own dear Caesar as it [leaves] his body" and carries it up to heaven, where "she [feels] it gather light and begin to burn." It then flies above the moon and shines as a star (15.843–850).

Barkan notes a "progression" in the successive apotheoses of Hercules, Aeneas, Romulus, and Julius Caesar "from the concretely physical" (Hercules) to the "purely abstract" (Caesar): in Caesar's apotheosis, Barkan says, "[t]here is no metamorphosis here at all. . . . Apotheosis has finally left the ruling image of the poem completely behind" (82–84). There is one remaining apotheosis, however, and it is both more abstract and more concrete, that of the poet himself, who, in his "better part," that is, his work, will "be carried up and fixed beyond the stars forever" (15.875–876).

Resuming the eulogy of Augustus, Ovid claims that the emperor surpasses his "father," just as Agamemnon, Theseus, Achilles—and Jupiter—surpassed their fathers. The comparison of Augustus to Jupiter here (15.858–860), with the poet's mention of the emperor by name (15.860), recalls the earlier comparison of Jupiter to Augustus at book 1.200–205 (Feeney 219–220), where (1.204) he also mentions the emperor by name. (Ovid refers to Augustus by name four times in the *Metamorphoses,* the two additional instances also occurring in books 1 [562] and 15 [869]. He uses the adjective *augustus,* which obviously suggests the emperor, three time in the poem: 6.73, 9.270, and 15.145 [Galinsky (1975) 257 with n. 61, 265]).

Ovid culminates his eulogy of Augustus with a prayer on his behalf (15.861–870). In his "roll-call" of the gods (Feeney 217), the poet invokes first Aeneas' Trojan household gods (15.861–862; Bömer at 15.861–863, 7.485); then the native Italian gods, called *di Indigetes* (15.862); then Quirinus, the deified Romulus (15.862–863); his father, Gradivus, or Mars (15.863); Vesta and Apollo, here said by the poet to be part of Augustus' household gods (15.864–865); Jupiter (15.866); and unnamed "other deities whom a poet has a sacred right to call upon" (15.867). Feeney notes that "the prayer is, so to speak, chronological," beginning with Aeneas' household gods and moving through Italian and Roman gods, to Vesta and Apollo, here said to be among Caesar's (that is, Augustus') household gods (15.861–865). Feeney adds that the prayer's focus "moves from the communal to the individual," that is, from Rome as a community to Augustus (215). But the prayer actually begins with the individual, that is, with the household gods of Aeneas; moves next to communal Italian and Roman gods; thence to Apollo and Vesta, "expropriated" by Augustus and placed among his household gods (as Ovid describes it); and then rises to a "climax" (Bömer at 15.866–867, 7.486) with Jupiter Optimus Maximus, whose temple was on the Capitoline hill, the location of the "Tarpeian citadel on high" (15.866); and concludes with a "poetical variation of a 'general-invocation'" formula (Bömer at 15.866–867, 7.486) to cover all unnamed gods.

Bömer notes that Augustus assumed the office of *pontifex maximus* in 12 B.C. and in this capacity was obligated to live in the Forum beside the temple of Vesta. In order to fulfill this duty but to avoid moving to the Forum, the emperor established in his palace on the Palatine hill a sanctuary for Vesta. Ovid can thus refer to Vesta as being among Augustus' household gods and can include Apollo among these gods as well, since a temple to Apollo beside Augustus' palace had been consecrated in 28 B.C. (see Bömer at 15.864–865, 7.486; and Due 178 n. 130). All these gods, "so vital and mesmerizing," as Feeney says, "have indeed now become 'august,' a cluster around the Princeps" (217). In this prayer as well as in the epilogue, the last nine lines of the poem (15.871–879), Ovid's model is the end of the *Aetia* of Callimachus, "the court poet of the Ptolemies," as Knox calls him, and "Augustus is for Ovid as much a literary motif as a political issue" (78–79), although for Feeney the prayer demonstrates "the privatization of communal cult and the communalization of private cult" as an "aspect of the evolution of the principate [Augustus' office] from an individual household [that of Augustus] into the state government" (216).

Ovid's epilogue begins, "I have now completed a work that neither Jupiter's wrath, nor fire, nor sword, nor time's corruption can ever destroy" (*Iamque opus exegi, quod* . . . , 15.871–872), evoking his predecessor, the Augustan poet Horace, whose *Odes* 3.30, the sixteen-line epilogue of his great collection of lyric poetry, begins, "I have completed a monument more lasting than bronze [*exegi monumentum aere perennius*, 3.30.1] . . . which corroding storms [*imber edax*, 3.3; cf. Ovid's *edax . . . vetustas*, "time's corruption" (15.872)] will not, which the violent north wind will not be able to destroy, or a numberless succession of years and flight of seasons" (3.30.1–5), written a little over thirty years before (24–23 B.C.). Similarities continue. For example, Horace claims, "I shall not totally die, and a large part of me will escape death" (*non omnis moriar, multaque pars mei / vitabit Libitinam*, 3.30.6–7), while Ovid declares, "The better part of me will be carried up and fixed beyond the stars forever, and my name will never die" (*parte tamen meliore mei super alta perennis / astra ferar, nomenque erit indelebile nostrum*, 15.875–876). But Ovid evokes the comparison only to distinguish his own epilogue by its differences: Horace says that his fame will grow (in time) as long as Rome—or Roman religion—lasts, and that he will be remembered (in space) in Apulia, his own small corner of Italy, where he was born, as the first to have adapted Greek lyric to Latin meters (3.30.7–14), both claims specific and limited. Ovid, however, declares that (as far as time goes), "[t]he better part of me will be carried up and fixed beyond the stars forever," and people will listen to and read his poetry (as far as space goes) "[w]herever Roman might extends, in all the lands beneath its rule" (15.875–878), claims that are, as Solodow says, "grander": "He enlarges considerably the extent of his fame in both time and space" (221). Moreover, while Horace describes his achievement as a *monumentum* (3.30.1), "Ovid, by contrast, presents a more abstract notion: he merely terms his poetry an *opus* [15.871], . . . while the forces of time which might harm it are divided between the natural . . . and the human [and] evoke no one particular image" (Solodow 222).

There is also a kind of odd reversal between the two poets: Horace closes his collection of personal lyrics with a statement, Solodow says, that "makes his achievement seem objective, nearly impersonal," while Ovid's epilogue to his epic (a genre that is objective and impersonal) is personal and private. "It originates in him, its sphere is himself, the glory that results will be his alone. Neither the poet nor his poem claims to speak for anything larger than the individual" (222).

Barkan, who has noted that the apotheoses in the latter books of the poem (Hercules, Romulus, Aeneas, Julius Caesar) become increasingly abstract (see above), observes that "motifs from the speech of Pythagoras (*edax . . . vetustas, incerti aevi* ["corroding age," translated as "time's corruption," 15.872; and "the uncertain (span of my) life," translated as "my life on earth," 15.874]) are united here with a reality of apotheosis, for the *pars melior* ["better part," 15.875], whose definition was increasingly vague in the Roman apotheoses, is now defined very specifically as the poem itself. . . . Ovid will become his poem" (88).

Not a few critics have wanted to read Ovid's statement that "Jupiter's wrath" (*Iovis ira,* 15.871) can never destroy his work as a reference to Augustus (for example, Fränkel 111, a "sharp clarion note of defiance"; Segal [1969b] 290; Kovacs [1987] 463–464 with n. 11; Feeney 222; and Barchiesi 194–195) and evidence that the epilogue was written in exile (for example, Haupt-Ehwald at 15.871, 2.489; Kenney says, "[I]t is tempting to guess that these words may have been added at Tomis," [1986] 466), for the poet has only a few lines earlier identified the emperor with Jupiter ("Jupiter rules the heavens . . . , the earth is under Augustus: Each is father and sovereign lord," 15.858–860). Moreover, in his late work *Tristia,* which was indeed written in exile, Ovid uses the phrase *Iovis ira* to refer to the wrath of Augustus that sent him to Tomis, his place of exile (1.5.78; 3.11.62; and a variation, *Caesaris ira,* at 3.11.72). But as Galinsky notes, at 15.858–860, "it is the distinctiveness of Jupiter and Augustus, and not their identification, that is foremost in his mind" ([1975] 254), that is, Ovid does not actually equate the two. Moreover, sixty lines earlier Jupiter described to Venus "the record of all that has ever happened in the world and that ever will happen, an archive indestructible and eternal, that fears neither collisions in heaven, nor raging thunderbolts, nor ruin of any kind" (15.810–812: *rerum tabularia . . . , / quae neque concursum caeli neque fulminis iram / nec metuunt ullas tuta atque aeterna ruinas*), and these lines are echoed now in what seems to be a formulaic variation describing the threats that Ovid says his similarly indestructible and eternal poem will be safe from. The phrase *fulminis iram* (15.811; literally, "wrath of the thunderbolt") is now varied by *Iovis ira* (15.871, "Jupiter's wrath"), and "collisions in heaven" and "ruin of any kind" (*concursum caeli,* 15.811; and *ullas . . . ruinas,* 812) are varied by "fire, . . . sword, . . . time's corruption" (15.871, *ignis;* 872, *ferrum* and *edax . . . vetustas*). Finally, it is at least as likely that Ovid in exile borrowed his phrase *Iovis ira* from the *Metamorphoses* and gave it a specific reference, that is, Augustus. In any case, as Little says, "We just do not know enough about Ovid's literary biography to be able to decide the question one way or the other" ([1976] 33).

The poet's future apotheosis foreseen in the epilogue is a "poetic" one, in contrast to the earlier apotheoses, particularly the "political" ones of Romulus, Aeneas, Julius Caesar, and (prospectively) Augustus, and, as Galinsky says, commenting on the epilogue, "Poetic fame is even more indestructible than the greatness of political order or empire"

([1975] 255). Curran, in fact, sees the contrast as deliberate: Ovid will be deified in his *pars melior* (15.875), by which "he means what he elsewhere calls his *ingenium* or, at the beginning of the poem, his *animus* [1.1–2]: his intellectual, imaginative, creative faculty. Augustus will be deified for his *actions,* his *public achievements,* his *bene facta* (15.850), his *acta* (15.852)" ([1972] 85).

Ovid concludes, "And if poets truly can foretell, in all centuries to come, I shall live" (15.878–879), that is, he will live in his poem, as it lives—and "in his personal destiny [he] at last escapes from the law of universal change" (Hardie [1995] 213). For the poem about change is itself—like the poet's "better part"—forever fixed, unlike the flux of this world's never-ending metamorphoses.

BIBLIOGRAPHY OF
WORKS CONSULTED

Albrecht, M. von. "Ovids Arachne-Erzählung." *Actes de VIIe Congrès de Fédération Inter-nationale d'Études Classiques* 1 (1984), 457–464.

————, and Ernst Zinn, eds. *Ovid.* Wege der Forschung 92. Darmstadt: Wissenschaft-liche Buchgesellschaft, 1968.

Altieri, Charles. "Ovid and the New Mythologists." In Anderson (1995a) 253–265.

American Heritage Dictionary of the English Language. See Morris, William.

Anderson, William S. 1963. "Multiple Changes in the *Metamorphoses.*" *Transactions of the American Philological Association* 94 (1963), 1–27.

————. 1968. Review of Brooks Otis, *Ovid as an Epic Poet* (Cambridge: Cambridge University Press, 1966). *American Journal of Philology* 89 (1968), 93–104.

————, ed., with intro. and comm. 1972. *Ovid's Metamorphoses, Books 6–10.* Norman: University of Oklahoma Press, 1972.

————, ed. 1982a. *Metamorphoses.* 2d edition. Bibliotheca Teubneriana. Leipzig: BSB B. G. Teubner Verlagsgesellschaft, 1977, 1982.

————. 1982b. "The Orpheus of Virgil and Ovid: *flebile nescio quid.*" In Warden 25–50.

————. 1989a. "Lycaon: Ovid's Deceptive Paradigm in *Metamorphoses* 1." *Illinois Clas-sical Studies* 14 (1989), 91–101.

————. 1989b. "The Artist's Limits in Ovid's Orpheus, Pygmalion, and Daedalus." *Syl-lecta Classica* 1 (1989), 1–11.

————. 1990. "The Example of Procris in the *Ars Amatoria.*" In Griffith and Mastro-narde 131–145.

————, ed. 1995a. *Ovid: The Classical Heritage.* New York: Garland Publishing, 1995.

————. 1995b. "First-Century Criticism on Ovid: The Senecas and Quintilian." In An-derson (1995a) 1–10.

————, ed., with intro and comm. 1997. *Ovid's Metamorphoses, Books 1–5.* Norman: University of Oklahoma Press, 1997.

Apollodorus. See Simpson, Michael.

Austin, R. G., ed., with comm. *P. Vergili Maronis Aeneidos Liber Sextus.* Oxford: Oxford University Press, 1977.

Barbu, Nicolao, Eugenio Dobroiu, and Michaele Nasta, eds., *Acta Conventus Omnium Gentium Ovidianis Studiis Fovendis.* Bucharest: University of Bucharest Press, 1976.

Barchiesi, Alessandro. "Endgames: Ovid's *Metamorphoses* 15 and *Fasti* 6." In Roberts, Dunn, and Fowler 181–208.

Barkan, Leonard. *The Gods Made Flesh: Metamorphoses and The Pursuit of Paganism.* New Haven: Yale University Press, 1986.

Barnard, Mary E. *The Myth of Apollo and Daphne from Ovid to Quevedo: Love, Agon, and the Grotesque.* Duke Monographs in Medieval and Renaissance Studies, No. 8. Durham: Duke University Press, 1987.

Barolsky, Paul. "A Very Brief History of Art from Narcissus to Picasso." *Classical Journal* 90 (1995), 255–259.

Barthes, Roland. *Mythologies.* Translated by Annette Lavers. New York: Hill and Wang, 1972.

Bauer, Douglas F. "The Function of Pygmalion in the *Metamorphoses* of Ovid." *Transactions of the American Philological Association* 93 (1962), 1–21.

Bömer, Franz, comm. *P. Ovidius Naso: Metamorphosen.* 7 vols. Heidelberg: Carl Winter Universitätsverlag, 1969–1986.

Buchheit, Vincenz. "Numa-Pythagoras in der Deutung Ovids." *Hermes* 121 (1993), 77–99.

Burnet, John, ed., with notes. *Plato's Euthyphro, Apology of Socrates, and Crito.* Oxford: Clarendon Press, 1924.

Cahoon, Leslie. "Shifting Narrators in Ovid, *Metamorphoses* 5." *Helios* 23.1 (1996), 43–66.

Claassen, Jo-Marie. "Ovid's Poetic Pontus." *Papers of the Leeds International Latin Seminar* 6 (1990), 65–94.

Coleman, Robert. "Structure and Intention in the *Metamorphoses.*" *Classical Quarterly* 21 (1971), 461–477.

Conte, Gian Biaggio. *Latin Literature: A History.* Translated by Joseph B. Solodow. Revised by Don Fowler and Glenn W. Most. Baltimore: Johns Hopkins University Press, 1994.

Crahay, Roland, and Jean Hubaux. "Sous le masque de Pythagore: à propos du livre 15 des 'Metamorphoses.'" In Herescu, 283–300.

Crump, M. Marjorie. *The Epyllion from Theocritus to Ovid.* Oxford: Basil Blackwell, 1931. Reprinted London: Bristol Classical Press, 1997.

Curran, Leo C. 1972. "Transformation and Anti-Augustanism in Ovid's *Metamorphoses.* *Arethusa* 5 (1972), 71–91.

———. 1978. "Rape and Rape Victims in the *Metamorphoses.*" *Arethusa* 11.1, 2 (1978), 213–241.

Davis, Gregson. 1980. "The Problem of Closure in a Carmen Perpetuum. Aspects of Thematic Recapitulation in Ovid Met. 15." *Grazer Beiträge* 9 (1980), 123–132.

———. 1983. *The Death of Procris: "Amor" and the Hunt in Ovid's Metamorphoses.* Rome: Edizioni dell' Ateneo, 1983.

Day Lewis, C., trans. *The Aeneid of Virgil.* Garden City, N.Y.: Doubleday & Company, 1953.

Due, Otto Steen. *Changing Forms: Studies in the Metamorphoses of Ovid.* Copenhagen: Gyldendal, 1974.

Ellsworth, James D. 1980. "Ovid's *Iliad* (*Metamorphoses* 12.1–13.622)." *Prudentia* 12 (1980), 23–29.

———. 1986. "Ovid's 'Aeneid' Reconsidered (*Met.* 13.623–14.608)." *Vergilius* 32 (1986), 27–32.

———. 1988. "Ovid's 'Odyssey': Met 13.623–14.608." *Mnemosyne* 41 (1988), 333–340.

Elsner, John, and Alison Sharrock. "Re-Viewing Pygmalion." *Ramus* 20 (1991), 149–182.

Evelyn-White, Hugh, ed. and trans. *Hesiod, the Homeric Hymns, and Homerica.* Cambridge, Mass.: Harvard University Press, and London: William Heinemann, 1914. Reprinted 1982.

Fagles, Robert, trans. *Homer: The Odyssey.* Introduction and notes by Bernard Knox. New York: Penguin Books, 1996.

Fantazzi, Carolus. "The Revindication of Roman Myth in the Pomona-Vertumnus Tale." In Barbu, Dobroiu, and Nasta 283–293.

Fantham, Elaine. 1979. "Ovid's Ceyx and Alcyone: The Metamorphosis of a Myth." *Phoenix* 33 (1979), 330–345.

———. 1993. *"Sunt Quibus in Plures Jus Est Transire Figuras:* Ovid's Self-Transformers in the *Metamorphoses." Classical World* 87 (1993), 21–36.

———, ed. 1998. *Ovid: Fasti, Book IV.* Cambridge: Cambridge University Press, 1998.

Farrell, Joseph. "Dialogue of Genres in Ovid's 'Lovesong of Polyphemus' (*Metamorphoses* 13.719–897)." *American Journal of Philology* 113 (1992), 235–268.

Feeney, D.C. *The Gods in Epic: Poets and Critics of the Classical Tradition.* Oxford: Clarendon Press, 1991.

Fränkel, Hermann. *Ovid: A Poet between Two Worlds.* Berkeley: University of California Press, 1945.

Fredericks, B. R. "Divine Wit vs. Divine Folly: Mercury and Apollo in *Metamorphoses* 1–2." *Classical Journal* 72 (1977), 244–249.

Galinsky, G. Karl. 1972. "Hercules Ovidianus (*Metamorphoses* 9, 1–272)." *Wiener Studien* 6 (1972), 93–116.

———. 1975. *Ovid's Metamorphoses: An Introduction to the Basic Aspects.* Berkeley: University of California Press, 1975.

———. 1998. "The Speech of Pythagoras at Ovid *Metamorphoses* 15.75–478." *Papers of the Leeds International Latin Seminar* 10 (1998), 313–336.

Gantz, Timothy. *Early Greek Myths: A Guide to Literary and Artistic Sources.* 2 vols. Baltimore: Johns Hopkins University Press, 1993.

Glare, P. G. W., ed. *Oxford Latin Dictionary.* Oxford: Oxford University Press, 1982.

Glenn, Edgar M. *The Metamorphoses: Ovid's Roman Games.* Lanham, N.Y.: University Press of America, 1986.

Griffin, Alan H. "Ovid's Treatment of Ceyx and Alcyone." In Barbu, Dobroiu, and Nasta 321–324.

Griffith, M., and D. J. Mastronarde, eds. *Cabinet of the Muses: Essays on Classical and Comparative Literature in Honor of Thomas G. Rosenmeyer.* Atlanta: Scholars Press, 1990.

Grimal, Pierre. *The Dictionary of Classical Mythology.* Translated by A. R. Maxwell-Hyslop. Oxford and New York: Basil Blackwell Publisher, Ltd., and Basil Blackwell, Inc., 1986.

Guthrie, W. K. C. *The Sophists.* First published as part 1 of *A History of Greek Philosophy.* Volume 3 (Cambridge University Press, 1969). Cambridge: Cambridge University Press, 1971.

Hardie, Philip. 1990. "Ovid's Theban History: The First 'Anti-*Aeneid*'?" *Classical Quarterly* 40 (1990), 224–235.

———. 1995. "The Speech of Pythagoras in Ovid *Metamorphoses* 15: Empedoclean Epos." *Classical Quarterly* 45 (1995), 204–214.

Hardy, Clara Shaw. "Ecphrasis and the Male Narrator in Ovid's Arachne." *Helios* 22.2 (1995), 140–147.

Haupt, M., and R. Ehwald, eds. and comm. *Metamorphosen.* Corrected and enlarged by M. von Albrecht. 2 vols., 9th and 5th editions (respectively). Dublin and Zurich: Weidmann, 1966.

Henderson, A. A. R., ed., with intro., notes, and vocabulary. *Ovid: Metamorphoses* III. Bristol: Bristol Classical Press, 1979.

Herescu, N. I., ed. *Ovidiana: recherches sur Ovide*. Paris: Société d'Édition "Les Belles Lettres," 1958.

Hill, D. E. "From Orpheus to Ass's Ears: Ovid, *Metamorphoses* 10.1–11.193." In Woodman and Powell 124–137.

Hinds, Stephen. 1987. *The Metamorphoses of Persephone: Ovid and the Self-Conscious Muse*. Cambridge: Cambridge University Press, 1987.

———. 1998. *Allusion and Intertext: Dynamics of Appropriation in Roman Poetry*. Cambridge: Cambridge University Press, 1998.

Hoefmans, Marjorie. "Myth into Reality: The Metamorphosis of Daedalus and Icarus (Ovid, *Metamorphoses*, VIII, 183–235)." *Antiquité Classique* 63 (1994), 137–160.

Hofmann, Heinz. "Ovid's *Metamorphoses: Carmen Perpetuum, Carmen Deductum*." *Papers of the Liverpool Latin Seminar* 5 (1985), 223–241.

Holland, Louise Adams. *Janus and the Bridge*. Papers and Monographs of the American Academy in Rome, vol. 21. American Academy in Rome, 1961.

Hollis, A. S., ed., with intro. and comm. *Ovid: Metamorphoses*. Book 8. Oxford: Oxford University Press, 1970.

Hopkins, David. "Nature's Laws and Man's: The Story of Cinyras and Myrrha in Ovid and Dryden." *Modern Language Review* 80 (1985), 786–801.

Hornblower, Simon and Antony Spawforth, eds. *The Oxford Classical Dictionary*. 3d edition. Oxford: Oxford University Press, 1996.

Horsfall, Nicholas. "Epic and Burlesque in Ovid, *MET*. viii. 260ff." *Classical Journal* 74 (1979), 319–332.

Humphries, Rolfe, trans. *Ovid: Metamorphoses*. Bloomington: Indiana University Press, 1955, 1983.

Janan, Micaela. 1988. "The Book of Good Love? Design versus Desire in *Metamorphoses* 10." *Ramus* 17 (1988), 110–137.

———. 1994. "'There Beneath the Roman Ruin Where the Purple Flowers Grow': Ovid's Minyeides and the Feminine Imagination." *American Journal of Philology* 115 (1994), 427–448.

Jebb, Sir Richard C., ed., with crit. notes, comm., and trans. in English prose. *Sophocles: The Plays and Fragments*. Part 4. *The Philoctetes*. Reprinted Amsterdam: Servio Publishers, 1962.

Johnson, Patricia. "Constructions of Venus in Ovid's *Metamorphoses* V." *Arethusa* 29 (1996), 125–149.

Johnson, W. R. 1970. "The Problem of the Counter-classical Sensibility and Its Critics." *California Studies in Classical Antiquity* 3 (1970), 123–151.

———. 1996. "The Rapes of Callisto." *Classical Journal* 92.1 (1996), 9–24.

Joyce, James. *A Portrait of the Artist as a Young Man*. Dublin: B. W. Huebsch, 1916. Reprinted Harmondsworth: Penguin Books, 1976.

Keith, A. M. *The Play of Fictions: Studies in Ovid's Metamorphoses, Book 2*. Ann Arbor: University of Michigan Press, 1992.

Kenney, E. J. 1973. "The Style of the *Metamorphoses*." In J. W. Binns, ed. *Ovid*. London: Routledge & Kegan Paul, 1973. 116–153.

———. 1976. "Ovidius Prooemians." *Proceedings of the Cambridge Philological Society* 22 (1976), 46–53.

———. 1982. "Ovid." In E. J. Kenney and W. V. Clausen, eds. *The Cambridge History of Classical Literature*. Volume 2. *Latin Literature*. Cambridge: Cambridge University Press, 1982. 420–457.

———. 1986. In A. D. Melville, trans., and E. J. Kenney, intro. and notes. *Ovid: Metamorphoses*. Oxford: Oxford University Press, 1986.

———. 1992. In A. D. Melville, trans., and E. J. Kenney, intro. and notes. *Ovid: Sorrows of an Exile: Tristia.* Oxford: Clarendon Press, 1992.

Kirk, G. S. 1962. *The Songs of Homer.* Cambridge: Cambridge University Press, 1962.

———, general ed. 1985a. *The Iliad: A Commentary.* 6 volumes. Cambridge: Cambridge University Press, 1985–1993.

———, ed. 1985b. *The Iliad: A Commentary.* Volume 1. Books 1–4. Cambridge: Cambridge University Press, 1985.

Kirk, G. S., J. E. Raven, and M. Schofield, eds. *The Presocratic Philosophers: A Critical History with a Selection of Texts.* 2d edition. Cambridge: Cambridge University Press, 1983.

Kleine Pauly, Der. See Ziegler, Konrat, and Walther Sontheimer.

Knox, Peter E. *Ovid's Metamorphoses and the Traditions of Augustan Poetry.* Cambridge: Cambridge Philological Society, 1986.

Konstan, David. "The Death of Argus, or What Stories Do: Audience Response in Ancient Fiction and Theory." *Helios* 18 (1991), 15–30.

Kovacs, David. 1987. "Ovid, *Metamorphoses* 1.2." *Classical Quarterly* 37 (1987), 458–465.

———. 1994. "Notes on Ovid's *Metamorphoses.*" *Museum Criticum* 29 (1994), 245–249.

Lafaye, Georges, ed. and trans. *Ovide: les Metamorphoses.* 3 vols. 3d edition revised and corrected (vols. 1 and 2), 2d edition revised and corrected (vol. 3). Paris: Société d'Édition "Les Belles Lettres," 1961, 1960, 1957.

Lanham, Richard A. *The Motives of Eloquence: Literary Rhetoric in the Renaissance.* New Haven: Yale University Press, 1976.

Lattimore, Richmond, trans. with intro. *The Odyssey of Homer.* New York: Harper & Row, 1965, 1967.

Leach, Eleanor. "Ekphrasis and the Theme of Artistic Failure in Ovid's *Metamorphoses.*" *Ramus* 3.1 (1974), 102–142.

Lee, A. G., ed. and comm. *Metamorphoses, Book I.* Cambridge: Cambridge University Press, 1953. Reprinted Bristol: Bristol Classical Press, and Chicago: Bolchazy-Carducci Publishers, 1984.

Lesky, Albin. *Greek Tragic Poetry.* Translated by Matthew Dillon. New Haven: Yale University Press, 1983.

Lewis, Charlton T., and Charles Short, eds. *A Latin Dictionary.* Oxford: Clarendon Press, 1879.

Liddell, Henry George, and Robert Scott. *A Greek-English Lexicon.* New edition revised and augmented throughout by Sir Stuart Henry Jones. Oxford: Clarendon Press, 1940.

Little, Douglas. 1970. "The Speech of Pythagoras in Metamorphoses 15 and the Structure of the Metamorphoses." *Hermes* 98 (1970), 340–360.

———. 1974. "Non-parody in *Metamorphoses* 15." *Prudentia* 6 (1974), 17–21.

———. 1976. "Ovid's Eulogy of Augustus: *Metamorphoses* 15.851–70." *Prudentia* 8 (1976), 19–35.

Littlefield, David J. "Pomona and Vertumnus: A Fruition of History in Ovid's *Metamorphoses.*" *Arion* 4 (1965), 465–473.

LSJ = Liddell, Scott–Jones. See Liddell, Henry George, and Robert Scott.

Mack, Sara. 1988. *Ovid.* New Haven: Yale University Press, 1988.

———. 1999. "Acis and Galatea or Metamorphosis of Tradition." *Arion,* 3d series, 6 (1999), 51–67.

Makowski, John F. "Bisexual Orpheus: Pederasty and Parody in Ovid." *Classical Journal* 92.1 (1996), 25–38.

Martindale, Charles, ed. *Ovid Renewed: Ovidian Influences on Literature and Art from the Middle Ages to the Twentieth Century.* Cambridge: Cambridge University Press, 1988.

McKeown, J. C. *Ovid: Amores: Text, Prolegomena, and Commentary in Four Volumes.* Volume 1. *Text and Prolegomena.* Liverpool: Francis Cairns Publications, 1987.

Melville, A. D., trans., and E. J. Kenney, intro. and notes. *Ovid: Metamorphoses.* Oxford: Oxford University Press, 1986.

Meriwether, James B., and Michael Millgate, eds. *Lion in the Garden: Interviews with William Faulkner (1926–1962).* Lincoln: University of Nebraska Press, 1968.

Miller, Frank J. "Some Features of Ovid's Style: III. Ovid's Methods of Ordering and Transition in the *Metamorphoses.*" *Classical Journal* 16.8 (1921), 464–476.

———, ed. and trans. Revised by G. P. Goold. *Metamorphoses.* Loeb Classical Library. 2 vols. 3d and 2d editions (respectively). Cambridge, Mass.: Harvard University Press, and London: William Heinemann, 1977, 1984.

Miller, Jane. "Some Versions of Pygmalion." In Martindale 205–214.

Miller, John F. "The Memories of Ovid's Pythagoras." *Mnemosyne* 47 (1994), 473–487.

Morris, William, ed. *The American Heritage Dictionary of the English Language.* Boston: Houghton Mifflin, 1979.

Murphy, G. M. H., ed., with intro. and comm. *Ovid: Metamorphoses: Book XI.* London: Oxford University Press, 1972.

Myers, Sara K. 1994a. *Ovid's Causes: Cosmogony and Aetiology in the Metamorphoses.* Ann Arbor: University of Michigan Press, 1994.

———. 1994b. "*Ultimus Ardor:* Pomona and Vertumnus in Ovid's *Met.* 14.623–771." *Classical Journal* 89 (1994), 225–250.

Nagle, Betty Rose. 1983. "Byblis and Myrrha: Two Incest Narratives in the *Metamorphoses.*" *Classical Journal* 78 (1983), 301–315.

———. 1988a. "Two Miniature Carmina Perpetua in the Metamorphoses: Calliope and Orpheus." *Grazer Beiträge* 15 (1988), 99–125.

———. 1988b. "A Trio of Love-Triangles in Ovid's *Metamorphoses.*" *Arethusa* 21 (1988), 75–98.

———. 1989a. "Ovid's Metamorphoses: A Narratological Catalogue." *Syllecta Classica* 1 (1989), 97–125.

———. 1989b. "Recent Structural Studies on Ovid." *Augustan Age* 9 (1989), 27–36.

Newlands, Carole. "The Simile of the Fractured Pipe in Ovid's Metamorphoses 4." *Ramus* 15 (1986), 143–153.

Nilsson, Martin P. *The Mycenaean Origin of Greek Mythology.* Berkeley: University of California Press, 1932, 1972.

Nugent, Georgia. "This Sex Which Is Not One: De-constructing Ovid's Hermaphrodite." *differences: A Journal of Feminist Cultural Studies* 2.1 (1990), 160–185.

Nuttall, A. D. "Ovid's Narcissus and Shakespeare's Richard II: The Reflected Self." In Martindale 137–150.

O'Bryhim, Shawn. "Ovid's Version of Callisto's Punishment." *Hermes* 118 (1990), 75–80.

OCD = *Oxford Classical Dictionary.* See Hornblower, Simon, and Antony Spawforth.

OLD = *Oxford Latin Dictionary.* See Glare, P. G. W.

Otis, Brooks. *Ovid as an Epic Poet.* 2d edition. Cambridge: Cambridge University Press, 1970.

Palmer, L. R. *The Greek Language.* Atlantic Highlands, N.J.: Humanities Press, 1980.

Parry, Hugh. "Ovid's *Metamorphoses:* Violence in a Pastoral Landscape." *Transactions of the American Philological Association* 95 (1964), 268–282.

Pöschl, Viktor. 1959. "Kephalos und Prokris in Ovids Metamorphosen." *Hermes* 87 (1959), 328–343.

———. 1968. "Der Katalog der Baüme in Ovids Metamorphosen." Originally published in *Medium Aevum Vivum*. Festschrift für W. Bulst, Heidelberg, 1960, 13–21. Reprinted in Albrecht and Zinn, 393–404.

Preussner, Arnold. "The Actaeon Myth in Ovid, Petrarch, Wyatt, and Sidney." *Bestia* 5 (1993), 95–108.

Primmer, Adolf. "Das Lied des Orpheus in Ovids 'Metamorphosen.'" *Sprachkunst: Beiträge zur Literaturwissenschaft* 10 (1979), 123–137.

Reinhold, Meyer. *Past and Present: The Continuity of Classical Myths*. Toronto: Hakkert, 1972.

Richardson, L., Jr. *A New Topographical Dictionary of Ancient Rome*. Baltimore: Johns Hopkins University Press, 1992.

Roberts, Deborah H., Francis M. Dunn, and Don Fowler, eds. *Classical Closure: Readings in the End in Greek and Latin Literature*. Princeton: Princeton University Press, 1997.

Segal, Charles. 1968. "Circean Temptations: Homer, Vergil, Ovid." *Transactions of the American Philological Association* 99 (1968), 419–442.

———. 1969a. *Landscape in Ovid's Metamorphoses: A Study in the Transformations of a Literary Symbol*. Hermes Einzelschriften 23. Wiesbaden: Franz Steiner Verlag, 1969.

———. 1969b. "Myth and Philosophy in the *Metamorphoses*: Ovid's Augustanism and the Augustan Conclusion of Book XV." *American Journal of Philology* 90 (1969), 257–292.

———. 1978. "Ovid's Cephalus and Procris: Myth and Tragedy." *Grazer Beiträge* 7 (1978), 175–205.

———. 1989. *Orpheus: The Myth of the Poet*. Baltimore: Johns Hopkins University Press, 1989.

———. 1992. "Philomela's Web and the Pleasures of the Text: Ovid's Myth of Tereus in the *Metamorphoses*." In Wilhelm and Jones 281–295.

Sharrock, A. R. "Womanufacture." *Journal of Roman Studies* 81 (1991), 36–49.

Simpson, Michael, trans., with intro and notes. *Gods and Heroes of the Greeks: The Library of Apollodorus*. Amherst: University of Massachusetts Press, 1976.

Skutsch, Otto, ed., with intro and comm. *The Annals of Q. Ennius*. Oxford: Oxford University Press, 1985.

Solodow, Joseph. *The World of Ovid's Metamorphoses*. Chapel Hill: University of North Carolina Press, 1988.

Stanford, W. B. *The Ulysses Theme: A Study of the Adaptability of a Traditional Hero*. 2d edition. Ann Arbor: University of Michigan Press, 1963.

Stephens, Wade C. 1957–1958. "Descent to the Underworld in Ovid's *Metamorphoses*." *Classical Journal* 53 (1957–1958), 177–183.

———. 1958a. "Two Stoic Heroes in the *Metamorphoses*: Hercules and Ulysses." In Herescu 273–282.

———. 1958b. "Cupid and Venus in Ovid's *Metamorphoses*." *Transactions of the American Philological Association* 89 (1958), 286–300.

Swanson, Roy Arthur. "Ovid's Pythagorean Essay." *Classical Journal* 54 (1958), 21–24.

Tarrant, R. J. "The Silence of Cephalus: Text and Narrative Technique in Ovid, *Metamorphoses* 7.685ff." *Transactions of the American Philological Association* 125 (1995), 99–111.

Thucydides. *The Complete Writings of Thucydides: The Peloponnesian War*. The unabridged Crawley translation with an introduction by John H. Finley, Jr. Modern Library Edition. New York: Random House, 1951.

Tissol, Garth. *The Face of Nature: Wit, Narrative, and Cosmic Origins in Ovid's Metamorphoses.* Princeton: Princeton University Press, 1997.

Viarre, Simone. "Pygmalion et Orphée chez Ovide (*Met.* X, 243–297)." *Revue des Études Latines* 46 (1968), 235–247.

Vincent, Michael. "Between Ovid and Barthes: *Ekphrasis,* Orality, Textuality in Ovid's 'Arachne.'" *Arethusa* 27 (1994), 361–386.

Vinge, Louise. *The Narcissus Theme in Western Literature up to the Early 19th Century.* Lund: Skånska Centraltryckeriet, 1967.

Warden, John, ed. *Orpheus: The Metamorphoses of a Myth.* Toronto: University of Toronto Press, 1982.

West, David. "Orpheus and Eurydice." *JACT Review* 4 (1986), 7–11.

West, M. L., ed., with prolegomena and comm. *Hesiod: Theogony.* Oxford: Oxford University Press, 1966.

Wheeler, Stephen M. "*Imago Mundi:* Another View of the Creation in Ovid's *Metamorphoses.*" *American Journal of Philology* 116 (1995), 95–121.

Wilhelm, Robert, and Howard Jones, eds. *The Two Worlds of the Poet: New Perspectives on Vergil.* Detroit: Wayne State University Press, 1992.

Wilkinson, L. P. 1955. *Ovid Recalled.* Cambridge: Cambridge University Press, 1955.

———. 1958. "The World of Ovid's *Metamorphoses.*" In Herescu 231–244.

Williams, Gordon. *Change and Decline: Roman Literature in the Early Empire.* Berkeley: University of California Press, 1978.

Williams, R. D., ed., with intro and notes. *The Aeneid of Virgil.* Books 1–6. Basingstoke and London: Macmillan/St. Martin's Press, 1972.

Wise, Valerie. "Flight Myths in Ovid's *Metamorphoses:* An Interpretation of Phaethon and Daedalus." *Ramus* 6 (1977), 44–59.

Woodman, Tony, and Jonathan Powell, eds. *Author and Audience in Latin Literature.* Cambridge: Cambridge University Press, 1992.

Ziegler, Konrat, and Walther Sontheimer, eds. *Der Kleine Pauly: Lexicon der Antike auf der Grundlage von Pauly's Realencyclopädie der Classischen Altertumswissenschaft unter Mitwirkung Zahlreicher Fachgelehrter Bearbeitet.* 5 volumes. Stuttgart: Alfred Druckenmüller Verlag, 1964–1975.

Index

MICHAEL SIMPSON was born in Winston-Salem, North Carolina, and educated in the public schools there and in Charlotte. He earned an A.B. degree in history at the University of North Carolina at Chapel Hill and a Ph.D. in classics at Yale University.

Mr. Simpson taught at Dartmouth, Amherst, and Smith colleges before joining the faculty of Bard College in Annandale-on-Hudson, New York, where he also served for two years as dean of Academic Affairs. In 1980 he was appointed professor of classics and associate dean and director of graduate studies in the Graduate Program in Humanities at The University of Texas at Dallas. He was dean of the School of Arts and Humanities there from 1992 to 1996.

Mr. Simpson resides in Dallas, Texas, with his daughter Hannah and his son Stephen.